FOR REFERENCE

Do Not Take From This Room

D0554282

HISTORICAL DICTIONARIES OF RELIGIONS, PHILOSOPHIES, AND MOVEMENTS
Edited by Jon Woronoff

1. *Buddhism,* by Charles S. Prebish, 1993
2. *Mormonism,* by Davis Bitton, 1994
3. *Ecumenical Christianity,* by Ans Joachim van der Bent, 1994
4. *Terrorism,* by Sean Anderson and Stephen Sloan, 1995
5. *Sikhism,* by W. H. McLeod, 1995
6. *Feminism,* by Janet K. Boles and Diane Long Hoeveler, 1995
7. *Olympic Movement,* by Ian Buchanan and Bill Mallon, 1995
8. *Methodism,* by Charles Yrigoyen Jr. and Susan E. Warrick, 1996
9. *Orthodox Church,* by Michael Projurat, Alexander Golitzin, and Michael D. Peterson, 1996
10. *Organized Labor,* by James C. Docherty, 1996
11. *Civil Rights Movement,* by Ralph E. Luker, 1997
12. *Catholicism,* by William J. Collinge, 1997
13. *Hinduism,* by Bruce M. Sullivan, 1997
14. *North American Environmentalism,* by Edward R. Wells and Alan M. Schwartz, 1997
15. *Welfare State,* by Bent Greve, 1998
16. *Socialism,* by James C. Docherty, 1997
17. *Bahá'í Faith,* by Hugh C. Adamson and Philip Hainsworth, 1998
18. *Taoism,* by Julian F. Pas in cooperation with Man Kam Leung, 1998
19. *Judaism,* by Norman Solomon, 1998
20. *Green Movement,* by Elim Papadakis, 1998
21. *Nietzscheanism,* by Carol Diethe, 1999
22. *Gay Liberation Movement,* by Ronald J. Hunt, 1999
23. *Islamic Fundamentalist Movements in the Arab World, Iran, and Turkey,* by Ahmad S. Moussalli, 1999
24. *Reformed Churches,* by Robert Benedetto, Donald McKim, and Darrell Guder, 1999
25. *Baptists,* by William H. Brackney, 1999
26. *Cooperative Movement,* by Jack Shaffer, 1999
27. *Reformation and Counter-Reformation,* by Hans J. Hillerbrand, 1999

Historical Dictionary of Islamic Fundamentalist Movements in the Arab World, Iran, and Turkey

Ahmad S. Moussalli

*Historical Dictionaries of Religions,
Philosophies, and Movements, No. 23*

The Scarecrow Press, Inc.
Lanham, Maryland, and London
1999

SCARECROW PRESS, INC.

Published in the United States of America
by Scarecrow Press, Inc.
4720 Boston Way
Lanham, Maryland 20706

4 Pleydell Gardens, Folkestone
Kent CT20 2DN, England

British Library Cataloguing in Publication Information Available

Library of Congress Cataloging-in-Publication Data

Mawṣililī, Aḥmad.
    Historical dictionary of Islamic fundamentalist movements in the
Arab world, Iran, and Turkey / Ahmad S. Moussalli.
      p.   cm. — (Historical dictionaries of religions,
philosophies, and movements ; no. 23)
   ISBN 0-8108-3609-2 (cloth : alk. paper)
    1. Islamic fundamentalism—Arab countries—History—Dictionaries.
2. Islamic fundamentalism—Middle East—History—Dictionaries.
3. Islamic fundamentalism—Turkey—History—Dictionaries.
I. Title. II. Series.
BP60.M36   1999
297'.09—dc21   98-45879
                                            CIP

Contents

Editor's Foreword

Islamic fundamentalism is one of those topics frequently emblazoned in feverish headlines rather than presented for sober analysis. News reports subject the public sensational descriptions of violent actions undertaken by shadowy groups and figures for seemingly futile causes. Without undertaking extensive research, it is nearly impossible to obtain a balanced presentation of the facts, a circumspect treatment of the groups and their goals or the individuals and their ideals. No wonder the topic remains so controversial and, what is worse, incomprehensible to most.

Fortunately, this *Historical Dictionary of Islamic Fundamentalist Movements in the Arab World, Iran, and Turkey* provides a solid foundation of fact. Much of it is devoted to the groups and their leaders, informing us not only of their origins and actions but also of the ideas and principles on which the groups are based. This is embedded in a broad description of Islamic fundamentalism, its underlying concepts, and the transformation (indeed, revolution) it seeks to bring about. In much of this, it must be remembered that terms do not always mean the same thing to those inside and outside of the movement. Equally important, fundamentalists do not necessarily agree with one another on goals, principles, and means of action. These are the kinds of nuances that rarely appear in the world media but are essential for understanding.

The author of this volume is Ahmad S. Moussalli, who was born, grew up, and was educated in the Middle East, earning a B.A. from the University of Al-Azhar in Cairo. His further studies took place in U.S. schools, including the University of Maryland, where he specialized in Islamic political theory and thought. This was followed by a decade as professor of Islamic thought, among other things, at the American University in Beirut. Dr. Moussalli's primary interest is Islamic fundamentalism, on which he has already written several books, the latest being *Islamic Fundamentalism: Myths and Realities* (Ithaca Press, 1998) and *Moderate and Radical Islamic Fundmentalism: The Quest for Modernity, Legitimacy and the Islamic State* (University Press of Florida, 1999). His background clearly qualifies him for compiling this historical dictionary, which presents the material in another form, one that is particularly handy for specialized researchers and general readers alike.

Jon Woronoff
Series Editor

Reader's Notes

The purpose of this historical dictionary is to provide essential information on and analytical discussion of basic ideas, notions, concepts, doctrines, ideologies, leaders, intellectuals, thinkers, ideologues, groups, and movements of Islamic fundamentalism, or Islamism, in the Arab world, Iran, and Turkey. It tends to focus on recent movements, groups, and leaders, although it does not neglect older and important ones.

The entries on the basic ideas, doctrines, and ideologies that make Islamic fundamentalism what it is, such as *shura* (consultation), *hakimiyya* (governance), *tawhid* (oneness of God), or *jahiliyya* (paganism), are treated at length in order to avoid repeated explanations. Thus, the dictionary is heavily cross-referenced, referring the reader to related entries to help explain the discourse of an ideologue or the ideology of a movement. When necessary, a distinction is made between radical and moderate fundamentalists in order to avoid confusion and generalization, because there are essential intellectual and political differences among fundamentalists in terms of their ideological discourses and political behavior.

More important, the entries are explained not in general Islamic terms or as understood by most contemporary Muslims today but from the fundamentalist points of view. Thus, when philosophy, the West, Islamic law, *shura*, or *jihad* is explained, it is the fundamentalist view and not the long-standing juridical, political, intellectual, religious traditions or modernist developments that are exposed. No attempt has been made to measure the divergence of fundamentalist views from traditional ones. The focuses of explanation are the purposes, justifications, and developments as well as the consequences of fundamentalists' reinterpretations of a particular notion, like freedom, or action, like revolution. The dictionary covers all the ideas, notions, and disciplines that distinguish Islamic fundamentalism from other modern manifestations of Islam, such as reformism and modernism.

Furthermore, some entries are not strictly "fundamentalist" but are included because of their relevance to Islamic fundamentalism. Such entries include, for example, Salman Rushdie. Other entries are not strictly related to the Arab countries, Iran, or Turkey but are included because of their influence over the Islamic fundamentalist movements of these countries. Such entries include, for instance, Abu al-A'la al-Mawdudi, the prominent Pakistani fundamentalist thinker and activist.

The amount of attention given to movements, groups, leaders, ideologues, and thinkers varies from one entry to another. Major Islamic movements, such as Muslim Brotherhood, Islamic Salvation Front, and *Hizbullah,* and major fundamentalist thinkers and leaders, such as Hasan al-Banna, Sayyid Qutb, Ayatollah Khomeini, and Hasan al-Turabi, occupy large spaces that range from a few paragraphs to a few pages. Entries on minor groups and movements, such as Islamic Amal or *al-'Ama'im al-Sawda'*, or politically and intellectually less important leaders or ideologues occupy less space that might range from a mere cross-reference to a few lines or a few paragraphs. The dictionary includes almost all major and minor figures of the Islamic movement as well as independent fundamentalists of importance. The movements and groups include well-known and obscure, legal and illegal organizations that range in size from a few individuals to massive popular followings. A special effort has been made to cross-reference entries in order to provide the reader with a more rounded picture of the item being reviewed.

All entries are listed alphabetically. The Arabic transliteration system used here has been kept to a minimum for the benefit of those educated readers who are not specialists in the fields of Islamic studies or the Middle East. Arabic words with an *al-* prefix are alphabetized according to their root words; for instance, to look for Jamal al-Din al-Afghani, one should look for the name under *A* (Afghani) in alphabetical order. The letter *ayn* is indicated by ' and the letter *hamza* is indicated by '. But the *hamza* as the first letter in a word is omitted and is replaced by an appropriate vowel. Again, these letters (*al*, ', ') are not used in the alphabetization of names; thus, Muhammad 'Abdu should be looked for under *A* (Abdu) in alphabetical order. Almost all names of individuals and movements are transliterated, with the exception of those names that are widely known in the English language; examples are Erbakan, Khomeini, and *Hizbullah*. Most doctrines and concepts are alphabetized according to their translated titles; thus, *al-dustur* should be looked for under constitution, *al-Shumuliyya* under comprehensiveness, *huquq al-insan*, under human rights, *al-hurriyya* under freedom, and *uluhiyya* under divinity. However, those doctrines and concepts that are known in English in their Arabic forms such as *jihad, hudud*, and *al-shari'a*, or that are specifically related to Islam, such as *dar al-harb*, *bid'a*, *fatwa*, and *fitra* are alphabetized under their transliterated forms. Some movements are alphabetized under their transliterated titles; thus, Islamic *Amal* Movement should be looked for under *Harakat Amal al-Islamiyya*, Renaissance Movement under *Harakat al-Nahda*, and Islamic Unification Movement under *Harakat al-Tawhid al-Islami*. Movements that are known in English in specific forms, whether transliterated or translated, are alphabetized accordingly. This includes in English, for instance, Islamic Salvation Front (*al-Jabha al-Islamiyya li al-Inqadh*), Muslim Brotherhood (*al-Ikhwan al-Muslimin*), and Islamic Youth Organization (*Munazzamat al-Shabiba al-Islamiyya*). Non-English titles are retained for movements that are known in English in their original forms, thus, there are entries for *Hizbullah* (Party of God), *Hamas* (Islamic Resistance Movement), *al-Jihad al-Islami* (Islamic *Jihad*), and *Refah Partisi*. However, because of cross-referencing, all entries, except proper names, can be looked up either in their translated or transliterated forms.

Chronology

This chronology is meant to provide dates of essential historical events, chronologically ordered, in order to provide the reader with a quick review of sequences of events that have or might have affected the rise and development of Islamic fundamentalist movements in the Arab world, Iran, and Turkey. The chronology is not meant to be comprehensive in a general sense, but comprehensive enough to include those events that might have some impact on or are formative in the making of Islamic fundamentalism. Specific dates and events can be found under various entries. Although the chronology covers events of the 19th and 20th centuries, it primarily focuses on the 20th century, because that is when most of the direct events that shaped the Islamic movements took place.

1804 Othman Dan Fodio established the Islamic State of Sokoto in Central Sudan.

1805 Muhammad Ibn Saud captured Medina, defeating the Turkish garrison.

1807 The Darqawi sect revolted against Turkish domination. Tunisia repudiated suzerainty of Algeria.

1812 Medina fell to the Egyptians.

1813 Mecca and Ta'if were captured by Egyptian forces, and the Saudis were expelled from Hijaz.

1814 Ibn Saud died. King Othman of Tunisia was assassinated by his cousin Mahmud.

1818 Under the caliphal instruction, Muhammad 'Ali Pasha launched a series of military attacks on Wahhabi-controlled territories. He reached Dar'iyya and captured the capital of the Wahhabi-Saudi alliance.

1828 Russia declared war against Turkey.

1829 The Treaty of Adrianople was concluded.

1830 French forces landed near Algiers, occupied Algeria, and ended Turkish rule.

1832 The Turks were defeated in the battle of Konia by Egyptian forces.

1834 Prince 'Abd al-Qadir was recognized as ruler of the area under his control in Algeria by the French.

1839 Turkey was defeated by the Egyptians in the battle of Nisibin.

1840 An alliance of the European powers forced Egypt to relinquish Syria. The British occupied Aden.

1842 Prince 'Abd al-Qadir, ousted from Algeria by the French, went to Morocco.

1847 Abd al-Qadir surrendered to French forces, but France violated its pledge and sent him as a captive to France.

1849 Muhammad 'Ali Pasha died.

1850 'Ali Muhammad Bab was arrested and executed by the Iranian government.

1852 'Abd al-Qadir was released by Napoleon III. He settled in Turkey.

1869 Jamal al-Din al-Afghani, exiled from Afghanistan, left for Egypt.

1871 Tunisia acknowledged the suzerainty of Turkey.

1876 Britain bought the shares of Khedive Isma'il in the Suez Canal and became privy to Egyptian affairs.

1878 Turkey handed over Cyprus to Britain. Adrianople fell to Russia.

1879 Jamal al-Din al-Afghani was exiled from Egypt. With the Treaty of Berlin, Turkey lost most of its territory in Europe.

1881 France invaded Tunisia and the Bey acknowledged the supremacy of France as a consequence of the treaty of Bardo. Muhammad Ahmad declared himself the Mahdi in Sudan.

1882 Egypt was placed under British occupation.

1883 'Abd al-Qadir died in Damascus.
Jamal al-Din al-Afghani was deported from Egypt and settled in Paris.

1885 Muhammad Ahmad declared the Government of Sudan free. The Mahdi died five months after the occupation of Khartoum.

1887 Muhammad 'Abdu was expelled from Egypt and joined Jamal al-Din al-Afghani in Paris. Together, they published *al-'Urwa al-Wuthqa*.

1895 Mirza Ghulam Ahmad of Qadian claimed prophethood.

1897 The World Zionist Organization was founded in Basel, Switzerland.

1899 The Mahdi State collapsed, and the British and the Egyptians jointly occupied Sudan. Muhammad 'Abdu became the Mufti of Egypt.

1901 'Abd al-'Aziz Ibn Saud entered Riyadh, and the Saudi dynasty regained authority while the regions of Najd, Hijaz, Mecca, Medina, and Jeddah were all captured. French forces occupied Morocco.

1903 The Pan-Islamic Society was founded in London by 'Abdullah Sharawardy.

1904 Morocco became a French protectorate.

1905 The *Salafiyya* movement began in Paris.

1906 The Persian constitution was promulgated.

1907 The Young Turks movement began in Turkey.

1912 The Muhammadiyya reform movement began in Indonesia.

1914 Under Ottoman rule, secret Arab nationalist societies were formed. World War I began.

1916 The Arabs announced their revolt against the Ottoman Islamic Empire at the instigation of the British who promised the Arabs an Arab Kingdom. The Arab revolt against Ottoman (Turkish) rule began. The Sykes-Picot Agreement divided the Middle East into Russian, British, and French spheres of influence.

1917 The British government issued the Balfour Declaration, which stated that Palestine would be a homeland for the Jews. Lawrence of Arabia led attacks on the Hijaz Railway.

1918 The British and their Arab nationalist allies defeated the Ottomans. The British dismembered the Ottoman Empire and occupied Palestine. They immediately began a campaign of letting European Jews immigrate to Palestine. 30 October, the armistice with the Ottomans was signed. 11 November, World War I ended. Syria became a French protectorate.

1921 'Abd Allah Bin Husayn was made King of Transjordan. Faysal Bin Husayn was made King of Iraq.

1922 Mustafa Kemal abolished the Turkish Sultanate.

1923 29 October, the Republic of Turkey was proclaimed, and Mustafa Kemal was elected the first President of the Republic.

1924 The Ottoman Caliphate was abolished. 'Abd al-'Aziz Ibn Saud conquered Mecca and Medina and unified Najd and Hijaz.

1925 Reza Khan seized the government in Persia and established the Pahlavi dynasty. Badi' al-Zaman Sa'id al-Nursi was arrested and exiled to a remote village in Turkey.

1926 'Abd al-'Aziz Ibn Saud assumed the title of King of Hijaz.

1927 'Abd al-'Aziz Ibn Saud assumed the title of King of both Najd and Hijaz. Sa'd Zaghlul, an Egyptian nationalist leader, died. *Jam'iyyat al-Shubban al-Muslimin* was founded in Egypt.

1928 Turkey was declared a secular state. Hasan al-Banna founded the Muslim Brotherhood in Egypt.

1932 Iraq was granted independence by the League of Nations.

1934 The war between King 'Abd al-'Aziz Ibn Saud and Imam Yahya of Yemen took place.

1935 The Muslim Brotherhood in Syria emerged when Syrian students returned from Egypt and established branches in different cities. The secret apparatus of the Muslim Brotherhood in Egypt was set up.

1936 Increased Jewish immigration provoked widespread Arab-Jewish fighting in Palestine. The Muslim Women's Association, a branch of the Muslim Brotherhood, was set up in Egypt.

1939 World War II began.

1940 The Warriors of Islam Society was founded in Iran.

1941 British and Russian forces invaded Iran and Reza Shah Pahlavi (Reza Khan) was forced to abdicate in favor of his son Muhammad Reza Shah in Iran. Mustapha al-Siba'i founded Muhammad's Youth in Syria.

1943 The violent Zionist campaign in Palestine began.

1945 World War II ended.

1946 Jordan, Lebanon, and Syria were granted independence from Britain and France. The Muslim Brotherhood in Jordan was established. The

Muslim Brotherhood in Palestine was established. The Muslim Brotherhood in Syria became public. The Islamic Liberation Movement in Sudan was established.

1947 Pakistan was founded from the Muslim majority area in India.

1948 Israel was founded. Arab armies were defeated in the war with Israel. Hundreds of thousands of Palestinians were forced out of Palestine under the military pressure of Jewish militant groups such as the Irgun, Levi, and Haganot. The first conference of the Islamic International was held by the Muslim Brotherhood in Mecca during the pilgrimage.

1949 Hasan al-Banna, the leader of the Muslim Brotherhood, was assassinated.

1951 Libya became an independent state. August, the Islamic Democratic Party was established in Turkey by Cevat Rifat Atilhan. A Pan-Islamic congress was held in Karachi.

1952 King Faruq of Egypt was forced to abdicate. The nationalist revolution of the Free officers, led by Colonel Jamal 'Abd al-Nasir, took place. *'Ibad al-Rahman* in Lebanon went public. *Hizb al-Tahrir al-Islami* was established in Palestine by Taqiy al-Din al-Nabahani.

1953 King 'Abd al-'Aziz Ibn Saud Arabia died. The CIA sponsored, through General Zahedi, a military coup against Dr. Muhammad Musaddaq and brought back the Shah of Iran. A Pan-Islamic congress was held in Jerusalem.

1954 An attempt on 'Abd al-Nasir's life while he was speaking to a crowd in Alexandria led to the arrest of hundreds of Muslim Brethren. The Muslim Brotherhood in Egypt was dissolved and went underground. The war of liberation against the French began in Algeria.

1956 *Jam'iyyat al-'Ulama' al-Muslimin* in Algeria was dissolved. Morocco became independent. Tunisia became independent.

1957 The Bey of Tunisia was deposed, and Habib Bourguiba became president. A Pan-Islamic congress was held in Lahore, Pakistan.

1958 14 July, General Karim Kasim led a coup against King Faysal II and the premier, Nuri al-Sa'id, who were killed, and Iraq became a republic. A Muslim uprising in Lebanon ended when American marines landed in Beirut.

1960   The Liberation Movement of Iran was founded by Mahdi Bazargan and Mahmud Talqani.

1962   Algeria became independent. Zaydi Imam of Yemen Ahmad died. Crown Prince Bahr succeeded him and took the title Imam Mansur Bi Allah Muhammad.

1964   The Islamic Action Organization was founded in Karbala', Iraq. Ayatollah Khomeini was deported from Iran. The Muslim Women's Association in Egypt was dissolved. *Al-Jama'a al-Islamiyya* in Lebanon was established by Fathi Yakan and others. The Islamic Charter Front in Sudan was established by Hasan al-Turabi.

1965   *Mujahidin Khalq* was founded in Iran. *Hizbullah* in Yemen was founded by Muhammad al-Zubayri, who was killed the same year.

1966   Sayyid Qutb, along with others, was executed in Egypt.

1967   The Democratic Constitutional Popular Movement in Morocco was founded in 1967 by 'Abd al-Karim al-Khatib. 5–11 June, in a war with Arab armies of Egypt, Jordan, and Syria, Israel seized control of West Bank and Gaza, as well as East Jerusalem, Sinai, and the Golan Heights.

1968   *Hizb al-Da'wa al-Islamiyya* was set up in Iraq. Israeli commandos blew up 13 airliners at Beirut International Airport. Israel justified the attack as a reprisal for an attack in Athens by Palestinian guerrillas. PLO members hijacked an Israeli (El Al) National Airliner. The International Islamic Union for Student Organizations was set up during the pilgrimage to Mecca.

1969   29 August, the flight of TWA 840 from Israel to Italy was hijacked. King Idris of Libya was overthrown by a coup led by Colonel Mu'ammar Qaddafi. The Islamic Youth Organization was founded in Morocco by 'Abd al-Karim Muti'. *Jama'at al-Muslimin*, or *al-Takfir wa al-Hijra,* was founded in Egypt by Shukri Mustapha.

1970   Egypt's President Jamal 'Abd al-Nasr died. *Jam'iyyat al-Hifadh 'ala al-Qur'an* in Tunisia came into existence. *Milli Nizam Partisi* was founded in Turkey by Necmettin Erbakan. *Mujahidin* Movement in Morocco was established by 'Abd al-'Aziz al-Na'mani. 16 September, five airliners were hijacked by five groups of PLO hijackers.

1971   Zaynab al-Ghazali was freed by President Anwar al-Sadat.

1972   *Milli Nizam Partisi* was dissolved in Turkey. *Milli Selamet Partisi* was founded by Necmettin Erbakan. 9 April, the Munich Massacre was carried out; the attack took place at the Olympic village.

1973 King Zahir Shah of Afghanistan was overthrown. The war between the Arab states and Israel took place. April, Israeli elite troops entered Beirut flats and shot dead three Palestinian guerrilla officials.

1974 Salih Sirriyya, the leader of *Tanzim al-Fanniyya al-'Askariyya*, was executed.

1976 Marwan Hadid, the leader of the Fighting Vanguards in Syria, was captured in Damascus. *Hizb al-Tahrir al-Islami* was banned in Jordan. April, a cease-fire was forced upon the two warring Lebanese sides when Syrian military forces intervened at the request of the Lebanese president, Suleiman Franjieh, and with the approval of the Arab League. 6 June, Air France flight 139 was hijacked by a PLO faction. Israeli commandos stormed the plane at Entebbe airport, Uganda, and all hijackers were killed.

1977 *Al-Jabha al-Qawmiyya al-Islamiyya* (the National Islamic Front) was founded in Sudan by Hasan al-Turabi. *Jama'at al-Muslimin* in Egypt kidnapped and killed a former *Awqaf* Minister, Mahmud al-Dhahabi. Shukri Mustapha, the leader of *Jama'at al-Muslimin*, was put to death in Egypt. Ali Shari'ati, the Iranian thinker, was found dead in England.

1978 Imam Musa al-Sadr, the leader of the Lebanese *Amal*, was apparently assassinated after he disappeared on a trip to Libya. January, an uprising in Qom, Iran, erupted to protest the publication of an article in a national daily insulting Ayatollah Khomeini. In February, demonstrations and rioting in Tabriz marked the 40th day of the Qom uprising. August, after demonstrations in Isfahan, and following the spread of national protests, the government of Amoozegar resigned and Sharif-Imami took office. September, *Eid al-Fitr* prayers turned into protests against the government; a large number of demonstrators were killed by army forces in Tehran, and the day became known as bloody Friday. October, Imam Khomeini decided to leave Iraq following the Iraqi government's prohibition of his political activities. He left for Kuwait first, but when refused an entry visa he resided temporarily in France; a number of political prisoners, including Ayatollah Muntazari and Taleqani, were released from prison. November, the students' demonstration in Tehran was violently suppressed by the military; a number of government buildings were set on fire in Tehran in the course of riots. The government of Sharif-Imami collapsed and the military government of General Az'hari took over. March, more than 30 bus riders were killed by Palestinian guerrillas near Tel Aviv; Israel attacked PLO positions in south Lebanon and occupied a 10 km-wide strip north of the Lebanese border. About 1,500 people were killed, mostly Lebanese and Palestinian civilians. UN Security Council resolution 425 stipulated the withdrawal of the Israeli forces. The United Nations set up UNIFIL, a 5,000-strong peace-keeping force to help restore Lebanese state authority. 17 September, the Camp David Accords established peace between Egypt and Israel; Israel agreed in principle to Palestinian autonomy in the West Bank and Gaza Strip.

1979   The Egyptian-Israeli Peace Accords were signed. The Islamic Front for the Liberation of Bahrain was founded by Hadi al-Mudarrasi. *Jama'at al-Jihad al-Islami* was founded by Muhammad 'Abd al-Salam Faraj in Egypt. Iraqi President Ahmad Hasan al-Bakr transferred power to Saddam Hussein. January, the Az'hari government collapsed and the Shah appointed Shapour Bakhtiar to form a government. Imam Khomeini announced the formation of the Council of the Islamic Revolution. 15 January, the Shah left Iran. February, Imam Khomeini arrived in Tehran to an unparalleled popular reception; he appointed Mehdi Bazargan as the head of his provisional government. The army surrendered to the revolutionary forces, the government of Bakhtiar fell, and the provisional government took office. The Islamic Republican Party was created. The majority of Iranians voted in favor of an Islamic Republic as opposed to the monarchy in a two-way referendum. 14 February, the U.S. Embassy in Tehran was seized by a group of Islamic student revolutionaries who took American hostages for 444 days. May, Ayatollah Mutahhari, then head of the Council of the Islamic Revolution, was assassinated. December, the draft constitution was endorsed in a referendum approved by Imam Khomeini. The Muslim People's Republican Party was founded in Iran by supporters of Ayatollah Muhammad Shari'atmadari. 21 November, militants led by students of the Theological University of Medina attempted to promote one of their group as Mahdi. They held the Haram of Mecca against the army for two weeks. Sixty-three of the 300 militants were captured alive, the mosque was recovered, and the conspirators were all put to death.

1980   Muhammad Baqir al-Sadr, the leader of *Hizb al-Da'wa al-Islami-yya*, and his sister were executed in Iraq. The Israelis attacked an Iraqi nuclear reactor. The Iran-Iraq war began. The Muslim People's Republican Party was closed down in Iran, and Ayatollah Muhammad Shari'atmadari was put under house arrest and was stripped of his titles. *Al-Jihad al-Islami* in the West bank and Gaza Strip was officially set up by Fathi al-Shiqaqi.

January, the first presidential election in Iran was held. Abu-Hasan Bani Sadr was elected. March, the general election for the first Islamic *Majlis* (parliament) was held. April, the bilateral relations with the United States were broken off. May, a Cultural Revolution was initiated, which led to the closure of all the universities and other higher education institutes for two years. December, the occupation of the United States Embassy came to an end, and the hostages were released after 444 days.

1981   Rashid al-Ghannushi, the leader of *Harakat al-Itijah al-Islami* in Tunisia, was arrested and sentenced to 10 years in prison but freed in 1984 by a presidential pardon. June, following a vote of the Islamic *Majlis*, Imam Khomeini dismissed Bani Sadr from the presidency. More than 70 politicians, including the highly influential Ayatollah Bahishti, were assassinated in a massive explosion at the headquarters of the Islamic Republican Party. The *Mujahidin Khalq* Organization claimed responsibility. July, Muhammad Ali Rajaie was elected President. August, Rajaie and Prime Minister Bahonar were assassinated in a massive explosion in the Prime Minister's office during a National Security Council meeting; the *Mujahidin Khalq* claimed responsibility. Bani Sadr escaped to France. October, the third presidential election was held and Ali Khamene'i was elected president. June, *Harakat al-Itijah al-Islami* in Tunisia came into existence and 93 of its members were arrested. 6 October, an army lieutenant, Khalid Islambuli, led a group of soldiers who assassinated President Anwar al-Sadat during a military parade. *Milli Selamet Partisi* was banned by the military regime in Turkey.

1982   Syrian forces suppressed the Islamist rebellion in Hama. The Islamic Movement for Algeria was set up by Mustapha Buya'li. The Iranian Foreign Minister, Sadiq Qutbzadah, was executed. During the Israeli invasion of Lebanon, a compound in Beirut where U.S. marines were housed was blown up by Muslim militants, killing over 200 marines. The Muslim Scholars' Association was set up during the Israeli invasion. *Harakat al-Tawhid al-Islami* in Lebanon was set up by Sa'id Sha'ban. April, the Iraqi forces retreated from large parts of the occupied territories of Iran, and the Iranians recaptured the port town of Khorramshahr. June, *Harakat Amal al-Islamiyya* in Lebanon came into existence. July, Israel invaded Lebanon with the declared aim of routing Palestinian guerrillas. The justification for that was the Palestinian attack that wounded the Israeli ambassador in London. After bitter fighting, PLO militiamen agreed to leave Beirut. September, Israeli forces stormed west Beirut after pro-Israeli Christian leader Bashir Gemayel, who was just elected president, was assassinated. Israeli troops ringing the Palestinian refugee camps of Sabra and Shatila allowed Christian militiamen into the camps. Over 1,500 refugees were slaughtered, and Israel was widely condemned.

1983 Syria crushed its Islamic fundamentalists in the *Hama* uprising. Around 20,000 people were killed. Earlier, fighters from the Muslim Brotherhood attacked a military training school in Aleppo and slaughtered a few young officers. In retaliation, the government killed hundreds of Islamist prisoners. May, the Tudeh party in Iran was outlawed. October, Yitzhak Shamir became Israel's new Prime Minister. 23 October, after 300 U.S. and French troops were killed, the Western forces pulled out of Lebanon. Factional fighting persisted and Westerners in Beirut became the targets of radical Shi'ite militants.

1985 *Hizbullah* in Lebanon was officially set up. Shi'ite militants hijacked a TWA airliner and forced it to land at Beirut International Airport. One U.S. navy sailor was killed. August, President Khamene'i was reelected in Iran for a second four-year term. November, the second Council of Experts selected Ayatollah Muntazari as Khomeini's successor.

1986 February, 39 passengers of a civilian Iranian aircraft, including several members of *Majlis*, were killed in an attack by an Iraqi fighter jet.

1987 Prime Minister Bin 'Ali overthrew President Bourguiba of Tunisia and released 608 prisoners, including Rashid al-Ghannushi, the leader of the Islamic Renaissance Movement (*Harakat al-Itijah al-Islami*). U.S. forces captured and sank an Iranian amphibious ship laying mines north of Bahrain, and U.S. ships bombarded an Iranian oil platform in the Gulf. Mustapha Buya'li, the leader of the Islamic Movement for Algeria who set up the Armed Islamic Movement, was killed. June, President Khamene'i and Speaker Rafsanjani, two prominent council members of the Islamic Republican Party, requested and obtained from Imam Khomeini the approval to dissolve the party. July, nearly 400 Iranian pilgrims were killed by Saudi security forces. 9 December, the Palestinians began an uprising (*Intifada*) that lasted for five years in the West Bank and Gaza Strip against Israeli occupation.

1988 The Islamic Salvation Front in Algeria was set up by Abbasi Madani, 'Ali Bilhaj, and others. The National Islamic Front was founded in Sudan by Hasan al-Turabi. March, Tehran was hit by Iraqi missiles for the first time during the war. The devastating missile attacks lasted for two months. August, a cease-fire was declared after eight years of war between

Iran and Iraq. 13 July, the American fleet's USS *Vincennes* blew up a civilian Iranian plane, Iran Air's Flight 655, killing all 290 passengers. 15 November, PLO Chairman Yasir Arafat proclaimed a Palestinian state.

1989 Ahmad Yasin, the leader of *Hamas* in Palestine, was arrested by Israeli forces. In 1991, he was sentenced to life imprisonment. Iran-Iraq war came officially to an end. *Harakat al-Itijah al-Islami* in Tunisia became *Harakat al-Nahda al-Islamiyya*. In the elections, it won between 14 and 30 percent of the vote, but the government cracked down on the movement. Between 1990 and 1992, the movement was dissolved. Shaykh 'Abd al-Salam Yasin was put under house arrest in Morocco. The Lebanese parliament accepted an Arab-brokered peace accord for national reconciliation in al-Ta'if. The parliament elected Rene Mu'awad as President, and he was assassinated 17 days later. The Islamist bloc in Jordan won 34 out of 80 seats in the country's first parliamentary elections held in a generation. The bloc lost some seats in the 1993 elections, when the Islamic Action Front won only 16 seats. In Sudan, a group of army officers, led by General 'Umar al-Bashir, seized power and ended three years of democracy and an elected parliament. Behind al-Bashir was the Islamic Salvation Front, led by Hasan al-Turabi. February, Imam Khomeini issued his *fatwa* (a decree) for a death sentence on Salman Rushdie, author of the *Satanic Verses*. March, Ayatollah Muntazari resigned his post as leader-designate and Imam Khomeini accepted his resignation. 4 June, the Council of Experts selected 'Ali Khamene'i to be the new leader of the Islamic Revolution after the death of Khomeini. Khomeini died, and Khamene'i became the leader of the Islamic Republic. July, 'Ali Akbar Rafsanjani was elected the fourth President of the Islamic Republic.

1990 Morocco's *Jama'at al-'Adl wa al-Ihsan* was dissolved by the government, and its leader 'Abd al-Salam Yasin was held under house arrest for six years. The Islamic Action Party was declared after the unification of Yemen by Ibrahim al-Wazir. 2 August, Iraqi forces invaded Kuwait. The United Nations Security Council passed resolution UNSC 660 condemning the invasion and demanding the immediate and unconditional withdrawal of Iraqi troops from Kuwait. Syrian, Moroccan, and Egyptian forces arrived in Saudi Arabia. Pakistan announced it had agreed to send troops to Saudi Arabia. 10 August, an Emergency Arab Summit meeting in Cairo voted to send Arab troops to Saudi Arabia and other Persian Gulf states to assist in defending them against possible Iraqi attack. Saudi religious scholars leading the Islamic revivalist movement, including Shaykhs Safar al-Howali and Salman al-Oda, rejected the official *'ulama*'s *fatwa* over the necessity to resort to employing non-Muslims to defend Arabia against an Iraqi threat created by the Americans themselves. 7 November, a women's demonstration takes place in Riyadh, supposedly organized in protest against their being banned from driving. The regime cracked down on the opposition to American assistance and permanent military presence in Saudi Arabia. 29 November, United Nations Security Council approved a resolution, UNSC 678, authorizing use of "all necessary means" to force Iraq from Kuwait if Iraq would not withdraw by 15 January 1991. September, *Hizb al-Tajammu' al-Yemeni li al-Islah* was established in Yemen by 'Abd Allah al-Ahmar. November, the Islamic Society Movement (*Hamas*) was founded in Algeria by Mahfoudh al-Nahnah. *Jama'at al-Nahda al-Islamiyya* in Algeria was founded by 'Abd Allah Jaballah.

1991 Abbasi Madani and 'Ali Bilhaj, the two leaders of the Islamic Salvation Front in Algeria, were arrested and tried by a military court and sentenced to 12 years in prison. A cease-fire in Western Sahara took place, and a UN referendum originally scheduled to take place a year later was postponed indefinitely. The Polisario Front threatened to go to war. The first congress of the Islamic International, organized by Hasan al-Turabi, was held in Khartoum. 16 January, the international coalition began air attacks on Iraqi targets. The Gulf War began and lasted for six weeks. 23 February, Coalition forces began a ground attack against Iraqi forces, after Iraq's offer on 15 February to withdraw from Kuwait was rejected by Coalition forces. 27–28 February, Iraq observed the cease-fire and accepted most coalition terms for a formal cease-fire. Coalition forces announced that Kuwait was liberated. President Bush announced a suspension of military operations at midnight on February 27. 30 October–1 November, the Middle East peace process was launched at the Madrid conference convened by the United States and the former Soviet Union, with Palestinian delegation confined to residents of Israeli-occupied territories, excluding the PLO from formal participation. November, a group of Islamist gunmen attacked Japanese tourists at Luxor.

1992 Iranian Culture and Guidance Minister Muhammad Khatami resigned. Iraq was accused of possessing weapons of mass destruction, and intense international pressure to eliminate them was brought to bear, in the shape of UN economic sanctions. With the help of Syria, the Lebanese army took control of Beirut, and under pressure from Iran and the United States, all the foreign hostages captured several years earlier were released. Rashid al-Ghannushi, the leader of *Harakat al-Nahda al-Islamiyya* in Tunisia, was sentenced to death. *Hizb Jabhat al-'Amal al-Islami* in Jordan was established. 11 January, Algeria's first free elections were canceled when it became apparent that the Islamic Salvation Front, Algeria's Islamic fundamentalist party, was expected to win. February, Israeli helicopter gunships rocketed the car of *Hizbullah* leader Shaykh 'Abbas al-Musawi, killing him, his wife, and his son. Rocket attacks into northern Israel followed, then Israeli forces stormed two villages north of the occupation zone. 23 June, Yitzhak Rabin's Labor coalition took control of Israeli government after winning the parliamentary elections on a platform that included negotiating self-rule with Palestinians.

1993 *Hizb Jabhat al-'Amal al-Islami* in Jordan won 16, or about one third, of all parliamentary seats. Hamid Nasr Abu Zayd was taken to court on charges of apostasy in Egypt. In 1994, his marriage was annulled but was later reinstituted. The Security Council voted to maintain the sanctions, despite attempts by Iraq to have them lifted. Yemen's *Hizb al-Tajammu' al-Yemeni li al-Islah* won 62 seats out of 301 in parliamentary elections and gained six cabinet posts. Iranian President Rafsanjani was reelected for a second term. The third congress of the Islamic International was held in Khartoum and was attended by 80 states. An explosion occurred at the World Trade Center in New York. 25 February, a suicide bombing of a bus in Jerusalem occurred. July, Israel unleashed "Operation Accountability," a week-long air, artillery, and naval bombardment in which 130 people, mostly Lebanese civilians, died, and 300,000 fled their homes. This was in response to the killing of seven Israeli soldiers by the *Hizbullah* resistance. 13 September, Israel and the PLO signed the Declaration of Principles on Interim Self-Government Arrangements outlining a plan for Palestinian self-rule in the occupied territories; PLO chairman Yasir Arafat and Israeli Prime Minister Yitzhak Rabin shook hands at a White House ceremony. 14 September, Israel and Jordan signed a substantive Common Agenda mapping out their approach to achieving peace. 1 October, the Conference to Support Middle East Peace was held in Washington, D.C.

1994 25 February, a Jewish settler killed 29 Palestinians who were praying at a Hebron mosque. The Gaza-Jericho talks stalled for five weeks as negotiators argued over Palestinian security in Hebron. April, violent attacks were carried out by *Hamas* in Afula and Hadera that preceded the signing by Israel and the PLO of the Cairo agreement. The attacks were also claimed to revenge the Hebron massacre of 29 people. 29 April, the Israel-PLO economic agreement was signed in Paris. 4 May, in Cairo, Prime Minister Rabin and Chairman Arafat signed the Agreement on the Gaza Strip and the Jericho Area. 13 May, Israel handed over Jericho to the Palestinians. 1 July, Arafat returned to the newly autonomous Gaza after more than a quarter century of Israeli occupation and took over as head of the Palestinian Authority. 13 April, Ahmad Ramzi Yusuf was convicted in the World Trade Center bombing in New York. 25 July, President Bill Clinton hosted a meeting between King Hussein and Prime Minister Rabin at the White House, which culminated in the signing of the Washington Declaration. 17 October, Israeli Prime Minister Rabin and Jordanian Prime Minister Majali initialed the text of a peace treaty. 18 October, some *Hamas* followers fired at Palestinian police near the Palestine Mosque in Gaza after the police had confiscated megaphones from them. Sixteen persons were killed and about 200 wounded. 26 October, Israel and Jordan signed a peace treaty in a ceremony at their border attended by U.S. President Bill Clinton. November, Islamists opposed King Hussein's policy of having peace with Israel. When the treaty was signed, they organized a march of 5,000 people at the center of the capital, Amman.

1995 The Syrian government released about 1,200 political prisoners, including leaders of the Muslim Brotherhood. The leader of the movement, 'Abd al-Fattah Abu Ghudda, returned from exile. Food riots took place in Morocco. The Supporters of Muhammadan *Sunna* in Sudan killed 16 people at a mosque in Um Durman. An assassination attempt on Egypt's President Hosni Mubarak took place in Ethiopia by Islamists who slipped away into Sudan. 25 July, Musa Abu Marzuq, head of the *Hamas's* political office, was arrested in the United States. August, violent attacks were perpetrated in Jerusalem. Disagreements over tactics evolved between *Hamas's* political leadership in the Territories and members of *'Izz a-Din al-Qassam.* 24 September, PLO Chairman Arafat and Israeli Foreign Minister Shimon Peres reached an agreement on details for implementing self-rule in most Palestinian-populated areas of the West Bank. 28 September, President Clinton hosted a White House ceremony for Israel and the Palestinians to sign the Interim Agreement on the West Bank and Gaza Strip, as provided for in the Declaration of Principles. 15 October, Saddam Hussein was reelected to another seven-year term as President of Iraq. 4 November, Prime Minister Rabin was assassinated as he was leaving a peace rally in Tel Aviv. A 23-year-old Jew, Yigal Amir, was arrested for the crime and, later, sentenced to life imprisonment. December, *Refah Partisi* in Turkey won 21 percent of the vote and gained more seats than any other party for parliament.

1996 *Hizb al-Da'wa al-Islamiyya* in Iraq claimed responsibility for the assassination attempt on Saddam Hussein's son, 'Uday. Necmettin Erbakan became prime minister of a coalition government led by the Islamists in Turkey. Riots in Tangier occurred, where hundreds of people set fire to one bank and ransacked another. The riot coincided with a general strike, which paralyzed much of the country's economic activity. Fathi al-Shiqaqi, the leader of *al-Jihad al-Islami*, was assassinated in Malta, allegedly by Israeli agents. Hasan al-Turabi, the leader of the Islamic Salvation Front in Sudan, became Speaker of the Parliament. 5 January, Yahya 'Ayyash, known as "the engineer," and the assumed mastermind behind several suicide bombings against Israel, was killed in the Gaza Strip when his cellular telephone blew up. The Islamist group *Hamas* threatened to avenge his death. 25 February, suspected Islamist bombers killed 26 people in separate attacks in Jerusalem and the southern town of Ashkelon. February–March, three extremely violent suicide attacks in Jerusalem by *Hamas* and in Tel Aviv by the Islamic *Jihad*, took place to avenge the 5 January killing of the *'Izz a-din al-Qassam*'s member, Yahya 'Ayyash. 23 February, Hussein and Saddam Kamel, Saddam's two sons-in-law who had taken asylum in Jordan in August 1995, returned to Baghdad on 20 February after receiving Iraqi government pardons. They were killed on 23 February. March, Muslim fundamentalists and leftist students clashed at Casablanca University of Law after 500 Islamist students interfered with a cultural show organized by a leftist group. March, 'Irfan Chiagharji, the leader of the Organization of the Islamic Movement in Turkey, was arrested. 11 April, Israel launched "Operation Grapes of Wrath." Between 160 and 170 Lebanese civilians were killed during the 16-day offensive, and over 350 were wounded. Fourteen *Hizbullah* fighters were killed. Estimates of the number of displaced civilians ranged from 300,000 to 500,000. The most violent event took place on 18 April when Israeli artillery shelled a UNIFIL compound near the village of Qana, where around 800 Lebanese civilians had taken shelter. Some 102 civilians were killed. 20 May, Iraq and the United Nations signed an "oil-for-food" deal, allowing Iraq to sell $2 billion worth of oil for food and medical supplies to be supplied to Iraqi civilians under UN supervision. 25 June, Islamic militants planted a bomb that killed 19 U.S. servicemen at al-Khobar Towers in Saudi Arabia. 15 August, an Egyptian military court sentenced civilians to prison for their attempt to form a political party, *al-Wasat*. The defendants in the *al-Wasat* Party case had all been arrested earlier on 3 April 1996, after a request to form a political party was presented to the Committee of Political Party Affairs on 16 January 1996. 3–4 September, U.S. military forces in the Persian Gulf region launched two missile attacks on Iraqi military and command positions in southern Iraq. Iraqi forces withdrew from Erbil. 12 September, the United States moved F-117A stealth bombers into position to prepare for possible air strikes against Iraq. Baghdad announced it had fired three missiles at allied planes.

1997   Abbasi Madani and 'Ali Bilhaj were released in Algeria. The Islamic Society Movement (*Hamas*), founded in Algeria by Mahfoudh Nahnah, became represented in the Parliament. 'Abd al-Fattah Abu Ghudda, the former leader of the Syrian Muslim Brotherhood, died in exile. Muhammad Khatami was elected as the new president of Iran, defeating the candidate of the religious right, Ali Akbar Natiq Nuri. Rafsanjani was appointed as the head of *Majlis Tashkhis Maslahat al-Nizam*. Ahmad Yasin, the leader of *Hamas*, was released from Israeli prisons in a deal between King Hussein and Israeli authorities after the Israeli attempt to assassinate Khalid Mash'al failed in Amman. *Jam'iyyat al-Islah* in Yemen lost all cabinet seats to the ruling party. 11 May, in Turkey's largest rally in decades, hundreds of thousands of people chanted verses from the Koran to protest the secular military's directives for closing Islamic schools. 26 May, Turkey's generals met with Prime Minister Necmettin Erbakan in a closed-door meeting and announced a purge of pro-Islamic officers from its ranks. 18 June, Necmettin Erbakan, the Islamist Turkish Prime Minister, resigned in response to threats by generals in the military to use force to overthrow the coalition government. 22–23 June, the first Arab Summit since 1990 was held. Iraq was the only Arab country that was excluded. 23 June, UNSC 1115 insisted on access to Iraqi sites. October, two brothers attacked a bus full of German tourists in Cairo, killing eight of them. 17 November, a group of Islamist gunmen attacked Japanese tourists at Luxor, one of Egypt's major tourist attractions on the Nile, killing 62 people.

1998   Subhi Tufayli, the former leader of *Hizbullah* in Lebanon, went underground after a military confrontation with the Lebanese army. Sa'id Sha'ban, the leader of *Harakat al-Tawhid al-Islami* in Lebanon, died. January, *Refah Partisi* in Turkey was dissolved by the Constitutional Court. January, Ahmad Ramzi Yusuf was sentenced to life imprisonment in the United States. 7 August, the bombings of the U.S. embassies in Nairobi, Kenya and Dar es Salaam, Tanzania, killed over 263 people and injured over five 5,000. Usama Bin Laden and Islamic *Jihad* were implicated in the bombings. 20 August, the United States avenged itself with two missile strikes. Over 75 Tomahawk cruise missiles were fired by U.S. vessels in the Red and Arabian Seas at two sites: Bin Laden's suspected military training and support camp, the Zhawar Kili al-Badr camp, 94 miles south of Kabul and near the Afghanistan-Pakistan border; al-Shifa pharmaceutical plant, northeast of Khartoum, Sudan, which was reportedly financed by Bin Laden to produce chemicals for the deadly VX nerve gas. The U.S. embassy in Khartoum was stormed by Sudanese militants.

Introduction

World War II constituted a turning point in the history of imperial Western powers that sought to dominate markets and raw materials. Oppression by the imperial powers led to nationalist and socialist orientations in the Third World. These imperial powers weakened the traditional and modernist Islamic responses while strengthening the secular but authoritarian responses. Egypt, which was under the British mandate, is a good example. Egyptians during that period were focusing on freeing their country from British colonial rule and were advocating democracy, whether secular or religious. However, the rise of Arab nationalism under Jamal 'Abd al-Nasir brought about secular and socialist authoritarian nationalism. The secular response was adopted, but democracy was rejected. Furthermore, while Jamal 'Abd al-Nasir accepted Islam as one of the three circles of Egyptian foreign policies, his acceptance did not amount in reality to more than lip service to Islam. Thus, the secular democratic response was aborted, and the Islamic modernist response was rejected.

In modern times, many Islamic movements that call for the return to the fundamentals of religion—hence the label fundamentalism—have flourished throughout the different regions of the Muslim world. These movements seem to be a continuation and development of the earlier Islamic response, or modernism, that was aborted. Leaders of such movements believed that the Islamic spiritual dimension could aid in developing a clear portrait of the enemy, condemn moral corruption, and mobilize Muslim societies. The contrast became brighter and sharper when the perceived corrupted present was contrasted with a perceived idealistic and glorious picture of a past full of ethical idealism. This ideal past is being used today to reactivate Muslims' energies to establish a new civilization, to reconstruct their identity, to absorb modernity, to revert their political subordination, and to achieve social justice.

In one way or another, and like any other intellectual and political product, the rise of Islamic fundamentalism must be located within a framework of educational, economic, political, and intellectual crises. That the reli-

1

gious and the political are interwoven and cannot be separated was upheld even by the *Khawarij* (seceders) in the seventh century. Similarly, and in modern times, the *Wahhabiyya*, following the great medieval thinker Ibn Taymiyya, has called for the purification of Islam by a return to the *usul* (fundamentals) of religion, that is, the Qur'an and the *Sunna* (way) of the Prophet. The movement followed a strict line of thinking in its attempts to reconstruct society and government on the basis of divine *tawhid* (oneness of God) and the doctrine of *al-salaf al-salih* (pious ancestors). Other important movements in modern times are *al-Sanusiyya* and *al-Mahdiyya*, which started as *sufi* (mystic) orders but were later transformed into political movements that struggled against Western intervention in Libya and the Sudan, respectively. The two perceived themselves as being movements of purification aiming at the restoration of genuine Islam and, thus, involving themselves in politics. Again, similar fundamental issues were raised and were looked at as the road to the salvation of the Islamic community.

At a more involved intellectual level, Jamal al-Din al-Afghani (1838–1897) stands out in terms of his intellectual and political influence as well as for setting forth a modern political agenda that is still more or less the essence of intellectual and political reform. At the intellectual level, he was ready to think over and adopt into Islamic thought any new intellectual, political, or scientific knowledge that could lead to the progress of the Islamic nation. On the political level, he was open and ready to adopt those Western institutions and systems that could serve the Islamic world and save it from crises. His follower and, later, colleague Muhammad 'Abdu (1849–1905) and Rashid Rida (1865–1935), the inspirer of Hasan al-Banna, were greatly affected by different aspects of his intellectual and political rigor. Whereas 'Abdu tilted more toward the modernist European aspect of al-Afghani's intellectual thought, Rida was more adamant about the necessity of returning to the fundamentals of religion to induce an intellectual revival and to develop new Islamic institutions for the establishment of an Islamic state. This would facilitate the renaissance of the *umma* (nation) and guarantee the ethical foundations of society.

Furthermore, both Muhammad Iqbal (1875–1938) and Abu A'la al-Mawdudi (1903–1979) have shown similar differences. Both tried to argue the traditions of Islam as they relate to knowledge and politics. However, through their attempts to reconceptualize the role of reason through *ijtihad* (reason and analogical deduction), al-Mawdudi, the founder of *Jama'at-i Islami* (Islamic Group) in Pakistan, was more puritanical in his call for the reestablishment of Islam as a whole on the purified roots of Islam and centered his efforts on establishing an Islamic state that could shoulder the implementation of Islam as a comprehensive way of life and a complete system. Iqbal, on the other hand, showed more liberal tendencies by trying to rework both Islamic tradition and Western modernity in his modernized system of Islam. For him, an Islamic state became of secondary importance when measured against the awesome intellectual task that Muslims must first undergo. Good politics for him was a by-product of a good intellectual edifice.

Like al-Mawdudi, the Egyptian Muslim Brotherhood, which had been greatly affected by Rida and al-Afghani, focused more on the political aspect of Islam for promoting a revival. It called for the dire need for the establishment of an Islamic state as the first important step in the implementation of the *Shari'a* (Islamic law). Although the Brotherhood focused its intellectual reinterpretation on returning to the fundamentals, it selectively accepted major Western political concepts, like constitutional rule and democracy, as necessary tools for overhauling the Islamic concept of state. However, the Brotherhood's extremely antagonistic dealings with the Egyptian government led some Brethren to splinter off under the leadership of Sayyid Qutb, who continued to uphold the need for the establishment of an Islamic state while, at the same time, rejecting any dealings or intellectual openness with the West or the secular Arab states.

Sayyid Qutb made the existence of an Islamic state an essential part of the creed. It was in fact, for him and his followers, the result of the community's submission to God on the basis of the *Shari'a*. It became representative of political and legal commitment to the *Shari'a* and was viewed as the basis of both social life and constitutional change. The absence of such basis removes any shred of legitimacy that the state may enjoy and brings it into *jahiliyya* (paganism). Ayatollah Khomeini, the leader of the Islamic Revolution of Iran, further restricted his concept of a legitimate Islamic government. He argued that although the *Shari'a* is the basis of government, it is only through the rule of the jurists that its existence is actualized. Within the Islamic world today, the mainstream fundamentalist movements in Algeria, Tunisia, Jordan, and Egypt follow al-Banna's discourse on the Islamic state, constitutional rule, and multi-party politics; radical Sunni movements follow that of Sayyid Qutb; and radical Shi'ite political movements follow that of Khomeini.

Tawhid has been developed by the fundamentalists as the cord that ties together all the doctrines of and views on politics, economics, ethics, theology, and all other aspects of life. Because God, as the Creator, is the source of every material and spiritual thing, the fundamentalists view him as the ultimate authority in political life as well. For the fundamentalists, man's theoretical, theological, and political submission should be directed only to God; and by this they go beyond the traditional theological submission as understood in the old, medieval, and modern history of Islam. In this sense, the fundamentalists could not but load this concept of *tawhid* with ultimate political significance. Thus, one can see why they insist on subordinating politics and political philosophy to the highest order of religious doctrines. This subordination has led to the confusion of religiosity with proper political behavior. The establishment of the state on the basis of God's governance (*hakimiyya*) becomes, therefore, a must for the legitimacy of any political regime.

The fundamentalists' rejection of the intellectual basis of Islamic modernism does not necessarily make their thought traditional. In fact, part of their criticism centers on the traditional establishment and its religious and political role. Traditional religious *'ulama'* (religious scholars) do not, according to fundamentalists, comprehend the true Qur'anic meaning because of their imitation of a defunct jurisprudence that is irrelevant to modern living and because of their complacency with political powers, which has led to the alienation of Islam from the populace. Also, the secular elites are criticized because of their marginalization of Islam from the administration of government. Thus, the rejection of both secular and religious elites makes the fundamentalists advocates of a new intellectual and political model that could lead to comprehending both religion and modernity in a new ethical and religious light. Although the fragility of Muslim civilization is underscored by al-Mawdudi, Qutb, and other thinkers, they believe that only an Islamic revival, not traditionalism, can be instrumental in the creation of an Islamic renaissance. Muslims must aim at founding a new science and philosophy to be developed from the essence of Islam. Otherwise there is no opportunity to recapture scientific and political supremacy.

Such a notion is very significant in the explication of the fundamentalist political projects, at both the theoretical and practical levels. Although the modernists' acceptance of the West led to their adoption of Western political theories, it precluded their claim to a new political theory and their ability to put forth the underpinnings for theory-building. Their attempts focused on the theoretical introduction of certain Western political doctrines, like democracy and republicanism, and on the practical exhortation of rulers to apply them. The nature of modernists' political thought was miscellaneously oriented and was developed for immediate political goals; it was not fully grounded in theoretical advancements. Even the modernists' criticism of traditionalism was not directed at traditions per se, but resulted from modernism's interpretation, which made it suitable to Western notions, especially on reading the harmonious nature of religion and science. History was not discredited as such but was used to show how the Muslims, through various states of their development, dealt with Islamic political powers, foreign political powers, and new scientific knowledge. One must keep in mind that the modernists themselves had no claim to any sort of theory-building but were very aware of the need to bring together the West and the East, both scientifically and religiously. This is why they did not shy away from adopting ideas from the West. The fact that they did not write a theory allowed the fundamentalists to use the adopted "Islamized" modernist notions to build their theory, such as the introduction of *shura* as democracy.

The fundamentalists in general see the Islamic and Western past and present disciplines of philosophy, jurisprudence, and theology as obsolete. From their point of view these disciplines were historically developed, and, as such, have no universal values. Though not aware of it—and probably they would reject such a "charge"—the fundamentalists are indirect historicists; for almost all old, medieval, and even modern interpretations are viewed as nothing more than social, and at times corrupt, readings of the religious text or the imposition of different meanings suitable to a multitude of readers into the religious text. The true meaning of the text is known only by the author, or God. The reader, any reader, cannot make a claim to have developed a universal reading of that text. Fundamentalists look at the divergent readings as the outcomes of a complex set of conditions that make a reader interpret a text in one way or another. Divergences of theological, juridical, philosophical and political schools and sects are the products of specific ways of living that may not necessarily fit contemporary societies and problems. Put differently, what is more important than the logic of a reading or its formal truth is its relevance to the conditions of the reading itself and its pragmatic aftermath. Qutb and other fundamentalists transmute their rejection of historical readings into the legitimacy of new readings that are relevant to the problems of this age. In general, the fundamentalists have produced a multitude of readings whose essential discourse converges on intellectual and political transformation that could be either moderate or radical. These readings are combining a number of doctrines in a new religious framework—explained below.

LEGISLATION

The fundamentalists' collective dismissal of historical readings has moved the fundamentalists from being just a political movement that aims at change through imposing some ideological orientations to a movement that must find alternative religious, political, and intellectual readings to traditional and modernist Islam and Western readings. Their alternative readings have been centered around the discourse on *tawhid* and *hakimiyya*. The fundamentalists view God as being not only the source of legislation but also the focus of establishing a new society that aims at obedience to Him. Thus, emphasizing the need to link even civic ethics to obedience to God follows suit; *tawhid* is not only the liberation of men from the need to submit to mundane laws and institutions, it is at the center of the formation of ethical and moral systems as well as those political institutions that serve the systems.

Because the fundamentalists believe that the moral and ethical systems are legislated by the divine, they argue that man cannot impose new ethical and moral doctrines on others. The Muslim society must follow the intuitive moral system in light of the universal divine Qur'anic norms. These norms are not humanly derived; and their application does not constitute an imposition on human nature. They are necessary for the well-being of man and for avoiding human misery. For the fundamentalists, Islamic *Shari'a* is not a social phenomenon but an eternal divine manifestation that postulates the duties and rights of individuals, society, and the state. Thus, legislating the basic principles of government, morality, and legality is sealed off from human calculation. However, this comprehensive, yet flexible, *Shari'a* is designed to suit all ages and societies; man's task is to codify from—or read into—it general principles that are appropriate for his life and society.

For the fundamentalists, any legal, political, or even personal deviation from *tawhid* is a violation of true Islam. Sovereignty in a strict sense and in a general sense belongs only to God and not to the individual. Radical fundamentalism considers any kind of submission to human, social, political, or individual pressures as *shirk* (polytheism) and *kufr* (unbelief). Human programs and systems must not contradict divine textual ordinances. Because divine sovereignty covers the mundane and the sublime, its implication is mostly related to politics, because it orders man's and society's life. The law of God is meaningful not only in terms of the afterlife but more equally in terms of the concrete life on earth. The law penetrates both the human conscience and, more significantly, man's political identity. Although the concern for the next life is part of religion, earthly existence is as important, because it is the bridge between the profane and the sacred. For the fundamentalists, the goal of *Shari'a* is to sanctify what is profane so that the duality between the other life and this life is, at least, softened and, at best, terminated. Consequently, human will must be consumed in the divine will, an act that makes the human will an expression of the divine, and, consequently, turns man's political actions and systems into divine actions and systems. The individual is capable only in this way of evaluating other's behaviors and thought.

REVOLUTION

Although the modernists reject numerous medieval Islamic theories of Islam, they are not theoretically antagonistic to Western principles and theories and do not pinpoint any basic inherent animosity between Islam and the West. This is why they had no hesitation in adopting Western political and scientific theories; al-Afghani, 'Abdu, and Iqbal, as well as some moderate fundamentalists, have no theoretical problem in accepting, for instance, republican democratic forms of government.

But to the radical fundamentalists, *tawhid* denies the theoretical and practical aspect of dialogue and compromise. For the radicals, *tawhid* is a revolution against all sorts of formal or informal entities that claim any authoritative or normative role; any such claim is considered to be an infringement on the divinity of God. Thus, for instance, a legislature that makes laws in its own name is seizing God's divine authority of legislation and therefore loses its legitimacy and should be changed. But such a change would be no less than a revolution against the system that produced the legislature, and should be turned into a conscious transformation of all social and political institutions. No local, regional or international institution has the right to disrupt or put obstacles to the development of a Muslim society or an Islamic state. The responsibility of developing a Muslim society or an Islamic state is universal. Therefore, the fundamentalists entertain no compromise on this issue. According to the radicals, compromise denies the possibility of a new reconstruction of the world and leads Muslims to give up some principles and to accommodate others. Thus, radical fundamentalists link theoretically radical change to creativity on the assumption that the old cannot be renovated, and, thus, must be destroyed.

Such a radical change, or revolution, requires for radical fundamentalists the transformation of the positive force of *tawhid* to a movement of realistic and active propagation that is ready to challenge, nationally, regionally, and internationally all sorts of powers, systems, ideologies, and philosophies. The foremost material obstacle is the governments and societies of the world. Therefore, an Islamic revolution must be set up in order to abolish the regimes that are essentially based on the government of man over man or simply *jahiliyya* (paganism). Individuals must be liberated from the shackles of the present and the past and given the choice for a new life. A new life, however, cannot be achieved without providing a new Islamic context within which the individual has a real choice to follow Islam or not.

CONSENSUS

The untraditional and revolutionary interpretations employed by the fundamentalists are more apparent when one studies their understanding of a major political doctrine, consensus *(ijma')*. Consensus, whose historical employment was theoretical in matters of jurisprudence and theology, is viewed by the fundamentalists as the source of political life. Whereas it has been traditionally used to arrive at one Qur'anic reading or another and has been relegated to the scholarly elites as means of convincing the community to follow one interpretation or another, now the fundamentalists view concensus as a source of freeing the community not only from the conservative traditional readings of scholars but, more importantly, also from the tyranny of both the rulers and political traditions. Thus, all fields of Islamic sciences and other aspects of life become the proper interest of ordinary Muslims and subject to their approval. No legitimate legal or political principles can be imposed on the community without its consent. The historically derived normative status of the scholars and of political authority is denied and replaced by a need for a continuous process of ratification and agreement by the community; no political leader or religious scholar has the right to impose his will on the people.

For the fundamentalists, such an act of reinterpretation relieves consensus from misuse and makes it a political tool used to evaluate the level of the Islamicity of the state rather than a tool to control the heretic views of the community. By freeing consensus from its historical limitations, the fundamentalists have opened the door to use it as a device to measure political behavior. This also leads to the need for communal involvement in political matters. Now it is only the community that can speak with authoritative voice; individuals have only opinions. The right to structure political institutions, to evaluate behavior, or to interpret the scripture is also communal. Equality in terms of rights and duties is postulated as a necessary condition for proper political behavior. This is why most moderate fundamentalists make a popular consensus a necessary condition for electing a legitimate Muslim ruler; and any ruler who comes to power without popular approval even while upholding the Islamic law is not legitimate. This view is opposite to the traditional notion of accepting any seizure of power out of fear that civil strife might break out. The fundamentalists believe that God's delegation of authority is embedded in the vicegerency of mankind, and is not bestowed on particular scholars, classes, or rulers. Therefore, any seizure of power cannot be legitimately justified.

According to most Sunni fundamentalists, the rule of Islam is by no means a theocracy but is the rule of Islamic law, however vaguely defined. They argue against the legitimate existence of a specific group that can be called clergy; such people are only scholars. Proper Islamic political rule is the systematic rule of Islam where Islamic ideas govern and where Islamic regulations define the forms of government and society. Thus, the inherent authority of the clergy is denied by all Sunni fundamentalists. Therefore, to describe the proper Islamic government as a theocracy is a misnomer, because doing so gives the wrong impression about the essence and manifestations of Islam. Neither theory nor practice lends credibility to the theocracy of Islam. However, the Shi'ite brand of Islamic fundamentalism as advocated by Ayatollah Khomeini may, more appropriately, be called theocratic. Khomeini advocates in his *Islamic Government* the legitimate rule of only the jurists, because a proper Islamic government must be based on jurisprudence and therefore must be supervised by jurists.

However, the majority of the fundamentalists rule out the need for the government of a specific group in order to bestow legitimacy on Islamic government. The government's authority springs from its adherence to divine governance and the execution of the *Shari'a*. Although for both Khomeini and Qutb the *Shari'a* forms the basis of government, Qutb views the right to rule as a matter of delegation from the people, whereas Khomeini views it as delegation, directly and indirectly, from the *Imam*.

Although the fundamentalists converge ideologically on many issues, there are still many differences, basic and essential. Generally speaking, the real issue and the decisive element in distinguishing radical fundamentalism from moderate fundamentalism revolves primarily around the conditions and principles of transforming a political agenda into daily life. Fundamentalisms employ diverse methodological and practical processes in their development of intellectual formulas and political agendas. One formula and agenda, radicalism, is based on conceptual exclusivity, and *otherness*. Because radical fundamentalism perceived its own real and imagined isolation to be a result of social disunity and exploitation, the political violence and illegitimacy of regimes, and personal impiety and corruption, it has reified, mostly under severe conditions of torture and mishandling, its political discourse into a purified theology of politics. Without its political contextualization, Islam cannot, from radical fundamentalism's point of view, survive in the consciousness of the individual and society.

For the radicals, *shura* (consultation) is not merely a religious doctrine or a mechanism for elections; rather it reflects the public will, a much more superior concept than individual freedom or social agreement. More importantly, it represents the divine will, and as such, any deviation from whatever is divine is a religious violation. The individual cannot but submit to this will; in fact, he is only an appendage to it, with his freedom depending on it. Although this will may opt for a political contract with a ruler, it cannot, because of what it represents, allow pluralism and basic differences that may lead to disunity. The establishment of an Islamic state becomes for radicalism the fulfillment of this divine will, and again, individuals and groups are consequently subordinated to the state.

Processed through the lenses of the *Shari'a*, the institutionalization of *shura* and *ijma'* provides the state, which expresses the general will, a normative role in making basic choices in people's lives. The formal legitimacy that the state acquires makes it in fact unaccountable to anyone but God, or obedience to *Shari'a*, itself institutionalized in the state. Thus, henceforth, legitimacy becomes an internal state affair and not a social and public issue, though originally it may have been so. Therefore, insofar as the state is not going against the *Shari'a*, no one can legitimately overthrow it, and it supervises in this context the morality of people and the application of *Shari'a*. Thus individual religiosity is transformed into a communal public will, itself transformed into state control, both moral and political. Parties, associations, and other civil institutions have no intrinsic validity in this hierarchy and may only operate in a supplementary manner. An elaboration like this seems to demand in the end exclusivity: no possibility of pluralistic understandings of religions and the politicization of Islam as the proper Islamic interpretation itself cannot be represented except by the state. In this context, the establishment of inclusive pluralistic civil democracies and ways of life seems unworkable for theoretical and practical reasons.

On the other hand, the absence of a pluralistic society and of democratic institutions is cited by the moderate trend as the real cause for violence. Although this trend has been excluded for a long time from political participation, it still calls for its inclusion as well as that of others in politics and formal institutions. Its involvement in civil society and its call for human rights, pluralism, and democracy are still seen as the road to salvation of the community and individuals. Their inclusionary views do not postulate an eternal or divine enmity between Islam's institutions and systems and the West's institutions and systems. Properly grounded, what is Western becomes indeed Islamic. The moderate fundamentalists as well as the modernists may blend the culture of the East with that of the West, because they are providing Islamic arguments for the adoption of human rights, pluralism and democracy, not mutual exclusivity—as some secular and religious radicals do in the East and West. The conflict between the East and the West is viewed as being primarily either political or economic but not religious or cultural. The East and the West have common monotheistic grounds upon which multicultural and religious cooperation and coexistence might be built.

Moderate fundamentalists' interpretative discourses on revivalism focus essentially on the termination of the normativeness of the past both as a history and a system. Of course, they exempt the Qur'an and the *Sunna* of the Prophet from such a termination, because they view the two sources metaphysically and metahistorically as formative and constitutive fundamentals of Islam and its main authentic sources. As such, they enjoy affirmative and negative interpretative and formative functions on a multitude of realities—such as *shura* is democracy or *shura* is not what has been practiced. In fact, they have to be superimposed on internal and external events in order to make sense of and evaluate those events as well. Thus, moderate fundamentalism conceives them as nonhistorical but eternal principles of Islam that must be used to create good societies and rectify evil ones. Again, moderate fundamentalists use the Qur'an and the *Sunna* to deny the existence, whether in the past or the present, of a perfect society—with the noted exemption of that of the Prophet—or complete collective Islamic self-awareness. But they employ them as well in order to push for achieving modern Islamic democratic and pluralistic societies and a newly developed self-awareness and human rights. The Qur'an and the *Sunna* permit an unending process of renewal based on interpretation and reinterpretation.

Moderate fundamentalist quests for reinterpretation rest on developing intellectual and formative discourses that rediscover the appropriate meanings and significance of the texts within the framework of a modern life: Such discourses must reformulate the fundamentals of religion (*usul al-din*). These discourses reformulate in turn a political theology loaded with political connotations, because it is directed not at a more substantive understanding of the divine but at more control of the mundane, in particular, the political. Questions related to divine theology are bypassed in favor of those related to political theology; for moderate fundamentalism, the former can only be realized in terms of the latter. Although obedience to God, for instance, is still an important demand for moderate fundamentalists, its most important manifestation is not mere individual religiosity but political doctrines such as the Islamic state, choice of the community, and rights of individuals. Again, the most important measure of divine oneness, or *tawhid*, manifests not in the private conscience of the individual but in his commitment and actions toward the Islamization of state and society, because deep theological commitment to Islam must involve the economic, social, and political concerns of society. Practical Islamic activism signifies the deep-rootedness of belief, whereas shallow and ceremonial nonactive commitment to Islam weakens belief, if not destroying it altogether.

Although divine governance has become for moderate fundamentalism an absolute political doctrine, so has the principle of *shura*. In fact, the good realization of the former becomes dependent on the good exercise of the latter. What moderate fundamentalism's development of *shura* has done is to absorb democracy within Islamic political and even epistemological thought, and consequently, to take the initiative from its advocates. It has also provided legitimate religious means toward the control of government, because legitimacy is linked to popular approval. By denying any contradiction between democracy and constitutional rule, on the one hand, and *shura* and divine law on the other, moderate fundamentalism became capable of postulating a correspondence between the doctrines. All of these have become parts of the fundamentalists' nonhistorical discourses that transform Islam into a system capable of absorbing what is best in philosophy, politics, economics, science, and history without the need to disclaim the validity of Islam itself.

What moderate fundamentalism has also done is to drive a wedge between the Muslims' understanding of history, history itself, and Islam. For our understanding of the history of Islam is not Islam itself. This understanding is only one discourse on Islam within specific spatiotemporal conditions. Therefore, according to moderate fundamentalism, history and people's understanding of it as well their understanding of Islam have no normative status in themselves. In fact, their correctness depends on their utility to society and to Islam. Moderate fundamentalism further considers any deformation as grounded in forcing Islam to yield to historical events and their justifications. But, although constitutional rule in the West and *shura* in Islamic history had quite different historical origins, moderate fundamentalism finds no theoretical problem in forcing a correspondence between the two. In fact, it has no hesitation in calling for the adoption of Western models of government. An act like this is not un-Islamic; rather it is Islamic, because it helps the Islamic state to run its affairs along divine postulates. Of course, moderate fundamentalism rejects secularism and communism, but not every Western doctrine is secular or communist. For moderate fundamentalism, Muslims can and should benefit from others and should update their thinking in order to keep pace with basic changes in the world.

Moderate fundamentalists' grounding of democracy in a metaphysically conceived composition reifies it into an act of worship. On the other hand, the application of *tawhid* in a democratically structured context makes it a justification for ruling. In this way, moderate fundamentalism transforms the substantive doctrine of *tawhid* into a form and formalizes *shura* into a substantive principle. Therefore, the discourse is interpreted by its form. Moderate fundamentalism thus condenses the religious discourse into no more than a political appendage and makes creedal belief and unbelief into political belief and unbelief. Political belief depends on sound application of the *hakimiyya* of the divinely ordained text; political unbelief results from depending alone on the governance of man. In this fashion, moderate fundamentalism negates the usefulness of traditional jurisprudence and transforms a modern religious jurisprudence into an ideologically derived political discourse. In such an explanation of the true essence of Islam one cannot fail to notice how politics informs all of religions.

The moderate trend adopts an Islamic interpretation of liberal democracy as opposed to the popular democracy of radical fundamentalism or the authoritarian nationalism of the Muslim world. Whereas radical fundamentalism proclaims the constitutionality of Islam even in non-Islamic states and as such requires no prior popular approval and excludes the possibility of its inclusion in dialogues and cooperation, whether with Arab regimes or the West, moderate fundamentalism seems more amenable and eager to be included in dialogue and compromise, whether in party formations or the general discourses about politics, ideology, and religion within the context of a civil society.

The Dictionary

-A-

'ABD AL-'AZIZ, 'ALI. See *AL-HARAKA AL-ISLAMIYYA AL-KUR-DIYYA.*

'ABD AL-'AZIZ, 'UTHMAN. See *AL-HARAKA AL-ISLAMIYYA AL-KURDIYYA.*

'ABD AL-'AZIZ, YASIN. See *HIZB AL-TAJAMMU' AL-YEMENI LI AL-ISLAH.*

'ABD AL-KARIM, AHMAD SALIH. See *AL-JIHAD* ORGANIZATION.

'ABD AL-MAHMUD, BABAKR. See POPULAR DEFENSE FORCES.

'ABD AL-MAJID, MAHMUD. See POPULAR DEFENSE FORCES.

'ABD AL-RAHMAN, 'UMAR (1938–). 'Abd al-Rahman was born to a poor family in Jamaliyya in Upper Egypt. He studied at traditional religious institutes and memorized the Qur'an at an early age. 'Abd al-Rahman graduated from al-Azhar University in 1965 and became a religious scholar. He was appointed as an *imam* in a state mosque, where his sharp speeches attracted people's interest. In 1968, he started moving into political Islam (q.v.); he described Jamal 'Abd al-Nasir as being a Pharaoh. The police secret intelligence as well as the administration of al-Azhar warned him against making provocative statements and threatened him with imprisonment and expulsion, respectively. 'Abd al-Rahman was imprisoned for eight months because he gave a *fatwa* (q.v.) (legal opinion) prohibiting the death prayer for 'Abd al-Nasir in 1970.

After he was released, he continued his graduate studies and received a Ph.D. In 1977, 'Abd al-Rahman was appointed a professor at al-Azhar

University in Asyut. Afterwards, he held a teaching position in Saudi Arabia for four years at Saud University. When he returned to Egypt, he was tried for instigating by a *fatwa* the murder of President Anwar Sadat but was released in 1984. In 1990, 'Abd al-Rahman emigrated to the United States, and in 1993 he was implicated in the World Trade Center explosion in New York. He was sentenced for this crime to life imprisonment in 1994.

Because 'Abd al-Rahman is blind, some fundamentalist activists rejected his "defective" leadership. He was asked to lead *al-Jama'a al-Islamiyya al-Jihadiyya* (Struggling Islamic Group), a branch of *al-Jihad* Organization (q.v.) (*Tanzim al-Jihad*), in upper Egypt.

'Abd al-Rahman divides the Islamic movements into two trends: one spearheaded by the Muslim Brotherhood (q.v.), which accepts the existing regime as legitimate and therefore accepts pluralism and democracy (qq.v.) as legitimate tools of political action as well as the establishment of the Islamic state (q.v.). The other trend, spearheaded by *al-Jama'a al-Islamiyya*, denies the legitimacy (q.v.) of the regime and publicly follows a course of total confrontation. 'Abd al-Rahman accuses the Brotherhood of complacency, because of its work with Sadat and Hosni Mubarak and its condemnation of the party behind Sadat's death and of violence (q.v.). He further rejects the Brotherhood's inclusive and compromising attitude in visiting the Coptic pope and allying itself with the *Wafd* party as well as *al-Amal* and *al-Ahrar*. He calls for replacing the inclusivity of the Brotherhood with the exclusivity of *al-Jama'a*, which rejects integration in democratic institutions and adopts a course of forceful resolution regarding basic issues of identity, ethics, value system, and the like. Also, in line with Sayyid Qutb's (q.v.) argument, 'Abd al-Rahman describes any system (q.v.) (*nizam*) that adopts Western principles as belonging to unbelief and paganism (qq.v.), which legalize its overthrow.

Such a view led *al-Jihad* to declare war against the Egyptian Parliament because the Parliament gave itself (Article 86 of the Constitution) the right to legislate and permitted democracy, a concept that treats the believer and nonbeliever equally as citizens. "The 'assumed democratic system' in Egypt wants the people to enter in party politics in order to equate Islam with other ideologies," 'Abd al-Rahman explains. However, his Islamic movement believes in its superiority and does not respect the *jahili* positive law. He further rejects any role for representative bodies as being an instrument of Qur'anic interpretation (q.v.) and adjudication. Qur'anic legitimacy stands on its own. Thus, any violation of the Qur'anic text (q.v.) leads a ruler to unbelief, punishable by death. 'Abd al-Rahman argues that illegitimate rulers deserve death.

'Abd al-Rahman also sanctioned the use of violence against the Copts of Egypt as well as taking their possessions. His group launched a sustained campaign against the leadership of the Copts, and this action has been part of the sectarian tensions in upper Egypt. The group also attacked and spoiled governmental sites and inventories. See also APOSTASY; CONSTITUTION; *FATWA*; *AL-JAMA'AT AL-ISLAMIYYA*; *JAMA'AT AL-JIHAD AL-ISLAMI*; RUSHDI, USAMA; TAHA, AHMAD.

'ABD, AL-SID, SALAH. See MUSLIM BROTHERHOOD IN SUDAN.

'ABD AL-WAHHAB, MUHAMMAD IBN (1703–1792). 'Abd al-Wahhab was the theoretician and founder of *al-Wahhabiyya* (q.v.) movement that aims to return to pure Islam (q.v.) as was practiced by the Prophet. He studied in Medina and lived abroad for many years, including four years in Basra, Iraq. 'Abd al-Wahhab preached against what he considered to constitute heresy and unbelief (q.v.) (*kufr*), such as the actions and doctrines of the Sufis. He wrote *Kitab al-Tawhid* (*Book on Oneness*), and his followers called themselves the *Ikhwan* (Brethren) or the *Muwahhidin* (Unitarians).

'Abd al-Wahhab was strictly against any innovation (q.v.) (*bid'a*) and insisted that the original practice and understanding of Islam were still possible. He was against positing any intermediary between God (q.v.) and man and was against any decoration of mosques. 'Abd al-Wahhab was expelled in 1744 from 'Uyaynah and settled in al-Dar'iyya, later the capital of Ibn Saud. Ibn Saud accepted the *Wahhabi* call and initiated conquests that his heirs continued and ended in the creation of modern Saudi Arabia. See also FARAJ, 'ABD AL-SALAM; *AL-IKHWAN*; *AL-SALAFIYYA*; *AL-WAHHABIYYA*.

'ABDU, GHANIM. See *HIZB AL-TAHRIR AL-ISLAMI*.

'ABDU, MUHAMMAD (1849–1905). 'Abdu was not a fundamentalist but was one of the leaders of the reformist movement that had tremendous impact on all Islamic movements. 'Abdu attended a religious school and later graduated from al-Azhar University. He met Jamal al-Din al-Afghani (q.v.) and became his friend and disciple. When al-Afghani was expelled from Egypt in 1879, 'Abdu was fired from his post at *Dar al-'Ulum*. In 1881, he became the editor of the *Gazette* in Egypt, but because he supported the 'Urabi revolution, he was expelled. He joined al-Afghani in Paris in 1887, and together they published *al-'Urwa al-Wuthqa*. In 1889, 'Abdu went back to Egypt and became a judge, and then in 1899 became the Mufti of Egypt. Some scholars attribute his appointment to this post to his friendship with the British.

After the period when he was under al-Afghani's influence, 'Abdu became disillusioned with political activism and started focusing on educational and intellectual reforms. He attempted to reinterpret Islam (q.v.) in the light of modernity (q.v.), which meant disregarding traditionally held interpretations. He freely promoted the exercise of reason (q.v.) (*ijtihad*) so that Islamic thought could benefit from the sciences and modernity. He believed that there was no essential contradiction between Islam and modern civilization. 'Abdu thought Islam should be the moral basis of social and political living. He, for instance, developed the dormant juridical principle of *maslaha* (interest) into utility, *shura* (q.v.) (consultation) into parliamentary democracy, and *ijma'* (q.v.) (consensus) into pubic opinion. He further called for the simplification or "purification" of Islam from the unnecessary theological, philosophical, and political complexities that had developed historically. 'Abdu accepted the basic role of reason in the interpretation (q.v.) (*tafsir*) of the Qur'an (q.v.), as opposed to past theological and juridical accumulations. See also AL-AFGHANI, JAMAL AL-DIN; IBN BADIS, 'ABD AL-HAMID; *JAM'I-YYAT AL-'ULAMA' AL-MUSLIMIN*; *AL-JIHAD AL-ISLAMI* IN THE WEST BANK AND GAZA STRIP; MODERNISM; RIDA, MUHAMMAD RASHID; *AL-SALAFIYYA*; THEOLOGY; *AL-WAHHABIYYA*.

ABODE OF ISLAM (*DAR AL-ISLAM*). See *DAR AL-HARB*.

ABODE OF PEACE (*DAR AL-SALAM*). See PEACE; UNIVERSALISM; WORLD ORDER.

ABODE OF WAR. See *DAR AL-HARB*.

ABRAQASH, HEDOU. See POPULAR MOVEMENT.

ABU BAKR, YUSUF. See DEMOCRATIC ISLAMIC ARAB MOVEMENT.

ABU FIRAS, MUHAMMAD (1940–   ). Abu Firas was a member of the executive council of the Muslim Brotherhood in Jordan (q.v.) between

1978 and 1990. He was born in al-Faluja and obtained a B.A. in law from the University of Damascus and an M.A. and a Ph.D. from the University of al-Azhar. Abu Firas taught in schools and practiced law. He represented the Muslim Brotherhood in the Lower House of the Jordanian Parliament from 1989 to 1993.

ABU GHUDDA, 'ABD AL-FATTAH (?–1997). This Shaykh died in February 1997 in exile. Abu Ghudda was the former supreme guide of the Muslim Brotherhood in Syria (q.v.) and a founding member of *Rabitat al-'Alam al-Islami* (Muslim World League). Abu Ghudda was born in Aleppo and studied with the well-known religious scholars of that age, like Ahmad Kurd 'Ali and Ahmad al-Shamma'. In 1944, Abu Ghudda began his studies in al-Azhar University in Egypt at the Faculty of *al-Shari'a*. He accompanied the Egyptian leader of the Muslim Brotherhood, Hasan al-Banna (qq.v.). After his return to Syria in 1951, Abu Ghudda taught at mosques and state schools.

In 1962, he became the fundamentalist representative in the parliament, then he taught at Damascus University. In 1963, Abu Ghudda was imprisoned for a short period because of his opposition to the government. In 1965, he was invited by the Saudi Mufti to help set up the Islamic University of al-Imam. Abu Ghudda had numerous followers and was considered, as a scholar, a safety valve from thinkers that are not well versed in Islamic traditions, for the Brotherhood had very few religious scholars.

ABU MARZUQ, MUSA. Until 1996, Dr. Abu Marzuq was the head of the political bureau of the Palestinian *Hamas*: *Harakat al-Muqawama al-Islamiyya* (q.v.) (Islamic Resistance Movement). The U.S. authorities arrested him as he entered the country in 1995 on charges of supporting terrorism. Earlier that year, Israel (q.v.) accused him of masterminding terrorist acts in Israel and demanded his extradition, and *Hamas* threatened to exact revenge if that extradition were to take place. Finally, a deal was struck: Abu Marzuq would give up his green card, or permit for residence, in exchange for his release. Upon his release, he was sent to Jordan in 1997, but the Jordanian government denied that its acceptance of Marzuq was part of a deal or that it had made conditions regarding his stay in Jordan. See also MUSLIM BROTHERHOOD IN PALESTINE; AL-SHIQAQI, FATHI.

ABU MUHAMMAD, SAMIH. Abu Muhammad is the leader of Muhammad's Army. See also *JAYSH MUHAMMAD*.

ABU QURAH, 'ABD AL-LATIF (1908–1967). Abu Qurah is the founder of the Muslim Brotherhood in Jordan (q.v.) and remained its supreme guide until 1953. Abu Qurah was born in Salt and participated in the 1948 Arab-Israeli war as the commander of a Brethren's battalion. Abu Qurah developed many voluntary and philanthropic foundations, such as the Jordanian Red Crescent and Palestinian Islamic Conference. See also INTERNATIONAL ORGANIZATION OF THE MUSLIM BROTHER-HOOD.

ABU AL-RUSHTA, 'ATA. Abu al-Rushta is the official spokesman for the Islamic Liberation Party in Jordan. See also *HIZB AL-TAHRIR AL-ISLAMI*.

ABU TAIR, MUHAMMAD. See *AL-JIHAD AL-ISLAMI* IN THE WEST BANK AND GAZA STRIP.

ABU ZAYD, HAMID NASR. Although this associate professor at Cairo University tried to get his promotion to full professorship in 1992, he was turned down in 1993 and was taken to court on the charge of apostasy (q.v.) (*ridda*). Dr. 'Abd al-Sabur Shahin (q.v.) accused Abu Zayd of blaspheming the Qur'an (q.v.), holding heretical beliefs, and of heresy and unbelief (q.v.) (*kufr*). Shahin equated Abu Zayd's writings to those of Salman Rushdie (q.v.) and further denounced Abu Zayd in his sermons at 'Amr Ibn al-'As Mosque.

Later, a lawsuit against Abu Zayd was brought to court, demanding the annulment of his marriage in line with the laws of apostasy. In 1994, after a long judicial process, his marriage was annulled. However, later Abu Zayd and his wife appealed and won the case. Later, Cairo University promoted him to the rank of professor. Nonetheless, he along with his wife sought political asylum in Holland, and he got a teaching position for one year at the University of Leiden. He has not returned to Egypt out of fear that he might be assassinated. See also APOSTASY; EXTREMISM; SHAHIN, 'ABD AL-SABUR.

ACTIVISM (*HARAKIYYA*). By neglecting the role of pure reason (q.v.), fundamentalists like Abu al-A'la al-Mawdudi, Hasan al-Banna, and Sayyid Qutb (qq.v.) highlight the importance of practical reason (praxis) or the interpretative discourse. Thus, a sign of any real knowledge (q.v.) is its production of concepts, leading to action. A correct discourse is therefore one that is based on action and the interpretation (q.v.) of the sacred text (q.v.) in conformity with that action.

For the fundamentalists, an activist political behavior takes precedence over submission to social and political traditions. Authoritative interpretations and authoritarian governments were dropped by fundamentalists as proper means of reading the text and dealing with reality, respectively. Of course certain values, especially the moral, are shared between fundamentalist Muslims and ordinary Muslims. However, for the fundamentalists, justification of these values lies only in the Qur'anic text and not in society or history (q.v.). See also 'ABDU, MUHAMMAD; EXTREMISM; FADLALLAH, MUHAMMAD HUSAYN; IRANIAN REVOLUTION OF 1979; ISLAMIC FUNDAMENTALISM; ISLAMIC REVOLUTION OF IRAN; ISLAMIC YOUTH ORGANIZATION; *JIHAD*; MARTYRDOM; RADICALISM; *RASA'IL AL-NUR*; RELIGION; REVOLUTION; VANGUARD.

AL-AFGHAN AL-'ARAB (AFGHAN ARABS). This is a name used for many groups of Arab volunteers who fought the Soviet invasion of Afghanistan and the Afghani communist government in the 1980s. The Afghan Arabs believed they were launching *jihad* (q.v.) (struggle) against the infidels. Most Muslim regimes and Islamic intellectuals as well as many countries in the West (q.v.) supported this movement at its beginning and before the collapse of the Soviet Union. After the end of the Soviet invasion, the Afghan Arabs split and supported different Afghani factions, which since have been jockeying for power. Many of them became catalysts in their own respective countries for armed revolt and activities against existing regimes. Some have gone to Pakistan to find a safe haven from their governments, which have been pursuing them and linking them to home terrorism. However, most of the Afghan Arabs are not involved in terrorist activities; many of them used to work in Islamic and Arab philanthropic and educational associations. The Afghan Arabs include citizens of most Arab states, especially Egypt, Jordan, Yemen, Saudi Arabia, and Iraq. Afghanistan's official number of Afghan Arabs is 6,170, but the actual number is much greater (about 20,000) because many of them did not register and entered Afghanistan without following procedures.

There are two notorious organizations that include many of the Afghan Arabs. One is *Jama'at al-Takfir wa al-Hijra*, or *Jama'at al-Muslimin* (q.v.) (The Group of Muslims), led by Dr. Ahmad al-Jaza'iri, which allied itself with and influenced the radical ideology of the Algerian Armed Islamic Group (q.v.) (*al-Jama'a al-Islamiyya al-Musallaha*). The other is *Jama'at al-Khilafa*, founded by Muhammad al-Rifa'i, who called for establishing an Islamic state (q.v.) on the borders with Pakistan. Other organizations include *al-'Ama'im al-Sawda'* (Black Turbans) and *Jama'at al-Fitra* (the Group of Pure Nature), which upheld naive principles like prohibiting the use of shoes or any footwear and cars. Some of the Afghan Arabs were implicated in the attempt on President Hosni Mubarak's life in Ethiopia, and two of the alleged assassins were Egyptian Afghan Arabs.

Also, Ahmad Ramzi Yusuf (q.v.), who has been accused of masterminding the World Trade Center bombing, has connections with the Afghan Arabs, and individuals who were accused of the 1995 bombing of the American mission headquarters in Riyadh in Saudi Arabia had been in Afghanistan. One should not attribute the increase of radical and violent Islamic groups in the Arab world to the Afghan Arabs alone because many of them—even the Algerian Armed Islamic Group or *al-Jama'a al-Islamiyya al-Musallaha*—grew up in countries other than Afghanistan. There is some circumstantial evidence that supports the claim that Afghan Arabs' return to their respective countries resulted in increased violence and radicalism (qq.v.).

In Jordan, *al-Afghan al-'Arab* are headed by 'Abd Allah Kamil al-Hashayka. Some observers say that this Jordanian group is made up of members from *Jaysh Muhammad* (q.v.) (Muhammad's Army) and the Muslim Brotherhood (q.v.). It is alleged that this group wanted to assassinate the Palestinian delegation to peace (q.v.) negotiations with Israel (q.v.), Jordanian Prime Minister 'Abd al-Salam al-Majali, as well as army and police officers and to blow up a large commercial center *(Majma' Amman al-Sakani)* and movie theaters. Its membership is estimated at around 1,000.

Al-Afghan al-'Arab have also been blamed for the explosion that took place at the American Military delegation barracks in Riyadh in Saudi Arabia. The four suspects were Saudi Afghans who had fought in the 1980s in Afghanistan against the Soviets. The suspects had been influenced by ideology of Usama Bin Laden and Muhammad al-Mas'ari (qq.v.) and the writings of Abu Muhammad al-Maqdisi (q.v.). See also BIN LADEN, USAMA; *AL-HARAKA AL-ISLAMIYYA AL-KURDIYYA*; *AL-JAMA'A AL-ISLAMIYYA AL-MUSALLAH*; *JAYSH MUHAMMAD*; AL-MAQDISI, ABU MUHAMMAD.

AL-AFGHANI, JA'FAR. See ARMED ISLAMIC GROUP.

AL-AFGHANI, JAMAL AL-DIN (1838–1897). Al-Afghani was a most outstanding Muslim thinker and activist who started the modern process of Islamic reform in the Muslim world. Al-Afghani has been called as *Hakim al-Sharq* (the Sage of the East) and the Awakener of the East. Some scholars argue that al-Afghani was born in Afghanistan, others, that he was born in Iran, then moved to Afghanistan. However, he himself claimed an Afghani birth. Although al-Afghani acted as a Sunni scholar, many scholars believed he was a Shi'ite. As a child, al-Afghani learned Arabic and memorized the Qur'an. His first trip was to India, and from there, he moved throughout the Islamic world.

In Afghanistan, al-Afghani was very active against the British and was expelled for that. Afterward he moved to Istanbul, Bombay, Cairo, and various other places. He looked to the Ottoman Caliphate (q.v.) as a source of unification for Muslims and for their defense. Although al-Afghani became well placed in Istanbul, he was again expelled and went to Cairo in 1871. There his career as a reformer flourished. Again he was very active in antagonizing the British and attracted a large following, including figures like Muhammad 'Abdu (q.v.), who would subsequently play prominent roles in society. Al-Afghani was exiled in 1879 to India, where he started working on the Pan-Islamic movement. Then he settled in Paris in 1883, where he published the very influential magazine *Al-'Urwa al-Wuthqa* (*The Tightest Bond*). In Iran, he worked against the Shah and ended up again in Istanbul where the Sultan promised him great influence. But al-Afghani died a lonely death after suffering two years with jaw cancer.

In response to a lecture by Ernest Renan on religion and science, al-Afghani argued that Islam and science were compatible, because Islam did not seek to stifle science or intellectual freedom (q.v.). He promoted the doctrine of free will as an avenue for religious and political freedom and for progress. Although the overall understanding of Islam became stagnant, al-Afghani viewed the fundamental principles of Islam as being compatible with modern science and development. He believed Islamic thought could use modernity (q.v.) effectively in order to revive Islam. He also called for a reworking of Islamic political thought that would include democracy and constitutional government (qq.v.) in a harmonious manner. Al-Afghani focused his political and ideological views on reforming the Islamic state (q.v.) through a call, Pan-Islamism (q.v.), and demanded adherence to justice and *shura* (qq.v.) (consultation) as two main pillars for modern rule. See also 'ABDU, MUHAMMAD; IBN BADIS, 'ABD AL-HAMID; MODERNISM; PAN-ISLAMISM; RIDA, MUHAMMAD RASHID; *AL-SALAFIYYA*.

AL-AHBASH (ETHIOPIANS). *Al-Ahbash,* legally known *as Jam'iyyat al-Mashari' al-Khairiyya al-Islamiyya* (Association of Islamic Philanthropic Projects), is a small Sunni group of the traditional fundamentalist thought. Its headquarters is in the area around Burj Abi Haydar mosque in Beirut. *Al-Ahbash* is spiritually headed by al-Shaykh 'Abd Allah al-Habashi, a former *mufti* from Ethiopia. The group is involved with theological issues and is anti-Shi'ite and very secretive. For the last few years, *al-Ahbash* has become very active against Islamic fundamentalist movements in Lebanon, and one of the presidents of the association, Shaykh Nizar al-Halabi, was assassinated in 1995 by a militant fundamentalist group. The group seems to be supported by Syria, which wants to further Syrian political objectives in Lebanon.

Al-Ahbash opposes the basic doctrines of modern fundamentalist movements, which it accuses of neglecting the Prophet's traditions. It harshly criticizes other Islamic movements and accuses their leaders, such as Sayyid Qutb and Hasan al-Banna (qq.v.), of unbelief (q.v.) (*kufr*). The group conceives itself as a moderate Islamic movement that is concerned with ethics. Its current president is Shaykh Husam al-Din Qaraqira, a graduate of an Islamic seminary in Syria. *Al-Ahbash*'s activities became more apparent when one of its members was elected to the Lebanese parliament in 1992. *Al-Ahbash* lost that seat during the 1996 elections, and the assassination of its leader by the Islamic Band of Helpers (q.v.) ('*Usbat al-Ansar al-Islamiyya*) reduced its activities. The group has an elaborate structure that includes schools, centers, sports, and scouts. It is unclear what the sources of *al-Ahbash* funding are, especially given its spending on activities in many parts of the world. See also ISLAMIC BAND OF HELPERS.

AL-AHMAR, 'ABD ALLAH. See *AL-HIZB AL-JUMHURI*; *HIZB AL-TAJAMMU' AL-YEMENI LI AL-ISLAH*; *AL-JIHAD* ORGANIZATION; *AL-TAJAMMU' AL-YEMENI LI AL-ISLAH*; ZANDANI, SHAYKH 'ABD AL-MAJID.

AL-AHMAR, SADIQ. See *AL-HIZB AL-JUMHURI*.

AHRADAN, MAHJUBI. See DEMOCRATIC CONSTITUTIONAL POPULAR MOVEMENT; POPULAR MOVEMENT.

AHZAB. See PARTIES.

'AKIF, MUHAMMAD MAHDI. See INTERNATIONAL ORGANIZA-
TION OF THE MUSLIM BROTHERHOOD.

'AKOUR, 'ABD AL-RAHIM (1939–). 'Akour is a member of the executive bureau of *Hizb Jabhat al-'Amal al-Islami* (q.v.) (Islamic Action
Front Party) in Jordan. He was born in Sarih and received his B.A. in
Islamic Law from the University of Damascus in 1966. He worked as the
director of religious endowment and guidance at the Ministry of Religious Affairs. 'Akour taught at many universities and was a deputy in the
Lower House of the Jordanian Parliament for the period of 1989–1993.

AL-ALBANI, SHAYKH NASIR AL-DIN. See *AL-SALAFIYYA*.

ALLAH. See GOD.

AL-'AMA'IM AL-SAWDA' (BLACK TURBANS). See *AL-AFGHAN AL-
'ARAB*.

AMIN AL-SAYYID, IBRAHIM (1950–). Amin al-Sayyid won a seat
in the Lebanese Parliament in 1992 and 1996 as a candidate for *Hizbullah* (q.v.) (Party of God) in the Biqa' and has been an active member of
its politburo. He is also a poet and scholar. He aims to change the parameters of the political game in Lebanon from sectarianism to party competition. Amin al-Sayyid denied that *Hizbullah* calls for the establishment
of an Islamic state (q.v.) in Lebanon. He believes that Islamic Resistance
in the south is not sectarian or related only to one party or the Shi'a sect;
all Lebanese participate in the resistance.

AMIR (GROUP'S COMMANDER). *Amir* (prince) is a term that denotes
either a prince or a commander in the military. The fundamentalists use
it as a title for the commanders of their groups. In traditionally structured
Islamic societies, there would be many *amir*s, but *amir al-jama'a* has
become identified with the head of fundamentalist movements and
groups. Many fundamentalists strictly obey the orders of their leaders
without question. See also *HARAKAT AL-ITIJAH AL-ISLAMI*; AL-IS-
LAMBULI, MUHAMMAD SHAWQI; ISLAMIC BAND OF HELP-
ERS; MUSLIM BROTHERHOOD IN JORDAN.

'AMMAR, 'ALI FADL (1956–). 'Ammar won a parliamentary seat in the elections of 1992 in Lebanon and lost it in 1996. He was the candidate of *Hizbullah* (q.v.) (Party of God) in Ba'abda District and is still a member of its politburo. 'Ammar believes that Lebanon should remain a country of guaranteed freedom (q.v.), including political opposition. Liberation of the south from Israeli occupation is a priority for him.

'AMUSH, BASSAM ALI SALAMA (1954–). 'Amush is a member of the executive bureau of *Hizb Jabhat al-'Amal al-Islami* (q.v.) (Islamic Action Front Party) in Jordan. He received his B.A. in Islamic Law from the University of al-Qarawiyyin in Morocco, and his M.A. and Ph.D. from the University of Imam Muhammad Ibn Saud in Saudi Arabia. 'Amush taught at the University of Riyadh and the University of Jordan. He represented his district in the Lower House of Parliament in 1993.

ANAS, 'ABD ALLAH. Anas is a member of the self-exiled executive committee of the Islamic Salvation Front (q.v.) (*Jabhat al-Inqadh al-Islamiyya*) whose members live abroad. He was one of many Algerians who volunteered in 1984 to fight in Afghanistan and has had a close relationship with the Afghani *Mujahidin*. Anas joined the Islamic Salvation Front and is very close to the Armed Islamic Group (q.v.) (*al-Jama'a al-Islamiyya al-Musallaha*). However, he opposes the violence (q.v.) of the Armed Islamic Group, which he regards as a danger to the mainstream movement. Anas now lives in Kabul, Afghanistan.

ANSAR AL-SUNNA AL-MUHAMMADIYYA. See SUPPORTERS OF MUHAMMADAN *SUNNA*.

APOSTASY (*RIDDA*). Radical fundamentalists believe that the teachings of the Qur'an (q.v.) and the regulations of *al-Shari'a* (q.v.) (Islamic Law) must be adhered to literally by all Muslims. Any deviation from, scorn, or misinterpretation of either is considered to constitute *ridda* (apostasy). This includes issues relating to theology, jurisprudence, reason (qq.v.), politics, or any field of knowledge (q.v.), and behavior. With certain exceptions, *ridda* was historically used by Muslims to describe those who denied their belief in Islam altogether or questioned one of its basic doctrines, and was less tied up with how a group of people view the behavior or belief of other individuals and groups. Usually, those Muslims who acknowledge that God (q.v.) exists and that Muhammad is

His messenger are not normally accused of apostasy; when they misbe-have or argue wrongly, they might be considered to be heretics.

Radical fundamentalists like Abu al-A'la al-Mawdudi, Sayyid Qutb, 'Umar 'Abd al-Rahman, and 'Abd al-Salam Faraj (qq.v.) endow apos-tasy with a meaning similar to unbelief (q.v.) (*kufr*). They further make it a concept that applies not only to creed but, more importantly, to be-havior and politics. For instance, a Muslim who believes in the Qur'an and the *Sunna* (way) of the Prophet but who follows a secular govern-ment and accepts the separation of politics from religion (q.v.) is consid-ered not only an apostate but also an unbeliever. Also, the usurpation of political sovereignty is considered unbelief. Issues relating to political sovereignty are turned into issues of belief, apostasy, and unbelief. Le-gitimacy (q.v.) of government is tied to divine governance (q.v.) (*hakimi-yya*) and human paganism (q.v.) (*jahiliyya*). Thus, a Muslim ruler who does not apply the Islamic Law but applies foreign laws and constitutions (q.v.) is an apostate because he does not apply the Law and a paganist because he applies foreign laws and constitutions.

Whereas moderate fundamentalism (q.v.) provides some space for all sorts of freedom (q.v.), radical fundamentalism applies a stiff formula for unbelief and apostasy. Two examples suffice here. The first is Salman Rushdie (q.v.) who was declared an apostate by Ayatollah Khomeini (q.v.) because of his perceived scorn of Islam (q.v.); the second, Hamid Nasr Abu Zayd (q.v.), who was accused of apostasy and taken to court by 'Abd al-Sabur Shahin (q.v.) because of the former's interpretative studies of the formative period of Islam.

For both trends, however, the human programs and systems must not contradict the divine *Shari'a*. Because divine sovereignty covers the mundane and the sublime, its implication is mostly related to politics, which orders man's and society's life. For the law of God is meaningful not only in terms of the beyond but more equally in terms of the here and now. It penetrates both the human conscience and, more signifi-cantly, man's political existence. Although the concern for the next life is part of religion, the earthly existence is as important, because it is the bridge between the profane and the sacred. See also ABU ZAYD, HAMID NASR; *FATWA*; GOD.

'AQAILEH, 'ABD ALLAH (1945–). 'Aqaileh is a member of the exec-utive bureau of *Hizb Jabhat al-'Amal al-Islami* (q.v.) (Islamic Action Front Party) in Jordan. 'Aqaileh was born and received his early educa-tion in Tafileh and received his secondary education in Aroub in Palestine. He received his B.A. in 1975 and his Ph.D. from the University of Southern California in 1982. 'Aqaileh was a professor at the University of Jordan and was elected to the Jordanian Parliament for the first time between 1984–1988 and for a second time in 1989. He became Minister of Education in 1991.

AL-'AQL. See REASON.

'ARABIYYAT, 'ABD AL-LATIF SULAYMAN (1933–). 'Arabiyyat was born in Salt in Jordan, and received his B.A. in Agronomy from Baghdad University in 1960, an M.A. in 1967, and a Ph.D. in vocational education from the University of Texas. He is a member and Deputy General Secretary of *Hizb Jabhat al-'Amal al-Islami* (q.v.) (Islamic Action Front Party) in Jordan. He became Secretary-General of the Ministry of Education. 'Arabiyyat served as speaker of the Jordanian Lower House of Parliament three times, ending in 1993. He has been a member of the Upper House of Parliament since 1993.

AL-'ARID, 'ALI. See *HARAKAT AL-ITIJAH AL-ISLAMI*.

'ARIF, SULAYMAN. See *MILLI NIZAMI PARTISI*; *MILLI SELAMET PARTISI*.

ARMED ISLAMIC GROUP (*AL-JAMA'A AL-ISLAMIYYA AL-MUSAL-LAHA*). Since the beginning of the civil war in Algeria, there have been two fundamentalist views on the need for armed activities. The first is represented by the Islamic Salvation Front (q.v.), which formed the Armed Islamic Movement (*al-Haraka al-Islamiyya al-Musallaha*). The movement was headed by 'Abd al-Qadir al-Shubuti who was assisted by Sa'id Makhlufi, Muhammad Sa'id, and 'Abd al-Raziq Rajjam. The movement limits the use of military activities to what it considers cases of self-defense against the armed forces and the police. It refuses to target civilian or foreign individuals and institutions.

The other trend is dominated by radical fundamentalists who belong to the Armed *Salafi* Islamic Group (*al-Haraka al-Islamiyya al-Sala⌐ 'ya al-Musallaha*), which was headed by Mansuri al-Miliani, a former member of the Salvation Front, who broke with Abbasi Madani (q.v.) and was executed in the summer of 1992. He was succeeded by Shaykh 'Abd al-Haqq al-'Ayayada, who was later arrested on charges of terrorism. Then Ja'far al-Afghani, a relative of al-Miliani, took over the leadership but was killed in 1994. He was succeeded by al-Sayih 'Atiyya who was followed by al-Sharif Qawasmi. Currently the leader is 29-year-old 'Antar al-Zawabri. The group became engaged in terrorist acts against foreigners in Algeria. Some observers accuse the movement of being part of the Algerian regime, and others consider it part of the Islamic Salvation Front.

The movement is made up of two groups: the followers of Mustapha Buya'li, the leader of the Islamic Movement for Algeria (q.v.), who was freed from prison by President al-Shadhili Bin Jadid and killed in 1987 after he declared *jihad* (q.v.) (struggle) against the regime. The second group is made up of former members of *al-Takfir wa al-Hijra*, or *Jama'at al-Muslimin* (q.v.) (The Group of Muslims), which is a branch of the Egyptian movement with the same name that was founded by Shukri Mustapha (q.v.). In Algeria, this group called for the establishment of the Islamic state (q.v.) and declared *jihad* (struggle) against the state.

Many members of this group were part of *al-Afghan al-'Arab* (q.v.) (Afghani Arabs) who joined the *Mujahidin* in Afghanistan, and upon their return they split with the Salvation Front because of its intention to participate in the legislative elections. After the cancellation of the elections in 1991, they set up their organization, *al-Jama'a al-Islamiyya al-Musallaha*. The group is concentrated in the suburbs of the capital, and its organizational structure is based on small units that act without referring to higher channels of authority.

The group's ideology allows violent acts against all non-Islamic governments all over the world. This includes the army, the police, ministers, state employees, political leaders, and others. It calls for armed *jihad* in order to establish the Islamic state. Even women who support such government can be taken as slaves. 'Abd al-Haqq published a collection of *fatwas* (q.v) calling for military attacks, and the group has been implicated in the assassination of former Prime Minister Qasidi Merbah and the murder of many French people residing in Algeria. The group has not denied the accusations. In its second declaration, the group threatened journalists who launch "wars" of revenge against the fundamentalists and it had, reportedly, killed over 30 journalists by 1995.

The group regards the Islamic Salvation Front as a popular force that has deviated from the path of Islam (q.v.) by entering into the democratic game when it knows that legislation (q.v.) is a divine matter and is not subject to human agreement. It has upheld the doctrines of divine governance (q.v.) (*hakimiyya*) and human paganism (*jahiliyya*) (q.v.). Pluralism (q.v.) is rejected, and dialogue (q.v.) with the regime is outlawed.

The group warned all foreigners not to stay in Algeria and the Algerian government blamed it for the slaughters that are taking place almost daily, resulting in the death of thousands of people. Certain observers and the Islamic movements accuse agencies of state security organizations of committing the massacres and penetrating some factions within the Armed Islamic Group. See also *AL-AFGHAN AL-'ARAB*; ANAS, 'ABD ALLAH; ISLAMIC SALVATION FRONT IN ALGERIA; *AL-JAYSH AL-ISLAMI LI AL-INQADH*; AL-NAHNAH, MAHFOUDH; YUSUF, AHMAD RAMZI.

ARMED ISLAMIC MOVEMENT (*AL-HARAKA AL-ISLAMIYYA AL-MUSALLAHA*). See ARMED ISLAMIC GROUP.

ARMED ISLAMIC *SALAFI* GROUP (*AL-JAMA'A AL-ISLAMIYYA AL-SALAFIYYA AL-MUSALLAHA*). See ARMED ISLAMIC GROUP; *AL-JAYSH AL-ISLAMI LI AL-INQADH*.

ASALA. See AUTHENTICITY.

ASLAMA. See ISLAMIZATION.

ASSOCIATION FOR THE DEFENSE OF ISLAMIC VALUES. See *TAYYAR AL-TAGHYIR*.

ASSOCIATION FOR SOCIAL REFORM IN KUWAIT. See *JAM'IY-YAT AL-ISLAH AL-IJTIMA'IYYA* IN KUWAIT.

ASSOCIATION FOR SOCIAL REFORM IN YEMEN. See *JAM'IY-YAT AL-ISLAH AL-IJTIMA'IYYA* IN YEMEN.

ASSOCIATION OF ALGERIAN ISLAMIC SOLIDARITY. See *JAM'-IYYAT AL-TADAMUN AL-ISLAMI AL-JAZA'IRI*.

ASSOCIATION OF ISLAMIC PHILANTHROPIC PROJECTS (*JAM'IYYAT AL-MASHARI' AL-KHAIRIYYA AL-ISLAMIYYA*). See *AL-AHBASH*.

ASSOCIATION OF MUSLIM SCHOLARS. See *JAM'IYYAT AL-'ULAMA' AL-MUSLIMIN*.

ASSOCIATION OF MUSLIM YOUNG MEN. See *JAM'IYYAT AL-SHUBBAN AL-MUSLIMIN.*

ASSOCIATION OF REFORM AND GUIDANCE (*JAM'IYYAT AL-ISLAH WA AL-IRSHAD*). See AL-NAHNAH, MAHFOUDH.

AL-ASWAD, MUHAMMAD HABIB. See VANGUARDS OF SACRIFICE.

ATILHAN, CEVAT RIFAT. See ISLAMIC DEMOCRATIC PARTY.

'ATIYYA, AL-SAYIH. See ARMED ISLAMIC GROUP; *AL-JAYSH AL-ISLAMI LI AL-INQADH.*

AL-'ATTAR, 'ISAM. See MUSLIM BROTHERHOOD IN SYRIA.

AUTHENTICITY (*ASALA*). Islamic fundamentalism (q.v.) advocates return to Islamic authenticity as a way of reviving Muslim communities. The call for authenticity is a demand for adhering to the fundamentals (q.v.) (*usul*) of Islamic religion (q.v.), foremost among which is the cultivation of Islamic morality (q.v.) of an Islamic society (q.v.) within an Islamic state (q.v.). Authenticity does not mean the rejection of modern living and science. It means, however, grounding such things in an Islamic framework, itself an act of disassociation from the perceived and actual domination of the West (q.v.).

For instance, *shura* (q.v.) (consultation) is an authentic Islamic doctrine; democracy (q.v.) is a foreign doctrine. The Islamization (q.v.) of the democracy, or its authentication, makes it an Islamic doctrine equivalent to *shura*. Again, science is adopted by fundamentalists, but is turned into an authentic field of study by linking it to *tawhid* (q.v.) (Oneness of God) and not to materialism. Implicit in the calls for authenticity is the need to distinguish the Muslim community from other communities in order to provide the Muslim community with a sense of superiority. Authenticity is a concept that touches on culture, politics, society, economics, metaphysics, and all fields of life. See also WESTERN CIVILIZATION.

AUTHORITY FOR IMITATION. See *MARJI' AL-TAQLID.*

'AWAYDA, MUHAMMAD (1947–   ). 'Awayda was a member of the executive council of the Muslim Brotherhood in Jordan (q.v.) for the period

1986–1990 and has been a member of the executive council of *Hizb Jab-hat al-'Amal al-Islami* (q.v.) (Islamic Action Front Party) in Jordan since 1993. He was born in al-Faluja, and obtained a B.A. in law from the University of Jordan in 1969. 'Awayda also obtained an M.A. in 1973 and a Ph.D. from the University of al-Azhar in 1977. He has worked in teaching and has represented the Muslim Brotherhood in the Lower House of Parliament since 1993.

'AWDA, 'ABD AL-'AZIZ (1948–   ). Shaykh 'Awda is a founding mem-ber of *al-Jihad al-Islami* in the West Bank and Gaza (q.v.). He was born in Bi'r al-Saba' in Palestine. His family left for the Gaza Strip and lived in Jabalayya Camp where he went to school. He received his B.A. in Arabic and Islamic studies and a diploma in Islamic Law from *Dar al-'Ulum*. 'Awda came back to the Gaza Strip in 1981 and was a lecturer at the Islamic University of Gaza and an *imam* for Shaykh 'Izz al-Din al-Hasan Mosque.

During his university years in Egypt, 'Awda was in contact with Is-lamic associations that did not belong to the Muslim Brethren (q.v.), for example, *al-Jihad* movement (q.v.) as well as *Jama'at* or *Tanzim al-Kuli-yya al-Fanniyya al-'Askariyya* Group, led by Salih 'Abd Allah Sirriyya (qq.v.). Besides this, he adhered to *Jama'at al-Jihad al-Islami* (q.v.) (the Islamic *Jihad* group), whose point of ideological reference is Shaykh 'Izz al-Din al-Qassam.

'Awda was among the first activists to call for getting rid of the "tradi-tional" ideas of the Muslim Brethren as well as for fighting the Israeli occupation. 'Awda was arrested by the Israeli forces in 1984 and was convicted of resisting and opposing the Israeli occupation. As a result, he was jailed for 11 months and was also exiled from his country. In 1993, 'Awda was one of the deportees to Southern Lebanon. See *AL-JIHAD AL-ISLAMI* IN THE WEST BANK AND GAZA STRIP.

'AWDA, 'ABD AL-QADIR (?-1955). 'Awda is one of the main ideolo-gists and writers for the Muslim Brotherhood (q.v.) in Egypt. 'Awda was executed along with five other Muslim Brethren in 1955 after accusing the Brotherhood of attempting to assassinate President Jamal 'Abd al-Nasir. See also BILHAJ, 'ALI; MUSLIM BROTHERHOOD, IDEOL-OGY OF; *AL-SALAFIYYA*.

AL-'AWWA, MUHAMMAD SALIM. Al-'Awwa is an Egyptian moder-ate fundamentalist thinker, lawyer, and university professor. He is now the head of the defense team for the fundamentalists on trial in Egypt. More importantly, he, as a former distinguished Egyptian member of the Muslim Brotherhood (q.v.), goes beyond general statements and directly addresses the standing issues of democracy (q.v.) and rights. Starting from al-Hasan al-Banna's (q.v.) discourse, al-'Awwa elaborates further the absolute necessity of both pluralism and democracy (qq.v.). According to al-'Awwa Islam (q.v.) has been falsely accused of being opposed to open societies and pluralism. For him, a society is civil when institutions aiming at effecting political life are free to function and to develop without interference from the state. In other words, the existence of particular forms of association is not in itself a guarantee that a civil society exists.

Because the institutions of society change from one time to another, al-'Awwa does not specify the kinds of institutions that make a Muslim society civil and pluralistic, instead he links this to the function of institutions. In the West (q.v.), unions, clubs, and parties (q.v.) ensure that society is civil and pluralistic; in the Muslim world, mosques, churches, religious endowments, teaching circles, professions, craft organizations, and the neighborhood serve the same purpose. These institutions are not wanted for themselves but instead are instruments for interaction. Muslims ought to develop what is conducive to a pluralistic life; their institutions do not have to be imitations of Western institutions in order to be civil.

Pluralism for al-'Awwa is the tolerance of diversity—political, economic, religious, linguistic, and others. Such diversity is a natural human tendency and an inalienable right, especially when considering that the Qur'an (q.v.) allows differences of identity and belonging. Al-'Awwa identifies six doctrines that make Islam tolerant and pluralistic. He argues that (1) Islam does not specify a particular social and political system (q.v.) (*nizam*) but provides general ideas; (2) the ruler must be elected by the people through *shura* (q.v.) (consultation); (3) because Islam permits religious freedom (q.v.), all other kinds of freedom are therefore legitimate; (4) all people are equal in terms of rights and duties; (5) God's command to enjoin good and to forbid evil is a communal religious duty; and finally, (6) rulers are accountable to their communities.

However, the legitimacy (q.v.) of pluralism hinges for al-'Awwa on two conditions. First, it should not contradict the bases of Islam, and, second, it should be made in the interest of the people. In all other respects, individuals and groups may associate with each other in any manner deemed necessary, especially in terms of political parties that could become a safety valve against limiting freedom and a means for limiting despotism. See also HUMAN RIGHTS; *AL-SHARI'A*.

'AYAYDA, 'ABD AL-HAQQ. See ARMED ISLAMIC GROUP.

'AYYASH, YAHYA (?-1996). 'Ayyash, who was born in Rafat in the West Bank, was trained as an electrical engineer at Bir Zayt University. He joined *Hamas*: *Harakat al-Muqawama al-Islamiyya* (q.v.) (Islamic Resistance Movement) and launched many armed attacks and suicide missions. His victims have been estimated at around 50 killed and 300 injured. Known as "the engineer" in Palestine, 'Ayyash became the most wanted on the lists of Israeli intelligence departments. He was nicknamed "the engineer" because of his expertise in explosives and their use. He eluded the Israeli government for many years, but was assassinated by Israelis in 1996 while answering a phone call. The phone earpiece was an explosive device. Fundamentalist militants threatened revenge. See also MUSLIM BROTHERHOOD IN PALESTINE.

AL-AZAYDAH, AHMAD (1948–1992). Al-Azaydah was the head of the fundamentalist bloc in the Jordanian Lower House of Parliament and the Secretary-General of *Hizb Jabhat al-'Amal al-Islami* (q.v.) (Islamic Action Front Party) during its preparatory stages. Al-Azaydah was also a member of the executive bureau of the Muslim Brotherhood in Jordan (q.v.).

AL-'AZM, YUSUF (1931–   ). Al-'Azm is a distinguished member of the Muslim Brotherhood in Jordan (q.v.). He was born in Ma'an, received his B.A. in Arabic from al-Azhar University in 1953, and received a graduate diploma in education from 'Ayn Sham University in 1954. He taught at the Islamic Scientific Faculty and became editor of *Majallat al-Kifah al-Islami* (*Journal of Islamic Struggle*) during the period 1954–1957 and later editor of the newspaper *al-Ribat*. He and others established a chain of schools, known as al-Aqsa. Al-'Azm became a member of the Lower House of Parliament during the period of 1963–1993. He published works on education and Sayyid Qutb (q.v.). See also MUSLIM BROTHERHOOD IN JORDAN; MUSLIM BROTHERHOOD IN PALESTINE.

AL-'AZMA, MAZHAR. See *AL-SALAFIYYA*.

'AZZAM, NAFIDH. 'Azzam is a member of the politburo of *Hamas*: *Harakat al-Muqawama al-Islamiyya* (q.v.) (Islamic Resistance Movement).

-B-

BABATI, 'ABD ALLAH. See *AL-JAMA'A AL-ISLAMIYYA FI LUBNAN*.

BADRI, YUSUF. See ORGANIZATION FOR ENJOINING GOOD AND FORBIDDING EVIL.

BAHA' AL-DIN, 'UMAR. See INTERNATIONAL ORGANIZATION OF THE MUSLIM BROTHERHOOD.

BAHI, MUHAMMAD. See *AL-SALAFIYYA*.

BAHISHTI, MUHAMMAD HUSAYN (1928–1981). This ayatollah was a disciple of Ayatollah Khomeini (q.v.) although he studied at Qum. Bahishti completed his graduate studies in Europe then worked for the Ministry of Education. He played an important role in solidifying the opposition of the clergy to the Shah and was imprisoned. After the Islamic Revolution (q.v.), he became the leader of the Islamic Republican Party (q.v.) and a member of the Revolutionary Council and the Council of Experts (qq.v.). Bahishti was appointed in 1980 head of the Supreme Court. He vigorously opposed the liberal politics of President Abul Hasan Bani Sadr (q.v.). Bahishti was killed in 1981 in a bomb explosion. See also ISLAMIC REPUBLICAN PARTY; KHAMENE'I, 'ALI; MUNTAZARI, HUSAYN 'ALI; REVOLUTIONARY COUNCIL.

BAHRAIN NATIONAL CONGRESS (*AL-MU'TAMAR AL-QAWMI AL-BAHRAINI*). This group is made up of important Sunnis in Bahrain who gathered together in 1923 in order to call for an end to British control of the country's affairs, the return of the ruler, and the organization of an advisory council or *Majlis al-Shura* (q.v.).

BALANCE (*TAWAZUN*). For the fundamentalists, the conceptual balance is essentially between the known and the unknown. Man surrenders to

God (q.v.) and accepts on faith issues like the nature of God's existence and the existence of the day of judgment, which are beyond human understanding. At the same time, man should free his mind to investigate those issues that are within the capability of human reason (q.v.). Because of his *fitra* (q.v.) (intuition) man possesses a natural inclination to submit to the unknown, and Islam (q.v.) satisfies that need by addressing his consciousness (q.v.) (*wa'iy*).

However, man also possesses the counterinclination to know and to make sense of this life, and Islam also meets this need by calling on humanity to extend its knowledge (q.v.) in the science (q.v.) that is within human reach. However, man must be careful not to confuse the two aspects of his life. For the investigation of the first is futile and impossible, and too much emphasis on the latter leads to confusion. Islam balances the two by giving man certain points of reference so that he is not led astray. See also DIVINITY; *FITRA*; ISLAM; PEACE; RELIGION; SCIENCE; *SHURA*; *TAWHID*; UNIVERSALISM.

BAND OF RIGHT (*'USBAT AL-HAQQ*). See *ITIHAD AL-QIWA AL-SHA'BIYYA*.

BANI SADR, ABUL HASAN (1933–   ). Bani Sadr was the first President of the Islamic Republic of Iran and was elected in January 1980 by a 75 percent majority. Bani Sadr was a close associate of Ayatollah Khomeini (q.v.) while he was in exile in France and returned with him on the same plane to Iran. He is regarded as a modernist Muslim, and radical forces rallied against him and Muhammad Shari'atmadari (q.v.). At the beginning of Bani Sadr's presidency, Khomeini transferred to him all executive powers, including command of the armed forces. His fall started with his opposition to the hostage taking and the seizure of the American Embassy in Tehran. Also, Bani Sadr, a Western-educated economist, surrounded himself with Western-educated technocrats and politicians who did not think highly of the clergy and sought some measure of freedom from the religious establishment.

When the modernist forces clashed with the conservative forces, Khomeini sided with Bani Sadr. But after much jockeying for power, in a speech at an air force base that attacked dictatorship, Khomeini removed Bani Sadr from the command of the armed forces. The *Majlis al-Shura* (q.v.) (*Shura* Council) impeached him with an overwhelming majority, and he was dismissed from the presidency in June 1981. Finally, Bani Sadr escaped to France in August 1981. See also BAHISHTI, MUHAM-

MAD; KHAMENE'I, 'ALI; QUTBZADAH, SADIQ; RAFSANJANI, 'ALI AKBAR; REVOLUTIONARY COUNCIL.

AL-BANNA, HASAN (1906–1949). Al-Banna is the founder and the first supreme guide of the Muslim Brotherhood (q.v.) in Egypt and one of the most charismatic leaders of modern Islamic movements. Al-Banna was not a traditional religious scholar but a thinker who propagated political Islam (q.v.) and an activist who established the most important Islamic fundamentalist movement in the Islamic world.

Al-Banna was born to Ahmad 'Abd al-Rahman, a watchmaker well known for his honesty and generosity. He was born in the district of Shamshirah in the center of West Fuh. He lived in a very religious atmosphere and learned religious jurisprudence and memorized the Qur'an. Al-Banna's father had an extensive religious education and had a good religious library, which al-Banna used to study. Because he was brought up in a religious environment, he developed a religious interest in life. He attended Sufi circles and visited faraway mosques. In 1920, he joined the junior teachers' college in Danaher and, upon receiving his degree, he went to Dar al-'Ulum, to study religious and linguistic sciences.

Al-Banna studied education, psychology, physiology, and other modern sciences. He was interested in social and political affairs as well as sports. As opposed to traditional religious schooling, al-Banna's scope of interest included other areas than religion (q.v.). As a teacher, al-Banna strove from the beginning to view political and economic issues from a religious point of view. As a child he was influenced by the Sufi order, and later al-Banna incorporated some of its principles in his teachings on education and ethics. The first movement he established, *al-Jam-'iyya al-Hasafiyya al-Khairiyya*, focused on developing good morality (q.v.). Al-Banna is famous for his good memory, which enabled him to remember faces, places, and years that he met people.

Al-Banna believed that Islam should deal with all aspects of society and that Islamic civilization (q.v.) includes the good of all other civilizations and even surpasses them. Both of these issues were addressed by al-Banna's ability to converse, lecture, and write.

Al-Banna founded the Muslim Brotherhood in 1928. Within five years, the movement reached from Alexandria to Aswan. His great physical strength allowed him to work very long hours, traveling, lecturing, writing, and participating in numerous sociopolitical activities. The Brotherhood became the largest and most influential religious movement in the Islamic world.

In 1933, al-Banna was transferred from his teaching post in Isma'ili-yya to Cairo, which proved to be a great opportunity to expand and strengthen his movement. He relied on such communication channels as magazines to spread his work and rally mass support. By 1938, his movement had become a well-developed organization that dealt with all aspects of life. During World War II, al-Banna's movement spread to university students who opposed Egypt's political policies. Al-Banna set up athletic programs, training students to build up support at the same time. The government confiscated the Brotherhood's magazines and ar-rested al-Banna. His arrest, however, increased his popularity.

By 1945, al-Banna directed his efforts toward undermining the gov-ernment. The Brotherhood criticized the government for persecuting its movement, nonetheless, it participated in the fighting in Palestine. Ten-sions between the Brotherhood and the government intensified when the government accused the Brotherhood of the assassination of al-Naqrashi Pasha. Al-Banna was assassinated in 1949, and the movement was dis-solved. With his death, a new era for fundamentalism (q.v.) was born, an era that found developing military capabilities to be a guarantee against the government repression.

The ideological and political discourse of the Muslim Brotherhood's founder and first supreme guide in Egypt, Hasan al-Banna, is the central discourse of most major and established Islamic movements. In other words, the Brotherhood is the mother organization for all other move-ments. Taking into account the circumstances of Egyptian society during the first half of the twentieth century, and given the relative freedom that the Egyptians had therein, the question of a forceful seizure of power was not on the agenda of the Muslim Brotherhood. Though interested in the Islamization (q.v.) of government, state, and society, al-Banna's main purpose was to be included in the existing political order and thus to compete politically with other parties (q.v.). Al-Banna himself ran twice for elections along with his party, the Brotherhood. Some of the Brotherhood's founding members were simultaneously members of other political parties; and the same applies to contemporary Brethren.

Al-Banna developed his organization into a political party with a spe-cific political agenda in order to compete with other parties that were, in his opinion, corrupt. In 1942, al-Banna along with other Brethren ran for elections, but the Prime Minister persuaded him to withdraw. In return, he was promised that his organization would receive more freedom and that liquor stores would be banned and prostitution prohibited. But later that year, Premier al-Nahhas closed down all of the Brotherhood branches, except its headquarters. Again, in 1945, al-Banna and five other Brethren ran for elections but lost. The Brotherhood competed with the *Wafd*, the communists, and others. Al-Banna became a powerful player; for instance, he was called to the palace in 1946 for consultation regarding the appointment of a new Prime Minister. At that time, the government encouraged the Brotherhood in order for the government to stand against the communists and the *Wafd*.

Again, al-Banna's condemnation of Egyptian parties was based not on their neglect of religion but on their widespread corruption and collaboration with the British. His denunciation of Egyptian pre-Nasir parliamentary experiences was therefore a rejection of Egyptian party life and not of the principle of constitutional life and multiparty politics. Al-Banna expressed his belief that Egypt's constitutional life had failed and was in need of reorientation. See also ABU GHUDDA, 'ABD AL-FATTAH; ACTIVISM; AL-BANNA, SAYF; CALIPHATE; DEMOCRACY; FARAJ, 'ABD AL-SALAM; GOVERNANCE; AL-HUDAYBI, HASAN; 'ISHMAWI, SALIH; ISLAMIC FUNDAMENTALISM; *AL-JIHAD AL-ISLAMI*; KNOWLEDGE; MUSLIM BROTHERHOOD; MUSLIM BROTHERHOOD, IDEOLOGY OF; RELIGION; REVOLUTION; RIDA, MUHAMMAD RASHID; SHADI, SALAH; *SHURA*; AL-SIBA'I, MUSTAPHA; SYSTEM; *TAQLID*; TEXT; UNIVERSALISM.

AL-BANNA, SAYF AL-ISLAM. Al-Banna is a very distinguished member of the Muslim Brotherhood (q.v.) and the son of its founder, Hasan al-Banna (q.v.). Al-Banna became the General Secretary of the Lawyers' Union. He was a member of the Egyptian Parliament in 1992, and he is supposedly a member of the Guidance Council of the Brotherhood.

AL-BARQAWI, SHAYKH YUSUF. See *AL-SALAFIYYA*.

AL-BASHIR, 'UMAR HASAN. Al-Bashir is an army general who led the coup, or *Thawrat al-Inqadh al-Watani* (National Salvation Revolution), in Sudan with the support of the National Islamic Front against Prime Minister Sadiq al-Mahdi in 1989. Al-Bashir established a military council, dissolved all parties (q.v.) and arrested most of their important leaders.

Since 1985, al-Bashir has been identified with the National Islamic Front, which was developed by the Muslim Brotherhood in Sudan (q.v.) and was headed by Hasan al-Turabi (q.v.). The military council did not include members of the front and did not function properly. The military council was later replaced by the *Majlis al-Shura* (q.v.) (*Shura* Council). Now, al-Bashir is the President of Sudan. See also MUSLIM BROTHERHOOD IN SUDAN; POPULAR DEFENSE FORCES; SUPPORTERS OF MUHAMMADAN *SUNNA*; TAHA, 'ALI 'UTHMAN; AL-TURABI, HASAN.

BAY'AT AL-IMAM (OATH OF ALLEGIANCE TO THE IMAM). See AL-AFGHAN AL-'ARAB.

AL-BAYNUNI, MUHAMMAD ABU AL-NASR. See MUSLIM BROTHERHOOD IN SYRIA.

BAZARGAN, MAHDI (1907–1996). Bazargan was born into a merchant family. In his early education, he combined traditional and modern studies and was later sent to the Central School in Paris, returning in 1935 with a doctorate. Bazargan subsequently joined the National Bank after completing his military service. He also became professor at the engineering faculty, Tehran University. He cooperated with Sayyid Mahmud Talqani (q.v.), a major figure of the opposition to the Shah's Iran, to spread the message of progressive Islam (q.v.). Bazargan became very active in founding and helping Islamic associations. He also joined the nationalist movement headed by Muhammad Musaddaq.

In 1951, he became Deputy Minister, supervising the nationalization of oil companies. After the coup of 1953, Bazargan joined the nationalist resistance and was imprisoned. Along with Talqani and Yadullah Sahabi, he set up the Liberation Movement of Iran (q.v.), but again he was imprisoned along with the other two. Bazargan later founded the Islamic Association of Teachers with Ayatollah Murtaza Mutahhari (q.v.) and Talqani. He also cofounded the Human Rights Association in 1977. Bazargan played an instrumental role in the Iranian Revolution of 1979 (q.v.), and Ayatollah Khomeini (q.v.) appointed him the first Prime Minister of the provisional government in 1979.

Bazargan, however, resigned over the issue of seizing the American Embassy in Tehran and taking American hostages. He later founded the Association for the Defense of the Freedom and Sovereignty of the Iranian Nation. Bazargan is regarded as a liberal Islamic reformer and not strictly a fundamentalist. See also LIBERATION MOVEMENT OF IRAN; QUTBZADAH, SADIQ; REVOLUTIONARY COUNCIL; TALQANI, SAYYID MAHMUD.

BEN KHEDDA, BENYOUCEF. See NATION'S PARTY.

BID'A. See INNOVATION.

BILHAJ, 'ALI (1955–). Bilhaj is the Vice President of the Islamic Salvation Front (q.v.) (*Jabhat al-Inqadh al-Islamiyya*) in Algeria. He was born in Tunisia. His father died during the revolution in Algeria. Bilhaj started his education in Wadi Souf, a town in southeastern Algeria, near the Tunisian border. He pursued his education in religion and Arabic language in al-Zaytuna Mosque, and later he taught Arabic language as well as religion in Algeria. Bilhaj was in contact with many Muslim Algerian personalities, such as 'Abd al-Latif Sultani, Ahmad Sahnun, and Abbasi Madani (qq.v.).

Bilhaj was exposed to many political fundamentalist writers like Hasan al-Banna, Sayyid Qutb and 'Abd al-Qadir 'Awda (qq.v.). Furthermore, he had some involvement with the Armed Islamic Group (q.v.) (*al-Jama'a al-Islamiyya al-Musallaha*) and enrolled in the Islamic Mission Organization. Early in his life, he was known for his political extremism (q.v.) and Islamic strictness. He was arrested and imprisoned during 1982–1983 because of his activities in the Algerian Islamic movement as well as for his contact with the Islamic Movement for Algeria (q.v.) of Mustapha Buya'li, an armed movement that worked against the Algerian system.

With the collaboration of others, Bilhaj founded the Islamic Salvation Front, and he was chosen Vice President for Abbasi Madani. Later in August 1991, both were arrested and transferred to a military court in Belida. They were sentenced to 12 years in prison. However, Bilhaj was released in 1997. See also ISLAMIC SALVATION FRONT; *JAMA'AT AL-NAHDA AL-ISLAMIYYA*; *AL-JAYSH AL-ISLAMI LI AL-INQADH*; KABIR, RABIH; MADANI, ABBASI.

BIN BAZ, 'ABD AL-'AZIZ. See *AL-SALAFIYYA*.

BIN LADEN, USAMA (1953–). He is one of the most internationally notorious fundamentalists. He was born to wealthy peasants in Saudi Arabia. His father established a construction business, the Bin Laden Group, valued at around five billion dollars. After graduating from an engineering school at King 'Abd al-'Aziz University in Jeddah in 1979, Bin Laden fought in Afghanistan and was one of the main leaders of *al-Afghan al-'Arab* (q.v.) (the Afghan Arabs), recruiting thousands of

Arabs and organizing training camps to fight the Soviets. In 1989, he returned to Saudi Arabia to run the family business. However, his anti-government activities led to his exile to Sudan in 1991. Because of his radical opposition to the Saudi regime, he was stripped of his Saudi citizenship. After the Gulf War, Bin Laden became very critical of the United States and viewed the American troops in the Gulf as an occupying army of infidels in the shadow of Islam's holiest shrines. In Sudan, he established and ran several businesses and employed hundreds of Afghan Arabs. Under heavy pressure from the American government, the Sudanese government expelled Bin Laden, who moved to Afghanistan in 1996. He issued a *fatwa* (q.v.) declaring war against U.S. presence in the Gulf. He currently lives in an elaborate hideout under the protection of the Taliban government and has established training camps for radical Arab fundamentalists. His followers are estimated at around 4,000 fighters in many countries.

Bin Laden's wealth, estimated at around $250 million, is mostly spent to fund Islamic activist movements that usually oppose their governments' regimes and the United States. He finds the means for distributing the funds to Muslim activists all over the Islamic world through companies in the United States, Europe, and the Middle East. He has been implicated in the attempts to assassinate Pope John Paul II and President Hosni Mubarak and in the 1995 bombings of World Trade Center in New York, and an American center for training National Guards in Riyadh, the bombing of al-Khobar Towers in Dhahran in 1996, and the bombing of the U.S. embassies in Kenya and Tanzania in 1998. He has set up the "Advice and Reformation Committee" and the "International Islamic Front for *Jihad* against Jews and Crusaders," the latter a shadowy organization made up of radical groups, pledged to launch severe retaliations against American forces and interests all over the world. U.S. and Saudi officials link Bin Laden to terrorist organizations and incidents in Algeria, Saudi Arabia, London, Egypt, Somalia, Philippines, Ethiopia, Yemen, and other places. The International Islamic Front is supposedly made up of Bin Laden's *al-Qaida*—Islamic Salvation Foundation—and Islamic *Jihad* and *al-Jama'a al-Islamiyya* (qq.v.).

BINKIRAN, 'ABD AL-ILAH. See AL-KHATIB, 'ABD AL-KARIM.

BIRJAWI, MUHAMMAD AHMAD (1959–). Birjawi won a seat on the Lebanese Parliament as a candidate for *Hizbullah* (q.v.) in Beirut. He participated in *Hizbullah*'s resistance to the Israeli invasion in 1992 and

was a member of the committee for supporting the resistance. He participated in founding the Lebanese branch of *Mu'assasat al-Shahid* in 1983
(the headquarters being in Tehran), *Bayt Mal al-Muslimin*, Khomeini's
cultural center, and *Hizbullah Manar* TV. Birjawi is interested in abolishing confessionalism because he believes it to be the main source for all
of Lebanon's problems. He lost his seat in the parliamentary elections
of 1996.

AL-BITAR, MUHAMMAD BAHJAT. See *AL-SALAFIYYA*.

BROTHERHOOD. See *IKHWAN*; MUSLIM BROTHERHOOD. See also
'ABD AL-WAHHAB, MUHAMMAD IBN; AL-BANNA, HASAN; *AL-
SALAFIYYA*; *AL-WAHHABIYYA*.

BULUSHI, 'ABD AL-BASIT. See YUSUF, AHMAD RAMZI.

BUYA'LI, MUSTAPHA (1940–1987). See ARMED ISLAMIC GROUP;
ISLAMIC MOVEMENT FOR ALGERIA; ISLAMIC SALVATION
FRONT IN ALGERIA; AL-NAHNAH, MAHFOUDH.

-C-

CALIPHATE (*AL-KHILAFA*). The Islamic Caliphate has been entertained
by Hasan al-Banna (q.v.) and the Islamic movement in general as being
the ultimate political establishment that can be set up on earth. As it has
been historically, the Caliphate is still viewed as the focus of any theoretical political discourse on government and politics. It represents the
highest goal of Islamic movements and the universalism (q.v.) of Islam
(q.v.) and constitutes the symbol of Islamic unity and power. It brings
together religion (q.v.) and politics, and therefore its field of study is not
only jurisprudence (q.v.) but also theology (q.v.) and the principles of
religion (*usul al-din*). In the history (q.v.) of Islam, great theoreticians,
such as al-Mawardi in *al-Ahkam al-Sultaniyya*, Ibn Taymiyya (q.v.) in
al-Siyasa al-Shar'iyya, Abu Yusuf in *Kitab al-Kharaj*, al-Ghazali in *al-
Iqtisad fi al-I'tiqad*, Ibn Jama'a in *Tahrir al-Ahkam*, and Ibn Khaldun in
the *Muqaddima*, retheorized the Caliphate's function as being of an
earthly nature, and therefore it must take into consideration the ups and
downs of history. The Caliphate is an institution that must be representative of the actualities of a given age. However, when it was al-Banna's

turn to discuss the Caliphate, it had, by then, already been abolished by the Turkish leader, Mustapha Ataturk. Thus, the symbol of Islamic unity in al-Banna's eyes was gone, and this is why the existence of the Caliphate is for him and other fundamentalists a nostalgic affinity with glory and power as well as the supremacy of Islam.

Because the existence of the Caliphate was a historical event, its regeneration was an awesome task. Regeneration would be nothing less than the unification of Muslims again in an international state, and al-Banna knew the difficulties that would be involved in achieving that task: A program of reforming the Muslims of his day should precede the Caliphate's revival. The program must include issues like the preparation of complete educational, social, and economic cooperation among Muslim peoples; the formation of alliances and conferences among these peoples; and finally, creation of a league of nations responsible for the choice of caliphs. Such issues, however, are not much easier than establishing the Caliphate itself. For this reason, an alternative institution was called for that seemed more practical and achievable.

As an indispensable step toward the reestablishment of the Caliphate, the concept of an Islamic state (q.v.) became as important, both theoretically and practically, as the Caliphate itself. Al-Banna and others have argued for the functional legitimacy (q.v.) of the state along the lines developed for that of *imarat al-isti'la'* (government by seizure) and the *sultanate*. Again, authoritative medieval thinkers such as al-Mawardi, Ibn Taymiyya, Ibn Jama'a, and Ibn Khaldun accepted the legitimacy of a government that can maintain Muslims under a unified umbrella and apply *al-Shari'a* (q.v.) (Islamic Law). But if the Caliphate were ever to come back, the functional legitimacy of the Islamic state would either be altogether abrogated or functionally subjected to the Caliphate.

The Muslim Brotherhood (q.v.) believes that the Caliphate is the symbol of Islamic unity and the sign of commitment to Islam. It is an institution that Muslims must think about and be concerned about achieving. For it is the caliph who is in charge of applying numerous commands of the divine law. Al-Banna shows the importance of the institution of the Caliphate by describing the happenings at the Prophet's death. Upon the Prophet's death, Muslims discussed the issue of political succession even before his burial. Today, because the Caliphate no longer exists, al-Banna calls for some rethinking about the issue of political rule, since it is the center of the political contract between the people and their unifying agency. This is why the Muslim Brotherhood makes the revival of Islam dependent on establishing an Islamic system (q.v.) (*nizam*) of government. However, Islam cannot flourish without the Qur'an (q.v.) and its language as well as a comprehensive political unity. Today, the Islamic political system of government can take many forms and structures, whether on the military, economic, or political level.

A fundamentalist like Abu al-Hasan al-Nadawi (q.v.) pictures this idea very clearly and states that man is God's vicegerent (*khalifa*), and his main objective in this life is to properly develop material things. Man is viewed by al-Nadawi as an active, not theoretical, vicegerent of God whose actions should aim ultimately at the good. Sayyid Qutb (q.v.) goes deeper and argues that Islam also aims at methodological changes as a first step toward substantive changes in life. Its method (q.v.) (*manhaj*) is to set up an *umma* (q.v.) (nation) through developing a creed; thus, Islam functions not only as a system of belief but also as a method and a discourse of change that goes against all human methods and discourses.

As an institution, the Caliphate was the highest religious and political body that survived in the Muslim world for about 14 centuries when it acted as the symbol of Muslim unity. See also *HIZB AL-TAHRIR AL-ISLAMI*; ISLAMIC STATE; *JAMA'AT AL-JIHAD AL-ISLAMI*; PAN-ISLAMISM; RIDA, MUHAMMAD RASHID; AL-SHAHRISTANI, HIBAT AL-DIN; AL-TURABI, HASAN; *AL-WAHHABIYYA*.

CALIPHATE GROUP (*JAMA'AT AL-KHILAFA*). See *AL-AFGHAN AL-'ARAB*.

CALL (*AL-DA'WA*). To call the world to the truth is part of the universalism (q.v.) of Islam (q.v.). It necessitates to fundamentalists like Abu al-Hasan al-Nadawi, Hasan al-Banna, Sayyid Qutb (qq.v.) and 'Abd al-Jawad Yasin the transfer of world leadership from the West (q.v.), which misused the trust, to the Muslims, who should struggle to induce that transfer. The struggle should take place first within the individual, the family, the society, and the state, and then the world. If the Muslims do that, the fundamentalists argue, then they constitute the only real power that can take away the leadership from the West, that can destroy the *jahili* (q.v.) system (*nizam*), and that can remove political persecution. Al-Banna, for instance, defends this notion from criticism of its practical impossibility by arguing that Muslims must start anew as the Prophet did: The Prophet had nothing but the truth and the will, which led to the defeat of many empires. See also AL-AFGHANI, JAMAL AL-DIN; AUTHENTICITY; *HIZB AL-TAHRIR AL-ISLAMI*; *HIZBULLAH*; ISLAMIC REVOLUTION OF IRAN; ISLAMIC SOCIETY; ISLAMIC

STATE; ISLAMIC YOUTH ORGANIZATION; *AL-JAMA'A AL-IS-LAMIYYA*; *JIHAD*; *AL-JIHAD AL-ISLAMI* IN THE WEST BANK AND GAZA STRIP; KHOMEINISM; *MILLI NIZAM PARTISI*; PAST; PEACE, AL-QUR'AN; RIDA, MUHAMMAD RASHID; *AL-SALAFI-YYA*; *AL-SALAFIYYA* FORCES IN EGYPT; *SHURA*; *TAWHID*; UNI-VERSALISM; *AL-WAHHABIYYA*.

CAPITALISM (*AL-RA'SIMALIYYA*). For radical fundamentalism (q.v.), capitalism, characterized by usury, monopoly, exploitation, and lack of justice (q.v.), is rejected as the model for Islam (q.v.) to imitate and follow. Moreover, capitalism has been linked closely to nationalism where states like England, France, Italy, Germany, and the United States, in the name of national interest, gave themselves the right to exploit, invade, and occupy other countries in the Middle East, India, Africa, and Latin America.

On the other hand, although socialism and Islam converge on many essential points, such as advocating guarantees of minimum standards of life, work, housing, and social justice (q.v.), Islam's economic system (q.v.) (*nizam*), according to radical fundamentalists, is an integral part of Islam and is based on *tawhid* (q.v.) (Oneness of God). See also MARX-ISM; MUSLIM BROTHERHOOD IN JORDAN; RELIGION, *SHURA*.

CHIAGHARJI, 'IRFAN. See ORGANIZATION OF THE ISLAMIC MOVEMENT.

CHRISTIANITY. The fundamentalists in general believe that Judaism (q.v.) and Christianity, the other two important monotheistic religions (q.v.) beside Islam (q.v.), are true revealed religions. However, Judaism and Christianity have been corrupted historically in a substantive way by their religious elites, and now political elites, for earthly and material interests. Thus, they lost their true meaning and, thereby, became human products that suit Western interests.

Although Christianity is viewed by the Qur'an (q.v.) as a true, authentic, and divine message, the Qur'an also speaks of the corruption of the original Christian view of God (q.v.) by associating God with nondivine elements. The Christian churches have historically manipulated their teachings for political and material interests, which led to their condemnation by God. Pure *tawhid* (q.v.) (Oneness of God) was vitiated by attributing divine attributes to a man and a prophet—Jesus.

For the fundamentalists, Christianity lost its true meaning because

Greek paganism (q.v.) (*jahiliyya*) and Roman veneration of power triumphed over the true spirit of Christianity. Finally, materialism and political interests triumphed over all forms of thought, and are still in the present a main feature of Western thought. These interests can be seen today, for instance, in Western imperialism and colonization, which manipulate and drain the Islamic world.

To the fundamentalists, current world order (q.v.) and recent modern history (q.v.), especially the occupation of Palestine and the occupation of Muslim land, testifies to the disregard of Christians and Europeans, who aided the Jews in settling Palestine, to the rights of others in the Holy Places and land in Palestine, and to their dependence on physical power and manipulation of other people.

Nonetheless, the fundamentalists argue that Muslims are ready to develop proper human relations with other religions in order to develop cooperation with other religions and people, on the condition that they do not stand against the Muslims' religion and rights. See also FADLAL-LAH, MUHAMMAD HUSAYN; ISRAEL; *JAHILI* SOCIETIES; JUDAISM; MONOTHEISTIC RELIGIONS; RELIGION; *TAWHID*; WESTERN CIVILIZATION.

CIVILIZATION (*AL-HADARA*). The fundamentalists, especially the radicals, underline the need for modern and new foundations of a civilization based on Islam (q.v.). Their deliberate dismissal of Western civilization (q.v.) and the Islamic civilization leads them to uphold the need for Islamic authenticity (q.v.) as a ground for developing new theories. This applies also to the formal aspect of government such as the proper forms of an Islamic state (q.v.). Although the moderate trend uses some Western notions like democracy (q.v.), the notions are always underpinned by Islamic concepts like *shura* (q.v.) (consultation).

The fundamentalists argue that a new Islamic civilization should be based on *tawhid* (q.v.) (Oneness of God) and its concomitant doctrines concerning paganism and governance (qq.v.) and institutions like Islamic society and state (qq.v.). It should also be based on an Islamic method and universalism (qq.v.) that lead to the development of an Islamic system (q.v.) (*nizam*) and a just world order (q.v.). Numerous fundamentalists condemn Western civilization for its materialism, use of power, and lack of morality (q.v.). They further criticize it for the unjust world order that it has built and the world conflicts that it has produced. See also 'ABDU, MUHAMMAD; AL-BANNA, HASAN; DIALOGUE; FUNDAMENTALISM; FUNDAMENTALS; *HARAKAT AL-NAHDA*

AL-ISLAMIYYA; HISTORY; *HIZB AL-TAHRIR AL-ISLAMI*; INTER-PRETATION; ISLAMIC CULTURAL HERITAGE SOCIETY; IS-RAEL; JUSTICE; LEGITIMACY; METHOD; MODERNISM; MO-DERNITY; PAGANISM; PAN-ISLAMISM; RIDA, MUHAMMAD RASHID; SCIENCE; WEST; WESTERN CIVILIZATION.

COMMITTEE FOR DEFENDING THE LEGITIMATE RIGHTS (*LAJNAT AL-DIFA' 'AN AL-HUQUQ AL-SHAR'IYYA*). See AL-MA-S'ARI, MUHAMMAD.

COMMUNITY (*AL-JAMA'A*). See *UMMA*.

COMPREHENSIVENESS (*AL-SHUMULIYYA*). For the fundamentalists, *al-shumuliyya* is formulated against the partiality of human thought. A divine, constant *tawhid* (q.v.) (Oneness of God) cannot but be comprehensive for fundamentalists, covering all aspects of life throughout history (q.v.) and transcending the particularities of time and place. Although man's knowledge (q.v.) and experience are limited, his weaknesses and desires are not.

It is therefore only the Islamic *tawhid* that gives humanity an intelligible interpretative discourse about the phenomena of life and the universe. Again, for fundamentalists the revealed religious discourse of the Qur'an (q.v.) should dominate all aspects of life because of its ability to provide humanity with a meaningful yet true discourse about the divine and the human, the social and the individual, the public and the private. See also *TAWHID*; UNIVERSALISM.

CONSCIOUSNESS (*AL-WA'IY*). For the fundamentalists, religious consciousness functions as the instrument of a proper religious life. It is needed for the establishment of an Islamic revolution, society, and state (qq.v.). It is further needed for developing morality, justice, and equality (qq.v.). Thus, it is the motivating force to develop all sorts of principles, including human rights (q.v.) that should not only be defined in terms of the material gain that an individual, society or state can obtain. In this sense, sheer power, or violence (q.v.), could not be the source of principles and rights, even of individuals. Rights are of a more fundamental, that is religious, nature.

The fundamentalists argue that if proper consciousness is developed at all levels, then political rights interact with political and social realities and transform the individual life into a social dimension and the social life into an individual dimension. Only through developing proper consciousness could the contradiction between different claims be resolved. The consciousness of an individual becomes representative of social consciousness, and social consciousness represents the will of the people. See also BALANCE; DEMOCRATIC ISLAMIC ARAB MOVEMENT; *HIZBULLAH*; KNOWLEDGE; LEGITIMACY; *MILLI SELAMET PARTISI*; MODERNITY; MUSLIM BROTHERHOOD; PAGANISM; RADICALISM; *SHURA*; AL-TURABI, HASAN; WESTERN CIVILIZATION.

CONSENSUS. See *IJMA'*.

CONSTITUTION (*AL-DUSTUR*). For most fundamentalist thinkers and activists the legally valid constitution is either the Qur'an (q.v.) or a compendium that is based on the Qur'an, because they view legislation (q.v.) as a divine matter. Whereas moderate fundamentalists, like Hasan al-Banna and Rashid al-Ghannushi (qq.v.), accept modern constitutional rule but require its grounding in the Qur'anic text and *al-Shari'a* (qq.v.) (Islamic Law) in general, radical fundamentalists like Sayyid Qutb and 'Umar 'Abd al-Rahman (qq.v.) deny any legitimate possibility of human legislation. The radicals consider human legislation to be aggression against divinity (q.v.) (*uluhiyya*). The only acceptable constitution for them is the Qur'an. See also 'ABD AL-RAHMAN, 'UMAR; APOSTASY; CONSTITUTIONAL RULE; COUNCIL FOR THE PRESERVATION OF THE CONSTITUTION; DEMOCRACY; *HIZB AL-HAQQ*; *HIZB JABHAT AL-'AMAL AL-ISLAMI*; *HIZB AL-TAHRIR AL-ISLAMI*; ISLAMIC REVOLUTION OF IRAN; ISLAMIC STATE; KHOMEINISM; *MAJLIS AL-SHURA*; *MAJLIS TASHKHIS MASLAHAT AL-NIZAM*; *MILLI NIZAM PARTISI*; MUSLIM BROTHERHOOD IN SUDAN; POPULAR MOVEMENT; QUTB, SAYYID; RELIGION.

CONSTITUTIONAL RULE (*AL-HUKM AL-DUSTURI*). For moderate fundamentalists, constitutional rule, or rule based on a public constitution (q.v.) is not merely a matter of copying Western practices but must be Islamized by undergoing a process of philosophical grounding in *al-Shari'a* (q.v.) (Islamic Law) as well as objective application. Hasan al-Banna (q.v.) and others, for instance, criticize Egypt's experimentation with constitutional rule and call for its reorientation toward Islamic Law, especially after constitutional rule failed to perform positively in Egypt's political life. On the theoretical level, fundamentalists base constitutional rule on *shura* (q.v.) (consultation). They claim *shura* to be the closest method (q.v.) (*manhaj*) of government to the nature of politics in Islam (q.v.). More importantly, fundamentalists find textual justifications for the adoption of constitutional rule as *shura* by grounding its necessity in a Qur'anic text (q.v.): "and consult them in affairs [of moment]. Then, when thou hast taken a decision, put thy trust in God." Such a derivation is possible because this Qur'anic revelation is interpreted as "the basic principle of rule of government and exercise of authority." The Qur'anic power is employed to highlight the power of the community in making and unmaking of political systems, governments, forms of government (q.v.), and political behavior. It provides the community with further power vis-à-vis the state, which must act in conformity with the ambitions and needs of the people. See also CONSTITUTION; ISLAMIC STATE; MODERNISM; MUSLIM BROTHERHOOD, IDEOLOGY OF; AL-SADR, MUHAMMAD BAQIR.

COUNCIL FOR CHARACTERIZING THE REGIME'S INTEREST. See *MAJLIS TASHKHIS MASLAHAT AL-NIZAM.*

COUNCIL FOR THE PRESERVATION OF THE CONSTITUTION (*MAJLIS AL-MUHAFAZA 'ALA AL-DUSTUR*). This Iranian council is composed of 12 individuals, of whom six are jurists appointed by the *waliy al-faqih* (q.v.) (the guardian of the jurist) and six jurists who are elected by *Majlis al-Shura* (q.v.) (the *Shura* Council). This council is the highest constitutional body in the Islamic Republic of Iran and supervises all electoral processes and studies the constitutionality of the laws passed by the *Shura* Council.

COUNCIL OF EXPERTS (*MAJLIS AL-KHUBARA'*). This Iranian council is made up of 83 experts who are elected every seven years from all districts of Iran in order to control and supervise the respect of the Iranian supreme guide or *waliy al-faqih* (q.v.) to the revolutionary course developed by Ayatollah Khomeini (q.v.). The council also reviews the mental and physical qualities of the guide, who could be removed from his post in the event of losing a quality such as reason (q.v.) or faith. The head of the Council is presently Ayatollah 'Ali Mashkini; former President 'Ali Akbar Rafsanjani (q.v.) was the first deputy. See also MUNTAZARI, HUSAYN 'ALI; TALQANI, SAYYID MAHMUD; *WALIY AL-FAQIH.*

-D-

DAKHIL, 'ABD AL-SAHIB (?-1970). Dakhil was a founding member of *al-Da'wa al-Islamiyya* in Iraq (q.v.). He died in prison in 1970 after undergoing torture when he refused to provide any information to the authorities about the party and its leaders.

DAR AL-HARB (ABODE OF WAR). For radical fundamentalists, the Islamic state (q.v.) is established on that land where the Islamic order and *al-Shari'a* (q.v) (Islamic Law) rule, regardless of whether all or only part of the population is Muslim. That land that is not ruled by Islam (q.v.) is *dar al-harb* (the abode of war), regardless of the religion (q.v.) of the people. What is significant here is that a Muslim society is Muslim not because it is composed of Muslims but rather because of the rule of Islamic Law. Thus, the application of Islamic Law in a society whether composed of a majority of Muslims or non-Muslims makes that society Muslim. The Islamic state is defined neither by specific territories nor by specific races, and a Muslim society can be established anywhere. On the other hand, those societies that claim to be Muslim are not so if they do not uphold the law of Islam. In practical terms, this means that most societies that exist now are not Islamic and, thus, must be changed. Moreover, *dar al-harb* includes any state that fights the religious orientations of Muslims. See also *HIZBULLAH*.

DAR AL-ISLAM (ABODE OF ISLAM). See *DAR AL-HARB*.

DAR AL-SALAM (ABODE OF PEACE). See PEACE; UNIVERSALISM; WORLD ORDER.

DARWISH, 'ABD ALLAH NIMR. See *AL-JIHAD AL-ISLAMI* IN THE WEST BANK AND GAZA STRIP.

DA'UR, AHMAD. See *HIZB AL-TAHRIR AL-ISLAMI*.

DA'WA. See CALL.

AL-DA'WA **IN JORDAN.** See DEMOCRATIC ISLAMIC ARAB MOVEMENT.

AL-DA'WA **(CALL) IN KUWAIT AND SAUDI ARABIA**. This is an underground Shi'ite political movement that was active in Kuwait and the eastern province of Saudi Arabia in the late 1970s and early 1980s. It called for overthrowing the existing regimes in these two states and for establishing Islamic republics modeled on the Islamic Republic of Iran. The movement was linked to Iran in the aftermath of the revolution of 1978–79. Although its secret operations were severely restricted by the security services of the two countries in the early 1980s, there are signs that it has continued to attract at least some degree of popular support, especially in Saudi Arabia in 1992.

AL-DA'WA AL-ISLAMIYYA **(ISLAMIC CALL) IN IRAQ**. *Hizb al-Da'wa al-Islamiyya* was formed in 1968 and is led by Shi'ite religious leaders with close ties to Iran. It was inspired by Ayatollah Muhammad Baqir al-Sadr (q.v.), who preached a return to Islamic precepts in government and social justice (qq.v.). In 1979, with riots in al-Najaf and Karbala, the government uncovered *al-Da'wa*, which is now dedicated to the overthrow of the regime with support from Iran. The party is suppressed by the government; Muhammad Baqir al-Sadr and his sister were arrested and executed in 1980, and the party went underground. Ayatollah Khomeini (q.v.) issued a legal decree in response to al-Sadr's execution in which he accused the Iraqi regime of unbelief (q.v.) (*kufr*) and called on the army to topple it. There seems to be a link between *Hizb al-Da'wa a*nd *Hizbullah* (q.v.), because Muhammad Husayn Fadlallah (q.v.), the spiritual leader of the latter, was a member of *Hizb al-Da'wa* during his study in Iraq. The party claimed responsibility for the assassination attempt in January 1996 on Saddam Hussein's son, 'Uday, who was severely injured. See also DAKHIL, 'ABD AL-SAHIB; *HIZBUL-LAH*; ISLAMIC FRONT FOR THE LIBERATION OF BAHRAIN; AL-SADR, MUHAMMAD BAQIR.

AL-DAWI, AL-HABIB. See ISLAMIC FRONT FOR SALVATION IN TUNISIA.

DAWLA (STATE). See CALIPHATE; GOVERNANCE; GOVERNMENT; ISLAMIC STATE.

DAWUDIYYA, 'ABD KHALAF (1922–). Dawudiyya was a leader and member of the Muslim Brotherhood in Jordan (q.v.). He was born in Tufiyleh and worked at the Ministry of Education. Dawudiyya became the governor of many districts. In 1984, he became Minister of Religious Endowment and Holy Places.

DEMOCRACY (*AL-DIMUCRATIYYA*). Some fundamentalists, such as Rashid al-Ghannushi (q.v.), the leader of *Harakat al-Nahda al-Islamiyya* (q.v.) (Islamic Renaissance Movement) in Tunisia, Dr. Hasan al-Turabi (q.v.) in Sudan, Shaykh Husayn Fadlallah (q.v.), the spiritual leader of *Hizbullah* (q.v.) (Party of God) in Lebanon, and even Hasan al-Banna (q.v.), the founder of the Muslim Brotherhood (q.v.) in Egypt, do argue for the adoption of democracy. But democracy to them does not include the concept of ultimate sovereignty. It means human sovereignty and the exercise of power. Particularly, it connotes election and not that the ultimate authority in political affairs belongs to the people. In Islam (q.v.), ultimate sovereignty is only God's (q.v.); man's sovereignty is related to the exercise of power within the limits of Islamic Law and consultation or *al-Shari'a* and *shura* (qq.v.).

Moderate fundamentalists argue that a popular liberating democracy, grounded in Islamic Law, is a political bridge between the East and the West (q.v.). Because authoritarianism and despotism are not specifically cultural or Islamic; they have existed in both the West and the East but are more prominent now in the Arab world. The moderate fundamentalist trend adopts an Islamic interpretation (q.v.) of liberal democracy as opposed to the popular democracy of radical fundamentalism (q.v.) and the authoritarian nationalism of the Arab world. Radical fundamentalism proclaims the constitutionality of Islam, even in non-Islamic states and as such requires no prior popular approval and excludes the possibility of its inclusion in dialogues and cooperation whether with Arab regimes or the West. Moderate fundamentalism seems more amenable and eager to be included in dialogue and compromise, whether in party formations or the general discourses about politics, ideology, and religion (qq.v.) within the context of a civil society.

Many fundamentalist theoreticians such as al-Turabi and al-Ghannushi argue that Islam is not opposed to democracy. On the contrary, al-Turabi explains that if *shura* and democracy were viewed outside their historical conditions, they might be used synonymously. Although it is true that ultimate sovereignty in Islam belongs to God, practical and political sovereignty is, however, the prerogative of the people. *Shura* does not therefore take away communal freedom (q.v.) to select an appropriate course of action and a set of rules or even representative bodies.

But al-Turabi cautions against breaking any fundamental principle of Islam provided by the Qur'an (q.v.).

Another reason for many fundamentalists' democratization of *shura* is related to their ability to distinguish divine governance (q.v.) (*hakimiyya*) from human governance: the first can never be properly represented; consequently no individual, group, or institution can properly claim to represent a specific mandate or a divine right to rule. However, the legitimacy (q.v.) of representing human governance must be sought in the fulfillment of and adherence to Qur'anic instructions and on the proper conditions for carrying out *shura*. This theoretical principle, the fulfillment of the Islamic constitution (q.v.), defines to the *umma* (q.v.) (nation) at large the kind of system (q.v.) (*nizam*) to be upheld; the practical principle, the fulfillment of the conditions of *shura*, makes the *umma* the sole legitimate *sulta* or authority for government. Most fundamentalists convert *al-amr bi al-ma'ruf wa al-nahy 'an al-munkar*, or enjoining good and forbidding evil, from an ethical concept into a formulation of public, legal, and political right to watch over the government. The ruler is accountable not only to God but to the *umma* as well. The belief that the exercise of authority requires the continuous ratification and approval of the *umma* transforms governance into nothing more than a contract between the ruled and the ruler, and politics is democratized. See also AL-AFGHANI, JAMAL AL-DIN; AUTHENTICITY; DIALOGUE; EQUALITY; GOVERNANCE; *IJMA'*; ISLAMIC FUNDAMENTALISM; ISLAMIC STATE; ISLAMIZATION; MODERNISM; MODERNITY; PARTIES; *SHURA*; *AL-SHUMULIYYA*; AL-TURABI, HASAN; WEST.

DEMOCRATIC CONSTITUTIONAL POPULAR MOVEMENT (*AL-HARAKA AL-SHA'BIYYA AL-DUSTURIYYA AL-DIMUCRATIYYA*). This movement was set up in the mid-1950s in Morocco by the Palace to counterbalance the power of the Independence Party (q.v.). It became popular and maintained a degree of stability and harmony within its leadership, especially between the two major leaders, al-Mahjubi Ahradan and 'Abd al-Karim al-Khatib (q.v.).

However, in February 1967, Dr. al-Khatib and his supporters announced the formation of the Democratic Constitutional Popular Movement Party, which followed an Islamic direction to support the monarchy. Because the party did not have an organizational structure or a popular base, it derived support from Palace and state authorities in Morocco and on the historical legitimacy of its leader, acquired during the period of armed resistance to the French. See also AL-KHATIB, 'ABD AL-KARIM; POPULAR MOVEMENT.

DEMOCRATIC ISLAMIC ARAB MOVEMENT (*AL-HARAKA AL-IS-LAMIYYA AL-'ARABIYYA AL-DIMUCRATIYYA*: *AL-DA'WA*). Established in Jordan in 1990 by Yusuf Abu Bakir, this movement rejected both Marxism and capitalism (qq.v.) and adhered to the Qur'an (q.v.) and the *Sunna* (way) of the Prophet as its only comprehensive sources for belief, political life, and solutions to socioeconomic problems. But the movement sharply criticized other Islamic groups for their rigid interpretations of Islam (q.v.) and their focus on "trivial" issues of Islamization (q.v.) of Jordan. It has also called for expanded political freedoms, the creation of an independent judicial system, and complete equality (q.v.) for women. In marked contrast to most Islamic parties (q.v.), which called for the immediate application of *Shari'a* (q.v.) (Islamic Law), the movement urged delaying its application until proper conditions have been met.

The constitution (q.v.) of the movement revolves around five principles: Arabism, Islam, democracy, *shura* (consultation), and reason (qq.v.). It believes that the Qur'an should be implemented in accordance with modernity (q.v.). It seeks to develop a solid working relationship with Christians through a process of refounding Muslim-Christian relations, because both aim at serving God, developing humanity, and raising religious consciousness (q.v.) (*wa'iy*), which has been destroyed by the tyranny (q.v.) of materialism.

DEVOTEES OF ISLAM. See *FADA'IYAN-I ISLAM*.

DHUNAYBAT, 'ABD AL-MAJID (1947–   ). Dhunaybat has been the general guide of the Muslim Brotherhood in Jordan (q.v.) since 1994. Dhunaybat was born in Karak and obtained a B.A. in law from the University of Damascus. He worked in teaching and law. Dhunaybat represented the Muslim Brotherhood in the Lower House of Parliament and was a member of the *Shura* (q.v.) Council of *Jabhat al-'Amal al-Islami* (q.v.) (Islamic Action Front Party). Dhunaybat became head of the *Shura* Council in 1993.

DIALOGUE (*AL-HIWAR*). For moderate fundamentalists, the modern Islamic movement, as the leader of revival in Islamic societies, must prepare itself to start a fruitful dialogue with the world and on all levels:

economic, social, political, and above all, intellectual. The universalism (q.v.) of Islam (q.v.) means that Muslims should deal with others in terms of others' discourses and languages. Both Muslim and Western societies should transcend their history (q.v.) of conflict and bloodshed in order to bring the diverse parts of the world closer to one another. Hasan al-Turabi and Rashid al-Ghannushi's (qq.v.) agenda for dialogue, for instance, includes the freedom (q.v.) to discuss all issues of culture, civilization (q.v.), politics, economics, information, society, arts, and even sports. The dialogue between the West (q.v.) and the Islamic movement on the political discourse should substantively deal with two main aspects: first, the Muslim political society and its political dimensions, including false representation of people, suppression of freedoms, political oppression, political unrest; second, the Islamic political system (*nizam*) and questions of change of man, society, and reality, *shura* (consultation) and democracy (qq.v.), Islamic revivalism, and the new world order (q.v.). For al-Turabi there is now no "end of history," and the "clash of civilizations" is not the destined fate of humanity, that is if humanity seeks salvation from its miseries and catastrophes. See also FADLAL-LAH, MUHAMMAD HUSAYN; AL-GHANNUSHI, RASHID; ISLAMIC SOCIETY MOVEMENT; MUSLIM BROTHERHOOD, IDEOLOGY OF; AL-TURABI, HASAN; UNION OF THE REVOLUTIONARY ISLAMIC FORCES; WEST.

AL-DIMUCRATIYYA. See DEMOCRACY.

AL-DIN. See RELIGION.

AL-DINNAWI, MUHAMMAD 'ALI. See *AL-JAMA'A AL-ISLAMIYYA FI LUBNAN*.

DIVINITY (*ULUHIYYA*). Divinity indicates to fundamentalists the unchangeability of the concept of *tawhid* (q.v.) (Oneness of God), because God (q.v.) is its author and source, and Prophet Muhammad is the agency of transmission, whose mission is essentially to faithfully preach divine doctrines. The Prophet, like other Muslims, is bound by the *Shari'a* (q.v.) (Islamic Law), but he is singled out as a messenger of God. Thus, the Prophet's function, according to Sayyid Qutb and Abu al-A'la al-Mawdudi (qq.v.), for instance, was not to philosophize and invent doctrines and philosophies but to literally adhere to the divine law. In this sense, they make the prophetic discourse a consequence of the Qur'anic discourse and dependent on it.

According to the fundamentalists, divine knowledge (q.v.) transmitted through the revealed text (q.v.) surpasses human knowledge, even that of the Prophet, insofar as the divine authority surpasses any human authority. If this is the case with the Prophet, it is rather easier for fundamentalists to deny any formative role or even more authentic understanding of religion (q.v.) by theologians and jurists.

The fundamentalists further argue that divinity of the universal Islamic concept *tawhid* also means that although it is eternal, the understanding of it is not, and understanding is subject to the conditions of the interpreter and the tools of interpretation (q.v.). A distinction is thus made between understanding the text and the text itself. The textually derived Islamic concept is eternally valid, human understanding is eternally fluid. Thus, the possibilities of understanding or reading the universal Islamic concept are extended throughout space and time. They become linked to the material, political, and economic conditions of the reader and interpreter. Thus, the basic text, or the Qur'an (q.v.), can be read, interpreted, and understood differently by different generations and individuals, therefore, past discourses on the meaning of Qur'an should not and must not be limiting to modern and contemporary human understanding of the text or of the past itself. The text cannot be contradicted by a past or present human discourse, only by another text. See also CONSTITUTION; GOD; GOVERNANCE; ISLAMIC STATE; *JIHAD*; PAGANISM; PEACE; REVOLUTION; *TAWHID*; AL-TURABI, HASAN; UNIVERSALISM.

AL-DUSTUR. See CONSTITUTION.

-E-

ECONOMIC THEORY. The first principle in Islamic economic theory is the right of private ownership, but Islam (q.v.), according to many fundamentalists, stipulates that ownership is nonexistent except by the authority of the Lawgiver, that is, God (q.v.). This is so because rights are not derived from the essence of things or a theory of natural rights but are derived from the permission of the Lawgiver as indicated in *Sha-ri'a* (q.v.) (Islamic Law). Because God is the owner of everything, man is His vicegerent. Man's vicegerency allows him to acquire private ownership, although the acquisition of private ownership is dependent on labor, physical or otherwise. And any ownership that is not based on the legal prescriptions of Islam and labor is a false possession, because Islam does not acknowledge or guarantee it. Therefore, the development of any financial enterprise should be within the framework of Islamic Laws. Thus, the benefits of gambling, cheating, monopoly, and excessive gain are illegal and cannot be guaranteed in an Islamic state (q.v.). In this way, the individual does not theoretically possess the thing itself but rather its benefits. Private ownership is a function of dispensation with conditions and limits.

EQUALITY (*AL-MUSAWAT*). Although most fundamentalists uphold the people's power over the government (q.v.) and democracy (q.v.), this view is not based on the philosophy (q.v.) of natural rights but is rather developed in light of a philosophy of equality and because of textual references to the *shura* (q.v.) (consultation) of the people and to the absence of legitimacy (q.v.) of unlimited governmental powers. However, the whole concept of people's choice is justified by the Qur'an by a reinterpretation of texts to conform to the democratic notion of popular governments. Although the role of reason (q.v.) is not denied in political matters, it is employed more at the theoretical level to extract political rights and duties. The equality of men is postulated by the Qur'an (q.v.); that this means equal political rights and duties is however the rational derivation of that. Again, this means that no individual or group can claim privileged positions, whether political or religious. Hasan al-Banna (q.v.) does not refer this issue again to any natural quality such as reason but refers to Qur'anic texts as a means of proving the necessity of people's rule, although within the governance (q.v.) (*hakimiyya*) of God (q.v.). See also CONSCIOUSNESS; DEMOCRATIC ISLAMIC ARAB MOVEMENT; *FITRA*; *HARAKAT AL-NAHDA AL-ISLAMIYYA* IN TUNISIA; *HIZBULLAH*; *IJMA'*; PEACE; REVOLUTION; *SHURA*; *AL-TAJAMMU' AL-YEMENI LI AL-ISLAH*; *TAWHID*; VIOLENCE; WORLD ORDER.

ERBAKAN, NECMETTIN (1926–   ). Erbakan is the most important figure in the fundamentalist movement in Turkey. Erbakan, who was brought up in a religious family, studied at the Technical University of Istanbul. In 1948 he graduated from the Faculty of Mechanics, and he received his Ph.D. in Mechanics from Aachen Techische Hochschule in Germany in 1953. From 1954 until 1966, Erbakan taught mechanics at the Technical University of Istanbul. Erbakan led the three very important fundamentalist parties (q.v.) in Turkey, *al-Refah Partisi*, *Milli Selamet Partisi*, and *Milli Nizam Partisi* (qq.v.). Erbakan led the *Refah* to its victory in the municipal elections in 1994–1995 and the parliamentary elections of 1996 and became the first fundamentalist Prime Minister in the Republic of Turkey. However, in 1997, he was forced to resign by the military and some secular parties. See also *MILLI NIZAM PARTISI*; *MILLI SELAMET PARTISI*; QAZAN, SHAWKAT; *RASA'IL AL-NUR*; *REFAH PARTISI*.

EXEGESIS (*TAFSIR*). See INTERPRETATION.

EXTREMISM (*TATARRUF*). Islamic extremism does not consist of one popular or organized movement. Rather, the extremist religious trend includes many small but well-organized and trained movements such as *Hizb al-Tahrir*, *al-jihad* organization, *Harakat al-Tawhid*, and *Jama'at al-Takfir wa al-Hijra* or *Jama'at al-Muslimin* (qq.v.). Extremism is the result of holding an ideology of radical and revolutionary nature that allows and sponsors violent acts and accuses regimes, societies, and individuals of unbelief (q.v.). More importantly, when mainstream movements are suppressed and are not given any say in the running of their government or allowed to play by the rules of the political game, splinter radical groups surface.

The radical religious trend began in Egypt in the shadow of the Muslim Brotherhood (q.v.) in the 1920s and 1930s and went through a repressive experience after 1952. This first led to the spread of the movement in the eastern and Gulf Arab countries, especially Saudi Arabia, Kuwait, Qatar, and the Emirates. Second, the extremists formed the nucleus of a new political behavior that was manifested in the activism (q.v.) (*harakiyya*) of extremist religious groups all over the Islamic world. They also derived hope for political change from the successful model of the Islamic Revolution of Iran (q.v.). See also BILHAJ, 'ALI; ISLAMIC YOUTH ORGANIZATION; AL-NAHNAH, MAHFOUDH.

-F-

FADA'IYAN-I ISLAM (DEVOTEES OF ISLAM). This secretive and clandestine mass movement emerged in the mid-1940s during a time of great fear in Iranian politics. Its major objectives were to work for the establishment of a theocratic regime that would implement *al-Shari'a* (q.v.) (Islamic Law) in all areas of life. This fundamentalist and dogmatic movement was founded by a young seminary student, Sayyid Mujtab Navvab Safavi (q.v.). Its first act was the assassination of the famous nationalist thinker Ahmad Kasravi who attacked the Shi'ite religious establishment for several years. Even Ayatollah Khomeini (q.v.) had written a rebuttal of one of his books.

The Devotees of Islam never created an organized, structured party, but they did exert influence in the streets. During the Musaddaq period, the Devotees tried hard to win the support of Ayatollah Kashani (q.v.), who rebuffed them. After the restoration of the shah in 1953, the government arrested many of the group's leaders. After the 1978–1979 revolution, the Devotees resurfaced, but once again the high-ranking clergy kept their distance. It fell to Shaykh Sadiq Khilkhali (known as the hanging judge) to become its leader. The Devotees, however, have not been successful in carrying out their own prescriptions. See also KASHANI, ABU AL-QASIM; SAFAVI, SAYYID MUJTAB NAVVAB; WARRIORS OF ISLAM SOCIETY.

FADILA PARTISI. See *REFAH PARTISI*.

FADLALLAH, MUHAMMAD HUSAYN (1936–). Fadlallah was born in the city of Najaf in Iraq. His father, Ayatollah 'Abd al-Rauf Fadlallah, and his uncle al-'Alama Muhammad Sayyid Fadlallah were clergymen. Fadlallah's family belonged to the lower class: his financial condition, which was close to the poverty line, affected his views of social justice (q.v.). His father and uncle, however, influenced his life. He respected Muhsin al-Hakim and his open mind to different ideas and beliefs. The Fadlallah family is considered by the Shi'ites as descendants of 'Ali Ibn Talib, and this is why today he holds the title of Sayyid.

At an early age, Fadlallah was sent to *Katatib* (traditional schools) where he learned the basics of readings and writing. Later on, he joined a secular school but left it to follow religious studies. Fadlallah believes that the religious environment that surrounded him is behind his commitment to a religious career. He joined the *Hawzat al-'Ilimiyya* (the religious circle) at the age of 11 (1947) and graduated after 22 years at the age of 33 (1966). His mentors, al-Imam Abu al-Hasan al-Khu'i, Sayyid Muhsin al-Hakim, Sayyid Muhammad al-Shahrudi, and Shaykh Husayn al-Hili, were very important Shi'ite religious figures. Fadlallah's encounter with Lebanese politics was through his uncle 'Ali Bazzi, a deputy and well-known political figure. From him, he learned some of the basics that characterize Lebanese political life. Fadlallah is married and has 11 children, seven boys and four girls.

Fadlallah's first activities in Najaf revolved around the Shi'ite political and religious revival that took place in the *Hawzat al-'Ilmiyya* led by Muhammad Baqir al-Sadr (q.v.), who established the *da'wa* Party in the 1960s. Fadlallah was close to al-Sadr and helped him in his political activities. He was one of the main editors of the journal, *al-Da'wa*. But due to the political conditions in Iraq, Fadlallah returned to Lebanon in 1966 and became active in the Eastern Suburb of Beirut.

In the late 1960s and early 1970s, Fadlallah helped Imam Musa al-Sadr (q.v.) establish the Higher Islamic Supreme Shi'ite Council but did not join it because he did not want to be in an institution that represented a faction of the nation. Fadlallah did not appear in the Lebanese political scene until the Israeli invasion of 1982. At that time, he was in Iran, and he came back although the Israelis were besieging Beirut. After the arrival of the Iranian Revolutionary Guards (q.v.), he helped establish *Hizbullah* (q.v.) (Party of God) and became its spiritual leader—a claim he rejects. In reality, he laid down the ideological bases of the party by advocating and spreading the idea of the Islamic state (q.v.) and other important doctrines.

Fadlallah's views are in line with the writings of Muhammad Baqir al-Sadr and Ayatollah Khomeini (q.v.) and the experience of the Iranian Revolution of 1979 (q.v.). The movement that *Hizbullah* led against the established rules was described by him as "rebellion against fear." Also, at that time, he advocated violence (q.v.). He described it as "a surgical operation that the doctor should only resort to after he has exhausted all other methods." His ideas on Islam (q.v.) and the logic of using force found receptive ears among Islamic activists.

Hizbullah began to launch suicide attacks against the Israelis in South Lebanon. After the expansion of these attacks, Fadlallah felt that some of these activities did not aim at the enemy and tried to draw a line between himself and *Hizbullah* after the kidnapping of foreign hostages in Lebanon. He warned *Hizbullah* about the deteriorating factors that turn any movement from its idealistic views. His attitude reflected his distinction between himself and *Hizbullah* in the period that preceded the political changes that took place in Iran as well as in *Hizbullah* after the death of Ayatollah Khomeini.

Fadlallah survived many attempts on his life. The most famous one occurred at the mosque of al-Imam al-Rida in Bir al-'Abd. According to him, the Saudi prince Bandar Bin Sultan and the CIA were involved.

Fadlallah called for the abolishment of confessionalism from the political system in Lebanon and believed that whereas Christianity (q.v.) called for the separation of religion (q.v.) from the state, Islam called for involvement in politics. Furthermore, he called for the Lebanonization of *Hizbullah* in an attempt to reconcile Islamic activism (q.v.) (*harakiyya*) with Lebanese realities after the establishment of the Ta'if Accord. It seems that *Hizbullah* now follows Fadlallah's attitude toward the Lebanese system and has, in fact, an important bloc in the Parliament. Moreover, he called for dialogue (q.v.) between Christians and Muslims and dropped his demand for an Islamic state. But after the death of Abbas al-Musawi, the relations between Fadlallah and *Hizbullah* cooled further, especially because of his disagreement about the issue of *al-Marji'iyya* (highest religious authority). Fadlallah believed that he was more qualified in religious matters than the leader of Iran, 'Ali Khamene'i (q.v.). See also *AL-DA'WA AL-ISLAMIYYA* IN IRAQ; DEMOCRACY; *HIZBULLAH*; ISLAMIC-ARAB CONGRESS; ISRAEL; *MARJI' AL-TAQLID*; SYSTEM.

FALSAFA. See PHILOSOPHY.

FAMILY OF *JIHAD* (*USRAT AL-JIHAD*). See *AL-JIHAD AL-ISLAMI* IN THE WEST BANK AND GAZA STRIP.

FAQIH, USAMA. See AL-MAS'ARI, MUHAMMAD.

FARAJ, 'ABD AL-SALAM (?–1982). Faraj graduated from the Faculty of Engineering, Cairo University and worked at the same university. His religious tendency was obvious from the time he was a child in the poor village of Aldilanjat. When Faraj arrived in Cairo, he joined *al-Jama'at al-Islamiyya* (q.v.) (Islamic Groups), which was active at the Faculty of Engineering. During that period he read the writings of Sayyid Qutb and Abu al-A'la al-Mawdudi (qq.v.). Faraj was also affected by the writings of Muhammad Ibn 'Abd al-Wahhab and Ibn Taymiyya (qq.v.). He focused his thoughts on toppling the government through a coup, although he recognized that most of the important fundamentalist leaders like Sayyid Qutb, Hasan al-Banna, Salih Sirriyya, Mustapha Shukri (qq.v.), and others had either been assassinated or executed. As a hobby, Faraj worked as an *imam* for a private mosque where he delivered sermons and speeches focusing on the plights of Muslims that were the consequences of un-Islamic political rule. He convinced Lieutenant Khalid Shawqi Islambuli to assassinate President Sadat.

Faraj was the master planner of *Jama'at al-Jihad al-Islami* (q.v.) (Islamic *Jihad* Group), including *Tanzim al-Jihad* (*Al-Jihad* Organization [q.v.]). His main views are contained in his little book, entitled *al-Farida al-Gha'iba* (the absent duty), that is, *jihad* (q.v.) (struggle). Faraj believed that Egypt was an Islamic country but that the Egyptian political rule was un-Islamic and infidel and fell with paganism (q.v.) (*al-jahiliyya*). See also APOSTASY; IBN TAYMIYYA, TAQIY AL-DIN; AL-IS-LAMBULI, MUHAMMAD SHAWQI; *JAMA'AT AL-JIHAD AL-IS-LAMI*; KISHK, NABIL 'ABD AL-HAMID; AL-MAGHRIBI, 'ABD AL-MAJID.

AL-FARHAN, ISHAQ AHMAD (1934–   ). Al-Farhan is the secretary-general of *Hizb Jabhat al-'Amal al-Islami* (q.v.) (Islamic Action Front Party) in Jordan. He was born in Jerusalem, Palestine, and got his primary education there. Al-Farhan continued his secondary education in Jordan, where his family lived in 1948. He got his science degree from the American University of Beirut in 1958. He taught in Jordan for many years, then he traveled to the United States, where he got his Ph.D. in education in 1964 from Columbia University, New York.

Since 1948, al-Farhan has been a member of the Muslim Brotherhood (q.v.), but his membership was frozen when he participated in Wasfi al-Tal's government in 1970. However, 10 years later he got back that membership and became an active member of the executive office. He later withdrew after establishing the Islamic Action Front Party in 1992.

Al-Farhan was in charge of many scientific, academic, administrative, and political cadres. He worked as professor at the Jordanian University and became its president. In addition, he worked at al-Yarmuk University and headed the Islamic Studies and Research departments. Also, from 1970–1973, al-Farhan held ministerial positions, that is, the Ministry of Education and the Ministry of Religious Endowments. He was elected to the National Council in 1987 and appointed a member of Jordanian *'Ayan* (senate) council.

Al-Farhan became the temporary Secretary-General for the party in 1992 and later was elected to that office. He has written and translated many books in scientific and educational topics, specifically in the fields of chemistry, physics, and other sciences. See also *HIZB JABHAT AL-'AMAL AL-ISLAMI*.

AL-FASI, MUHAMMAD 'ALLAL (1906–1973). Al-Fasi was a well-known Moroccan political leader and thinker and the founder of Independence Party (q.v.) (*Hizb Istiqlal*). Al-Fasi studied Islamic Law at Qarawiyyin University. He was very critical of the French Protectorate and developed his view along the lines of Islamic modernism (q.v.) and reformism. Al-Fasi was arrested in 1936 after organizing public protests, and he reorganized his political group into the National Reform Party, which again was reorganized into the *Istiqlal* Party. In 1947, he fled to Cairo until independence in 1956, from where he traveled to many cities in the Arab world, the Islamic world, and North America and published many of his important writings. After returning to Morocco, al-Fasi became Minister of Religious Affairs in 1961 and resigned in 1963 over differences with the King.

FATWA (LEGAL OPINION). Historically, legal opinions were used to resolve legal and social problems that were not known textually or had arisen in new contexts. In modern times, many fundamentalists use legal opinions as a way of fighting the government or evaluating people's behavior and views. One of the most outstanding *fatwas* is the view of Ayatollah Khomeini (q.v.) that Salman Rushdie (q.v.) should be killed for his scorn of Islam (q.v.) and the Prophet. According to Khomeini, Rushdie has committed apostasy (q.v.) (*ridda*). Another important theoretical *fatwa* is the view of 'Umar 'Abd al-Rahman (q.v.) that those rulers who do not rule by the Qur'an (q.v.) are infidels and, therefore, should be killed—an opinion that was employed by the assassins of President Sadat to defend their actions during their trial.

FIGHTING VANGUARDS (*AL-TALA'I' AL-MUQATILA*). These secret cells of militant members of the Muslim Brotherhood in Syria (q.v.) emerged under the leadership of Marwan Hadid of Hama Province in the late 1960s. Hadid, who had studied in Cairo under the radical ideologist of the Egyptian Muslim Brotherhood (q.v.), Sayyid Qutb (q.v.), argued that the Muslim Brotherhood faced ultimate extinction at the hands of the state unless it defended itself through armed struggle or *jihad* (q.v.). Although this message did not appeal to the mainstream leaders of the Brotherhood in Damascus, who favored nonviolent means of undermining the power and legitimacy (q.v.) of the Ba'th regime, younger members in the north-central cities, particularly Hama and Aleppo, rallied to his side.

Hadid's followers organized into clandestine cells of a dozen or so members, supported by artisans and trades people who made up the majority of the membership of the northern branches of the Syrian Brotherhood. These cells organized a series of anti-Ba'thi uprisings in Aleppo, Hama, Homs, and Idlib in 1968 and 1969. In the early 1970s, they united under the rubric of Fighting Vanguards, attracting the support of one of Syria's most prominent fundamentalist ideologues, Sa'id Hawwa (q.v.).

Throughout the 1970s, the Fighting Vanguards carried on a campaign of assassination and intimidation against Ba'th officials. Marwan Hadid was captured in the course of one of these operations in Damascus in 1976, and he died in prison shortly thereafter. Leadership was then disputed among several rivals, including Hawwa and Adnan 'Uqla. But the organization continued its campaign to destabilize the regime, striking at more and more targets. These attacks culminated in a brief but bloody civil war in the north-central cities in 1980.

During this period, state security services decimated the Fighting Vanguards, capturing or killing most of its leaders. Remnants of the organization, led by 'Uqla, cooperated with the Islamic Front (q.v.) during the 1982 rebellion in Hama but refused to join the front in setting up the National Alliance for the Liberation of Syria. In 1983, 'Uqla ended three years of fruitless clandestine agitation against the regime by surrendering to the authorities under the terms of a general amnesty. See also MUSLIM BROTHERHOOD IN SYRIA.

FINAYSH, MUHAMMAD 'ABD (1953–). Finaysh became a member of the Lebanese Parliament in 1992 and was the candidate of *Hizbullah* (q.v.) for Tyre. He called for the abolition of the confessional system in Lebanon.

FIS. See ISLAMIC SALVATION FRONT.

FITRA (INTUITION; LAW OF NATURE). In Islam (q.v.) *fitra* directs man to the good, according to fundamentalists. For man diverted his natural drive and forgot the *fitra* and replaced it with philosophy (q.v.) and desire. Man has involved himself in philosophy that, although supported by argumentative reason (q.v.), has led humanity to wrong conclusions, symbolized in man's worship of ungodly things and abstract ideas or, simply, paganism (q.v.) (*jahiliyya*). Nonetheless, man looks naturally for God (q.v.) as much as he seeks water and shelter. Put simply, moral laws residing in the *fitra* are intuitive and are as natural as physical laws. Abu al-A'la al-Mawdudi (q.v.), for instance, contends that humans agree that a well-administered society enjoys social justice, equality (qq.v.), cooperation, mutuality, and advice. Also humans agree that theft, adultery, murder, spying, jealousy, and so forth are evil. The fundamentalists use this doctrine as a replacement for philosophy. See also *AL-AFGHAN AL-'ARAB*; GOVERNMENT, FUNCTION OF; LIBERATION; MORALITY; ISLAM; ISLAMIC FUNDAMENTALISM; LIBERATION; MODERNISM; MODERNITY; RELIGION; *TAWHID*; UNIVERSALISM.

FREEDOM (*AL-HURRIYYA*). Freedom is such a central doctrine in modern Islamic thought that almost all fundamentalists have called for its development. Radicals have, however, related it to paganism (q.v.) (*jahiliyya*). In the last quarter of the 20th century, the issue has taken a different track and has been identified by many thinkers like Rashid al-Ghannushi and Hasan al-Turabi (qq.v.) as a comprehensive and fundamental right and formative principle in the life of people and according to Islam (q.v.). More specifically, al-Turabi, for instance, denies the government any right to impose recognized legal views on the community. Such an action constitutes an uncalled-for interference by the state in the life of the community and a breach of *shura* (q.v.) (consultation). See also APOSTASY; AL-'AWWA, MUHAMMAD SALIM; DEMOCRACY; DIALOGUE; AL-GHANNUSHI, RASHID; HAWWA, SAID; IBN BADIS, 'ABD AL-HAMID; *IJMA'*; *JIHAD*; JURISPRUDENCE; LEGITIMACY; LIBERATION; MODERNITY; MUSLIM BROTHERHOOD, IDEOLOGY OF; PEACE; RADICALISM; REASON; *SHURA*; TURABI, HASAN; TYRANNY; UNBELIEF.

FREEDOM MOVEMENT OF IRAN (*NEHZATE-E AZAI-YE IRAN*). See LIBERATION MOVEMENT OF IRAN.

FUNDAMENTALISM (*USULIYYA*). In origin, fundamentalism is a term that was developed in the West (q.v.) in order to describe the beliefs of some Evangelists in the Bible as the literal and eternal word of God (q.v.). Later, this meaning was expanded to include all sorts of religious groups that attempt to live according to their revelations, thus, there are Jewish fundamentalism, Christian fundamentalism, and Islamic fundamentalism. Although fundamentalism has been loaded with negative connotations, it is employed in this Dictionary to describe that movement that calls for the return to the fundamentals (q.v.) (*usul*) of Islam (q.v.), that is, the Holy Qur'an (q.v.) and the *Sunna* (way) of the Prophet. Of course, fundamentalism can and has been studied from historical and socioeconomic perspectives, but such perspectives alone have not led to in-depth understanding of fundamentalist discourses and their appeal to large sections of Muslims.

In modern times, many movements that call for a return to the fundamentals (*usul*) of religion (q.v.) have flourished throughout the Muslim world. Leaders of such movements feel that the Islamic spiritual dimension can aid in developing a clear portrait of the enemy and condemn moral corruption—especially when the perceived corrupted present is contrasted with a perceived idealistic and glorious picture of a past full of ethical idealism. This moral dimension in turn may be used to urge Muslims to establish anew their civilization (q.v.), reconstruct their identity, and absorb modernity (q.v.) and change.

In one way or another, and like any other intellectual and political product, the rise of Islamic fundamentalism must be located within a framework of reacting to educational, political, and intellectual crises in line with certain cultural and historical perspectives. See also APOSTASY; AUTHENTICITY; AL-BANNA, HASAN; CAPITALISM; CHRISTIANITY; DEMOCRACY; ISLAMIC FUNDAMENTALISM; ISRAEL; JUDAISM; KHOMEINISM; LIBERATION; MODERNISM; MODERNITY; MORALITY; QUTB, SAYYID; RADICALISM; RELIGION; REVOLUTION; SCIENCE; THEOLOGY; AL-TURABI, HASAN; UNBELIEF.

FUNDAMENTALS (*USUL*). The fundamentalists ask for a return to the fundamentals (*usul*) of religion (q.v.), that is, the Qur'an (q.v.) and the *Sunna* (way) of the Prophet. They argue that earlier Muslims were free and able to construct a major civilization (q.v.) by directing their focus toward constructing the fundamentals, or *usul*, of religion through the development of the roots of jurisprudence (q.v.) (*fiqh*).

Later periods witnessed lesser interest in the need to reexamine *usul* of law in relation to changing circumstances and focused instead on the specifics, or the *furu'*, as if they were of divine origin. For Hasan al-Turabi (q.v.), this is an indication that political priorities of Islamic discourses, such as the form of political order or the legitimacy (q.v.) of representative government, which were originally directed at the service of the Islamic civilization, have been misplaced. This act in turn made Islamic discourses obsolete and incapable of serving Muslim societies, which necessitated as well borrowing from Western positive laws that are in tune with modernity (q.v.). Such a misplaced political prioritization led to the glorification of jurisprudence instead of religion. What happened is that Muslims became the servants of a thought that could not serve them any more. This act led to weakening free thought and the domination of *taqlid* (q.v.) (traditionalism), which became identical to religion itself.

According to the fundamentalists, the overall inherited Islamic thought and system (q.v.) (*nizam*) have proved their incapability of advancement, and what is needed instead is a new and modern Islamic thought that takes into account modernity but simultaneously grounds it in the divine text (q.v.) and not in new or inherited authorities. Individual *ijtihadat*, or reasoning, should deal with profound issues and not merely with unfounded assumptions, linguistic interests, or details that have plagued the history (q.v.) of Islam (q.v.). Theoretical sciences (*al-'ulum al-'aqliyya*) are of utmost importance for recreating a viable Islamic thought, because only such sciences are capable of proper interaction with the *usul*, especially the divine text, and the transformation of *al-Shari'a* (q.v.) (Islamic Law) stipulates an unfolding embodiment of law and faith.

Because, for the fundamentalists, only the *usul* carries within it any normative or eternal value for Muslims, they look down at the perceived nonchangeability of Islamic traditions and describe them as being no more than historical accumulations without any solid normative status. See also AUTHENTICITY; FUNDAMENTALISM; ISLAMIC SOCIETY; ISLAMIC STATE; PAST; SYSTEM; AL-TURABI, HASAN; *AL-WAHHABIYYA*.

FURQAN (PROOF). This political group was founded in 1978 and disappeared shortly after that. *Furqan* came into the headlines in 1979 when it claimed responsibility for the assassination of Ayatollah Murtaza Mutahhari (q.v.), one of the Islamic Republic of Iran's leading intellectuals. It justified its action by claiming that the Iranian Revolution of 1979 (q.v.) had been hijacked by reactionary clergymen, rich merchants, liberal political figures, and Marxists.

-G-

AL-GHANNUSHI, RASHID (1939–). Al-Ghannushi is the leader of *Harakat al-Nahda al-Islamiyya* (q.v.) (Islamic Renaissance Movement) in Tunisia and is an open and liberal thinker. He was born in Tunisia and received his primary and secondary education in Cairo. Later, al-

Ghannushi went to Damascus and received a diploma in philosophy in 1968. He did not finish graduate studies in France and was obliged to return to Tunisia because of family problems.

Al-Ghannushi came into contact with the Muslim Brotherhood (q.v.) and its ideas during his university years in Syria. When he returned to Tunisia, al-Ghannushi founded, with 'Abd al-Fattah Moro, the Islamic Group, composed of subgroups selected from mosques and al-Ghannushi's students. In 1979, he became the leader of the Islamic Group.

In June 1981, al-Ghannushi participated with 'Abd al-Fattah Moro and others in spreading *Harakat al-Itijah al-Islami* (q.v.) (the Islamic Tendency Movement) under his leadership. A month later, he was arrested for the first time and tried for forming an illegal organization. Al-Ghannushi was sentenced to 10 years in jail, but after three years, in August 1984, he was set free by a presidential pardon. In August 1987, al-Ghannushi was arrested again when the Tunisian government held members of his organization responsible for explosions, and al-Ghannushi as well as other leaders of the movement were tried on the charge of cooperating with a foreign state, that is, Iran. They were sentenced to life imprisonment, however, President Zayn al-'Abidin Bin 'Ali set them free by a presidential pardon in May 1988. Al-Ghannushi left for London and did not return to Tunisia. In 1989, the Islamic Tendency Movement became *Harakat al-Nahda al-Islamiyya* (Islamic Renaissance Movement), and al-Ghannushi was named its leader although he was in exile. In 1992, the authorities charged him with many crimes, which led to his case being transferred to a military court where he was sentenced in absentia.

Al-Ghannushi was one of the most innovative thinkers in political Islam; he is the example of an extrovert. In 1982, Ghannushi's articles were collected in a book published in France by Karawan Publishing and in another book published in 1993 by the Arab Unity Studies Center in Beirut. He argues for the need of maintaining both public and private freedom (q.v.) as well as human rights (q.v.), which are called for by the Qur'an (q.v.) and ratified by international covenants. These covenants are not contradictory to Islam (q.v.) and involve primarily the freedom of expression and association as well as political participation, independence, and the condemnation of violence (q.v.) and the suppression of free opinion. Such principles for al-Ghannushi may become the center of peaceful coexistence and dialogue between society and the state and between rulers and the ruled.

However, al-Ghannushi ties the political legitimacy (q.v.) of a political system (q.v.) (*nizam*) to its provision of freedom for political parties (q.v.) and segments of society that could compete peacefully on social, political, and ideological agendas. Such a system must provide free elections to all representative councils and institutions so that they may contribute to state administration. If this takes place, the Islamic movement lends its popular support to any such system that carries out political legitimacy, because the popular authority, grounded in God's governance (q.v.) (*hakimiyya*), is the highest authority in society. Accepting freedom of association leads al-Ghannushi to accept even those parties that do not believe in God (q.v.), such as the communists. Some citizens may find it in their best interest to form parties and other institutions that might be irreligious. This kind of political diversity does not constitute a breach of religion and unbelief (qq.v.), because pluralism (q.v.) is sanctioned by religion. The sacred text (q.v.) represents a source for, a reference to, and an absorption of the truth, whereas its human interpretations are grounded in diverse methods, representing different understandings of changing social, economic, political, and intellectual complexities. See also CONSTITUTION; DEMOCRACY; DIALOGUE; FREEDOM; *HARAKAT AL-ITIJAH AL-ISLAMI*; *HARAKAT AL-NAHDA AL-ISLAM-IYYA*; HUMAN RIGHTS; ISLAMIC FRONT FOR SALVATION IN TUNISIA; ISLAMIC FUNDAMENTALISM; ISLAMIZATION; *JAM'I-YYAT AL-HIFADH 'ALA AL-QUR'AN*; PARTIES; PROGRESSIVE MUSLIMS; SCIENCE; *AL-SHARI'A*; *SHURA*; *AL-TAJAMMU' AL-YE-MENI LI AL-ISLAH*; *TAQLID*; *TAWHID*; TEXT; THEOCRACY; THE-OLOGY.

AL-GHAZALI, MUHAMMAD (1917–1996). Al-Ghazali was originally a religious scholar from al-Azhar University who joined the Muslim Brotherhood (q.v.) in Egypt and became a leading member. He joined the Brotherhood in 1938 and was active in the 1940s. He was imprisoned in 1949 after the assassination of Hasan al-Banna (q.v.). He supported the revolution of Jamal 'Abd al-Nasir in its earlier stages and argued the reason for the split between the Brotherhood and 'Abd al-Nasir was the latter's authoritarianism. In 1965, al-Ghazali was imprisoned along with Sayyid Qutb (q.v.), although he censored Qutb's books.

Al-Ghazali held many important positions, including Director of the Mosque Department, Director General of Islamic *da'wa* (call), and Undersecretary of the Ministry of *Awqaf* (religious endowment). He is one of the most renowned moderate fundamentalist thinkers, whose prolific writings influenced many generations. Al-Ghazali taught at al-Azhar

University and later resided in Saudi Arabia after the great ordeal of the Muslim Brotherhood in Egypt in the 1950s. He taught at King 'Abd al-'Aziz University and Umm al-Qura. In 1953, al-Ghazali was dismissed from the Political Body of the Muslim Brotherhood because of his attempt to unseat Hasan al-Hudaybi (q.v.).

Al-Ghazali wrote extensively on all of the contemporary issues of the Muslim world. He was considered to be a moderate fundamentalist who commanded numerous followers and advocated *shura* (q.v.) (consultation) and tolerance. During the presidency of Anwar al-Sadat, al-Ghazali used to come from Saudi Arabia to Egypt in order to speak in the religious ceremonies that were attended by thousands of fundamentalists. See also *AL-SALAFIYYA*; AL-SHIQAQI, FATHI.

AL-GHAZALI, ZAYNAB. Zaynab al-Ghazali was the leader and founder of the Muslim Women's Association (1936–1964) and later became the leader of the Muslim Sisters, the women's branch of the Muslim Brotherhood (q.v.) in Egypt. Al-Ghazali gave weekly lectures that commanded large attendance, published a magazine, maintained an orphanage, and provided the poor and the needy with help. In 1956 and during the great trial of the Muslim Brethren, al-Ghazali was very instrumental in collecting money for and maintaining the families of the thousands of jailed Muslim Brethren. She visited the Brethren in jails and played an important role in sneaking out the writings of Sayyid Qutb (q.v.) when she visited him with his sisters. Al-Ghazali distributed Qutb's manuscripts to other Brethren, who in turn later published them. She was instrumental in the reorganization of the Muslim Brotherhood in the 1960s. She was imprisoned in 1965 and sentenced to 25 years of hard labor. Al-Ghazali was released under President Anwar al-Sadat in 1971 and started teaching and writing in *al-Da'wa*, which was banned in 1981, and then in *al-Liwa' al-Islami*. Although al-Ghazali supported the Iranian Revolution of 1979 (q.v.) at its beginning, she later denounced the sectarianism and violence (q.v.) of the Iranian state. She divorced her first husband, and her second husband divorced her while she was in prison. See also SIRRIYYA, SALIH.

GHOUSHA, IBRAHIM. Ghousha is the official spokesman for *Hamas*: *Harakat al-Muqawama al-Islamiyya* (q.v.) (Islamic Resistance Movement).

GHUNGHUR, FIDAN. See *HIZBULLAH* IN TURKEY.

GIA. See ARMED ISLAMIC GROUP.

GOD (*ALLAH*). For the fundamentalists, God's essence, *tawhid* (q.v.) (Oneness of God), is beyond the comprehension of human reason (q.v.), because His essence is not limited in time and space, and man's reason is situated in time and space. This is a characteristic that precludes human understanding of God's essence. Man can only interact with the divine text (q.v.) and act accordingly. Therefore, a direct interaction between man and God is precluded because of differences between the divine and the human. This is why the fundamentalists reject any method (q.v.) (*manhaj*) of knowledge (q.v.), like philosophy and theology (qq.v.) and Sufism, that claims to arrive at an absolute understanding of God.

The fundamentalists argue that God should be made the source of all legitimacy and legislation (qq.v.), politics, and society, as well as philosophy and reason (qq.v.). For them, there is no correct interpretation (q.v.) of governance, knowledge, religion, morality, and democracy (qq.v.) without their linkage to God. Issues like morality and freedom (q.v.) and religions like Christianity and Judaism (qq.v.) have been corrupted by a wrong understanding of God. This wrong understanding led to the rise of a wide range of dangerous doctrines about divinity (q.v.) (*uluhiyya*), like paganism, apostasy, and unbelief (qq.v.), because it became dependent on human thought that is not grounded in a correct text, or the Qur'an (q.v.). Thus, a true belief in God, for the fundamentalists, requires a revolution (q.v.) that implements the divine law and establishes the Islamic state and society (qq.v.). See also APOSTASY; BALANCE; CALIPHATE; CHRISTIANITY; DIVINITY; FUNDAMENTALISM; *IJMA'*; ISLAMIC FUNDAMENTALISM; ISRAEL; *JIHAD*; JUDAISM; MARTYRDOM; MARXISM; MONOTHEISTIC RELIGIONS; REASON; RADICALISM; *AL-SHARI'A*; *SHURA*; THEOCRACY; THEOLOGY; *TAWHID*; WESTERN CIVILIZATION.

GOVERNANCE (*HAKIMIYYA*). The universalism (q.v.) of Islam (q.v.) is underpinned by the doctrine of divine *hakimiyya* (governance) that postulates the absolute sovereignty of God (q.v.) in the universe; thus, no legitimate lawgiver exists but Him. For almost all fundamentalists, this view is not identical to theocracy (q.v.). Man should apply His divine legislation (q.v.) and *al-Shari'a* (q.v.) (Islamic Law) and refrain from philosophy (q.v.) that postulates the basic principles of what is right or wrong; humanity should simply be ruled by basic principles of *al-Shari'a*. Furthermore, because the doctrine of *hakimiyya* is a derivative of *tawhid* (q.v.) (Oneness of God), the latter spreads into all aspects of life and constitutes the only acceptable political basis for any system (q.v.) (*nizam*).

Abu al-A'la al-Mawdudi (q.v.) elaborates this by saying that ultimate sovereignty is God's. God alone has the right to command or forbid, and worship and obedience is due to him. God is the only true divinity (q.v.) (*uluhiyya*). Al-Mawdudi adds further that there is no individual, institution, or even mankind that can claim sovereignty. God alone is the sovereign, and the law of Islam are His commandments. Any individual or institution that claims such a sovereignty lives a life of paganism (q.v.) (*jahiliyya*).

Such a view allows radical fundamentalists such as Abu al-Hasan al-Nadawi, Sayyid Qutb, al-Mawdudi, and Ayatollah al-Khomeini (qq.v.) to call for fighting any human, philosophical, or political system that does not make *tawhid* its fountainhead. As a philosophical system, Islam stands against unbelief (q.v.) (*kufr*) and atheism, and as a political order, it stands against Western democracy (q.v.) and communism. Thus, radical fundamentalists like al-Mawdudi, Qutb, and al-Nadawi make this division. Human beings follow God's method (q.v.) (*manhaj*) and system, and, therefore, are the followers of God or *hizb Allah* (q.v.) (party of God). Or human beings follow the method and system of a king or a people, and, therefore, are the followers of a king or nondivine human systems or *hizb al-Shaytan*. The first group constitutes the virtuous society, the second, the nonvirtuous, or the *jahili*, society (q.v.).

Hasan al-Banna (q.v.), unlike al-Mawdudi and Qutb, does not comprehensively apply the doctrine of divine *hakimiyya*. Rather, he favors compromise and dealing with governments, instead of isolating and charging them with religious unbelief. He does not see any further need to push the doctrine to its divisive limits and, instead, focuses on its unitary aspects. He also has no reservations about his organization's infiltration of official apparatuses and state control. Believing in the *hakimiyya* as the substantial underpinning of his political discourse does not make his method impractical. To put it differently, his political discourse is abstract and uncompromising as in proposing the necessity and legitimacy (q.v.) of God's *hakimiyya*, however, his method, itself conducted by humans, is practical and compromising, because no one individual can claim finality for his interpretation (q.v.). Interpretations are always tentative and subject to review and correction.

The disavowal of any legitimate theoretical possibility of legislation and political action without proper grounding in the "comprehensive flexible, and total Islamic legislation" leads Hasan al-Banna to ground the appropriateness of action in correct doctrines. That is why he calls for the derivation of all civil, criminal, international, and commercial affairs from Islamic Law. For al-Banna, it is self-defeating in the Islamic view to ground laws for Muslims in non-Islamic laws whose infrastructure and sources are full of other cultures' particularities, not to mention their contravening of Islamic Law. This becomes more acute because Islamic law, along with its eternal and comprehensive principles, has not precluded the possibilities of individual and collective reformations in order to make legislation suitable to time and place. According to al-Banna and other fundamentalists, the sayings and behavior of *al-Salaf al-Salih*, or the good ancestors, as well as other great jurists support the relationship between Islamic Law, on the one hand, and rules of government, of conduct, and of judicial and civil contracts, on the other. In fact, the history (q.v.) of Islam shows that legislation has essentially covered people's beliefs and the political dimension of Islam, that is, when Islam was the dominant ideology and when both the government and the people adhered to it. See also APOSTASY; CIVILIZATION; DEMOCRACY; EQUALITY; AL-GHANNUSHI, RASHID; GOD; *HIZBUL-LAH*; *IJMA'*; ISLAMIC FUNDAMENTALISM; ISLAMIC GOVERNMENT; *AL-JAMA'AT AL-ISLAMIYYA*; *JAMA'AT AL-JIHAD AL-ISLAMI*; *JAMA'AT AL-MUSLIMIN*; *JIHAD*; JUDAISM; KHOMEINI, AYATOLLAH; LEGISLATION; LIBERATION; AL-MAWDUDI, ABU AL-A'LA; MUSLIM BROTHERHOOD, IDEOLOGY OF; MUSTAPHA, SHUKRI; ORGANIZATION OF SHAYKH 'ABD ALLAH AL-SIMAWI; QUTB, SAYYID; *SHURA*; SYSTEM; *TAWHID*; THEOCRACY; AL-TURABI, HASAN; UNBELIEF; WORLD ORDER.

GOVERNMENT, FORMS OF. Most fundamentalist elaborations on the forms of government make formal legitimacy (q.v.) dependent on public choice and deny all elitist forms, especially theocracy (q.v.). Representative government becomes, because of its substantive principle of *shura* (q.v.) (consultation), the cornerstone in the formation of any state.

In one way or another, the fundamentalists postulate the need for public participation and demand the right of electing political rulers. *Shura* is not specifically defined; its form is an organizational matter depending on the needs of every age. *Shura* has been historically the domain of scholars who advised the ruler and suggested a course of action to be followed. See also CONSTITUTIONAL RULE; ISLAMIC GOVERN-MENT; MUSLIM BROTHERHOOD, IDEOLOGY OF; THEOCRACY.

GOVERNMENT, FUNCTION OF. Radical fundamentalists argue that the function of the government is the enforcement of *fitra* (q.v.) (the law of nature) and *Shari'a* (q.v.) (Islamic Law) as advocated by the Qur'an (q.v.). On the other hand, they accept the doctrine of natural rights, including property. Moderate fundamentalists argue that the function of government is to represent the interests of people within the limits of Islamic Law. It is not theocracy (q.v.). However, they downplay the importance of state religious power to supervise social and individual conduct and leave more room to individuals and institutions. See also *HIZB AL-TAHRIR AL-ISLAMI*; *IJMA'*; ISLAMIC GOVERNMENT; ISLAMIC SALVATION FRONT IN ALGERIA; ISLAMIC STATE; *AL-SHARI'A*.

GROUP OF ISLAMIC RENAISSANCE. See *JAMA'AT AL-NAHDA AL-ISLAMIYYA*.

GROUP OF LEGITIMATE ISOLATION (*JAMA'AT AL-'UZLA AL-SHAR'IYYA*). This Egyptian fundamentalist group believes in the doctrines of paganism and governance (qq.v.) (*hakimiyya*) but refuses to sanction the use of violence for political and religious ends. It believes that its members must not live in society but must isolate themselves psychologically from the ills of society. Its members believe in the need to hide the real aims of the group in order to protect and allow it to develop and fulfill the divine commands. This was the main difference with the organization of Shukri Mustapha (q.v.), who believed in the need to pronounce the unbelief (q.v.) (*kufr*) of society.

GROUP PURE NATURE (*JAMA'AT AL-FITRA*). See *AL-AFGHAN AL-'ARAB*.

GROUP OF *SUNNA* SUPPORTERS (*JAMA'AT ANSAR AL-SUNNA*). See *AL-SALAFIYYA* FORCES IN EGYPT.

GROUP'S COMMANDER. See *AMIR*.

GUARDIANSHIP (*WILAYA*). See *WALIY AL-FAQIH*. See also KHA-MENE'I, 'ALI; KHOMEINI, AYATOLLAH; *MARJI' AL-TAQLID*.

GUARDIANSHIP OF THE JURIST (*WILAYAT AL-FAQIH*). See *WALIY AL-FAQIH*.

H

HADATHA. See MODERNITY.

HADDAM, ANWAR. Haddam is the head of the Algerian "Parliamentary Delegation" that runs the Islamic Salvation Front (q.v.) from abroad after the arrest of its leadership and the cancellation of the 1991 elections. Since 1996, Haddam has been awaiting trial in the United States after the French government accused him of supporting the assassins of seven French citizens in Algeria.

HADID, MARWAN. See FIGHTING VANGUARDS; MUSLIM BROTHERHOOD IN SYRIA.

HADJ, MESSALI. See PARTY OF THE ALGERIAN PEOPLE.

AL-HAKIM, MUHSIN. See ISLAMIC PARTY.

HAKIMIYYA. See GOVERNANCE.

HAMAS **IN ALGERIA.** See ISLAMIC SOCIETY MOVEMENT.

HAMAS: HARAKAT AL-MUQAWAMA AL-ISLAMIYYA (ISLAMIC RESISTANCE MOVEMENT) **IN PALESTINE.** During the early 1980s, the Muslim Brotherhood in Palestine (q.v.) developed its center at the Islamic University of Gaza and continuously clashed with secular forces of the Palestine Liberation Organization. Shaykh Ahmad Yasin (q.v.) became the leader of *Hamas: Harakat al-Muqawama al-Islamiyya*, and was held for years in an Israeli jail to serve a life sentence. But he was released in 1997 in a deal between King Hussein of Jordan and Israeli authorities after the failed attempt to assassinate Khalid Mash'al (q.v.), head of *Hamas* Political Bureau, in Amman.

The Brotherhood's platform in the Israeli-occupied territories since 1967 revolved around social and economic reform through a return to authentic Islamic value and living rather than overt military struggle. When the *intifada* started in 1987, the Brotherhood initially did not take part in the anti-Israeli activities, although other fundamentalists did. However, popular support won by the uprising in the occupied territories led to a revision of the Brotherhood's traditional reluctance to engage in military resistance activities and to join in the activities of the secular nationalists.

Hamas became the Brotherhood organization that participated in resisting Israeli occupation and launching military attacks against Israelis and Israeli establishment. It became popular because of the many social institutions that it set up to serve the needs of the people. Furthermore, *Hamas* has rejected the Arab-Israeli peace (q.v.) process and has tried its utmost to subvert it. However, it has refrained from confronting the Palestinian National authority. *Hamas* has many offices throughout the capitals of the Islamic world, in Damascus, Amman, Tehran, and elsewhere. See also ABU MARZUQ, MUSA; 'AYYASH, YAHYA; 'AZZAM, NAFIDH; ISRAEL; JARRAR, BASSAM; MASH'AL, KHALID; MUSLIM BROTHERHOOD IN PALESTINE; NAZZAL, KHALID; SALAMA, SALIM; VIOLENCE; YASIN, AHMAD; ZAHHAR, MAHMUD.

HAMDAN, YUSUF. See *HIZB AL-TAHRIR AL-ISLAMI.*

AL-HAMIDI, MUHAMMAD AL-HASHIMI. See *HARAKAT AL-NAHDA AL-ISLAMIYYA* IN TUNISIA.

HAMMUD, MAHIR. See MUSLIM SCHOLARS' ASSOCIATION.

HANIFNEZHAD, MUHAMMAD. See *MUJAHIDIN KHALQ.*

AL-HARAKA AL-AL-DUSTURIYYA AL-ISLAMIYYA (ISLAMIC CONSTITUTIONAL MOVEMENT). See *JAM'IYYAT AL-ISLAH AL-IJTIMA'IYYA* IN KUWAIT.

AL-HARAKA AL-ISLAMIYYA AL-'ARABIYYA AL-DIMUCRATIYYA. See DEMOCRATIC ISLAMIC ARAB MOVEMENT.

AL-HARAKA AL-ISLAMIYYA FI LUBNAN (ISLAMIC MOVEMENT IN LEBANON). This underground movement declared its existence in a leaflet in 1983, but its leader, Sadiq al-Musawi, had been active in militant Shi'ite political life since the 1970s. This obscure movement preceded *Hizbullah* (q.v.) (Party of God) in its call for the immediate establishment of the Islamic state (q.v.) in Lebanon. It considered *Hizbullah* very moderate because it was incompletely dedicated to the goal of establishing an Islamic state in Lebanon. The movement is very active in distributing publications demanding the election of a Muslim Shaykh as President of Lebanon. Al-Musawi had close ties to the Iranian government, had been frequently visible in the Iranian press, and had sometimes written commentaries on Lebanese issues.

AL-HARAKA AL-ISLAMIYYA AL-KURDIYYA (KURDISH ISLAMIC MOVEMENT). Many observers believe that the growth of the Kurdish Islamic Movement came as a consequence of Saddam Hussein's destruction of the city of Hilbaja in Kurdistan in 1988, where chemical weapons were used, which led to the death of 5,000 Kurds after the end of the Iran-Iraq war. When the major Kurdish parties withdrew from Kurdistan in the face of the regime's attack during the period of 1988–1991, the religious feeling intensified, and membership in the Islamic movement grew as a result. The leaders of the movement, like Mulla 'Uthman 'Abd al-'Aziz and his brother Mulla 'Ali, exerted tremendous efforts to coordinate their actions with the Kurdish political movements. However, the movement did not join the Kurdish Front that was set up in 1988, although it participated in military actions against the Iraqi regime. Some attribute the increase in the power of the Islamic movement to the return of *al-Afghan al-'Arab* (q.v.) (the Afghan Arabs), although the movement is very careful not to be identified with Iran. In the Kurdish elections of 1992, the movement came in third but did not get the 5 percent needed for entering the Parliament.

AL-HARAKA AL-ISLAMIYYA LI AL-JAZA'IR. See ISLAMIC MOVEMENT FOR ALGERIA.

AL-HARAKA AL-ISLAMIYYA LI TAHRIR AL-BAHRAIN. See ISLAMIC FRONT FOR THE LIBERATION OF BAHRAIN.

AL-HARAKA AL-ISLAMIYYA AL-MUSALLAHA (ARMED ISLAMIC MOVEMENT). See ARMED ISLAMIC GROUP.

AL-HARAKA AL-SHA'BIYYA. See POPULAR MOVEMENT.

AL-HARAKA AL-SHA'BIYYA AL-DUSTURIYYA AL-DIMUCRATI-YYA. See DEMOCRATIC CONSTITUTIONAL POPULAR MOVEMENT.

HARAKAT AMAL AL-ISLAMIYYA (ISLAMIC *AMAL* MOVEMENT). The Islamic *Amal* Movement, headed by Husayn al-Musawi, is an off-shoot of the *Amal* Movement. It splintered from the mother organization in June 1982 when Nabih Berri, head of *Amal*, agreed to participate along with the leader of the Lebanese Forces, Bashir Jumayyil, in the Salvation Committee, formed by the Lebanese government after the Israeli invasion. Al-Musawi considered Berri's participation as tantamount to treason, given Bashir's relations with the Israelis and his anti-Muslim attitudes. Islamic *Amal* rejects the secular orientation of *Amal*.

Al-Musawi came from a middle-class prestigious family that claims descent from the Prophet. He is a former schoolteacher whom Imam Musa al-Sadr (q.v.) had expelled from *Amal* in the mid-1970s because of his insistence on establishing an Islamic state (q.v.) in Lebanon. Al-Musawi denied his expulsion, although he acknowledges some differences with al-Sadr at the time.

Islamic *Amal* has been strongly supported by the Islamic Republic of Iran, but the movement is still confined to areas near Ba'albak, the area from which al-Musawi started. His relations with *Hizbullah* (q.v.) (Party of God) have been obscure. Iran pressured him to unify Shi'ite militia movements in Lebanon. Although al-Musawi insisted upon maintaining his separate organizational existence, he later became one of the leaders of *Hizbullah*. He is reported to have become a member of the highest ruling body of *Hizbullah*. See also *HIZBULLAH*; IRANIAN REVOLUTION OF 1979; NASRALLAH, SAYYID HASAN; AL-SADR, MUSA.

HARAKAT AL-DAWLA AL-ISLAMIYYA (MOVEMENT OF THE ISLAMIC STATE). See *AL-JAYSH AL-ISLAMI LI AL-INQADH*.

HARAKAT AL-INQADH. See SALVATION MOVEMENT.

HARAKAT AL-ITIJAH AL-ISLAMI (ISLAMIC TENDENCY MOVEMENT). The predecessor of *Harakat al-Nahda al-Islamiyya* (q.v.) (Islamic Renaissance Movement) dates back to 1970 when Rashid al-Ghannushi (q.v.) and 'Abd al-Fattah Moro founded an Islamic group as an Islamic educational movement. It is the most important fundamentalist movement in Tunisia. The movement went through three essential phases:

- 1970–1981: In order to face the revolutionary socialist ideas, the government allowed in 1970 the formation of *Jam'iyyat al-Hifadh 'ala al-*

Qur'an (q.v.) (Qur'anic Preservation Society). At the beginning, the Association had cultural and missionary objectives and attracted young militants, including 'Abd al-Fattah Moro and Rashid al-Ghannushi. In its 1990 congress the Association decided to transform itself into a political movement: the Islamic Tendency Movement (*Harakat al-Itijah al-Islami*). When the Islamic group was transformed into *Harakat al-Itijah al-Islami* in June 1981 it was committed to the foundation of an Islamic system (q.v.) (*nizam*) and the spreading of a political Islamic ideology on both the local and national levels.

- 1981–1988: The Tendency did not gain recognition from the government. In 1981, 93 cadres of the Tendency were arrested and given jail sentences; al-Ghannushi and Moro were sentenced to 18 years. In 1987, Tunisia severed diplomatic relations with Iran after its accusation of helping the Tendency. Al-Ghannushi and 38 other leaders were imprisoned because the Islamic Tendency Movement was considered to be an Islamic political party. However, it failed to obtain a legal license to practice its activities. Between 1981 and the end of 1987, the Tendency went underground. In 1982 and 1983, the Tendency recruited young militants from mosques and universities. Each new member paid 5 percent of his income to the movement. Other financial support came from commercial activities like selling publications and contributions from foreign organizations. In 1985, the Tendency created both the general union of the Tunisian students, which became the most important student syndicate in Tunisia, and the general union of Tunisian workers. It was supposed in 1988 that membership reached 10,000 and its budget reached over 1.6 million French francs. Following several incidents that proved the inability of President Habib Bourguiba to control peace in the country, Prime Minister General Zayn al-'Abidin Bin 'Ali overthrew the President in 1987 and released 608 members of the Tendency. Al-Ghannushi was freed in 1988. President Bin 'Ali tried to court the fundamentalists by stressing the Islamic identity of Tunisia and inaugurating religious centers.

- 1989–present: In 1989, a new law was promulgated that forbade forming parties whose names referred to a race, religion (q.v.), language, or region. The Islamic Tendency became *Harakat al-Nahda al-Islamiyya* (q.v.) (Islamic Renaissance Movement). The major changes of this period were related to changing the nature of its activities to include political activities that turned it into an Islamic political party in 1988 under the leadership of Rashid al-Ghannushi and 'Abd al-Fattah Moro, the General Secretary. Also, *al-Fajr* newspaper, directed by

Hamadi al-Jabali, began publications and served as a mouthpiece for *al-Nahda*.

The structure of Tendency was simple. The head of the pyramid was the *amir* (q.v.) (commander) who was assisted by a consultative council or *majlis shura* (q.v.). The movement had a regional structure in the 14 regions of Tunisia, the *amir* appointed the leaders of the regions who were assisted also by consultative councils. See also AL-GHANNUSHI, RASHID; *HARAKAT AL-NAHDA AL-ISLAMIYYA*; PROGRESSIVE MUSLIMS; VIOLENCE.

HARAKAT AL-JIHAD AL-ISLAMI (ISLAMIC STRUGGLE MOVEMENT). See *AL-JIHAD AL-ISLAMI* IN THE WEST BANK AND GAZA STRIP.

HARAKAT AL-JIHAD AL-ISLAMI: BAYT AL-MAQDIS (ISLAMIC STRUGGLE MOVEMENT: JERUSALEM). This movement surfaced in early 1990 and has been headed by Shaykh As'ad al-Tamimi. It is a militant group, and the Jordanian authorities arrested many of its members, who were accused of committing terrorist acts against foreign tourists. The leadership of the movement denied any such involvement, except in the West Bank and Gaza Strip. It has also denied any relation to Islamic *Jihad* in Lebanon. However, Jordanian security sources link this movement to the Lebanese Islamic *Jihad*.

HARAKAT AL-MUJTAMA' AL-ISLAMI. See ISLAMIC SOCIETY MOVEMENT.

HARAKAT AL-MUQAWAMA AL-ISLAMIYYA: HAMAS. (ISLAMIC RESISTANCE MOVEMENT). See *HAMAS*; MUSLIM BROTHERHOOD IN PALESTINE.

HARAKAT AL-NAHDA AL-ISLAMIYYA (ISLAMIC RENAISSANCE MOVEMENT) **IN ALGERIA**. See *JAMA'AT AL-NAHDA AL-ISLAMIYYA*.

HARAKAT AL-NAHDA AL-ISLAMIYYA (ISLAMIC RENAISSANCE MOVEMENT) **IN TUNISIA**. After its encouragement of *Jam'iyyat al-Hifadh 'Ala al-Qur'an* (q.v.) (Qur'anic Preservation Society), the Tunisian government refused the movement's request to be organized as a political party. In 1980, however, a group broke away from *Jam'iyyat al-Hifadh* and in 1980 set up *Harakat al-Itijah al-Islami* (q.v.) (Islamic Tendency Movement). Its members sought to establish their movement as a political party based on the regulations stipulated by the Tunisian authorities. They organized committees, for the most part, in cities, and they developed very rapidly into a significant force in Tunisian politics.

From the time of the movement's establishment, the government cracked down on its leaders and members, a confrontation that culminated in massive arrests in 1987 and the dismantling of much of the movement's organizational structures. Habib Bourguiba's decision to sentence some of the leaders to death led to his eviction from power by Zayn al-'Abidin Bin 'Ali, the Prime Minister, who felt that such an action might end up in social polarization and civil strife in Tunisian society.

In December 1987, the new Tunisian leader, Bin 'Ali, granted amnesty to 2,487 prisoners, including 608 members of the movement and dropped the charges against another 60 members. Rashid al-Ghannushi (q.v.) was pardoned and set free in 1988 with many members of the movement who had been imprisoned on charges of having committed crimes against public rights. The Secretary-General of the movement, 'Abd al-Fattah Moro, was also allowed to return from exile in September of that year.

During the last few years, the movement, which became *Harakat al-Nahda al-Islamiyya* (q.v.) (the Islamic Renaissance Movement) in 1989, has been in conflict with the President Bin 'Ali's authorities and has been accused of endangering national security and the regime, establishing an illegal organization, and possessing weapons in addition to many other charges. Many members of the movement are either in prison or outside the country.

Moreover, the last few years have witnessed several conflicts within the Islamic movement. 'Abd al-Fattah Moro, for instance, left *al-Nahda* as a result of differences with Rashid al-Ghannushi, the leader of the movement. Furthermore, leaders like Muhammad al-Hashimi al-Hamidi resigned—al-Hamidi now lives in London and publishes *al-Mustaqila* from there. *Al-Nahda* published many newspapers that expressed its views. These included *al-Habib*, *al-Ma'rifa*, *al-Mujtama'*, and *al-Fajr*, which were banned in 1992. Important figures of the movement are Salih Qarqar, Sadiq Shoro, Hamadi al-Jabali, and 'Ali al-'Arid.

The relations between *al-Nahda* and the government have never been smooth. Six hundred student activists were arrested during antigovernment protests that demanded the end of secular education and the resignation of the Education Minister. These protests turned violent at the end of February 1990, and the students were forced to serve in the armed forces. President Bin 'Ali has refused to legalize *al-Nahda* because he fears it will end the current political system. Again, in 1992, 265 supporters of *al-Nahda* were imprisoned after charges of attempting to overthrow the regime. The government still forbids *al-Nahda* to participate in elections.

Rashid al-Ghannushi, the movement's principal leader and ideologue, argued then that Westernization was destroying Islamic civilization (q.v.), and that it was imperative to establish an Islamic state (q.v.), by means of *jihad* (q.v.) (struggle) if necessary, to liberate the land of Islam (q.v.) and save all Muslims from domination by the West (q.v.). He also called for a more equitable distribution of the wealth of Islamic countries to resolve their economic problems. The political discourse of *al-Nahda* calls for diversity and pluralism (q.v.), encourages the recruitment of women to the highest institutions of the movement, and rejects sectarianism. It calls for the establishment of a modern Islamic state (q.v.) or at least a state where an Islamic and other parties (q.v.) are allowed to compete politically. See also DEMOCRACY; AL-GHANNUSHI, RASHID; *HARAKAT AL-ITIJAH AL-ISLAMI*; ISLAMIC FRONT FOR SALVATION IN TUNISIA; *JAM'IYYAT AL-HIFADH 'ALA AL-QUR'AN*; *AL-TAJAMMU' AL-YEMENI LI AL-ISLAH*.

HARAKAT AL-NAHDA AL-ISLAMIYYA (MOVEMENT OF ISLAMIC RENAISSANCE) **IN YEMEN**. See *AL-TAJAMMU' AL-YEMENI LI AL-ISLAH*.

HARAKAT AL-TAHRIR AL-ISLAMI (ISLAMIC LIBERATION MOVEMENT) **IN SUDAN**. See MUSLIM BROTHERHOOD IN SUDAN.

HARAKAT AL-TAJADDUD AL-ISLAMI. See MOVEMENT OF ISLAMIC RENEWAL.

HARAKAT AL-TAWHID AL-ISLAMI (ISLAMIC UNIFICATION MOVEMENT) **IN LEBANON**. This is the most important radical Sunni movement in Tripoli, Lebanon. It was founded in 1982, and its leader is Shaykh Sa'id Sha'ban, a former member of *al-Jama'a al-Islamiyya fi Lubnan* (q.v.) (Islamic Group in Lebanon). He was able to assert his power over the city in 1983 against Syria's wishes. Sha'ban, who comes from a lower-middle-class family, has been successful in attracting the poor classes of Tripoli. Originally, Sha'ban was a member of the pro-Saudi Muslim Brotherhood (q.v.) before setting up his movement in 1982. It was the outcome of unifying three fundamentalist groups: Soldiers of God (q.v.) (*Jundullah*), *al-Muqawama al-Sha'biyya* (Popular Resistance), founded by Khalil 'Ikawi, and the Movement for Arab Lebanon (*Harakat Lubnan al-'Arabi*), founded by Dr. 'Ismat Murad. However, the first two groups split from the Islamic Unification Movement by the summer of 1984, denying Sha'ban an important power base. *Al-Muqawama al-Sha'biyya* formed *al-Lijan al-Islamiyya* (Islamic Committees), and the Movement for Arab Lebanon formed *Lijan al-Masajid wa al-Ahya'* (Committees for Mosques and Neighborhoods).

Sha'ban believed the civil war could end only when *al-Shari'a* (q.v.) (Islamic Law) would be applied in Lebanon under an Islamic government (q.v.). He was very antagonistic to the communists, and his movement engaged in deadly massacres of communists in Tripoli. The movement controlled the city for a few years and imposed strict Islamic Laws on the people. But when Syrian forces entered the city, the movement was defeated. In recent years, Sha'ban has become a close ally of Iran, and he has improved his ties with Syria. See also EXTREMISM.

HARAKAT AL-TAWHID WA AL-ISLAH (MOVEMENT OF UNIFICATION AND REFORM). See AL-KHATIB, 'ABD AL-KARIM.

HARAKIYYA. See ACTIVISM.

AL-HARB (WAR). See *DAR AL-HARB*.

AL-HARRANI, MUHAMMAD. See ISLAMIC FRONT FOR SALVATION IN TUNISIA.

HASHAYKA, 'ABD ALLAH KAMIL. See *AL-AFGHAN AL-'ARAB*.

HASHIMI-RAFSANJANI, 'ALI AKBAR. See RAFSANJANI, 'ALI AKBAR.

HASHSHANI, 'ABD AL-QADIR (1957–). See *JAMA'AT AL-NAHDA AL-ISLAMIYYA*; ISLAMIC SALVATION FRONT IN ALGERIA.

HASSAN, 'ABD AL-RAQIB. See UNION OF POPULAR FORCES.

AL-HAWAMDA, 'ALI (1932–). Al-Hawamda is a member of the executive bureau of the Muslim Brotherhood in Jordan (q.v.). Al-Hawamda was born in Karak and obtained a degree in medicine from the University of 'Ayn Shams in Egypt. He has practiced medicine in many hospitals. Al-Hawamda also headed many philanthropic associations. He represented the Muslim Brotherhood in the Lower House of Parliament during the 1989–1993 term.

HAWWA, SA'ID. Sa'id Hawwa, the Syrian Muslim Brotherhood's (q.v.) leader and thinker, argues that in an Islamic state (q.v.) all citizens are equal and protected from despotism and arbitrariness. The distinction between one individual and another should not center around race or belief. As to the exercise of power, it should be based on *shura* and freedom (qq.v.) of association, specifically the freedom to set up political parties (q.v.), unions, minority associations, and civil institutions. The one-party system is unworkable in an Islamic state. Furthermore, Hawwa adds that the rule of law should reign supreme, and people should be able to have access to courts to redress their grievances. More importantly, freedom of expression should be guaranteed, whether on the personal or the public level.

In particular, Hawwa shows sensitivity to the importance of arguing for equal rights for Syrian minorities with the majority. Although ultimate authority should be within the confines of Islamic teachings, and although individuals from minorities can be members of cabinets and parliaments, political representation must be proportionate. But, the administration of their internal affairs and the construction of educational institutions and religious courts is the domain of the minorities themselves and should not be subjected to others. See also FIGHTING VANGUARDS; MUSLIM BROTHERHOOD IN SYRIA.

HERITAGE REVIVAL ASSOCIATION. See *JAM'IYYAT IHYA' AL-TURATH*.

HIJRA (MIGRATION). See *JAMA'AT AL-MUSLIMIN*.

AL-HILAL, TAQIY AL-DIN. See *AL-SALAFIYYA*.

HISTORICISM (*TARIKHANIYYAH*). Because of fundamentalist emphasis on the historicism of man's intellectual development in relation to the text (q.v.), man's reading and interpretation (q.v.) of the text cannot but be historically tentative and incapable of claiming eternal utility. Its truth is relative to its usefulness to social needs and man's development. Even then, such usefulness to humanity cannot transform a humanly developed doctrine into an absolute certainty or a categorical imperative that should be applied universally or eternally. Its truth is relative to its social and political conditions. In addition, Hasan al-Turabi, Sayyid Qutb (qq.v.), and Abu al-Hasan Nadawi's historicist analyses of intellectual human products require the restriction of any religious interpretation to the conditions of the interpreter who, regardless of his intellectual powers, cannot capture the original message of the scripture or the Qur'an (q.v.). Put differently, man may produce relative and tentative readings and interpretations, which may be good or not, depending on their practicability and usefulness. But man can never proclaim finality for any human product, including an interpretation that is derived from history (q.v.).

The fundamentalists further argue that man's conditions do change, and changes require new readings and interpretations. The eternal divine text, specifically divine revelation, remains eternal and valid for all ages and places, because its truth stems not from its correspondence to specific conditions of a particular society, but rather from its provision of a set of principles that can be interpreted and reinterpreted to suit different ages and places. Because the divine text itself remains unaffected by changes in human conditions for most fundamentalists, it should therefore be the source for organizing the philosophies of life, society, and the state. It functions, therefore, both as a unifying text based on which Muslims need to construct society and the state and as an ultimate canonical reference of probable readings and interpretations. In other words, because man's understanding of the text's ultimate meaning is always imperfect, the perfection of the text becomes itself a guarantee that Muslims have a metahistorical continuity that acts on the unification of Muslims. See also HISTORY.

HISTORY (*AL-TARIKH*). Because history may further the distance between the individual and the text (q.v.)—the Qur'an (q.v.) and the *Sunna* (way) of the Prophet—that man is to model himself upon, the fundamentalists dismiss the normative status of history. For them, as opposed to the modernists, history, which has prevented a direct understanding and reading of the Qur'an and the *Sunna* (way) of the Prophet, becomes a source of obscurity and dilution. It is situated in the past (q.v.) (*al-madi*) and not in revelation. No possible advancement for them is possible without a disruption of the historically developed past discourses, a disruption that permits a more "authentic" and direct understanding of the text. Thus all previously widely used disciplines of knowledge (q.v.), like theology and jurisprudence (qq.v.), must be substituted by new ones. Again, a new political philosophy (q.v.) and a new political art and behavior become necessary for the reevaluation and verification of this textual reading, itself nothing more than a political reading.

Such a claim becomes all the more necessary for the justification of rejecting past history. The fundamentalist view of historical or scientific movements as containing unquestionable principles, first, deflates their call for a new history or a new science (q.v.). Second, it forces them to continue the development of the older disciplines like jurisprudence. Thus, third, it denies the legitimacy (q.v.) of their claim for the need for introducing radical changes to current societies. Consequently, their denial of the Islamic basis of sciences and philosophies makes their claim for developing new Islamic sciences and philosophies rather reasonable. The fundamentalists participate indirectly in historicism (q.v.) by relating all interpretations to material, social, and political conditions.

Again, the radical fundamentalists go a step further and argue that these two aspects of life ought to be independent of both past Islamic civilization (q.v.) and foreign civilizations. This argument is made in order to vindicate the fundamentalists' call for nonreconciliation with Western thought because of the perceived basic incongruence between Islamic ideals and the ideals of others. See also ACTIVISM; CALIPHATE; CHRISTIANITY; COMPREHENSIVENESS; DIALOGUE; FUNDAMENTALS; HISTORICISM; GOVERNANCE; *IJMA'*; ISLAMIC STATE; JURISPRUDENCE; MODERNISM; MODERNITY; PAST; AL-QUR'AN; REVOLUTION; *AL-SALAFIYYA*; *AL-SHARI'A*; *SHURA*; *TAQLID*; *TAWHID*.

AL-HIWAR. See DIALOGUE.

HIZB (PARTY). See PARTIES.

HIZB AL-'AMAL AL-ISLAMI. See ISLAMIC ACTION PARTY.

HIZB AL-DA'WA AL-ISLAMIYYA (ISLAMIC CALL PARTY). See *AL-DA'WA AL-ISLAMIYYA* IN IRAQ; AL-SADR, MUHAMMAD BAQIR.

HIZB AL-HAQQ (RIGHT PARTY) **IN YEMEN**. This party was established by Ahmad al-Shami after the unification of Yemen in 1990 by a group of religious scholars and judges. *Hizb al-Haqq* views itself as a party that aims at the implementation of Islamic Law (q.v.) and the realization of justice (q.v.), Islamic unity, Islamic revival, and reverence to religious authorities. However, *al-Hizb al-Haqq* opposes the Muslim Brotherhood in Yemen (q.v.), especially because it considers the Yemeni Constitution (q.v.) to be in line with Islam (q.v.) whereas the Muslim Brotherhood views it as being un-Islamic. Furthermore, *Hizb al-Haqq* believes in the important role of the *'ulama'* (religious scholars) who are given the final say in all matters. During the 1993 election, the party won two seats in the Parliament.

HIZB AL-HAQQ AL-ISLAMI (ISLAMIC RIGHT PARTY). The party was founded in September 1990, and its spokesman is lawyer Jamal al-Malawani. *Hizb al-Haqq al-Islami* does not consider itself to be in competition with other Islamic parties (q.v.). However, its major ideological reference is the complete support for the comprehensive unity of the Islamic and Arab *umma* (nation). *Hizb al-Haqq al-Islami* legitimizes both peaceful and violent means to achieve this unity.

HIZB AL-ISLAM (PARTY OF ISLAM). This Turkish group, which was supported by the Soviet Union, flourished among the Kurds in the 1980s.

AL-HIZB AL-ISLAMI **IN IRAQ**. See ISLAMIC PARTY.

HIZB AL-ISTIQLAL. See INDEPENDENCE PARTY.

HIZB JABHAT AL-'AMAL AL-ISLAMI (ISLAMIC ACTION FRONT PARTY). This Jordanian party was established in 1992 as the political wing of the Muslim Brotherhood (q.v.). Its first Secretary-General was Ishaq Ahmad al-Farhan (q.v.). The party's platform resembled that of the Brotherhood, calling for the application of Islamic precepts, respect for democratic principles, pluralism, and human rights (q.v.), and the creation of a national economy based on Islamic principles of social justice (q.v.). *Hizb Jabhat al-'Amal* did not publish a newspaper, but its views were expressed in *al-Rabat* newspaper of the Brotherhood. The front ran in the 1993 elections, winning 16, or about one-third of all parliamentary seats.

The Secretary-General outlined the objectives of the party: to adhere to the basic teachings of Islam (q.v.), the constitution (q.v.), the law, and the national pact and to compete democratically in the political arena. The Deputy Secretary-General, Ra'if Najm, announced that the party would work to introduce *al-Shari'a* (q.v.) (Islamic Law) into the Jordanian constitution and that the party's general strategic objective was to liberate all of Palestine through *jihad* (q.v.) (struggle) because the conflict with Israel (q.v.) is a war for survival. *Hizb Jabhat al-'Amal* upholds the principle of women's rights within the framework of Islam. It also accepts women as members and aims at setting up a female leadership. See also 'AKOUR, 'ABD AL-RAHIM; 'AMUSH, BASSAM; AQAILEH, 'ABD ALLAH; 'ARABIYYAT, 'ABD AL-LATIF; 'AWAYDA, MUHAMMAD; AL-AZAYDAH, AHMAD; DHUNAYBAT, 'ABD AL-MAJID; AL-FARHAN, ISHAQ AHMAD; KAFAWIN, AHMAD; KASASBA, AHMAD; KHALIFA, MAJID; KHATTAB, DHIB; AL-KILANI, IBRAHIM; KUFAHI, AHMAD; MANSUR, HAMZA; MUSLIM BROTHERHOOD IN JORDAN; AL-NITCHA, HAFIZ; RAGHIB, ZUHAYR; AL-RIYATI, BADR; SA'ID, HAMMAM; SHAKIR, QANDIL; AL-TAL, HASAN; ZAWAHRA, 'ABD AL-BARI.

AL-HIZB AL-JUMHURI (REPUBLICAN PARTY). This party is led by Shaykh Sadiq al-Ahmar, son of Shaykh 'Abd Allah al-Ahmar. *Al-Hizb al-Jumhuri* was part of another group known as *al-Ahzab al-Muwaqi'a 'ala al-'Ilan* (The Parties that Signed the Declaration), which was made up of parties that signed a declaration to try to limit the civil debates on the future of the new Republic of Yemen. That is, they committed themselves to refraining from taking extremist positions in an attempt to curry favor or to gain votes from disaffected elements and to concentrate their efforts on the establishment of a democratic system (q.v.) (*nizam*). See also *HIZB AL-HAQQ*.

AL-HIZB AL-JUMHURI AL-ISLAMI. See ISLAMIC REPUBLICAN PARTY.

HIZB AL-NAHDA. See *HARAKAT AL-NAHDA AL-ISLAMIYYA*.

HIZB AL-SALAMA AL-WATANI (NATIONAL SAFETY PARTY). See *MILLI SELAMET PARTISI*.

HIZB AL-SHA'B AL-JAZA'IRI. See PARTY OF THE ALGERIAN PEOPLE.

HIZB AL-SHAYTAN (PARTY OF SATAN). See *HIZBULLAH*.

HIZB AL-SHURA. See UNION OF POPULAR FORCES.

HIZB AL-TAHRIR (LIBERATION PARTY) **IN TURKEY**. This very secretive party is one of the oldest radical fundamentalist groups in Turkey.

HIZB AL-TAHRIR AL-ISLAMI (ISLAMIC LIBERATION PARTY). The Muslim Brotherhood (q.v.) was fully in control of the political as well as the intellectual scene in Jordan, in the East and West banks. The Ba'thists and Communists felt they had no presence in Jordan because of the Muslim Brotherhood's involvement in politics, two members of which became Prime Ministers and 74 became Ministers. When *Hizb al-Tahrir al-Islami* (Islamic Liberation Party) began spreading its call, the Brotherhood tried in vain to draw to its side Shaykh Taqiy al-Din al-Nabahani (q.v.).

A group of religious clerks established *Hizb al-Tahrir al-Islami* in Jerusalem after it split from the *Ikhwan*. This division was initiated in early 1952 by Shaykh Taqiy al-Din al-Nabahani, one of the followers of Haj Amin al-Husayni. Although the former taught at a high school, he was joined by three of his colleagues: Shaykhs As'ad and Rajab Bayyudi al-Tamimi and 'Abd al-Qadim Zallum—who became the leader after al-Nabahani's death. The group met frequently in Jerusalem and Hebron to exchange views and recruit new members. Initially, the emphasis was on religious discussions; however, by the end of 1952, the group began to assume the form of a political party. The split with the Brotherhood stemmed from al-Nabahani's links with Haj Amin al-Husayni, a violently anti-Hashimite Palestinian nationalist figure, and al-Nabahani's criticism of the Brotherhood for its pro-Hashimite position. Al-Nabahani also criticized the Muslim Brotherhood for presenting what he felt was an inauthentic picture of Islam (q.v.).

On 17 November 1952, five members of the group—Taqiy al-Din al-Nabahani, Yusuf Hamdan, Munir Shuqayr, 'Adil al-Nabulsi, and Ghanim 'Abdu—presented the Jordanian Ministry of the Interior with an official request to form a political party. This request, after being examined personally by Sa'id al-Mufti, the Minister of the Interior and Deputy Prime Minister at that time, was turned down. The group was informed of the Minister's decision through the office of the Mayor of Jerusalem in March 1953. The group informed the Mayor of Jerusalem of its intention of establishing a society rather than a political party, yet the authorities arrested the group's members on 2 March 1953. They were released after two weeks and placed under house arrest. During its first year, the group's activities were focused in Jerusalem, Hebron, Nablus, and refugee camps around Jericho. People referred to them as *al-Nabahaniyyun*.

The party spread its call through speeches delivered at mosques. Gradually the speakers of the party became less restrained with respect to the political nature of their speeches, and this became one of the most effective weapons of the party, regarded with increasing concern by the authorities. The party began to publicly instigate the masses against the regime, and the regime responded directly and effectively. The government passed a bill on preaching and guidance in late 1954, which restricted speeches in mosques by requiring written permission of the chief Judge or his representative. This law was in effect as of January 1955. As a result, this law ended the public political speeches and deprived the party of the advantage that it enjoyed over its political competitors. The party now had to depend solely on the circles for spreading its call and gaining new recruits, yet the circles had limited success in achieving these goals, which led to the party's decline in the following years. The Liberation Party participated in the general elections in Jordan like any other political party in the West Bank. In 1951 Shaykh Taqiy al-Din al-Nabahani lost against the Ba'th candidate, 'Abd Allah Na'was.

In 1956, members of the party ran for election as independents. The candidates were Yusuf Hamdan (Jerusalem), 'Abd al-Qadim Zallum (Hebron), As'ad Bayyudi al-Tamimi (Hebron), 'Abd al-Ghaffar al-Khatib (Hebron), Ahmad al-Da'ur (Tulkarm), and Muhammad Musa 'Abd al-Hadi (Janin). Only Ahmad al-Da'ur, who cooperated with the *Ikhwan*, won. Shaykh al-Da'ur played an effective role in the parliamentary opposition.

In the 1956 elections, the Liberation Party struggled to win the seats of Jerusalem, Hebron, Janin, and Tulkarm, and al-Da'ur was again elected, the only candidate of the party who succeeded. Al-Da'ur maintained his policy of strict opposition. Consequently, he was dismissed from the Parliament in 1958, accused of antiregime activities, and was sentenced to two years in jail. The party did not take part in the following elections, and its influence in Westernized cities like Ramallah and Bethlehem, where the majority of the citizens were Christians, was insignificant, nor could it compete with the secular nationalist and leftist parties in Jerusalem and Nablus.

The Liberation Party exerted much more influence in the conservative areas of the West Bank, especially Hebron in the south and the Janin-

Tulkarm region in the north. The party attempted to establish itself among the students, as many party members were teachers. Yet, in mid-1955, the teachers were strictly forbidden to discuss any political issues. Consequently, beginning in 1956, the party's activities among students became secret, and students were organized in circles of five, with the head of the group receiving instructions from a party instructor.

The party's attempt to recruit members of the armed forces and police was of special significance. Direct messages were sent to army officers and, in the mid-1950s, a special agent was appointed to contact army members. Owing to the sensitivity of any political action in the army, the party replaced its circles with individual instruction. Such actions had relative success, but were more effective among the members of the National Guard.

The Liberation Party competed with other parties in the West Bank for the loyalties of the Muslim population, their main competitors being the Muslim Brotherhood. As a result, the party launched its fiercest attack against the *Ikhwan* by declaring them to be followers of the King and accusing them of providing an inaccurate picture of Islam. Nonetheless, the party also attempted sometimes to form an alliance with the Muslim Brotherhood because of their common commitment to political Islam. Several unsuccessful attempts at cooperation were undertaken between the two parties between 1953 and 1955. The supreme guide of the Egyptian Muslim Brotherhood, Hasan al-Hudaybi (q.v.), attempted to persuade the leadership of the Liberation Party not to divide the fundamentalist position, but the Liberation Party refused to cooperate.

In addition to organizational reasons, the fundamental intellectual differences between them might account for the failure of any productive cooperation between the *Ikhwan* and the Liberation Party. One of the reasons behind the collapse of the 1953 negotiations was the *Ikhwan*'s insistence on keeping the secrecy of the alliance; yet the Liberation Party, which was seeking legitimacy (q.v.), felt that such an alliance could support their legitimacy. Negotiations for unity resumed in early 1955 and reached an advanced stage, yet the party in Jordan could not take the responsibility for such a major decision and referred it to the central leadership in Syria, where Shaykh Taqiy al-Din al-Nabahani resided. Unity, however, did not take place because the Liberation Party did not want to lose its distinctive identity.

The Liberation Party made several attempts at organizing secretly to avoid the authority's surveillance. It soon became clear that Yusuf Hamdan was mistaken in thinking that the party needed three months to be ready to displace the regime. As a result, efforts were made to increase the party's followers, especially in the countryside. In 1954, Shaykh Ahmad Da'ur ran for election to the Parliament, and his membership in the Parliament boosted the party's self-confidence. The party was now ready to openly declare its views, especially in mosques and during the month of Ramadan. Jerusalem, Tulkarm, and Hebron were the centers of the party's activities.

In the following decade, 1955–1965, the party's activities declined because of several things, including internal differences, such as Shaykh Taqiy al-Din's move to Beirut and his disagreement with several party members in the West Bank. Also, the authorities expelled many prominent members in mid-1956, which temporarily stopped the party's activities in Jerusalem.

The logic behind not legalizing the party, as the Jordanian Ministry of the Interior declared, had to do with the party's proposed program and not with its membership. The party called for the comprehensive application of Islam in Jordan, including the establishment of a democratic, Islamic state (q.v.), and advocated the revival of the Arab-Islamic civilization (q.v.) and the rejection of foreign ideologies.

Unlike the Muslim Brotherhood, the Liberation Party incurred the regime's wrath from its inception because it advocated replacing the Hashimite regime with a religiously based government as the first step toward Pan-Islamic world unity and because it criticized the regime's pro-Western position. Those individuals concerned with the request were informed that the principles of their suggested program were in contradiction not only with the spirit of the Jordanian constitution but with its articles as well. It was explained, for instance, that the suggested program did not accept the principle of hereditary rule as stated in the Jordanian constitution, and, instead, it called for the election of the ruler. The program also denied nationalism as the basis of the state and viewed Islam as the alternative. Consequently, the program imposed a challenge to the legitimacy of the Jordanian regime and was viewed as intending to promote divisions among the citizens.

The party was not allowed to register legally, and its publications, *al-Raya* and *al-Sarih*, were banned in 1954. Despite the harassment, the party was able to operate underground and to popularize its views through Friday sermons, secret pamphlets, and underground cells. The party participated in the legislative elections of 1954 and won eight seats in 1956, mainly through the support of conservative West Bank towns, such as Hebron, Janin, and Tulkarm. Led by 'Atta Abu Rashta, the party at last emerged in public during the liberalization of 1989.

The practice of organizing "circles" was the distinctive feature of the Liberation Party. The local leadership made the decisions on vital questions, such as which topics were to be discussed and the manner in which they would be discussed, and the leaders of the various circles were instructed and guided as to how they should conduct their circles. Each circle consisted of 5 to 10 members, although for security purposes, a "one-man" circle also existed for statesmen and army officers. New members did not join the circles until they passed a trial period, usually of one or several months and, sometimes, even a year. During this period the newcomers got acquainted with the goals and ideas of the party, and they did not swear the oath of membership or join a circle until they understood the basic philosophy (q.v.) and ideology of the party.

The party advocated the liberation (q.v.) of occupied Palestine through clandestine action, and it viewed its struggle as part of a larger Islamic revolution (q.v.). As a pan-fundamentalist organization, it was strongly opposed to secular Arab movements. It was also strongly anti-Western because it perceived the West (q.v.) as fundamentally opposed to Islam. See also EXTREMISM; *HIZB AL-TAHRIR AL-ISLAMI* IN LIBYA; *HIZB AL-TAHRIR AL-ISLAMI* IN TUNISIA; *JAMA'AT AL-FANNIYYA AL-'ASKARIYYA*; KHAYYAT, 'ABD AL-'AZIZ; AL-NABAHANI, TAQIY AL-DIN; SHAFIQ, MUNIR; SIRRIYYA, SALIH.

HIZB AL-TAHRIR AL-ISLAMI (ISLAMIC LIBERATION PARTY) **IN LIBYA**. This party is a branch of the Jordanian *Hizb al-Tahrir al-Islami* (q.v.) (Islamic Liberation Party). It is probably the most powerful, covert Islamic fundamentalist political organization in Libya. In 1984, Mu'ammar al-Qaddafi publicly hanged student leaders who belonged to the party on the campus of al-Fatih University.

HIZB AL-TAHRIR AL-ISLAMI (ISLAMIC LIBERATION PARTY) **IN TUNISIA**. This secret Islamic organization traces its origins to the Palestinian leader, Taqiy al-Din al-Nabahani (q.v.) and his party, *Hizb al-Tahrir al-Islami* (q.v.) (Islamic Liberation Party), whose objectives include the establishment of the Caliphate (q.v.). Some of its members were arrested and tried in 1983 and 1985 for belonging to an illegal organization. A number of those members were military officers.

HIZB AL-TAJAMMU' AL-YEMENI LI AL-ISLAH (PARTY OF YEMENI GROUPING FOR REFORM). This party, which is headed by Shaykh 'Abd Allah al-Ahmar, a great tribal super-chief, was able in three years, from the time of its foundation in September 1990 to 1993, to penetrate the state system, and al-Ahmar became Speaker of the Parliament. The party was established on the membership of the Muslim Brotherhood (q.v.), which was founded in the early 1960s, and which has played an important role for three decades in North Yemen. *Al-Islah* became the second strongest party in Yemen after the elections of 1993. Two other groups, tribal chiefs and merchants, made the party very strong. However, the leadership of the Muslim Brotherhood did not fully participate in the leadership of the party and some uneasiness still taints the relationship between the leaderships of *al-Islah* and the Brotherhood. Yet, the deputy head of *al-Islah* is the supreme guide of the Brotherhood, Shaykh Yasin 'Abd al-'Aziz. In addition, the Brotherhood's former supreme guide, 'Abd al-Majid al-Zandani (q.v.), is the head of the *Islah Shura* Council.

The leadership of *al-Islah* has decided to participate in the political process in Yemen and has been critical of the violent acts in 1992 that were committed by radical fundamentalists like *al-Salafiyyin* and *Jama'at al-Jihad*. The radical groups describe both the Brotherhood and *al-Islah* as infidel because of their participation in the democratic elections. Al-Zandani refused the radical reduction of all others into only the party of God and the party of the Devil or *Hizb Allah* and *Hizb al-Shaytan* (qq.v.). The party is very active in educational and religious affairs as well as political life. See also *AL-TAJAMMU' AL-YEMENI LI AL-ISLAH*; AL-WARTALANI, FUDAYL; ZANDANI, SHAYKH 'ABD AL-MAJID.

HIZB AL-UMMA. See NATION'S PARTY IN ALGERIA; NATION'S PARTY IN EGYPT.

HIZB-E JOMHURI-YE KHALQ-E MUSALMANE-E IRAN. See MUSLIM PEOPLE'S REPUBLICAN PARTY IN IRAN.

HIZBULLAH (PARTY OF GOD). *Hizbullah* is a Qur'anic term that is employed by the fundamentalists to describe themselves in opposition to *Hizb al-Shaytan* (party of Satan). The basic distinction between *Hizbullah* and *Hizb al-Shaytan* is that the former adheres to the doctrines of *tawhid* (Oneness of God), *al-Shari'a* (Islamic Law), and divine governance (qq.v.), whereas the later adheres to unbelief (*kufr*), human legislation, and paganism (qq.v.).

The term is essentially a political and not a theological one. Radical fundamentalists regard most Muslims and Islamic societies and states as *Hizb al-Shaytan* because they live a paganistic life and away from true *tawhid*. But a condition to be included in *Hizbullah* is Islam (q.v.). In fact, the fundamentalists legitimize *jihad* (q.v.) (struggle) against *Hizb al-Shaytan* because they belong to *dar al-harb* (q.v.) (abode of war). See also RELIGION.

HIZBULLAH (PARTY OF GOD) **IN IRAN**. See ISLAMIC REPUBLI-CAN PARTY.

HIZBULLAH (PARTY OF GOD) **IN LEBANON**. *Hizbullah* is the leading fundamentalist movement in Lebanon. It emerged as a result of the convergence of Lebanese Shi'ite interests with Iranian foreign policy. It surfaced after the Israeli invasion of Lebanon in 1982. Its origin can be traced to several Shi'ite militants who were displeased with the agenda of Imam Musa al-Sadr (q.v.) in the 1960s. Muhammad Husayn Fadlallah (q.v.) is regarded as the spiritual guide of the party. After his active involvement in Iraq, Fadlallah settled in al-Nab'a, a suburb of Beirut and promoted his Islamic vision through his own organization, *Usrat al-Ta'akhi* (Family of Brotherhood). The Iranian Revolution of 1979 (q.v.) led him to believe in the efficacy of the notion of *waliy al-faqih* (q.v.) (the guardian of the jurist) as a model for a political system (q.v.) (*nizam*) and consequently in the necessity of establishing an Islamic state (q.v.). The call for an Islamic system in the absence of the Twelfth Imam is the main feature of Ayatollah Khomeini's (q.v.) political outlook. It is a revolutionary idea because it constitutes an active response after centuries of Shi'ite tolerance of Sunni rule. In Lebanon, advocates of *waliy al-faqih* opposed the Christian domination of the government.

The single most important event in the history of Shi'ite militant groups in Lebanon was the creation of the Salvation Committee by President Ilyas Sarkis in 1982 to deal with the repercussions of the Israeli invasion. The membership of *Amal*'s leader, Nabih Berri, in that committee along with Bashir Jumayyil, a radical Christian, alienated many the Shi'ites who were pushing for a more hard-line Islamic path. Husayn al-Musawi, a leading figure in *Amal* movement at the time, objected to Berri's acceptance of membership in the committee and called for Iranian arbitration of the matter. The dispute was referred to the Iranian ambassador in Damascus at the time, 'Ali Akbar Muhtashimi (q.v.), later Minister of Interior and member of the *Majlis al-Shura* (q.v.) (*Shura* Council), who ruled against Berri's participation in the committee. Berri did not abide by the ruling, and Musawi decided to resign from *Amal* and to form his own *Harakat Amal al-Islamiyya* (q.v.) (Islamic *Amal* Movement).

In Iran, Shaykh Ibrahim Amin al-Sayyid (q.v.), the *Amal* representative, attacked the committee. It was then that the organization of *Hizbullah* was formed under the sponsorship of the Iranian Revolutionary Guards (q.v.) stationed in the Biqa'. The organization became official in 1994 when a statement commemorating the massacre of Sabra and Shatila was issued with the party's signature.

The role of Muhammad Husayn Fadlallah in the establishment of the party is unclear. One account maintained that Fadlallah preferred to have Muslim Shi'ite fundamentalists working within the body of *Amal* in order to reach the broadest possible audience within the Shi'ite community. But the tide of pro-Iranian sentiments within the community was growing at a pace that could not be restrained within the confines of *Amal*'s alliance with the Syrian regime. Furthermore, Iran preferred to have a loyal organization to further its influence among the Shi'ites and to fight its enemies. The presence of Israeli troops and U.S. marines in Lebanon added another incentive for direct Iranian involvement in Lebanon.

Hizbullah's ideology emphasizes the Qur'anic origin of its terminology. Almost all the terms that the party uses in its political literature are derived from the Qur'an (q.v.). One party leader stated that most of the activities and movements of Muslims should be based on Qur'anic verses. But this does not mean that the ideology and practices of *Hizbullah* are necessarily Qur'anic, even although they are justified as such.

The ideology of *Hizbullah* is also based on the attachment to the leadership of the religious scholars in Muslim society. The task of citing religious texts in Islam to prove that religion (q.v.) required Muslims to abide by the rulings and orders of their religious leaders is not difficult. The party restricts the interpretation (q.v.) of the sources of its ideology to a select few. The *'ulama'* (religious scholars) of Islam are viewed as the best qualified to perform the duty of leading the *umma* (q.v.) (nation) toward Islam.

Moreover, the leadership of the party, in accordance with Shi'ism, does not leave the interpretation of religious texts to the average Muslim. Every Shi'ite has to follow strictly the theological pronouncements of a *marji'* (authority). The mechanical process of fellowship is termed *taqlid* (q.v.) (traditionalism), which literally means imitation. The leaders of the party believe that the *'ulama'* alone can bring about Islamic consciousness (q.v.) (*wa'iy*) of unification. The model of Leninist party organization was convenient to all those groups in the Arab world that favored one-party rule and that are based on absolute self-righteousness and intolerance. In *Hizbullah*, power flows from the *'ulama'*, who are led by the *'alim-qa'id* (scholar-leader) down through the entire community. The centralism of *Hizbullah* is less intense than that of *al-Da'wa al-Islamiyya* (q.v.) (Islamic Call) in Iraq. However, the manner in which a certain act is executed is left to the initiative of the people, provided that the *'alim* intervenes when it is necessary. Typically, *Hizbullah* traces its centralism to the style of leadership of the Prophet Muhammad. Moreover, the centralism of *Hizbullah* prevents the elimination of the party structure by one blow from the regime and requires the creation of different organizational formations to provide the party with durability and to avoid the control of the regime under which that party operates. *Hizbullah* regards the entire *umma* as a framework for the party. The ideology of *Hizbullah* also contains features of class analysis, for the rise of Islamic fundamentalism (q.v.) in Lebanon is a product of the failure of the Lebanese Left.

Hizbullah adheres to the doctrines of *al-jihad* (q.v.) *al-akbar* (greater struggle) and *al-jihad al-asghar* (smaller struggle). Whereas the smaller *jihad* denotes the combating activities against the enemies of Islam, the greater *jihad* was defined by the Prophet as that which encompasses the individual's service to the cause of religion. *Hizbullah* broadens the notion of greater *jihad* to include all efforts that an individual exerts to complete his duty as a believer.

In *Hizbullah*'s ideology, justice and equality (qq.v.) can be achieved through human efforts and through a revolutionary process. Its ideology represents a radical and revolutionary strand of Shi'ite theology (q.v.). The conservative and orthodox Shi'ite theological school believes that justice and equality can be achieved only with the return of the Twelfth Imam. The doctrine of *wilayat al-faqih* calls for a political revolution (q.v.) to establish an Islamic order headed by the deputy of the Imam on earth, a title that Ayatollah Khomeini (q.v.) held first in recent times. The ideology also introduces a new distinction between revolutionary *'ulama'* and *fuqaha' al-salatin* (state's jurists).

It is clear that the Iranian influence among members and leaders of the party stems primarily from the moral and political standing of Khomeini in the Shi'ite world. He was the link between the Shi'ite community and the blood lineage of the Prophet. His death led to more political independence of the party vis-à-vis the Iranian government, which was perceived by an earlier leadership of the party as being too moderate.

The leadership body was initially called the *Majlis al-Shura* (*Shura* Council), which has been converted into a Politburo whose decisions are reached by either *ijma'* (q.v.) (consensus) or by a majority vote. The leadership may also decide to refer matters to the Iranian government. Responsibility is divided according to typical party functions. There are seven committees: ideology, finance, political affairs, information, military affairs, judicial affairs, and social affairs. The party organization in Lebanon is also divided geographically into three regions: Beirut and its suburbs, the Biqa', and the South.

The rise of *Hizbullah* occurred after 1984 and benefited from its firm confrontational stance vis-à-vis the U.S. Marine presence in Lebanon and the Israeli occupation in the South. The bombing of the U.S. Marine barracks in Lebanon and the series of hostage takings boosted the radical credentials of the party. The party originally maintained a low profile and focused on the slow formation of cells, but the TWA airliner hijacking in 1985 focused more attention on the party. The party, however, has denied any association with these acts. The party thus became visibly active in the Lebanese political and military arena. It declared its manifesto in 1985, which called for the establishment of an Islamic state and an end to Maronite domination and refused to associate itself with the conventional Lebanese political game. It further emphasized its ideological uniqueness within the context of Islamic thinking.

During the war between *Amal* and *Hizbullah* in 1988–1990, the party scored some successes on both the political and military fronts. Whereas *Amal* was discredited, the party intensified its attacks against Israel (q.v.) and its allies in the South of Lebanon. *Amal* has entered the government, whereas *Hizbullah* has asserted the need for a radical overthrow of the Lebanese political system and stressed the urgency of establishing an Islamic order in Lebanon. More importantly, the party proved to be far more sophisticated in its recruitment procedures and its propaganda campaigns than *Amal*. The party takes seriously the indoctrination of its members and holds lectures and seminars for members and sympathizers alike. It also publishes a large number of periodicals that are aimed at children, women, and militant youths. *Hizbullah* reportedly has benefited for years from generous financial aid from Iran, but there is no solid information on this subject.

The party has also created a variety of social services for desperately impoverished Shi'ites in various parts of Lebanon. It tried to provide services that the Lebanese government would not deliver in predominately Shi'ite areas after the outbreak of civil war. Party speakers use the crucial platform of the Friday prayer sermon to spread the party message to large sectors of the population. It has effectively used its radio and television stations to influence more followers in Lebanon. Significantly, the party has grown up from the style that characterized its military success against *Amal*.

The end of the inter-Shi'ite war in 1991, as well as the disarming of militias, posed a challenge to the party. The party had to adjust to the change of government and the rise of the Hashimi Rafsanjani's (q.v.) line in Iran, which focused less on the immediate creation of an Islamic state in Lebanon. Furthermore, the Rafsanjani government seemed more interested in maintaining good relations with Damascus than in furthering Islamic revolutionary goals in Lebanon.

Whereas the party has not abandoned the armed struggle and has indeed moved most of its weapons to safe areas in the Biqa', the leadership appears prepared to engage in conventional political battles. Leaders now hold meetings with various Lebanese political factions, including bitter enemies of yesterday, like the Phalangists and the Communists. They have even met with representatives of the Lebanese government and its army. This would have been inconceivable until recently.

After years of postponement, the party held its second national congress in May 1991. The congress, which was attended by members and cadres from all segments of the party, elected a new leadership. The Secretary-General of the party, Subhi al-Tufayli, was replaced by 'Abbas al-Musawi, who was killed by an Israeli raid in 1992. Sayyid Hasan Nasrallah (q.v.) was elected General Secretary, and Ibrahim al-Amin was elected his deputy. The new leadership could very well prepare the party for the new and difficult stage of post-militia politics.

The 1992 parliamentary elections allowed the party to win eight seats and, along with other fundamentalist deputies, it constituted the largest parliamentary bloc. As to the relationship with the Lebanese state, many positive steps have been taken, and the party now endorses the legitimacy (q.v.) of the Lebanese state. Also, the party participated in the 1996 parliamentary elections and won a few seats. See also AMIN AL-SAYYID, IBRAHIM; 'AMMAR, 'ALI; BIRJAWI, MUHAMMAD; FADLALLAH, MUHAMMAD HUSAYN; FINAYSH, MUHAMMAD; *AL-HARAKA AL-ISLAMIYYA FI LUBNAN*; *HARAKAT AMAL AL-IS-LAMIYYA*; *HIZBULLAH* IN LIBYA, *HIZBULLAH* IN SAUDI ARABIA; IRANIAN REVOLUTION OF 1979; ISLAMIC *JIHAD* IN SAUDI ARABIA; ISLAMIC REPUBLICAN PARTY; ISLAMIC REVOLU-TIONARY ORGANIZATION OF THE ARABIAN PENINSULA; IS-

RAEL; *AL-JIHAD AL-ISLAMI FI LUBNAN*; KHOMEINISM; *MARJI'*
AL-TAQLID; NASRALLAH, SAYYID HASAN; RA'D, MUHAM-
MAD; AL-SADR, MUSA; TAHA, 'ALI HASAN; TULAYS, 'ALI;
TWA HIJACK; VIOLENCE, YAGHI, MUHAMMAD.

HIZBULLAH (PARTY OF GOD) **IN LIBYA**. *Hizbullah* in Libya is a fundamentalist party that is engulfed in secrecy. No solid information is available.

HIZBULLAH (PARTY OF GOD) **IN SAUDI ARABIA**. Implications suggest that *Hizbullah* (q.v.) (Party of God) in Lebanon had a branch, which is also known as *al-Jihad al-Islami* (Islamic *Jihad*) that was also active in the predominantly Shi'ite eastern province of Saudi Arabia at the end of the 1980s. See also *AL-JIHAD AL-ISLAMI* IN SAUDI ARABIA.

HIZBULLAH (PARTY OF GOD) **IN TURKEY**. This Turkish organization is not well known. Two organizations, or groups, use the same name. The first is called Manzil's group and is led by Fidan Ghunghur. Turkish intelligence links this organization to Iran because it wants to establish a similar political system (q.v.) (*nizam*) and believes in armed revolt. Husayn Wali Oghlo, a graduate in political science in Ankara, leads the other group. It is believed that the latter group is progovernment and commits atrocious acts that are attributed to the first group. The two groups have fought against each other, and in 1994, approximately 94 individuals were victims of the fights.

HIZBULLAH (PARTY OF GOD) **IN YEMEN**. See *AL-TAJAMMU' AL-YEMENI LI AL-ISLAH*.

HOJJATIYEH ORGANIZATION (*SAZMAN-E HOJJATIYEH*). This organization was set up in the mid-1950s to fight against the Bahà'ì society and launched anti-Bahà'ì campaigns. After the Iranian Revolution of 1979 (q.v.), it challenged the clergy's single party, the Islamic Republican Party (q.v.). For example, the *Hojjatiyeh* Organization urged Iranian Shi'ites to emulate the teaching of highest religious authorities and to refrain from participating in the struggle for power and await the return of the Hidden *Imam*. Some critics believe that the society, in the postrevolutionary period, has not been a genuine social force but simply a group of clergymen and their supporters without an important social program beyond their anti-Bahà'ì campaign. Others say that its followers joined the Islamic Republican Party and worked from within to undermine its doctrine of *waliy al-faqih* (q.v.) (the guardian of the jurist).

AL-HUDAYBI, HASAN (?–1973). After the assassination of Hasan al-Banna (q.v.) in 1949, the Muslim Brotherhood (q.v.) selected Judge Hasan al-Hudaybi as the new supreme guide. He was not well known as being among the leadership of the Brotherhood, but was the compromise choice between the radical and moderate wings of the Brotherhood—some say dictated by the Egyptian Palace. Al-Hudaybi did not seem to be very popular with many members of the movement because of his compromising attitude. During the Brotherhood's ordeal with the 'Abd al-Nasir regime, the leadership seemed to have lost its ability to lead politically and to develop ideologically. This allowed Sayyid Qutb (q.v.) to become the leading theoretician. Al-Hudaybi appointed Qutb as a member of the highest council in the Brotherhood, *Maktab al-Irshad* (Guidance Bureau), and editor in chief of the newspaper *al-Ikwan al-Muslimin* (*Muslim Brethren*). Al-Hudaybi disagreed with Qutb over his radical interpretation (q.v.) of Islam (q.v.), as elaborated in *Ma'alim fi al-Tariq* (*Signposts on the Road*), and al-Hudaybi wrote his book, *Du'at La Qudat* (*Callers, Not Judges*) in response. Al-Hudaybi and Qutb were arrested and sentenced to death, but al-Hudaybi's sentence was reduced to life imprisonment. See also AL-GHAZALI, MUHAMMAD; *HIZB AL-TAHRIR AL-ISLAMI*; 'ISHMAWI, SALIH; *AL-SALAFIYYA*.

AL-HUDAYBI, MA'MUN. Currently, Ma'mun al-Hudaybi is the Deputy General Secretary and spokesman for the Egyptian Muslim Brotherhood (q.v.).

HUDAYTHA, MASHHUR. See SALVATION MOVEMENT.

HUDUD (DETERRENTS). Because most fundamentalists consider the *umma* (q.v.) (nation) as one body, Islam (q.v.) has set up legal deterrents (*hudud*) for social crimes, because cooperation requires the protection of individuals. Every individual is responsible for guarding the interests of the community. By this, Islam secures complete social justice (q.v.) in the large Islamic countries, not only for its adherents but also for all its inhabitants regardless of their religion (q.v.), race, or language. *Hudud* are seen as not only legal but also as social and political deterrents that help maintain peace (q.v.) in society. See also SOCIAL JUSTICE.

AL-HUKM AL-DUSTURI. See CONSTITUTIONAL RULE.

AL-HUKM AL-ISLAMI (ISLAMIC RULE). See ISLAMIC GOVERN-MENT.

HUKUMA (GOVERNMENT). See ISLAMIC GOVERNMENT. See also CALIPHATE; GOVERNANCE; GOVERNMENT, FORMS OF; GOV-ERNMENT, FUNCTION OF; ISLAMIC STATE.

AL-HUKUMA AL-'ALAMIYYA LI AL-ISLAM (INTERNATIONAL GOVERNMENT OF ISLAM). See SECOND ISLAMIC INTERNA-TIONAL.

HUMAN RIGHTS (*HUQUQ AL-INSAN*). Radical fundamentalists like Sayyid Qutb and Abu al-A'la al-Mawdudi (qq.v.) refuse to acknowledge the existence of rights other than those that are postulated by *al-Shari'a* (q.v.) (Islamic Law). They insist that the only rights are those that are derived from *al-Shari'a* and not from any philosophical system (q.v.) (*nizam*) or secular political system. They believe that the issue of human rights is being used politically against the Muslims and Islamic states in order to force them to yield to Western interests.

Moderate fundamentalists, like Rashid al-Ghannushi and Muhammad Salim al-'Awwa (qq.v.), believe not only that Islamic thought accepts these rights as basic rights but that Islam was the first system to provide man qua man with rights. They revise the legal theory of *Maqasid al-Shari'a* (objectives of Islamic Law) and *al-huquq al-Shar'iyya* (legal rights) in order to show that currently accepted schemes of natural human rights could be developed from an Islamic perspective and could be incorporated into the main body of modern Islamic thought. See also CONSCIOUSNESS; AL-GHANNUSHI, RASHID; *HIZB JABHAT AL-'AMAL AL-ISLAMI*; ISLAMIC CULTURAL HERITAGE SOCIETY; *MUJAHIDIN KHALQ*; SHAFIQ, MUNIR; AL-TURABI, HASAN.

HUQUQ AL-INSAN. See HUMAN RIGHTS.

AL-HUQUQ AL-SHAR'IYYA (LEGAL RIGHTS). See HUMAN RIGHTS.

HURRAS AL-THAWRA. See REVOLUTIONARY GUARDS.

AL-HURRIYYA. See FREEDOM.

AL-HUWAIDI, FAHMI. Al-Huwaidi is the deputy editor in chief of *al-Ahram* in Egypt. He is a very well known moderate fundamentalist writer and journalist who has defended many fundamentalist positions and views. Al-Huwaidi has further advocated tolerance, democracy, and pluralism (qq.v.).

AL-HUWAIDI, HASAN. See INTERNATIONAL ORGANIZATION OF THE MUSLIM BROTHERHOOD.

I

'IBAD AL-RAHMAN (WORSHIPPERS OF THE MERCIFUL). This society was founded by Muhammad 'Umar al-Da'uq in Beirut immediately after the creation of Israel (q.v.) and became official in 1952. Founding members include Muhammad 'Ali al-Zamini, 'Umar Huri, Mustapha Huri, and Ibrahim Qatirji, and it followed in the footsteps of the Muslim Brotherhood (q.v.) in Egypt, but was less political and more concerned with cultural, moral, and philanthropic activities. Before it was licensed, it functioned within the association of *al-Bir wa al-Ihsan* (Good and Benevolence). A group of younger members who wanted to be politically involved split and founded *al-Haraka al-Islamiyya fi Lubnan* (q.v.) (Islamic Movement in Lebanon). See also *AL-HARAKA AL-ISLAMIYYA FI LUBNAN*.

IBN BADIS, 'ABD AL-HAMID (1889–1940). Ibn Badis is one of the best-known reformers of the first half of the 20th century and the founder of *Jam'iyyat al-'Ulama' al-Muslimin* (q.v.) (Association of Muslim Scholars). Born in Constantine in Algeria to a well-known Berber family, he received a religious education at the Zaytuna Mosque in Tunisia. Ibn Badis was influenced by the teachings of Jamal al-Din al-Afghani and Muhammad 'Abdu (qq.v.). His main goal was to reform Islam (q.v.). Ibn Badis started a reform movement to assert the Islamic identity of Algeria against French colonization. Part of his reform centered around criticizing the Sufi orders for their un-Islamic rituals. The association that he founded in 1931 advocated the revival of Islam, religious freedom, (q.v.) and the recognition of Arabic as the national language. In 1938, the Association of Muslim Scholars declared naturalized Algerians in France to be non-Muslims. The French tried to limit its influence. Although he shared many of the views of *al-Salafiyya* (q.v.), Ibn Badis thought his mission was one of education and improvement of Islamic conditions. He stressed the importance of free will and reason (q.v.). For him, the Algerian identity is composed of Arabism, Islam, and nationalism. See also *JAM'IYYAT AL-'ULAMA' AL-MUSLIMIN.*

IBN SAUD. See 'ABD AL-WAHHAB, MUHAMMAD IBN; *AL-WAHHABIYYA.*

IBN TAYMIYYA, TAQIY AL-DIN AHMAD (1263–1328). Ibn Taymiyya was the most influential medieval thinker among the fundamentalists, especially the radicals. Ibn Taymiyya was a Hanbali scholar and exerted a tremendous influence on Sunnism. In most of his writings, he was reacting to the Mongol invasions and disruption of normal life in the Islamic world. Ibn Taymiyya was imprisoned in Syria and Egypt. His legal views in deciding whether or not the Mongol rulers were Muslims have been used today by many fundamentalist thinkers like Sayyid Qutb and 'Abd al-Salam Faraj (qq.v.). Ibn Taymiyya built his whole intellectual and religious discourse on the absolute supremacy of the Qur'an (q.v.) and the *Sunna* (way) of the Prophet as well as on the *salaf al-Salih* (the pious ancestors). Thus, for instance, he denied the legitimacy (q.v.) of theology (q.v.), as the modern fundamentalists do. His logic for accusing the Mongol rulers of unbelief (q.v.) (*kufr*) has been used by modern fundamentalists to designate the status of modern rulers. Furthermore, his thought was based on extreme literalism in terms of reading the Qur'anic text (q.v.), but, at the same time, he was against *taqlid* (q.v.) (traditionalism). *Al-Wahhabiyya* movement, the Muslim Brotherhood (qq.v.), and many other Islamic movements have accepted and reinterpreted many of his political and religious views, like *tawhid* (q.v.), *taqlid* (traditionalism), or reason (q.v.) (*ijtihad*) and others. See also CALIPHATE; FARAJ, 'ABD AL-SALAM; ISLAMIC STATE; *AL-WAHHABIYYA.*

AL-IBRAHIMI, BASHIR (1889–1965). He struggled, along with 'Abd al-Hamid Bin Badis (q.v.) in *Jam'iyyat al-'Ulama' al-Muslimin* (q.v.) (Association of Muslim Scholars), to free Algeria from French occupation under the banner of Islam and the Arabic language. Al-Ibrahimi worked as well for the revival of Arabic, which he considered to be the vehicle for Algerian unity and Islamic supremacy. See also ISLAMIC SALVATION FRONT; *JAM'IYYAT AL-'ULAMA' AL-MUSLIMIN;* KABIR, RABIH; *AL-WAHHABIYYA.*

IJMA' (CONSENSUS). *Ijma'* has been seen in the history (q.v.) of Islam (q.v.) by Muslim scholars as the source of political authority, whose legitimate continuation depends on popular *shura* (q.v.) (consultation). This is what is historically referred to as *'aqd al-bay'a* (the contract of allegiance) between the people and their designated ruler. In fact, fundamentalists like Abu al-A'la al-Mawdudi, Sayyid Qutb, and Hasan al-Turabi (qq.v.) argue that Western philosophy (q.v.) could not have developed the concept of universal equality (q.v.) and the need for *ijma'* (consensus) or a contract between the ruler and the ruled, without external references and experience. The development of the Western view of contract was not historically derived but rather advocated as a means toward reducing the rulers' absolute powers and increasing the people's limited power. The issue of freedom (q.v.) was originally a political doctrine that aimed at liberating the people economically and politically, but democracy (q.v.) developed to mean the free exchange of opinions and the interaction of free wills. Consequently, the theory of social contract in liberal democracy became the source of compromise and interdependency between the government (q.v.) and the people. However, the uneven distribution of power and wealth led to another breed of democracy, the socialist, which attempted to redistribute the capital held by the few and to reintroduce the essence of democracy, that is, political equality.

Muslim societies are facing major problems, and *ijma'* has been partly seen as a necessary means for resolving these problems. First, societies are still traditional and not easily open to change. Second, poor economic conditions, exploitation, and unequal distribution prevented the transition to democracy. Third, military institutions are by nature undemocratic, not to mention the long-standing cultural, military, and political imperialism, which have not been conducive to the establishment of a democratic environment. The fourth and last reason is related more to the psychology of the people themselves, who became conditioned to tyranny (q.v.) and, consequently, the absence of individual political awareness of the need for consensus and democracy. All these factors together led to a deep-rooted conviction that, although democracy might be a good political ideal, real politics rested on actual power, itself dependent on the use of force, coercion, and the monopoly of authority.

Therefore, moderate fundamentalists wanted to remodel democracy in a new form based on *ijma'* and *shura* that could do away with the historicity and misuse of Islamic political doctrines. They call on Muslims for adaptation of democracy after having redefined it in terms of Islamic terminology and after having reformulated it within the conditions of contemporary Islamic life. Thus, it may become both *ijma'* and *shura*. The fundamentalists see that a mere *taqlid* (q.v.) (imitation) of Western democracy, without proper consideration of the conditions of its new environment, may lead to a faulty situation, be it social, philosophical, political, or ethical. A situation like this makes democracy more of an alien doctrine superimposed by a foreign culture and, consequently, a sign of foreign hegemony and imposition. What is needed then is the reacquisition of democracy and its Islamization (q.v.) so that it becomes self-induced, native, natural, and beneficial.

Consensus (*ijma'*), whose employment was theoretical in matters of jurisprudence and theology (qq.v.), is viewed as the source of political transformation and democratization. Although it has been traditionally used to arrive at one Qur'anic interpretation (q.v.) or another and has been relegated to the scholarly elites in order to convince the *umma* (q.v.) (nation) to follow one interpretation or another, now the fundamentalists view it not only as a source of freeing the nation from the conservative scholarly traditional readings but, more importantly, as a source of the community's liberation (q.v.) from the tyranny of both the rulers and political traditions. Thus, all fields of Islamic sciences and of other aspects of life become the proper interest of ordinary Muslims and subject to their approval. No legitimate legal or political principles can be imposed on the community without its consent through *shura* and consensus. The historically derived normative status of scholars and of political authority is denied and replaced by a need for a continuous consensus of ratification and agreement by the community; no political leader or religious scholar has the right to impose his will on the people. Now it is only the community that can speak with an authoritative voice, individuals have only opinions. The right to structure political institutions, to evaluate behavior, or to interpret the scripture is communal. Equality in terms of rights and duties is postulated as a necessary condition for proper political behavior. This is why most fundamentalists make popular *ijma'* a necessary condition for electing a legitimate Muslim ruler, and any ruler who comes to power without popular approval even though upholding *al-Shari'a* (q.v.) (Islamic Law) is not legitimate.

This view is opposite to medieval thinkers' acceptance of seizure of power. But the fundamentalists see such an acceptance as yielding to political power and betraying God's (q.v.) trust, which is, again, communal in nature. God's delegation of authority is to all humanity as his vicegerent and is not bestowed on particular scholars, classes, or rulers. Therefore, any seizure of power cannot be legitimately justified. Whereas historically the elites looked at themselves as *ipso facto* representatives of the community, the fundamentalists turn down any suggestion to the particular privileges of any elite, be it political or religious. Although the fundamentalists acknowledge differences among individuals, they are nonetheless against the institutionalization of intellectual and political elitism. No group of people, regardless of its special gifts, can claim legally to have more rights or enjoy special prerogatives than any other group.

Most fundamentalists downplay the importance of *ijma'* in theology—which was the main goal of traditional theology. As said previously, people should be capable of reading and interpreting the text (q.v.) without an authoritative body. Legitimate interpretations must not contradict the text, on the one hand, and must be grounded in *tawhid* (q.v.) (Oneness of God), on the other. The governance (q.v.) (*hakimiyya*) of God, which is the practical embodiment of *tawhid*, must appear in the unity of Muslims and must be the principle of revival. Otherwise any revival that lacks such governance is indistinguishable from un-Islamic ones. For the moral grounds for an Islamic revival must always be present and embodied in the creation of a Muslim society and an Islamic state (q.v.). See also 'ABDU, MUHAMMAD; *HIZBULLAH*; ISLAMIC ACTION PARTY; ISLAMIC GOVERNMENT; *JAMA'AT AL-MUS-LIMIN*; JURISPRUDENCE; KHOMEINISM; *AL-MADI*; MODERNISM; RADICALISM; RIDA, MUHAMMAD RASHID; SYSTEM; THEOCRACY; AL-TURABI, HASAN.

IJTIHAD. See REASON.

'IKAWI, KHALIL. See *HARAKAT AL-TAWHID AL-ISLAMI* IN LEBANON.

AL-IKHWAN (BRETHREN). This group is made up of *Wahhabi* activists who follow the ideological theology (q.v.) of Muhammad Ibn 'Abd al-Wahhab (q.v.). The *Wahhabi* activists (*Ikhwan*) were employed by 'Abd al-'Aziz Ibn Sa'ud, who set up the Kingdom of Saudi Arabia in the first quarter of the 20th century. Suppressed by the government of the new state in the mid-1930s, they provided the inspiration for contemporary proponents of strict social and cultural practices in the kingdom. The *Ikwan* are still active in contemporary times. They prefer to call themselves *al-Muwahhidin* (the monotheists). See also 'ABD AL-WAHHAB, MUHAMMAD IBN; MUSLIM BROTHERHOOD IN THE GULF; *AL-WAHHABIYYA*.

AL-IKHWAN AL-MUSLIMIN. See MUSLIM BROTHERHOOD; MUSLIM BROTHERHOOD, IDEOLOGY OF. See also AL-BANNA, HASAN; INTERNATIONAL ORGANIZATION OF THE MUSLIM BROTHERHOOD; QUTB, SAYYID.

'ILM. See SCIENCE.

'ILM AL-KALAM. See THEOLOGY.

AL-'ILMANIYYA (SECULARISM). See DIVINITY.

IMAM, SHAYKH 'ABD AL-FATTAH. See *AL-SALAFIYYA*.

IMITATION. See *TAQLID*.

INDEPENDENCE PARTY (*HIZB AL-ISTIQLAL*). The Independence Party was initially characterized by its struggle against imperialist presence in Morocco and its attempts to realize independence and the return of the Sultan. As a result, the internal contradictions in the party did not appear until after independence when the party split up. In 1960, Muhammad 'Allal al-Fasi (q.v.) was elected as the head of the party. Al-Fasi introduced several ideological changes, including "Islamic socialism" as the basis of the party's political program.

Because of the Independence Party's historical and religious Arab-Islamic foundations, its intellectual basis, as manifested in the writings of its spiritual leader, 'Allal al-Fasi, mainly depended on Islam (q.v.) and Arabism in order to achieve the unity of Morocco. For the Independents, the concept of Islam is organically related to Arab Nationalism and was employed as their unifying force and the basis of the party's ideas and future course. See also DEMOCRATIC CONSTITUTIONAL POPULAR MOVEMENT; AL-FASI, MUHAMMAD 'ALLAL; POPULAR MOVEMENT.

INNOVATION (*BID'A*). The term *bid'a* for the fundamentalists does not mean just inventing something and developing a concept and a doctrine. In fact, it connotes the un-Islamic development of doctrines and concepts as opposed to earlier developments that have been accepted by the Islamic community or the general rule of religion (q.v.). A radical fundamentalist, for instance, may consider democracy (q.v.) as a *bid'a*, whereas a moderate fundamentalist may think it is a good innovation, and thus, not strictly a *bid'a*.

INTERNATIONAL GOVERNMENT OF ISLAM (*AL-HUKUMA AL-'ALAMIYYA LI AL-ISLAM*). See SECOND ISLAMIC INTERNATIONAL.

INTERNATIONAL ISLAMIC FRONT FOR *JIHAD* AGAINST JEWS AND CRUSADERS. See BIN LADEN, USAMA.

INTERNATIONAL ORGANIZATION OF THE MUSLIM BROTHERHOOD (*AL-TANZIM AL-'ALAMI LI AL-IKHWAN AL-MUSLIMIN*). The International Organization of the Muslim Brotherhood was set by the Muslim Brotherhood in Egypt (q.v.) in a meeting of the *Majlis al-Shura* (q.v.) (*Shura* Council). It was founded in order to make known general decisions relating to the objectives and goals of the Brotherhood, especially in times of crisis and trouble that might surround a specific branch in one country or another.

In the 1940s, Hasan al-Banna (q.v.), the founder of the Muslim Brotherhood, developed a branch for communicating with the Islamic world. This branch was headed first by Dr. Tawfiq al-Shawi and then 'Abd al-Hafiz al-Sayfi. By the end of the 1940s, the Brotherhood expanded this branch into Damascus and Iran as well as Yemen. The first conference of the Islamic International (*al-Umamiyya al-Islamiyya*) took place in 1948 in Mecca during pilgrimage time. During the conference, it was decided that the Brotherhood would participate in fighting the Jews in Palestine through *al-Nizam al-Sirri* (q.v.) (Secret Apparatus).

After the dissolution of the Brotherhood in 1954, this branch turned into an international organization, because many members of the leadership spread throughout the Islamic world and Europe. The international organization assumed more importance because it was the channel that facilitated communication and organization. Dr. Sa'id Ramadan, al-Banna's son-in-law, was instrumental in developing the organization. He went first to Jordan and then to Switzerland, where the first branch of the

Brotherhood was set up in Europe. Then other centers spread, the most important of which was in Munich, headed for a long time by Muhammad Mahdi 'Akif. Ramadan died in 1995, and the leadership of the Brotherhood negotiated his burial in Egypt with the Egyptian government. Earlier, the President of Egypt, Jamal 'Abd al-Nasir, had forfeited Ramadan's Egyptian citizenship, but President Anwar al-Sadat returned it to him. However, Ramadan refused to return to Egypt. His son Tariq is still managing some of his father's functions. Other important members of this organization included Yusuf Nada, Yusuf al-Qaradawi, and Mustapha Mashhur (qq.v.), the current supreme guide of the Brotherhood, who stayed in Germany from 1981 to 1986.

The organization not only established branches in many states but also gave a lot of attention to youth and student unions, like the International Islamic Union for Student Organizations (*al-Itihad al-Islami al-'Alami li al-Munazzamat al-Tullabiyya*), which was established during the pilgrimage of 1968 and included Muslim Students from Canada, the United States, Europe, and Sudan. The most important branch of this Union is the Muslim Student Association in the United States and Canada. The Union has published some writings of Sa'id Ramadan, Mustapha Mashhur, Yusuf al-Qaradawi, and others. It has also set up Bank *al-Taqwa*.

The International organization brings together leaders of the different branches in order to consult on current affairs. Every country branch is given leeway to conduct its local affairs, although it must uphold the general policies, principles, and teachings of the Brotherhood. 'Abd al-Latif Abu Qurah, 'Umar Baha' al-Din, Hasan al-Huwaidi, Salih 'Ishmawi, Muhammad Khalifa, Mustapha al-Siba'i, 'Abd al-'Aziz Mutawi' (qq.v.), and others have played central roles in this organization.

In terms of the decision-making, the Brotherhood in Egypt dominates the leadership. The Guidance Council of the Brotherhood is made up of 13 members, eight from Egypt, and five from other countries. Differences between the Egyptian leadership with others led to the rise of the Second Islamic International (q.v.) headed by Hasan al-Turabi (q.v.). See also MUSLIM BROTHERHOOD; SECOND ISLAMIC INTERNATIONAL.

INTERPRETATION (*TAFSIR*). For Islamism, Qur'anic interpretation is no more than the attempts of human beings to read and reread the divine text (q.v.) of the Qur'an (q.v.) or, at times, the superimposition of human conditions and culture on the text, according to the fundamentalists. The overall intellectual and historical experience of Muslims has regrettably failed them at all levels, in military confrontations as well as intellectual rigor, and, consequently, Islam (q.v.) has become rather incapable of keeping pace with modernity (q.v.). This situation is the outcome of the failure of Muslim thinkers and their intellectual edifices like traditional *tafsir*, or interpretation and theology (q.v.) to positively influence development. These edifices have failed to solve Muslims' problems and meet their dire needs. Muslims, nowadays, live on the margins of both Islam and the West (q.v.). Their lives lack both Islamic religious spirit and Western technological advancement. Lacking in philosophical and scientific sciences, Islamic culture and civilization, according to the fundamentalists, have reached bankruptcy. It is high time to introduce modern interpretations of Islam that are free of historical and theological views. See also 'ABD AL-RAHMAN, 'UMAR; 'ABDU, MUHAMMAD; ACTIVISM; DEMOCRACY; DIVINITY; GOD; GOVERNANCE; HISTORICISM; *IJMA'*; ISLAM; JURISPRUDENCE; KHOMEINISM; MODERNISM; MUSLIM BROTHERHOOD, IDEOLOGY OF; AL-QUR'AN; QUTB, SAYYID; REASON; RELIGION; *AL-SHARI'A*; *SHURA*; THEOLOGY; *AL-WAHHABIYYA*.

INTIFADA. See *AL-JIHAD AL-ISLAMI* IN THE WEST BANK AND GAZA STRIP.

INTUITION. See *FITRA*.

IQBAL, MUHAMMAD (1877–1938). Iqbal was a Pakistani reformer and modernist whose religious and intellectual impact has reached all over the Islamic world. He was both a poet and a philosopher. Iqbal was born in Sialkot and was raised in a religious family. When he finished high school, he joined the Scottish Mission College and then joined the Government College in Lahore. He was intellectually influenced by Sayyid Ahmad Khan and Thomas Arnold. After receiving his master's degree, Iqbal became a reader at the University of Oriental College in Lahore. In 1905, he went to Europe and studied at Trinity College of Cambridge, receiving his Ph.D. in Munich in 1907. He was deeply involved in the politics of India and was elected to Parliament from 1930–1936. Iqbal was also a member of the All-India Muslim League, which became instrumental in the creation of Pakistan. See also *JAM'IYYAT AL-'ULAMA' AL-MUSLIMIN*; MODERNISM; *AL-WAHHABIYYA*.

IRANIAN REVOLUTION OF 1979. This revolution is considered to be the most practical outstanding example of Islamic activism (q.v.) (*hara-*

kiyya) in this century. It was led by Ayatollah Khomeini (q.v.), who mobilized the clergy as well as the general public against the Shah of Iran. The revolution brought about some kind of Islamic awakening all over the Islamic world. The revolution aimed not only at changing the conditions of Iranian political, economic, and religious life but also at spreading its Shi'ite views all over the Islamic world, of which the majority is Sunni. The Shi'ite communities were extremely mobilized and became active politically. *Hizbullah* and *Harakat Amal al-Islamiyya* (qq.v.), or Party of God and Islamic *Amal* Movement, respectively, were two of the most important international manifestations of the spread of the Iranian revolution. See also *HIZBULLAH*; ISLAMIC REPUBLICAN PARTY; ISLAMIC REVOLUTION OF IRAN; KHOMEINI, AYATOLLAH; KHOMEINISM; *MUJAHIDIN KHALQ*; MUSLIM PEOPLE'S REPUBLICAN PARTY; MUTAHHARI, MURTAZA; REVOLUTIONARY GUARDS; SHARI'ATMADARI, AYATOLLAH; *HOJJATIYEH* ORGANIZATION; *WALIY AL-FAQIH*.

'IRYAN, 'ISAM. See *AL-JAMA'AT AL-ISLAMIYYA*.

'ISHMAWI, SALIH. 'Ishmawi was a member of the Muslim Brotherhood (q.v.) in Egypt and was one of its main ideologists. He both founded and edited the famous fundamentalist Journal *al-Da'wa* in the 1940s upon the request of Hasan al-Banna (q.v.). The journal was very successful and played a central role in the life of the Brotherhood. When Hasan al-Hudaybi (q.v.) became the supreme guide, 'Ishmawi joined the radical wing. Jamal 'Abd al-Nasir tried to lure 'Ishmawi into joining the government, to which al-Hudaybi reacted by firing him from the Brotherhood. 'Ishmawi recruited Sayyid Qutb (q.v.) into the Muslim Brotherhood. The journal was then to continue being published, not as a mouthpiece for the Brotherhood but as an independent fundamentalist journal. When Hudaybi died in 1973, 'Umar al-Tilmisani (q.v.) became the supreme guide, and 'Ishmawi joined the new leadership and gave back the license of the journal to the Brotherhood. See also ISMA'IL, 'ABD AL-FATTAH; INTERNATIONAL ORGANIZATION OF THE MUSLIM BROTHERHOOD; *AL-NIZAM AL-SIRRI*.

ISLAM. For the fundamentalists, Islam's main doctrine, *tawhid* (q.v.) (Oneness of God) is the ultimate manifestation of the divine message, because it totally conforms to *fitra* (q.v.) (law of nature), and, more importantly, is in conformity with the universe, because everything is part of the divine creation. For the fundamentalists, Islam is not only a religion (q.v.) based on the Qur'an (q.v.) but a total system (q.v.) (*nizam*) and a comprehensive method (q.v.) (*manhaj*) upon which the good fate of humanity depends. It includes metaphysics, politics, economics, ethics, and all other branches of knowledge (q.v.). This is why the happiness of humanity depends on obeying the totality of Islam and its law, *al-Shari'a* (q.v.). Conversely, unhappiness is the consequence of disunity: mind against body, man against man, man against society, and ultimately man against nature, which constitutes the adoption of a nondivine system, that is, paganism (q.v.) (*jahiliyya*).

Because of the flexible nature of Islam, radical fundamentalists argue against those thinkers who accuse Islam of being a reactionary thought. The fundamentalists argue that the nature of Islam could not be reactionary, because the method and system of Islam themselves allow individual and collective adaptations to progress in order to meet the needs of changing living conditions. Alhough Islam postulates specific eternal doctrines and specific punishments, this does not mean that everything considered Islamic is divine and thus not subject to change. Any thought or ideology includes basic unchanging doctrines, but this does not make others reactionary. Interpretation (q.v.) is to be used to modify Islamic thought in accordance with modernity (q.v.). In this sense, Hasan al-Banna (q.v.) felt that labeling Islam as reactionary exemplified ignorance of the nature of both divine law and Islamic jurisprudence (q.v.). The focus on a fraction of Islamic Law and the neglect of the overall organization and fundamental roots of religion corrupts the real meaning of Islam by restricting it to a few juristic stipulations applied here and there.

Islam provides certain fundamental rights that might encourage other individuals and peoples to accept or, at least, to tolerate such a situation. Thus, fundamentalists argue that Islam provides man as man, regardless of his religion, basic rights, such as life, that cannot be taken away without due process. They state, also, that Islam develops relations with other religions and attempts to open the possibility of cooperation on the condition that other religions do not stand against Islam.

The truth of the matter is that one has to see the multilayered substantive meanings of Islam as religion and society, mosque, and state. It belongs both to this life and to the hereafter. Furthermore, it pays attention to worship and behavior, both of which are parts of a more substantive system of life. Religious beliefs constitute only part of the Islamic system, and Islam regulates both religion—in the narrow sense—and life—in a general sense. For fundamentalists, true Muslims could not but subject all aspects of their life to the total method and system of Islam. See also DIVINITY; *FITRA*; GOD; GOVERNANCE; INTERPRETA-TION; ISLAMIC FUNDAMENTALISM; ISLAMIC STATE; KNOWL-EDGE; METHOD; MONOTHEISTIC RELIGIONS; PAGANISM; AL-QUR'AN; RELIGION; *AL-SHARI'A*; *SHURA*; SYSTEM; *TAWHID*; TEXT; THEOLOGY.

ISLAM DEMOKRAT PARTISI. See ISLAMIC DEMOCRATIC PARTY.

ISLAM KORUMA PARTISI. See PARTY FOR THE DEFENSE OF ISLAM.

AL-ISLAMBULI, KHALID SHAWQI. See AL-ISLAMBULI, MU-HAMMAD SHAWQI.

AL-ISLAMBULI, MUHAMMAD SHAWQI. Al-Islambuli was the *amir* (q.v.) (commander) of *al-Jama'a al-Islamiyya* (q.v.) (Islamic Group) at the Faculty of Commerce, University of Asyut in Egypt and one of the leaders of *al-Jihad* (q.v.). Muhammad al-Islambuli was recruited by 'Abd al-Salam Faraj (q.v.). His brother, First Lieutenant Khalid, assassi-nated President Anwar al-Sadat. Their father, who was a member of the Muslim Brotherhood (q.v.), believed that Egypt's loss of the war with Israel (q.v.) in 1967 was the divine revenge for the execution of Sayyid Qutb (q.v.) by President Jamal 'Abd al-Nasir.

ISLAMIC ACTION FRONT (*JABHAT AL-'AMAL AL-ISLAMI*). See *HIZB JABHAT AL-'AMAL AL-ISLAMI.*

ISLAMIC ACTION FRONT PARTY. See *HIZB JABHAT AL-'AMAL AL-ISLAMI.*

ISLAMIC ACTION ORGANIZATION (*MUNAZZAMAT AL-'AMAL AL-ISLAMI*) **IN BAHRAIN.** This Bahraini Shi'ite political organization played an active political role in Bahraini politics during the late 1970s and 1980s. The organization called for the radical transformation of the local social and economic order. See also ISLAMIC ACTION ORGANI-ZATION IN IRAQ; KHOMEINISM.

ISLAMIC ACTION ORGANIZATION (*MUNAZZAMAT AL-'AMAL AL-ISLAMI*) **IN IRAQ.** This Shi'ite political organization was founded in 1964 in Karbala'. It started its political actions under the name *al-Shiraziyun*, because the leader of the organization's family name was *al-Shirazi*. Muhammad al-Shirazi founded the organization after not being accepted to the rank of *mujtahid* because of his young age. He was born in al-Najaf in 1947 and studied at Karbala'. Al-Shirazi taught there, then he moved to Kuwait and finally settled in Qum. He is an important authority on Islamic jurisprudence (q.v.); although he accepts the doctrine of *waliy al-faqih* (q.v.) (the guardian of the jurist), he argues that it should be collective and democratic. Al-Shirazi moved into political action early in the 1960s. Although he rejected the establishment of political parties (q.v.), he thought he was setting up an authoritative organization that could advise all of society on the proper conduct that should be followed.

During the communist rule in Iraq, the organization did not forcefully fight the regime, but it increased its religious activities like teaching the Qur'an (q.v.) and renovating mosques. In the 1960s, it elaborated its organizational structure and functioned under the guise of educational institutes and conferences. Al-Shirazi accepted the leadership, or *marji'i-yya* of Ayatollah Khomeini (q.v.), even before the Iranian Revolution of 1979 (q.v.). The Islamic Action Front also moved into adopting armed struggle (q.v.) (*jihad*) against the regime. It was persecuted severely by the regime, and many of its members were arrested. Some of its influential ideologues are Muhammad Taqiy al-Mudarrisi and his brother Hadi al-Mudarrisi, two nephews of al-Shirazi, who along with al-Shirazi, were deported to Kuwait in 1970. The two were among the five leaders who set up the Revolutionary Guards (q.v.) in Iran. Al-Shirazi, who maintained excellent relations with Khomeini, finally settled in Qum in Iran.

After the success of the Islamic Revolution of Iran (q.v.) in 1979, the term *Munazzamat* (organization) was used more systematically. The organization holds that Islam (q.v.) is a total system (q.v.) (*nizam*) of life and that the nature of Islam is revolutionary. Today, the organization is surrounded by secrecy.

ISLAMIC ACTION PARTY (*HIZB AL-'AMAL AL-ISLAMI*) **IN YEMEN.** This party was declared immediately after the unification of Yemen in 1990. It was founded by Ibrahim Bin Muhammad al-Wazir, and aims at observing the teachings of Islam (q.v.) and linking the understanding of religion (q.v.) to progress in order to establish a good society.

Its points of reference in terms of interpreting Islam are the Qur'an (q.v.), the valid *Hadith*, *ijma'* (q.v.) (consensus), and the general spirit of religion. It calls for implementing an Islamic economy and reducing the role of the state to a minimum. It further accepts pluralism (q.v.) as an outcome of *shura* (q.v.) (consultation), which is understood as being equivalent to democracy (q.v.).

ISLAMIC *AMAL* MOVEMENT. See *HARAKAT AMAL AL-ISLAMIYYA*. See also *HIZBULLAH*.

ISLAMIC-ARAB CONGRESS (*AL-MU'TAMAR AL-QAWMI AL-IS-LAMI*). The congress is a loose organization that attempts to find working programs between Arab nationalists and fundamentalists. Its first yearly conference was held in October 1994 in Beirut and was attended by representatives of Islamic and nationalist movements from all over the Arab world. Ahmad Sudqi al-Dajani outlined the program of the nationalists, and Muhammad Husayn Fadlallah (q.v.) outlined the fundamentalist program.

ISLAMIC ARMY OF SALVATION. See *AL-JAYSH AL-ISLAMI LI AL-INQADH*.

ISLAMIC AWAKENING (*AL-SAHWA AL-ISLAMIYYA*). See FUNDAMENTALISM; ISLAMIC FUNDAMENTALISM; REVOLUTION.

ISLAMIC BAND OF HELPERS (*'USBAT AL-ANSAR AL-ISLAMIYYA*). This group was unknown until 1995 when it was condemned for assassinating the head of *al-Ahbash* (q.v.), Nizar al-Halabi. Three of the assailants were executed. The leader of the group, the Palestinian Ahmad 'Abd al-Karim al-Sa'di (nicknamed Abu Muhjan), is still free in one of the Palestinian camps in southern Lebanon. This group is not active socially, and its members live away from society. It is active in Palestinian camps.

The group was founded by Shaykh Hisham Sharidi in 1985 and was allied with Palestinian organizations that opposed Yasir Arafat. It set up a training camp east of Sidon. When Sharidi was killed in 1991, Abu Muhjan became the *amir* (q.v.) (commander) of the group. The group takes a very strict position against those who do not follow exactly the *Sunna* (way) of the Prophet. It believes that all political systems are living the life of paganism (q.v.) (*jahiliyya*). *Al-Ahbash* is targeted as its foremost enemy because of its justification of un-Islamic governments and of its very strong opposition to Islamic fundamentalism (q.v.). See also *AL-AHBASH*.

ISLAMIC CALL IN IRAQ. See *AL-DA'WA AL-ISLAMIYYA*; AL-SADR, MUHAMMAD BAQIR.

ISLAMIC CHARTER FRONT (*JABHAT AL-MITHAQ AL-ISLAMI*). See MUSLIM BROTHERHOOD IN SUDAN.

ISLAMIC CONSTITUTIONAL MOVEMENT (*AL-HARAKA AL-AL-DUSTURIYYA AL-ISLAMIYYA*). See *JAM'IYYAT AL-ISLAH AL-IJTI-MA'IYYA* IN KUWAIT.

ISLAMIC CULTURAL HERITAGE SOCIETY (*JAM'IYYAT AL-TUR-ATH AL-THAQAFI AL-ISLAMI*). This society worked toward rejecting Westernization and the Western attitudes of the political leadership. It views Western leadership as leading to weakening self-control. The society distinguished between the need for inspiring religious adherence and freedom (q.v.) and the need for using Western sciences for practical purposes.

Although the society accepts the existence of a political system (q.v.) (*nizam*) grounded in democratic practices, freedom, social justice (q.v.), and human rights (q.v.), it aims at grounding them within Islam (q.v.). Thus, it wants to choose selectively from Western civilization (q.v.) what could fit into Islamic heritage.

ISLAMIC DEMOCRATIC PARTY (*ISLAM DEMOKRAT PARTISI*). Cevat Rifat Atilhan, an anti-Semitic writer who had already established the Turkish Conservative Party in 1947, established this party in Istanbul, in August 1951. Zuhtu Bilmer, a doctor who had been one of the founders of the Party for Land, Real Estate, and Free Enterprise in 1949, joined the party. The party claimed to have 2,000 members, organized in 150 branches in 10 provinces. The party was traditional, voicing a high regard for Turkey's past and Islam (q.v.) and equally strong disapproval of such clandestine groups as the Communists and Freemasons. Although it claimed to speak for freedom of conscience and for the progress of Turkey, the party was brought to court in 1952 for stirring up intercommunal troubles, and its activity seems to have ceased since that time.

ISLAMIC FRONT IN SYRIA (*AL-JABHA AL-ISLAMIYYA*). See MUSLIM BROTHERHOOD IN SYRIA.

ISLAMIC FRONT FOR THE LIBERATION OF BAHRAIN (*AL-JABHA AL-ISLAMIYYA LI TAHRIR AL-BAHRAIN*). This front was founded in 1979 by Hadi al-Mudarrisi, who was a close associate of Ayatollah Khomeini (q.v.) during his stay in Iraq. This front is assumed to be sponsored by the Islamic Republic of Iran as well as by *al-Da'wa al-Islamiyya* in Iraq (q.v.) (Islamic Call) in order to encourage the Shi'ites to overthrow al-Khalifa family's rule in Bahrain and to set up an Islamic state (q.v.). It has carried out three attempts to overthrow the government. Its members received military training in Iran—which Iran denies. After the government cracked down on the front and arrested many of its members, it was renamed *al-Haraka al-Islamiyya li Tahrir al-Bahrain* (Islamic Movement for the Liberation of Bahrain) in 1993 in order to recruit new members. See also KHOMEINISM.

ISLAMIC FRONT FOR SALVATION IN TUNISIA (*AL-JABHA AL-IS-LAMIYYA LI AL-INQADH*). This is a relatively new Tunisian radical fundamentalist group that calls for armed action and adopts radical views that oppose the moderate program of *Harakat al-Nahda al-Islamiyya* (q.v.) (Islamic Renaissance Movement). It has a publication, *al-Raja'*, that is printed in Vienna and distributed all over Europe through E-mail. It adopts the way of *al-Sunna wa al-Jama'a* and calls for armed *jihad* (q.v.) (struggle). Some observers attribute the rise of this group to al-Habib al-Dawi, who committed many violent acts against the tourist establishment but was proven not to be a member of *Harakat al-Nahda al-Islamiyya* in Tunisia. The front is very critical of the moderate line of Rashid al-Ghannushi (q.v.), the leader of *al-Nahda*. It is rumored that the new leading figure is Muhammad al-Harrani, a *Salafi*, who is very active in European cities.

ISLAMIC FUNDAMENTALISM (*AL-USULIYYA AL-ISLAMIYYA*). Islamic fundamentalism is not just a set of political movements but carries also a spectrum of moderate and radical intellectual and political discourses. These discourses constitute a critique of philosophy (q.v.), political ideology, and science (q.v.). In a philosophical sense, although believing in the existence of objective and ultimate truth, fundamentalism (q.v.) claims that no individual can understand it, thus all of our knowledge (q.v.) is relative. More substantially, it attempts to offer a way of life and thought based on its understanding of both God's law, *al-Shari'a* (q.v.), and the phenomenon of nature. Both constitute what religion (q.v.) is about. Fundamentalist political ideologies depend on adhering to divine governance (q.v.) (*hakimiyya*) and on refuting paganism (q.v.) (*jahiliyya*) and the notion of people's ultimate authority and man's natural possessiveness. Instead, it relegates that ultimate authority to God (q.v.). Fundamentalist world views revolve around setting up virtuous, just, and equal societies that are regulated by Islam (q.v.).

Although the fundamentalists look instrumentally at reason (q.v.), they make the existence of morality (q.v.) a natural objective reality. However, the fundamentalists underline the insufficiency of human reason for acquiring absolute knowledge. A view like this obviously necessitates the existence of revelation so that humanity may live in harmony with the universal system (q.v.) (*nizam*). For Abu al-A'la al-Mawdudi and Sayyid Qutb (qq.v.), God has created in man a *fitra* (q.v.) (intuition) that acts as the recipient of *wahy* (revelation) and assures obedience to God, who created the universal laws in both their physical and moral forms. Universal natural laws are not value-free but aim at the well-being of this universe. Both universal moral and natural laws are created by God to serve man.

Islamic fundamentalism is an umbrella term for a wide range of discourses and activism (q.v.) that tends to and moves from a high level of moderate pluralism (q.v.), and thus inclusive democracy (q.v.), to extreme radicalism (q.v.), intolerant unitarianism, and thus exclusive majority rule. Whereas some fundamentalist groups are pluralistic in terms of inter-Muslim relations and between Muslims and minorities, others are not. Again, whereas some fundamentalists are politically pluralistic but theologically exclusive, others are accommodating religiously, but direct their exclusivist programs to the outside, the West (q.v.) and imperialism. Even at the scientific level, Western science (q.v.) and technology are argued for by some fundamentalists as having sound Islamic basis, whereas others exclude them, because of their assumed un-Islamic nature.

For instance, the discourses of Sayyid Qutb, Abu al-A'la al-Mawdudi, and Ayatollah al-Khomeini (q.v.) on the nature of politics and the Islamic state (q.v.) are more radical than those of Hasan al-Banna, Hasan al-Turabi, and Rashid al-Ghannushi (qq.v.). The first three ideologists have no notion of gradual change and possible compromise. They emphasize the need to overthrow secular governments as being a religious must that cannot be negotiated. Their discourses hold tightly and uncompromisingly to both the divine governance of God and paganism of the world. However, al-Banna's discourse is more open and less particular about the forceful overthrow of un-Islamic regimes. In fact, his discourse shows readiness to compromise, both practically and theoretically, and relegates ultimate earthly authority to the community, whose agreement is in itself an embodiment of the divine will. If the community is not willing to adopt an Islamic state, then its imposition does not reflect the essence of Islam. See also AUTHENTICITY; FUNDAMENTALISM; *HIZBULLAH*; ISLAMIC BAND OF HELPERS; ISRAEL; JUDAISM; KHOMEINISM; MODERNIZATION; AL-TURABI, HASAN; AL-'UTAYBI, JUHAYMAN.

ISLAMIC GOVERNMENT (*AL-HUKUMA AL-ISLAMIYYA*). For the fundamentalists, the Islamic government, which is sometimes used interchangeably with the Islamic state (q.v.), represents the central organ of an Islamic system (q.v.) (*nizam*) of governance (q.v.) (*hakimiyya*). It derives its legitimacy (q.v.) to exercise power from the people through exercising *shura* (q.v.) (consultation) and conducting *ijma'* (q.v.) (consensus), and its responsibility is twofold: religious and political, before God (q.v.) and the people. Furthermore, it is morally and politically responsible for the community's unity and therefore must be responsive and defer its preferences and wishes. For the fundamentalists, the ruler's power over and responsibility before his people derives from the fact that Islam (q.v.) views the establishment of government as a social contract between the ruler and the ruled so that the interests of the latter are taken care of. The ruler's reward and punishment must depend on people's views. The community enjoys moral supremacy over the ruler in matters of general and partial concerns. Therefore, a legitimate ruler or government must always refer to *shura* with the community and yield to its will. Forms of government (q.v.) may change from one to another and from one locality to another, but the basic rules of Islam must always be adhered to. See also *HARAKAT AL-TAWHID AL-ISLAMI*; *AL-SHARI'A*; SOCIAL JUSTICE; THEOCRACY; AL-TURABI, HASAN; *UMMA*.

ISLAMIC GROUP (*AL-JAMA'A AL-ISLAMIYYA*) **IN EGYPT**. See *AL-JAMA'A AL-ISLAMIYYA*; 'ABD AL-RAHMAN, 'UMAR.

ISLAMIC GROUP IN LEBANON. See *AL-JAMA'A AL-ISLAMIYYA FI LUBNAN*.

ISLAMIC GROUP (*AL-JAMA'A AL-ISLAMIYYA*) **IN TUNISIA**. See AL-GHANNUSHI, RASHID.

ISLAMIC GROUPS. See *AL-JAMA'AT AL-ISLAMIYYA*.

ISLAMIC HISTORY. See HISTORICISM; HISTORY; PAST.

ISLAMIC *JIHAD*. See *AL-JIHAD AL-ISLAMI* IN THE WEST BANK AND GAZA STRIP.

ISLAMIC *JIHAD* IN LEBANON. See *AL-JIHAD AL-ISLAMI FI LUBNAN*.

ISLAMIC *JIHAD* IN SAUDI ARABIA (*AL-JIHAD AL-ISLAMI*). Also known as *Hizbullah*, it is a party supported by Iran in order to overthrow the Saudi Kingdom and to establish a revolutionary Islamic state (q.v.). Some observers assume that it has some links to *Hizbullah* (q.v.) (Party of God) in Lebanon as well as other Shi'ite political groups in the Gulf. It has threatened to attack American and Saudi interests all over the world. See also *HIZBULLAH* IN SAUDI ARABIA.

ISLAMIC LAW. See *AL-SHARI'A*.

ISLAMIC LIBERATION FRONT (*JABHAT AL-TAHRIR AL-ISLAMI-YYA*). The Islamic Liberation Front is a Jordanian secret organization that claimed responsibility for the 5 July 1990 explosion of an American chemical factory in Texas. The Liberation Front has threatened to subvert Israeli and American interests all over the world. It considers this to be an act of revenge against the massacre that was committed by an Israeli soldier against seven Palestinians near Tel Aviv on 2 May 1990.

ISLAMIC LIBERATION MOVEMENT (*HARAKAT AL-TAHRIR AL-ISLAMI*) **IN SUDAN**. See MUSLIM BROTHERHOOD IN SUDAN.

ISLAMIC LIBERATION PARTY. See *HIZB AL-TAHRIR AL-ISLAMI*.

ISLAMIC LIBERATION PARTY IN LIBYA. See *HIZB AL-TAHRIR AL-ISLAMI* IN LIBYA.

ISLAMIC LIBERATION PARTY IN TUNISIA. See *HIZB AL-TAHRIR AL-ISLAMI* IN TUNISIA.

ISLAMIC MOVEMENT FOR ALGERIA (*AL-HARAKA AL-ISLAMI-YYA LI AL-JAZA'IR*). This fundamentalist Algerian movement followed a violent course toward the regime and worked underground from 1982–1987. It was led by Mustapha Buya'li (1940–1987). In fact, the Islamic movement was the first radical political fundamentalist movement in Algeria. It set up armed cells and carried out attacks against police stations. During the early and mid-1980s, hundreds of people associated with the movement were arrested but some were given reduced sentences and others were acquitted. Many of these people played important roles in the Islamic Salvation Front in Algeria (q.v.). In 1987, the movement ended when Buya'li was killed. See also ARMED ISLAMIC GROUP; ISLAMIC MOVEMENT FOR ALGERIA; ISLAMIC SALVATION FRONT IN ALGERIA.

ISLAMIC MOVEMENT FOR THE LIBERATION OF BAHRAIN (*AL-HARAKA AL-ISLAMIYYA LI TAHRIR AL-BAHRAIN*). See ISLAMIC FRONT FOR THE LIBERATION OF BAHRAIN.

ISLAMIC MOVEMENT IN LEBANON. See *AL-HARAKA AL-ISLAMIYYA FI LUBNAN.*

ISLAMIC PARTY (*AL-HIZB AL-ISLAMI*). This is an anti-Communist Iraqi party supported by the Shi'ite religious scholar Muhsin al-Hakim. The Islamic party opposed the rule of 'Abd al-Karim Qasim, who first refused but later agreed to license it.

ISLAMIC POPULAR ALLIANCE (*AL-TAHALUF AL-SHA'BI AL-ISLAMI*). See *JAM'IYYAT AL-ISLAH AL-IJTIMA'IYYA* IN KUWAIT.

ISLAMIC RENAISSANCE MOVEMENT. See *HARAKAT AL-NAHDA AL-ISLAMIYYA.*

ISLAMIC RENAISSANCE MOVEMENT (*HARAKAT AL-NAHDA AL-ISLAMIYYA*) **IN ALGERIA.** See *JAMA'AT AL-NAHDA AL-ISLAMIYYA.*

ISLAMIC REPUBLIC OF IRAN. See BANI SADR, ABUL HASAN; CONSTITUTION; *FURQAN*; *HARAKAT AMAL AL-ISLAMIYYA*; ISLAMIC FRONT FOR THE LIBERATION OF BAHRAIN; IRANIAN REVOLUTION OF 1979; ISLAMIC REVOLUTION OF IRAN; ISLAMIC STATE; KHAMENE'I, 'ALI; KHOMEINI, AYATOLLAH;

KHOMEINISM; *MARJI' AL-TAQLID*; MUHTASHIMI, 'ALI AKBAR; MUNTAZARI, HUSAYN.

ISLAMIC REPUBLICAN PARTY (*AL-HIZB AL-JUMHURI AL-ISLAMI*). Since the Iranian Revolution of 1979 (q.v.), Iran has become an Islamic state (q.v.) and has been ruled by the Islamic Republican Party. The party was established in 1979, a week after the revolution and was led by Ayatollah Bahishti, Hashimi Rafsanjani, the former President of Iran, and Ayatollah Ali Khamene'i, the current Spiritual Leader of Iran (qq.v.). Its supporters are in control of the executive, the legislative, and the judicial branches and are composed of the followers of Ayatollah Khomeini (q.v.) whose ideological orientations constituted the ideology of the party. Since 1981, the party has infiltrated state institutions. After Bahishti's death, Rafsanjani and Khamene'i took over the leadership of the party.

The doctrine of *waliy al-faqih* (q.v.) (the guardian of the jurist) constitutes the ideological underpinning of the party. However, there are many different tendencies within it in terms of social and educational policies. Its organization was loose until 1981 when a committee of five members was formed. It is worth mentioning that Khomeini stayed away from the daily administration of the party.

The party rallied supporters mainly from public meetings organized by Ayatollah Muntazari (q.v.) and held on Fridays at the University of Tehran. Its social base consisted of religious groups like the poor and petite bourgeoisie. The government workers, around 1.5 million, constituted the party's voting power. In addition, the party created parallel institutions to the government like *Hizbullah* (Party of God), the Revolutionary Guards (q.v.), and others. *Hizbullah*, for instance, is not a political party in the usual sense. It is made up of groups of people that are tied to and led by the clergy and perform a moral and political supervision of life in Iran. However, the party was dissolved in 1987 owing to the opposition of the high-ranking clergy and fear of its power. See also BAHISHTI, MUHAMMAD; *HOJJATIYEH* ORGANIZATION; ISLAMIC REVOLUTION OF IRAN; KHAMENE'I, 'ALI; MUNTAZARI, HUSAYN; MUSLIM PEOPLE'S REPUBLICAN PARTY; RAFSANJANI, 'ALI AKBAR.

ISLAMIC RESISTANCE MOVEMENT: *HAMAS* (*HARAKAT AL-MU-QAWAMA AL-ISLAMIYYA: HAMAS*). See *HARAKAT AL-MUQAWAMA*

AL-ISLAMIYYA: HAMAS; MUSLIM BROTHERHOOD IN PALES-
TINE.

ISLAMIC REVIVAL (*AL-SAHWA AL-ISLAMIYYA*). See FUNDAMEN-
TALISM; ISLAM; ISLAMIC FUNDAMENTALISM; KHOMEINISM;
REVOLUTION.

ISLAMIC REVOLUTION OF IRAN. The opposition to the Shah of Iran
centered on three main groups, the *'ulama'* (religious scholars), guerrilla
organizations and parties, and a great number of the intelligentsia. Major
political parties were the Communist Tudeh party, the *Mujahidin Khalq*
(q.v.), and *Fida'iyyin*. But it was the religious clerics who played the
most important role, acted as guardians of the new political system (q.v.)
(*nizam*) and advocated political activism (q.v.) (*harakiyya*).

Many factors helped the revolution, among which was the people's
dislike for both the Shah and the United States. Also, the Carter administration's human rights policy, by preventing the regime from further suppression during 1978–1979, enabled the revolution to increase momentum.

A 75-year-old religious man, Ayatollah Khomeini (q.v.), led the revolution. He relied heavily on Islam (q.v.) to activate the Islamic movement
and destroy the Pahlavi dynasty. His emergence as the undisputed leader
of the revolutionary movement was a major surprise. He had been in
exile for 13 years when political agitation began in Iran.

Ayatollah Khomeini was a most charismatic leader, who united the
diverse opposition forces and dethroned the Shah. The traditional middle
class, especially the bazar (the marketplace), supported him because he
upheld the right for private property and Islamic values. The modern
middle class supported him as a nationalist who revived Muhammed
Musaddaq's legacy, which centered on fighting foreign interference. The
working classes accepted his call for social justice (q.v.), and the rural
class believed that he would give them the needed infrastructure for agriculture.

To mobilize people, Ayatollah Khomeini employed religious symbols
like martyrdom (q.v.) and the month of Ramadan and transforming
'Ashura into a political demonstration. He dominated the leadership of
the political opposition, and his appeal cut through all social strata. The
movement of 1977–1979 was a political revolution that resulted in overthrowing the Shah's regime. The coalition of diverse secular and religious forces to overthrow the Shah broke up immediately after the revo-

lution in 1979, after which the Islamic Revolutionary Council (q.v.) and the provisional Revolutionary Government and the Islamic Republican Party (q.v.) were set up.

However, the security apparatuses were not dissolved but were purged and were overshadowed by the Revolutionary Guards (q.v.). More importantly, the religious clergy took over the government, and an Assembly of Experts (q.v.), mostly composed of theologians and devout Muslims was created. A new constitution (q.v.), based on the Shi'ite school of *Shari'a* (Islamic Law), was drafted; Khomeini's powers were sweeping and centered on *waliy al-faqih* (q.v.) (the guardian of the jurist). The Islamic movement in Iran produced more surprises in 1979 than most countries did in the 1960s. It sprang up at a time of economic prosperity, military strength, and political stability.

On the international scene, Iran challenged the United States by seizing its diplomats in Iran for 14 months, but it experienced economic difficulties because of the Western boycott imposed in 1980. Iran was also dragged into a war with Iraq in 1980 that lasted until 1989. This allowed the nascent revolution to consolidate itself and to mobilize the Iranian people. See also BAHISHTI, MUHAMMAD; EXTREMISM; IRANIAN REVOLUTION OF 1979; ISLAMIC ACTION ORGANIZATION; ISLAMIC YOUTH ORGANIZATION; ISRAEL; *AL-JIHAD AL-ISLAMI* IN THE WEST BANK AND GAZA STRIP; KHATAMI, MUHAMMAD; KHOMEINISM; LIBERATION MOVEMENT OF IRAN; MUSLIM SCHOLARS' ASSOCIATION; MUTAHHARI, MURTAZA; REVOLUTIONARY GUARDS; TABATABA'I, MUHAMMAD.

ISLAMIC REVOLUTIONARY ORGANIZATION OF THE ARABIAN PENINSULA (*AL-MUNAZZAMA AL-THAWRIYYA AL-ISLAMIYYA FI SHIBH AL-JAZIRA AL-'ARABIYYA*). This secretive Shi'ite organization was active in the eastern province of Saudi Arabia in the months following the Iranian revolution of 1979 (q.v.). Some observers assume that it has, like Islamic *Jihad* (q.v.) in Saudi Arabia, some links to *Hizbullah* (q.v.) (Party of God) in Lebanon as well as other Shi'ite political groups in the Gulf.

ISLAMIC RIGHT PARTY. See *HIZB AL-HAQQ AL-ISLAMI.*

ISLAMIC RULE (*AL-HUKM AL-ISLAMI*). See ISLAMIC GOVERNMENT. See also CALIPHATE; CONSTITUTION; CONSTITUTIONAL RULE; GOVERNANCE; ISLAMIC STATE; THEOCRACY.

ISLAMIC SALVATION FRONT IN ALGERIA (*AL-JABHA AL-IS-LAMIYYA LI AL-INQADH*, FRONT DE SALUT ISLAMIQUE [FIS]). The Algerian Islamic movement is not a new political movement but played an important role in the war of liberation and independence of Algeria from French colonialism. Ahmad Bin Bella became President of Algeria and opposed *Jam'iyyat al-'Ulama' al-Muslimin* (q.v.) (Association of Muslim Scholars) and especially Shaykh Bashir al-Ibrahimi (q.v.) as well as the program for Arabization and Islamization (q.v.). Then Bin Bella dissolved the organization. Another organization, the Value Society, was headed by Shaykh Tijani and other Shaykhs such as Sultanti, Arabawi, and Sahnun—a group of individuals who were influenced by the thinking of Malik Bin Nabi. The society and these personalities worked at the mosques of the universities and worked against Westernization. By 1975, the *imam*s of the mosques criticized the policies of the authorities. During the presidency of Bin Jadid, the Islamic movement tried to convene its first mass conference, but its leaders were jailed. As a result, the first armed movement that appeared was the Armed Islamic Movement, headed by Mustapha Buya'li, the leader of the Islamic Movement for Algeria (q.v.), who was supported by Shaykh Sahnun and others. Buya'li was killed by the government in 1987.

In 1988, the Algerian economy was in bad shape because of strikes against the government. Shaykh 'Ali Bilhaj (q.v.) declared that the cause of the country's problems was the nonapplication of *al-Shari'a* (q.v.) (Islamic Law). The government's plebiscite to change one-party rule received a favorable result, and Islam (q.v.) was considered for the first time the religion (q.v.) of the state, and Arabic, the official language. The Algerian Islamic movement was divided into three main currents: the Islamic Salvation Front (FIS), Islamic Society Movement: *Hamas* (q.v.), and the Algerianization Party. These parties were nonviolent. *Hamas* belonged to the Muslim Brotherhood (q.v.), and the Islamic Salvation Front was headed by Abbasi Madani (q.v.). The differences between the diverse currents started in 1980, reflecting great differences within the Muslim Brotherhood in Egypt. As a result, a majority within the Algerian Islamic movement abandoned the Brotherhood and opted for an Algerian model.

The Islamic Salvation Front was the first movement to publicly propose a political program after the eruption of violence (q.v.). In February 1989, the leadership consisted of Bilhaj, Madani, and others, and in March the birth of the Front was announced. The Front won a sweeping victory of 60 percent in the municipal elections. The confrontation with the state arose after the Front called for a strike that turned into a bloody conflict with the security apparatuses. The FIS leaders were arrested in 1991. Also, in 1991, the Islamic Salvation Front had a sweeping victory in the first round of elections through the efforts of Shaykh 'Abd al-Qadir Hashshani, who received the support of Madani and Bilhaj, who were still in prison. However, the results led Bin Jadid to resign, and the election results were then nullified and the FIS dissolved. Since then the Algerian regime has entered into a cycle of violent conflicts with the Armed Islamic Group (q.v.) (*al-Jama'a al-Islamiyya al-Musallaha*). Although the FIS leadership was still in prison, it did call for a peaceful and democratic solution to Algeria's problems.

The directing agencies of the Islamic Salvation Front are its national Executive Bureau and *Majlis al-Shura* (q.v.) (*Shura* Council), which includes from 35 to 40 members. The composition of these two bodies was never revealed, and until the summer of 1991 the identities of most figures were unknown to the greater public. The secretiveness of the FIS is well known. It is structured in a hierarchical manner with almost all actions decided by the leadership. Until 1991, the only FIS leaders to give interviews to the media and issue formal public statements were Abbasi Madani and, occasionally, 'Ali Bilhaj.

The support for the Islamic Salvation Front comes from many educated classes, including engineers and technicians and university students at technical faculties. Also, commercial strata and sections of the private sector help the FIS financially. Still the marginalized and the unemployed constitute a large and volatile segment of the population. The Islamic Salvation Front provides this segment with a way to express its views and frustrations.

In 1991, the Islamic Salvation Front was harassed, and Abbasi Madani and Ali Bilhaj were arrested as were other Front officials. Also, internal division within the FIS leadership became public. 'Abd al-Qadir Hashshani (b. 1957) emerged as the new spokesman, after some important members were suspended from *Majlis al-Shura*.

The Islamic Salvation Front was divided into two main tendencies: the *Jaza'ira*, led by Hashshani who controlled the party leadership, and *al-Salafiyya* (q.v.), represented by those ousted from *Majlis al-Shura*. *Al-Salafiyya* movement follows the Hanbalite legal school, whereas the *Jaza'ira* called for the Algerianization of the fundamentalist movement. The second tendency called for participation in the 1991 election. However, the army canceled the electoral process in 1992; Hashshani and other main figures were arrested, and the party was outlawed. Hashshani was released in July 1997, and Madani was released later that year.

The Islamic Salvation Front believes that the establishment of an Islamic state (q.v.) is obligatory and that Islam deals with the affairs of this world and the afterlife. *Shura* (q.v.) (consultation) and *al-Shari'a* are essential doctrines of the state that lead to representative governments and prevent dictatorial governments. Thus, the basic function of the government is to apply *al-Shari'a*. The front also calls for economic self-sufficiency and the prohibition of exploitation and usury.

This religious trend is less a party and more a social protest movement. Its discourse centers more on moral and religious issues and less on a coherent program. It aims at mobilizing the people to act according to Islamic *Shari'a*, which is thought to be capable of resolving the economic and moral as well as the political problems that are facing the Algerian people. It picked up the issue of economic justice and made its base of support the urban popular classes, for the most part consisting of rural migrants. The FIS calls for a return to cultural authenticity (q.v.) and includes among its adherents a counter-elite to the one that has been dominant since 1962. Its leader, Abbasi Madani, argues that the war of liberation (q.v.) was fought in the name of Islam.

The political program of the Islamic Salvation Front in Algeria calls for adherence to *shura* in order to avoid tyranny (q.v.) and to eradicate all forms of monopoly, whether political, social, or economic. Political pluralism (q.v.), elections, and other democratic methods in politics and social life are called for as the means for the salvation of the community. Despite using the slogan of *al-Shari'a*, the Islamic Salvation Front program is moderate, accepting the multiparty system. See also ANAS, 'ABD ALLAH; ARMED ISLAMIC GROUP; BILHAJ, 'ALI; HADDAM, ANWAR; ISLAMIC MOVEMENT FOR ALGERIA; ISLAMIC SOCIETY MOVEMENT; *JAMA'AT AL-NAHDA AL-ISLAMIYYA*; *JAM-'IYYAT AL-TADAMUN AL-ISLAMI AL-JAZA'IRI*; *AL-JAYSH AL-ISLAMI LI AL-INQADH*; KABIR, RABIH; MADANI, ABBASI; MUSLIM BROTHERHOOD; AL-NAHNAH, MAHFOUDH.

ISLAMIC SOCIALIST FRONT (*AL-JABHA AL-ISHTIRAKIYYA AL-ISLAMIYYA*). See MUSLIM BROTHERHOOD IN SYRIA.

ISLAMIC SOCIETY (*AL-MUJTAMA' AL-ISLAMI*). Sayyid Qutb, Hasan al-Banna, Ayatollah al-Khomeini, and Abu al-Hasan al-Nadawi (qq.v.) believe that *al-Shari'a* (q.v.) (Islamic Law) contains the fundamentals (q.v.) (*usul*) of a complete, virtuous social and political structure that touches on the individual, the family, society, the *umma* (q.v.) (nation), and the state. Islamic Law is capable, because of its moral, social, and political superiority, according to fundamentalists like Hasan al-Banna, Sayyid Qutb, Abu al-Hasan al-Nadawi, and Ayatollah al-Khomeini, to claim the right and the duty of Muslims to call the world to the truth and to establish their Islamic society. Morality (q.v.) is the distinguishing mark between Islamic societies and non-Islamic ones.

Al-Khomeini's argument is very straightforward. He argues that although darkness overshadowed the West (q.v.), when America's population was still then Indians and the Roman and Persian empires suffered from tyrannical and racial rules, Islam (q.v.) put forward divine laws that the Prophet submitted to as well. These laws, which cover human affairs from birth to death and from politics to social affairs and worship, can establish a modern Islamic society. Those thinkers who dwell on the imperfection of Islamic societies and the need to borrow the bases of social existence from the West are either ignorant or imperialist. See also AUTHENTICITY; CIVILIZATION; ISLAMIC STATE; *JAHILI* SOCIETIES; JURISPRUDENCE; LEGISLATION; LIBERATION; PAN-ISLAMISM; PARTIES; PAST; RELIGION; *AL-SHARI'A*; *TAWHID* WEST.

ISLAMIC SOCIETY MOVEMENT (*HARAKAT AL-MUJTAMA' AL-ISLAMI* [*HAMAS*]). This is an Algerian fundamentalist party that was founded in 1990 by Mahfoudh Nahnah (q.v.) and expresses the views of *Jam'iyyat al-Irshad wa al-Islah*. Nahnah is one of the most outstanding figures of the Islamic movement in Algeria. His movement competes for the Islamic audience with the Islamic Salvation Front (FIS) (q.v.) and follows more accommodating policies toward the state.

Nahnah did not support the FIS bid for power in the legislative elections because the Front refused to join the Islamic alliance that Nahnah had called for. Nahnah argued that numerous parties (q.v.) could exist within the Islamic movement and called for a dialogue with nonfundamentalist parties. The main difference was that Nahnah insisted that from an Islamic perspective society should be prepared morally and spiritually before a party moves to control the political affairs.

Nahnah decided to enter the political arena after the success of the FIS in 1991. He enjoyed good relations with the regime, which seemingly used him to draw attention and support away from the Islamic Salvation Front. That is why he received good media coverage by the state apparatus.

The support base for the Society is the educated classes and middle-

and upper-level cadres in the state administration, and among the private sector, entrepreneurs, who are an influential force in Nahnah's town of Blida. *Hamas* won 5.3 percent of the vote, which was disappointing to the movement. In 1997, Nahnah was elected to the Parliament. This movement is not linked to the Palestinian *Hamas*. See also ISLAMIC SALVATION FRONT; JABALLAH, 'ABD ALLAH; *JAMA'AT AL-NAHDA AL-ISLAMIYYA*; AL-NAHNAH, MAHFOUDH.

ISLAMIC STATE (*AL-DAWLA AL-ISLAMIYYA*). Before modern times, specifically during the 6th and 7th centuries of *Hijra*, when the Caliphate (q.v.) entered into a phase of weakness and challenge, the state as an independent conceptual Islamic polity was seriously entertained, although the Caliphate was perceived more as a symbol of unity. Later on, and with the rise of moral, political and economic crises, not to mention the invasion of Muslim lands by foreign powers, Muslim communities have witnessed many revivalist movements that oscillated between radical revolution (q.v.) and conservative reform.

That religious dogma and the state are interwoven together and cannot be separated was upheld even by the *Khawarij* (seceders) in the 7th century. They were the first to postulate the doctrine of divine governance (q.v.) (*hakimiyya*) and rule (*hukm*) and the ultimate authority of the Qur'an (q.v.) as the sole point of reference that may have any obligation on the Muslim. Furthermore, they denied the legitimacy (q.v.) of human arbitration, unless it could be textually supported. They were not ready to submit to the ruling of the community and instead, isolated themselves from the mainstream and advocated fighting those who did not adhere to the textual ruling of the Qur'an. They gave themselves, moreover, the right to judge others' beliefs and behaviors and endowed all aspects of human existence with religious connotations. More importantly, they were uncompromising when it came to either principles or actions. But the general community fought them as renegades who did not accept the arbitration of the community.

Similarly, in modern times, *al-Wahhabiyya* (q.v.), following the great medieval thinker Ibn Taymiyya (q.v.), has called for the purification of Islam by a return to the fundamentals of religion (q.v.), that is, the Qur'an and the *Sunna* (way) of the Prophet. It has followed a strict line of thinking in its attempts to reconstruct society and state on the basis of divine *tawhid* (q.v.) (Oneness of God) and the doctrine of *al-Salaf al-Salih* (righteous ancestors). What is important about the ancestors is their reluctance to engage in philosophical and intellectual argumentation and their adherence to the basic texts (q.v.) without any major attempt at reinterpretation or reworking of the principles of Islam (q.v.).

Other important movements in modern times are *al-Sanusiyya* and *al-Mahdiyya* (qq.v.), which started basically as Sufi orders but were later transformed into political movements that struggled against Western intervention in Libya and the Sudan respectively, and wanted to set up Islamic states. The two perceived themselves as being movements of purification, aiming at the restoration of genuine Islam and thus involving themselves in politics. Again, similar fundamentals were raised and were looked at as the road to the salvation of the Islamic community.

The Muslim Brotherhood (q.v.) in Egypt, like the Islamic Group of Abu al-A'la al-Mawdudi (q.v.) in Pakistan, focused more on the political aspect of Islam for promoting a revival. It called for the urgent need to establish an Islamic state as the first step in the implementation of *al-Shari'a* (q.v.) (Islamic Law). Although the Brotherhood focused its intellectual reinterpretation on going back to the fundamentals (q.v.) (*usul*), nevertheless, it selectively accepted major Western political concepts such as constitutional rule and democracy as necessary tools for overhauling the Islamic concept of state. However, the Brotherhood's extremely antagonistic dealings with the Egyptian government led some Brethren to splinter off under the leadership of Sayyid Qutb (q.v.). Qutb continued to uphold the need for the establishment of an Islamic state although rejecting any dealing and intellectual openness with the West (q.v.) and others. Qutb made the existence of an Islamic state an essential part of creed. It was in fact, for him and his followers, the community's submission to God (q.v.) on the basis of *al-Shari'a*. It became representative of political and legal abidance to *al-Shari'a*, which should be the bases of both legal rules and constitution. The absence of such bases removes any shred of legitimacy that the state may enjoy and brings it into paganism (q.v.) (*jahiliyya*).

Ayatollah al-Khomeini (q.v.) further restricts the concept of a legitimate Islamic state. Although *al-Shari'a* is the basis of government, it is only through the rule of the jurists that its existence is actualized. Within the Islamic world today, the demands of the mainstream fundamentalist movements in Algeria, Tunisia, Jordan, and Egypt follow Hasan al-Banna's (q.v.) discourse on the Islamic state, constitutional rule, and multiparty politics. Radical Sunni movements follow the discourse of Sayyid Qutb and Shi'ite political movements follow that of al-Khomeini, whose view of Islamic state borders on being a theocracy (q.v.).

A prerequisite to understanding the fundamentalist demand for an Islamic state requires an in-depth study of al-Banna's concept of Islamic state, which is the main organizing idea and driving force behind the movement of the Muslim Brotherhood and other movements throughout the Arab world. Al-Banna and the Brotherhood believed that the impurity of politics has resulted from the unethical exercise of power as well as from the mishandling of the multilayered social, economic, and educational crises. A mere change of government does not seem to be what is required or desired for the revival of the ethical spirit of the community. The state is not only an agency that organizes people's affairs but transcends such a description to be morally involved in the protection of creed and of religion's supremacy so that a human regeneration is affected and humanity's lifestyle is amended in accordance with the spirit of religion. The state's function, although limited, should be to help people live a virtuous life by, for example, redirecting the course of education toward God. A view of life that is accepted by the people becomes the conditioning ground for the establishment of the desired state. The legitimate exercise of authority and the withdrawal of legitimacy depend on the same conditions, and, once the Islamic state is established, the state cannot annul the original contract between the people and the ruler.

Furthermore, the state function is extended worldwide, especially because geographical limitations are not, in al-Banna's view, applicable to the Islamic call (q.v.) or therefore to the state that universalizes that call. Therefore, the well-being of humanity as a concern of the Islamic call makes the role of the Islamic state moral, even at the international level. In turn, the universality of the call makes the existence of a universal Caliphate a necessity on the international level, because it is the institution that transcends localities, borders, and the like. However, and for the time being, al-Banna looks at the geographic Islamic entity, the state, as more pivotal in terms of instituting the Islamic system (q.v.) (*nizam*). Practically speaking, and for the fundamentalists, it is more possible to achieve the Islamic state than the Islamic Caliphate.

For the fundamentalists, an Islamic state is an essential beginning for the achievement of the good Islamic society. Without its existence, it is very impractical for society to organize itself voluntarily on an Islamic basis. The very nature of essential Islamic doctrines requires a first rate agency of organization. It is only the state that functions as the executive corrective institution as well as the modern juridical agency for the development of *al-Shari'a*. Furthermore, an Islamic state could not be conceptually and functionally compartmentalized, at one time functioning as a secular agency, at another, as religious. The state, by following the demands of a virtuous society, does not produce conflicting claims but becomes the popular guiding social power in charge of executing just law and order. Only through such a role is the necessary condition for the legitimacy of state developed and accepted.

Hasan al-Banna goes back to the state that was founded by the Prophet in order to derive the best prototype of an Islamic state and society. This has nothing to do with the individuals themselves and their social and political settings, but rather it is a matter of attitude and philosophy (q.v.). The principal foundation of that state was unity, which became the backbone of the Qur'anic social system, leading to authentic phenomena and dimensions. The Qur'anic discourse and its language achieved social unity, the caliphs' unified ideological orientations led to political unity, even at a time when decentralization of government took the form of local governors, army commanders, and tax collectors. But the overall structure of the state was built on a solid infrastructure, that is, creed and belief, that goes beyond today's understanding of government and politics.

For the fundamentalists, Qur'anic scriptural references constitute the legitimacy of the Islamic state, which is largely based on its function: the spiritual and political uplifting and the defense and well-being of the community. Intellectually, the legitimacy of the state is built on a reinterpretation of the doctrine of God's *rububiyya* (lordship) and its political consequence, *al-hakimiyya*, or governance (q.v.). God's universal *rububiyya* makes Islamic revelation the basic text in matters relating to both politics and political philosophy. Theoretically speaking, all conceptions of an Islamic state developed according to Islam have to refer to similar ideological postulates and principles. These conceptions include the need to ground the Islamic state in the divine law that serves as the main source of constitutional framework; Islam's integration of religious and political substance; theoretical opposition to derive Islamic principles from non-Islamic philosophies and systems; viewing religious and ideological compromises as religious concessions; and Islam's inclusion of eternal principles that could deal with modern socioeconomic, political, and philosophical crises.

For the fundamentalists, the history (q.v.) of Islam shows testimonies to the Muslims' subordination of politics to religion, for instance, all political expansions were made in the name of Islam. Insofar as Muslims did that, they were victorious, but when they disassociated politics from true religion and their expansions lost religious zeal, they became losers, and consequently, Islam lost the role it had played throughout history.

In other words, only through a true revival of the Islamic spirit could contemporary Muslims regain both political power and international recognition. For Islam requires from its adherents not only the adherence to rituals but also, more importantly, the embodiment of Islam in the active lives of Muslims. What is also required from the state is not only a symbolic embracing of Islam but an active involvement on its behalf, which constitutes the main source for the legitimacy of government. The government, or the state, can rework the principles of *al-Shari'a* in terms of the changing needs and demands of society. However, the government's objectives should not neglect the general and guiding principles of *al-Shari'a*.

Issues relating to such principles as the universal unity of the Muslim community cannot be forever replaced by narrow bonds of patriotism and nationalism, although the two can be used to strengthen the universal principles of Islam. Such an act of replacement would distort the true spirit of the Qur'anic discourse, which essentially aims at unity, not disunity. For al-Banna, denying God's divinity (q.v.) (*uluhiyya*) over this life and the concomitant disavowal of universal unity leads simply to unbelief (q.v.) (*kufr*). Therefore, fundamentalists believe that one of the essential functions of the Islamic state is not to yield to those ideologies and philosophies that disrupt the unity of humanity—Muslims in particular. In fact, it should counterattack any political or philosophical endeavor that would limit the scope of Islam by imposing humanly developed systems over God's system. If the Islamic state were to yield to such an act, it would be solidifying paganism (q.v.) and contributing to the disunity of humanity, and, thus breaking the postulates of *al-Shari'a*. However Abu al-Hasan al-Nadawi (q.v.), Sayyid Qutb, and Abu al-A'la al-Mawdudi see the establishment of an Islamic state as a religious duty.

Al-Mawdudi also portrays similar views and explains the difference between an Islamic and non-Islamic state in the following way. First of all, the Islamic state is not just an administration. It is an entity that seeks the fulfillment of a high ideal, including purity, goodness, success, and prosperity. Impartial justice (q.v.), objective truth, and honesty are the bases of politics, whether between states or individuals. Power is only a trust from God that is used for fulfilling obligation and the establishment of justice and morality (q.v.).

The doctrine of an Islamic state, as put forward by a variety of scholars, ranges from complete conservatism, such as that of Saudi Arabia, to total revolution, such as that of the Islamic Republic of Iran as elaborated by Ayatollah Khomeini, or those of Sayyid Qutb, Hasan al-Banna, and

Hasan al-Turabi (q.v.). See also 'ABD AL-RAHMAN, 'UMAR; AL-AF-GHANI, JAMAL AL-DIN; ARMED ISLAMIC GROUP; AUTHEN-TICITY; CALIPHATE; CIVILIZATION; *DAR AL-HARB*; ECONOMIC THEORY; FADLALLAH, MUHAMMAD HUSAYN; GOD; *AL-HAR-AKA AL-ISLAMIYYA FI LUBNAN*; *HARAKAT AMAL AL-ISLAMIYYA*; *HARAKAT AL-NAHDA AL-ISLAMIYYA*; HAWWA, SA'ID; *HIZB AL-TAHRIR AL-ISLAMI*; *HIZBULLAH*; *IJMA'*; ISLAMIC FRONT FOR THE LIBERATION OF BAHRAIN; ISLAMIC FUNDAMENTALISM; ISLAMIC *JIHAD* IN SAUDI ARABIA; ISLAMIC REPUBLICAN PARTY; ISLAMIC SALVATION FRONT IN ALGERIA; ISLAMIC YOUTH ORGANIZATION; ISLAMIZATION; JABALLAH, 'ABD ALLAH; *AL-JAMA'A AL-ISLAMIYYA FI LUBNAN*; *JAMA'AT AL-FAN-NIYYA AL-'ASKARIYYA*; *JAMA'AT AL-JIHAD AL-ISLAMI*; *AL-JIHAD AL-ISLAMI* IN THE WEST BANK AND GAZA STRIP; JURISPRU-DENCE; JUSTICE; KHALID, KHALID MUHAMMAD; KHOMEINI, AYATOLLAH; *MARJI' AL-TAQLID*; *MILLI SELAMET PARTISI*; MO-DERNITY; *MUJAHIDIN KHALQ*; MUSLIM BROTHERHOOD, IDE-OLOGY OF; MUSLIM BROTHERHOOD IN SUDAN; NASRALLAH, SAYYID HASAN; QUTB, SAYYID; RADICALISM; REVOLUTION; RIDA, MUHAMMAD RASHID; SIRRIYYA, SALIH; AL-TURABI, HASAN; UNION OF THE ISLAMIC ASSOCIATIONS AND GROUPS; UNION OF POPULAR FORCES; UNION OF THE REVO-LUTIONARY ISLAMIC FORCES; *AL-WAHHABIYYA*; WORLD ORDER; AL-ZUMAR, 'ABBUD.

ISLAMIC STRUGGLE MOVEMENT: JERUSALEM. See *HARAKAT AL-JIHAD AL-ISLAMI: BAYT AL-MAQDIS.*

ISLAMIC TENDENCY MOVEMENT. See *HARAKAT AL-ITIJAH AL-ISLAMI.*

ISLAMIC UNIFICATION MOVEMENT. See *HARAKAT AL-TAWHID AL-ISLAMI.*

ISLAMIC YOUTH ORGANIZATION (*MUNAZZAMAT AL-SHABIBA AL-ISLAMIYYA*). This organization grew out of religious expansion in Morocco and the weakness of national forces as well as mounting inter-nal problems. In 1969, 'Abd al-Karim Muti' (q.v.) along with a religious group established the Islamic Youth Organization as "the mother and pi-oneer of the modern Islamic revival in Morocco." After some years of involvement in politico-religious activities, the organization applied for a license from the Moroccan government, and it was granted in November 1972.

The Islamic Youth Organization's religious ideology aims at achieving the well-being of the social system (q.v.) (*nizam*) and spreading morality (q.v.) through the application of God's law. It does not allow its leadership to participate in un-Islamic institutions. To achieve its goal, the organization works through a program of Islamic reeducation and activism (q.v.) (*harakiyya*): fighting illiteracy, undertaking public campaigns to preserve health, holding lectures, arranging tours, and conducting educational, religious, artistic, and athletic activities.

The organization has its own Islamic view, which is derived from the Qur'an (q.v.) and the *Sunna* (way) of the Prophet and the recognized legal schools. Thus, the organization takes it upon itself to rid the Moroccan society of corrupt ideas through the clarification of Islamic doctrines. The organization claims that it is aware of all the plots and conspiracies that aim at destroying its position as a good representative of Islamic principles. The organization calls upon its members to continue their adherence to wisdom and patience and expects that a sincere Islamic call (q.v.) (*da'wa*) will face serious opposition by authoritarian governments and tyrants.

A ferocious campaign was launched against the Islamic Youth in the early 1970s by the *al-Bayan* journal, the mouthpiece of the socialist party, and *al-Anba'*, the governmental magazine. This was supplemented by governmental efforts that aimed at attracting the organization's leadership, especially 'Abd al-Karim Muti', and at pressuring the organization's leadership to accept the policies of the government and the Palace.

However, the secretary-general of the organization claims that the efforts of the Palace and the government to dominate the organization and its leadership were not successful. They led, instead, to implicating the organization and some of its members in the assassination of 'Umar Bin Jallun, a member of the political office of the Socialist Union of the Morocco's Popular Forces and the editor of *al-Muharrir* journal. The Moroccan security forces made several arrests, including those of Ibrahim Kamal, the deputy of 'Abd al-Karim Muti', and a few other members of the organization. They were accused of planning and participating in the murder of Bin Jallun in December 1975. On 20 February 1977, the organization issued a statement published in *al-Balagh*, a Kuwaiti journal, denying that it had anything to do with the assassination. In a later statement published in Kuwait, the organization declared that it was not involved in any political struggle among the national parties (q.v.) and that it did not include among its members anyone who might attack another individual or any action that contradicts Islamic ethics. It condemned all acts of violence and extremism (qq.v.) and denied any connections to the "Moroccan Assembly of the Islamic Organizations."

Despite this, after the victory of the Islamic Revolution of Iran (q.v.), the Iranian model gained considerable attention with the leadership of the Islamic Youth Organization. The organization adopted the course of the Islamic revolution in Iran and began to call for the overthrow of the Moroccan monarchical regime, the establishment of an Islamic state (q.v.), and the implementation of the *Shari'a* (q.v.) (Islamic Law). The organization also resorted to armed violence (q.v.) as a means of reaching its goal and started assassination operations and attacks against state figures and symbols as well as the opposition forces, both leftist and rightist.

The organization began training its members and cadres for military operations as well. In the 1970s and early 1980s, the organization continued its activities. One of the main developments affecting the organization was the outbreak of the "bread revolution" early in 1984. The authorities declared at that time that the Islamic Youth Organization was among the forces behind the popular uprising against the decision to raise food prices.

Official Moroccan sources stated that the Islamic Youth Organization was an armed extremist religious organization that had adopted a Khomeini course and that had participated in provoking the bloody events and demonstrations against the government. The organization distributed radical Islamic pamphlets and pictures of the Shi'ite Iranian leader Imam Ayatollah Khomeini (q.v.). It also took advantage of the events to proclaim the moral deterioration in Morocco.

As a result of these events, the organization issued a declaration in which it condemned the practices of the Moroccan regime and its repression of the masses. The declaration also stated that the regime had taken several measures to confront the mass opposition movement represented by the Islamic Youth.

The regime's reaction, according to the organization, consisted of shooting at mass rallies; killing, wounding, and arresting hundreds of people and accusing the opposition of having communist, Zionist, and Iranian forces behind it. But the organization rejected these accusations, stating that the regime was provoking tensions among Muslims and was attempting to raise the Sunni majority of the Moroccan population against the Islamic revolution by highlighting its Shi'ite nature.

In June 1984, the government put 71 individuals accused of belonging to the Islamic Youth Organization on trial. Of these, 20 were sentenced in absentia, among them, 'Abd al-Karim Muti', who was given a death sentence. In July 1985, the Moroccan security forces arrested an armed group that came from Algerian territories to conduct military operations and assassinations in Morocco. The 27 individuals arrested were accused of belonging to the Islamic Youth Organization and were put on trial. In September 1985, 15 of them were put to death.

The organization publishes *al-Mujahid* newspaper, which represents the organization's position and policies and its views on the political conditions of Morocco. See also MUJAHIDIN MOVEMENT IN MOROCCO; MUTI', 'ABD AL-KARIM; AL-NA'MANI, 'ABD AL-'AZIZ.

AL-ISLAMIYUN AL-TAQADDUMIYUN. See PROGRESSIVE MUSLIMS.

ISLAMIZATION (*ASLAMA*). *Islamization* is a term used to describe arguments, discussions, and processes employed by the fundamentalists to adopt disciplines, doctrines, principles, and concepts into Islamic thought. Thus, Islamization refers to turning foreign concepts like human rights and democracy (q.v.), for instance, into Islamic concepts like legitimate rights and consultation, or *al-huquq al-Shar'iyya* and *shura* (qq.v.). Islamization includes numerous disciplines, like social sciences and economics, and doctrines, like pluralism and Islamic state (qq.v.). It is massive in terms of its scope and substance and includes knowledge, philosophy, religion, world order (qq.v.), and even technology.

This process of Islamization depends on the possibility of deconstructing the histories of the borrowed and new terms and on developing their new connotations and functions. Thus, although the history (q.v.) of democracy is different from that of *shura*, both are linked and made equal by focusing on the function of both and neglecting their past (q.v.). In that sense, democracy and *shura* become the instruments for involving the public in the creation of their political life. This process is, then, linked to a historicist and socioeconomic understanding of human thought and philosophy.

Many fundamentalists, such as Rashid al-Ghannushi and Hasan al-Turabi (qq.v.), have directly and indirectly participated in the Islamization process. Institutionally, the International Institute for Islamic

Thought (IIIT) is leading the project of Islamization and has published numerous volumes and articles on Islamized disciplines and subjects. See also AUTHENTICITY; AL-BANNA, HASAN; DEMOCRATIC IS-LAMIC ARAB MOVEMENT; *IJMA'*; ISLAMIC SALVATION FRONT IN ALGERIA; ISRAEL; MODERNISM; POPULAR DEFENSE FORCES; AL-TURABI, HASAN; *UMMA* PARTY; WEST; AL-ZUMAR, 'ABBUD.

ISMA'IL, 'ABD AL-FATTAH (1924–1966). After the release of Sayyid Qutb (q.v.) in May 1964, 'Abd al-Fattah Isma'il organized many meet-ings for some Muslim Brethren in Egypt and built a secret organization. In the beginning, the organization was seen as an instrument of revenge for the massacres of 1954, but later it became an instrument against the regime. Sayyid Qutb became its ideologue, and he urged these Brethren to take the strongest possible actions against the regime. His followers became known as *al-Qutbiyyin* (the Qutbists).

Isma'il had earlier arranged the escape of many members of the Mus-lim Brotherhood (q.v.) to Saudi Arabia and the Gulf States. Isma'il, who was known as the dynamo of the Muslim Brotherhood in Egypt, was arrested in August 1965 and was accused of being part of the Secret Ap-paratus. In 1966, he, Sayyid Qutb, and Salih 'Ishmawi (q.v.) were sen-tenced to death. See also MUSLIM BROTHERHOOD; *AL-NIZAM AL-SIRRI*.

ISRAEL. One of the lasting demands and formative events in the life and expansion of Islamic fundamentalism (q.v.) was the creation of Israel and the deportation of millions of Palestinians to places all over the world. Celebrating Jerusalem Day (q.v.) (*Yawm al-Quds*), which was in-augurated by the Islamic Revolution of Iran and Ayatollah Khomeini (qq.v.), in particular confirms the religious nature of the Arab-Israeli conflict, for the Aqsa Mosque would always be "a thorn in the occupier's throat;" for Muslims Jerusalem is and will forever remain Islamic and the capital of Palestine. The Muslim Brotherhood (q.v.) in Egypt became a military movement with the immigration of Jews and expulsion of Pal-estinians from Palestine, followed by the creation of Israel.

The Arab-Israeli conflict has been seen by almost all fundamentalists as a struggle between not only Arabism and Zionism but also between Islam and Judaism (q.v.) and, therefore, is not subject to appeasement or concessions. As is known, *Hamas* (q.v.) is considered the central Islamic organization in Gaza and the West Bank that aims at the Islamization of (q.v.) the conflict. The Islamization of the conflict with Israel transforms it into a two-sided religious duty: first, the elimination of the state of Israel; and second, the establishment of an Islamic state (q.v.). Today's fundamentalist ideologies present themselves as the alternative to nationalist and secular ideologies. For instance, since the late 1980s, *Hamas*, the military wing of the Muslim Brotherhood in Palestine (q.v.), has come to portray the Arab-Israeli conflict as a struggle between not only the forces of Zionism and Arabism but also those of Judaism and Islam, with Zionism and Judaism being regarded as the source of evil and the symbol of Western civilization (q.v.).

Both *Hamas* and *al-Jihad al-Islami* (q.v.) as well as *Hizbullah* in Lebanon (q.v.) have launched many military operations against the Israeli army, of which the most famous was that which has led to the deportation of more than 400 people affiliated with Islamic movements. Moreover, *Hamas* has declined to join the Palestinian National Council and declared in its Covenant (*al-Mithaq*) of 1988 its rejection of UN resolution 242 and the recognition of Israel. It has also developed its security apparatuses significantly and refused to join the unified leadership of the *intifada*. It has rejected the Oslo accords and any peace (q.v.) agreement with Israel.

Hamas, first of all, is the main Sunni fundamentalist movement in the Gaza Strip and the West Bank. It is deeply rooted in the famous Muslim Brotherhood, which is known as an international umbrella for many sorts of fundamentalist movements that call for the reinstitution of Islam as a universal ideology and for the application of Islamic divine law as the law of the land. *Hamas* was started as the military wing of the Muslim Brotherhood with the inception of the *intifada*. The ideology of *Hamas* is therefore based on religious principles that have transformed the Arab-Israeli or Arab-Zionist conflict into a religious war between Islam and Judaism.

The ideology of *Hamas*—and almost all other fundamentalist movements as regards the Arab-Israeli conflict—can be outlined from its *Mithaq* (pact). The *Mithaq* states that loyalty is to God (q.v.) only and Islam (q.v.) is the method of life and action. God's banner should be spread over every inch of Palestine. It is only in the shadow of Islam that followers of all religions can coexist in security and peace as relates to their persons, money, and rights. In the absence of Islam, struggle will arise, injustice will dominate, corruption will spread, and conflicts and wars will break out. As to the goals, the *Mithaq* states that the land of Palestine is a land of religious endowment *(waqf)* for all Muslim generations until the Day of Resurrection; neither all of it nor part of it can be given away or conceded by any state or individual or a combination thereof.

Peaceful solutions and international conferences directed at resolving the Palestinian problem contradict the creed of the Islamic resistance movement. Struggle against secular Judaism or Zionism is a must for liberation. Muslims must, therefore, exercise *jihad* (q.v.) (struggle) because it is a religious duty. Palestine includes Islamic sacred places, and the Aqsa Mosque has been linked unconditionally and forever to *al-Haram* Mosque in Saudi Arabia for so long as the earth and heavens exist; it is the location where the Prophet's travel and ascension took place.

The fundamentalists further argue that only under Islam can the three religions, Islam, Christianity (q.v.), and Judaism coexist peacefully in Palestine. Therefore, the followers of other religions must give up their contest with Islam over the sovereignty of this area, because since the day that they have ruled, there has been nothing but killing, torture, and diaspora.

Al-Jihad al-Islami in Palestine represents as well a challenge to both Israel and the Palestine Liberation Organization (PLO). From one aspect, *al-Jihad*, as declared by one of its leaders, As'ad al-Tamimi, in his book *The Liquidation of Israel: A Qur'anic Duty* (1990), does not recognize the establishment of a Jewish state in Palestine, because the struggle between the Islamic movement and Israel is not a temporary nationalist struggle between Zionism and Arabism but is an everlasting religious duty. Consequently, there is no possible compromise to settle the conflict in a way that will satisfy the two parties. Jews must therefore go back to their original lands in Europe and elsewhere. Furthermore, and as a challenge to the PLO, *al-Jihad* has rejected the Palestinian National Council resolutions and compromises and demanded withdrawal from the peace process. It has further rejected the peace agreement between the Palestinian National Authority and the Arab states with Israel. See also ABU MARZUQ, MUSA; *AL-AFGHAN AL-'ARAB*; *HARAKAT AMAL AL-ISLAMIYYA*; *HIZB JABHAT AL-'AMAL AL-ISLAMI*; *HIZBULLAH*; AL-ISLAMBULI, MUHAMMAD SHAWQI; *AL-JAMA'A AL-ISLAMIYYA FI LUBNAN*; *JAMA'AT AL-MUSLIMIN*; *AL-JIHAD AL-ISLAMI* IN THE WEST BANK AND GAZA STRIP; KASHANI, ABU AL-QASIM; KHOMEINISM; MADI, ABU AL-'ULA; MONOTHEISTIC RELIGIONS; MUSLIM BROTHERHOOD IN PALESTINE; NASRALLAH, SAYYID HASAN; YUSUF, AHMAD RAMZI.

AL-ISTI'MAR AL-GHARBI. See WESTERN COLONIZATION.

AL-ITIHAD AL-ISHTIRAKI AL-ISLAMI AL-MURITANI. See MAURI-TANIAN MUSLIM SOCIALIST UNION.

AL-ITIHAD AL-ISLAMI AL-'ALAMI LI AL-MUNAZZAMAT AL-TULLABIYYA (INTERNATIONAL ISLAMIC UNION FOR STU-DENTS ORGANIZATIONS). See INTERNATIONAL ORGANIZA-TION OF THE MUSLIM BROTHERHOOD.

ITIHAD AL-JAM'IYYAT WA AL-JAMA'AT AL-ISLAMIYYA. See UNION OF THE ISLAMIC ASSOCIATIONS AND GROUPS.

ITIHAD AL-QIWA AL-ISLAMIYYA AL-THAWRIYYA. See UNION OF THE REVOLUTIONARY ISLAMIC FORCES.

ITIHAD AL-QIWA AL-SHA'BIYYA. See UNION OF POPULAR FORCES.

-J-

AL-JABALI, HAMADI. See *HARAKAT AL-NAHDA AL-ISLAMIYYA*.

JABALLAH, 'ABD ALLAH (1956–). Jaballah is the head of *Jama'at al-Nahda al-Islamiyya* in Algeria (q.v.) (Islamic Renaissance Group). Ja-ballah was born in Qustantiniyya, Algeria, to a poor family. He got his religious education when he was young and later continued his study of Islamic Law in Saudi Arabia. He returned to Algeria in 1979 and joined the Islamic Group (*al-Jama'a al-Islamiyya*) forming good relationships with its leaders. He then set up *Jam'iyyat al-Nahda li al-Islah al-Thaqafi wa al-Ijtima'i*. Jaballah was arrested many times, including one time when he was imprisoned for a year and a half with Abbasi Madani (q.v.), beginning in 1982. At that time, he lost his job and housing.

In December 1988 Jaballah and others founded the Islamic Renais-sance Movement (*Harakat al-Nahda al-Islamiyya*) as an extension of the Islamic Group, and he was chosen as its leader. The movement is consid-ered by many observers as being more moderate than the Islamic Society Movement, or *Hamas*, headed by Mahfoudh Nahnah (qq.v.). The Islamic Renaissance Movement follows a moderate social cultural program and upholds the principle of peaceful transfer of power and democracy (q.v.). Although it believes in the necessity of the Islamic state (q.v.), it uses democratic elections as a means of achieving it and opposes violence (q.v.). See also *JAMA'AT AL-NAHDA AL-ISLAMIYYA.*

AL-JABHA AL-ISHTIRAKIYYA AL-ISLAMIYYA (ISLAMIC SOCIAL-IST FRONT). See MUSLIM BROTHERHOOD IN SYRIA.

AL-JABHA AL-ISLAMIYYA FI SURIYYA (ISLAMIC FRONT IN SYRIA). See FIGHTING VANGUARDS; MUSLIM BROTHERHOOD IN SYRIA.

AL-JABHA AL-ISLAMIYYA LI AL-INQADH. See ISLAMIC FRONT FOR SALVATION IN TUNISIA.

AL-JABHA AL-ISLAMIYYA LI TAHRIR AL-BAHRAIN. See ISLAMIC FRONT FOR THE LIBERATION OF BAHRAIN.

AL-JABHA AL-QAWMIYYA AL-ISLAMIYYA (NATIONAL ISLAMIC FRONT). See MUSLIM BROTHERHOOD IN SUDAN.

AL-JABHA AL-WATANIYYA LI INQADH LIBYA. See NATIONAL FRONT FOR THE SALVATION OF LIBYA.

JABHAT AL-'AMAL AL-ISLAMI (ISLAMIC ACTION FRONT). See *HIZB JABHAT AL-'AMAL AL-ISLAMI.*

JABHAT AL-INQADH (FIS). See ISLAMIC SALVATION FRONT.

JABHAT AL-MITHAQ AL-ISLAMI (ISLAMIC CHARTER FRONT). See MUSLIM BROTHERHOOD IN THE SUDAN.

JABHAT AL-TAHRIR AL-ISLAMIYYA. See ISLAMIC LIBERATION FRONT.

JAHILI SOCIETIES. For the radical fundamentalists, the very definition of a true *umma* (q.v.) (nation) involves a group of people who are connected by religion (q.v.), which is its nationality. Otherwise there is no religiously real nation because land, race, language, and material interests are not adequate for establishing a righteous nation. For Sayyid Qutb and Abu al-A'la al-Mawdudi (qq.v.) the importance of Islam (q.v.) is its ability to unite humanity on religious bases and do away with race, language, territories, and cultures. An Islamic society (q.v.) is basically constructed on *al-Shari'a* (q.v.) (Islamic Law). Religion should be the nationality of and the focal point for Muslims. Therefore, Muslims must not imitate Christians, who have separated the political from the religious, because the European experience differs from the Islamic. Islam is different from Christianity (q.v.) in that the latter does not postulate a political code.

Muslim societies turn into *jahili* societies when they rule themselves in accordance with human governance (q.v.) (*hakimiyya*) and shun divine governance. Paganism (q.v.) (*jahiliyya*) is reached when human beings follow a human system or philosophy (qq.v.) (religion). A society that is constructed on human, and not divine, bases, is a *jahili* society, according to radical fundamentalists. See also *JAMA'AT AL-JIHAD AL-ISLAMI*; *JAMA'AT AL-MUSLIMIN*; *JIHAD*; LIBERATION; PAGANISM; VANGUARD.

JAHILIYYA. See PAGANISM.

AL-JAMA'A AL-ISLAMIYYA FI LUBNAN (ISLAMIC GROUP IN LEBANON). This fundamentalist group was established in 1964 in Tripoli by young members of '*Ibad al-Rahman* (the Worshippers of the Merciful). According to one of its leaders, 'Abd Allah Babati, the split took place because some younger members wanted to be involved in politics. The movement was led by the influential Sunni fundamentalist thinker Fathi Yakan (q.v.), Judge Faysal al-Mawlawi, and writer Muhammad 'Ali al-Dinnawi. It called for an Islamic society and state (qq.v.) whose bases were derived from *al-Shari'a* (q.v.) (Islamic Law). This call (q.v.) led to its advocating and using political violence and radicalism (qq.v.) and to the establishment of its own military wing in 1976.

The group fought during the civil war on the side of the leftist-Islamic coalition in Tripoli. Although it opposes secularism (q.v.) and communism, it considers Islam (q.v.) to be the best solution to the Lebanese crisis. Later on, however, some of its members, like Yakan and Zuhayr 'Abd al-Rahman al-'Ubaydi (q.v.), became members of the secular, although confessional, Lebanese Parliament. The group still calls for the abolition of confessionalism.

During the Israeli invasion of 1982, the group launched military activities against the Israelis. The group, however, is not, for the time being, trying to set up an Islamic state (q.v.) in Lebanon, because it believes that the Islamic state should be the natural outcome of a particular environment, which Lebanon lacks, because it is composed of groups that have different religions and sects. Its participation in the electoral process has reduced its original claims and led to its moderation. See also *'IBAD AL-RAHMAN*; YAKAN, FATHI.

AL-JAMA'A AL-ISLAMIYYA (ISLAMIC GROUP) **IN EGYPT**. See *AL-JAMA'AT AL-ISLAMIYYA*; 'ABD AL-RAHMAN, 'UMAR.

AL-JAMA'A AL-ISLAMIYYA (ISLAMIC GROUP) **IN TUNISIA**. See AL-GHANNUSHI, RASHID.

AL-JAMA'A AL-ISLAMIYYA AL-MUSALLAHA. See ARMED ISLAMIC GROUP.

AL-JAMA'A AL-ISLAMIYYA AL-SALAFIYYA AL-MUSALLAHA (ARMED ISLAMIC *SALAFI* GROUP). See ARMED ISLAMIC GROUP.

AL-JAMA'A AL-SIMAWIYYA (*AL-SIMAWIYYA GROUP*). See ORGANIZATION OF SHAYKH 'ABD ALLAH AL-SIMAWI. See also *JAMA'AT AL-MUSLIMIN*.

JAMA'AT AL-'ADL WA AL-IHSAN. See JUSTICE AND CHARITY GROUP.

JAMA'AT ANSAR AL-SUNNA (GROUP OF *SUNNA* SUPPORTERS). See *AL-SALAFIYYA* FORCES IN EGYPT.

JAMA'AT AL-FANNIYYA AL-'ASKARIYYA (GROUP OF THE MILITARY TECHNICAL [SCHOOL]). This group was led by Salih Sirriyya (q.v.), who aimed at toppling the Egyptian regime. He was born in Palestine and joined *Hizb al-Tahrir al-Islami* (q.v.) (Islamic Liberation Party), which was set up by Taqiy al-Din al-Nabahani (q.v.) in 1950 as a reaction to the assassination of Hasan al-Banna (q.v.), the leader and founder of the Muslim Brotherhood (q.v.). Sirriyya went to Cairo in 1971 and received a Ph.D. in education from 'Ayn Shams University. He then went to Baghdad and taught there but left suddenly after he was accused of being a member of the Islamic Liberation Party. He settled in Cairo again where he organized a group of university students, including students from the Military Technical School. Sirriyya drew up a plan to attack the school and assassinate the officials of the Egyptian regime, a way to help the government of Anwar al-Sadat. His plan failed because of its primitiveness and weakness.

The group believes in armed struggle, or *jihad* (q.v.), against the Egyptian regime, which it considers un-Islamic. It also sanctions violence (q.v.) in order to establish the Islamic state (q.v.). Any Muslim who belongs to any secular or philosophical school is considered an unbeliever. The group's radicalism (q.v.) leads it to adhere to the doctrine of total revolution (q.v.) against the governments of the world and to have as a goal the unification of the world under the Islamic banner. See also 'AWDA, 'ABD AL-'AZIZ; MUSTAPHA, SHUKRI; SIRRIYYA, SALIH.

JAMA'AT AL-FITRA (GROUP OF PURE NATURE). See *AL-AFGHAN AL-'ARAB.*

JAMA'AT 'IBAD AL-RAHMAN. SEE *'IBAD AL-RAHMAN.*

AL-JAMA'AT AL-ISLAMIYYA (ISLAMIC GROUPS). The radical ideas developed by Sayyid Qutb (q.v.) have been influential among many fundamentalists. These ideas pushed many groups beyond the opposition of the Muslim Brotherhood (q.v.) to advocacy of revolution (q.v.). Because these groups have been illegal and have constantly clashed with security forces, they have remained underground. At times, repression of the radical groups led to the disappearance of the mainstream figures.

The writings of certain intellectual figures associated with radical movements have gained some circulation; such writings claim that Egypt's government and even its society lead lives of paganism (q.v.) (*jahiliyya*) and are against divine governance (q.v.) (*hakimiyya*). They are therefore a legitimate, even mandatory, target for political violence (q.v.). The actions of these groups include physical and violent attacks on videotape stores, police officials, Copts, and foreign tourists.

The major issues raised by these groups are domestic and center around the claim that the current Egyptian political system is inimical to Islam and must be changed. The nature of their support base is difficult to gauge, but their intellectual influence is greater than their small numbers would suggest. They have a reputation for militant and uncompromising insistence on adherence to Islamic principles. They seem to have the greatest appeal among students and the middle class, primarily in urban areas.

These groups are not allowed to publish openly, although some of their ideas infiltrate the legal press, where more mainstream fundamentalist groups sometimes attack them. Recent leading radical figures include Shaykh 'Umar 'Abd al-Rahman (q.v.), who was sentenced for his involvement in the World Trade Center bombing in New York, Hafiz Salama, and Shaykh Jalal Kishk.

These groups include the organizations that appeared in Egyptian universities in the early 1970s where the regime wanted to fight and counterbalance leftist organizations. These organizations have engaged in many social and educational activities, including organizing trips to Mecca, summer camps, publications, and the like. They have been very active in teaching the religious sciences, holding lecture activities, and prohibiting parties and dancing. During 1978 and until Anwar al-Sadat's assassination, these groups dominated student unions and were particularly active in the faculties of engineering, medicine, and sciences. *Al-Jama'at al-Islamiyya* has been the dominant political power in the universities and the means of protest against the regime since 1977. During its rallies, it attacked the regime, called for the application of *al-Shari'a* (q.v.) (Islamic Law), and rejected peace (q.v.) negotiations and agreements with Israel (q.v.). During the 1980s, it expanded the borders of its activities to include all of Egypt and set up a union, *al-Jama'a al-Islamiyya*. Important figures in this union were Hilmi al-Jazar, the General Secretary, and 'Isam al-'Aryan, the Treasurer, who took part in the group's meetings to condemn "the conspiracy of the Copts for controlling Egypt and expelling the Muslims." Dr. 'Isam al-'Aryan, who is now in prison, was allegedly one of the most outstanding figures of the groups at Cairo University and was on good terms with 'Abbud al-Zumar (q.v.).

One of the groups is the Qutbian forces (*al-Qiwa al-Qutbiyya*), which refers to individuals in different organizations who have adopted the views of Sayyid Qutb, especially the doctrines of paganism and governance. Most of these forces are made up of individuals who where jailed with Qutb and who tried to push Qutb's brother, Muhammad, to follow in his footsteps. Included in these forces are Mustapha al-Khudayri, 'Abd al-Majid al-Shadhili, the author of *Had al-Islam and Haqiqat al-Iman*, and 'Abd al-Jawad Yasin, the author of *Fiqh al-Jahiliyya al-Mu'asira*. See also FARAJ, 'ABD AL-SALAM; *JAMA'AT AL-FAN-NIYYA AL-'ASKARIYYA*; *JAMA'AT AL-JIHAD AL-ISLAMI*; *JAMA'AT AL-MUSLIMIN*; AL-ZAYAT, MUNTASIR.

JAMA'AT AL-JIHAD AL-ISLAMI (ISLAMIC *JIHAD* GROUP). The group was founded by Muhammad 'Abd al-Salam Faraj (q.v.) in 1979. It became the center of three groups: those of Karam Zuhdi, Salim al-Rahhal, and Faraj. The first *Majlis al-Shura* (q.v.) (*Shura* Council) was established in 1981, and was headed by Faraj himself. The group allowed itself to loot Christian shops in order to finance its activities.

The group believed, as is clear from Faraj's *al-Farida al-Gha'iba* (The Absent Duty), that its basic objective was the establishment of the Islamic state and then the Caliphate (qq.v.) and the abolition of the governments of the world as a religious duty, for which every Muslim should struggle or exercise *jihad* (q.v.). Today, Muslims are ruled by *jahili* laws and have turned to unbelief (q.v.) (*kufr*) as a way of life. Muslims are now subjects of Zionism, imperialism, and communism. The rulers of today are like the Tatars who usurped the government of the Islamic world. That is why the group attempted to assassinate President Anwar al-Sadat, who accepted the Israeli occupation of Islamic land under the pretext of peace (q.v.). Thus, the group adopts the doctrines of governance, paganism, and *jahili* societies (qq.v.).

Another important figure in the group was 'Abbud al-Zumar (q.v.), who also believed that all Islamic governments of today are un-Islamic. He further described all Muslim societies as *jahili* societies. However, he exempted individuals from the paganism, insofar as they participated in armed struggle or renounced paganism. Al-Zumar aimed at establishing the Islamic state in Egypt and considered Ayatollah Khomeini (q.v.) as his ideal example. He called for armed popular revolution (q.v.) against the regimes.

Also important in this group was 'Umar 'Abd al-Rahman (q.v.), who represented the ideological leadership of the group and who later became very instrumental in the maintenance of the group. 'Abd al-Rahman had allegedly given a *fatwa* (q.v.) for the assassination of President Sadat in response to a question on the rulers who do not rule according to *al-Shari'a* (q.v.) (Islamic Law). The Islamic alternative for 'Abd al-Rahman and his group was the reestablishment of the Islamic Caliphate as a distinctive political institution whose foundations must spring from *shura* (consultation), *'adl* (justice), and religion (qq.v.). See also 'AWDA, 'ABD AL-'AZIZ; FARAJ, 'ABD AL-SALAM; *AL-JIHAD AL-ISLAMI* IN THE WEST BANK AND GAZA STRIP; AL-ZUMAR, 'ABBUD.

JAMA'AT AL-JIHAD (*JIHAD* GROUP) **IN YEMEN**. See *HIZB AL-TA-JAMMU' AL-YEMENI LI AL-ISLAH*.

JAMA'AT AL-KHILAFA (CALIPHATE GROUP). See *AL-AFGHAN AL-'ARAB*.

JAMA'AT AL-MUSLIMIN (GROUP OF MUSLIMS). This group, which is better known as *al-Takfir wa al-Hijra*, was founded in 1969 out of the Egyptian Muslim Brotherhood (q.v.) by Shukri Mustapha (q.v.). It has been one of the most notorious Islamic splinter groups in Egypt since the 1970s. This group assassinated a former Minister of Endowment, for which Mustapha and four other members of the group were executed.

Its views are radical because it calls for the establishment of the Islamic society (q.v.) through avoidance of positive interaction with society and it sanctions the use of violence (q.v.). It also holds the view that all societies on earth are *jahili* societies (q.v.) and consequently un-Islamic. Any individual who does not belong to the group is considered to be an infidel as well. Mustapha delineated a two-stage development for the movement: the stage of weakness *(al-istid'af)* where the group leaves the Egyptian society to live in deserted areas like caves and mountains and builds itself, and the "enabling stage" *(al-tamkin)*, where the group becomes strong and faces the *jahili* society and ultimately rules. In other words, the group believes in the doctrines of paganism and governance (qq.v.).

Some attribute the group's adoption of violence to the effect that the views of 'Abd al-Fattah Isma'il and Sayyid Qutb (qq.v.) had on the inmates in prison. When Mustapha was released in 1971, he began to actively apply his radical program. The group rejects past Islamic culture, even isolates itself religiously, rejects *ijma'* (q.v.) (consultation), reason (q.v.) (*ijtihad*), and other principles of law. It believes that *jihad* (q.v.) (struggle) should be the singular attitude toward Israel (q.v.) and the United Nations as well as the Islamic states. See *AL-AFGHAN AL-'ARAB*; ARMED ISLAMIC GROUP; EXTREMISM; *AL-JIHAD AL-ISLAMI* IN THE WEST BANK AND GAZA STRIP; MUSTAPHA, SHUKRI; VIOLENCE.

JAMA'AT AL-NAHDA AL-ISLAMIYYA (GROUP OF ISLAMIC RENAISSANCE). This Algerian fundamentalist group, which was founded in 1988, is a branch of the Muslim Brotherhood in Algeria (q.v.) and is led by 'Abd Allah Jaballah (q.v.). When the Islamic Salvation Front (FIS) (q.v.) rejected Mahfoudh Nahnah's (q.v.) call (q.v.) for an Islamic alliance, Jaballah founded this movement. It follows a middle ground between the Islamic Society Movement: *Hamas* (q.v.) and the Islamic

Salvation Front. For instance, it takes harder positions against the government than *Hamas*. Many of its members, like 'Abd al-Qadir Hashshani, who became the head of the temporary leadership when Abbasi Madani and 'Ali Bilhaj (qq.v.) were arrested, joined the FIS.

Jaballah's differences with the FIS centered around different conceptions of reason (q.v.) (*ijtihad*), use of mosques in political affairs, and the manner of applying the *al-Shari'a* (q.v.) (Islamic Law). Jaballah drew his inspiration from the Muslim Brotherhood in Egypt (q.v.) and considered the Islamic Salvation Front to be a hard-line movement. The movement won 2.2 percent of the votes of the legislative election in Algeria in 1991. See also JABALLAH, 'ABD ALLAH.

JAMA'AT AL-'UZLA AL-SHAR'IYYA. See GROUP OF LEGITIMATE ISOLATION.

AL-JAM'IYYA AL-THAQAFIYYA AL-IJTIMA'IYYA. See SOCIAL CULTURAL SOCIETY.

JAM'IYYAT AL-HIFADH 'ALA AL-QUR'AN (QUR'ANIC PRESERVATION ASSOCIATION). This cultural association was founded in 1970 in al-Zaytuna Mosque in Tunisia. It turned out to be a launching stage for the Islamic movement and party that played an important political role during the 1980s and 1990s, that is, *Harakat al-Nahda al-Islamiyya* (q.v.) (Islamic Renaissance Movement), which is headed by Rashid al-Ghannushi (q.v.). At the beginning, the state favorably supported its creation in order to counteract the influences of leftist groups on university campuses. See also *HARAKAT AL-ITIJAH AL-ISLAMI*; *HARAKAT AL-NAHDA AL-ISLAMIYYA*; MOVEMENT OF ISLAMIC RENEWAL.

JAM'IYYAT IHYA' AL-TURATH (HERITAGE REVIVAL ASSOCIATION). During the 1980s, this fundamentalist association adopted a moderate reform agenda in Kuwait. As opposed to many Shi'ite groups, this association dealt peacefully with its political demands. See also *JAM'IYYAT AL-ISLAH AL-IJTIMA'IYYA*.

JAM'IYYAT AL-ISLAH AL-IJTIMA'IYYA (SOCIAL REFORM ASSOCIATION) **IN KUWAIT**. This association grew out of the Muslim Brotherhood in Kuwait in the early 1960s. The Muslim Brotherhood in Kuwait is a branch of the Muslim Brotherhood in the United Arab Emirates and was founded in 1951 by Egyptian teachers. The association was active in the 1980s. Candidates of fundamentalists parties (q.v.), including *Jam'iyyat Ihya' Turath*, ran as individual candidates and in the 1992 elections won 18 seats out of 50 in the National Assembly. The fundamentalists formed two blocs, the moderate Islamic Constitutional Movement and a conservative Islamic Popular Alliance. However, both blocs advocated the institution of *al-Shari'a* (q.v.) (Islamic Law) to reform Kuwait's legal system. See also MUSLIM BROTHERHOOD; MUSLIM BROTHERHOOD IN THE GULF.

JAM'IYYAT AL-ISLAH AL-IJTIMA'IYYA (SOCIAL REFORM ASSOCIATION) **IN YEMEN**. This association became active during the 1980s in Yemen and advocated a moderate platform. It grew out of the Muslim Brotherhood in Yemen (q.v.) during the 1960s and was founded by old Adeni merchant families. Many members of these families played important political roles from the 1930s until independence in 1976.

Some of the important family names include Luqman, al-Makkawi, al-Asnaj, Bayumi and al-Jifri. *Nadi al-Sha'b* (People's Club) in Lahij, *al-Hizb al-Watani* (Nationalist Party) in the Qu'ayti Sultanate, as well as the *Lajnat al-'Amal li Wihdat Hadhramaut* (Committee for Working for the Unification of Hadhramaut) and *Jam'iyyat al-Ihsan* (Benevolence Association) give a measurement of the widespread discontent with the British at that time.

JAM'IYYAT AL-ISLAH WA AL-IRSHAD (ASSOCIATION OF REFORM AND GUIDANCE). See AL-NAHNAH, MAHFOUDH.

JAM'IYYAT AL-MASHARI' AL-KHAIRIYYA AL-ISLAMIYYA (ASSOCIATION OF ISLAMIC PHILANTHROPIC PROJECTS). See *AL-AHBASH*.

JAM'IYYAT AL-SHABAB AL-HUR. See SOCIETY OF FREE YOUTH.

AL-JAM'IYYAT AL-SHAR'IYYA. See *AL-SALAFIYYA* FORCES IN EGYPT.

JAM'IYYAT AL-SHUBBAN AL-MUSLIMIN (ASSOCIATION OF MUSLIM YOUNG MEN). The association was founded in 1927 on the model of the Young Men's Christian Association (YMCA). It was a protest over Christian domination of civil service jobs in Palestine, which it blamed on divisive British policy. The association became vocally radical in the early 1930s, and it turned into a major political actor in Palestine.

JAM'IYYAT AL-TADAMUN AL-ISLAMI AL-JAZA'IRI (ASSOCIATION OF ALGERIAN ISLAMIC SOLIDARITY). The president of the association is Ahmad Sahnun, and it is made up of a coalition of the Islamic Algerian Party and other minor Islamic groups. It was formed after the dissolution of the Islamic Salvation Front (q.v.).

JAM'IYYAT TAHRIR AL-ARAD AL-MUQADDASA. See SOCIETY FOR THE LIBERATION OF THE HOLY SOIL.

JAM'IYYAT AL-TURATH AL-THAQAFI AL-ISLAMI. See ISLAMIC CULTURAL HERITAGE SOCIETY.

JAM'IYYAT AL-'ULAMA' AL-MUSLIMIN (ASSOCIATION OF MUSLIM SCHOLARS). This association, established as a reformist movement in the 1920s, focused on Algerian religious and culture affairs. It was dissolved in 1956. The majority of leaders had Arabic educations and middle-class backgrounds. It was founded by a group of graduates from traditional learning institutions such as al-Azhar and al-Zaytuna. They followed in the footsteps of Jamal al-Din Afghani, Muhammad Iqbal, and Muhammad 'Abdu (qq.v.). The most important leaders of the movement are 'Abd al-Hamid Ibn Badis and his successor, Bashir al-Ibrahimi (qq.v.). The association sought to uphold Islam (q.v.) and the Arabic language and fought the practices of Sufi orders. Furthermore, Islam was viewed as the national ideology that could lead to unity and independence from France. See also IBN BADIS, 'ABD AL-HAMID; AL-IBRAHIMI, BASHIR; KABIR, RABIH; AL-WARTALANI, FUDAYL.

JAMMU, 'ABD AL-BAQI (1922–). Jummu is a member of the Muslim Brotherhood in Jordan (q.v.) and has been a member of the Parliament since 1956. He was born in al-Zarqa and graduated from al-Azhar University in Egypt. Jammu headed many voluntary associations, such as the Islamic Education Society, and became the Mayor of al-Zarqa. He became State Minister for Parliamentary Affairs in 1993.

JARRAR, BASSAM. Jarrar is a leading figure of *Hamas* (q.v.) *(Harakat al-Muqawama al-Islamiyya)* in the Gaza District.

AL-JAYSH AL-ISLAMI LI AL-INQADH (ISLAMIC ARMY OF SAL-VATION). This Algerian fundamentalist group came about as a result of the unification of different fundamentalist forces under the leadership of Abbasi Madani and 'Ali Bilhaj (qq.v.), who became the leaders of the Islamic Salvation Front (FIS) (q.v.). It is formed of three main groups. The first is the Armed Islamic Movement, which is headed by 'Abd al-Qadir Shubuti, and this movement is loyal to the FIS. The second is the *Harakat al-Dawla al-Islamiyya* (The Movement of the Islamic State), which is led by a former army officer, Sa'id Makhlufi, who called for civil disobedience—a demand that led to the arrest of the Salvation leadership in June 1991. The third group is the Armed Islamic Group (q.v.) (*al-Jama'a al-Islamiyya al-Musallaha*), which, for the most part, is made up of Algerians who fought in Afghanistan, and has lost many of its leaders, like al-Sayih 'Atiyya.

JAYSH MUHAMMAD (MUHAMMAD'S ARMY). Jaysh Muhammad is an underground militant group that appeared in 1991 in Jordan and is headed by Samih Abu Muhammad. One hundred and fifty of its members were arrested for planning terrorist activities, including the assassination of public figures. According to Jordanian government sources, *Jaysh Muhammad* receives financial support from the Islamic movement and from funds donated to *al-Afghan al-'Arab* (q.v.) in Afghanistan and Palestine. See also *AL-AFGHAN AL-'ARAB*.

AL-JAZA'I, AHMAD. See *AL-AFGHAN AL-'ARAB*.

JERUSALEM DAY (*YAWM AL-QUDS*). The celebration of the Muslims' right over Jerusalem was inaugurated by Ayatollah Khomeini (q.v.) as a national day in Iran to support the revolutionary Palestinian Islamic movements that work toward liberating Jerusalem. It is celebrated every year on the last Friday of Ramadan, and huge numbers of demonstrators attend it. It is celebrated by many Islamic movements, especially Shi'ite, all over the Islamic world. See also ISRAEL.

JIHAD (STRUGGLE). Although struggle (*jihad*) aims at transforming any institution that opposes and does not allow Islam (q.v.) to be freely practiced, it is neither suicide nor a campaign of atrocities. Hasan al-Banna (q.v.), although not as radical as Sayyid Qutb (q.v.), argues that Islamic *jihad* is not a message of aggression and ambition. Its universalism (q.v.)

is for the protection of *da'wa* (call [q.v.]), and a guarantee for peace (q.v.), and a fulfillment of the divine mission of justice (q.v.) and right.

Jihad has basic characteristics like realism, which means that Islam faces with *da'wa* and refutation incorrect conceptions and belief. It also faces with power and *jihad* those regimes and authorities based on such incorrect conceptions. For the fundamentalists *jihad* is a movement that can operate in stages and may need a long period of time and numerous efforts as well as good organization. Another characteristic is the need for continuity, which may take many forms of activism (q.v.) (*haraki-yya*) when not in contradiction with Islam, like writing, assisting others, teaching, self-discipline, and other activities. The last characteristic is that relations between Muslim and non-Muslim societies occur only if two conditions are met: first, that Islam is the basis of international relations, second, that Islam is permitted peacefully to propagate its call without barriers imposed by any political regime or power. The freedom (q.v.) to accept or reject Islam is central for tolerating non-Muslim societies.

Radical fundamentalists cannot accept the argument that Islam launches *jihad* only for defensive purposes, because Islam is not defensive but rather a defense of man. The fundamentalists argue that the thinkers who claim that *jihad* is only defensive have been defeated spiritually and mentally and do not distinguish between the method (q.v.) of this religion (q.v.) in rejecting compulsion to embrace Islam and its method in destroying those material and political forces which stand between man and his God (q.v.). Those who see *jihad* as being only defensive do not understand Islam. They argue that it is true that Islam defends the land on which it exists, but it also struggles to establish the Islamic order wherever possible and to abolish the *jahili* societies (q.v.). *Jihad* is then launched to eradicate paganism (q.v.) (*jahiliyya*) and to uphold divine governance (q.v.) (*hakimiyya*).

In particular, the fundamentalists are concerned with the state's denial of the activists' right to propagate their understanding of Islam and to educate people in political Islam. Thus, freedom of propagation is basic to the fundamentalists, because it is the natural way to call people to their ideas. Any obstruction of the propagation is thus interpreted as standing against Islam itself, because Islam is essentially a call for change. Such a situation leads to the necessity of setting up a vanguard (q.v.) whose raison d'être is struggle (*jihad*) against the institutions standing against the propagation of Islam. Such a vanguard, for Hasan al-Banna, Abu al-A'la al-Mawdudi (q.v.), and Sayyid Qutb, is responsible for making people aware of the existing inhuman conditions of humanity and the need to reorganize human institutions on the principles of *tawhid* (q.v.) and justice. Assumption of power should ideally be the result of popular conviction. Fundamentalists' insistence on the freedom of the people to adopt this philosophy (q.v.) of life springs from their confidence that Islam is more natural than other religions and consequently will triumph.

Radicals like Sayyid Qutb, Abu al-A'la al-Mawdudi, Abu al-Hasan al-Nadawi (q.v.), and 'Abd al-Jawad Yasin argue that *jihad* is launched in order to establish God's divinity (q.v.) (*uluhiyya*) and to negate any other *uluhiyya*. Those individuals, methods, and systems that stand against the establishment of God's *uluhiyya* are therefore aggressors against God and live in paganism. Their removal becomes a must for the fulfillment of God's governance and *rububiyya* (lordship). The role of revolution (q.v.) is, then, the liberation (q.v.) of humanity from the governments and societies and systems that are structured on positive laws and legislation (q.v.), instead of *al-Shari'a* (q.v.) (Islamic Law) and legislation. The alternative must, therefore, be a pure and uncompromising Islamic form of government, a Muslim society and an Islamic system (q.v.) (*nizam*).

The practical agenda set by radical fundamentalists like Abu al-A'la al-Mawdudi, Sayyid Qutb, and Ayatollah Khomeini (q.v.) is to "struggle" to include the following: material and moral defense of the *umma* (q.v.) as the first task of the revolution, annihilation of any obstacle before the Islamic *da'wa* as the second, and the establishment of God's governance and fighting the aggressors who have usurped this governance as the third. Hence, every system that is based on unbelief (q.v.) and tyranny (q.v.) (*taghut*) must be destroyed. No justification of the status quo is allowed by the fundamentalists because the task of Islam is to effect change. The fundamentalists stress the importance of *tawhid* (q.v.) as a political principle and turn, like *al-Khawarij* (q.v.), its fundamental formula, "no God but Allah," into a revolution against worldly authorities that apply their own laws and legislation.

Ayatollah Khomeini, Qutb, and others use the Qur'anic text (q.v.) in order to make their point and argue that the Qur'an (q.v.) is full of descriptions such as *shirk* (polytheism) and *taghut* (tyranny) for those systems and governments that are not Islamic. Muslims are therefore responsible for eliminating them and for preparing the proper environment where a new virtuous generation can destroy the thrones of the tyrants. This is an obligation of all Muslims, wherever they are, so that an Islamicly inspired political revolution can be induced. See also ISLAMIC ACTION ORGANIZATION; ISRAEL; *AL-JIHAD AL-ISLAMI* IN THE

WEST BANK AND GAZA STRIP; KHOMEINISM; *AL-MAHDIYYA*; MONOTHEISTIC RELIGIONS; *MUJAHIDIN KHALQ*; MUSLIM BROTHERHOOD.

JIHAD **GROUP IN EGYPT.** See *JAMA'AT AL-JIHAD AL-ISLAMI*.

JIHAD **GROUP** (*JAMA'AT AL-JIHAD*) **IN YEMEN.** See *HIZB AL-TA-JAMMU' AL-YEMENI LI AL-ISLAH*.

AL-JIHAD AL-ISLAMI FI LUBNAN. This organization, *al-Jihad al-Islami*, is considered to be part of *Hizbullah* (q.v.) in Lebanon and is used by it to conduct violent actions. It has been implicated in the bombings of the U.S. embassy in Beirut and the U.S. Marine headquarters of the Multinational Forces as well as in the kidnapping of foreign nationals. See also *HIZBULLAH*; TWA HIJACK.

AL-JIHAD AL-ISLAMI (ISLAMIC *JIHAD*) **IN LIBYA.** This party was formed in the early 1970s with an ideology similar to that of the Islamic *Jihad* in Egypt (q.v.). Mu'ammar al-Qaddafi tried in 1973 and 1986–1987 to undermine its underground structure after it launched many terrorist acts. Now, it seems to be gathering more ground than before and is becoming more active.

AL-JIHAD AL-ISLAMI **IN THE WEST BANK AND GAZA STRIP.** The 1967 Arab-Israeli war was a turning point in the development of Islamic movements. This war not only questioned the legitimacy (q.v.) of the secular and nationalistic tendencies and states but even challenged the authority of the long-standing religious movements led by the Muslim Brotherhood (q.v.) (*al-Ikhwan al-Muslimin*). From the perspective of the Islamic *Jihad* movement, the *Ikhwan* experienced three phases: (1) the phase of Hasan al-Banna (q.v.), the phase of revitalization, (2) the second phase, "the phase of crisis and retreat," which was the period following al-Banna's assassination until 1967, and (3) the phase of differentiation from other movements that started in 1976 and continues to the present.

   In the mid-1970s, out of the ranks of the *Ikhwan* there emerged *al-Takfir wa al-Hijra*, or *Jama'at al-Muslimin* (q.v.), Islamic *Jihad* group, or *Jama'at al-Jihad al-Islami* (q.v.), and Salih Sirriyya's (q.v.) group. Shaykh Ya'qub Qarash, who maintained good relations with the Palestine Liberation Organization (PLO), was one of the first people to posit the necessity of facing the Israeli occupation in the Occupied Territories and called for *jihad* (q.v.) (struggle).

Shaykh Muhammad Abu Tair of Jerusalem, a fundamentalist closely related to the Palestinian Fatah, was an active member of the movement. In 1985, he was freed in a prisoner exchange between the Palestinians and the Israelis. Also Shaykh As'ad al-Tamimi, who was deported to Jordan in 1970, had called to eliminate the state of the Jews and to launch *jihad* against it.

In Israel (q.v.), a trend within the ranks of the *Ikhwan* that called itself *Usrat al-Jihad* appeared in 1979 and was led by Shaykh 'Abd Allah Nimr Darwish, who, after being imprisoned for three years gave up his revolutionary Islamic vision and called for an Israeli-Palestinian coexistence. After 1970, several Palestinian students of Gaza joined Egyptian universities. Their presence in Egypt close to the *Ikhwan* played a major role in the creation of new ideas. The *Ikhwan*'s lack of sufficient response to the Palestinian cause was the main reason behind these students' decision to leave the *Ikhwan*. During the period 1967–1970, questions started arising concerning both the *Ikhwan*'s position with respect to the occupation and the practical steps the *Ikhwan* have taken to weaken it. The *Ikhwan* justified its noninvolvement in the armed resistance of the occupation by stating that the leadership of the struggle was not in Islamic hands.

There is no supranational organization of the Islamic *Jihad*, and it does not have any one central organization in the Islamic world, this despite the ideological closeness and cooperation among the various *Jihad* organizations. Nineteen eighty is considered the official year for the establishment of the Islamic *Jihad* movement in Palestine, founded by Fathi al-Shiqaqi and 'Abd al-'Aziz 'Awda (qq.v.) from the Gaza Strip. Whereas Shiqaqi is considered the military leader of the Islamic *Jihad*, 'Awda (q.v.) is its spiritual leader. 'Awda has a very charismatic personality and is a very respectable religious figure. Shiqaqi and 'Awda come from the new Muslim generation, men in their thirties or early forties, who are mainly professionals and come from poor social backgrounds. Their activities are characterized by tight organization, strict discipline, and total secrecy.

Members of *Jihad* are religious fundamentalists who are ready to risk their lives. The Israeli prisons played a vital role in recruiting followers because although several *Jihad* leaders were imprisoned, they indoctrinated other prisoners. The main geographical concentration of *Jihad* is in the Gaza Strip, yet its presence in the West Bank is constantly increasing. Also, there is a growing presence for *al-Jihad* within the body of the students of the universities in the Occupied Territories.

Jihad derives its thought and ideology from the Islamic tradition in general. Nevertheless, three Islamic personalities are of special importance: first, Hasan al-Banna (q.v.), who is considered to be the Islamic leader who founded a new Islamic revivalist movement that united reformist and the *Salafi* movements; second, Sayyid Qutb (q.v.), who occupied a special role because of his intellectual and ideological discourse, especially on revolution (q.v.) and armed revolt. Qutb, who embodies radical opposition to authority and rejection of compromise, became the real symbol of Islamic revolution; and third, Shaykh 'Izz al-Din al-Qassam, who became the first symbol of the ideology of *jihad* in the Islamic *Jihad* movement. The movement considers Qassam to be the first leader of the Palestinian armed *Intifada* in the modern history (q.v.) of Palestine and the real father of the Palestinian armed revolution. Al-Qassam was born in Syria in 1881 and was taught in al-Azhar by Shaykh Muhammad 'Abdu (q.v.).

From the beginning, al-Qassam called for confronting British imperialism and Zionist settlements in Palestine. There are similarities between what al-Qassam did to the British and what *al-Jihad* is doing to the Israeli occupation. Al-Qassam combined the call (q.v.) for *jihad* with real *jihad* activities. Again, al-Qassam chose his followers carefully from the poor and adopted strict organizational methods, and so did *al-Jihad*. In both cases a new member had to go through a period of rigorous testing before he was recruited to join the secret cells or circles, which know nothing about each other. Al-Qassam trusted the poor of Palestine, and *al-Jihad* has followed suit. Nevertheless, *al-Jihad*, like al-Qassam, refuses to include the notion of class in its ideology. Just as al-Qassam treated the British and Zionists in Palestine equally, similarly the Islamic *Jihad* views Israel and America as two sides of the same coin.

The Islamic *Jihad* took its basic positions with respect to exercising *jihad* in Palestine from several sources, including the Iranian Revolution of 1979 (q.v.), the radical tradition of the Muslim Brotherhood (Sayyid Qutb), and the experience of the Islamic *Jihad* in Egypt (q.v.). The Iranian Revolution of 1979 made it possible to view the Palestinian cause as an Islamic cause; *al-Jihad* group in Egypt legitimized resisting an infidel authority as a religious duty. Israel is treated not only as an occupier of land but also as part of *Dar al-Islam*, with the aim of dividing the Islamic world.

Suicidal, or martyr, operations are considered a major way of fighting

Israel. The particularity of the Islamic *Jihad* is its emphasis on the dialectical relationships between *jihad* and true religion (q.v.). Its ideology clearly combines religion and nationalism and aims to establish an Islamic state (q.v.) and to eradicate Israel. Palestine is viewed as the central cause for the entire Muslim world.

Al-Jihad gives priority to the elimination of Israel, refuses any form of recognition of Israel, and opposes all the proposed political solutions. The main factor that has focused attention on the Islamic *Jihad* has been its armed struggle against Israeli occupation, and *al-Jihad* differs in this domain from the other factions that practice *jihad*. Up until the *Intifada* took place, *al-Jihad* and the PLO did not cooperate, because *al-Jihad* views the PLO's goal of establishing a secular state in Palestine as contradictory to the Islamic view of history.

As to Fatah, it views the relationship between itself and the Islamic *Jihad* as a relationship of independence and intersection. And since 1982, a trend within the Fatah began to support the movement of Islamic *Jihad*. This movement formed a parallel wing to *al-Jihad* inside the Fatah movement, and it was called the Islamic *Jihad* as well. It provided political, military, and economic support to *al-Jihad* in the Occupied Territories. It was led by Muhammad Bassam al-Tamimi (al-Hamidi), one of the major military figures in Fatah who was, along with two other Palestinians, assassinated in Cyprus on 14 February 1988 by the Israeli intelligence. After the outbreak of the *Intifada* in 1987, *al-Jihad* admitted the existence of some coordination with Fatah. It has been careful not to clash with any other Palestinian force, whether Islamic or secular.

Owing to the continuous blows that *al-Jihad* received from the Israeli authorities, it could not keep up its leading role. The opposition between *al-Jihad* and the PLO concerning Israel began appearing clearly during and after the decision of the 19th round of the National Palestinian Council to accept UN Resolution 242, Oslo agreements, and the establishment of the Palestinian National Authority. See also 'AWDA, 'ABD AL-'AZIZ; ISRAEL; AL-SHIQAQI, FATHI; VIOLENCE.

AL-JIHAD ORGANIZATION (*MUNAZZAMAT AL-JIHAD*). *Al-Jihad* Organization is one of the radical fundamentalist organizations in Yemen that tried to carry out violent attacks against its political opponents like Salih 'Abbad Muqbil, a member of the politburo of *al-Hizb al-Ishtiraki*. Three of its members acknowledged membership in this secretive organization (*Munazzamat al-Jihad*). This organization has many branches in different districts, and its members have received intensive training in camps near San'a. Their main targets were the members of the Socialist Party. The government of South Yemen chased it in 1991 when 500 members were jailed. Many members of the organization who fought in Afghanistan in the mid-1980s then received the support of 'Abd Allah al-Ahmar (q.v.) before the unity of the two Yemens in 1990. The leader of *al-Jihad* is Ahmad Salih 'Abd al-Karim. Some observers link this organization to *Tajammu' al-Islah* (q.v.), but the organization moved on its own toward political assassination and violence (q.v.). See also EXTREMISM.

JUDAISM. According to Islamic fundamentalism (q.v.), Judaism and Christianity (q.v.), which were originally monotheistic religions, have lost their true meaning, and humans have changed and corrupted the religions' divine meaning to suit their own interests. Although Judaism is true in principle, and the Qur'an (q.v.) speaks of Jews as having a divine message, it also speaks of their disobedience to God (q.v.) and of manipulating their divine laws for political and material interests, which led to their condemnation by God. Fundamentalism further explains that modern history, especially the occupation of Palestine, testifies to the disregard of Jews to the rights of others, to Muslims and Christians in the Holy Places in Palestine, and to their dependence on physical power and manipulation of other people. See also CHRISTIANITY; GOD; ISRAEL; MONOTHEISTIC RELIGIONS; *TAWHID*; WESTERN CIVILIZATION.

JUNDULLAH. See SOLDIERS OF GOD IN LEBANON; SOLDIERS OF GOD IN EGYPT.

JURISPRUDENCE (*AL-FIQH*). Many fundamentalists call for developing jurisprudence in order to make Islam workable with modernity (q.v.). Some thinkers, like Hasan al-Turabi (q.v.), even call for the founding of a modern jurisprudence that is not based on history (q.v.) but rather on modern experience. The fundamentalists believe that a modern Islamic jurisprudence that is based on freedom (q.v.) of research and is not hindered by past restrictions imposed by the jurists and state interference seems capable of providing Muslims with the necessary instruments for the onset of revival. The fundamentalists in general do not view Islamic jurisprudence as normative in nature but as a reflection of historical needs that may not suit modern Islamic society (q.v.). The normative science for the fundamentalists is only *al-Shari'a* (q.v.) (Islamic Law), and not its interpretation (q.v.), that is, jurisprudence.

In the process of writing a modern jurisprudence, the Islamic state's (q.v.) role should be formal, that is, to conduct *shura* (q.v.) (consultation) and *ijma'* (q.v.) (consensus), and therefore to codify communal opinions. It must refrain from forcing a specific view of jurisprudence on the public. It must also allow a new breed of scholars to develop and restructure Islamic jurisprudence. Official institutions and jurists have no right to seize the communal rights of legislating and thinking. See also APOSTASY; CALIPHATE; FUNDAMENTALS; HISTORY; *IJMA'*; ISLAM; PAST; *SHURA*; *TAQLID*; THEOCRACY; AL-TURABI, HASAN.

JURIST'S GUARDIAN. See *WALIY AL-FAQIH.*

JUSTICE (*AL-'ADALA*). To fundamentalists like Sayyid Qutb and Hasan al-Banna (qq.v.), but not to Abu al-A'la al-Mawdudi (q.v.), the revolutionary role of Islam (q.v.) does not end with the establishment of an Islamic state (q.v.), but extends itself to the realization of justice on the whole earth. For them, social, legal, and international justice must replace all existing kinds of injustice. Because Islam's target is humanity and the world, fundamentalists aim at spreading justice and providing security to all peoples and religions. As such, Islam must become the overall basis of the world order (q.v.).

From this point of view, the fundamentalists make it an Islamic duty to enjoin good and forbid evil (*al-amr bi al-ma'ruf wa al-nahy 'an al-munkar*), which includes spreading justice and protecting the weak from injustice. Such moral idealism makes Islam clearly distinguishable from all other systems. Al-Banna outlines this idealism under four characteristics: unwavering will, fixed commitment, great sacrifice, and correct knowledge (q.v.). This makes the *umma* (q.v.) (nation) a great moral and psychological force that is just internally and externally. Every nation that enjoys these characteristics can set up a high civilization (q.v.) of freedom and justice and renew itself. But the nation that lacks any of these characteristics is doomed to injustice and nothingness. Al-Banna makes justice a condition for any future success and even for correct worship. Sheer numbers without appropriate feelings of solidarity leads the nation to be overcome by other nations. Weak morality (q.v.) ends up in material and political loss.

For Sayyid Qutb the absence of justice leads to aggravating self-interest. Self-interest weakens communal solidarity, whereas mutual responsibility (q.v.) (*takaful*) strengthens that solidarity, itself a religious duty on all of the society. Although Qutb, for instance, argues that justice is social in nature, it may turn into a political responsibility carried out by the state—such a responsibility includes education, health, proper jobs, and so forth. Although the state's interference must be limited, in reality and in practice, any failure of society to be just would lead to the state's moral responsibility to distribute justice in society.

For radical fundamentalists, although the state's actions are of a supplementary nature, they ultimately replace as well as exclude institutions of civil society. Interest groups are allowed only if their objectives are broad like the spreading of justice. Women's liberation (q.v.) movements along Western models are not welcomed or included, because their freedom (q.v.) to pursue their narrow personal interests away from the family weakens society. A good society is then composed of groups sharing similar interests and perceptions of life as well as unified political orientations. Its fountainhead is justice. See also AL-AFGHANI, JAMAL AL-DIN; CAPITALISM; CONSCIOUSNESS; *AL-DA'WA AL-ISLAMI-YYA*; FADLALLAH, MUHAMMAD HUSAYN; *HIZB AL-HAQQ*; *HIZB JABHAT AL-'AMAL AL-ISLAMI*; *HIZBULLAH*; ISLAMIC REVOLUTION OF IRAN; ISLAMIC STATE; *JIHAD*; JUSTICE AND CHARITY GROUP; METHOD; MORALITY; PAGANISM; PEACE; POPULAR MOVEMENT; REVOLUTION; *AL-SHARI'A*; SOCIAL JUSTICE; *AL-TAJAMMU' AL-YEMENI LI AL-ISLAH*; *TAWHID*; UNION OF POPULAR FORCES; UNIVERSALISM; WORLD ORDER.

JUSTICE AND CHARITY GROUP (*JAMA'AT AL-'ADL WA AL-IHSAN*). This group, which is headed by 'Abd al-Salam Yasin, believes that justice (q.v.) is a popular demand and a divine command. Charity should be an educational program that takes care of the individual and the community. Yasin has been influenced by the radical political discourse of Sayyid Qutb (q.v.). Although Yasin does not call for violent actions because a religious call does not fit with violence (q.v.), and although he does not employ the doctrine of paganism (q.v.) (*jahiliyya*) between 1988–1991, the Moroccan government nonetheless suspended the work of 25 Friday-prayer preachers who were suspected of being close to the group. Yasin himself was arrested and released and was called upon to participate in the construction of the state.

The group does not reject democracy (q.v.), although it does not think that democracy as practiced in Morocco provides Moroccans with appropriate rights. It also calls for freedom (q.v.) of expression and the establishment of the Islamic society (q.v.).

-K-

KABIR, RABIH (1954–   ). Kabir is one of the leaders of the Islamic Salvation Front (FIS) in Algeria (q.v.). Kabir was born to a religious family that opposed French domination, and his father was part of the Algerian liberation movement. During his childhood, he met many important scholars, including 'Abd al-Hamid Ibn Badis (q.v.), the leader of *Jam'iyyat al-'ulama' al-Muslimin* (q.v.), Bashir al-Ibrahimi (q.v.), and 'Abd al-Latif Sultanti. Kabir entered the university in 1975, at a time when the devout were too shy to pray at the university. He became acquainted with the emerging Islamic movement at the university and finally joined it.

During the elections of 1991, this physics teacher became assistant to 'Abd al-Qadir Hashshani, and together they led the "Temporary Executive National Council" although the elected leadership was in prison. But Kabir was also arrested suddenly along with Abbasi Madani and 'Ali Bilhaj (qq.v.), although he was released in 1992. He then went abroad and presently lives in exile in Germany, where he has been given political asylum, and serves as the Front's official spokesman. He is very active in representing the objectives of the FIS.

KAFAWIN, AHMAD (1948–   ). Kafawin has been a member of the politburo of *Hizb Jabhat al-'Amal al-Islami* (q.v.) (Islamic Action Front Party in Jordan) since 1994. Kafawin was a member of the Lower House of Parliament between 1989 and 1993. He received his degree in literature and geography from the University of Damascus, then worked at the Ministry of Transportation. Kafawin later became a director of a religious school. Since 1970, he has given speeches and lessons at mosques.

KAJAR, KAMAL. See *AL-SULAYMANIYYA*.

KANJ, ZUHAYR. See MUSLIM SCHOLARS' ASSOCIATION.

KASASBA, AHMAD (1948–   ). Kasasba has been a member of the executive bureau of *Hizb Jabhat al-'Amal al-Islami* in Jordan (q.v.) (Islamic

Action Front Party) since 1994. He was also a member of the fundamentalist bloc in the Lower House of Parliament in 1993.

KASHANI, ABU AL-QASIM (1882–1962). Kashani was one of the leading religious leaders of Iran during the national movement of the 1950s. He studied in al-Najaf, Iraq, and became a *mujtahid* in his twenties. Also, he fought the British colonization and was sentenced to death but escaped to Iraq in 1921. He worked against the Shah of Iran and founded along with others the Movement of Iranian Nationalists. This time, Kashani was exiled. After World War II, he worked with Palestinians against the establishment of Israel (q.v.). In Iran, *Fada'iyan-i Islam* (q.v.) assassinated two Prime Ministers, and Kashani was implicated. After an attempt on the Shah's life, he was exiled to Lebanon. In 1950, he went back to Iran and became a member of the Parliament. He had numerous followers, including the National Front, headed by Muhammad Musaddaq. When Musaddaq came to power in 1952 Kashani broke with him over the issue of control. Kashani wanted to give more power to the clergy. His political power ended with the fall of Musaddaq.

Kashani called for the combination of the political and the religious. Some analysts believe that he was the precursor to Ayatollah Khomeini's (q.v.) ideas and actions, because he argued that the '*ulama*' had a political role to play, and *al-Shari'a* (q.v.) (Islamic Law) had a social role in society. See also *FADA'IYAN-I ISLAM*; WARRIORS OF ISLAM SOCIETY.

KAWADIR AL-BINA' (BUILDING CADRES). This is one of the existing political trends in Iran today. *Kawadir al-Bina'* usually refers to the supporters of the former President 'Ali Akbar Rafsanjani (q.v.). Rafsanjani grouped together different segments of society during the elections of 1996 in order to support current development policies. *Kawadir al-Bina'* focuses on the need for heavy industrialization.

Its base of support includes the commercial community, and some university circles, and a great number of state employees and shopkeepers. It has not taken its final form or developed its platform.

KAWJAQ, DAWUD (1926–). Kawjaq was born in Na'ur and obtained his B.A. in geography and literature from the University of Damascus in 1960. Kawjaq has worked in educational institutes and was elected to the Jordanian Lower House of Parliament in 1989. He is a member of the executive bureau of the Muslim Brotherhood in Jordan (q.v.).

KHALID, KHALID MUHAMMAD (1920–1997). Khalid graduated from the Faculty of *al Shari'a* of al-Azhar University in 1947. He worked as a teacher then in the Directorate of Culture at the Ministry of Culture, where Khalid later became a supervisor. He has written dozens of books and published articles in many newspapers and magazines. Although Khalid started as a reformer and was concerned primarily with the issue of social justice (q.v.), he moved closer to the fundamentalist camp and became concerned with the establishment of the Islamic state (q.v.) on the basis of *shura* (q.v.) (consultation), which he considered to be a force of liberation (q.v.).

KHALIFA, ABU AL-'ABBAS. See POPULAR DEFENSE FORCES.

KHALIFA, MAJID (1948–). Majid Khalifa is a member of the executive bureau of *Hizb Jabhat al-'Amal al-Islam* (q.v.) (Islamic Action Front Party). Khalifa was born in Salt and received his B.A. in law from the University of Damascus. He also received an M.A. and a Ph.D. from Cairo University and was the Dean of the Faculty of Law at the University of Jordan from 1982–1993. Khalifa was appointed Minister of Justice in 1991 and was elected to the Lower House of Parliament for the period of 1989–1993.

KHALIFA, MUHAMMAD 'ABD AL-RAHMAN (1919–). Muhammad Khalifa was the General Guide of the Muslim Brotherhood in Jordan (q.v.) during the period of 1953–1994. Khalifa was born in Salt and received a diploma in agriculture from Tulkarm and a B.A. in law from a law institute in Jerusalem. He worked as a prosecutor and judge and became Deputy General Guide of the Brotherhood. Khalifa was a member of the Lower House of Parliament from 1956 to 1961. Since 1953, he has worked as an independent lawyer. See also INTERNATIONAL ORGANIZATION OF THE MUSLIM BROTHERHOOD; MUSLIM BROTHERHOOD IN JORDAN.

KHAMENE'I, 'ALI (1939–). Ayatollah Khamene'i became the third President of the Islamic Republic of Iran in 1981 and the second *waliy al-faqih* (q.v.), or supreme spiritual and political guide, after the death of Ayatollah Khomeini (q.v.) in 1989. As a student and associate of Khomeini, he opposed the Shah and was arrested many times. After the revolution he dropped his membership in the Revolutionary Council (q.v.) and presided over the Council of Defense. Khamene'i was also a founding member and Secretary-General of the Islamic Republican Party (q.v.). He along with 'Ali Akbar Rafsanjani and Muhammad Bahishti (qq.v.) played a central role in the dismissal of President Abul Hasan Bani Sadr (q.v.) from the Presidency of the Republic and the collapse of the power of Muhammad Shari'atmadari (q.v.). See also FADLALLAH, MU-HAMMAD HUSAYN; ISLAMIC REPUBLICAN PARTY; KHATAMI, MUHAMMAD; *MAJLIS TASHKHIS MASLAHAT AL-NIZAM*; *MARJI' AL-TAQLID*; MUNTAZARI, HUSAYN 'ALI; *WALIY AL-FAQIH*.

KHATAMI, MUHAMMAD (1943–). This religious Shi'ite Iranian clerk was elected as President of Iran in 1997, defeating 'Ali Akbar Natiq Nuri (q.v.), who received the blessing of the religious establishment, including supposedly Iran's supreme guide, Ayatollah Khamene'i (q.v.). Khatami received 69.7 percent of the 29.7 million votes cast. He is considered a moderate and liberal intellectual.

In 1982, Khatami became the Minister for Culture and Guidance, and then was removed in 1990 from the ministry because of his views as a liberal theologian and politician who advocated some measure of freedom. He later became the director of the Library of Tehran. He also supervised, under Ayatollah Khomeini (q.v.), the *Kihan* Newspaper. He was removed under the pretext of the "invasion of decadent ideas from the U.S. and Europe." He became advisor to President 'Ali Akbar Rafsanjani (q.v.).

Khatami attended the seminary in Qum, yet he studied Western philosophy. He has mastered many languages, including Arabic, English, and German, and has numerous publications on scientific, political, and religious topics. He is the first President to lack revolutionary credentials. His campaign speeches, which he wrote himself, promised the activation of civil society, freedom (q.v.), and tolerance. Khatami intends to control the extremist elements, especially the Revolutionary Guards (q.v.) and intelligence services. His election has been considered by most world observers as an extremely significant event in the modern history of Iran and its Islamic Revolution (q.v.). See also MUNTAZARI, HUSAYN 'ALI; NURI, 'ALI NATIQ; RAFSANJANI, 'ALI AKBAR; *RUHANIYYAT MUBARIZ*; *RUHANIYYUN MUBARIZ*; SORUSH, 'ABD AL-KARIM.

AL-KHATIB, 'ABD AL-KARIM. Al-Khatib is the General Secretary of the Democratic Constitutional Popular Movement (q.v.), which is an umbrella organization for the fundamentalists. He held many important posts in the Moroccan government, including Speaker of the Parliament. He is a well-known doctor and is a respected international figure. He has entertained many well-known figures, like Nelson Mandela of South Africa and 'Abbasi Madani (q.v.), head of the Islamic Salvation of Algeria Front (q.v.), whom he received at his home.

The movement started in 1967 after splitting from the Popular Movement (q.v.). Since then it has followed fundamentalist views and refused to participate in the parliamentary elections, which al-Khatib considered to be more like appointments. In 1997, al-Khatib and his movement participated in the Moroccan elections because he felt the 1997 elections would be freer than those held before. He argues that the candidates of his party, which number 142, including three women, are not fundamentalists or Islamists but Muslims. They are not extremist or violent and accept a moderate version of Islam and the parameters of the state—the constitutional monarchy.

Al-Khatib acknowledges that the candidates of the illegal fundamentalist party, *Harakat al-Tawhid wa al-Islah* (Movement for Unification and Reform), headed by Muhammad Yatim and 'Abd al-Ilah Binkiran, are running under the Democratic Constitutional Popular Party. But he said that these people and others from *Harakat al-Tawhid* have joined his party. However, al-Khatib rejects any connection with the Justice and Charity Group (q.v.) (*Jama'at al-'Adl wa al-Ihsan*), headed by 'Abd al-Salam Yasin, because it views participation in the electoral process as against Islam and, instead, seeks isolation. See also DEMOCRATIC CONSTITUTIONAL POPULAR MOVEMENT; POPULAR MOVEMENT.

AL-KHATIB, MUHAMMAD. Al-Khatib is considered to be the strongman and one of the old guard of the Muslim Brotherhood (q.v.) in Egypt. Currently, he heads the *da'wa* (call [q.v.]) section.

KHATTAB, DHIB 'ABD ALLAH (1948–). Khattab was born in Amman, and studied medicine at the University of Cairo, and then continued his specialization as an ophthalmologist at the University of London. He worked as a physician at the medical city of Husayn. Khattab was elected to Jordan's Lower House of Parliament in 1993. He is a member of the Muslim Brotherhood and *Hizb Jabhat al-'Amal al-Islami* (qq.v.) (the Islamic Action Front Party) in Jordan. Khattab resigned from the front and the fundamentalist bloc in the Parliament in 1996.

KHAWARIJ. See ISLAMIC STATE.

KHAYYAT, 'ABD AL-'AZIZ (1924–). Dr. Khayyat was born in Nablus in the West Bank. He joined the University of al-Azhar in Cairo in 1939 and became a close associate of Hasan al-Banna (q.v.), leader of the Muslim Brotherhood (q.v.). Khayyat along with others, including Mustapha al-Siba'i (q.v.), distributed pamphlets in Egypt against foreign intervention in Iraq. The others were arrested for three months, and he collected funds to help them. He officially joined the Muslim Brotherhood in 1942 and worked in the Department of Communication with the Islamic World. Khayyat left Cairo in 1947 on a mission from al-Banna to educate the youth in Palestine, Jordan, and Syria. During that period, he became one of the representatives of the Brotherhood in Palestine.

Ten years later, he split with the Brotherhood because he did not like the way it spread its message after the death of al-Banna. Later, he joined Taqiy al-Din al-Nabahani (q.v.), the leader of *Hizb al-Tahrir al-Islami* (q.v.) (Islamic Liberation Party), and became one of its important members. He was imprisoned by the Jordanian government but was later appointed Minister of Religious Endowment and the Holy Places for times during the period of 1973–1989.

AL-KHILAFA. See CALIPHATE.

KHILKHALI, SHAYKH SADIQ. See *FADA'IYAN-I ISLAM*.

KHOMEINI, AYATOLLAH RUHOLLAH AL-MUSAWI (1902–1989). Khomeini was the leader of the Iranian Revolution of 1979 (q.v.). Khomeini was born in Khomein, the prestigious Shi'ite religious center. His family was religious, and his father was killed because of his opposition to Shah Reza when Khomeini was a few months old. His brother educated him, and Khomeini studied jurisprudence (q.v.) in the established schools of the time.

Khomeini opposed the Shah's rule and criticized it openly in 1944. His main opposition was to the economic conditions, because he wanted the weak to revolt against the system (q.v.) (*nizam*), and he criticized the influence of foreign powers in Iran. The Shah's terror was carried out by his infamous SAVAK, which was reputed to be aided by the CIA. Moreover, Khomeini created an ideology that focused on the governance (q.v.) (*hakimiyya*) of God (q.v.), *jihad* (q.v.) (struggle), unity, interpretation (q.v.) of religion (q.v.) through politics and reason (q.v.) (*ijtihad*) and the Islamic state (q.v.). Thus, he encouraged the people to revolt. His confrontations with the regime began in 1963 when Khomeini was arrested and imprisoned. Later, he was released under popular and clerical protests. However, he told his followers to boycott the parliamentary elections of that year. He was arrested again and exiled to Turkey in 1964 and later to Iraq. Finally he left for France.

Even when he was in exile, Khomeini mobilized the masses in Iran through writings and speeches that were spread by the clerical network that he established and maintained. All his teachings against the West (q.v.) and the regime were taped on cassettes and smuggled into Iran. At weekly Friday-prayers, Khomeini's speeches were played on tapes and distributed to the people. He was very charismatic and appealed to the masses. Moreover, the villagers supported Khomeini because he lived and talked like them. He was viewed as an honest and moral man who promised to help the poor and the farmers. These characteristics of Khomeini helped enhance his influence over the Iranian masses. He was actually the most supported leader. Later he commanded many followers outside Iran, such as Lebanon's *Hizbullah* (q.v.).

All these factors contributed to the spread of Islamic revival, culminating in the mass revolution of 1978–1979 that toppled the Shah's regime and established the Islamic state in Iran. After the revolution, Khomeini led Iran until his death in 1989. To the present day, he is viewed as the one who led a successful revolution to set up the Islamic state. See also APOSTASY; BAHISHTI, MUHAMMAD; BANI SADR, ABUL HASAN; BAZARGAN, MAHDI; COUNCIL OF EXPERTS; *AL-DA'WA AL-ISLAMIYYA* IN IRAQ; *FADA'IYAN-I ISLAM*; FADLALLAH, MUHAMMAD HUSAYN; *FATWA*; GOVERNANCE; *HIZBULLAH*; IRANIAN REVOLUTION OF 1979; ISLAMIC ACTION ORGANIZATION; ISLAMIC FRONT FOR THE LIBERATION OF BAHRAIN; ISLAMIC FUNDAMENTALISM; ISLAMIC REPUBLICAN PARTY; ISLAMIC REVOLUTION OF IRAN; ISLAMIC SOCIETY; ISLAMIC STATE; ISLAMIC YOUTH ORGANIZATION; ISRAEL; *JAMA'AT AL-JIHAD AL-ISLAMI*; JERUSALEM DAY; *JIHAD*; KHAMENE'I, 'ALI; KHATAMI, MUHAMMAD; KHOMEINISM; LIBERATION; LIBERATION MOVEMENT OF IRAN; *MAJLIS TASHKHIS MASLAHAT AL-NIZAM*; *MARJI' AL-TAQLID*; *MUJAHIDIN KHALQ*; MUSLIM PEOPLE'S REPUBLICAN PARTY; MUTAHHARI, MURTAZA; QUTBZADAH, SADIQ; RAFSANJANI, 'ALI AKBAR; REVOLUTION; REVOLUTIONARY GUARDS; RUSHDIE, SALMAN; SHARI'ATI, 'ALI; SHARI'ATMADARI, AYATOLLAH

MUHAMMAD; AL-SHIQAQI, FATHI; SYSTEM; THEOCRACY; UNIVERSALISM; *WALIY AL-FAQIH*.

KHOMEINISM (*KHOMEINIYYA*). During its first decade and a half, the Islamic Republic of Iran remained committed to the double aims of the Ayatollah Khomeini's (q.v.) regime and the institutionalization of the revolution (q.v.) at home and its export abroad. The first goal was largely achieved in a relatively short time. A constitution (q.v.) was adopted, providing for an elected parliamentary form of government under the guidance of *al-Shari'a* (q.v.) (Islamic Law). Khomeini became the ultimate legal authority and the supreme religious and political guide for the state and society in accordance with his stipulation of *waliy al-faqih* (q.v.) (the guardian of the jurist). The export of the revolution, or Khomeinism, became a cornerstone of Iran's foreign policy. The export of the Iranian Revolution of 1979 (q.v.) is embedded in the ideological worldview and religious interpretations of the Imam Khomeini and his ideologues, who have combined a religiously rooted brand of Iranian nationalism with a belief in a transitional mission to spread their version of revolutionary Islam (q.v.), thus paving the way for global Islamic fundamentalism (q.v.). Iran's foreign policy is rooted in Khomeini's understanding of Islam.

However, after 'Ali Akbar Hashimi Rafsanjani (q.v.) was elected President in July 1989, a broadly based *ijma'* (q.v.) (consensus) on the fundamental principles, institutions, and politics of an Islamic policy began to emerge. Muslim activists all over the world were inspired by the success of the Iranian Revolution of 1979, so they made it a springboard in their struggle against unjust regimes. In this way, Iran acted both as a catalyst and initiator of Islamic revolution. Shi'ite uprisings erupted in Saudi Arabia, Bahrain, Kuwait, Pakistan, and Iraq. The tendency in those countries was toward the revitalization of Islamic resurgence and mobilization in line with Khomeini's call.

In Saudi Arabia, communal riots and bombing attacks in November 1995 targeted the American Military Cooperation program headquarters, where a few people were killed, including two Americans. The incident took place along with the stationing of 5,000 U.S. troops in Saudi Arabia. Immediately fingers pointed toward Iran, Sudan, and Iraq.

In Bahrain, communal riots and several coup attempts took place that were directly linked to Iran. Also, terrorist acts, like hijacking, which were attributed to Iranian militants, took place in Kuwait. During the 1970s, Hadi al-Mudarrisi created a network in Bahrain to support Khomeini, who was exiled. Soon after Khomeini's return to Iran, several hundreds of Shi'ite Bahrainis demonstrated in favor of Iran's revolution and clashed with the authorities in August 1979. Muhammad Mudarrisi, who had been expelled from Bahrain in 1980, made regular broadcast appeals from Tehran for an uprising against the ruling dynasty. In 1981, the government thwarted a coup d'état and arrested several members of the Islamic Front for the Liberation of Bahrain (q.v.), a movement inspired by Mudarrisi and financed by Iran. It is worth mentioning that the impact of the Iranian Revolution of 1979 is most noticeable in Bahrain because of its Shi'ite majority and because it was at the Shah's time an Iranian province until 1971 when he formally gave up Iran's long-standing claim to sovereignty over Bahrain.

However, Iran's influence was less dangerous to other Sunnite Gulf states, especially during the Iran-Iraq war, which lasted until 1989. In Iraq, Saddam Hussein was successful in blocking the impact of the Iranian Revolution of 1979, although he is a Sunni ruling a Shi'ite majority (60 percent) predominantly in the south.

The most direct and sustained influence was and still is in Lebanon, a country with a large Shi'ite minority. Imam Musa al-Sadr (q.v.), an Iranian born clergy and the nephew of Muhammad Baqir al-Sadr (q.v.), led the Shi'a into mobilization throughout the 1960s and the 1970s until his "disappearance" in Libya in 1978. Musa al-Sadr was as influential in his revolutionary interpretation of Shi'ite symbolism in Lebanon, as Khomeini was in his revolutionary interpretation (q.v.) of Islam. He established the movement of the *Mahrumin* and *Amal*, which aimed at social, economic, and political reforms. Moreover, the second Israeli invasion of Lebanon in 1982 witnessed the establishment of *Hizbullah* (q.v.). Posters of Khomeini appeared on houses and in streets, and *Hizbullah*'s publications were decorated with his picture.

Egypt, a predominantly Sunnite country, has experienced an indirect Iranian influence because the inspiration of the revolution has reinforced existing Islamic political opportunities without significant intervention by the Iranian government. However, following the Iranian revolution, more radical Islamic groups stepped up violent revolutionary actions against the regime and its accommodation to Israel (q.v.). This culminated in the assassination of President Anwar al-Sadat, who was regarded as a traitor by those movements.

The Iranian influence in Tunisia and Libya was indirect because it only confirmed and accelerated preexisting Islamic trends. Although the Libyan leader Mu'ammar al-Qaddafi supported the Iranian Revolution of 1979, and Tunisian President al-Habib Bourguiba opposed it, both considered it a threat to their regimes. However, in Tunisia, for instance, the Iranian example encouraged Muslim activists to assert their own demands and led to the emergence of *Harakat al-Itijah al-Islami* (q.v.) (Islamic Tendency Movement).

KHOMEINIYYA. See KHOMEINISM.

KHUDAYRI, MUSTAPHA. See *AL-JAMA'AT AL-ISLAMIYYA.*

KHURAYSAT, IBRAHIM (1941–   ). Khuraysat was born in Salt, Jordan, and received a master's degree in Islamic studies from Pakistan. Khuraysat became a Dean of Islamic Society in Zarqa and a member of many philanthropic associations. He is a member of the executive committee of the Muslim Brotherhood (q.v.) and was a member of the Lower House of Parliament in Jordan.

AL-KILANI, IBRAHIM (1937–   ). Al-Kilani is a member of the executive bureau of *Hizb Jabhat al-'Amal al-Islami* in Jordan (q.v.) (the Islamic Action Front Party). He was born in Salt, Jordan, and received his B.A. from the university of Baghdad and a Ph.D. from the University of al-Azhar in 1978. Al-Kilani became Minister of Religious Endowment in 1991 and a member of the Lower House of the Parliament in 1993.

KINI, AYATOLLAH MAHDAWI. See MUHTASHIMI, 'ALI AKBAR.

KISHK, 'ABD AL-HAMID (1933–1996). Kishk is a religious Azharite scholar and a most renowned Egyptian fundamentalist orator, whose speeches on Fridays attracted tens of thousands of people. Kishk was imprisoned and tortured during 'Abd al-Nasir's era and jailed during Anwar al-Sadat's in 1981. He attacked President Sadat for corruption of the army and for his "indecent" wife. His recorded tapes were sold by the tens of thousands. Kishk especially attacked the radical ideologies of Shukri Mustapha and 'Abd al-Salam Faraj (qq.v.). See also *AL-JA-MA'AT AL-ISLAMIYYA.*

KNOWLEDGE (*MA'RIFA*). For the fundamentalists, knowledge is not seen as an end in itself but must be turned into a motivating force for action. Hasan al-Banna (q.v.) puts this relationship in the following manner: The revival of religion (q.v.) aims first at the individual who should become a model for others. Knowledge aims also at developing a consciousness (q.v.) (*wa'iy*) capable by nature of differentiating between what is good and what is bad and of standing against what is unjust so that it becomes a good instrument for achieving the good life and the triumph of good over evil. In the proper ordering and disciplining of the conscience in accordance with the Islamic worldview lies, according to al-Banna, both the true interpretative discourse on knowledge and the secrets of existence. Knowledge like this leads to total commitment to an Islamic way of life.

The fundamentalists like Sayyid Qutb, Abu al-A'la al-Mawdudi, Hasan al-Turabi, 'Umar 'Abd al-Rahman (qq.v.), however, reject human claims to gaining ultimate knowledge, which belongs only to God (q.v.). Human knowledge consists of interpretations of revelation: the text (q.v.) or the Qur'an (qq.v.). For humans cannot understand ultimate causes and, therefore, knowledge. What man can understand philosophically and metaphysically must be grounded in the text. However, science (q.v.) is viewed by the fundamentalist as an instrument of power and livelihood that should not be given interpretative power of ultimate knowledge. The possible knowledge that man can attain must be employed in practical, not theoretical, matters. See also ACTIVISM; APOSTASY; BALANCE; COMPREHENSIVENESS; DIVINITY; GOD; HISTORY; ISLAM; ISLAMIC FUNDAMENTALISM; ISLAMIZATION; JUSTICE; *MARJI' AL-TAQLID*; METHOD; MODERNISM; PAN-ISLAMISM; AL-QUR'AN; QUTB, SAYYID; REASON; RELIGION; REVOLUTION; SYSTEM; TEXT.

KUFAHI, AHMAD MUJALLI (1939–). Kufahi is a member of the executive Bureau of *Hizb Jabhat al-'Amal al-Islami* (q.v.) (the Islamic Action Front Party) in Jordan. Kufahi was born in Irbid and received his B.A. in Islamic Law from the University of Damascus and an M.A. and a Ph.D. in Islamic Law from the University of al-Azhar. He became a lecturer at some Jordanian universities and was elected to the Lower House of Parliament for the period 1989–1993.

KUFR. See UNBELIEF.

KURDISH ISLAMIC MOVEMENT. See *AL-HARAKA AL-ISLAMIYYA AL-KURDIYYA.*

KUSHAN, MUHAMMAD AS'AD. See *AL-NAQSHABANDIYYA*.

AL-KUTLA AL-ISLAMIYYA. See RELIGIOUS BLOC.

-L-

LAJNAT AL-DIFA' 'AN AL-HUQUQ AL-SHAR'IYYA (COMMITTEE FOR DEFENDING THE LEGITIMATE RIGHTS). See AL-MAS'ARI, MUHAMMAD.

LAW OF NATURE. See *FITRA*.

LEAGUE OF ISLAMIC PROPAGATION (*RABITAT AL-DA'WA AL-IS-LAMIYYA*). See AL-NAHNAH, MAHFOUDH.

LEGISLATION (*TASHRI'*). A collective dismissal of the normativeness of past theological readings has moved the fundamentalists from just a political movement that aims at change through ideological orientations to a movement that must find alternative religious, political, and intellectual readings to traditional and modernist Islam (q.v.) and Western readings. Their alternative readings have been centered around the discourse on *tawhid* (q.v.) (Oneness of God) and governance (q.v.) (*hakimiyya*) of God (q.v.). Hasan al-Banna, Sayyid Qutb, and Abu al-A'la al-Mawdudi (qq.v.), for instance, view God as the only mandatory source of legislation, because the goal of an Islamic society (q.v.) must be obedience to Him within the spirit and legislation of Islam.

Thus, emphasizing the need to link even civic ethics to obedience to God, it follows suit, for Qutb, that *tawhid* is not only the liberation (q.v.) of men from bowing to each other, but the center of forming ethical and moral systems as well as the political institutions that serve them. Because Qutb believes that the legislation of moral and ethical systems is a divine matter, man should not impose new ethical or moral values or legislate values. The Muslim society must follow the intuitive moral system (q.v.) (*nizam*) in light of the universal divine Qur'anic norms and legislation. These norms are not humanly derived, and their application does not constitute an imposition on human nature and is therefore necessary for the well-being of man and to avoid human misery.

For Qutb, *al-Shari'a* (q.v.) (Islamic Law) is not a social phenomenon but an eternal phenomenon of postulating the duties and rights of individuals and the state. Thus, the legislation of the basic principles of government, morality (q.v.), and legality is sealed off from human calculation. However, these comprehensive, yet flexible principles are designed to suit all ages and societies, and man's task is to codify from these general principles what is appropriate for his life and society. See also CONSTITUTION; GOD; GOVERNANCE; *HIZBULLAH*; *JIHAD*; AL-QUR'AN; REVOLUTION; *AL-SHARI'A*; *UMMA*.

LEGITIMACY (*AL-SHAR'IYYA*). The fundamentalists employ the lack of human liberation (q.v.) to cast doubt on the legitimacy of modern governments of the Muslim world, because most, if not all, lack religious liberation, political freedom, and consciousness (*wa'iy*) (qq.v.). They argue that contemporary Muslim societies are as well in need of a process of reification of the political and social to the metaphysical. The posing of today's problems away from religious *wa'iy* (consciousness) and in terms of economic and political difficulties may lead to wrong and unsatisfactory solutions. Thus, human governments lack the essential legitimacy to lead and rule.

The fundamentalists view modern Islamic societies as the result of both *taqlid* (traditionalism) and modernism (qq.v.). They are more or less combinations of both because the traditional way of thinking is identified by the people with religion (q.v.). They are modern not because they are developed but in the sense that they are beset by the transported problems of the modern West (q.v.). Doing away with *taqlid* (traditionalism) by renewing the roots and understanding of religion may resolve major problems. The fundamentalists in general do not downplay the importance of acquiring the skills necessary for the creation of an advanced civilization (q.v.). Mere religious consciousness alone cannot trigger a process of working toward the elimination of underdevelopment and the setting up of an efficient administration. See also 'ABD AL-RAHMAN, 'UMAR; APOSTASY; AL-'AWWA, MUHAMMAD SALIM; CALIPHATE; DEMOCRACY; DEMOCRATIC CONSTITUTIONAL POPULAR MOVEMENT; EQUALITY; FIGHTING VANGUARDS; FUNDAMENTALS; AL-GHANNUSHI, RASHID; GOD; GOVERNANCE; GOVERNMENT, FORMS OF; HISTORY; *HIZB AL-TAHRIR AL-ISLAMI*; *HIZBULLAH*; IBN TAYMIYYA, TAQIY AL-DIN; ISLAMIC GOVERNMENT; ISLAMIC SATE; *AL-JIHAD AL-ISLAMI* IN THE WEST BANK AND GAZA STRIP; *MAJLIS AL-SHURA*; METHOD; MUSLIM BROTHERHOOD; MUSLIM BROTHERHOOD, IDEOLOGY OF; MUSTAPHA, SHUKRI; AL-NABAHANI, TAQIY AL-DIN;

PAST; RADICALISM; *AL-SHARI'A*; *SHURA*; *TAWHID*; THEOC-
RACY; WORLD ORDER.

LIBERATION (*AL-TAHRIR*). Liberation for fundamentalism (q.v.) is central to its political thought. It is advocated in order to bring about the
forces of change to effect major transformation in people's lives, without
of course weakening the essence of creed. However, any change must
take into consideration different kinds of social, economic, and political
freedoms (q.v.), which are themselves directed at abolishing materialism
and submissiveness to individuals or things.

For Islamic fundamentalism (q.v.), man's submission to divine *tawhid*
(q.v.) (Oneness of God) makes freedom meaningful and paves the way
for individuals to liberate themselves from enslavement to others. Without *tawhid* man has no superior concept to liberate himself, because a
human-liberating philosophy (q.v.) serves to free him from one ideology
only to have him enslaved to another. *Tawhid* is then a doctrine that liber-
ates man from man and connects him to a higher level of responsibility.
The doctrine of *tawhid*, which could not be metaphysically compre-
hended by man, becomes most important in terms of its function as a
unifying doctrine. For the fundamentalists, freedom grounded in the philosophy of man is materialistic, unjust, relative, and falls shorts of man's
pure nature, or *fitra* (q.v.). *Tawhid* anchors positively divine governance
(q.v.) (*hakimiyya*) in Islamic society (q.v.) and makes revolution (q.v.)
against the paganism (q.v.) (*jahiliyya*) of human rule a necessity. This
gives liberation a different meaning than is practiced by non-Muslim, or
jahili, societies (q.v.).

On the other hand, freedom could be perfected when it is based on a
fitra (intuition) that is liberated from submission to human things, carries
within it correct beliefs, and is motivated by objectives that go beyond
everyday living. For the fundamentalist, although individual pursuit of
things is legitimate, freedom must not mean animalistic or individualis-
tic actions to attain particular earthly gains; in fact, this poses a danger
to society. An act like this constitutes the very opposite of freedom and
enslaves man to his lower instincts and obscures his vision of true freedom. An individual whose main goal in life is pleasure cannot claim to
be free; because freedom only comes from liberty whose essence is the
individual's foregoing animalistic pleasure and living the life of *tawhid*.
See also *IJMA'*; ISLAMIC SALVATION FRONT; ISRAEL; *JIHAD*;
JUSTICE; LEGISLATION; LEGITIMACY; MODERNISM; MODER-

NITY; MORALITY; *AL-SHARI'A*; *SHURA*; SOCIAL JUSTICE; AL-
TURABI, HASAN; WORLD ORDER.

LIBERATION MOVEMENT OF IRAN (*NEHZATE-E AZAI-YE IRAN*).
The movement was sometimes called Freedom Movement of Iran. It was
established in 1960 by the supporters of Muhammad Musaddaq's National Front coalition, Mahdi Bazargan and Sayyid Mahmud Talqani
(qq.v.). This organization was made up of four groups: the Iran Party,
the National Party, the Society of Iranian Socialists, and Liberation
Movement of Iran. In affiliating the movement with the Second National
Front, Bazargan and Talqani added a specifically Islamic coloring to it,
which distinguished it from other political forces. The movement was
willing to accept members from the clergy who criticized the Shah's autocracy yet opposed land reform and women's suffrage, whereas the rest
of the National Front supported such reforms.

However, a split in the second National Front took place, and leaders
of the movement were mostly under arrest or in exile during the period
between 1965 and 1978. However, when the Islamic Revolution of Iran
(q.v.) broke out, the movement was a major player. Mahdi Bazargan became Ayatollah Khomeini's (q.v.) emissary in the southwestern oil
fields. He was able to mobilize people in massive protests on behalf of
the revolutionaries. In 1979, Ayatollah Khomeini appointed Bazargan as
the first Prime Minister after the revolution. However, Bazargan clashed
with hard-line clergymen and their secular allies in the Revolutionary
Council (q.v.), which was the real center of power. While Bazargan was
meeting with the U.S. national security advisor in Algiers, Iranian students overran the U.S. embassy in Tehran and took hostages. Bazargan
resigned, and his liberal supporters lost their bid for power. He accused
Khomeini of misleading him on the role of the clergy, who he felt should
have retired to mosques and left the government to politicians.

Talqani had been widely respected at the time of the revolution, because he had been imprisoned several times under the monarchy. He was
an independent clergy, although he joined the powerful Revolutionary
Council. However, he finally boycotted its meetings because he disagreed with its policies, even although he was its chairman. He died suddenly in 1979. After that, the movement fought a losing battle and was
reduced in influence and role. *Hizbullah* (q.v.) attacked its offices, beat
its members, and arrested some of them. Yet, it continued to issue statements critical of the regime. See also BAZARGAN, MAHDI; *MUJAHI-
DIN KHALQ*; TALQANI, SAYYID MAHMUD.

AL-LIJAN AL-ISLAMIYYA (ISLAMIC COMMITTEES). See *HARAKAT AL-TAWHID AL-ISLAMI.*

LIJAN AL-MASAJID WA AL-AHYA' (COMMITTEES FOR MOSQUES AND NEIGHBORHOOD). See *HARAKAT AL-TAWHID* IN LEBANON.

-M-

MADANI, ABBASI (1931–   ). Madani is the president of the Islamic Salvation Front (FIS) in Algeria (q.v.). Madani was born in Algeria (Biskra area). He studied in Qur'anic schools, then he continued his education at the school of the Association of Algerian Scholars.

Madani joined the National Liberation Front when it started in 1954 and was arrested because of his attacks on the French. He was imprisoned for eight years. Later, Madani joined the Value Society, established in 1963 and abolished in 1966 because of its protests against the execution of Sayyid Qutb (q.v.).

Madani continued his higher education in Great Britain (1975–1977), studying philosophy and psychology, and got his Ph.D. in education from London University. He later worked as professor at the University of Algiers.

Madani was jailed during 1982–1984, because he supported a religious political opposition trend and signed a letter in 1982 that criticized the secular government and asked for the maintenance of Islam (q.v.). Following the October 1988 events, he founded with others the Islamic Salvation Front and was elected its leader.

During his leadership, the FIS became legal and won a large majority of seats in the municipal elections. In 1991, the FIS organized a strike to protest the new electoral law and to push for early parliamentary and presidential elections. When the front seemed to be winning during the first round of elections, the government canceled the results of the first round and did not permit the holding of the second round. Madani, along with 'Ali Bilhaj (q.v.), was arrested and tried before a military court. He was accused of conspiracy to subvert state security then was transferred to the military tribunal of al-Belida where he was sentenced for a period of 12 years. He was released in 1997, supposedly as a result of a deal with the government.

Abbasi Madani published several works on the intellectual and religious aspects of Islam. He is considered to be a moderate fundamentalist who calls for political competition through democracy (q.v.). The FIS presented itself as the popular alternative to the elitist political leadership of Algeria. See also ARMED ISLAMIC GROUP; BILHAJ, 'ALI; IS-LAMIC SALVATION FRONT IN ALGERIA; JABALLAH, 'ABD ALLAH; *JAMA'AT AL-NAHDA AL-ISLAMIYYA*; *AL-JAYSH AL-IS-LAMI LI AL-INQADH*; KABIR, RABIH; AL-KHATIB, 'ABD AL-KARIM.

MADANI, MUKHTAR. See POPULAR DEFENSE FORCES.

AL-MADI. See PAST.

MADI, ABU AL-'ULA (1958–). Madi is a well-known fundamentalist who tried recently to found a new party, *al-Wasat*. Madi was born in Minya in Upper Egypt. During his primary schooling, he distinguished himself and showed special interest in mathematics. His father was not a fundamentalist, and Madi had acquaintance with Sufi traditions. In secondary school, Madi did not show any particular interest in politics. Only after the war of 1976 with Israel (q.v.) and the defeat of Egypt did he entertain political action and revenge. At that time, he thought of joining the military but ended up studying engineering in 1976.

During his university life, Madi became very devout and grew his beard and joined *al-Jama'a al-Islamiyya* (q.v.) (Islamic Group). In 1977, he joined the student union and won its presidency. This was the first union that the Islamic movement controlled. Later on, the fundamentalists controlled the unions of eight out of 12 universities. Madi became the vice president of the national student union. He stood against President Anwar al-Sadat's policies toward Iran and the Shah and Israel, as did the Islamic movement. He was imprisoned, and during that period he joined the Muslim Brotherhood (q.v.). Madi was opposed to the violent trend among the Islamic movements and tried to reconcile the different branches of the Islamic trend. He later joined the union of engineers and became its Vice President.

Because he disagreed with the policies of the Brotherhood, Madi tried along with others to set up *al-Wasat* party. He was fired from the Brotherhood in 1996.

AL-MAGHRIBI, NABIL 'ABD AL-MAJID (1951–). Al-Maghribi was born in the governorate of Buhayra, Egypt. Al-Maghribi graduated in 1973 from the Faculty of Languages, and during his university study, he became devout and studied Islam. He entered the compulsory military service, for which he shaved his beard. In 1977, al-Maghribi left the army and worked in a cultural center, once again growing his beard.

Al-Maghribi was recruited by 'Abbud al-Zumar (q.v.) in 1981. He is a leading member of the Egyptian *Jihad al-Islami* (q.v.) (Islamic *Jihad*) and is ranked equally with 'Abbud al-Zumar and Muhammad 'Abd al-Salam Faraj (q.v.). His job includes training and recruiting military members in addition to special missions. Al-Maghribi planned many assassination attempts and participated in planning Anwar al-Sadat's assassination by recruiting Khalid al-Islambuli, who killed Sadat. Al-Maghribi was arrested 11 days before Sadat's assassination. With the exile of Ayman al-Zawahiri in Switzerland, al-Maghribi became the leading member of *al-Jihad*.

AL-MAHDI, MUHAMMAD IBN 'ABD ALLAH. See *AL-MAHDIYYA*.

AL-MAHDIYYA. This movement was founded by Muhammad Ahmad Ibn 'Abd Allah al-Mahdi al-Sudani (1843–1885), who was born to a religious family. He memorized the Qur'an when he was 12 years old, went to Khartoum and studied jurisprudence (q.v.) and exegesis, then withdrew from society for 15 years and devoted himself to worship, studying, and teaching. He attracted numerous followers, and through marriage, he strengthened tribal loyalty. He was viewed by his followers as *al-Mahdi al-Muntathar*—the awaited guide. He wrote to the jurists of Sudan, urging them to support him, and his Sufi supporters urged the tribes to launch the *jihad* (q.v.) (struggle). When the General Governor of Egypt summoned him to Khartoum and al-Mahdi refused, an army was sent to bring him but was defeated. Another military campaign also failed to capture him. His followers then attacked Khartoum, and the Sudan fell under his control.

Al-Mahdiyya called for freeing the mind by going back to the roots of religion (q.v.) and by dropping traditional interpretations and abolishing the tradition of legal schools. Al-Mahdi wrote legal pronouncements without adhering to any specific school. He also abolished Sufi orders and called for a return to the Qur'an (q.v.) and the *Sunna* (way) of the Prophet. Al-Mahdi gave the doctrine of interest a role in dealing with issues of the world and found in the collective nature of social thought in Islam the answer for the needs of the Sudanese society. For instance, in terms of private property, al-Mahdi limited property to the owner's ability to plant it. Institutions like ports, gardens, commercial agencies, and others were considered public and could not be privately owned. See also ISLAMIC STATE; *AL-WAHHABIYYA*.

MAJLIS AL-KHUBARA'. See COUNCIL OF EXPERTS.

MAJLIS AL-MUHAFAZA 'ALA AL-DUSTUR. See COUNCIL FOR THE PRESERVATION OF THE CONSTITUTION.

MAJLIS AL-SHURA (CONSULTATION COUNCIL). *Majlis al-Shura* has been a demand for most fundamentalist movements, especially in the countries of the Arabian Peninsula and the Gulf States. Liberal reform movements called for setting up representative advisory councils during the 1920s and 1930s. Although these movements were suppressed, the call for their establishment under the guise of *shura* (q.v.) (consultation) is being revived now. Also, many fundamentalist movements describe their politburos or general councils as *Majlis al-Shura*.

After the Second Gulf War, Saudi Arabia, for instance, established an advisory body as *Majlis al-Shura*, which ties political legitimacy (q.v.) to *al-Shari'a* (q.v.) (Islamic Law) and kinship. *Majlis al-Shura* functions for the fundamentalists as an indigenous alternative to the Parliament. See also BAHRAIN NATIONAL CONGRESS; BANI SADR, ABUL HASAN; AL-BASHIR, 'UMAR; CONSTITUTION; *HIZBULLAH*; INTERNATIONAL ORGANIZATION OF THE MUSLIM BROTHERHOOD; ISLAMIC SALVATION FRONT; *JAMA'AT AL-JIHAD AL-ISLAMI*; *MAJLIS AL-SHURA* IN IRAN; *MAJLIS TASHKHIS MASLAHAT AL-NIZAM*; MUSADDAQ'S TREND; AL-NABAHANI, TAQIY AL-DIN; NURI, 'ALI AKBAR; RAFSANJANI, 'ALI AKBAR; *RUHANIYYAT MUBARIZ*; YAGHI, MUHAMMAD HUSAYN.

MAJLIS AL-SHURA (*SHURA* COUNCIL) **IN IRAN**. The Iranian constitution (q.v.) provides several powers to this council. It is the center of the legislative processes and lawmaking as well as the center for approving appointments and supervising the actions of the government. It also can investigate the activities and policies of the President of the Republic as well as call for his removal pending the approval of *waliy al-faqih* (q.v.) (the guardian of the jurist). The council is also responsible for ratifying treaties with foreign countries. It is composed of 270 members who are directly elected by the people. Currently, the Speaker is 'Ali Akbar Natiq Nuri (q.v.). See also *MAJLIS AL-SHURA*; *MAJLIS TASHKHIS MASLA-*

HAT AL-NIZAM; MUSADDAQ'S TREND; NURI, 'ALI AKBAR; RAFSANJANI, 'ALI AKBAR; *RUHANIYYAT MUBARIZ.*

MAJLIS TASHKHIS MASLAHAT AL-NIZAM (COUNCIL FOR CHARACTERIZING THE REGIME'S INTEREST). Ayatollah Khomeini (q.v.) started developing this council, but it came to full existence with Ayatollah 'Ali Khamene'i (q.v.), who issued a decree in 1997 appointing outgoing President Rafsanjani (q.v.) as the head of this highest state council.

Its original task was to settle conflicts between the legislative and other constitutional and legal bodies, but it is being developed as the central decision-making body in the Republic of Iran. It will include the President of the Republic, the Speaker of *Majlis al-Shura* (q.v.), and the President of the Supreme Court. This means in effect that Rafsanjani is to hold, after leaving the presidency, the second authority in the Republic, after Khamene'i. The President of this council is to become the second man in the Iranian system. The council is composed of 25 permanent members, in addition to ex officio members who are the heads of the executive, legislative, and judicial branches, and some members of the Council for the Preservation of the Constitution (q.v.). See also RAFSANJANI, 'ALI AKBAR.

MAKHLUFI, SA'ID. See ARMED ISLAMIC GROUP; *AL-JAYSH AL-ISLAMI LI AL-INQADH.*

MANHAJ. See METHOD.

MANSUR, HAMZA 'ABBAS (1944–   ). Mansur is a member of the executive committee of *Hizb Jabhat al-'Amal al-Islami* in Jordan (q.v.) (Islamic Action Front Party). Mansur was born in Haifa and in 1975 received his B.A. in Arabic language and in 1984 an M.A. in education from the University of Jordan. He worked first as a teacher and then joined the Ministry of Education. Mansur as well preached in mosques during the 1970s and was a member of the Lower House of Parliament for the 1989–1993 period. He presided over the Red Crescent Association in 1991.

AL-MAQDISI, ABU MUHAMMAD. Al-Maqdisi, whose real name is 'Isam Muhammad Tahir, is now in a Jordanian jail on charges of forming an illegal organization, *Bay'at al-Imam* (Oath of Allegiance to the

Imam), and planning terrorist activities. He is Palestinian but was brought up in Kuwait and was influenced by *Jam'iyyat Ihya' al-Turath al-Islami* (q.v.), a cover organization for the *Salafi* trend in Kuwait and the Gulf. His book, *Millat Ibrahim* (*Abraham's Sect*), espouses radical *Salafiyya*, paganism, and violence (qq.v.). Al-Maqdisi accused the mainstream fundamentalist movements of unbelief (q.v.) and had numerous differences with other Afghan Arabs. Some young people from the Gulf joined al-Maqdisi, who moved them away from the mainstream fundamentalists trend because of the Muslim Brotherhood's influence over it.

Al-Maqdisi was very critical of the Muslim Brotherhood in Jordan and of its acceptance of democracy. He considers democracy and parliaments as forms of unbelief because they seize God's governance and legislation (qq.v.), which he believes should be God's alone. Al-Maqdisi used to spread his message in a mosque. In Jordan, many former members of Muhammad's Army joined him. In 1995, members of his group, who were tried on charges of terrorism and possessing weapons, accused everyone in the courtroom, the judge, the lawyers, and the police, of unbelief. Some of the Saudi suspects in the Riyadh explosion had been members of al-Maqdisi's group and had undergone training with him in Afghanistan. See also *AL-AFGHAN AL-'ARAB*.

MAQRIF, MUHAMMAD YUSUF. See NATIONAL FRONT FOR THE SALVATION OF LIBYA.

MA'RIFA. See KNOWLEDGE.

MARJI' AL-TAQLID (AUTHORITY FOR IMITATION). *Marji' al-taqlid* is a title used to describe the highest-ranking clergymen of the Twelvers' Shi'ite community. The number of *marji'* is limited. At one time and during this century, there were four *maraji'* (plural of *marji'*). Ayatollah Khomeini (q.v.) was considered to be one. The *marji'* reaches this rank by having a large following who look to him for legal opinions and judgments and who imitate his actions and follow his opinions on religious issues.

The *maraji'* do not have to hold the same views; for instance, whereas Imam Khomeini called for the establishment of the Islamic state (q.v.), another *marji'*, Ayatollah Abu al-Qasim al-Khu'i (1899–1992), called for separating politics from religion (q.v.). Today, for instance, the Shi'ite community disagrees on whether Ayatollah Khamene'i (q.v.), the current leader of the Islamic Republic of Iran, has the scholarly credentials, such as the knowledge (q.v.) and ability to exercise reason (q.v.) (*ijtihad*), to be named a *marji'*.

The *marji'iyya* (source of authority) is not officially institutionalized. There is no specific council that chooses the *marji'*. The need for the *marji'* is dictated by some Shi'ites' view that the Shi'a should not follow the opinion of a dead *mujtahid* (legal thinker) but instead should seek the guidance of a living *mujtahid*, who is superior to other religious scholars by his knowledge, virtue, and piety. When a *mujtahid* like this is found, he must be imitated. To move from the rank of *ijtihad* (legal reasoning) to *marji'iyya*, the *mujtahid* must receive the approval of the other *mujtahid*s and the religious circles, the acceptance of the common people of his reputation as being modest, virtuous, knowledgeable, and otherwise virtuous, and the nonexistence of other *maraji'*, which in practice means the need to live many years to arrive at that stage.

In addition the *marji'* should command a large public following. When Khomeini died, the Great *Marji'iyya* was represented in four Great Ayatollahs, who generally commanded the respect of the Shi'ite community. Iran has attempted to consolidate the religious and political *marji'iyya* in *waliy al-faqih* (q.v.), that is, Khamene'i; this much led to friction between the religious establishments in Iran and the Arab world. Also, a few religious Iranian scholars were arrested because of their opposition to the *marji'iyya* of Khamene'i.

The religious establishment in Qum has nominated Khamene'i to the position of the greatest *marji'iyya* in addition to six others. He was ranked third. The Iranian plan has been to make his *marji'iyya* acceptable within the ranks of *Hizbullah* (q.v.) in Lebanon and the Gulf States. The religiously conservative Right in Iran wants him to combine *waliy al-faqih* and the *marji'iyya* or, in other words, to make Iran the highest political and religious center for the Shiites. *Hizbullah* has accepted this except for Muhammad Sayyid Fadlallah (q.v.), who prefers Ayatollah 'Ali al-Sistani.

MARTYRDOM (*ISTISHHAD*; *SHAHADA*). The martyr has a special place in Islam, because he is not punished on the day of judgment and is promised Paradise. Although historically and theoretically Muslims have practiced martyrdom in defending their existence and land, it is not normally considered something that was acquired through fighting fellow Muslims.

The fundamentalists believe that Islam (q.v.) has commended martyrdom as a way of uplifting the community and defending the weak and the community. For them, it is considered to be a sign of ultimate belief in God (q.v.). Today, it is mostly practiced by the fundamentalists, especially radicals, who use it as a distinguishing mark of their activism (q.v.) (*harakiyya*). See also ACTIVISM; EXTREMISM; RADICALISM; RELIGION; VIOLENCE.

MARXISM. For most fundamentalists, Marxism and Islam (q.v.) clash head-on, because Islam founds its system (q.v.) (*nizam*) on belief in God (q.v.), and Marxism on denying God. Dialectical materialism dominates Marxism, whereas Islam is dominated by the Creator.

Ultimately, whereas for Marxism any conflict is presented in economic terms (capitalist, communist, and socialist), for the fundamentalists all conflicts are between spiritualism and materialism. The former is represented by Islam and religion (q.v.) in general, the latter by capitalism (q.v.), socialism, and communism. Marxism is the most advanced level of mechanical and intellectual materialism, and although the two camps, the capitalist and the socialist, disagree and wage wars for their own benefit, their difference is a matter of degree, of organization, and of method (q.v.) (*manhaj*).

Although some fundamentalists, such as Mustapha al-Siba'i and Sayyid Qutb (qq.v.), adopted some Marxist and socialist concepts, such as equal distribution of wealth and state control of production, they attribute these concepts to Islam. See also CAPITALISM; JUSTICE; METHOD; MUTUAL RESPONSIBILITY; QUTB, SAYYID; SHARI'-ATI, ALI; SOCIAL JUSTICE.

AL-MAS'ARI, MUHAMMAD. Mas'ari is one of the most outspoken Saudi fundamentalists against the Saudi government. Dr. Mas'ari founded *Lajnat al-Difa' 'An al-Huquq al-Shar'iyya* (Committee for Defending the Legitimate Rights). He was expelled from Saudi Arabia and now lives in England as a political refugee. He was subject to deportation from England to the Dominican Republic because his case was harming British interests with the Saudi Kingdom. Differences arose between him and the Secretary of the Committee, Dr. Usama al-Faqih, because al-Mas'ari was "falling under the influence" of *Hizb al-Tahrir al-Islami* (q.v.) (Islamic Liberation Party) and its radical ideology. Some observers point out that al-Mas'ari receives financial aid from Iranian sources.

MASH'AL, KHALID. Mah'al is the current head of the political bureau of *Hamas* (q.v.) (*Harakat al-Muqawama al-Islamiyya*). See also MUSLIM BROTHERHOOD IN PALESTINE.

MASHHUR, MUSTAPHA (1924–   ). The 74-year-old Mashhur is the current supreme guide of the Muslim Brotherhood (q.v.) in Egypt, who took up his post in 1996. Previously, he had been the deputy to the supreme guide, Muhammad Hamid Abu al-Nasr. Mashhur tends to be less accommodating and more antagonistic to the government than was Abu al-Nasr.

In an interview in 1997, his views brought about a storm in Egypt because of a "misunderstood" statement he made, allegedly calling Christians and minorities in the army second-class citizens. What he was saying is that if there were an Islamic army, then Christians would not be obliged to fight in it, because such fighting would be of a religious nature. Instead they should pay *jizya* (poll tax). See also MUSLIM BROTHERHOOD; MUSLIM BROTHERHOOD, IDEOLOGY OF.

MASHKINI, 'ALI. See COUNCIL OF EXPERTS.

MAURITANIAN MUSLIM SOCIALIST UNION (*AL-ITIHAD AL-ISH-TIRAKI AL-ISLAMI AL-MURITANI*). The Party of Mauritanian People joined this union, which was created in 1961. It was banned in 1978, and many of its leaders went into exile. Although its leaders were from important tribal families, its power base is limited to ethnic and religious groups. Its main ideological character was the emphasis on Arab and Muslim identity as opposed to Black African identity.

AL-MAWDUDI, ABU AL-A'LA (1903–1979). Al-Mawdudi was a Pakistani fundamentalist and one of the most outstanding fundamentalist thinkers in the 20th century, whose impact on the ideologies of Islamic and radical movements cannot be underestimated. Al-Mawdudi influenced thinkers like Sayyid Qutb (q.v.), especially on the doctrines of governance and paganism (qq.v.), and large numbers of radical thinkers. He founded *Jama'at-i Islami*, which played a very important role in the politics of Pakistan and India and became a model for many Islamic movements. Al-Mawdudi's works have been translated into many languages.

AL-MAWLAWANI, JAMAL. See *HIZB AL-HAQQ AL-ISLAMI*.

AL-MAWLAWI, FAYSAL. See *AL-JAMA'A AL-ISLAMIYYA*.

METHOD (*MANHAJ*). Fundamentalists, like Abu al-A'la al-Mawdudi, Abu al-Hasan al-Nadawi, Hasan al-Banna, Sayyid Qutb, and Hadi al-

Mudarrisi (qq.v.), transform Islam (q.v.) into the most perfect method of knowledge (q.v.). They argue that this method subsumes under the concept of unity (*wahda*), the unity of the intellectual and the spiritual with the material, and the unity of the known with the unknown. They argue that the Islamic method, which is grounded in *tawhid* (q.v.) (Oneness of God), the concept of unity denies the legitimacy (q.v.) of any theoretical or practical disunity and views the whole of existence as one creation. Any individual or state that negates this method is branded by many fundamentalists as being in a state of paganism (q.v.) (*jahiliyya*).

For the fundamentalists, if Muslims do not follow the Islamic method, their life is then ruled by a jungle mentality. A nondivine and human method undermines humanity and pushes it backward, notwithstanding the high technology of the 20th century. The fundamentalists in general argue that both the method and philosophy of Western thought lead to the centrality of the concepts of power and matter in the making of Western civilization (q.v.). Both the Marxist and the capitalist are charged with the same crime, domination—Vietnam is cited as an instance. Contrary to this, an Islamic method and philosophy leads to the centrality of the concepts of justice (q.v.) and brotherhood in the making of Islamic civilization (q.v.). See also CALIPHATE; CIVILIZATION; CONSTITUTIONAL RULE; GOD; GOVERNANCE; ISLAM; ISRAEL; MARXISM; PAGANISM; RELIGION; *TAWHID*; THEOLOGY; AL-TURABI, HASAN; WESTERN CIVILIZATION.

MILIANI, AL-MANSURI. See ARMED ISLAMIC GROUP.

MILLI NIZAM PARTISI (PARTY FOR NATIONAL ORDER). This party was the first legal party in Republican Turkey that was committed to the promotion of Islam (q.v.). It was established and headed in January 1970 by Necmettin Erbakan (q.v.), an independent member of the Grand National Assembly from Konya, a former professor of automotive engineering at Istanbul Technical University. The party's first general convention, held in Ankara in February 1970, proved a starting point for establishing branches in other metropolitan areas. Erbakan and his Secretary-General, Sulayman Arif Emre, were particularly active in recruitment.

The party's public promotion of Islam led the Attorney-General's office to prosecute it before the Constitutional Court, on the charge of exploiting religion for political objectives. The court dissolved the party in 1971. Some of its leaders subsequently established the *Milli Selamet*

Partisi (q.v.), with the same ideological orientation. The attempt to resurrect the party in Ankara in 1976 did not lead to practical outcomes.

The party's ideology represented a basic alternative to secularism, which is the main ideology of the Turkish Republic and has been enshrined in its constitution (q.v.). Although the party could not oppose secularism in public, it criticized any interpretation (q.v.) that was opposed to religion. Furthermore, although it could not include Islam as a guiding principle within its program, its call for Islamic morality (q.v.) was highly visible. The party identified moral revival with the application of social justice (q.v.) and the promotion of happiness and peace (q.v.). It argued that Islam was not only progressive but in harmony with Turkey's welfare.

An important part of its program was the reinstitution and encouragement of religious education in all Turkish schools. Because of the party founder's distinction as an automotive engineer, the party's position in favor of technological progress was credible. Other leaders were more orthodox Muslim than the founder, and the traditional circles, looked down on by the ruling classes, provided supporters of the party. Although the party did not have its own newspaper, it was supported by the periodicals that had advocated Islam during the 1960s. See ERBAKAN, NECMETTIN; *MILLI SELAMET PARTISI*; *REFAH PARTISI*.

MILLI SELAMET PARTISI (NATIONAL SALVATION PARTY). This Turkish Islamic party was the outcome of restructuring the *Milli Nizam Partisi* (q.v.) (Party for National Order), which was banned in 1971. The Salvation Party was established in October 1971, by 19 persons, most of whom had been involved with the National Order. Its founder, Necmettin Erbakan (q.v.), kept a low profile for a while. By 1973, the party had branches all over the country. This party is the new formation that Necmettin Erbakan used to mobilize the Islamic movement in Turkey. After the dissolution of the National Order by the constitutional court, because of its antagonistic activities to secularism, Erbakan founded this party. Sulayman 'Arif Emre, the former Secretary-General of the National Order, helped Erbakan in the reorganization of the party in 67 districts.

The National Salvation Party derived its power during 1972–1980 from the general sympathy of Islamic public opinion, and it developed further after 1979. Its newspaper, *Tali Carteh*, started a process of criticizing secularism in Turkey. The newspaper even upheld the slogan of establishing an Islamic state and the return to *al-Shari'a* (Islamic Law) (qq.v.). Furthermore, the party opposed the American military presence in Turkey, which was viewed as being directed against Middle Eastern states. It stressed that the spread of Islamic principles should not be brought about by force but through creating a free environment for the Muslim that allows him to return to Islam (q.v.).

Within the political life of Turkey, the party stood in the middle between the Liberals and the Leftists. One achievement that the party was proud of was its ability in 1980, in cooperation with *Hizb al-Sha'b*, to have the vote of confidence withdrawn from the Minister of Foreign Affairs, Khayr al-Din Arkaman, for his Zionist tendencies.

All of the Salvation Party's resources were mobilized in the campaign for general elections of 1973. The party's leaders traveled widely and spoke earnestly. The party won 11.8 percent of the vote of the Grand National Assembly, 48 of 450 seats, and 12.3 percent of the vote for the Senate, for three of the 52 contested seats. Thus, it came in third after the Republican People's Party and the Justice Party.

The party joined the cabinet and focused on educational and economic policies, all in the name of Islamic morals and virtues. It strove to promote religious education, to disburse funds for religious purposes, to ban alcohol, to oppose Turkey's joining the European Economic Community, to which it preferred a common market for Islamic states. The party was banned by the military regime in 1981.

The ideology of the Salvation Party is anti-Kemalist and aimed at eliminating secularism and establishing an Islamic state in Turkey. Its religiosity was mixed with a strongly nationalist ingredient, to identify Turkish patriotism with Islam. Furthermore, it was based on a fairly sophisticated economic program, which was aimed at bringing the *umma* (q.v.) (nation) happiness and security via moral and material progress. Moral progress postulated the need for a virtuous society: one based on the ideals of Islam enforced by Turkey's glorious heritage. Material progress required general development, speedy industrialization, and balanced socioeconomic progress. For example, the party argued that Turkey's much-needed industrialization should not be at the expense of the little man, such as the artisan. It was this combination of morals and religion (q.v.) with the advocacy of industrialization that shaped the party's ideological image and probably differentiated it from other religiously based parties (q.v.). This was partially because of the personal character of the party leadership.

The party's program underlines the following points: the need for a virtuous society with secularism as a guarantee for freedom (q.v.) of thought and consciousness (q.v.) (*wa'iy*) and a deterrent of conflicts. But secularism should not be used to suppress specific religious beliefs. Freedom of belief is part of freedom of thought. However, after the party's success in the 1973 elections, it showed basic changes concerning its views of liberties.

The leadership, especially Erbakan, and a few of his former students at the Technical University of Istanbul, and several orthodox Muslims, was a dedicated group that used modern methods of political organization and propaganda well. The party included numerous religiously minded persons, who, for the first time in 50 years, were given an opportunity to come out of the political wilderness, as well as many small artisans, who made and sold their own products and were economically threatened by major manufacturers. The party emerged as a protector of this large group in its opposition to Turkish membership in the European Economic Community. The party's main electoral support came from Turkey's less-developed areas and smaller towns. In addition to Islamic-oriented newspapers, which supported the party, the party published a daily, *Milli Gazette*, in Istanbul and had many other periodicals throughout the country. See also ERBAKAN, NECMETTIN; *MILLI NIZAM PARTISI*; *REFAH PARTISI*.

MINHAJ (METHOD). See METHOD.

MODERNISM (*AL-TAHDITH* [TREND]). Modernism focuses its endeavor to interpret Islam (q.v.) on the central role that reason (q.v.) can play in reworking Islamic doctrines within a universal civilization (q.v.). Although fundamentalism (q.v.), in line with Hasan al-Banna and Sayyid Qutb (qq.v.), views, for instance, moral laws as natural, it still insists on grounding them in *al-Shari'a* (q.v.) (Islamic Law). However, modernism in the line of Jamal al-Din al-Afghani, Muhammad Iqbal, and Muhammad 'Abdu (qq.v.) argues that all true laws can be authenticated and demonstrated by reason.

Ali Shari'ati (q.v.), for instance, argues that Islam is opposed to Marxism (q.v.) because the latter equates moral laws with social customs by relating them to social and economic materialism. However, Islam attempts to attribute moral laws to the primordial nature of man, or *fitra* (q.v.). But reason is the instrument that locates them. Although Jamal al-Din al-Afghani insists on the existence in man of an urge to rise above bestiality and lust and to improve his life, he tells us that following the *fitra* without reason cannot be the primary instrument needed for the pursuit of knowledge (q.v.) and the cultivation of the necessary tools for the development of civilization.

That is why Islamic modernism accepts the fruits of reason along Western lines. It attempts to interpret religion (q.v.) in terms of philosophy (q.v.). Reason is manifested primarily in the cultivation of science (q.v.) and development of technology. It adopts, for instance, Western philosophical and political theories because they are both rational and scientific. Islamic modernism has preceded and opened the way for Islamic fundamentalism (q.v.) to adopt Western doctrines like democracy and constitutional rule (qq.v.) and to Islamize them by using Islamic terms like *shura* and *ijma'* (qq.v.).

Such a notion is very significant in the explication of the fundamentalist political project, at both the theoretical level and the practical level. Although the modernist's acceptance of the West (q.v.) led to their adoption of Western political theories, it precluded both the claim to a new political theory and putting forth the underpinnings for theory-building. Their attempts focused on the theoretical introduction of certain Western political doctrines like democracy and republicanism and on the practical exhortation of rulers to apply them. The nature of their political thought was miscellaneously oriented, not fully grounded in theoretical advancements, and for immediate political goals. Even the modernist criticism of traditionalism was not directed at traditions per se, but at its interpretation (q.v.) in order to make it suitable to Western notions, especially on the harmonious nature of religion and science.

History (q.v.) again was not discredited as such but used to show how the Muslims through various stages of their development dealt with foreigners and their compendium of knowledge. We must keep in mind that the modernists themselves had no claim to any sort of theory-building but were very keen on the need to bring together the West and the East, both scientifically and religiously. This is why they did not shy away from adoption from the West. The fact that they did not write a theory allowed the fundamentalists to use the adopted modernist notions to build their theory, such as the introduction of *shura* as being equivalent to democracy. The modernists should in any case be credited for the open-mindedness and for the Islamization (q.v.) of essential concepts such as democracy and pluralism (q.v.). The revival of an intellectual atmosphere in the Muslim world is also due to them, and the belief in the possible congruence between Islam and the West is also theirs. See also 'ABDU, MUHAMMAD; AFGHANI, JAMAL AL-DIN; AL-FASI, MUHAMMAD 'ALLAL; IQBAL, MUHAMMAD; MUTAHHARI, MURTAZA; SHARI'ATI, ALI; MODERNITY; SCIENCE.

MODERNITY (*HADATHA*). For the fundamentalists, modernity is entangled with the problems of Western living and history. The modern Western society therefore cannot be a model for regenerating Islamic societies. The main problems with Western civilization (q.v.) include its focus on materialism and power. Although Islamic societies are in dire need of change, Hasan al-Turabi (q.v.) does not, for instance, perceive the West (q.v.) as being the model that would lead to peaceful living.

The West, the fundamentalists argue, is suffering more than the Islamic world from all sorts of philosophical, economic, and, to a lesser extent, political problems. Whereas modern Islamic states should have adopted only what is good and relevant to the Islamic world, they borrowed the West as a complete model. Along with this, they also inherited its inherent troubles and tensions, which led to ending *al-Shari'a* (q.v.) (Islamic Law) as the model that Muslims could work on and develop from within. A new political life, characterized by sharp economic, political, and ideological tensions and conflicting claims between the individual, the state, and society (q.v.), has become a main feature of Islamic societies.

Therefore, what has actually occurred is the transportation from the West to the East of problems that did not exist initially in the East. Islamic societies lost their original powers without gaining the powers of their Western counterparts. In other words, contemporary Islamic societies suffer doubly: first, by the negative aspects of their history (q.v.), intellectual backwardness and *taqlid* (q.v.) (traditionalism), and second, by the emergence of new and "modern" tyrannical states and comprehensive conflicts as well as the states' control of individual and social life.

Modern Islamic societies are therefore in need of a major reshuffling of priorities to turn upside down the social and political agenda by making liberation (q.v.) the immediate objective of change for the benefit of religion (q.v.). Such a liberation requires a force that will redraw the parameters of conflict, from a mere problem of personal freedom (q.v.) to man's corruption of his original nature or *fitra* (q.v.) and the reduction of freedom to a personal objective.

The fundamentalists believe that true liberation and freedom should be directed at the elimination of the root cause of modern crisis, that is, *shirk* (polytheism). True belief eliminates the narrow problem of freedom and brings about true liberation for all: the individual, the society, and the state. Religious liberation leads to political liberation from *salatin al-ard* (lords of the earth). Without this, the proper functioning of the Islamic state (q.v.) through the spread of free religious consciousness (q.v.) (*wa'iy*) would be encumbered. The imposition of a state's political objectives on the believers without a proper Islamic philosophy (q.v.) of life would lead the state into outright paganism (q.v.) (*jahiliyya*).

The fundamentalists in general accept, however, technical and scientific developments and argue for their adoption. They attempt to separate science (q.v.), for instance, from its philosophical background. Thus, they accept science without its philosophy. The same could be said of democracy (q.v.). To do this, the fundamentalists Islamize the adopted doctrines and tie them to the commandments of the *al-Shari'a* (Islamic Law). The difference between fundamentalism and modernism (qq.v.) is that the former does not view reason (q.v.) as providing categorical results, whereas the latter grounds Islamic doctrines in reason as well as Islamic Law. See also 'ABDU, MUHAMMAD; AL-AFGHANI, JAMAL AL-DIN; DEMOCRATIC ISLAMIC ARAB MOVEMENT; FUNDAMENTALISM; FUNDAMENTALS; INTERPRETATION; ISLAM; MUSLIM BROTHERHOOD, IDEOLOGY OF; NATION'S PARTY; POPULAR MOVEMENT; RIDA, MUHAMMAD RASHID; SHARI'ATI, 'ALI; *SHURA*; *TAQLID*; TEXT; AL-TURABI, HASAN.

MONOTHEISM. See *TAWHID*.

MONOTHEISTIC RELIGIONS. For the fundamentalists, *tawhid* (q.v.) (Oneness of God) is the basic principle of all religions, especially the monotheistic ones like Christianity and Judaism (qq.v.). Monotheism therefore means submission to *tawhid*, which requires following God's path in every aspect of life, whether ritualistic, like prostrating before God (q.v.), or political, like obeying His laws and orders.

Like other revealed religions, specifically Christianity and Judaism, the fundamentalists argue that Islam (q.v.) includes a complete creed. However, Islam does not negate others' ethics and personal attitudes toward God. Islam contains most of the teachings of other religions and views their rights as God's rights. What constitutes a good religion (q.v.) is good behavior toward the self, the other, the community, and God, and not necessarily better argumentation.

Islamic fundamentalists believe other religions have deviated from the essence of their messages and used them for acquiring more power, increasing their worldly interests, and suppressing the peoples of the world. Both Christianity and Judaism of today are not the true religions that God revealed but are their corrupted forms. Nonetheless, the fundamentalists are ready to coexist with these forms if a peaceful way of existence that guarantees Muslims' rights can be established.

However, the fundamentalists in general look at the current world order and the West (qq.v.) as well as Israel (q.v.) as being aggressive and unfair to the Muslim world. Radical fundamentalists even uphold the need for struggling or *jihad* (q.v.) against them as a necessary condition for the rise of Islam and the attainment of Muslims' rights, as is the case in Palestine and Bosnia-Herzegovina. See also CHRISTIANITY; JUDAISM.

MORALITY. For the fundamentalists, morality is seen as the distinguishing mark between Islam (q.v.) and other philosophies. Islam's most important function is the calculation of morality. Although *tawhid* (q.v.) (Oneness of God) is the fundamental comprehensive metaphysical doctrine, it becomes the linchpin in the process of the unification and liberation (q.v.) of humanity. Social morality is the outer manifestation of Muslims' commitment to Islam, and immorality is the outer manifestation of its disobedience.

Fundamentalism (q.v.) looks at *tawhid* not only as a doctrine of political government but as a moral doctrine necessary for good living. *Tawhid* leads man to uplift himself over material things and engage himself with other humans as fellows who share the same destiny and interests. When human beings believe in God (q.v.) and follow His *fitra* (q.v.) (law of nature) and *Shari'a* (q.v.) (Islamic Law), they tend to focus less on selfish interests and more on the common interests of the community. Without a religious morality, humans tend to exploit each other and to use them as means toward success and power. Thus, justice (q.v.) is linked to the domination of morality, and injustice to its absence.

Abu al-Hasan al-Nadawi (q.v.) describes in detail how Europe has lost its morality and diverted the world toward paganism (q.v.) (*jahiliyya*). For him, Christian Europe has turned into materialist paganism and left aside all sorts of spiritual teachings and religious morality. Now, it rests its beliefs at the individual level in pleasure and material interest, in pragmatic life, in power and domination, in political life, and in aggressive nationalism and unjust citizenship. Europe has revolted against human nature and moral principles and has lost sight of valuable goals. It has also lost religious conscientiousness and fallen into materialism. It is, according to al-Nadawi, like an unbridled elephant that steps over the weak and destroys whatever comes before it. The whole world looks as if it is a train pulled by paganism and materialism. The Muslims, like many others, are only passengers who control nothing; the faster the train moves, the faster humanity moves into paganism, moral degradation, and spiritual bankruptcy. See also AUTHENTICITY; AL-BANNA, HASAN; CIVILIZATION; CONSCIOUSNESS; GOD; ISLAMIC FUNDAMENTALISM; ISLAMIC SOCIETY; ISLAMIC STATE; ISLAMIC YOUTH ORGANIZATION; JUSTICE; LEGISLATION; *MILLI NIZAM PARTISI*; RADICALISM; RELIGION; *AL-SHARI'A*; WORLD ORDER.

MORO, 'ABD AL-FATTAH. See AL-GHANNUSHI, RASHID.

MOROCCAN ASSEMBLY OF ISLAMIC ORGANIZATIONS. See ISLAMIC YOUTH ORGANIZATION.

MOVEMENT OF ISLAMIC RENEWAL (*HARAKAT AL-TAJADDUD AL-ISLAMI*). As an offshoot of *Jam'iyyat al-Hifadh 'Ala al-Qur'an* (q.v.) (the Qur'anic Preservation Society), this movement was created in 1978 by a loose coalition of fundamentalists who began voicing the economic and political grievances of many Tunisians, defining the framework of their opposition to government politics in religious terms.

MOVEMENT OF THE ISLAMIC STATE (*HARAKAT AL-DAWLA AL-ISLAMIYYA*). See *AL-JAYSH AL-ISLAMI LI AL-INQADH*.

MOVEMENT OF UNIFICATION AND REFORM (*HARAKAT AL-TAWHID WA AL-ISLAH*). See AL-KHATIB, 'ABD AL-KARIM.

MUDARRISI, HADI. See ISLAMIC ACTION ORGANIZATION IN IRAQ; ISLAMIC FRONT FOR THE LIBERATION OF BAHRAIN; KHOMEINISM.

MUDARRISI, MUHAMMAD TAQIY. See ISLAMIC ACTION ORGANIZATION IN IRAQ; KHOMEINISM.

MUHAMMAD, AL-NKADI. See *MUJAHIDIN* MOVEMENT IN MOROCCO.

MUHAMMAD'S ARMY. See *JAYSH MUHAMMAD*.

MUHAMMAD'S YOUTH (*SHABAB MUHAMMAD*). Muhammad's Youth is a splinter group from the Egyptian Muslim Brotherhood (q.v.)

created in the 1940s. It adopted the use of violence (q.v.) for political ends.

MUHSIN, SA'ID. See *MUJAHIDIN KHALQ.*

MUHTASHIMI, 'ALI AKBAR. Muhtashimi is the former Minister of Interior of the Islamic Republic of Iran and one of the leaders of the Iranian Radical Left, or the opposition from within the establishment (the Conservative Right has been in control of government). The religious cover for this left is *Rahaniyyun Mubariz* (q.v.), which is headed by Ayatollah Mahdawi Kini (q.v.), and for the right, *Ruhaniyyat Mubariz* (q.v.), which is headed by Parliament Speaker Shaykh 'Ali Akbar Natiq Nuri (q.v.). Muhtashimi and the left call for redressing the social and political problems through reducing the role of the clergy and increasing the role of the technocrats and liberals. See also *HIZBULLAH.*

MUJAHIDIN KHALQ (SAZIMAN-I MOJAHEDIN-I KHALQ IRAN). In 1965, the people's *Mujahidin* organization in Iran was established. It was founded by Muhammad Hanifnezhad and Sa'id Muhsin, who split from the Liberation Movement of Iran (q.v.), and four other graduates from the University of Tehran. It mixes Islam (q.v.) with Marxism (q.v.). *Mujahidin* contributed to the victory of the Iranian Revolution of 1979 (q.v.). But after the Revolution, it opposed Imam Khomeini (q.v.) and became an opposition force.

After 1963 Hanifnezhad, an Azeri agricultural engineer from Tabriz, concluded that all other movements had failed and decided to continue challenging the Shah's regime. This organization came about as a real attempt to develop a revolutionary Shi'ite ideology prior to the revolution of 1978–1979 that gave Islam a highly radical and revolutionary shape. It interpreted doctrines like *tawhid, jihad* (qq.v.) and *shahada*, or monotheism, struggle, and martyrdom (q.v.), as revolutionary political doctrines. Furthermore, it combined an activist program within a secret society and emphasized a leftist interpretation (q.v.) of Islam that was based on Marxism as well as the history (q.v.) of revolutionary movements in the world.

Later on, it adhered to and advocated Marxist Leninism, which led to a split in the movement in 1975, thus creating two factions, one Marxist and the other Islamic. The communist faction was later called Peykar; the Islamic one maintained the name *Mujahidin*. To the latter faction, Iran's Shi'ite culture embodies great revolutionary potential. It believes that original Islam, as practiced by the Prophet, would lead to a united community. It assumes that all oppression and exploitation would vanish with the establishment of the Islamic society (q.v.). The organization was very much helped by the political discourse and support of Ali Shari'ati (q.v.).

In 1970 and up until 1979, the *Mujahidin* started the military training of its members and in 1970 launched covert operations against the regime. In 1972, about 100 of the top leaders were jailed, of whom 10 were sentenced to death. After 1978 these detainees were released. The *Mujahidin* launched a campaign of assassination and bombing. The regime was able in the mid-1970s to control the activities of the organization.

Meanwhile, the organization established contact with Ayatollah Khomeini (q.v.), who was in Iraq, but failed to reach an agreement with him because of Khomeini's insistence on leadership. However, it is argued that Khomeini adopted some of their doctrines, such as *al-mustad 'afin* (the oppressed) and *al-mustakbirin* (the oppressors). Nonetheless, the organization contributed to the revolution of 1978. Because of basic ideological differences with Khomeini, namely, his views on the Islamic state (q.v.) as well as his call for nationalization of natural resources and equal rights for women, the organization became the main opposition force to the newly established regime.

In 1981, the *Mujahidin* launched riots protesting the policies of the new regime and formed a government in exile. Since then it has been involved in guerrilla warfare with the regime. It is based today in Kurdistan, an area adjacent to both Iran and Iraq. One of its demands is local autonomy for minorities.

The *Mujahidin* felt strong enough in June 1981 to attempt popular protests against the regime. But it failed to undermine the regime and had to establish itself in Iraq. The *Mujahidin* was at that time under the control of Mas'ud Rajavi who tended to tone down his attacks on imperialism and social revolution and instead stressed democracy, political parties, pluralism, and human rights (qq.v.) (*huquq al-insan*). Rajavi later lived in Europe.

The organization did not appeal much to the public because of its elitist policy. Membership was given to university students and middle-class professionals. Furthermore, it advocated guerrilla warfare and the creation of a people's army to fight the Shah. It called as well for purifying Iran from Western influence in order to protect traditional Shi'ite values. See also ISLAMIC REVOLUTION OF IRAN; REVOLUTIONARY GUARDS.

MUJAHIDIN **MOVEMENT IN MOROCCO.** The *Mujahidin* movement in Morocco is considered to be one of the extremist branches of the armed religious movement that became active in the late 1960s as a reaction to the expansion of the Moroccan democratic and nationalistic movement opposed to the regime.

The movement, according to its own press, was established late in 1970 by 'Abd al-'Aziz al-Na'mani (q.v.) and other fundamentalists who were implicated in 'Umar Bin Jallun's assassination. It appears that the *Mujahidin* movement has worked under different covers, which has resulted in some overlapping with other Islamic organizations, especially the Islamic Youth Organization (q.v.).

The movement began issuing its own journal, *al-Saraya*, in 1984, which revealed its course of action and regional and international alliances. The movement's political program can be summarized as two goals: first, to overthrow the monarchy and second, to establish an Islamic state (q.v.) on the Iranian model.

The movement has strong ties with Iran and Algeria, and the latter trains and arms the movement's members, who are smuggled into Morocco to conduct violent operations. Several violent groups belonging to the *Mujahidin* movement have been arrested. In August 1986, the most significant of these groups was captured, and 13 of its members were put on trial. The prosecutor based his case on the accusations that they were working to overthrow the monarchy and replace it with an Islamic republic on the Iranian model, distributing pamphlets of *al-Saraya* that encouraged disorder, organizing secret cells and motivating demonstrations, and forging documents. The court's verdicts included imprisonment, ranging from one year to 30 years for 16 people. In March 1984 authorities in Morocco arrested two Muslim extremists, Muhammad Haji and Muhammad al-Awan, who admitted belonging to the *Mujahidin* movement. The arrests revealed that the majority of the *Mujahidin* members were young individuals from Moroccan working classes.

Al-Saraya launched fierce attacks on the Moroccan authorities, especially King Hasan II, who was accused of "drowning the country in corruption, tyranny (q.v.) and repression," and condemned his pro-Western policies.

The movement is led by 'Abd al-'Aziz al-Na'mani, who was an inspector in the Moroccan educational system. Al-Na'mani lives in exile and has been sentenced to death in the case of Bin-Jallun's assassination. Al-Nkadi Muhammad participates in the movement's leadership. See also NA'MANI, 'ABD AL-'AZIZ.

AL-MUMNI, DAYF (1940–). Al-Mumni is a member of the Muslim Brotherhood in Jordan (q.v.). Al-Mumni was born in 'Abiyn and obtained a B.A. in history from the University of Yarmuk. He worked as a teacher at the Ministry of Education for 27 years and was elected to the Lower House of the Parliament in 1993.

AL-MUNAZZAMA AL-THAWRIYYA AL-ISLAMIYYA FI SHIBH AL-JAZIRA AL-'ARABIYYA. See ISLAMIC REVOLUTIONARY ORGANIZATION OF THE ARABIAN PENINSULA.

MUNAZZAMAT AL-'AMAL AL-ISLAMI. See ISLAMIC ACTION ORGANIZATION IN BAHRAIN; ISLAMIC ACTION ORGANIZATION IN IRAQ.

MUNAZZAMAT AL-HARAKA AL-ISLAMIYYA. See ORGANIZATION OF THE ISLAMIC MOVEMENT.

MUNAZZAMAT AL-JIHAD. See *AL-JIHAD* ORGANIZATION.

MUNAZZAMAT AL-JIHAD AL-ISLAMI (ORGANIZATION OF ISLAMIC *JIHAD*) **IN LEBANON.** See *AL-JIHAD AL-ISLAMI FI LUBNAN.*

MUNAZZAMAT MUQATILU AL-SHARQ AL-KABIR AL-ISLAMI. See ORGANIZATION OF THE FIGHTERS FOR THE GREATER ISLAMIC EAST.

MUNAZZAMAT AL-SHABIBA AL-ISLAMIYYA. See ISLAMIC YOUTH ORGANIZATION.

MUNTAZARI, HUSAYN 'ALI (1933–). Muntazari is one of the main personalities of the Islamic Republic of Iran. He is a grand Ayatollah who is very much respected and honored. He studied at Qum where he met and supported Ayatollah Khomeini (q.v.). Muntazari was a member of the Freedom Movement, was active in his opposition to the Shah's regime, and was a key figure in the informal organization that propagated Khomeini's messages and tapes.

After the revolution, Muntazari became a member of the Islamic Republican Party (q.v.), the Council of Experts (q.v.), and the designated successor to Khomeini. However, his "radical" views, including his support for land reform as well as jockeying for power against a powerful right-wing group that included 'Ali Khamene'i, 'Ali Rafsanjani, and Muhammad Bahishti (qq.v.), brought him into disfavor with Khomeini. He resigned his posts, and Khomeini removed him as his successor. But Muntazari is still a powerful figure to contend with. When Muhammad Khatami (q.v.) was elected President of Iran in 1996, Muntazari wrote him a very critical letter against the regime, pointing out that his election was a vote against the current regime. He also confronted Ayatollah Khamene'i, the supreme guide of the Republic of Iran, about the issue of *waliy al-faqih* (q.v.) (guardian of the jurist), which led to Muntazari's being publicly censured and persecuted by groups of the regime's supporters. See also ISLAMIC REPUBLICAN PARTY.

MUQBIL, SALIH 'ABBAD. See *AL-JIHAD* ORGANIZATION.

MURAD, 'ISMAT. See *HARAKAT AL-TAWHID AL-ISLAMI.*

MURSHID AL-THAWRA (REVOLUTION'S GUIDE). See *WALIY AL-FAQIH.*

MUSADDAQ'S TREND (*AL-TAYYAR AL-MUSADDAQI'S*). This is a liberal national trend that adheres to the view of the late Prime Minister Muhammad Musaddaq who ruled Iran in the early 1950s and nationalized the oil industry. Although this trend lacks solid popular support, it enjoys popularity among intellectuals, university circles, and some middle-class groups of state employees.

One of its leaders is the engineer 'Izzat Allah al-Sihabi, a member of the former Iranian Revolutionary Council (q.v.) and a former member of *Majlis al-Shura* (q.v.) in Iran. Along with Sayyid Mahmud Talqani (q.v.), he is considered to be one of the important figures of the National Front that fought the Shah's regime. In 1996, Sihabi competed as an independent candidate for the presidency of the Republic.

AL-MUSAWAT. See EQUALITY.

AL-MUSAWI, 'ABBAS. See *HIZBULLAH.*

AL-MUSAWI, HUSAYN. See *HARAKAT AMAL AL-ISLAMIYYA.*

AL-MUSAWI, SADIQ. See *AL-HARAKAT AL-ISLAMIYYA FI LUBNAN.*

MUSLIM BRETHREN. See MUSLIM BROTHERHOOD.

MUSLIM BROTHERHOOD (*AL-IKHWAN AL-MUSLIMIN*). The Muslim Brotherhood was founded in Egypt in 1928 by Hasan al-Banna (q.v.). Upon completing his studies at Dar al-'Ulum, al-Banna returned to Isma'iliyya to begin his job as a teacher in a governmental school. In March 1928, he founded the Association of the Muslim Brethren, which was supported by a few of his students and proponents of his earlier mission to Isma'iliyya as a religious student. He set up sermons at large coffeehouses and preached to thousands of people, thereby gaining immense popularity. Within a few years, the movement spread to many regions of Egypt and attained great power. The movement's growth, however, has been largely accomplished through concealment from the government.

In 1933, al-Banna was transferred as a teacher to Cairo. He saw this as an opportunity to expand and strengthen the movement. He created special magazines for the organization, which circulated articles and amassed widespread support. The organization went beyond Egypt's border, reaching Sudan, Syria, Lebanon, and North Africa. Still, the Brethren did not attract the attention of the government because their activities were well hidden behind the veil of religion.

By 1938, the movement had assumed its mature phase as an "orthodox organization," a political body, a scientific and cultural society, and a social idea. During World War II, the movement's efforts were doubled, and it was supported by university students. It set up athletic and physical training centers in regions across Egypt during summer vacations.

Politically, the state ultimately became aware of the Brotherhood's far-reaching abilities. Under the rule of Sirri Pasha, their weekly magazines were confiscated and they were prohibited from printing any new material. Both al-Banna and his Secretary-General were arrested and later on released. Al-Banna ran for election, but al-Nahhas asked him to withdraw and, instead, allowed him to circulate his magazines and printed material under government regulations. The peaceful involvement of the Muslim Brotherhood in Egypt's political life has been well documented. It was involved in the struggle of the Azhar during the 1920s and 1930s and sided as well with the King against the government.

By 1945, the Brethren were directing all their efforts and their activities against the government, where their interests and demands would reach a far greater number of people. They set up commerical companies that yielded profits and hence support from the working classes. They also set up camps for military training. The Brethren devoted themselves to stirring up the consciousness (q.v.) (wa'iy) of the people, calling for jihad (q.v.) (struggle) and for the complete independence of the country.

The Brotherhood built its headquarters from voluntary donations, after which it built a mosque and schools for boys and girls. In 1946, the government provided financial aid, free books, and stationery to the Brotherhood schools, with the Ministry of Education having paid all their educational and administrative expenses. Al-Banna established holding companies for schools, and this became a success, because most of the Brotherhood's membership was composed of middle-class professionals and businessmen.

Only a year after the establishment of the Brotherhood in Cairo, it had 50 branches all over Egypt. Worried about the spread of Christian missionary schools in Egypt, the Brotherhood called on King Faruq to subject this activity to governmental supervision. But after a meeting with a Christian preacher in the church, al-Banna wrote about the necessity for men of religion (q.v.) to unite against atheism. During the same year, the Brotherhood decided to set up a press and publish a weekly, *al-Ikhwan al-Muslimun*.

During the rule of al-Naqrashi Pasha (1946), the Brethren called for a nationwide *jihad* and published articles criticizing the government for persecuting and oppressing the movement. With the Palestine question, the Brethren's active support intensified the tensions between the movement and the government. In 1948, the Brethren participated in the battle of the Arab armies for the liberation of Palestine, thereby arming themselves and gaining valuable combat training. The Egyptian government feared this newly found power and led a series of seizures and arrests against the organization and all its branches. The Brethren's position grew weaker with the assassination of al-Naqrashi and the government's consequent blame of members of the group as the murderers. The association was officially dissolved in 1947, and a year later al-Banna was assassinated.

The Brotherhood was able to mobilize the Egyptian masses. Al-Banna, for instance, included Boy Scouts in his organization. The Scouts' pledge was essentially of a moral tone, and not political and revolutionary but rather centered around faith, virtue, work, and the family. But al-Banna never denied that the Brotherhood was a movement that sought the revival of religion (q.v.) and had its own political, educational, and economic aspirations. This, however, did not mean that the Brotherhood would isolate itself from society. In 1936, the Brotherhood participated, for instance, in the coronation of King Faruq. During 1948, the membership of its youth scouts exceeded 40,000 and had spread by then all over Egypt, working to eliminate illiteracy, cholera, and malaria epidemics. In 1948, the Brotherhood had set up 500 branches for social services and established as well medical clinics and hospitals, treating about 51,000 patients. Al-Banna set up a women's organization in the 1940s whose membership in 1948 reached 5,000—a high number according to the standards of the time. It played a central role in what is referred to as *al-mihna al-ula* (First Ordeal) during 1948–1950 when it catered to the families of the thousands of Brethren who were jailed. The active membership of the Brotherhood was around half a million, and the supporters numbered another half million. The Brotherhood had, by the time of its dissolution, one thousand branches in Egypt.

By 1951, the Brethren were picking up the pieces and slowly rebuilding all that had been lost. In October 1951, they made their presence felt by participating in the liberation movement against the British. They regained some of their political voice only when the government saw that they did not violate any laws.

During the 'Abd al-Nasir period, the Brethren suffered a severe blow when they came face-to-face with 'Abd al-Nasir and were accused of an attempt on his life. The government then destroyed the organization and imprisoned its leaders. In the concentration camp, Sayyid Qutb (q.v.) wrote an analysis of the state's relationship to society based upon the suffering and pain that had been endured. This analysis was expounded in his book *Ma'alim fi al-Tariq*, which played a major role in the radicalization of many fundamentalist movements. In 1965, the detainees were released and began creating an organized plan to topple the government. The Brotherhood was again persecuted.

Qutb's work was interpreted in two ways, as an invitation to denounce the government and as a call to return to al-Banna's objectives. Those who adhered to the latter interpretation (q.v.) asked President Anwar al-Sadat for recognition. Although their request was denied, they were granted permission to publish a monthly, *al-Da'wa*, headed by 'Umar al-Tilmisani (q.v.). This monthly reached university students in 1977, and that year witnessed student elections that produced a fundamentalist victory.

At the same time, the *Jama'a al-Islamiyya* (q.v.) (Islamic Group) was establishing an infrastructure to work against the government. This group split into various competing groups, however, the students continued to challenge the government, even though it closed the General Union of Students. The arrests following the dissolution of the *Jama'a* broke down the movement.

The importance of the Brotherhood was that during the 1970s, the

Brethren were used by Sadat to add legitimacy (q.v.) to his government, even though they were still not allowed to form their own political party. They broke with him over his trip to Jerusalem in 1977 and the Camp David Accord. Their protest led to the imprisonment of hundreds of Brethren in addition to members of other radical groups. But the Muslim Brethren have not officially sanctioned and used violence (q.v.) to achieve any political and religious objective. In October 1981, a fundamentalist group, *al-Jihad al-Islami* (Islamic *Jihad*), assassinated President Sadat. This was seen as a great success for the movement, because Sadat was at the peak of unpopularity, and so his assassin was seen as a spokesman for the people. However, Sadat's death did not dissolve the regime.

Since 1984, the Brotherhood in Egypt and elsewhere and similar movements, like *Harakat al-Nahda al-Islamiyya* (q.v.) (Islamic Renaissance Movement) in Tunisia and the Islamic Salvation Front in Algeria (q.v.), have sought to be included in the political process and have been involved in setting up civil institutions. Because the Muslim Brotherhood in Jordan (q.v.) has functioned since the 1950s as a political party, some of its members have become well placed in the government and the Parliament.

The Muslim Brotherhood has undergone many trials and has gone through periods of success and failure, but it is gaining momentum. It has infiltrated much of the Egyptian society and other Islamic societies. It has branches all over the world, including the Gulf States, Algeria, Jordan, Palestine, Lebanon, Libya, Mauritania, Sudan, Syria, and others. See also 'ABD AL-RAHMAN, 'UMAR; ABU GHUDDA, 'ABD AL-FATTAH; 'AWDA, 'ABD AL-QADIR; AL-'AWWA, MUHAMMAD SALIM; AL-BANNA, HASAN; AL-BANNA, SAYF; AL-GHAN-NUSHI, RASHID; AL-GHAZALI, MUHAMMAD; AL-GHAZALI, ZAYNAB; AL-HUDAYBI, HASAN; AL-HUDAYBI, MA'MUN; IBN TAYMIYYA, TAQIY AL-DIN; INTERNATIONAL ORGANIZATION OF THE MUSLIM BROTHERHOOD; 'ISHMAWI, SALIH; AL-IS-LAMBULI, MUHAMMAD SHAWQI; ISLAMIC SALVATION FRONT IN ALGERIA; ISMA'IL, 'ABD AL-FATTAH; ISRAEL; JA-BALLAH, 'ABD ALLAH; *JAMA'AT AL-FANNIYYA AL-'ASKARIYYA*; *AL-JAMA'AT AL-ISLAMIYYA*; *JAMA'AT AL-MUSLIMIN*; *JAMA'AT AL-JIHAD*; MADI, ABU AL-'ULA; MASHHUR, MUSTAPHA; MU-HAMMAD'S YOUTH; MUSLIM BROTHERHOOD, IDEOLOGY OF; MUSLIM BROTHERHOOD, IN THE GULF, JORDAN, PALESTINE, SUDAN, SYRIA; AL-NABAHANI, TAQIY AL-DIN; AL-NADAWI,

ABU AL-HASAN; AL-NAHNAH, MAHFOUDH; *AL-NIZAM AL-SIRRI*; AL-QARADAWI, YUSUF; QUTB, MUHAMMAD; QUTB, SAYYID; RIDA, MUHAMMAD RASHID; *AL-SALAFIYYA*; *AL-SALAFIYYA* FORCES IN EGYPT; SECOND ISLAMIC INTERNATIONAL; AL-SIBA'I, MUSTAPHA; SIRRIYYA, SALIH; *AL-TAJAMMU' AL-YEMENI LI AL-ISLAH*; *AL-WAHHABIYYA*; AL-WARTALANI, FUDAYL; YAKAN, FATHI; YASIN, AHMAD.

MUSLIM BROTHERHOOD, IDEOLOGY OF. The peaceful involvement of the Muslim Brotherhood (q.v.) in Egypt's political life is well documented. It was involved in the struggle of the Azhar during the 1920s and 1930s and sided as well with the King against the government. During that period, Hasan al-Banna (q.v.) cooperated at times with Isma'il Sidqi, who was periodically Prime Minister, and engaged in teaching and lecturing.

In politics, the Brotherhood did not originally resort to violence (q.v.) but played according to the rules of the game, as long as it was allowed to do so, and then resorted to violence when it became the name of the game. It was not only the Brotherhood that established striking secret apparatuses—that was a common practice with other parties (q.v.) as well as the state, which used political assassination to resolve many problems. This violence manifested itself against the Brethren in jailing thousands of them, dissolving the organization, liquidating its assets, as well as assassinating al-Banna.

Al-Banna's emphasis on the proper grounding of political ideology does not exclude individual and collective social and political reformulations of Islamic political doctrines in accordance with modern society's needs, aspirations, and beliefs. More importantly, al-Banna attempts to show that political ideology must account for and deal with modernity (q.v.) as a world view, not only as a law. Both the law and world view must deal with the real world, not in abstract terms, but essentially in practical terms and, therefore, must take into account and include other interpretations, political ideologies, and philosophies. Because Islam (q.v.) is both religion (q.v.) and society and a mosque and a state, it must deal effectively with religion and the world by the inclusion of diverse substantive and methodological pluralistic interpretations, although maintaining the basic doctrines of religion.

Because *al-Shari'a* (q.v.) (Islamic Law) is viewed as a social norm, al-Banna frees its application from past specific methods and links its good practice to the maintenance of freedom (q.v.) and popular authority over the government and the delineation of the competence of the executive, the legislative, and the judiciary. Western constitutional forms of government do not contradict Islam if grounded in both constitutionality of *al-Shari'a* and objectivity. Constitutional rule (q.v.) is transformed into *shura* (q.v.) (consultation) by a subtle reinterpretation in light of modernity and in a spirit not contradictory to the Qur'an (q.v.). *Shura*, as the basic principle of government and the exercise of power by society, becomes inclusionary by definition and is employed to empower the people to set the course of their political actions and ideology.

If the ultimate source of the *shura*'s legitimacy (q.v.) is the people, its representation cannot be restricted to one party that may represent only a fraction of the people. Continuous ratification by the community is required because governance (q.v.) (*hakimiyya*) is a contract between the ruled and the ruler. Al-Banna's theoretical acceptance of political pluralistic, democratic, and inclusionary interpretations plants the future seeds for further acceptance by the Muslim Brotherhood of political pluralism and democracy (qq.v.), not withstanding its link to *tawhid* (q.v.) (Oneness of God) and its political connotation, unity. This acceptance does not exclude even the existence of many states. Party politics and political systems do not preclude for al-Banna the acceptance of substantial differences in ideologies, policies, and programs. But an Islamic state (q.v.) does exclude parties that contradict the Oneness of God.

Again, al-Banna's system (q.v.) (*nizam*) includes different social and religious groups such as Christians and Jews, who along with Muslims are united by interest, human good, and belief in God and the holy books. Where religion is acknowledged as an essential component of the state, political conflicts ought not to be turned into religious wars and must be resolved by dialogue. Individuals enjoy as well equal religious, civil, political, social, and economic rights and duties. This principle of individual involvement, to enjoin the good and forbid evil, is the origin of pluralism leading to the formation of political parties and social organizations or, simply, the democratization of the social and political process. See also AL-BANNA, HASAN; CALIPHATE; DEMOCRACY; EXTREMISM; MUSLIM BROTHERHOOD; QUTB, SAYYID; VIOLENCE; WESTERN CIVILIZATION.

MUSLIM BROTHERHOOD (*AL-IKHWAN AL-MUSLIMIN*) **IN ALGERIA.** See ISLAMIC SOCIETY MOVEMENT: *HAMAS*.

MUSLIM BROTHERHOOD (*AL-IKHWAN AL-MUSLIMIN*) **IN THE GULF.** This Sunni fundamentalist organization was founded in Egypt in

1928. Offshoots spread throughout the Gulf as Egyptian teachers and professionals took up residence in the region during the 1950s. The Brotherhood inspired the reformist fundamentalist movements that emerged in the Arab Gulf states in the 1970s and 1980s, particularly in Kuwait, but it, supposedly, is not related to the *Ikhwan* (q.v.) of Saudi Arabia. See also *JAM'IYYAT AL-ISLAH AL-IJTIMA'IYYA*; *JAM'IYYAT IHYA' AL-TURATH.*

MUSLIM BROTHERHOOD (*AL-IKHWAN AL-MUSLIMIN*) **IN JORDAN.** The Brotherhood was established in 1946 by 'Abd al-Latif Abu Qura (q.v.) as a branch of the Muslim Brotherhood (q.v.) in Egypt; the Brotherhood has been very active in the politics of Jordan since the 1950s. Although it is registered as a charitable society, a great deal of its program is political. Islam (q.v.) is viewed not only as a religion (q.v.) but also as an ethical guideline. Its program addresses spiritual, political, and socioeconomic issues. It urges the return of Jordan to Islamic principles and the application of *al-Shari'a* (q.v.) (Islamic Law) as the basis for society. Only in this way can Jordan move toward social justice (q.v.) and progress. Issues such as banning the sale of alcohol and gender separation in the workplace hold more than just symbolic importance.

The organization has presented itself as a nonthreatening socioreligious movement and has maintained a workable relationship with the regime. During the late 1940s, and under the mandate, it received the support of Amir 'Abd Allah. Later King Husayn also lent his support and used it to counterbalance the leftist challenges in the 1950s. After 1957, although all other parties were banned, the Brotherhood played a central political role. In the 1990s the party did not totally support the regime, which had started to view the Brotherhood with suspicion because of the diverging political platform regarding the Gulf War and the Arab-Israeli peace (q.v.) process.

During the 1950s and 1960s, the Brotherhood, led by Muhammad Khalifa (q.v.), had scored major electoral successes. However, in the 1989 elections for the Parliament, the Brotherhood staged a vigorous campaign under the slogan "Islam Is the Solution" and scored a major victory, an act that irritated the establishment. The Brotherhood won 22 of 80 seats, more than any other party, then it allied itself with 10 independent fundamentalists and formed an Islamic bloc. Thus, it was rewarded with five of the 24 ministries in the government of Mudar Badran. However, it boycotted the government of Tahir al-Masri (1991) because of his support of peace negotiations in the Middle East.

The Brotherhood's popular success has been based on its addressing people's grievances, including the abolition of martial law, protection of civil liberties, rejection of Western influence, support of the Palestinian cause, and rejection of both Marxism and capitalism (qq.v.). The Brotherhood also joined with the Left in supporting Iraq during the 1991 Gulf War, a popular stance at the time in Jordan.

Several other factors account for its success. For years it operated as an association. The Brotherhood was thus able to establish effective organizational structures and reach the masses through use of the mosques, Friday sermons, and publications such as *al-Kifah al-Islami* in the 1950s, *al-Manar* in the 1960s, and *al-Rabat* in the 1990s. In 1992, the Brotherhood formed *Jabhat al-'Amal al-Islami* (q.v.) (Islamic Action Front Party). See also ABU FIRAS, MUHAMMAD; ABU QURAH, 'ABD AL-LATIF; 'AWAYDA, MUHAMMAD; AZAYDAH, AHMAD; AL-'AZM, YUSUF; DAWUDIYYA, 'ABD KHALAF; DHUNAYBAT, 'ABD AL-MAJID; AL-FARHAN, ISHAQ; AL-HAWAMDA, 'ALI; *HIZB JABHAT AL-'AMAL AL-ISLAMI*; *HIZB AL-TAHRIR AL-ISLAMI*; JAMMU, 'ABD AL-BAQI; *JAYSH MUHAMMAD*; KAWJAQ, DAWUD; KHALIFA, MUHAMMAD; KHATTAB, DHIB; KHURAYSAT, IBRAHIM; AL-MUMNI, DAYF; SA'ID, HAMMAM; SA'ID, SULAYMAN; AL-SHARIF, KAMIL.

MUSLIM BROTHERHOOD (*AL-IKHWAN AL-MUSLIMIN*) **IN KUWAIT**. See *JAM'IYYAT AL-ISLAH AL-IJTIMA'IYYA*; MUSLIM BROTHERHOOD IN THE GULF.

MUSLIM BROTHERHOOD (*AL-IKHWAN AL-MUSLIMIN*) **IN LEBANON**. See *AL-JAMA'A AL-ISLAMIYYA FI LUBNAN*.

MUSLIM BROTHERHOOD (*AL-IKHWAN AL-MUSLIMIN*) **IN LIBYA**. The influence of the Muslim Brotherhood in Libya goes back to the early 1950s, owing to the impact of the powerful Egyptian Muslim Brotherhood (q.v.). In Libya, the Muslim Brethren appealed to students and graduates of both religious and modern schools. The organization broke into three factions, one that became Nasirite and a second faction that distanced itself from any political activity and confined itself to the practice of religion. The third faction continued in the same tradition as the Muslim Brethren. With Mu'ammar al-Qaddafi's anticlerical and Islamic reformist polices, the Muslim Brotherhood has become one of the major political opposition forces against the revolutionary regime under the rubric of the National Front for the Salvation of Libya (q.v.) (*al-Jabha al-Wataniyya li Inqadh Libya*). See also NATIONAL FRONT FOR THE SALVATION OF LIBYA.

MUSLIM BROTHERHOOD (*AL-IKHWAN AL-MUSLIMIN*) **IN MAURITANIA**. See *UMMA* PARTY IN MAURITANIA.

MUSLIM BROTHERHOOD (*AL-IKHWAN AL-MUSLIMIN*) **IN PALESTINE**. A strong Egyptian initiative was behind the setting up of the Muslim Brotherhood in Palestine. As a result the first branch was established in May 1946 under British Mandate in Jerusalem. This branch was important because of the major role played by Jamal al-Husseini in its establishment. Jamal al-Husseini was the Vice President of the High Islamic Council and its President by proxy while Haj Amin al-Husseini was in exile. During the same year, branches were established in Jaffa, Lid, and Haifa.

Other branches were also established in Nablus and Tulkarm as well as the branches in Jordan. In October 1946, the movement gained official approval and recognition in a conference attended by Lebanon, Jordan, and Palestine. As an outcome of the 1948 Arab-Israeli war, several branches under Israeli occupation were closed, yet others appeared in the villages of the West Bank, which fell under Jordanian jurisdiction. Initially very little cooperation and coordination was present among the various branches, especially after Jamal 'Abd al-Nasir became the dominant figure in Egypt, where the Brotherhood's public activities came to an end.

It was obvious that the creation of Israel (q.v.) in 1948 divided Palestine. Whereas the Brotherhood flourished in the West Bank, where Jordanian authorities made it a legal party despite the 1957 ban on all other political organizations, it became an underground party in Egyptian-controlled Gaza. Following the Israeli occupation of Gaza and the West Bank in 1967, Gaza emerged as the center of Muslim Brotherhood activities.

Haj 'Abd al-Latif Abu Qura (q.v.) led the movement in Jordan until 1956. His successor was Muhammad 'Abd al-Rahman Khalifa (q.v.), under whose leadership the movement began showing more cooperation and organization among the various branches. In 1954, he was succeeded by Sa'id Ramadan, yet the latter was expelled from Jordan the following year. Khalifa returned to lead the movement a decade later in 1965. Muhammad 'Abd al-Rahman Khalifa remained the leader of the movement from 1954 until the mid-1960s, although sometime in mid-1963 Yusuf al-'Azm became its leader.

The movement wanted Jordanian permission to establish its branches in Jerusalem, Bethlehem, and Jericho. In 1956, the Brotherhood's branch in Hebron organized a powerful campaign for that year's elections to support its candidate, Dr. Hafiz 'Abd al-Nabi al-Nitcha.

Also, the Brotherhood in Palestine was very loyal to the movement in Egypt, which was characterized as being very active politically. But the lack of trust of some Egyptian officials was clear from the start when the government refused to allow the Brotherhood to establish a branch in Hebron right after the 1948 war, even although the *Ikhwan* joined the Egyptian forces in that war. The officials feared that the movement was assisted by Haj Amin al-Husseini, who was then living in exile.

The government also stopped granting permissions to establish new branches because the Brotherhood had criticized some governmental policies, especially those considered to deviate from the moral values of Islam. It also used to call the masses to support the King against Communist and Ba'thist forces, although criticizing the state policies and demanding reform according to Islamic principles. The Brotherhood also condemned the strong ties that the government maintained with the West, mainly Great Britain. In 1954, the Brotherhood demonstrated against the presence of British officers in the army and called for their evacuation. From its establishment, the movement was very anti-imperialistic, and the general guide was arrested several times.

Their anti-imperialism caused them to support Jamal 'Abd al-Nasir in his anti-Western policies. However, mutual skepticism between the Brotherhood and the Free Officers was clear at times of crisis, as in 1955. In that year, the Brotherhood was placed under close surveillance: Leaders' speeches were monitored and the general guide clashed frequently with the authorities. The Brotherhood's position with respect to the regime showed considerable fluctuations because of changing local factors and external political ones. However, it was severely suppressed by the Egyptian government.

Since the mid-1950s, the *Ikhwan* has used its deputies in the Jordanian Parliament to object to certain state policies, in particular its failure to implement Islamic Law and failure to remove Jordan from the West's sphere of influence. Also, the government did not do much in the way of struggling against Israel. At that time, those deputies spoke out publicly against the performance and policies of Prime Minister Samir al-Rifa'i.

The Brotherhood became active again during the Palestinian *Intifada* and sat up *Harakat al-Muqawama al-Islamiyya: Hamas* (q.v.) under the leadership of Ahmad Yasin (q.v.). Since then the movement has been very active in fighting the Israeli occupation of the Territories and has launched many violent attacks. It has been active as well in providing social and medical services to the Palestinians. It has rejected the Oslo Accords and all of the agreements between the Palestinian National Authority and Israel. See also *HARAKAT AL-MUQAWAMA AL-ISLAMIYYA: HAMAS*; *HIZB AL-TAHRIR AL-ISLAMI*; ISRAEL; *AL-JIHAD AL-ISLAMI* IN THE WEST BANK AND GAZA STRIP; KHAYYAT, 'ABD AL-'AZIZ; SHIQAQI, FATHI.

MUSLIM BROTHERHOOD (*AL-IKHWAN AL-MUSLIMIN*) **IN SUDAN.** In 1946, a group of Sudanese students who studied in Egypt or were affected by the Muslim Brotherhood (q.v.) in Egypt organized the Islamic Liberation Movement (*Harakat al-Tahrir al-Islamiyya*) to counter the influence of the Communist Party. This happened after a delegation of the Muslim Brotherhood headed by the Egyptian lawyer Salah 'Abd al-Sid visited Sudan, which was followed by an official delegation in 1946.

The movement changed its name to the Muslim Brotherhood at a conference held at Khartoum University in 1954 and centered its demands on the implementation of Islamic Law. The movement went through two stages with President Ja'afa al-Numayri: first, one of struggle against the regime, 1969–1977; then, one of reconciliation with the regime, 1977–1984. It even participated in government from 1984 to 1989. It was instrumental in the revolt against the government of Sadiq al-Mahdi and the establishment of the current regime of 'Umar Hasan al-Bashir (q.v.).

The Brotherhood formed the Islamic Charter Front, which was led by Hasan al-Turabi (q.v.), after the October Revolution of 1964 to recruit followers into its political program and to contest parliamentary elections. The front became active in the Transitional Government of 1964–1965 and an opponent of the Communist Party. During the period 1964–1969, the front was very active politically and socially and benefited from the regime's conflicts with the communists. The front also fought with traditional parties, that is, *Umma* Party and Democratic Unionist Party. Later on, the Islamic Charter Front was dissolved by al-Turabi and was reorganized as the National Islamic Front around 1977.

The National Front infiltrated the armed forces, the banking sector by establishing Islamic banks, and Islamic cultural organizations as well as many segments of civil society. Because the social base of the Islamic movement included students and graduates, the Muslim Brotherhood, as well as the two fronts, viewed itself as an alternative to the *Umma* Party and the People's Democratic Party. Its power base included nontraditional forces in society and a good number of the intelligentsia. The front has developed a sophisticated organization, with branches that deal with all aspects of life. It has established numerous newspapers, including *al-Ra'y* and *al-Sudan*. The Islamic movement has historically participated in elections under all regimes.

In 1988, the National Islamic Front joined the coalition government headed by Sadiq al-Mahdi. The front was behind the army's *Thawrat al-Inqadh* (Salvation Revolution), headed by General 'Umar al-Bashir in 1989.

The Muslim Brotherhood is split today; one branch is led by Sulayman Abu Naro, who has disconnected his organization from al-Turabi's and has repeatedly described the current regime as non-Islamic; the other is led by Shaykh 'Abd al-Majid, who is the representative of the International Organization of the Muslim Brotherhood (q.v.), and who supports the current regime.

Sudan is considered today as an Islamic state (q.v.), and Hasan al-Turabi has dominated intellectually and politically the Islamic movement in Sudan as well as the ideology of the state. The Islamic movement called for the revival of Islamic society (q.v.), the establishment of an Islamic state, the adoption of an Islamic constitution (q.v.) and the application of *al-Shari'a* (q.v.) (Islamic Law), and the attainment of worldwide Muslim unity. See also INTERNATIONAL ORGANIZATION OF THE MUSLIM BROTHERHOOD; SECOND ISLAMIC INTERNATIONAL; AL-TURABI, HASAN.

MUSLIM BROTHERHOOD (*AL-IKHWAN AL-MUSLIMIN*) **IN SYRIA**. The Muslim Brotherhood in Syria was established in 1945–1946 by Mustapha al-Siba'i (q.v.) of Homs. Students and religious *'ulama'* that were influenced by the Egyptian Muslim Brotherhood (q.v.) returned to Syria during the late 1930s and 1940s. They set up local fundamentalist benevolent societies that aimed at social and moral improvement. The Brotherhood also had exercised pressure on the National Bloc to provide aid to the Palestinian Arabs during the 1936 rebellion. It further directed mass demonstrations against the French-induced reforms relating to the educational system during World War II. With the close of the war, these societies united into a national organization. In 1946, al-Siba'i was elected to be general guide of the Syrian branches of the

Muslim Brotherhood. The organization set up its headquarters in Damascus and was close to the Egyptian Muslim Brotherhood, guided by Hasan al-Banna (q.v.).

During the 1940s and 1950s, the Syrian Brotherhood took a very active role in local politics and competed with the Communist Party and the Ba'th Party. Because al-Siba'i refused to characterize the organization as a formal party, the national leadership did not sponsor candidates in the parliamentary elections of September 1954. Instead, the organization formed a short-lived Islamic socialist front at the end of 1949 to oppose the People's Party's attempt to unite Syria with Iraq.

The Brotherhood also opposed, eight years later, Syria's unity with Egypt, or what became the United Arab Republic (UAR). This unity convinced the leaders of the need to be more active in politics, which resulted in popular demonstrations against the post-UAR regime in 1963–1964. As a result of these activities, al-Siba'i's successor as general guide, 'Isam al-'Attar, was expelled and sent to Germany in 1964.

During the 1960s, the Brotherhood in Syria gradually split into a relatively quietist branch centered in Damascus and a comparatively militant northern branch. Northerners, who were organized into the Fighting Vanguards (q.v.) (*al-Tala'i' al-Muqatila*) and led by Marwan Hadid, launched a campaign to overthrow the Ba'th regime by force. This campaign precipitated a crisis in the organization's leadership, which ended up by splitting into two distinct entities.

The northern branch escalated its campaign of assassination and sabotage in the early 1970s, culminating in a virtual civil war in the north-central cities in the spring of 1989. After a forcible suppression of rebellion, the leaders of various factions of the Muslim Brotherhood created the Islamic Front (q.v.) in Syria. In 1980, the front elected as its Secretary-General Shaykh Muhammad Abu al-Nasr al-Baynuni of Aleppo. A month later, it published a comprehensive manifesto calling for the overthrow of the regime and its replacement by a liberal democratic system firmly rooted in the principles of Islam (q.v.).

Continuing action against the Islamic Front by state security forces in 1981 and 1982 heightened antiregime sentiment in the cities and towns of north-central Syria. The front advised the inhabitants of these areas not to resist the operations of the security services, lest overt resistance provide the government with a pretext for obliterating the Muslim Brotherhood. When a large-scale rebellion broke out in Hama in 1982, Islamic Front militants joined the fighting. They resisted the Syrian army's efforts to dislodge them for three weeks but eventually were crushed by furious artillery and air strikes that reduced whole districts of the city to rubble.

After the suppression of the Hama uprising, the exiled leadership of the Islamic Front joined liberal and socialist opponents of the regime to form a national alliance for the liberation of Syria. This step was criticized by militants led by 'Adnan 'Uqla of *al-Tala'i' al-Muqatila*, who vowed to continue to struggle against the regime from within Syria. In response, the Islamic Front leaders expelled 'Uqla and appointed Sa'id Hawwa (q.v.) as commander of the organization's military formations. In 1985, 'Uqla's surrender to the authorities under a general amnesty ended any significant political activity by members of the Syrian Brotherhood. See also ABU GHUDDA, 'ABD AL-FATTAH; FIGHTING VANGUARDS; HAWWA, SA'ID; AL-SIBA'I, MUSTAPHA.

MUSLIM BROTHERHOOD (*AL-IKHWAN AL-MUSLIMIN*) **IN YEMEN**. See *AL-TAJAMMU' AL-YEMENI LI AL-ISLAH*; AL-WARTALANI, FUDAYL; AL-ZANDANI, SHAYKH 'ABD AL-MAJID.

MUSLIM PEOPLE'S REPUBLICAN PARTY IN IRAN (*HIZB-E JOMHURI-YE KHALQ-E MUSALMANE-E IRAN*). The party was founded in 1979 by supporters of Ayatollah Muhammad Shari'atmadari (q.v.), the main clerical rival of Ayatollah Khomeini (q.v.) in the Iranian Revolution of 1979 (q.v.). Although the party supported the notion of an Islamic republic, it disagreed strongly with the doctrinal principle of *waliy al-faqih* (q.v.) (guardian of the jurists). Arguing the importance of tolerating diverse points of view, Shari'atmadari was frequently interviewed by reporters seeking his opinions on public policy in the 1979–1980 period.

The party base was in Azerbaijan, and its membership was active in combating what it believed to be the abuses of the pro-Khomeini Islamic Republican Party (q.v.). After a number of attacks were made on the party offices and supporters, the party was closed in 1980, and Shari'atmadari was placed under virtual house arrest. He was later charged with masterminding an assassination plot against Khomeini. He was stripped of his religious titles and stayed in Qum until he died in 1986. See also SHARI'ATMADARI, AYATOLLAH MUHAMMAD.

MUSLIM SCHOLARS' ASSOCIATION (*TAJAMMU' AL-'ULAMA' AL-MUSLIMIN*). The Muslim Scholars' Association was originally set up in Lebanon in order to further Sunni-Shi'ite understanding after the victory of the Islamic Revolution of Iran (q.v.) and to serve the Iranian agenda. It appeared during the Israeli invasion of Lebanon in 1982. Some of its leading members are Shaykh Mahir Hammud and Zuhayr Kanj.

However, many individuals have broken with or frozen their membership in the association, including Shaykh 'Abd al-Nasir Jabri, who thinks that this association is not useful anymore. Also, Shaykh Hammud, who expected to be appointed President of this association, froze his membership after his disagreement with the Iranian ambassador to Syria. Shaykh Kanj refuses to obey the orders of the ambassador and attacked him publicly. The association has a center in Southern Beirut and is funded by Iran. The most outspoken member of this association is Shaykh Ahmad al-Zayn.

MUSLIM SISTERS. See AL-GHAZALI, ZAYNAB; MUSLIM BROTHERHOOD.

MUSLIM WOMEN'S ASSOCIATION. See AL-GHAZALI, ZAYNAB; MUSLIM BROTHERHOOD.

MUSTAPHA, SHUKRI (1942–1977). Mustapha was born in Abu Khruz village in Asyut, and his father had influence in Upper Egypt. But Mustapha left the village early, because his father deserted his mother, who took him along to her family. Mustapha entered the Benevolent Islamic school, and his high school grades allowed him to enter only the Faculty of Agriculture. He was arrested in 1965 while distributing pamphlets against the regime at the Asyut University. Mustapha was released in 1971 and continued his studies.

As an inmate with Sayyid Qutb (q.v.), Shukri Mustapha accepted the former's views and established the exclusivist radical *Jama'at al-Muslimin* (q.v.) (the Community of the Muslims), notoriously known a *al-Takfir wa al-Hijra* (Apostasy and Migration) as a fulfillment of the Qutbian vanguard (q.v.). In 1977, his group kidnapped a former *Awqaf* Minister, Shaykh Mahmud al-Dhahabi, who had earlier criticized its ideology. It asked for money and the release of some fundamentalist prisoners from *Jama'at al-Fanniyya al-'Askariyya* (q.v.). When its demands were not met, the ex-minister was executed. Mustapha and others were tried by the Higher State Security Court, found guilty, and executed.

Mustapha denied the legitimacy (q.v.) of pluralism (q.v.) and called on people to adhere to only the Qur'an (q.v.) and the *Sunna* (way) of the

Prophet. In his trial before a martial court in Egypt, he explained the exclusivity of his group in its rejection of theories and philosophies that are not textually derived from the Qur'an and the *Sunna* (way) of the Prophet, which he believed were the only criteria of legitimacy and truth. Therefore, the government was in violation of God's governance (q.v.) (*hakimiyya*). Furthermore, Mustapha brands as unbelievers all other Muslims who did not view Islam (q.v.) in his own manner and turned migration (*Hijra*) from the Egyptian society into a religious duty— making by this his isolated community the only true Muslim society.

MUTAHHARI, MURTAZA (1920–1979). Ayatollah Mutahhari, who was born in Mashhad, studied at the religious circles of Qum and became very close to Ayatollah Khomeini (q.v.). Mutahhari was a religious clergyman and author. He met Muhammad Husayn Tabtaba'i, a renowned scholar and thinker. Mutahhari moved to Tehran in 1952 and later taught at the Faculty of Theology at Tehran University. As a professor of theology, Mutahhari expressed well his views opposing the Shah's regime, which led to his imprisonment twice, once in 1964 and again in 1975.

Mutahhari was a founding member of *Husayniyyat al-Irshad*, where Ali Shari'ati (q.v.) became active and took over. He was associated with Sayyid Mahmud Talqani (q.v.) and promoted Islamic modernism (q.v.). He later joined more militant organizations, like *Jami'ah-yi Ruhaniyat-i Mubariz* (Society of the Militant Clergy). During the Iranian Revolution of 1979 (q.v.), Mutahhari stayed with Khomeini in France and was later appointed to the Council of the Islamic Revolution (q.v.). Mutahhari was assassinated in May 1979. As a thinker, Mutahhari promoted the Islamic revolution and criticized philosophically the materialism (q.v.) of the West (q.v.). See also *FURQAN*.

AL-MU'TAMAR AL-QAWMI AL-ISLAMI. See ISLAMIC-ARAB CONGRESS.

AL-MU'TAMAR AL-SHA'BI AL-'ARABI AL-ISLAMI (POPULAR ARAB ISLAMIC CONGRESS). See SECOND ISLAMIC INTERNATIONAL.

AL-MU'TAMAR AL-WATANI AL-BAHRAINI. See BAHRAIN NATIONAL CONGRESS.

MUTAWI', 'ABD AL-'AZIZ. See INTERNATIONAL ORGANIZATION OF THE MUSLIM BROTHERHOOD.

MUTI', 'ABD AL-KARIM (1936–). Al-Muti' is the leader of the Islamic Youth Organization (q.v.). In the early 1950s, 'Abd al-Karim joined the Moroccan resistance movement, which was under the leadership of Haman al-Ftwaki. After independence, he worked as an inspector in the field of education in Morocco.

Muti' established the Islamic Youth Organization in 1969 and has been its leader since then. However, because of his father's activity in opposing the government, he was dismissed from the National Teaching Union that was related, at that time, to the National Union People Forces. In 1972, he obtained a legal permit for the organization. Muti' participated in many Islamic activities related to the state and was elected a few times to different positions in Islamic state organizations.

In 1975, while Muti' was abroad attending an Islamic conference, a campaign was launched against the Islamic Youth, and since then he has been living in exile after having been condemned to death several times. He was accused of plotting to murder 'Umar bin Jallun. Muti' has survived several assassination attempts since he has been in exile. He is still leading the Islamic Youth Organization from abroad. See also ISLAMIC YOUTH ORGANIZATION.

MUTUAL RESPONSIBILITY *(TAKAFUL)*. Most fundamentalists view Islamic mutual responsibility not merely as charity and mercy but also as a system (q.v.) *(nizam)* of preparing people for work and of guaranteeing basic necessities to those who cannot work. Mutual responsibility is not only an individual duty, it is a public duty as well. Fundamentalists state that Islam (q.v.) considers acquiring education, with which one can earn and deserve his livelihood, a duty for every individual. The community has a responsibility to facilitate the fulfillment of this duty. If the community proves incapable, it becomes a state responsibility.

Fundamentalists in general stress the importance of society over the state (qq.v.); the state intervenes only where the voluntary efforts of individuals and of society fail. Therefore, the state, in theory at least, is supplementary to individual and social efforts, and as long as individuals and societies can get along without the state, the state should not interfere. See CALL; CAPITALISM; ECONOMIC THEORY; ISLAM; JUSTICE; MARXISM; MORALITY; RELIGION; SOCIAL JUSTICE.

AL-MUWAHHIDUN. See *AL-JAMA'A AL-ISLAMIYYA.*

-N-

AL-NABAHANI, TAQIY AL-DIN (1909–1977). Al-Nabahani was the founder of *Hizb al-Tahrir al-Islami* in Jordan (q.v.) (the Islamic Liberation Party) and Palestine. Al-Nabahani studied at the University of al-Azhar in 1932. He was a schoolteacher from the West Bank, worked at the *Shari'a* court, and became a judge in Ramelah in 1945. He fled to Syria in 1948 after the war in Palestine. He returned to Jerusalem as Judge in the Appeals Court, where he stayed until 1950, when he resigned. He flirted for some time with Ba'th ideology and wrote his *In-qadh Filistin* (*Liberation of Palestine*). He was a member of the Muslim Brotherhood (q.v.) in Palestine but later established his own party, *Hizb al-Tahrir al-Islami*, in 1952.

As a matter of fact, *Hizb al-Tahrir al-Islami* has not been able or enabled since the 1950s, either in the East or West Bank, to act according to its program and play its designated role. In 1976, the Jordanian government banned the party because its actions were perceived as threatening the stability of the monarchy, especially its emphasis on the necessity of elections for the legitimacy (q.v.) of government. As a result of persecution, al-Nabahani went to Damascus and then to Beirut. His party did not get a license, because the Jordanian government viewed the party as trying to end the monarchy.

Al-Nabahani accepted in his *al-Takattul al-Hizbi* (Party Formation) multiparty politics as a contemporary synonym to the duty of "enjoining good and forbidding evil." Also, he lamented the loss by political movements of many opportunities because of the lack of proper awareness of the role of parties (q.v.) in communal renaissance. A good party life must be based on a set of principles that commit the community to act. Only in this manner can a real party arise first and then represent the people and push for a major positive development. Without popular support civil actors cannot work properly.

Al-Nabahani imagined a gradual process of development that centered on a threefold program: first, propagating the party's platform where people become aware of the party and its principles; second, social interaction to sharpen the awareness of the people on essential issues; and third, the quest for power in order to rule in the name of the people. The party should always play the role of watchdog and should not dissolve itself into the structure and machinery of the state. Its independence of the government is essential for its credibility. Whereas the government's role is executive and should represent the people, the party's role is ideological. In this sense, the party should always watch the government. The government should not, therefore, isolate itself from society, but must be responsive. The party must stay—even if it is represented in government—as a social force that supervises governmental actions. Put differently, the civil institutions of society are above the government, which must yield to public demands and interests. Nonetheless, this situation must not be in contradiction to any Islamic principle.

Al-Nabahani viewed the institutions of the community at large as the legal source of authority. The government therefore should respect the wishes of the community and enact its will. The people were free to give or to withdraw authority, especially because a consultative council or *majlis al-shura* (q.v.) should be the consequence of elections and not appointment. Al-Nabahani downplayed the importance of the executive power and highlighted the pivotal function of elected bodies, because of their representation of the people and the protection of their "natural rights," including the right to form parties. See also *HIZB AL-TAHRIR*; *HIZB AL-TAHRIR AL-ISLAMI* IN TUNISIA; *JAMA'AT AL-FANNIYYA AL-'ASKARIYYA*; KHAYYAT, 'ABD AL-'AZIZ; VANGUARD.

AL-NABAHANIYUN. See *HIZB AL-TAHRIR AL-ISLAMI.*

NABULSI, 'ADIL. See *HIZB AL-TAHRIR AL-ISLAMI.*

AL-NADAWI, ABU AL-HASAN (1914–). Al-Nadawi is one of the most renowned Islamist thinkers in the Islamic world. He was born to a very religiously distinguished family in India. He received a B.A. in Arabic literature in 1929. In Lahore, he met Muhammad Iqbal and joined *Nadwat al-'Ulama'*. In 1934, he became a teacher in Dar al-'Ulum and started writing religious books and articles. He met Abu al-A'la al-Mawdudi (q.v.) and became a member of *al-Jama'a al-Islamiyya* in 1941, from which he resigned in 1978. In 1944, al-Nadawi published his very important book, *Madha Khasir al-'Alam bi Inhitat al-Muslimin* (*What the World Lost by Muslims' Deterioration*), which has had tremendous influence all over the Islamic world. Since then he has written extensively on most topics of interest to Muslims.

In 1951, al-Nadawi visited Egypt and met Sayyid Qutb (q.v.) and many members of the Muslim Brotherhood (q.v.), including Muhammad al-Ghazali (q.v.), with whom he toured Egypt. Since then, he has traveled widely and visited most of the Arab world as well as the United States. He received the prestigious International King Faysal Award in 1979 and now resides in England.

His intellectual impact on the Arab world is equalled only by that of Abu al-A'la al-Mawdudi. The two thinkers have given fundamentalist movements basic notions in their intellectual heritage. Al-Nadawi's extensive writings have been translated into many languages. The major idea that al-Nadawi propagates is the importance of Islam (q.v.) for any world order (q.v.), and he does this by drawing comparisons and contrasts between the "balanced" Islamic views on the world, society, and man with the "unbalanced" Western paganist and materialist views. See also CALIPHATE; CALL; GOVERNANCE; ISLAMIC SOCIETY; ISLAMIC STATE; *JIHAD*; METHOD; MORALITY; PAGANISM; TEXT; UNIVERSALISM; WESTERN CIVILIZATION.

AL-NAHNAH, MAHFOUDH (1942–). Al-Nahnah is the head of Islamic Society Movement: *Hamas* (q.v.), in Algeria. Al-Nahnah was born in Algeria (Blida District) into a very poor family but worked for the Arabization of Algeria and defending Islam (q.v.). He got his primary education at the Irshad school. Al-Nahnah enrolled in the Liberation Party, then, after independence, he studied Arabic literature, learned about the ideology and writings of the Egyptian Muslim Brotherhood (q.v.), moved to the extremist Islamic groups, and got involved in armed actions that led to his arrest in 1976. Al-Nahnah was sentenced to 15 years in prison, but served only five years.

In 1981, President al-Shadhili Bin Jadid set al-Nahnah free. After this, he became more rigid in his attitude toward the Mustapha Buya'li grouping in Armed Islamic Group (q.v.). He was against armed political Islam as well as political extremism (q.v.). He founded and became the leader of Islamic Society Movement, or *Hamas*, in November 1990, a period that can be considered one of Algerian expansion of the Muslim Brotherhood. His movement was licensed to practice its activities publicly.

Al-Nahnah is now professor of religious studies at the University of Algeria. He is also the founder of *Rabitat al-Da'wa al-Islamiyya* and *Jam'iyyat al-Irshad wa al-Islah*. His movement, *Hamas*, is considered a moderate fundamentalist organization and received over 600,000 votes in the parliamentary election of 1991. He calls for a peaceful democratic solution to the crisis of Algeria. Today, al-Nahnah and his movement are represented in the Parliament after the elections of 1997 and in the absence of the Islamic Salvation Front (q.v.). See also ISLAMIC SOCIETY MOVEMENT: *HAMAS*; JABALLAH, 'ABD ALLAH; *JAMA'AT AL-NAHDA AL-ISLAMIYYA*.

NAJAM, RA'IF. See *HIZB JABHAT AL-'AMAL AL-ISLAMI*.

AL-NAJUN MIN AL-NAR. See *JAMA'AT AL-MUSLIMIN*.

AL-NA'MANI, 'ABD AL-'AZIZ. Al-Na'mani headed the breakaway faction of the Islamic Youth Organization, the *Mujahidin* Movement in Morocco (qq.v.). It is a clandestine movement seeking the overthrow of the Moroccan monarchy and the establishment of a more leftist regime based on Islam (q.v.). The group has been involved in violent disputes with other radical movements on Moroccan university campuses. Because it has been repressed by the government, its strength and influence are difficult to ascertain. As the name suggests, the *Mujahidin* has been thought to have closer ties to Iran than Morocco's fundamentalist groups. See also *MUJAHIDIN* MOVEMENT IN MOROCCO.

AL-NAQSHABANDIYYA. *Al-Naqshabandiyya* was originally a Sufi movement founded by Muhammad Baha' al-Din al-Naqshabandi in Bukhara, Turkey. It backed *Hizb al-Salama al-Watani* (q.v.), then before the military Coup of 1990, supported the Turkish party of *al-Watan al-Umm*, and finally moved to support the *Refah Partisi* (q.v.), which it has done since 1986. *Al-Naqshabandiyya* was introduced to Turkey during the Ottoman Empire by Shaykh Ahmad Hindi, who had a reputation as a great religious scholar. Hindi turned down all public offices offered to him by the state, and his call spread in India. Today's leading figure of the movement in Turkey is Professor Muhammad As'ad Kushan.

AL-NAS. See TEXT.

NASR, 'ALI 'ABD AL-'AZIZ. See UNION OF POPULAR FORCES.

NASRALLAH, SAYYID HASAN (1960–   ). Nasrallah is one of the notable figures to exert weight and impose their presence on the Lebanese political scene. He has been the General Secretary of *Hizbullah* (q.v.) since 1992. He was born in a poor family of the poor area of Karantina where a mixture of Armenians, Kurds, and Shi'ites settled. There he stayed until 1974 when he and his family moved to Sin al-Fil so that he could continue his secondary education. At that time, Nasrallah had no political tendencies, but he had been religiously committed since the age of nine. As soon as the civil war broke out in Beirut, the Nasrallahs returned to their native village, Bazuriyya in the south. There he felt alienated from the leftist and nationalist presence that dominated the village. Nasrallah helped set up a library, where he started giving lectures and founded his religious group.

At the age of 15, Nasrallah joined the Shi'ite *Amal* movement and became its organizing chief in Bazuriyya. However, he left for Najaf to continue his studies in 1976 where he met his future guardian, Muhammad Baqir al-Sadr (q.v.) and instructor, 'Abbas al-Musawi. He stayed there until 1987 and fled the country out of fear of Iraqi intelligence. As Nasrallah and others arrived in Lebanon, 'Abbas al-Musawi established his own school for Islamic theology in Ba'albak. Nasrallah later taught there, while he studied and gave public speeches in the surrounding area. He also became actively involved in *Amal*, where he was appointed to high positions and resisted the Israeli occupation.

But Nasrallah left *Amal* for internal reasons, and he along with Husayn al-Musawi and others began establishing a substitute organization that trained people militarily and ideologically, *Harakat Amal al-Islamiyya* (q.v.) (Islamic *Amal* Movement). Its main focus was fighting Israeli occupation. In 1985, Nasrallah moved to Beirut to organize the party of *Hizbullah* (q.v.), and in 1987 he became the head of the newly established Executive Committee. However, he left for Iran to continue his studies, but returned after the bloody confrontations between *Hizbullah* and *Amal*. In 1992, he became the General Secretary of *Hizbullah* after the assassination of 'Abbas al-Musawi by the Israelis.

Intellectually, Nasrallah states that *Hizbullah* is a national party, whose main objective is to fight against occupation and to establish relationships with other political sectors and civil groups, including Christians. He believes in *Hizbullah's* need to participate in the Lebanese political system and to refrain from violence (q.v.). Under his leadership, *Hizbullah* has become represented officially in the Parliament. Mostly, he justifies violence (q.v.) against Israel (q.v.) as a way of national struggle and defense against Israel.

As to the issue of the Islamic state (q.v.), Nasrallah does not deny its idealistic importance but rejects the validity of imposing an Islamic state because such a state should imply social justice and freedom (qq.v.) and consent. An Islamic state, he argues, should not be established by a party or an army, but rather by the people. In Lebanon, there exists a majority of Christians and Muslims who might reject the establishment of an Islamic state. He also calls for the abolition of the Lebanese confessional system and the adoption of democracy (q.v.).

NATION. See *UMMA*.

NATION'S PARTY IN MAURITANIA. See *UMMA* PARTY.

NATIONAL FRONT FOR THE SALVATION OF LIBYA (*AL-JABHA AL-WATANIYYA LI INQADH LIBYA*). The front was set up in 1981 and is led by Muhammad Yusuf Maqrif. It is one of the largest and most militant opposition organizations. The front is made up of members of diverse political views, including those with Islamic leanings, especially the supporters of the Muslim Brotherhood (q.v.). Others are followers of *al-Sanusiyya* (q.v.). See also MUSLIM BROTHERHOOD IN LIBYA.

NATIONAL ISLAMIC FRONT (*AL-JABHA AL-QAWMIYYA AL-IS-LAMIYYA*). See MUSLIM BROTHERHOOD IN SUDAN; AL-TUR-ABI, HASAN.

NATIONAL SAFETY PARTY (*HIZB AL-SALAMA AL-WATANI*). See *MILLI SELAMET PARTISI.*

NATIONAL SALVATION PARTY. See *MILLI SELAMET PARTISI.*

NATION'S PARTY (*HIZB AL-UMMA*) **IN ALGERIA.** Nation's Party is an Algerian fundamentalist group that was founded in 1989. It did not participate in the 1991 elections. The movement is involved in few public activities and does not seem to have a strong militant base. One of its founders and its leader, Benyoucef Ben Khedda, was a director of a government agency. The movement is critical of socialism and calls for a return to cultural authenticity (q.v.) through adopting Islamic values. It believes that Islam and modernity (qq.v.) are compatible through the development of *shura* (q.v.) (consultation).

NATION'S PARTY (*HIZB AL-UMMA*) **IN EGYPT.** Nation's Party was founded shortly before the 1984 Egyptian parliamentary elections by Ahmad al-Sibahi. It was believed at the time that he wished to form a party that would allow the candidates of the Egyptian Muslim Brotherhood (q.v.) to run under its banner. The Brotherhood's surprise alliance with the *Wafd* Party made the *Umma* Party superfluous and led al-Sibahi to launch periodic attacks on the Brotherhood. Although quiescent, the party remains in existence, calling for the implementation of *al-Shari'a* (q.v.) (Islamic Law) and political liberalization.

NAZZAL, KHALID. Nazzal is the representative of *Hamas* (q.v.) (*Harakat al-Muqawama al-Islamiyya*) in Jordan. See also MUSLIM BROTHERHOOD IN PALESTINE.

NEHZATE-E AZAI-YE IRAN. See LIBERATION MOVEMENT OF IRAN.

AL-NITCHA, HAFIZ (1922–   ). Al-Nitcha was born in Hebron and is a physician and surgeon by training. Al-Nitcha became a member of *Hizb Jabhat al-'Amal al-Islami* in Jordan (q.v.) (Islamic Action Front Party) and was a member of the Lower House of Parliament in Jordan from 1956–1961 and 1984–1989.

NIZAM. See SYSTEM.

AL-NIZAM AL-SIRRI (SECRET APPARATUS). The secret apparatus of the Muslim Brotherhood (q.v.) in Egypt was originally set up in 1935 to fight British occupation in Palestine. It was structured on the basis of cells of five members, and each cell did not know the members of other cells, which worked independently. Its members were rigorously trained in Islamic sciences and military operations.

But the apparatus conducted violent acts in Egypt itself, such as killing al-Naqrashi Pasha, the Prime Minister. The members of the apparatus had to swear an oath of allegiance in an awesome and dark setting. A pistol and a Qur'an (q.v.) were used on this occasion; the member put his hand over the two. This apparatus was headed first by Salih 'Ishmawi (q.v.) and 'Abd al-Rahman al-Sindi and was liquidated by the Egyptian government under Jamal 'Abd al-Nasir.

NURI, 'ALI AKBAR NATIQ. Nuri has been the speaker of *Majlis al-Shura* (q.v.) in Iran since 1992 and leader of the conservative right. In 1996, Nuri lost his bid for the presidency of the Republic to Muhammad Khatami (q.v.). See also KHATAMI, MUHAMMAD; *MAJLIS AL-SHURA* IN IRAN; MUHTASHIMI, 'ALI AKBAR; *RUHANIYYAT MUBARIZ*.

AL-NURSI, BADI' AL-ZAMAN SA'ID (1873–1960). Al-Nursi was born in the village of Nuris. Al-Nursi studied with his brother, 'Abd Allah, then left his village to seek knowledge. He accompanied Sultan Muhammad Rashad on his trip to Rumali and suggested building a university. But World War II stopped that project. Al-Nursi fought against the Russians, was captured and exiled to Siberia, and was released after the Russian Revolution.

When the Allied forces occupied Turkey, al-Nursi joined the Resistance. Al-Nursi himself was injured and detained by the Russians. After two years and after the Bolshevik Revolution, he escaped from his detention camp in Russia and arrived in Germany, then went to Leningrad,

Vienna, and Istanbul. In 1918, he was appointed a member of Islamic *Dar al-Hikma*, the Highest Religious Council for *Fatwa* (q.v.), and he headed the religious bloc of the Shaykhs at the Greater National Assembly (the Parliament). Because of this and his advocacy of public calls for prayers, he clashed with Mustapha Kemal Ataturk. Al-Nursi resigned from the Assembly and left Ankara to visit other parts of Turkey to urge the implementation of Islam (q.v.) and the fight against Westernization.

Al-Nursi commanded a large following and became a problem for the regime. In 1925, he was arrested and exiled to a remote village, where he lived for eight years. There he wrote his epistles, *Rasa'il al-Nur* (q.v.), which were copied by hand by many of his followers.

Al-Nursi left the village for a year but was arrested again and exiled for another eight years. Because of al-Nursi's activism, the Turkish security apparatuses watched him, and he was arrested in 1935 because of his attempt to set up a secret organization that aimed at demolishing the secularism of the Republic. He was imprisoned twice, in 1943 and 1948. He wrote over 100 epistles, *Rasa'il al-Nur*, where he called for coexistence between science (q.v.) and belief.

His followers supported 'Adnan Mandris who headed the Democratic Party and allowed the building of new religious schools. He died on 23 March 1960. See also *RASA'IL AL-NUR*.

-O-

OGHLO, HUSAYN ALI. See *HIZBULLAH* IN TURKEY.

OGHLO, KAMAL BILLO. See *AL-TIJANIYYA*.

OGHLO, SALIH MIRZA. See ORGANIZATION OF THE FIGHTERS FOR THE GREATER ISLAMIC EAST.

ONENESS OF GOD. See *TAWHID*.

ORGANIZATION FOR ENJOINING GOOD AND FORBIDDING EVIL (*TANZIM AL-AMR BI AL-MA'RUF WA AL-NAHY 'AN AL-MUNKAR*). This organization is led by Shaykh Yusuf al-Badri in Ma'adi and Hilwan, suburbs of Cairo. Twenty of its members were arrested in the September events of 1981 on charges of sectarianism. It is one of the marginal radical fundamentalist groups that are still active.

ORGANIZATION OF THE FIGHTERS FOR THE GREATER IS-LAMIC EAST (*MUNAZZAMAT MUQATILU AL-SHARQ AL-KABIR AL-ISLAMI*). The organization's acronym is IBDA and sometimes IBDA-C. This Turkish organization started in 1975 and supported the *Milli Selamet Partisi* (q.v.). Its leader is Salih Mirza Bay Oghlo, who called for an Islamic public revolution (q.v.).

ORGANIZATION OF ISLAMIC *JIHAD* IN LEBANON. See *AL-JIHAD AL-ISLAMI* IN LEBANON.

ORGANIZATION OF THE ISLAMIC MOVEMENT (*MUNAZZAMAT AL-HARAKA AL-ISLAMIYYA*). The Turkish government alleged that this organization committed many assassinations of well-known journalists and intellectuals. The organization's leader, 'Irfan Chiagharji, was arrested in March 1996.

ORGANIZATION OF SHAYKH 'ABD ALLAH AL-SIMAWI (*TAN-ZIM AL-SHAYKH 'ABD ALLAH AL-SIMAWI*). The Shaykh was known for his close contacts and activities with most leaders of the radical and militant fundamentalist groups that use violence (q.v.) to change the status quo. His doctrines of governance, paganism, and *tawhid* (qq.v.) (Oneness of God) are very much derived from Sayyid Qutb and Abu al-A'la al-Mawdudi (qq.v.).

-P-

PAGANISM (*JAHILIYYA*). Many fundamentalists argue that modern ideologies and their production of system-conflicts have reduced man to living again a life of the jungle. To the fundamentalists, modern life is based on the philosophy (q.v.) of power and the logic of dominance and exploitation, leading to barbaric and bloody wars. In fact, fundamentalists such as Hasan al-Banna, Sayyid Qutb, and Hadi al-Mudarrisi (qq.v.) believe that Europe and the West (q.v.) in general have given up high ideals, virtues, and humanitarian principles. And all of these have been replaced with materialistic paganism or paganism based on lust and desire and the loss of religious consciousness (q.v.) (*wa'iy*) and the teachings of the messengers of God (q.v.). This paganism has resulted in physical destruction, social confusion, moral degeneration, economic tension, political conflict, and spiritual bankruptcy.

Abu al-Hasan al-Nadawi (q.v.) even laments Europe's loss of its high Christian moral objectives, including Christ's message of justice (q.v.). These objectives, al-Nadawi believes, are contrary to the modern spirit of Europe and America as well as Africa and Asia. All of the ongoing international political conflicts are the result of competition for material things, and there are no substantive differences between the competing parties. Even "communist Russia," al-Nadawi goes on, is nothing more than a consequence of Western civilization (q.v.), and is in fact more honest than other Western countries, because it stopped using religion (q.v.) and has publicly replaced it with unbelief (q.v.) (*kufr*) and materialism. Asian nations are following suit, but their conflict with the West is on the leadership of the world.

From this angle, radical fundamentalists, such as Abu al-A'la al-Mawdudi (q.v.), Sayyid Qutb, and Hadi al-Mudarrisi, include all existing societies on earth as living in paganism, or *jahili* societies (q.v.). It becomes the main task of fundamentalists to use *tawhid* (q.v.) (Oneness of God) as a device to evaluate the Islamicity or the paganism of any economic, social, or political order. What worries the fundamentalists most is that Muslims are imitating Western civilization in its worst forms: destruction, degeneration, sectarian divisions, civil wars, and racial discrimination. Al-Nadawi sees that *taqlid* (q.v.) (the imitation) of the West goes beyond these characteristics and subjects the Muslim world to the scientific, industrial, commercial, and political dominance of the West. Muslims as well have become allies and soldiers of Western paganism, and even some Muslim people look to the West, which has led the new wave of paganism, as their protector and the enforcer of justice in the world.

Notwithstanding this, many—but not all—fundamentalists take upon themselves and other Muslims the task of saving humanity by, first, removing themselves from paganism. In its political form this means repudiating any political order that is disharmonious with *al-Shari'a* (q.v.) (Islamic Law). Any political or social order that has this characteristic is in violation of God's teachings. In fact, any political or social order that has this characteristic is in violation of God's *Shari'a* and is in a state of transgression against His divinity (q.v.) (*uluhiyya*).

The *jahili* society, which is erected on any principle that does not take into account divine guidance, must be confronted and modified in accordance with God's method (q.v.) (*manhaj*) and system (q.v.) (*nizam*). Qutb has no qualms about calling for subjecting at any cost the realities of the world to Islamic standards, because submission to such realities goes against the spirit of Islam (q.v.), whose main focus is the destruction of paganism. See also 'ABD AL-RAHMAN, 'UMAR; APOSTASY; ARMED ISLAMIC GROUP; CHRISTIANITY; CIVILIZATION; *FITRA*; FREEDOM; GOD; GOVERNANCE; GROUP OF LEGITIMATE ISOLATION; *HIZBULLAH*; ISLAM; ISLAMIC BAND OF HELPERS; ISLAMIC FUNDAMENTALISM; ISLAMIC STATE; *JAHILI* SOCIETIES; *AL-JAMA'AT AL-ISLAMIYYA*; *JAMA'AT AL-JIHAD AL-ISLAMI*; *JAMA'AT AL-MUSLIMIN*; *JIHAD*; JUSTICE AND CHARITY GROUP; LIBERATION; AL-MAWDUDI, ABU AL-A'LA; METHOD; MODERNITY; MORALITY; ORGANIZATION OF SHAYKH 'ABD ALLAH AL-SIMAWI; QUTB, SAYYID; REVOLUTION; *SHURA*; UNBELIEF; UNIVERSALISM; WESTERN CIVILIZATION; WORLD ORDER.

PAN-ISLAMISM. Pan-Islamism is an ideology that aims at a comprehensive union of all Muslims into one political entity. However, it is a movement that grew out of the East's confrontation with the Western colonialism and imperialism. Pan-Islamist propaganda began in the 1880s and reached its prime before the end of the 19th century.

Its chief ideologist and philosopher was Jamal al-Din al-Afghani (1838–1897) (q.v.). Until he adopted Pan-Islamism, it was only a vague idea. He made it equivalent to the revival of Islamic civilization (q.v.) that was opposed to European domination and called for the necessity of Islamic unity. Al-Afghani became the leading figure behind the movement. In 1884, he published the anti-British journal, *al-'Urwa al-Wuthqa*, which called for the unity of all Islamic peoples and states against Western domination. In 1892, Turkish Arabs in London invited Jamal al-Din al-Afghani to settle in Constantinople on a life pension as guest of the sultan.

Al-Afghani proposed the combination of all religions, politics, and cultures in one all-embracing civilization. He urged Muslims to awake. They must liberate themselves from Western domination, they must support necessary reforms, they must insist on popular and stable governments, and they must cultivate modern scientific and philosophic knowledge (q.v.). In Constantinople, al-Afghani was unhappy and was kept nearly the rest of his life under house arrest, until he died in 1897 from cancer.

The patron of Pan-Islamism was Sultan Abdulhamid II who appropriated the movement as a means of justifying his own tyrannical rule over the Turkish Empire. He proclaimed himself to be the defender of the Islamic social system (q.v.) (*nizam*) against Western imperialism, especially against the British in the Near East and the French in Morocco. It was an article of faith, he said, for all Muslims to combine in a holy war for the spread of Islamic ideals.

In 1903, 'Abdullah al-Sharawardy founded the Pan-Islamic Society in London. His journal, *Pan Islamism*, emphasized opposition to Western society and used humanitarian and socialist concepts in order to contrast "European vice" with "Asian virtue." It also dedicated itself to mending the relationship between Sunnis and Shi'ites.

Abdulhamid II supported the great annual conference of Muslims at Mecca. He provided Turkish troops as escorts for pilgrim caravans to Mecca. Abdulhamid helped to build the Hijaz railway, which was the sole practical achievement of Pan-Islamism. The Young Turk Revolution not only put an end to the regime of Abdulhamid but also ended the early stage of Pan-Islamism. Moreover, the alliance between Turkish nationalism and German militarism could not be reconciled with Islamic ideology. When, in November 1914, the caliph proclaimed a holy war against the Allied Powers, the response in Egypt, India, and Arabia was to enlist in the ranks of his enemies. The attempt of the Berlin war office to arouse Pan-Islamic union against the Allied Powers turned out to be altogether ineffective.

When the Turkish Empire collapsed at the end of World War I, it meant the end of the original Pan-Islamic movement. A second wave of Pan-Islamism rising in India was even less enduring than the first. Several Pan-Islamic congresses held between 1920 and 1931 were unsuccessful. On 8 July 1937, representatives of Turkey, Persia, Iraq, and Afghanistan signed a pact at Tehran designed to preserve their common frontiers. Some observers believed that this amounted to a return by Turkey to Pan-Islamism. However, Kamal Ataturk had already cut his country off from its Islamic links.

After World War II, there was a modest revival of Pan-Islamism, when Pakistan began a center for Pan-Islamist activities. However, this new Pan-Islamism represented a common attitude of Islamic states in meeting their economic, cultural, and social problems with emphasis on political rather than religious questions. There were further Pan-Islamic congresses at Karachi (1951), Jerusalem (1953), and Lahore (1957–1958). By then the religious liberty that Pan-Islamism advocated had become subordinated to political and national goals.

Pan-Islamism turned out to be a utopian idea. It was never implemented as a working ideology. Pan-Islamists were not able to overcome the rivalry between Sunnism and Shi'ism. The leadership of Pan-Islamism was weak. Efforts to revive the Caliphate (q.v.) as well as the Pan-Islamic movement proved to be unsuccessful. The masses were inclined to accept religious leadership from Mecca but not political control from any one Islamic country. See also AFGHANI, JAMAL AL-DIN.

PARTIES (*AHZAB*). As a sign of pluralism (q.v.), the existence of parties is rejected by radical fundamentalists. A particular problem for radical fundamentalists in adopting Western models of parties, unions, and federations is their "selfish and materialistic" nature. But in Islam (q.v.) *al-naqabat* (unions), which were originally the models for their Western counterparts, are based on brotherhood and solidarity. Thus, they reject those parties or organizations that may express substantive differences between groups in society, especially if they are un-Islamic. They replace them with the idea of a vanguard (q.v.) (*al-tali'a*) that should lead the Islamic society (q.v.). Thus, fundamentalists like Sayyid Qutb (q.v.) see only mutual exclusivity between Western philosophies, ideologies, and institutions and those of Islam. The former are *jahili* (paganist) and, as such, belong to *hizb al-shaytan* (the party of Satan); the other are Islamic and, as such, belong to *hizb Allah* (the party of God).

On the other hand, moderate fundamentalists like Rashid al-Ghannushi (q.v.) accept the existence of parties as an expression of different social, political, philosophical and ideological views. They legitimize their existence by the command to enjoin good and forbid evil (*al-amr bi al-ma'ruf wa al-nahy 'an al-munkar*). In fact, the moderate accept not only parties but democracy (q.v.) as being warranted by Islam. The moderate fundamentalists do not see any essential contradiction between Western political organizations and philosophies and those of Islam. See also AL-'AWWA, MUHAMMAD; AL-BANNA, HASAN; AL-BASHIR, 'UMAR; ERBAKAN, NECMETTIN; GHANNUSHI, RASHID; *HARAKAT AL-NAHDA AL-ISLAMIYYA*; HAWWA, SA'ID; *HIZB AL-HAQQ AL-ISLAMI*; ISLAMIC ACTION ORGANIZATION; ISLAMIC YOUTH ORGANIZATION; *AL-JAMA'AT AL-ISLAMIYYA*; *JAM'IYYAT AL-IHYA' AL-TURATH*; *MILLI SELAMET PARTISI*; *MUJAHIDIN KHALQ*; MUSLIM BROTHERHOOD, IDEOLOGY OF; AL-NABAHANI, TAQIY AL-DIN; NAHNAH, MAHFOUDH; RADICALISM; SIRRIYYA, SALIH; VANGUARD.

PARTY (*HIZB*). See PARTIES.

PARTY FOR THE DEFENSE OF ISLAM (*ISLAM KORUMA PARTISI*). This party was established in Istanbul in July 1946. It aims at supporting

Islamic activities. Because it mixed religion (q.v.) with politics, and thus broke Turkish laws, the Turkish authorities disbanded it in September 1946, less than two months after its foundation.

PARTY FOR NATIONAL ORDER. See *MILLI NIZAM PARTISI.*

PARTY OF THE ALGERIAN PEOPLE (*HIZB AL-SHA'B AL-JA-ZA'IRI*). This was the first Algerian party to call for Algerian independence. It dominated Algerian Muslim political life during 1937–1956 and focused its attention on the development of Islamic topics and supported the efforts to revive the Arabic language. However, it relied heavily on folk Islam of the Sufi order, which brought it into conflict with *Jam'iyyat al-'Ulama' al-Muslimin* (q.v.). It called for *jihad* (q.v.) (struggle) against the colonial power.

The party's founder was Messali Hadj, who was the first leader to unequivocally call for complete independence. He developed an Islamic populist discourse. This party took over after the *Etoile Nord-Africaine*, which had also been founded by Messali in 1926.

PARTY OF GOD. See *HIZBULLAH.*

PARTY OF ISLAM. See *HIZB AL-ISLAM.*

PARTY OF SATAN (*HIZB AL-SHAYTAN*). See *HIZBULLAH.*

PARTY OF YEMENI GROUPING FOR REFORM. See *HIZB AL-TA-JAMMU' AL-YEMENI LI AL-ISLAH.*

PAST (*AL-MADI*). Dismissing the normative view of the past is, in one way or another, one of the features of Islamism. This feature involves the rejection of jurisprudence, theology (qq.v.), politics, and other disciplines. It neglects, for instance, that traditional jurisprudence (q.v.) did not originally view itself as an eternal normative interpretation (q.v.) of the eternal text (q.v.) and postulated the possibility of radical change within its structure. That one *ijma'* (q.v.) (consensus) abrogates an older one is a traditional argument, and is not new.

Fundamentalists like al-Hasan Turabi (q.v.) move beyond the general call (q.v.) to renew jurisprudence to renew its foundations and bases. Al-Turabi, for instance, does not take into account that the longevity of the accepted four schools of law is due not to any particular claims on their part but to people's adoption of these schools. Earlier scholars and founders of schools never claimed everlasting status for their arguments, although they had, as al-Turabi has done, upheld the eternal legitimacy (q.v.) of the source materials, the Qur'an (q.v.) and the *Sunna* (way) of the Prophet, and the few political models represented by the first four rightly guided caliphs. However, al-Turabi's argument, and the fundamentalists, endeavor in general to personify a juristic transformation of historical reconceptualization of fundamentals (q.v.) (*usul*) from the text and the rebirth of primordial models.

Thus, the fundamentalists summon again similar discussions, and their improvements remain within the traditional juristic processes resulting in the very same *usul*: the Qur'an, the *Sunna* (way) of the Prophet, *ijma'*, and *al-ra'i* (opinion). The innovation lies, however, in that whereas juristic models were constructed for specific societies, the fundamentalist reformations aim at constructing an imagined and hoped-for society. Again, whereas traditional jurisprudence historically reflected the formative power of *umma's* (q.v.) *ijma'*, the fundamentalists' reconceptualization of jurisprudence serves as a prescriptive model for a new political theory that might propel Muslims to redirect the course of their history (q.v.) and set up a modern Islamic society (q.v.). See also HISTORY.

PEACE (*AL-SALAM*). The establishment of justice (q.v.) requires peace; and peace requires the dominance of one over others. Though not all fundamentalists picture it in this crude way, radicals nonetheless say the same thing. In fact, before world peace is realized, peace must be found first in the individual, family, and society. The peace of the individual, which is the real seed of positive peace, gives the supreme power to the spiritual part of man to discipline its desires and purify the soul. As such desires are balanced and controlled by spiritual yearnings, thus, equilibrium between the spiritual and the material is made. This peace extends to the family and becomes the focal point of love, mercy, and tranquillity. In turn, the peace of the family constitutes a building block for a peaceful society.

Hasan al-Banna (q.v.) argues in his *Peace in Islam* that Islam (q.v.) holds to the notion of the organic unity of humanity and preaches its call to it without distinction. Citing Qur'anic verses on the topic, he concludes that Islam does acknowledge distinctive differences between peoples, but this must be viewed as an avenue for cooperation, not enmity.

Islam is described by al-Banna as the law of peace and the religion (q.v.) of mercy.

In a similar manner, the true peace of the world should revolve around the moral precepts of Islam, including justice. Hence, Islam's peaceful coexistence with others depends on the fulfillment of basic conditions, foremost among which are freedom (q.v.) of worship, nonaggression against Muslims' propagation, the nonexistence of any authority that stands against the call (q.v.) (*da'wa*), and the realization of comprehensive justice.

Peace to the fundamentalists, then, cannot be dealt with outside Islam's metaphysical foundations such as divinity and *tawhid* (qq.v.) (Oneness of God), its political bases such as equality (q.v.) and freedom, and its social doctrines such as social justice, balance (qq.v.), integration, and cooperation. See also *AL-AFGHAN AL-'ARAB*; *HAMAS*; *HUDUD*; ISLAMIC SALVATION FRONT; *AL-JAMA'AT AL-ISLAMIYYA*; *JAMA'AT AL-JIHAD AL-ISLAMI*; *JIHAD*; *MILLI NIZAM PARTISI*; MUSLIM BROTHERHOOD IN JORDAN; RUSHDI, USAMA; AL-SHIQAQI, FATHI; TAHA, HASAN; UNION OF POPULAR FORCES.

PEOPLE'S MOJAHEDIN ORGANIZATION OF IRAN. See *MUJAHIDIN KHALQ*.

PHILOSOPHY (*FALSAFA*). Sayyid Qutb (q.v.) explains the fundamentalists' problem with philosophy in the following way. When some Muslim philosophers were enticed by Greek philosophy, especially that of Aristotle, they thought that the Greek discourse reached maturity and perfection. Instead of constructing an Islamic discourse, according to the general rules of religion and the text (qq.v.), they used the general rules of philosophy and reason (q.v.) in order to construct the Islamic discourse. This allowed philosophy to corrupt the harmony of religion: first, by introducing different theological disputations into Islamic literature; second, by including in their teachings diverse paganistic and Christian elements that did not fit the *tawhid* (q.v.) (Oneness of God) of Islam (q.v.); and third, by using their arguments to support different political trends that were turned into theological schools. See also EQUALITY; *FITRA*; GOD; GOVERNANCE; HISTORY; *IJMA'*; ISLAMIC FUNDAMENTALISM; ISLAMIC STATE; ISLAMIZATION; *JAHILI* SOCIETIES; *JIHAD*; LIBERATION; METHOD; MODERNISM; MODERNITY; PAGANISM; RELIGION; SCIENCE; *SHURA*; *TAWHID*; VANGUARD.

PLURALISM (*TA'ADDUDIYYA*). The absence of a pluralistic society and of democratic institutions is cited by the moderate fundamentalist trend as the real cause for violence (q.v.). Although this trend has for long been excluded from political participation, it still calls for its inclusion as well as of others in politics and formal institutions. Its involvement in civil society and its call (q.v.) for pluralism are still seen as the road to salvation of the community and individuals. Their inclusionary views do not postulate an eternal and divine enmity between Islam's institutions and systems, and the West's institutions and systems. Properly grounded, what is Western becomes indeed Islamic. The conflict between the East and West (q.v.) is viewed as being primarily political and economic but not religious and cultural. The two have common monotheistic grounds upon which multicultural and religious cooperation and coexistence might be built. See also 'ABD AL-RAHMAN, 'UMAR; ARMED IS-LAMIC GROUP; AL-'AWWA, MUHAMMAD; AL-GHANNUSHI, RASHID; *HARAKAT AL-NAHDA AL-ISLAMIYYA*; AL-HUWAIDI, FAHMI; ISLAMIC ACTION PARTY; ISLAMIC FUNDAMENTAL-ISM; ISLAMIC SALVATION MOVEMENT; MODERNISM; *MUJAH-IDIN KHALQ*; MUSLIM BROTHERHOOD, IDEOLOGY OF; MUS-TAPHA, SHUKRI; PARTIES; RADICALISM, AL-TURABI, HASAN; UNION OF POPULAR FORCES.

POLITICAL ISLAM. See FUNDAMENTALISM; ISLAMIC FUNDA-MENTALISM.

POPULAR ARAB ISLAMIC CONGRESS (*AL-MU'TAMAR AL-SHA'BI AL-'ARABI AL-ISLAMI*). See SECOND ISLAMIC INTERNA-TIONAL.

POPULAR DEFENSE FORCES (*QUWWAT AL-DIFA' AL-SHA'BI*). The Popular Defense Forces are the Sudanese militia that were set up by the government of 'Umar al-Bashir (q.v.) in October 1989, three years after the military coup. General Faysal Mukhtar Madani, who later became Minister of Health and who is a member of the Revolutionary Council of *Thawrat al-Inqadh* (Salvation Revolution), headed the Forces. These Forces have participated in the civil war in southern Sudan.

It is alleged that the Forces' camps are training bases for terrorists although the government claims that their role is to strengthen the internal solidarity and help the armed forces to dedicate their activities to the south. The first official commander was General Babakr 'Abd al-Mahmud who commanded the Forces until 1993. He was followed by General Abu al-'Abbas Khalifa, who retired a year later. Now, the forces are commanded by General 'Abd al-Majid Mahmud, who believes that the role of the Defense Forces is to bring about changes through the Islamization (q.v.) of society and the exercise of *jihad* (q.v.) (struggle).

The members of the Forces are selected from individuals who received their high school diplomas and are about to join universities. Individuals from specific professions, like medicine, are recruited. The Forces are estimated at around 100,000 men and women, of whom 50,000 have been put through heavy military training. These Forces started fighting in 1991 in southern Sudan, and the first brigade was nicknamed *al-ahwal* (difficulties). See also AL-BASHIR, 'UMAR MUSLIM BROTHERHOOD IN SUDAN.

POPULAR MOVEMENT (*AL-HARAKA AL-SHA'BIYYA*). Hedou Abraqash established the Popular Movement, considered to be a Berber party, in Morocco in October 1957. The movement enjoyed the support of the heir apparent (Hasan II) in order to confront the increasing influence of the Independence Party (q.v.). The movement was legally recognized in February 1959, after the Public Freedoms Law that legalized multiparty politics in Morocco was issued.

In its second national convention in October 1962, the movement adopted the slogan of "Islamic Socialism" as the basis for its future political program. The movement's basic goal became the establishment of "justice (q.v.) in the context of Islamic socialism."

Dr. 'Abd al-Karim al-Khatib (q.v.), one of the leaders of the movement, described the movement's program as attempting to prevent people from moving toward materialism, especially Marxism (q.v.). The party wants to establish a state that, despite its modernity (q.v.), still has its roots firmly in Islam (q.v.). It does not believe that it is in people's ability, either in terms of innate disposition or moral constitution, to modernize without religion (q.v.). And it is Islam that forces people to liberate women and solves the problems of ownership and land distribution as well as those arising from money and commerce.

In the following years, because of differences among its leadership, especially between al-Mahjubi Ahradan and Dr. 'Abd al-Karim al-Khatib, the movement split into the traditional trend, led by al-Mahjubi Ahradan, that preserved the movement's name. The opposing trend, led by 'Abd al-Karim al-Khatib, formed in 1967 a new party, the Democratic Constitutional Popular Movement (q.v.). Following this division, al-Mahjubi Ahradan, who was elected to the post of Secretary-General of the movement, rearranged and reorganized it and increased its Berber constituency. See also DEMOCRATIC CONSTITUTIONAL POPU-LAR MOVEMENT; AL-KHATIB, 'ABD AL-KARIM.

PROGRESSIVE MUSLIMS (*AL-ISLAMIYUN AL-TAQADDUMIYUN*). The Progressive Muslims are a group of Tunisian Muslim intellectuals who were members of *Harakat al-Itijah al-Islami* (q.v.) (Islamic Tendency Movement) in the early 1970s. They spread their views in mosques, schools, and universities until the early 1980s when Rashid al-Ghannushi (q.v.) and 'Abd al-Fattah Moro decided to transform Islamic Trend into a political organization. Some members, like Salah al-Din Jourshi and Ziad Krishan, objected to this action and resigned. They decided to focus their attention on intellectual and educational progressive activities. The Progressive Muslims are mostly found in cities and university areas and the "15–21" newspaper used to express the Progressive Muslims' attitudes and political concepts.

-Q-

QABALAN, JAMAL AL-DIN (1926–1995). Qabalan is the founder of the Union of the Isalmic Associations and Groups (q.v.), which is considered an extemely radical Turkish Islamic movement. He graduated from the University of Ankara. He held many religious posts and became the Deputy Head of Religious Affairs, but he resigned and left for Europe and supported *Munazzamat al-Nazra al-Wataniyya*, which is considered part of the *Milli Selamet Partisi* (q.v.), headed by Necmettin Erbakan (q.v.).

Qabalan visited Iran and met Ayatollah Khomeini (q.v.) in 1984. He was nicknamed the "Black Voice." In 1978, he declared an Islamic state (q.v.) in Anatolia and became the caliph and established an Islamic "embassy" in Germany. Qabalan called for the destruction of the secular system (q.v.) (*nizam*) and for the establishment of the Islamic state. He considered all Turkish leaders, including Erbakan, infidels. He was regarded as Turkey's Khomeini, although he lived in isolation in Germany. See UNION OF THE ISLAMIC ASSOCIATIONS AND GROUPS.

AL-QALQAYLI, SHAYKH 'ABD ALLAH. See *AL-SALAFIYYA*.

QANATABADI, SHAMS AL-DIN. See WARRIORS OF ISLAM SOCIETY.

AL-QARADAWI, YUSUF. Al-Qaradawi is a religious scholar from the University of al-Azhar who joined the Muslim Brotherhood (q.v.) in Egypt. Al-Qaradawi is one of the most renowned moderate fundamentalist thinkers, and his writings have had some impact all over the Islamic world.

After the great ordeal of the Muslim Brotherhood in Egypt in the 1950s, al-Qaradawi resided in Qatar and became the Dean of the Faculty of Law at Qatar University. During the presidency of Anwar al-Sadat, al-Qaradawi would come to Egypt from Qatar to speak in religious ceremonies that were attended by thousands of people.

QARASH, YAQUB. See *AL-JIHAD AL-ISLAMI* IN THE WEST BANK AND GAZA STRIP.

QARQAR, SALIH. See *HARAKAT AL-NAHDA AL-ISLAMIYYA*.

AL-QASSAM, 'IZZ AL-DIN. See *AL-JIHAD AL-ISLAMI* IN THE WEST BANK AND THE GAZA STRIP.

QAWASMI, AL-SHARIF. See ARMED ISLAMIC GROUP.

QAZAN, SHAWKAT. Qazan is the deputy leader of the Turkish fundamentalist party, *Refah Partisi* (q.v.). Qazan was elected to the Parliament in 1995 and is the party whip in the Parliament. He is also responsible for the party's public relations.

Qazan participated in setting up *Hizb al-Salama al-Watani* in the early 1970s and participated in the coalition government of 1974 as the Minister of Justice. After the military coup, Qazan was tried along with the party's leader, Necmettin Erbakan (q.v.).

AL-QULAYBI, SHAYKH MUHIY AL-DIN. See *AL-SALAFIYYA*.

AL-QUR'AN. For the fundamentalists, the revealed word of God (q.v.), the Qur'an, is the only authoritative text (q.v.) of both creed and social foundations. It also provides general codes of earthly legislation (q.v.)

and *al-Shari'a* (q.v.) (Islamic Law). It is a text that aims at guiding humanity to the truth and the good, as the Qur'an makes Muslims custodians of humanity until it reaches maturity. The believer does not attempt to reform humanity for any material gains but is rather a guide that leads others to follow God's path. As such, the Muslim does not limit his call (q.v.) to any geographical area but extends his efforts to encompass the world as a whole.

Although fundamentalists make the Qur'an the ultimate source of knowledge (q.v.), they find that differences regarding worldly matters is a natural outcome when it comes to political and practical issues. One of the reasons they allow diversity is that the power of reason (q.v.) differs from one individual to another. And because reason is the source of interpretation (q.v.), many divergent interpretations may be postulated. In addition, the level of one's knowledge affects his level of understanding, and the environment of the interpreter and of reason itself affects understanding and knowledge. It is very difficult for man to transcend his own environment even when he wishes to do so.

Moreover, the fundamentalists argue that the credible sources of knowledge may differ from one interpreter to another: Whereas one person may accept a specific science (q.v.) and a particular history (q.v.) as being true beyond doubt, another may find no cause for trusting that specific science or history. Again, the sciences and histories may be the same, but their significance may differ from one individual to another. The Qur'an is then the only credible and lasting source of inspiration and revelation that Muslims should adhere to. If they do not adhere to the Qur'an, Muslims and humanity will be lost. See also 'ABDU, MUHAMMAD; ABU ZAYD, NASR; APOSTASY; AL-'AWWA, MUHAMMAD SALIM; CALIPHATE; CHRISTIANITY; COMPREHENSIVENESS; CONSTITUTION; DEMOCRACY; DEMOCRATIC ISLAMIC ARAB MOVEMENT; DIVINITY; EQUALITY; *FATWA*; FUNDAMENTALISM; FUNDAMENTALS; AL-GHANNUSHI, RASHID; GOD; GOVERNMENT, FUNCTION OF; HISTORICISM; HISTORY; *HIZBULLAH*; IBN TAYMIYYA, TAQIY AL-DIN; INTERPRETATION; ISLAM; ISLAMIC ACTION ORGANIZATION; ISLAMIC ACTION PARTY; ISLAMIC STATE; ISLAMIC YOUTH ORGANIZATION IN IRAQ; *JIHAD*; JUDAISM; KNOWLEDGE; *AL-MAHDIYYA*; MUSLIM BROTHERHOOD, IDEOLOGY OF; *AL-NIZAM AL-SIRRI*; PAST; QUTB, SAYYID; RIDA, MUHAMMAD RASHID; *AL-SHARI'A*; SYSTEM; TEXT; AL-TURABI, HASAN; UNION OF POPULAR FORCES; *UMMA*; *AL-WAHHABIYYA*.

QUR'ANIC PRESERVATION SOCIETY. See *JAM'IYYAT AL-HIFADH 'ALA AL-QUR'AN.*

QUTB, MUHAMMAD. Qutb is one of the leading thinkers among the Egyptian fundamentalists. Qutb is the brother of the famous Sayyid Qutb (q.v.). He was also a member of the Muslim Brotherhood (q.v.) and was arrested in 1965. Qutb was one of the authors of Sayyid Qutb's *al-Atyaf al-Arba'a.* He now resides in Saudi Arabia and teaches in Mecca. See also *AL-JAMA'AT AL-ISLAMIYYA.*

QUTB, SAYYID (1906–1966). Qutb, born in Musha in the district of Asyut to a middle-class family, received, like Hasan al-Banna (q.v.), his B.A. from Dar al-'Ulum. After that, he worked as a teacher and columnist and was associated with Taha Hussein, 'Abbas Mahmud al-'Aqqad, and other liberal thinkers. When he started writing in journals and magazines, Qutb showed a general tendency to be in opposition to the government and critical of Egypt's state of affairs.

Qutb was very daring in his opposition to the government and in his "radical liberalism," which was manifested in stories he wrote of free love and in his call for nudity. His writings revealed existential, skeptical, and liberal bents. Because of his opposition to government, he was first sent away to the countryside, and the two journals of which he was editor in chief, *al-'Alam al-'Arabi* and *al-Fikr al-Jadid*, were closed down. Then, in 1948, Qutb was sent by the Ministry of Education to the United States of America to continue his studies on education.

Qutb's first book adopting fundamentalism (q.v.) as a way of life along with a political agenda, *al-'Adala al-Ijtima'iyya fi al-Islam*, which appeared during his stay in the United States, was far removed from radicalism (q.v.) and closer to al-Banna's discourse. His stay in the United States, 1948–1951, made him review his previous attitude and adoption of Westernization. His dislike of materialism, racism, and the pro-Zionist feelings of the West (q.v.), which he personally experienced in the United States, seems to have been the beginning of his alienation from Western culture and his return to the roots of the culture he was brought up in.

Upon his return to Egypt, that is, after the assassination of Hasan al-Banna and the First Ordeal of the Brotherhood, Qutb joined the Muslim Brotherhood (q.v.) and became very active in its intellectual and publishing activities, writing numerous books on "Islam as the solution." However, until that point, no radicalism or violence (q.v.) had been involved in his writings. His priority was to rewrite a modern understanding of Islam (q.v.) and the solutions that Islam provides to the basic political, economic, social and individual problems of Egypt and the Arab and Islamic worlds.

In 1953, Qutb was appointed editor in chief of the weekly *al-Ikhwan al-Muslimun*, which was banned along with the dissolution of the Muslim Brotherhood in 1954 after the falling out between the Brethren and the Free Officers' regime. He was put in jail then released. In fact, the Brotherhood in general, and Qutb in particular, was instrumental to the Free Officers in paving the way for the Revolution of 1952. But the Brotherhood refused to accept the absolute power of the Officers and called for a referendum that would show the kind of constitution (q.v.) that the people want. Furthermore, the Brotherhood supported General Muhammad Najib against Colonel 'Abd al-Nasir. After major disagreements between the Brotherhood and 'Abd al-Nasir, the Muslim Brethren were accused of cooperating with the communists to overthrow the government. Their movement was dissolved again in 1954, and many Brethren were jailed, including Qutb. He was released later that year and arrested again after the *Manshiyya* incident, where an attempt was made on 'Abd al-Nasir's life. Qutb and others were accused of being affiliated with the movement's secret military section.

In 1955, Qutb, sentenced by then to 15 years in prison, along with thousands of the Brethren and their supporters, was subjected to ferocious torture. In some ways, that left unhealed scars to this very day. As a result of the torture, Qutb shifted to radical fundamentalism and exclusiveness. His most important books, or the gospels of radicalism, *Fi Zilal al-Qur'an, Ma'alim fi al-Tariq, Hadha al-Din, al-Mustaqbal li Hadha al-Din* and others, were written because of and despite the torture that he and others were subjected to year after year. Qutb was released in 1965, then was later arrested on charges of attempting to overthrow the government. He was executed in 1966.

Qutb was the founder of radicalism. The study of his thought, which is based on paganism and governance (qq.v.) in the Arab world, would show us why many Islamic groups moved to radicalism and "uncompromise." Qutb himself was its first victim; he was transformed under 'Abd al-Nasir's regime from a very liberal writer in Egypt to the most radical fundamentalist thinker in the Arab world. His imprisonment and ferocious torture have been reified into a radical political theology (q.v.) of violence and isolation. It may be that this was his psychological compensation for the violence and repression inflicted by the regime.

Most of the radical fundamentalist groups in the Arab world, and specifically in Egypt, have been influenced both directly and indirectly by this Qutbian radical exclusivist discourse and by his notions of the governance (q.v.) of God (q.v.) and paganism (q.v.) of the "other" at all levels: personally, socially, politically, culturally and philosophically. A few examples may suffice here.

For Qutb, Islam (q.v.) is a comprehensive way of life that includes all of the aspects of this life and the life to come. It is so inclusive that it is difficult to imagine a main issue that is not covered by Islam. It includes both religious and worldly affairs, the spiritual and the physical, the ordinary and the extraordinary. All of this, however, is linked to the universal Islamic concept (*al-mafhum al-kawni al-Islami*) that functions as the constitutive block for Islam and engulfs all aspects of life. Furthermore, it provides the essentials for building the Islamic discourse on life, truth, knowledge (q.v.), man's role in the universe, values, and, above all, an interpretation (q.v.) of the meaning of life. See also ACTIVISM; *AL-AHBASH*; APOSTASY; AL-'AZM, YUSUF; BILHAJ, 'ALI; CALIPHATE; CONSTITUTION; DEMOCRACY; DIVINITY; FARAJ, 'ABD AL-SALAM; FIGHTING VANGUARDS; AL-GHAZALI, MUHAMMAD; AL-GHAZALI, ZAYNAB; GOVERNANCE; HISTORICISM; AL-HUDAYBI, HASAN; HUMAN RIGHTS; IBN TAYMIYYA, TAQIY AL-DIN; *IJMA'*; 'ISHMAWI, SALIH; AL-ISLAMBULI, MUHAMMAD SHAWQI; ISLAMIC FUNDAMENTALISM; ISLAMIC SOCIETY; ISLAMIC STATE; ISMA'IL, 'ABD AL-FATTAH; *JAHILI* SOCIETIES; *AL-JAMA'AT AL-ISLAMIYYA*; *JAMA'AT AL-MUSLIMIN*; *JIHAD*; *AL-JIHAD AL-ISLAMI* IN THE WEST BANK AND GAZA STRIP; JUSTICE; JUSTICE AND CHARITY GROUP; KNOWLEDGE; LEGISLATION; MADANI, 'ABBASI; MARXISM; AL-MAWDUDI, ABU AL-A'LA; METHOD; MODERNISM; MUSLIM BROTHERHOOD; MUSTAPHA, SHUKRI; AL-NADAWI, ABU AL-HASAN; ORGANIZATION OF SHAYKH 'ABD ALLAH AL-SIMAWI; PAGANISM; PARTIES; PHILOSOPHY; QUTB, MUHAMMAD; RADICALISM; RELIGION; REVOLUTION; *AL-SALAFIYYA*; SCIENCE; *AL-SHARI'A*; AL-SHIQAQI, FATHI; *SHURA*; SIRRIYYA, SALIH; SOCIAL JUSTICE; SYSTEM; *AL-TAJAMMU' AL-YEMENI LI AL-ISLAH*; *TAQLID*; *TAWHID*; TEXT; THEOCRACY; THEOLOGY; UNIVERSALISM; VANGUARD.

QUTBISTS (*QUTBIYYIN*). See ISMA'IL, 'ABD AL-FATTAH; QUTB, SAYYID.

QUTBIYYIN (QUTBISTS). See ISMA'IL, 'ABD AL-FATTAH; QUTB, SAYYID.

QUTBZADAH, SADIQ (1936–1982). Qutbzadah was a harsh critic of the Shah's regime and a staunch supporter of Ayatollah Khomeini (q.v.). Qutbzadah studied at Georgetown University in Washington, D.C., where he led a campaign against the Shah. He joined Khomeini in Paris along with Abul Hasan Bani Sadr (q.v.).

After the Iranian Revolution of 1979 (q.v.), Qutbzadah became the head of the National Radio and TV stations in the government of Mahdi Bazargan (q.v.). He became Foreign Minister during the seizure of the American embassy in Tehran. As was the case with President Abul Hasan Bani Sadr, Qutbzadah fought with the conservative forces. Accused of plotting against the revolution and overthrowing the government, he was executed in 1982.

QUWWAT AL-DIFA' AL-SHA'BI. See POPULAR DEFENSE FORCES.

-R-

RABITAT AL-DA'WA AL-ISLAMIYYA (LEAGUE OF ISLAMIC PROPAGATION). See AL-NAHNAH, MAHFOUDH.

RABITAT KIBAR 'ULAMA' AL-DIN AL-MUNADILUN (THE ASSOCIATION OF THE STRUGGLING RELIGIOUS SCHOLARS). See *RUHANIYYAT MUBARIZ.*

RA'D, MUHAMMAD HASAN (1955–   ). Ra'd won a seat in the Lebanese Parliament in 1992 and 1996 as a candidate for *Hizbullah* (q.v.) in al-Nabatiyya District. Ra'd is a member of the party's political bureau.

RADICALISM (*TATARRUF*). The real issue and the decisive element in distinguishing a radical fundamentalist program from a moderate one revolves primarily around the conditions and principles of transforming a political agenda into daily life. Fundamentalism (q.v.) employs diverse methodological and practical processes to intellectual and political formulas. One of these is based on conceptual exclusivity and *otherness*, whether philosophically, morally, or politically, that permits all unusual means to fulfill the real "I." Because radical fundamentalism perceived its own real and imagined isolation to be a result of social disunity and exploitation, the political violence (q.v.) and illegitimacy of regimes, personal impiety, and corruption, it has reified, mostly under severe conditions of torture and mishandling, its political discourse into a purified theology (q.v.) of politics. Without its political contextualization, Islam (q.v.) cannot, from radical fundamentalism's point of view, survive in the consciousness (q.v.) (*wa'iy*) of the individual and society.

Shura (q.v.) (consultation), for instance, is not merely a religious concept or a mechanism for elections. It reflects for the radicals the public will, a far superior concept than individual freedom (q.v.) or social agreement. More importantly, it represents the divine will, and as such, any deviation from whatever is divine is a religious violation. The individual cannot but submit to this will, in fact, he is only an appendage to it, with his freedom depending on it. Although this will may opt for a political contract with a ruler, it cannot, because of what it represents, allow pluralism (q.v.) and basic differences that may lead to disunity. The establishment of an Islamic state (q.v.) becomes for radicalism the fulfillment of this divine will, and again, individuals and groups are consequently subordinated to the state.

Processed through the lenses of *al-Shari'a* (q.v.) (Islamic Law), the institutionalization of *shura* and *ijma'* (q.v.), or consultation and consensus, provides the state, which expresses the general will, a normative role in making basic choices in people's life. For the radical fundamentalists, the formal legitimacy (q.v.) that the state acquires makes it in fact unaccountable to anyone but God (q.v.) and obedience to *al-Shari'a*, itself institutionalized in the state. Thus, henceforth, legitimacy becomes an internal state affair and not a social and public issue, although originally it may have been so. Therefore, insofar as the state is not going against *al-Shari'a* no one can legitimately overthrow it, and it supervises in this context the morality (q.v.) of people and the application of *al-Shari'a*.

Thus, radical fundamentalists transform individual religiosity into a communal public will, itself transformed into state control, both moral and political. Parties (q.v.), associations, and other civil institutions have no intrinsic validity in this hierarchy and may only operate in a supplementary manner. An elaboration like this seems to demand in the end exclusivity: no possibility of pluralistic understandings of religions and the politicization of Islam as the proper Islamic interpretation (q.v.) itself cannot be represented but by the state. In this context, the establishment of inclusive pluralistic civil democracies and ways of life seems unworkable for theoretical and practical reasons. See also *AL-AFGHAN AL-*

'ARAB; EXTREMISM; ISLAMIC FUNDAMENTALISM; *AL-JAMA'A AL-ISLAMIYYA FI LUBNAN*; *JAMA'AT AL-FANNIYYA AL-'ASKARI-YYA*; QUTB, SAYYID.

RAFSANJANI, 'ALI AKBAR (1934–   ). Rafsanjani was born in Rafsanjan and studied at Qum with Ayatollah Khomeini (q.v.) and others. Rafsanjani fought the Shah's regime and was frequently arrested. He played an important role in organizing the clerical opposition and was one of the main personalities who opposed the liberalism of the first President of the Republic, Abul Hasan Bani Sadr (q.v.).

Rafsanjani was a founding member of the Islamic Republican Party (q.v.) and a member of the Revolutionary Council (q.v.). He became Speaker of *Majlis al-Shura* (q.v.) and was elected President of the Republic of Iran in 1989 and reelected in 1993. Rafsanjani tends to be very pragmatic and capable of manipulating the political game. In 1997, he became the President of *Majlis Tashkhis Maslahat al-Nizam* (q.v.). See also COUNCIL OF EXPERTS; *HIZBULLAH*; ISLAMIC REPUBLICAN PARTY; *KAWADIR AL-BINA'*; KHAMENE'I, 'ALI; KHATAMI, MUHAMMAD; KHOMEINISM; *MAJLIS TASHKHIS MASLAHAT AL-NIZAM*; MUNTAZARI, HUSAYN; REVOLUTIONARY COUNCIL; TUFAYLI, SUBHI.

RAGHIB, ZUHAYR SHARIF ABU (1942–   ). Raghib is a member of the executive bureau of *Hizb Jabhat al-'Amal al-Islami* in Jordan (q.v.) (Islamic Action Front Party). Raghib was born in Amman, Jordan, and received a B.A. in Law from Cairo University in 1968. He is a member of the Lawyers' Association and became its Deputy President in 1988. Raghib is also a member of the Arab Organization for Human Rights and Solidarity with the Palestinian People's Committee.

RAHHAL, SALIM. See *JAMA'AT AL-JIHAD.*

RAJJAM, 'ABD AL-RAZIQ. See ARMED ISLAMIC GROUP.

RASA'IL AL-NUR. A Turkish Islamic movement founded by Badi' al-Zaman Sa'id al-Nursi (q.v.), which viewed itself not as a movement but as a group of Muslims who called others to God (q.v.). They did not espouse separation from the community and called for introducing Islamic teachings into the school curriculum. Its membership reached around one and a half million, spread within all classes of the Turkish society. Al-Nursi's movement was a Sufi movement that stood against Russian aggression.

The followers of al-Nursi affirmed that the Turkish society, which was formed according to the philosophy of Kemalism, defaced Turkey. After the Coup of 1980, they refused to join *Hizb al-Salama al-Watani* (q.v.), with which they sympathized earlier and which is now known as *Refah Partisi* (q.v.). They viewed the public activities of Necmettin Erbakan (q.v.) as the cause for the military takeover.

Al-Nursi died on 23 March 1960, and his place of burial is unknown. His followers went public after their teachings were considered nonpolitical by the authorities. They focused their activities on the publication of newspapers and magazines. The movement split into many factions over the issue of the relationship of the movement to political affairs. Erbakan led the faction that focused on the political relevance of Nursi's teachings. The leader of the movement granted Erbakan permission to set up a political party. See also AL-NURSI, BADI' AL-ZAMAN.

AL-RA'SIMALIYYA. See CAPITALISM.

REASON (*IJTIHAD/AL-'AQL*). Although the fundamentalists do not deny the role of reason in understanding the universe and life, they preclude its understanding of God's (q.v.) essence. Thus, Islam (q.v.) is not in favor of limiting the function of reason but makes it the instrument of knowledge (q.v.) and provides it with a framework so that it does not go astray. This is a characteristic that precludes human understanding of God's essence.

According to the fundamentalists, this does not mean that Islam is against freedom (q.v.) of thought or obstructs the search for truth, but it warns man against falling into falsehood and total dependence on human reason. This is why human reason for the fundamentalists cannot provide everlasting truth but rather partial interpretation (q.v.) that depends on man's situation and power of reason.

It is only through reason that a Muslim must exert his understanding, but such an *ijtihad* cannot be said to constitute categorical understanding. When humans disagree they must always fall back on the basic religious texts, which constitute the ultimate source of justification. But the metaphysical realm is beyond man's reason and *ijtihad*, and the Qur'anic discourse leaves man with few ideas on that issue. See also ACTIVISM; APOSTASY; BALANCE; EQUALITY; *FITRA*; GOD; INTERPRETATION; ISLAMIC FUNDAMENTALISM; *MARJI' AL-TAQLID*; MOD-

ERNISM; MODERNITY; PHILOSOPHY; AL-QUR'AN; RELIGION; *SHURA*; SYSTEM; *TAQLID*; *TAWHID*.

REFAH PARTISI (WELFARE PARTY). *Refah Partisi* was established in 1983, and its first chairman was 'Ali Turkmen, a lawyer. When the National Security Council vetoed him, Ahmad Tekdal, a businessman and former religious official, succeeded him. In 1987, after the ban on pre-1980 political leaders had been lifted, Necmettin Erbakan (q.v.), the former head of the *Milli Selamet Partisi* (q.v.) became its chairman.

The party came in sixth in the local election of 1984, with 4.8 percent of the vote. It improved on this result in the 1987 parliamentary elections, when it received 7.16 percent but no seats (due to the 10 percent barrier). It entered the 1991 elections in a joint list with the Nationalist Work Party, obtaining 43 seats for itself. Its ideology is close to that of the Salvation Party, but it is more cautiously expressed, in a coating of Kemalist slogans (except in the domain of secularism). There is strong emphasis on development in an atmosphere of freedom (q.v.) of thought and increase in prosperity.

It is the most important Turkish fundamentalist party, and in the last 1996 elections it received 158 seats out of 550, which made it the strongest party and allowed its leader, Necmettin Erbakan, to become the Prime Minister and to form a coalition party with *al-Tariq al-Qawim*. In February 1997, the army forced Erbakan and his party out of government. Then in January 1998, the Constitutional Court dissolved the party. The political rights and parliamentary terms of Erbakan, Shawkat Qazan (q.v.), Ahmad Takdal, and three other members of his party in the Turkish Parliament were suspended for five years. Preparations are being made to launch a new Islamist party, *Fadila Partisi* (Virtue Party). A few names were circulating as possible candidates for heading the new party, including Rajab al-Tayib Ardughan, Mayor of Istanbul, Malih Kutchak, Mayor of Ankara, 'Abd Allah Ghuyl, the responsible person for foreign relations in the party, and Buland Ajawid, member of the Parliament. The most likely candidate is, however, former Minister of Energy, Raja'i Tukan, who is now in his sixties and commands the respect of all parties.

Refah's parliamentary experience is considered to be one of the foremost fundamentalist attempts to reconcile modern Islamic movements with democracy (q.v.) and elections. See also ERBAKAN, NECMETTIN; *MILLI NIZAM PARTISI*; *MILLI SELAMET PARTISI*; *AL-NAQ-SHABANDIYYA*; QAZAN, SHAWKAT; *RASA'IL AL-NUR*.

REFORM ASSOCIATION. See *JAM'IYYAT AL-ISLAH.*

RELIGION (*AL-DIN*). Abu al-A'la al-Mawdudi, Hasan al-Banna, Sayyid Qutb (qq.v.), and others present religion as the alternative to philosophy (q.v.) because its method (q.v.) (*manhaj*) and system (q.v.) (*nizam*) are harmonious with the universe. By this presentation, fundamentalism (q.v.), especially the radical trend, reduces all methods and systems of life and action into a basic twofold division: what is God-given and what is man-made. The God-given is derived from a divine origin, and those individuals and institutions that organize their lives and actions accordingly are the followers of God (q.v.), or *Hizbullah* (q.v.) (the party of God). But the man-made is derived from human systems, their followers are the followers of the people, not God. Or simply, they constitute *hizb al-Shaytan* (the party of Satan).

Religion in this sense is a method of belief that includes a system of metaphysics, politics, society, and morality (q.v.). Hasan al-Banna believes that God has provided Islam (q.v.) with all of the necessary rules for the life of a nation as well as for its renaissance and happiness. Whereas world ideologies, specifically socialism and capitalism (q.v.), have some benefits and many harmful effects, Islam has captured what is beneficial and shunned what is harmful in both. But imitating other nations or adopting other ideologies cannot rekindle the renaissance of the East.

Every *umma* (q.v.) (nation), according to al-Banna, has a constitution, and the fountain of the Islamic constitution is the Qur'an (q.v.). Again, every *umma* has a law, and Islamic laws must be derivatives of *Shari'a* (q.v.) (Islamic Law) and in accordance with its constitutive principles and universalism (q.v.). The same idea, Islamicity, is expanded by al-Banna to include all aspects of life, the social, the moral, the ethical, the educational, the political, and the economic.

In fact, the fundamentalists, led by Abu al-A'la al-Mawdudi and Sayyid Qutb as well as Hasan al-Banna, conceive of religion as a system of life defined by both concepts and doctrines and, more substantively, by political, social, and individual conducts and behaviors. Because the religion of a people is not a mere profession of faith but the way they act, conduct becomes therefore the yardstick of faith and Islam. True faith must then include both the realms of conscience and public life. It is simply a living motivating force: Islam is not a theory that deals with postulates, it is more importantly a method that deals with the real.

For fundamentalists religion replaces philosophy, whereas ancient and medieval philosophers argue that the good state, knowledge (q.v.), and happiness depend on correct metaphysics attained and justified by reason (q.v.), Qutb, for instance, views the good state, knowledge, and happiness as derivatives of correct doctrines. This kind of linkage, which makes the validity of any political system dependent on its ability to produce and promote happiness, shows that politics is the art that must seek the fulfillment of the divine purpose for the creation of man. It is a fulfillment that requires a correct understanding of nature. Any social order that is incapable of fulfilling human *fitra* (q.v.) is therefore unnatural, unjust, and unsuitable to the movement of man and the divine design.

The fundamentalists' interpretation (q.v.) of religion focuses on praxis rather than theory for the deepening and developing of belief—action being the sign of true belief. Defined in this way, religion is used to encourage activism (q.v.) (*harakiyya*) in social and political matters and for rejecting systems, philosophies, and ways of life that are not derived from Islam. Islam is superior to other religious and nonreligious systems for fundamentalists because its discourse is characterized by vital and direct allusions to the great truths that are incomprehensible by any other human methods. The discourse addresses the innermost aspects of humanity in terms of theory and praxis. Although human philosophies limit the truth, because most human and essential encounters cannot be properly expressed and are beyond the comprehension of human thought, philosophies become for fundamentalists full of unnecessary complication, confusion, and dryness.

The role of religion for the fundamentalists is not to set forth a detailed discourse on metaphysics. It aims at, first, the revival of a conscious awareness of the self and its powers; second, the cultivation of virtue that uplifts the self; third, the sacrifice in quest for the truth and guidance toward God; fourth, the removal of man from ephemeral material "happiness" and the provision of ways for achieving real happiness; fifth, the establishment of religion as the ultimate goal of the soul; sixth, being the source for unity and the resolution of conflicts; seventh, the encouragement of sacrifice for the sake of humanity; and eighth, being the focus of development of the individual, society, the *umma*, and the world. See also APOSTASY; AUTHENTICITY; CALIPHATE; *DAR AL-HARB*; DEMOCRACY; DIVINITY; FUNDAMENTALISM; FUNDAMENTALS; GOD; *HIZBULLAH*; *HUDUD*; INNOVATION; ISLAM; ISLAMIC FUNDAMENTALISM; ISLAMIC STATE; ISLAMIZATION; *JAHILI* SOCIETIES; *JIHAD*; KNOWLEDGE; LEGITIMACY; *MARJI' AL-TAQLID*; MARXISM; MODERNISM; MODER-

NITY; MONOTHEISTIC RELIGIONS; PAGANISM; PEACE; PHILOSOPHY; REVOLUTION; *AL-SHARI'A*; SYSTEM; *TAQLID*; *TAWHID*; THEOLOGY; UNBELIEF; UNIVERSALISM.

RELIGIOUS BLOC (*AL-KUTLA AL-ISLAMIYYA*). The religious bloc was made up of an informal group of Shi'ite representatives in the Bahraini National Assembly, which was active in 1970s. It is not active anymore.

REPUBLIC. See ISLAMIC GOVERNMENT; ISLAMIC STATE; THEOCRACY.

REPUBLICAN PARTY. See *AL-HIZB AL-JUMHURI*.

REVELATION (*AL-WAHY*). See AL-QUR'AN; TEXT.

REVIVAL. See FUNDAMENTALISM; ISLAMIC FUNDAMENTALISM; MODERNISM; PAN-ISLAMISM; REFORMISM; *AL-SALAF-IYYA*.

REVOLUTION (*AL-THAWRA*). Fundamentalists, the radicals in particular, argue that *tawhid* (q.v.) (Oneness of God) is a revolution against all sorts of formal and informal entities that claim any authoritative and normative role, an act that is considered to be an infringement on the divinity (q.v.) (*uluhiyya*) of God (q.v.). Thus for instance, a legislature that legislates in its own name is seizing God's divine authority of legislation (q.v.).

A massive infringement on this level must lead to the eradication of the institution that committed it. But such a change, according to Sayyid Qutb (q.v.), is no less than a revolution that has the ultimate aim of conscious transformation of social and political institutions within the universalism (q.v.) of Islam (q.v.). This notwithstanding, individuals are not forced to become Muslims, although they must not disrupt or place obstacles in the way of the development of a Muslim society and an Islamic state (q.v.). For these two institutions shoulder the responsibility of ending man's enslavement to man and to material things. This responsibility is, however, not limited to Muslim countries, but is universal and includes the world.

Therefore, no compromise on this issue is entertained. According to Qutb and Abu Al-A'la al-Mawdudi (q.v.) compromise denies the possibility of a new reconstruction of the world and leads Muslims to give up some principles and to accommodate others. Thus, radical fundamentalists link theoretically radical change to creativity on the assumption that the old cannot be renovated and thus, must be destroyed. Therefore, an Islamic revolution must be launched whose objective must be the total abolishment of the regimes that are essentially based on the government of man over man or, simply, paganism (q.v.) (*jahiliyya*). Individuals must be liberated from the shackles of the present and the past and be given the choice for a new life.

In particular, the view of Islam as a revolution as disseminated by Sayyid Qutb in the second half of the 20th century represents a radical development within the history (q.v.) of Islamic political thought. Revolution is now loaded with political, ethical, theological, and metaphysical connotations whose fulfillment becomes a synonym to righteous application of Islamic teachings. Thus, Qutb and al-Mawdudi postulate Islam as a total revolution against ungodly human conditions whose rectification requires nothing less than total annihilation of human delusions of knowledge (q.v.) and power.

Again, al-Mawdudi makes God's messengers advocates of radical comprehensive transformation of all existing institutions. It becomes for Qutb, Hasan al-Banna (q.v.), al-Mawdudi, and Ayatollah Khomeini (q.v.) a quest for universal change to bring about justice (q.v.), and happiness and must not be hindered by any authority. Revolution aims then at translating *tawhid* and *wahda* (unity) into a social and political movement against the universal state of moral and political bankruptcy that justifies itself by the materialistic progress that has been attained.

The fundamentalist line of thinking sees that revolution is both a moral and social duty. It is not restricted to fighting the enemies of Islam but is also embodied in political, ideological, and metaphysical dimensions. Thus, Islam is turned into a religion (q.v.) of revolution, covering all aspects of life and of metaphysics, ethics, politics, and economics. Its discourse becomes revolutionary. The prophets of God are made into advocates of revolution, renewal, and change of metaphysical, moral, social, economic, and political systems and orders. Hence, revolution is a world claim that calls for justice for all and equality (qq.v.) for all.

The enormity of this responsibility leads the fundamentalists to adopt measures such as *jihad* (struggle) and call (qq.v.) (*da'wa*). Qutb argues that the mission of Islam is not to reconcile itself with paganist conceptions and situations; in fact, no reconciliation is possible with paganism. One sort of paganism is human legislation for humans without divine sanctions. Islam's mission is therefore to establish a human life in accordance with the Islamic conception and to set up an earthly system (q.v.) (*nizam*) where such a life can exist.

For the radical fundamentalists, revolution is the main tool in the attainment of a Muslim society that is based on *al-Shari'a* (Islamic Law) and social justice (qq.v.). A revolution is the road to a conscious transformation of current existing societies. Although it is not meant to convert people into Islam, it still aims at creating the Muslim individual, the Muslim society, and the Islamic state. As such, this revolution is not directed at a particular society but essentially at those societies that yield to human laws and orders.

For radical fundamentalists, a proper Islamic revolution does not, for Qutb, compromise with non-Islamic doctrines and orders. The road to change necessitates creative activism (q.v.) (*harakiyya*) that demands total development and not mere patching up of ways of life and orders and even philosophies and ideologies. Again, although aiming at a gradual Islamic revolution that could first spread out the message of Islam, the highest aim for radical fundamentalism (q.v.) is a total revolution that sweeps away the governments of the time as well as establishes new revolutionary Muslim societies instead of the un-Islamic, patched-up societies. It should shake and destroy the old society in order to build a new one. Not believing in the viability of mild change for a society erected on false or immoral foundations, radicals insist on the necessity of revolution as the only proper remedy for decaying societies. And for Qutb, al-Mawdudi, and other radicals, all societies are, in one way or another, decaying and *jahili* (paganist). See also CONSCIOUSNESS; GOD; *HIZB AL-TAHRIR AL-ISLAMI*; *HIZBULLAH*; IRANIAN REVOLUTION OF 1979; ISLAMIC ACTION ORGANIZATION; ISLAMIC REVOLUTION; ISLAMIC STATE; ISLAMIC YOUTH ORGANIZATION; *JAMA'AT AL-FANNIYYA AL-'ASKARIYYA*; *AL-JAMA'AT AL-ISLAMIYYA*; *JAMA'AT AL-JIHAD AL-ISLAMI*; *JIHAD*; *AL-JIHAD AL-ISLAMI* IN THE WEST BANK AND GAZA STRIP; KHOMEINISM; LIBERATION; *MUJAHIDIN KHALQ*; *MUNAZZAMAT MUQATILU AL-SHARQ AL-AKBAR AL-ISLAMI*; MUSLIM BROTHERHOOD IN SUDAN; POPULAR DEFENSE FORCES; REVOLUTIONARY GUARDS; *AL-SHARI'A*; SORUSH, 'ABD AL-KARIM; *TAWHID*.

REVOLUTIONARY COUNCIL. After Ayatollah Khomeini's (q.v.) return to Iran from France in 1979, he formed the Revolutionary Council to fill the vacuum left by the departure of the Shah. It became the most powerful institution to rule Iran and was responsible for the activities of the newly developed institutions like the Revolutionary Guards (q.v.) and the Revolutionary Courts. It was composed of 15 members, the majority of whom were members of the clergy, like Hashimi-Rafsanjani, Muhammad Husayn Bahishti (qq.v.), and liberals, like Abul Hasan Bani Sadr and Mahdi Bazargan (qq.v.). The Council was dissolved in 1980 after a constitutional government was set up. See also BAHISHTI, MUHAMMAD; ISLAMIC REVOLUTION OF IRAN; KHAMENE'I, 'ALI; LIBERATION MOVEMENT OF IRAN; MUSADDAQ'S TREND; RAFSANJANI, 'ALI AKBAR.

REVOLUTIONARY GUARDS (*HURRAS AL-THAWRA*). This is an organization that was established to protect the Iranian Revolution of 1979 (q.v.) and has become the most influential organization in Iran. It emerged as a militia and helped Ayatollah Khomeini (q.v.) achieve power. It has been institutionalized as the representative of the revolution. In the post-revolutionary period, the Guards developed into a very strong institution concerned with society, military matters, and politics. Although now it is integrated in the military system, it still enjoys some independence and freedom (q.v.).

The Guards have incorporated different social groups that were in opposition to the Shah. Meanwhile, the Guards have taken over most of the role of the Iranian regular military, especially during the Iran-Iraq War that ended in 1989. Even today, the Guards maintain a defensive military role together with a civilian role to reconstruct Iran. Furthermore, there were other guerrillas and organizations involved in Iranian politics, such as *Mujahidin Khalq* (q.v.), the pro-Communist Tudeh party, and the *Mujahidin* of the Islamic Revolution of Iran (q.v.). The Guards also exert influence in politics through the appointment of their members to important posts in the Iranian bureaucracy, military, and political leadership. They influence the parliament, the Council of Guardians, and many other institutions.

The organization itself is complex. It maintains an internal security apparatus, a military structure, and a network of services like army, air force, and navy. All of this was represented in the Ministry of Revolutionary Guards that was abolished after the death of Khomeini in 1989. More importantly, the Guards expanded beyond Iranian borders and became the arm for carrying the revolution to other countries like Lebanon, where they conducted actions against the United States and Arabs present in Lebanon. See also FADLALLAH, MUHAMMAD HUSAYN;

HIZBULLAH; ISLAMIC ACTION ORGANIZATION; ISLAMIC RE-PUBLICAN PARTY; ISLAMIC REVOLUTION OF IRAN; KHATAMI, MUHAMMAD; REVOLUTIONARY COUNCIL; *WALIY AL-FAQIH.*

REVOLUTION'S GUIDE (*MURSHID AL-THAWRA*). See *WALIY AL-FAQIH.*

RIDA, MUHAMMAD RASHID (1865–1935). Rida was one of the Muslim reformers whose influence spread all over the Islamic world. He was born in a village in northern Lebanon. After attending a religious school, he joined the reformist movement headed by Jamal al-Din al-Afghani and later Muhammad 'Abdu (qq.v.). In 1897, Rida went to Egypt to join al-Afghani but ended up joining 'Abdu because of Afghani's death. He became one of 'Abdu's closet students and associates. Rida published the influential magazine, *al-Manar*, which lasted till 1935.

Rida, as one of the thinkers of the reformist and modernist movement, advocated the capability of modernity (q.v.) and Islam (q.v.) through a process of reinterpretation of the text (q.v.) that is based on reason (q.v.) (*ijtihad*). Nonetheless, he was against secularism and argued that the return to the teaching of the ancestors and the employment of the Qur'an (q.v.), the *Sunna* (way) of the Prophet, and *ijma'* (q.v.) (consensus) would lead to the reworking of the role of Islam within modernity. Rida thought that the deterioration of the Muslim *umma* (q.v.) (nation) was not because of the essence of Islam but because of the ignorance and negligence of the Muslim elites. He called for the introduction of the rule of law and adoption of democratic means into *shura* (q.v.) (consultation) and other aspects of Western civilization (q.v.) in order to do away with tyrannical rules.

Although Rida upheld the necessity of the Caliphate (q.v.), which was abolished in 1923, he nonetheless was one of the first Muslim thinkers to call for the establishment of the Islamic state (q.v.) as a temporary political entity. This call was picked up later by Hasan al-Banna and his Muslim Brotherhood (qq.v.). See also *AL-SALAFIYYA.*

RIDDA. See APOSTASY.

RIFA'I, MUHAMMAD. See *AL-AFGHAN AL-'ARAB.*

RIGHT PARTY. See *HIZB AL-HAQQ.*

AL-RIYATI, BADR (1947–). Al-Riyati is a founding member of *Hizb Jabhat al-'Amal al-Islami* (Islamic Action Front Party) in Jordan (q.v.).

Al-Riyati was born in Bir al-Sab' in Palestine, and received his B.A. in commerce from the University of Damascus. He became a member of the Lower House of Parliament in 1993.

RUBUBIYYA (LORDSHIP). See ISLAMIC STATE.

RUHANIYYAT MUBARIZ (ASSOCIATION OF THE STRUGGLING RELIGIOUS SCHOLARS). *Ruhaniyyat Mubariz* is the Iranian traditional Right-wing political group that derives its ideology from *Rabitat Kibar 'Ulama' al-Din al-Munadilun* or *Ruhaniyyat Mubariz* (Association of the Struggling Religious Scholars). Its base of support includes older religious scholars, the bazaar, traditional technocrats, and middle class traditional groups. Its leader is 'Ali Natiq Nuri (q.v.), the current Speaker of *Majlis al-Shura* (q.v.). It lost its bid for the presidency of the Republic when Muhammad Khatami (q.v.) won the election in 1997. See also MUHTASHIMI, 'ALI AKBAR.

RUHANIYYUN MUBARIZ (RALLY OF THE STRUGGLING RELIGIOUS SCHOLARS). *Ruhaniyyun Mubariz* is the traditional Left, which derives its ideology from *Tajammu' 'Ulama' al-Din al-Munadilin* or *Ruhaniyyun Mubariz* (Rally of the Struggling Religious Scholars). Its base of support includes students of religious sciences from the middle class and a few older religious scholars. It is also popular among intellectuals and university students as well as poor and lower middle classes. This group is more liberal than the Right, and President Muhammad Khatami (q.v.), who holds "controversial" liberal views about the relationship between government and society, is one of its members. See also *TAYYAR AL-TAGHYIR*.

RUSHDI, USAMA. Rushdi is one of the leaders of *al-Jama'a al-Islamiyya* (q.v.) (Islamic Groups) in Egypt, which was headed by 'Umar 'Abd al-Rahman (q.v.), who is now living abroad. He supported the peace (q.v.) initiative between the Egyptian government and *al-Jama'a*, which was drawn up by Muntasir al-Zayat (q.v.). Rushdi attributes the continuation of military operations that take place within Egypt, like the one in Luxor in 1997, to the leadership of *al-Jama'a*, like Ahmad Taha (q.v.). After that operation, Rushdi apologized for the military operations against tourism in Egypt.

RUSHDIE, SALMAN. Rushdie is a literary British author of Indian Islamic origin. His book *The Satanic Verses* (1988), which Muslims generally viewed as a blasphemy to Islam (q.v.), brought him both fame and infamy, depending on the perspective of the reader. According to Rushdie, *Satanic Verses* is a fiction about an imaginary revered religious personality in Islam. However, Iran's Ayatollah Khomeini (q.v.) and others accused him of insulting the Qur'an and making ironic remarks against such basic principles of Islam as *tawhid* (q.v.) and the wives and companions of the prophet Muhammad. Although almost all Muslim countries condemned the book, it was Khomeini who issued a *fatwa* (q.v.) (legal opinion) in 1989 calling for the death of the author, and one million dollars was offered as a reward for killing him. This *fatwa* further worsened the relationship of Iran with the West (q.v.). The Western world saw Khomeini's *fatwa* against Rushdie as a topic that relates to freedom (q.v.) of expression—but that was employed politically.

Rushdie's book brought about protests and demonstrations all over the Muslim world. In 1989, even Muslims in Bradford, England, burned copies of the book, and demonstrations in Bombay led to the deaths of 12 people. Reactions to the book in the Muslim world differed from one country to another, but it was certainly not viewed favorably or sympathetically. In 1998 the Iranian leadership announced that it is no longer seeking the implementation of Khomeini's *fatwa*. However, radicals have increased the amount of money earmarked for Rushdie's assassination. See also APOSTASY; *FATWA*; KHOMEINI, AYATOLLAH; KHOMEINISM.

-S-

SABIQ, SAYYID. See *AL-SALAFIYYA*.

AL-SA'DI, AHMAD 'ABD AL-KARIM. See ISLAMIC BAND OF HELPERS.

AL-SADR, MUHAMMAD BAQIR (1935–1980). Al-Sadr was born in Iraq and was brought up in al-Najaf. Al-Sadr is considered one of the most distinguished fundamentalist Shi'ite thinkers. His thought has spread all over the Islamic world, especially in the Shi'ite communities. Al-Sadr combined both scholarship in *al-Shari'a* (q.v.) (Islamic Law) and political leadership through setting up his *Hizb al-Da'wa al-Islamiyya* (q.v.) (Islamic Call Party). He fought both communist influences and Ba'th domination.

The *'ulama'* (religious scholars) of Iraq came under the watchful eyes of the regime, and a process of taming and repression took place, especially after the Iranian Revolution of 1979 (q.v.) and al-Sadr's active support for it. The struggle between the Shi'ite community and the regime led to many dramatic events, which included the execution of al-Sadr and his sister in 1980. Al-Sadr's intellectual influence however increased, and many of his ideological and philosophical views are widely held or discussed, especially in matters related to constitutional rule (q.v.) and economics. See also *AL-DA'WA AL-ISLAMIYYA* IN IRAQ; FADLALLAH, MUHAMMAD HUSAYN; *HIZBULLAH*.

AL-SADR, MUSA (1928–1978). Although al-Sadr is not strictly a fundamentalist, he set up *Amal* Movement in Lebanon, from which *Harakat Amal al-Islamiyya* (Islamic *Amal* Movement) and *Hizbullah* (qq.v.) sprang, and activated Shi'ite political mobilization.

Al-Sadr was born in Qum to an Ayatollah and attended religious schools and seminaries. He then studied political economy and law at Tehran University. In 1953, he went to al-Najaf in Iraq and continued his religious studies. In 1960, he moved to Lebanon and became the highest Shi'ite authority. Al-Sadr was granted Lebanese citizenship in 1963. He "disappeared" in 1978 while on a trip between Tripoli (Libya) and Rome. Libya has been accused of having disposed of him. See also FADLALLAH, MUHAMMAD HUSAYN; *HIZBULLAH*; ISLAMIC *AMAL* MOVEMENT.

SAFAVI, SAYYID MUJTAB NAVVAB (1932–1956). Safavi was the leader of *Fada'iyan-i Islam* (q.v.), which was set up in 1954. He joined a theological school in Najaf in Iraq. Two of his followers killed Ahmad Kasravi, a religious clerk, because Safavi found his writings heretical. After the Shah's return to the throne in 1953, the *Fada'iyan* attempted to assassinate the Prime Minister in 1955. Safavi and three other leaders of the movement were sentenced to death and executed in 1956. See also *FADA'IYAN-I ISLAM*.

SAHNUN, AHMAD. See *JAM'IYYAT AL-TADAMUN AL-ISLAMI AL-JA-ZA'IRI*.

AL-SAHWA AL-ISLAMIYYA See FUNDAMENTALISM; ISLAMIC FUNDAMENTALISM; MUSLIM BROTHERHOOD; PAN-ISLAMISM; *AL-SALAFIYYA*; *AL-WAHHABIYYA*.

SA'ID, HAMMAM 'ABD AL-RAHIM (1944–   ). Sa'id was a member of the executive council of the Muslim Brotherhood in Jordan (q.v.) during 1978–1992 and has been a member of the executive bureau of *Hizb Jabhat al-'Amal al-Islami* (Islamic Action Front Party) in Jordan (q.v.) since 1996.

Sa'id was born in Jenin in Palestine and received his B.A. in Islamic Law from the University of Damascus, an M.A. in education from the University of Jordan in 1970, and a Ph.D. in *Hadith* (Prophetic sayings) from the University of al-Azhar in 1974. Sa'id became the dean of the Faculty of Islamic Law at the University of Jordan. He was elected to the House of Jordanian Parliament for the period 1989–1993.

SA'ID, MUHAMMAD. See ARMED ISLAMIC GROUP.

SA'ID, RAMADAN. See INTERNATIONAL ORGANIZATION OF THE MUSLIM BROTHERHOOD; MUSLIM BROTHERHOOD IN JORDAN.

SA'ID, SULAYMAN (1949–   ). Sa'id is a member of the Muslim Brotherhood in Jordan (q.v.) and a founding member of *Hizb Jabhat al-'Amal al-Islami* (q.v.) (Islamic Action Front Party) in Jordan. Sa'id was born in Jarash and obtained a B.A. in Islamic Law from the University of Jordan. He worked at the Ministry of Endowment and was elected to the Lower House of the Parliament in 1993.

AL-SALAFIYYA. Some believe that the *Salafi* movement is the result of the increased Saudi influence following the oil boom, yet the reality is otherwise. For instance, the *Rashid* has existed in Jordan since the days of the emirate under the direct influence of some of *al-Salafiyya* symbols and the students of Shaykh Jamal al-Din al-Afghani and Shaykh Muhammad Rashid Rida (qq.v.).

The *Salafi* school is not a defined doctrine like the "Hanafi" doctrine, and it is not an established group like *al-Ikhwan* (q.v.) in Saudi Arabia. Rather it is a general set of ideas and has adherents throughout the Islamic world. What the *Salafis* call for is the return to the early formative period of Islam (q.v.) and to the basic texts of Islam.

Al-Salafiyya movement also called for reform and renovation. It was not directly connected to the movement of Shaykh Muhammad Ibn 'Abd al-Wahhab (q.v.) in Najd. Among the movement's notables were Shaykh Jamal al-Din al-Qasimi, Shaykh 'Abd al-Razzaq al-Bitar, and Shaykh

Tahir Bin al-Tazairy. The *Salafi* call (q.v.) in the Arab East was secretive until the end of World War I. After that, the *Salafi* ideas spread and were established among the intelligentsia. *Al-Salafiyya* entered Jordan in a later period but spread first from Damascus to Saudi Arabia and finally, Egypt, with the Muslim Brotherhood (q.v.).

In Damascus, many Jordanian students were influenced by the Muslim Brotherhood's Shaykh Mustapha al-Siba'i (q.v.) and 'Isam al-'Attar, both with a long history in *al-Salafiyya*. In Damascus, the movement had a large following, including Allama Shaykh Muhammad Bahjat al-Bitar, 'Ali al-Tantawi, Shaykh Nasir al-Din al-Albani, Shaykh 'Abd al-Fattah al-Imam, Mazhar al-'Azma, Shaykh al-Bashir al-Ibrahimi (q.v.), Dr. Taqiy al-Din al-Hilal, Shaykh Muhiy al-Din al-Qulaybi, and Shaykh 'Abd Allah al-Qalqayli. The Islamic Bookstore in Lebanon, owned by Zuhayr Shawish, printed many of the movement's books.

In Jordan, two *Salafi* trends exist: One is related to the followers of Shaykh Nasir al-Albani, and another is led by Shaykh Yusuf al-Barqawi and Shaykh 'Abd al-Fattah 'Umar. In Saudi Arabia the *Salafiyyin* are people who studied in Saudi institutes and were influenced by Shaykh 'Abd al-'Aziz Bin Baz.

Al-Salafiyya, a call for return to the fundamental religious roots, was picked up by the Muslim Brotherhood in Egypt. It included a wide range of thinkers like Hasan al-Banna, Hasan al-Hudaybi, Sayyid Sabiq, Sayyid Qutb (qq.v.), 'Abd al-Qadir 'Awda, Muhammad Mitwali al-Shi'r- awi, and Muhammad al-Ghazali (q.v.). And this *Salafi* school dates back to the efforts of Muhammad 'Abdu (q.v.) and his vision of Islam.

The doctrine of the "righteous ancestors" (*al-Salaf al-Salih*) was in- vented by historians and scholars in order to create a romantic picture of the early Islamic period and to compare that period with a later period of corruption. See also 'ABDU, MUHAMMAD; AL-AFGHANI, JAMAL AL-DIN; MUSLIM BROTHERHOOD; PAN-ISLAMISM; RIDA, MUHAMMAD RASHID; *AL-SALAFIYYA* FORCES IN EGYPT.

AL-SALAFIYYA **FORCES IN EGYPT**. This Islamic group is the second major group in Egypt after the Muslim Brotherhood (q.v.), but strictly speaking, it is not a fundamentalist group. *Al-Salafiyya*'s call (q.v.) refers back to *Jama'at Ansar al-Sunna*, which split from *al-Jam'iyyat al-Shar- 'iyya* over the means of Islamic propagation during the 1950s. Its ideol- ogy is very traditional. See also *AL-SALAFIYYA*.

SALAFIYYIN **IN YEMEN**. See *HIZB AL-TAJAMMU' AL-YEMENI LI AL-ISLAH*.

AL-SALAM. See PEACE.

SALAMA, HAFIZ. See *AL-JAMA'AT AL-ISLAMIYYA*.

SALAMA, SALIM. Salama is the president of Gaza University and an important leading member of Palestinian *Hamas*: *Harakat al-Muqawama al-Islamiyya* (q.v.).

SALVATION MOVEMENT (*HARAKAT AL-INQADH*). The Salvation was founded by retired general Mashhur Hudaytha in April 1990. This Jordanian party views itself as an Islamic Arab movement that holds Islam (q.v.) as its ideology. It functions publicly and receives contributions from supporters and membership fees. In its basic declaration of principles, it announced the following objectives: to solidify independence and to get rid of foreign domination by capitalist states, to maintain a strong army, to support the Palestinian *Intifada* and liberation of Palestine, to provide a job to every individual, to provide free education and medication, and to give women their rights and encourage their participation in all kinds of activities.

AL-SANUSI, MUHAMMAD IBN 'ALI. See *AL-SANUSIYYA*.

AL-SANUSIYYA. This movement is attributed to Muhammad Ibn 'Ali al-Sanusi (1791–1859) who was born to a very respectable and religious family. Al-Sanusi studied at Fas as well as al-Azhar in 1839 in Cairo. At one time, a Shaykh accused al-Sanusi of heresy because of his tendency to exercise reason (q.v.) (*ijtihad*). Al-Sanusi is well known for setting up a stronghold for fighting the Westerners in North Africa. But later he called for focusing on religious and intellectual reforms. His main doctrine, which he exposed in his books, was the necessity of *ijtihad* and the need to reduce the dependence on traditional schools and to modernize Islam (q.v.) from within.

    Al-Sanusiyya was a religious movement that united some tribes and played a fundamental role in resisting the Italians in Libya. Through the mediation of the British, the Italians recognized the autonomy of *al-Sanusiyya* in 1917. Its other headquarters was in Misrata. See also ISLAMIC STATE; NATIONAL FRONT FOR THE SALVATION OF LIBYA; *AL-WAHHABIYYA*.

SAUDI ARABIA. See 'ABD AL-WAHHAB, MUHAMMAD IBN; *AL-WAHHABIYYA*.

AL-SAYFI, 'ABD AL-HAFIZ. See INTERNATIONAL ORGANIZA-TION OF THE MUSLIM BROTHERHOOD.

SAZIMAN-I MOJAHEDIN-I KHALQ IRAN. See *MUJAHIDIN KHALQ.*

SAZMAN-E HOJJATIYEH. See HOJJATIYEH ORGANIZATION.

SAZMANE-E MOJAHEDIN-E ISLAM. See WARRIORS OF ISLAM SOCIETY.

SCIENCE (*'ILM*). Islamic fundamentalism (q.v.) conceptualizes the function of science in a special manner. Abu al-A'la al-Mawdudi, Hasan al-Banna, Sayyid Qutb, Hasan al-Turabi, and Rashid al-Ghannushi (qq.v.) assert that Islam (q.v.) encourages benefiting from human experiments. However, the bias of experimental science, which is essentially developed in the West (q.v.), makes it lacking in universality and makes it a slave in the service of nationalism, immorality, and unbelief (q.v.) (*kufr*).

However, although al-Hasan al-Banna and Sayyid Qutb agree with al-Mawdudi on his opinion about the direction of science, they nonetheless view science, which they consider as a historical part of Islamic contribution to civilization (q.v.), as universal.

The fundamentalist rejection of the bases of modernism (q.v.) does not make their thought traditional as a matter of necessity. Although the fragility of Muslim civilization is underscored by al-Mawdudi, Qutb, and other thinkers, they believe that only an Islamic revival, not *taqlid* (q.v.) (traditionalism), can be instrumental in motivating an Islamic renaissance. Muslims must aim at founding a new science and philosophy (q.v.) to be developed from the essence of Islam, or else there will be no opportunity to recapture scientific and political supremacy. See also AUTHENTICITY; INTERPRETATION; ISLAMIZATION; KNOWLEDGE; MODERNISM; MODERNITY; PHILOSOPHY; AL-QUR'AN; REASON; RELIGION; TEXT.

SECOND ISLAMIC INTERNATIONAL (*AL-UMAMIYYA AL-ISLAMI-YYA AL-THANIYYA*). Hasan al-Turabi (q.v.), the leader of the Muslim Brotherhood in Sudan (q.v.) since 1964, led the first major split with the International Organization of the Muslim Brotherhood (q.v.). This was the beginning of the Second Islamic International. Al-Turabi set up *al-Mu'tamar al-Sha'bi al-'Arabi al-Islami* (Popular Arab Islamic Congress) to loosely represent all major Islamic movements, and this Congress was opposed by Iran, which proposed the idea of *al-hukuma al-'Alamiyya li al-Islam* (the International Government of Islam) in order to support radical Islamist movements.

This body took solid shape in 1991 when the first conference of the Congress was held in Khartoum; the second Congress was held in 1993 when many differences with Iran became obvious because the Congress upheld the word "Arab," which was considered racist by the Iranians. The third Congress took place in 1995, and 300 representatives from 80 states attended, including the delegations of the Muslim Brotherhood that was headed by Mustapha Mashhur (q.v.), the Islamic Salvation Front (q.v.), *Harakat al-Nahda* (q.v.), *Hizb al-'Amal*, and Iran. The third conference decided to set up branches all over the Islamic world.

The main difference between the International Organization of the Muslim Brotherhood and the Congress is that the Congress gives more leeway to local movements and does not believe in centralization. Islamic movements should cooperate as independent units that function in different socioeconomic and political environments. Thus, what is useful and helpful to one movement may not be appropriate for another. In other words, the Congress defends the "localism" of Islamic movements. The Brotherhood tends more to adhere to the decisions of central authorities. See INTERNATIONAL ORGANIZATION OF THE MUSLIM BROTHERHOOD; AL-TURABI, HASAN.

SECULARISM (*'ILMANIYYA*). See DIVINITY; GOVERNANCE; HISTORY; ISLAM; PAGANISM; RELIGION; SCIENCE; *TAWHID*; UNIVERSALISM.

SHABAB MUHAMMAD. See MUHAMMAD'S YOUTH.

SHA'BAN, SA'ID. See *HARAKAT AL-TAWHID AL-ISLAMI*.

AL-SHABIBA AL-ISLAMIYYA. See ISLAMIC YOUTH ORGANIZATION.

AL-SHADHILI, 'ABD AL-MAJID. See *AL-JAMA'AT AL-ISLAMIYYA*.

SHADI, SALAH. Shadi was one of the most important members of the Muslim Brotherhood (q.v.) and very close to its founder, Hasan al-Banna (q.v.). Shadi was a police lieutenant when he met al-Banna and became

the Brotherhood's man on the police force. See also MUSLIM BROTH-
ERHOOD.

SHAFIQ, MUNIR. He is a fundamentalist thinker previously linked to
Hizb al-Tahrir al-Islami (q.v.) (Islamic Liberation Party). Munir Shafiq
argues that the relationships between governments and society face
major obstacles, foremost among which is the lack of social justice
(q.v.), human dignity, and *shura* (q.v.) (consultation). These issues transcend the Western ideas of human rights (q.v.) (*huquq al-insan*), the sovereignty of law, and democracy (q.v.) and form the base for a proper
relationship between the ruler and the ruled. Shafiq does not accept any
justification for the conditions that beset Muslim life, such as the absence
of political freedom in the interest of the ruling elite and the existence of
widespread economic injustice that ruins the people. Thus, any modern
resurgence must address these issues by spreading social justice, uplifting human dignity, maintaining man's basic rights and the sovereignty
of law, and extending the meaning of *shura* and popular political participation through the development of representative institutions.

SHAHIN, 'ABD AL-SABUR. Shahin is a professor at Cairo University.
He has been the main Friday-prayer speaker of 'Amr Ibn al-'As Mosque.
It is he who brought a lawsuit against another professor, Hamid Nasir
Abu Zayd (q.v.), on unbelief (q.v.) (*kufr*) charges. See also ABU ZAYD,
HAMID; APOSTASY.

AL-SHAHRISTANI, HIBAT AL-DIN (1883–1967). Al-Shahristani was
born in Samirra' in Iraq to a religious family. Al-Shahristani moved to
Karbala' and then to Najaf to study with, among others, Kazim al-Khura-
sani. The latter headed the movement for constitutionalism (*al-Mash-
ruta*). Al-Shahristani became very well versed in religious and philosophical sciences and connected himself to major centers of religious
knowledge. After the outbreak of World War I, al-Shahristani struggled
against the British who launched their invasion of Iraq. The Shi'ite religious scholars declared *jihad* (q.v.) (struggle) against the British and defended the Ottoman Caliphate (q.v.). Al-Shahristani led forces against
the British and lost. Then al-Shahristani helped the Ottomans fight the
British. After the British occupation of Iraq, he returned to teaching
while at the same time trying to resist the British. He was imprisoned for
nine months for his activities. Al-Shahristani became, under King Faysal, the head of the Appeals Court in Iraq. He lost his sight and resigned

from his post. He became a member of the Parliament until his death in 1967.

SHAKIR, QANDIL (1931–   ). Shakir is a member of the executive councils of both the Muslim Brotherhood in Jordan (q.v.) and *Hizb Jabhat al-'Amal al-Islami* (q.v.) (Islamic Action Front Party) in Jordan since 1994. Shakir was born in Nuayran and obtained medical degrees from the universities of Baghdad, Liverpool (England), and Illinois and practiced at many hospitals in Egypt, England, Baghdad, and Jordan. Shakir translated medical books into Arabic.

SHALLAH, 'ABD AL-RAHMAN. See *HARAKAT AL-JIHAD AL-ISLAMI*.

SHALTUT, MAHMUD (1893–1963). Shaltut was the Shaykh of al-Azhar during the period 1958–1963. Shaltut took some measures to reform al-Azhar and to modernize *al-Shari'a* (q.v.) (Islamic Law). Although he supported the law of 1961 to reform al-Azhar, he opposed subjecting al-Azhar to state authority.

Shaltut's thought has two basic characteristics: first, his interpretations of the legal opinion attempting to relate religion (q.v.) to the contemporary economic and political realities, especially with respect to interest; second, his support of the idea of reconciling and bringing together the various religious schools of law and sects, especially the Sunnis and the Shi'ites. Some of his disciples are Dr. Muhammad Fu'ad al-Sarraf, Ahmad 'Abdu al-Sharbaci, Ahmad Hasan al-Baquri, Muhammad Abu Zahra, Dr. Zakariya Albara, and Dr. 'Abd al-'Aziz Kamal.

AL-SHAMI, AHMAD. See *HIZB AL-HAQQ*.

AL-SHARI'A (ISLAMIC LAW). Although *al-Shari'a* is pivotal to Hasan al-Turabi, Rashid al-Ghannushi, Muhammad Salim al-'Awwa, Hasan al-Banna (qq.v.), and others, it does not exclude non-Islamic doctrines and institutions, especially if an Islamic society (q.v.) needs them. Al-Turabi, for instance, exhorts the Muslims of the need to keep in mind the objectives of religion (q.v.). Justice (q.v.), for instance, does not mean one thing throughout history (q.v.), and therefore individual interpretations of it may change with the change of time and space, insofar as there is no direct opposition to a Qur'anic text (q.v.).

For the fundamentalists, *al-Shari'a* plays the role of harmonizing the different aspects of life, from setting up a government over which it rules to prohibiting the legislation (q.v.) of normative values and doctrines. The revealed Islamic *Shari'a* takes away the possibility of human control through legislation and sets both social and political systems on broader moral order and on universal divine laws as outlined in the Qur'an (q.v.). Because divine laws are not woven into the interests and customs of peculiar groups, they do not function, as do human laws, in an alienating manner.

The fundamentalists further argue that Muslims can at the same time base their "legislation" and its development on the general roots of the divine law or *usul al-fiqh*. Although the articulation or interpretation (q.v.) of particular doctrines depends on the conditions of the interpreter, this is tentative in the case of Islamic Law. On the other hand, human law has no true reference but the people, whose desires and ambitions dictate the principles to be followed. For fundamentalists, Islamic Law is not a social phenomenon but an eternal manifestation of God's (q.v.) will that defines the moral, social, and political order. In this sense, humanity should not but follow the order because it represents the meta-historical and universal basis. In this sense, any human legislation or rule that goes against the order or its underpinnings has no positive or legal standing. Therefore, human legislation should be limited to codification and recodification, as required by different conditions and circumstances of societies.

Radical fundamentalists argue that moral and political sovereignty is a divine right; man's duty is therefore to submit before it, or else man falls prey to *shirk* (polytheism). Human action or thinking is correct insofar as it involves no contradiction to the divine law. Sovereignty in principle and legislation in fact belong to God, and their significance goes beyond rituals and beliefs to include politics and government. Although the objective of the law is salvation in the next life, still that cannot be achieved without proper living now. The two lives should be integrated, and the instrument for that is *al-Shari'a*. Because it harmonizes the life of man with the divine will, its universal application becomes a duty for all Muslims in order to attain the Islamic order.

Furthermore, radical fundamentalists in general link morality (q.v.) and *al-Shari'a* and underscore the need for their obedience by the ruler and the ruled. Nonadherence to *al-Shari'a* by any government, whether democratic or autocratic, removes legitimacy (q.v.) as well as morality. Sayyid Qutb (q.v.) views the Islamic government (q.v.) as the government of law and of the ruled; rulers are still no more than servants to

Islamic Law. Thus, at this level, legitimacy is substantive and not only formal. Although the formal aspect of the government's function is to regulate human affairs in accordance with *shura* (q.v.) (consultation) and the individual is obliged to obey the government, obedience cannot be unconditional and absolute. Nonadherence to Islamic Law removes formal legitimacy and creates sufficient grounds for disobedience and revolution (q.v.).

Therefore, legitimacy and *Shari'a* become synonyms for radical fundamentalists who argue that even the formal aspect of legitimacy, *shura*, is part of the law and hence is substantive like any other aspect. This is why legitimacy functionally starts with the choice of Muslims but continues through the application of the law. That people should continue obeying the ruler stems from his adherence to *al-Shari'a*.

Thus, Sayyid Qutb makes the distinction between the ruler's function as the executive of the divine law and the initial source of authority that is based on his merits. The ruler derives initial authority and legitimacy from the people in general; their perpetuation is linked to proper application of *al-Shari'a*. But the ruler, as an individual, has no intrinsic religious authority as a divine right derived from heaven or through mediation. He derives the power to exercise authority from the choice of Muslims. See also APOSTASY; CALIPHATE; CONSTITUTION; CONSTITUTIONAL RULE; DEMOCRACY; *FADA'IYAN-I ISLAM*; FUNDAMENTALS; GOVERNANCE; *HARAKAT AL-TAWHID AL-IS-LAMI*; HUMAN RIGHTS; *IJMA'*; ISLAM; ISLAMIC FUNDAMEN-TALISM; ISLAMIC SALVATION FRONT; ISLAMIC SOCIETY; IS-LAMIC STATE; *JABHAT AL-'AMAL AL-ISLAMI*; *JAHILI* SOCIETIES; *AL-JAMA'A AL-ISLAMIYYA FI LUBNAN*; *AL-JAMA'AT AL-ISLAMI-YYA*; *JAMA'AT AL-JIHAD AL-ISLAMI*; *JAMA'AT AL-NAHDA AL-IS-LAMIYYA*; *JAM'IYYAT AL-ISLAH AL-IJTIMA'IYYA*; *JIHAD*; JURIS-PRUDENCE; KASHANI, ABU AL-QASIM; KHOMEINISM; MODERNISM; MODERNITY; MUSLIM BROTHERHOOD, IDEOL-OGY OF; MUSLIM BROTHERHOOD IN JORDAN; MUSLIM BROTHERHOOD IN SUDAN; NATION'S PARTY IN EGYPT; PA-GANISM; AL-QUR'AN; RADICALISM; REVOLUTION; SHALTUT, MAHMUD; *SHURA*; THEOCRACY; AL-TURABI; *UMMA* PARTY; UNION OF THE REVOLUTIONARY ISLAMIC FORCES; AL-ZAN-DANI, SHAYKH 'ABD AL-MAJID; AL-ZUMAR, 'ABBUD.

SHARI'ATI, ALI (1933–1977). Shari'ati was one of the most renowned social Islamic thinkers, whose influence has spread beyond Iran to all of the Islamic world. Although not strictly a fundamentalist, he nonetheless exhibited many tendencies in that direction. Shari'ati was born to a well-known family. One of his grandfathers was a respected scholar. His father was a religious scholar as well with modernist bents. Shari'ati benefited intellectually from his father's library as well as from studying under him. In 1949, Shari'ati joined a teacher's college for two years and started teaching in the villages. He and his father participated in pro-National Front rallies. In 1957, he was arrested for his political activities and was imprisoned until 1958.

Shari'ati received a B.A. from Mashhad University in 1960 and left for France to study at the Sorbonne, where he received his doctorate. In 1964, he returned to Iran and was arrested and jailed for six months. After being released, Shari'ati went to Mashhad and became instructor of humanities at Mashhad University. His lectures there attracted many people. He also joined *Husayniyah-yi Irshad*, an organization that focused on intellectual and educational activities. His activities were not popular among the religious circles or the government. By the early 1970s, Shari'ati was watched carefully by the government and was imprisoned again in 1973 for his radical views. He was released in 1975 because of the mediation of the Algerian government. He studied mainly under house arrest and was allowed to leave the country in 1977. Shari'-ati was found dead in England from a heart attack, but many rumors spread concerning his possible assassination by Iranian intelligence agents.

Shari'ati's main intellectual heritage was his attempt to reinterpret Islam (q.v.) in terms of modernity (q.v.). He believed in the necessity of popular revolutions as a fulfillment of the divine message of Islam. Religion (q.v.) for him could not be only a personal issue but must spread throughout all walks of life. Islam is a philosophy (q.v.) and ideology of liberation (q.v.) where the people are freed to pursue the implementation of the divine message and self-fulfillment. Shari'ati used many Marxist doctrines, such as dialectical materialism, that he Islamized to argue his views. Paramount among these views was the issue of social justice (q.v.) and the need of the Shi'ite community to be mobilized politically. As opposed to the traditionally held Shi'ite view of waiting for the Hidden Imam to spread justice (q.v.), Shari'ati called on the people to do so. This view he shared with Ayatollah Khomeini (q.v.). He, as opposed to the latter, allowed the exercise of reason (q.v.) (*ijtihad*) by laymen. See also MODERNISM; *MUJAHIDIN KHALQ*; MUTAHHARI, MURTAZA.

SHARI'ATMADARI, AYATOLLAH MUHAMMAD (1899–1986). He was born in Azerbaijan. Shari'atmadari founded along with others the Muslim People's Republican Party (q.v.). This Ayatollah led the forces that challenged the authority of the clergy after the Iranian Revolution of 1979 (q.v.). Though he later amended his relations with Ayatollah Khomeini (q.v.), he was still a modernist Muslim intellectual and a powerful figure whose advice was sought by many groups.

For instance, the Muslim People's Republican Party is alleged to have had his approval when it controlled Tabriz and seized the radio and TV stations and other places after Islamic militants occupied the U.S. embassy and took hostages. Four members from the Republican Party were executed by the new regime, and Khomeini visited Shari'atmadari in order to prove to him that the executed individuals were counterrevolutionaries. The party was closed down, and two years later, Shari'atmadari was put under house arrest for an alleged attempt to overthrow the regime, and his title of grand Ayatollah was removed. See also BANI SADR, ABUL HASAN; KHAMENE'I, 'ALI; MUSLIM PEOPLE'S REPUBLICAN PARTY.

AL-SHARIDI, SHAYKH HISHAM. See ISLAMIC BAND OF HELPERS.

AL-SHARIF, KAMIL (1926–   ). Al-Sharif was one of the leaders of the Muslim Brotherhood in Jordan (q.v.) during the 1948 war in Palestine. Al-Sharif was born in 'Ariysh, Egypt. He became a member of the Jordanian Senate in 1993. Earlier, he had been Minister of Religious Endowment and Ambassador to Nigeria, Pakistan, and Indonisia. Al-Sharif headed the Jordanian Company for Journalism and Publication.

AL-SHAWI, TAWFIQ. See INTERNATIONAL ORGANIZATION OF THE MUSLIM BROTHERHOOD.

SHAWISH, ZUHAYR. See *AL-SALAFIYYA*.

AL-SHAWQIYYIN. See *JAMA'AT AL-MUSLIMIN*.

SHIHRI, MUHAMMADI RIY. See *TAYYAR AL-TAGHYIR*.

AL-SHIQAQI, FATHI (1951–1996). Al-Shiqaqi was born into a poor family in Ramallah in Palestine then moved to a refugee camp in Gaza.

His mother died when he was 15 years old. Al-Shiqaqi got his school education at UNRWA schools. Al-Shiqaqi joined Bir Zayt University on a German fellowship to study mathematics, then he moved to Jerusalem where he taught mathematics until 1964.

Subsequently, al-Shiqaqi went to Cairo and studied medicine at Zaqaziq University and became a pediatrician. He was an admirer of Jamal 'Abd al-Nasir's nationalist ideology. In 1966, he and two friends set up a small Nasirite group. After 1967, he moved to Islamism and started reading books by Muhammad al-Ghazali, Sayyid Qutb (qq.v.), and others. Al-Shiqaqi met Shaykh Ahmad Yasin (q.v.), the future leader of *Hamas* (q.v.): *Harakat al-Muqawama al-Islamiyya* (Islamic Resistance Movement), but they did not get along. Later, he worked as a doctor between Jerusalem and Gaza. Al-Shiqaqi started his political life in 1964 with the Muslim Brotherhood (q.v.) and left it in 1968 after disagreeing with its policies toward the Israeli occupation forces.

During his presence in Egypt, Al-Shiqaqi contacted some radical Islamic opposition groups and was arrested twice in 1979 because of his strong oppositional Islamic activity. He was arrested the first time because he wrote a book, *Khomeini, al-Hal al-Badil* (*Khomeini, the Alternative Solution*), the second time, because of his political activities. During his stay in Egypt, al-Shiqaqi met Musa Abu Marzuq (q.v.), the future politburo representative of *Hamas* in the United States and Ramadan 'Abd Allah Shallah, who later became a university professor in the United States. Shallah eventually became the General Secretary of *Harakat al-Jihad al-Islami* (q.v.) (Islamic *Jihad*) after al-Shiqaqi's death.

Al-Shiqaqi started building up *Harakat al-Jihad al-Islami* militarily but only publicly declared the rise of *Harakat al-Jihad* in 1980, although it became known in 1978. It depended on Zaqaziq graduates who moved later to the Occupied Territories; al-Shiqaqi organized the cells of his movements, especially in Gaza. He started practicing medicine in Victoria Hospital in Jerusalem but was arrested in 1983 and imprisoned for 11 months on charges of organizing *al-Jihad*. In 1986, he was arrested again and sentenced to four years. In 1988, he was deported to southern Lebanon. In his exile, which lasted for seven years, al-Shiqaqi moved throughout the Arab and Islamic world. His movement participated in the Palestinian Uprising. He was against the Palestinian-Israeli peace (q.v.) treaties, but tried not to antagonize the Palestinian authority. In 1996, al-Shiqaqi was assassinated in Malta, allegedly by Israeli intelligence. See also *AL-JIHAD AL-ISLAMI* IN THE WEST BANK AND GAZA STRIP.

SHI'RAWI, MUHAMMAD MITWALI. See *AL-SALAFIYYA*.

SHIRAZI, MUHAMMAD. See ISLAMIC ACTION ORGANIZATION IN IRAQ.

AL-SHIRAZIYYUN. See ISLAMIC ACTION ORGANIZATION IN IRAQ.

SHUBUTI, 'ABD AL-QADIR. See ARMED ISLAMIC GROUP; *AL-JAYSH AL-ISLAMI LI AL-INQADH*.

AL-SHUMULIYYA. See COMPREHENSIVENESS.

SHUQAYR, MUNIR. See *HIZB AL-TAHRIR AL-ISLAMI*.

SHURA (CONSULTATION). A modern *shura*, as advocated by Hasan al-Banna, Hasan Turabi, Rashid al-Ghannushi (qq.v.), and other fundamentalists, postulates the necessity of people's involvement, not only in political matters but also in all issues concerning the community. *Shura* denies the legitimacy (q.v.) of authoritarian rule or political monopoly over the community and makes the community the source of executive power. The ruler, regardless of his social or religious position, cannot single-handedly regulate state affairs: In the final analysis, he must resort and yield to the choices of the people. Again, *shura* makes the ruler sensitive to, or at least accommodating of, popular attitudes and views.

Hasan al-Banna, for example, gives us the example of courts in Egypt and argues that if the government takes into consideration people's views and upholds *al-Shari'a* (q.v.) (Islamic Law) as the ultimate authority in making and amending laws, the dual judicial system of Egypt must then be amended. Uniting the court systems, both the secular and the religious, under the banner of *al-Shari'a* is a religious must and is in accordance with the nature of the Egyptian people. From an Islamic point of view, the supremacy of God's (q.v.) law must be maintained in all aspects, whether relating to political, economic, personal, or social matters. But current laws are against people's consciousness (q.v.) (*wa'iy*).

The authority of Islamic Law over society and people is grounded in the Qur'anic verses (V: 49, IV: 65). These verses not only indicate the supremacy of Islamic Law but have also provided fundamentalists since Hasan al-Banna with textual references to political governance (q.v.)

(*hakimiyya*) as the major political doctrine of fundamentalist ideologies. These verses are now interpreted by fundamentalists in general and the radicals in particular to indicate the non-Islamicity of most of the world's contemporary governments. Nonadherence to this political governance has been viewed by the radicals as unbelief (q.v.) (*kufr*) and *shirk* (polytheism). However, the possibility of such a charge has arisen because the fundamentalists have removed these verses from their social and political contexts and have universalized their use metahistorically to include every age and every country.

Most fundamentalists attempt to introduce *shura* as the main central and legitimizing doctrine of political rule. Not only this, but the whole question of *al-Shari'a*, for them, must be separated from its development and history (q.v.) and reworked in modern times through *shura*, itself in need of a modern interpretation (q.v.). Put differently, a modern Islamic political discourse cannot flourish on the underpinnings of medieval discourses. Although *al-Shari'a*'s derivative interpretations were seen as absolutes, medieval social and political practices conditioned such interpretations.

The fundamentalists call for the grounding of *al-Shari'a* today in modernity (q.v.) and 20th century conditions of existence. Thus, although *shura* has been perceived as a supporting principle in political life, there is no text (q.v.) to limit its interpretation as such. The limitations are social and political, not textual. In modern times, it is closer to democracy (q.v.). But although *shura* and democracy are denotatively similar, that is, calling for public participation and representation in the making of political affairs, nevertheless, they are connotatively different. Democracy grounds its ultimate reference in the people who become the sovereign, in contrast, *shura* grounds its reference in God's revelation, thus making God the supreme sovereign.

The advantage that *shura* has over democracy for Hasan al-Turabi, Sayyid Qutb (q.v.) and Hasan al-Banna is that although human thinking is always fluid there is a divine text that is always present and unifies the consciousness of the people. On the other hand, democracy has no text, but that of human reason (q.v.), which leads to the establishment of equal discourses that are equally full of shortcomings. When *shura* tackles or arrives at, for instance, constitutional, legal, social, and economic principles, it is always made in view of *al-Shari'a*, and not only in the interest of this group or that. Even when a particular claim is made by a majority, it could be counterbalanced by *al-Shari'a*.

Shura also differs from liberal democracy where the enjoyment of political rights is mostly figurative and essentially controlled by economic structures, according to al-Turabi. Without the grounding of human reason in what is beyond reason itself, it produces defective, sectional, and partial theories and doctrines. One example is capitalism (q.v.), which concentrates wealth in a few hands; another example is communism, which places real authority with the few, although theoretically dispersing personal wealth. This dialectical result stems from the conditionality of human theories that precludes the possibility of arriving at any absolute, whether in society, economics, or politics.

Thus, the fundamentalist view that any discourse that disrupts the connection between *shura* and *tawhid* (q.v.) derails the objective of the divinely ordained discourse. This also applies to other doctrines as well: Tyranny (q.v.) is unity without *shura*; the severance of unity from freedom (q.v.) makes it tyranny; the disengagement of freedom from unity turns it into licentiousness. Islamic liberation (q.v.), grounded in *shura*, is the balance (q.v.) (*tawazun*) of both and is the instrument that frees the people from intellectual paganism (q.v.) (*jahiliyya*), religious *shirk*, and political tyranny (*taghut*).

Again, a liberating *shura* based on Islam becomes for al-Turabi, Qutb, and al-Banna the instrument of change and of searching for the true meaning of *tawhid* and constant transcendence of human intransigence. Thus, a new discourse based on the ideology of a liberating *shura* must be adopted and advocated in order to redirect both the course of religiosity and political action. It should be treated as an essential part of a modern Islamic philosophy (q.v.) of transcendence, negation, and challenge.

However, such a reformulation of democracy and *shura*, al-Turabi argues, has some Islamic roots, for democracy in the West (q.v.) developed under the indirect impact of Islamic political thought and, specifically, under the Islamic doctrine of religious and political equality (q.v.) of Muslims. See also 'ABDU, MUHAMMAD; AL-AFGHANI, JAMAL AL-DIN; AUTHENTICITY; AL-'AWWA, MUHAMMAD; CIVILIZATION; CONSTITUTIONAL RULE; DEMOCRACY; DEMOCRATIC ISLAMIC ARAB MOVEMENT; DIALOGUE; EQUALITY; FREEDOM; AL-GHAZALI, MUHAMMAD; GOVERNMENT, FORMS OF; HAWWA, SA'ID; *IJMA'*; ISLAMIC ACTION PARTY; ISLAMIC GOVERNMENT; ISLAMIC SALVATION FRONT; ISLAMIZATION; *JAMA'AT AL-JIHAD AL-ISLAMI*; JURISPRUDENCE; KHALID, KHALID MUHAMMAD; *MAJLIS AL-SHURA*; MODERNITY; MUSLIM BROTHERHOOD, IDEOLOGY OF; AL-NABAHANI, TAQIY AL-DIN; NATION'S PARTY; RADICALISM; RIDA, MUHAMMAD

RASHID; SHAFIQ, MUNIR; *AL-SHARI'A*; UNION OF POPULAR FORCES; UNION OF THE REVOLUTIONARY ISLAMIC FORCES.

AL-SIBAHI, AHMAD. See NATION'S PARTY IN EGYPT.

AL-SIBA'I, MUSTAPHA (1915–1964). Al-Siba'i is one of the most outstanding Syrian fundamentalist thinkers and the founder of the Muslim Brotherhood in Syria (q.v.). Al-Siba'i was born in Homs to a family noted for its scholars. At 18 he studied in Egypt at al-Azhar University and became involved with the Egyptian Muslim Brotherhood (q.v.). Al-Siba'i became a close associate of Hasan al-Banna (q.v.) and was jailed in 1934 because he demonstrated against the British. In 1940, the British sent him to a camp in Palestine, and after his release in 1941, al-Siba'i established Muhammad's Youth (q.v.). But soon he was arrested again by the French and jailed for over two years. In 1964, he brought together different Islamic groups and founded the Muslim Brotherhood in Syria.

His intellectual heritage is mainly his attempt to rework social justice (q.v.) within the basic doctrines of Islam (q.v.). For God (q.v.) is the ultimate owner of things, and humans hold things as a trust from God. The state should only regulate the essential means of production and services and supervise the proper implementation of social mutual responsibility (q.v.). See also FIGHTING VANGUARDS; INTERNATIONAL ORGANIZATION OF THE MUSLIM BROTHERHOOD; MUHAMMAD'S YOUTH; MUSLIM BROTHERHOOD IN SYRIA; *AL-SALAF-IYYA*.

SIHABI, 'IZZAT ALLAH. See MUSADDAQ'S TREND.

AL-SIMAWI, SHAYKH 'ABD ALLAH. See ORGANIZATION OF SHAYKH 'ABD ALLAH AL-SIMAWI.

AL-SIMAWIYYA **GROUP** (*AL-JAMA'A AL-SIMAWIYYA*). See ORGANIZATION OF SHAYKH 'ABD ALLAH AL-SIMAWI. See also *JA-MA'AT AL-MUSLIMIN*.

AL-SINDI, 'ABD AL-RAHMAN. See *AL-NIZAM AL-SIRRI*.

SIPAH-I PASDARAN-I INQILAB-I ISLAMI. See REVOLUTIONARY GUARDS.

SIRRIYYA, SALIH (1947–1974). Dr. Sirriyya was born in Yafa in Palestine and moved with his family to Iraq in 1948. He escaped to Egypt in 1972, and Zaynab al-Ghazali (q.v.) arranged for his meetings with active members of the Muslim Brotherhood in Egypt (q.v.). Although originally associated with *Hizb al-Tahrir al-Islami* (q.v.) (Islamic Liberation Party), Sirriyya became the leader of *Jama'at al-Fanniyya al-'Askariyya* (q.v.), a radical and militant fundamentalist group. Ideologically, he adopted the ideological and political discourse of Sayyid Qutb (q.v.).

His exclusivity can be seen in his categorization of humanity into three groups only: Muslims, infidels, and hypocrites. Any neglect of an Islamic duty makes the individual an apostate and subject to death. Multiparty systems and diverse legal schools negate unity and lead to substantive conflicts. Sirriyya permits the temporary use of democracy (q.v.) in order to set up an Islamic state (q.v.). If the activists are persecuted, then it is possible for such activists to secretly infiltrate the political system and even become cabinet ministers. For the struggle to topple un-Islamic governments and any irreligious entity is a religious duty until the day of judgment.

The defense of un-Islamic governments, participation in un-Islamic ideological parties (q.v.), and adhering to foreign philosophies and ways of life are cited by Sirriyya as obvious instances of unbelief (q.v.), which incurs death. The sovereignty that belongs to God (q.v.) is used by him to divide humanity into the exclusive *hizb al-Shaytan* (party of Satan), consisting of all individuals and institutions that do not believe in or even practice Islam (q.v.), and the exclusive *hizb al-Allah* (q.v.) (party of God), consisting of those who struggle to establish the Islamic state. Out of this logic, Sirriyya attempted a coup d'état against Anwar al-Sadat, which resulted in the former's execution in 1974. This also happened later to Shukri Mustapha (q.v.) in 1977. See also 'ABD AL-RAHMAN, 'UMAR; EXTREMISM; *JAMA'AT AL-FANNIYYA AL-'ASKARIYYA*; *AL-JAMA'AT AL-ISLAMIYYA*; RADICALISM.

SOCIAL CULTURAL SOCIETY (*AL-JAM'IYYA AL-THAQAFIYYA AL-IJTIMA'IYYA*). This Shi'ite fundamentalist organization was active in Kuwait during the 1980s and was critical of the regime.

SOCIAL JUSTICE (*AL-'ADALA AL-IJTIMA'IYYA*). For thinkers like Mustapha al-Siba'i and Sayyid Qutb (qq.v.), Islam (q.v.) stipulates for the fundamentalists the principle of equal opportunity and makes basic values things other than material possession. Although Islam has set forth the right of individual possession and has made it the basis of its economic system (q.v.) (*nizam*), it simultaneously imposes legal and moral *hudud* (q.v.) (limits). The Islamic economic system is neither capitalist nor socialist, it is Islamic. What is essential in the Islamic economic system is social justice, which calls for the harmonious, balanced, and absolute unity between the individuals and groups and the general mutual responsibility (q.v.) between the individuals and groups.

The importance of justice (q.v.) stems from its being an ethical concept as well as one of the bases of Islamic government (q.v.). However, economic liberation (q.v.) is not seen as sufficient by itself for realizing a good society. Liberation cannot be guaranteed by laws alone, because man is affected by needs and inclinations. What is equally, if not more, important than economic liberation is the liberation of consciousness (q.v.) (*al-wa'iy*). See also CAPITALISM; *AL-DA'WA AL-ISLAMIYYA* IN IRAQ; FADLALLAH, MUHAMMAD HUSAYN; *HIZB JABHAT AL-'AMAL AL-ISLAMI*; *HUDUD*; ISLAMIC CULTURAL HERITAGE SOCIETY; ISLAMIC REVOLUTION OF IRAN; KHALID, KHALID MUHAMMAD; *MILLI NIZAM PARTISI*; MUSLIM BROTHERHOOD IN JORDAN; NASRALLAH, SAYYID HASAN; PEACE; REVOLUTION; SHAFIQ, MUNIR; SHARI'ATI, 'ALI; AL-SIBA'I, MUSTAPHA.

SOCIAL REFORM PARTY. See *JAM'IYYAT AL-ISLAH AL-IJTIMA'IYYA*.

SOCIETY FOR THE LIBERATION OF THE HOLY SOIL (*JAM'IYYAT TAHRIR AL-ARAD AL-MUQADDASA*). This clandestine political organization was active in Saudi Arabia during the mid-1960s. Its members carried out armed attacks on government installations and facilities of the Arabian-American Oil Company.

SOCIETY OF FREE YOUTH (*JAM'IYYAT AL-SHABAB AL-HUR*). This clandestine political organization was active in Bahrain following the suppression of the reform movement of 1938.

SOLDIERS OF GOD (*JUNDULLAH*) **IN EGYPT.** Soldiers of God is one of the radical fundamentalist groups in Egypt. See *AL-AFGHAN AL-'ARAB*.

SOLDIERS OF GOD (*JUNDULLAH*) **IN LEBANON.** Soldiers of God is a small and armed group in the quarter of Abu Samra in Tripoli, Lebanon. This militia stood for the establishment of an Islamic state (q.v.), and its fighters have acted on their own, refusing to cooperate with the Lebanese National Movement. See also *HARAKAT AL-TAWHID AL-ISLAMI*.

SORUSH, 'ABD AL-KARIM (1945–   ). Sorush was born in Tehran and studied chemistry first at Tehran University then at the University of London. Sorush became interested in the philosophy of science and history. After the Iranian Revolution of 1979 (q.v.), he became a member of the High Council of Cultural Revolution, along with Muhammad Khatami (q.v.). Sorush also became a university professor as well as a member of the boards of many cultural institutes. His main job was as a researcher at the Institute for Cultural Research and Studies. Later, he directed his criticism at the clerical role in political affairs and produced writings that the religious and political establishment did not concur with. Sorush has been stripped of his official positions and has frequently been prevented from traveling abroad. In his religious and political views, he is a liberal and anticlerical.

Sorush argues that the religious establishment has become intellectually superficial, politicized, and materialistic. He opposes the theory that the Islamic revolution should continue and argues that ideological interpretation (q.v.) does not fit the stage where the state is being built. Such an interpretation is not religious. Sorush called on the clergy to withdraw from state institutions. He was removed from his teaching post at the University of Tehran.

SOVEREIGNTY. See GOVERNANCE.

STATE (*DAWLA*). See ISLAMIC STATE.

AL-SULAYMANIYYA. *Al-Sulaymaniyya* is one of the Islamic groups that were formed in the 1960s by Sulayman Hilmi Tunhan. *Al-Sulaymaniyya* considered the law of Turkey to be exported laws of the devil. It, along with *al-Nur* group, continued their Islamic propagation or call (q.v.), although it was illegal. It was confronted by the two important parties of *Hizb al-Sha'b al-Jumhuri* and *al-Hizb al-Dimocrati*. Sulayman Hilmi Tunhan was arrested along with his two children and held for three days in 1939. Then again he was arrested in 1948. In 1957, the general prosecutor called for his detention for 100 years, and Sulayman died in 1959 of diabetes. The authorities refused to bury him in the Mosque of Muhammad al-Fatih.

Kamal Kajar, a relative of Sulayman, led the movement and allied himself with *Hizb al-'Adala*, whose representative he became in the Parliament. The strength of this movement was in the southern parts of Turkey and among the commercial class. See also *RASA'IL AL-NUR*.

SULTANI, 'ABD AL-LATIF. See *JAM'IYYAT AL-'ULAMA' AL-MUS-LIMIN*.

SUNNA ([PROPHETIC] WAY). See FUNDAMENTALS; TEXT.

SUPPORTERS OF MUHAMMADAN *SUNNA* (*ANSAR AL-SUNNA AL-MUHAMMADIYYA*). This Sudanese group opposes Hasan al-Turabi's (q.v.) movement in Sudan. When *Thawrat al-Inqadh* (Salvation Revolution) took place, this group supported the Islamist takeover. Later, it turned against the regime and al-Turabi. The Sudanese government has persecuted and arrested many of its members and accused it of terrorist activities inside Sudan. An important example is the incident that took place at the Mosque of *Ansar al-Sunna al-Muhammadiyya* in 1995 in Um Durman, where 16 individuals were killed and about 20 others were injured during prayers. This incident was attributed to a radical wing within the group *Jama'at al-Takfir wa al-Hijra*.

SYSTEM (*NIZAM*). What distinguishes Islam (q.v.) from most other religions, according to Hasan al-Banna, Sayyid Qutb, Hasan al-Turabi, Ayatollah Khomeini, Muhammad Husayn Fadlallah (qq.v.), and others, is that it concerns itself not only with worship but more importantly with social system. Islam is thus composed of creed, worship, and governance (q.v.) (*hakimiyya*), for Islam is a collective and state religion (q.v.), and Muslims therefore must derive their principles from it.

Again, for fundamentalist's Islam as a social system means that it deals with all the phenomena of life, and as such the Qur'an (q.v.) and the *Sunna* (way) of the Prophet must represent the highest fundamental authorities and points of reference, which ought to be interpreted through exercising analogical reason (q.v.) (*ijtihad*) and conducting *ijma'* (q.v.) (consensus) as well as *shura* (q.v.) (consultation). In brief, Islam is concerned with all aspects of life and postulates precise methods, fundamentals (q.v.) (*usul*), and foundations in order to solve humanity's problems.

This comprehensive religion for al-Banna is a general code for all races, peoples, and nations.

To the fundamentalists there is no other system of life that provides nations with the necessary tools needed for renaissance as Islam does. Islam, first of all, provides hope which is needed in the building of nations, second, national pride which is needed to create a good image of the self, third, power, which is needed for defense and which Islam asks its adherents to cultivate. Furthermore, Islam calls for the preservation of the self and the community through earthly and religious knowledge (q.v.), ethics, and economy. This is but a fraction of Islam's regulations for the renaissance of nations. See also 'ABD AL-RAHMAN, 'UMAR; AL-'AWWA, MUHAMMAD; CALIPHATE; CAPITALISM; CIVILIZATION; DEMOCRACY; DIALOGUE; FUNDAMENTALS; AL-GHANNUSHI, RASHID; GOVERNANCE; HUMAN RIGHTS; ISLAMIC FUNDAMENTALISM; ISLAMIC GOVERNMENT; *JAHILI* SOCIETIES; MARXISM; PAGANISM; QUTB, SAYYID; RELIGION; REVOLUTION; SOCIAL JUSTICE; *TAWHID*; AL-TURABI, HASAN; UNIVERSALISM.

-T-

TA'ADDUDIYYA. See PLURALISM.

TABATABA'I, MUHAMMAD HUSAYN (1903–1981). Tabataba'i is one of the leading Shi'ite Qur'anic commentators and philosophers. Tabataba'i was born to a famous family of religious scholars in Tabriz. He studied at Najaf in Iraq, specializing in religious and philosophical sciences. He returned to Tabriz in 1934, and after World War II, he became important because of his opposition to communist domination of Azerbaijan. Tabataba'i spent his life devoted to writing and teaching at Qum, Iran.

His main philosophical contribution rests on his attempt to rebut the foundations of Marxism (q.v.). His students included important individuals, like Murtaza Mutahhari (q.v.), who played a significant role in bringing about the Islamic Revolution of Iran (q.v.).

TAFSIR. See INTERPRETATION.

TAGHUT. See TYRANNY.

TAHA, AHMAD. Taha is one of the leaders of *al-Jama'a al-Islamiyya* (q.v.) (Islamic Group) in Egypt that is headed by 'Umar 'Abd al-Rahman. He is now living abroad. He supported the peace (q.v.) initiative between the Egyptian government and *al-Jama'a*, which was drawn up by Muntasir al-Zayat (q.v.). But Taha has not in fact delivered on his promise to al-Zayat to declare that *al-Jama'a* would cease its armed activities. He seems to be planning from abroad the military attacks of *al-Jama'a* and gives declarations of support for the operations that take place within Egypt, like the one in Luxor in 1997. After that operation, he declared that military operations against tourism in Egypt will continue.

TAHA, 'ALI HASAN (1949–). As a candidate for *Hizbullah* (q.v.) (Party of God) in the Biqa', he became a member of the Lebanese Parliament in 1992. Taha is a member of the party's politburo and has been very active in the Islamic Resistance activities against the Israelis. He believes that Muslims and Christians should find common national grounds for joint actions and Lebanon should not be based on confessionalism.

TAHA, 'ALI 'UTHMAN. He is the second most important individual in the Islamic Movement in Sudan after Hasan al-Turabi (q.v.). Taha was a member of the transitional national council (the Parliament) then became minister under 'Umar al-Bashir's (q.v.) regime. Previously, he was the head of the fundamentalist bloc in the Parliament and head of the opposition against the coalition between the other parties (q.v.), that is, *al-Umma* and *al-Itihadi*. Taha is one of the most distinguished figures in the National Islamic Front.

AL-TAHALUF AL-SHA'BI AL-ISLAMI (ISLAMIC POPULAR ALLIANCE). See *JAM'IYYAT AL-ISLAH AL-IJTIMA'IYYA* IN KUWAIT.

AL-TAHDITH [TREND]. See MODERNISM.

TAHIR, 'ISAM MUHAMMAD. See *AL-AFGHAN AL-'ARAB*.

AL-TAHRIR. See LIBERATION.

TAJAMMU' 'ULAMA' AL-DIN AL-MUNADILIN (THE RALLY OF THE STRUGGLING RELIGIOUS SCHOLARS). See *RUHANIYYUN MUBARIZ*.

TAJAMMU' AL-'ULAMA' AL-MUSLIMIN. See MUSLIM SCHOLARS' ASSOCIATION.

AL-TAJAMMU' AL-YEMENI LI AL-ISLAH (YEMENI ASSOCIATION FOR REFORM). This group represents a marriage of convenience of many of the tribal leaders of North Yemen, including Shaykh 'Abd Allah al-Ahmar (q.v.), the paramount Shaykh of the Hashid Confederation, as well as the more conservative elements of Zaydi clergy like 'Abd al-Majid Zandani (q.v.). However, the tribal elements of the party appeared to be divided into at least two factions (the second led by Shaykh Naji 'Abd al-'Aziz Shayif). It was clearly one of the three most important parties in the run-up to the elections originally scheduled for late 1992. Its newspaper, *al-Nahda*, is edited by Faris al-Saqqaf, who is the Deputy Director of the Information Committee of the Association. Its overwhelming emphasis is on Islamic issues, with constitutional reform as the first priority.

The Muslim Brotherhood (q.v.), which became an organized party in the 1970s, is part of the association. It was set up in order to counterbalance radical and leftist forces in Yemen. The Brotherhood regards itself as part of the national movement before the Revolution of 1962. It further considers itself to be part of the movement that led to the Revolution of 1948 because the Muslim Brotherhood in Egypt (q.v.) participated in leading the revolutionary movement and setting up its programs. The Brotherhood views Muhammad Mahmud al-Zubayri as its spiritual father and links its current organization to his attempt to set up the Yemeni *Hizbullah* (q.v.) (party of God) in the mid-1960s.

The Algerian Fudayl al-Wartalani (q.v.) played an important role in convincing al-Zubayri, who was visiting Egypt, to follow in the footsteps of the Egyptian Brotherhood. Al-Zubayri was recruited by the Brotherhood in 1941. In the mid-1940s, the Brotherhood became very influential and interfered in local and regional Yemeni affairs. Al-Zubayri set up *Hizbullah* in Yemen in 1965 following the ideological orientations of Sayyid Qutb (q.v.). But the movement did not last long, and al-Zubayri was killed in 1965. Al-Zubayri had called for justice, equality, and *shura* (qq.v.) (consultation). The movement did not then materialize into an organization.

After the unification of Yemen in 1990, the Brotherhood was represented in *al-Tajammu' al-Yemeni li al-Islah* and has been led by Shaykh 'Abd al-Majid al-Zandani. It has participated publicly in the political affairs of Yemen, entered the electoral process, and worked for expanding religious education and schools. Because of the Brotherhood's alliance with the tribal chief, 'Abd Allah al-Ahmar, groups of young Brethren split away and founded *Harakat al-Nahda al-Islamiyya* (q.v.) (Islamic Renaissance Movement) and followed the political views of Rashid al-Ghannushi (q.v.). See also *JAM'IYYAT AL-ISLAH AL-IJTIMA'IYYA*; AL-WARTALANI, FUDAYL; AL-ZANDANI, SHAYKH 'ABD AL-MAJID.

TAJDID (RENEWAL). See FUNDAMENTALISM; INTERPRETATION; ISLAMIC FUNDAMENTALISM; REVOLUTION; *TAWHID*; UNIVERSALISM.

AL-TAKFIR AL-JADID. See *JAMA'AT AL-MUSLIMIN*.

AL-TAKFIR WA AL-HIJRA. See ARMED ISLAMIC GROUP; *JAMA'AT AL-MUSLIMIN*; MUSTAPHA, SHUKRI.

AL-TAL, HASAN (1932–). Al-Tal is a member of the executive bureau of *Hizb Jabhat al-'Amal al-Islami* (q.v.) (Islamic Action Front Party) in Jordan. Al-Tal was born in Irbid in Jordan and graduated from the Teachers' Center in 1955. He worked at the Ministries of Education and Information. In 1972, he set up the fundamentalist weekly, *al-Liwa'*. Currently, al-Tal serves as Deputy President for *al-Dustur* newspaper.

TALA'I' AL-FIDA'. See VANGUARDS OF SACRIFICE.

AL-TALA'I' AL-MUQATILA. See FIGHTING VANGUARDS.

TALQANI, SAYYID MAHMUD (1910–1979). Talqani was one of the important theoreticians for the Islamic Revolution of Iran (q.v.). Talqani was born to a religious family in Talqan Valley and was brought up in Tehran. He studied at both Qum and al-Najaf and returned to Tehran in 1939. In 1939, Talqani opposed the Shah and was jailed for a few months. He also opposed the quietism of the religious clerks and set up sessions for Qur'anic teaching. Talqani collaborated with Mahdi Bazargan (q.v.) to develop a strategy against the communists after the abdication of the Shah in 1941.

Talqani became very involved in political activities. His writings analyze political and social issues from an Islamic perspective. He became part of the National Resistance Movement of Iran. Later, Talqani spent many years in both jail and exile and was freed in 1978. He was elected to the Council of Experts (q.v.). Different groups in Iran claim intellectual and political affiliations with him, such as the liberal Muslims of the Liberation Movement of Iran and *Mujahidin Khalq* (qq.v.). See also BAZARGAN, MAHDI; LIBERATION MOVEMENT OF IRAN; MUSADDAQ'S TREND.

TAMIMI, AS'AD. See *HARAKAT AL-JIHAD AL-ISLAMI: BAYT AL-MAQDIS*.

TANTAWI, 'ALI. See *AL-SALAFIYYA*.

AL-TANZIM AL-'ALAMI LI AL-IKHWAN AL-MUSLIMIN (INTERNATIONAL ORGANIZATION OF THE MUSLIM BROTHERHOOD).

TANZIM AL-AMR BI AL-MA'RUF WA AL-NAHY 'AN AL-MUNKAR. See ORGANIZATION FOR ENJOINING GOOD AND FORBIDDING EVIL.

TANZIM AL-SHAYKH 'ABD ALLAH AL-SIMAWI. See ORGANIZATION OF SHAYKH 'ABD ALLAH AL-SIMAWI.

TAQLID (IMITATION; TRADITIONALISM). Most fundamentalists, including Hasan al-Banna, Hasan al-Turabi, and Rashid al-Ghannushi (qq.v.), validate borrowing only from the generations of the Prophet Muhammad and the first two caliphs—for Sayyid Qutb (q.v.), or the first four caliphs—for Abu al-A'la al-Mawdudi (q.v.) and others. The reason for the exemption of these caliphs from the frailty of human existence is that they paid due attention to the real meaning of Islam (q.v.). Although they do not deny the existence of some occasional good guidelines, nonetheless they essentially view history (q.v.) as being corrupt and falling short of the ideal Islamic worldview.

Demystification of history is by and large a profound threat to the orthodox establishment of Sunnism as well as Shi'ism whose authorities lie in the historical development of both doctrines and sects. Those traditionally viewed imperatives, such as the doctrines of great founders of theological and law schools like Abu Hanifa, al-Shafi'i, Ibn Hanbal, and Malik or al-Ghazali and al-Baqillani, have been turned into possible historical interpretations but lack the quintessential meanings that have been attached to them. Their doctrines are turned into nothing more than reason (q.v.) (*ijtihad*) that could easily be modified or eradicated by another *ijtihad*.

In fact, part of the fundamentalist criticism centers on the traditional establishment and its religious and political role. Traditional religious *'ulama'* do not, according to Sayyid Qutb, comprehend the true Qur'anic spirit because of their *taqlid* (q.v.), or the imitation of defunct jurisprudence (q.v.) that is irrelevant to modern living and because of their complacency to political power, which leads to the alienation of Islam from the populace. Also, the secular elites are not spared criticism, which revolves around their marginalization of Islam from the administration of Islamic affairs and government. Thus, the rejection of both secular and religious elites makes the fundamentalists advocates of a new model for Muslims who properly comprehend both religion and modernity (qq.v.) and make them congruent. See also FUNDAMENTALS; *HIZBULLAH*; IBN TAYMIYYA, TAQIY AL-DIN; *IJMA'*; LEGITIMACY; *MARJI' AL-TAQLID*; MODERNITY; PAGANISM; SCIENCE; AL-TURABI, HASAN; *AL-WAHHABIYYA*.

TAQWA (PIETY). See MORALITY; ISLAM; RELIGION; UNIVERSALISM.

TAQWA **BANK** (PIETY BANK). See INTERNATIONAL ORGANIZATION OF THE MUSLIM BROTHERHOOD.

AL-TARIKH. See HISTORY.

TARIKHANIYYAH. See HISTORICISM.

TATARRUF. See EXTREMISM; RADICALISM. See also REVOLUTION.

TAWAZUN. See BALANCE.

TAWHID (ONENESS OF GOD). Abu al-A'la al-Mawdudi, Hasan al-Banna, Hasan al-Turabi, Rashid al-Ghannushi, and Sayyid Qutb (qq.v.) define Islam (q.v.) as an active program for life in conformity with God-given laws of nature and as a discourse aiming at the construction of a worldwide superstructure on the governance (q.v.) (*hakimiyya*) of God (q.v.). *Tawhid*, as the fundamental component of Islam and embodiment of its universalism (q.v.), becomes not only a religious principle but, more importantly, the elimination of independent earthly human systems that are not derived form divine governance and a complete transformation in the life of individuals.

For the fundamentalists, what is also indicated is, then, that God's control and governance of this universe negate the legitimacy (q.v.) of humanly independent governments. Thus, an essential part of the fundamentalists' conception of *tawhid* is turned into a process of negation of and opposition to any man-made system (q.v.) (*nizam*) that is not ultimately grounded in divine *hakimiyya*. Any meaningful search for ultimate truths in this universe is therefore denied, if it is unrelated to God.

Tawhid has been developed by the fundamentalists as the cord that ties together all the substance of politics, economics, ethics, theology (q.v.), and all other aspects of life. Because God, as the Creator, is the fountain of every material and spiritual thing, He is viewed as the ultimate authority in political life as well. Man's theoretical, theological, and political submission, to the fundamentalists, should be directed only to God, and by this they go beyond the traditional theological submission as understood in the old, medieval, and modern history (q.v.) of Islam.

In this sense, the fundamentalists could not but load this concept of *tawhid* with ultimate political importance. Thus one can see why they insist on subordinating politics and political philosophy (q.v.) to the highest kind of religious doctrines, which have led to confusing religiosity with proper political behavior. Thus, the establishment or the maintenance of the state on the basis of God's governance becomes a must for the legitimacy of any political regime. What happens is that fundamentalists like al-Banna and Qutb, who turn down medieval philosophy, which pursued a similar kind of polity, should not benefit from its pioneering efforts.

The testimony that there is "no god but God" is for Hasan al-Banna a call to the establishment of God's governance on earth. The perfection of a Muslim's creed must lead him to act on behalf of society. Furthermore, Islam's comprehensiveness (q.v.) (*al-shumuliyya*) makes it fit for human *fitra* (intuition) and capable of influencing not only the majority of people but elites as well. Because Islam is assumed to provide the worldly most just principles and the straightest of divine codes of law, al-Banna, for instance, views that it uplifts the human soul and sanctifies world brotherhood. It also draws practical ways to all of this in the people's daily life, social living, education, and political aspirations. It is also on these bases that Islam sets its state and establishes its call to the benefit of all humanity, thus making religion (q.v.) universal.

For although Islam asks man to satisfy himself spiritually and materially, it provides him with regulations that prevent extreme behaviors so that a state of balanced fulfillment is attained. Such a balance is important for the fundamentalists because man does not live in isolation, he is, by necessity, a member of a community, and the community has its "collective reason" (q.v.), which differs from the individual's. Thus, Islam's diverse regulations satisfy different needs, the economic, for material well-being, the political, for justice (q.v.), and the social, for equality (q.v.). All these regulations are but parts of a whole Islamic method (q.v.) that is authentic, unified, and integral. Only such a method can lead humanity to escape from the miseries of its existence.

Tawhid is the central doctrine in the formulation of the fundamentalists' political discourse as well as their epistemological discourse. Because their political discourse is constructed around the concept of *tawhid*, their ideology is transformed into a doctrinal one. And insofar as *tawhid* is a political doctrine, it entails political submission. Such a rendering provides the fundamentalists with a doctrinal yardstick to evaluate political behavior and to produce political doctrines.

Because *tawhid* is a movement of continuous development of life, Islam, for the fundamentalists, does not accept an evil reality as such because its main mission is to eradicate evil and to improve the quality of life. For the radical fundamentalists *tawhid* involves freedom from subordination to anyone or anything but divine law, revolution (q.v.) against the authority of tyrannical lords, and the rejection of negating human individuality. An act like this is a crime because God, having created man free, forbade the subordination of oneself. "No god but God," declares Qutb, is a revolution against the worldly authority that seizes the first characteristic of divinity (q.v.) (*uluhiyya*) and a revolution against the situations based on this seizure and against the authorities that rule by human and un-Islamic Laws.

For the fundamentalists, it is the basic principle of all religions, especially the monotheistic religions like Christianity and Judaism (qq.v.). Islam therefore means submission to *tawhid*, which requires following God's path in every aspect of life, whether ritualistic, like prostrating before God, or political, like obeying His laws and order. It further indicates the need for positive submission to God and the negative revolt against submitting to anything else, be it concrete or metaphorical, metaphysical, or political. Therefore, the only truly Islamic way of life for Qutb and other radical fundamentalists is the one that ties together all differentiated aspects of life into one solid unit organized around *tawhid*.

This is the basic foundation for any Islamic society and state (qq.v.) as well as economy. All aspects of life should be finally grounded in the text (q.v.) of revelation and not in the traditions and hearsay. A Muslim's belief that there is no ruler and legislator but God should mean that He is the ultimate organizer of life and the universe. The radical fundamentalist political discourse is dominated by this idea to the extent that it extends into all aspects of life, the personal as well as the public, the individual as well as the social and, of course, the political. See also AUTHENTICITY; CAPITALISM; CHRISTIANITY; COMPREHENSIVENESS; DIVINITY; EXTREMISM; GOD; GOVERNANCE; *HIZBULLAH*; IBN TAYMIYYA, TAQIY AL-DIN; *IJMA'*; ISLAM; ISLAMIC STATE; *JIHAD*; LEGISLATION; LIBERATION; METHOD; MONOTHEISTIC RELIGIONS; MORALITY; MUSLIM BROTHERHOOD, IDEOLOGY OF; PAGANISM; PEACE; PHILOSOPHY; REVOLUTION; RELIGION; THEOLOGY; UNBELIEF; UNIVERSALISM; *AL-WAHHABIYYA*.

AL-TAYYAR AL-MUSADDAQI. See MUSADDAQ'S TREND.

TAYYAR AL-TAGHYIR (TREND FOR CHANGE). *Tayyar al-Taghyir* is one of the emerging Iranian political trends that call for change. It has an attractive appeal for the youth, which is represented by the Association for the Defense of Islamic Values. It is closer to the traditional Left, or *Ruhaniyyun Mubariz* (q.v.), but has fundamentalist ambitions. Its leader is Hujjat al-Islam Muhammadi Riy Shihri who was head of courts, Minister of Intelligence and head of the pilgrimage delegation to Mecca. Shihri is a distinguished, controversial, yet respected religious clergyman trusted by revolutionary forces.

TERRORISM. See ACTIVISM; EXTREMISM; RADICALISM; VIOLENCE.

TEKDAL, AHMAD. See *REFAH PARTISI*.

TEXT (*AL-NAS*). Text usually refers to the Qur'an (q.v.) and, at times, to the *Sunna* (way) of the Prophet. It constitutes for the fundamentalists the only categorical interpretive substance and quintessential Islam (q.v.). Unlike traditional views, for the fundamentalists, Qur'anic exegeses are, therefore, tentative and should be subject to continuous review. In this sense, the Qur'an, whose practical usefulness to modernity (q.v.) is untapped, must be functionally rejoined to the *umma's* (q.v.) (nation) life. According to Hasan al-Turabi, Rashid al-Ghannushi, Sayyid Qutb, Hasan al-Banna, and Abu al-Hasan al-Nadawi (qq.v.), the society's separation from its fundamental foundation, that is, the Qur'an, is a major hindrance to any viable renaissance. Thus, the reworking of the text into all facets of life is a must for any future development or for the establishment of sound political and philosophical systems.

Historically, the "isolation" of the divine text from the people's life has transformed human thinking into a functional replacement of the divine. The fundamentalists argue that although people may believe in Islam, true outcomes of belief, however, cannot be limited to the realm of the conscience or creed but must, more importantly, involve the practical aspects of life as well as the intellectual. In other words, the neglect of the divine text in the real life of the people makes them come closer to polytheism (q.v.) (*shirk*).

Thus, for many other fundamentalists, any deviation from the divine text or man's dismissal from his conscience of the actualization of the divine commands leads to life within an impious context, regardless of the knowledge (q.v.) and technology that have been accumulated. Those societies that do not rule by God's (q.v.) commands live in unbelief (q.v.) (*kufr*), where God's commands are associated with those of others. See also 'ABD AL-RAHMAN, 'UMAR; ACTIVISM; CONSTITU-TION; CONSTITUTIONAL RULE; DIVINITY; FUNDAMENTALS; AL-GHANNUSHI, RASHID; GOD; HISTORICISM; HISTORY; IBN TAYMIYYA; *IJMA'*; INTERPRETATION; ISLAMIC STATE; *JIHAD*; KNOWLEDGE; PAST; AL-QUR'AN; RIDA, MUHAMMAD RAS-HID; *AL-SHARI'A*; *SHURA*; *TAWHID*; THEOLOGY; AL-TURABI, HASAN.

AL-THAWRA. See REVOLUTION.

THAWRAT AL-INQADH. See AL-BASHIR, 'UMAR. See also POPU-LAR DEFENSE FORCES; AL-TURABI, HASAN.

THEOCRACY. The rule of Islam (q.v.) is by no means the rule of theoc-racy but is the rule of *al-Shari'a* (q.v.) (Islamic Law), however vaguely defined. Sayyid Qutb and Hasan al-Banna (qq.v.) argue against the legit-imate existence of a specific group that can be called clergy; such people are only scholars. Proper Islamic government (q.v.) is more generally the systematic rule of Islam where Islamic ideas govern and where *al-Shari'a* defines the forms of government (q.v.) and society.

Thus, the inherent authority of the clergy is denied by all Sunni fundamentalists. Therefore to describe the proper Islamic government as a theocracy is a misnomer, because it gives the wrong impression about the essence and manifestations of Islam. Neither theory nor practice lends credibility to the theocracy of Islam.

However, the Shi'ite brand of Islamic fundamentalism (q.v.), as advocated by Ayatollah Khomeini (q.v.), may more appropriately be called theocratic. Khomeini advocates in his *Islamic Government* the legitimate rule of only the jurists because a proper Islamic government must be based on jurisprudence (q.v.), and the ruler must represent functionally the Hidden *Imam*.

However, the majority of the fundamentalists rule out the need for a specific group in order to bestow legitimacy (q.v.) on Islamic government. Its authority springs from adhering to divine governance (q.v.) (*hakimiyya*) and the execution of *al-Shari'a*. Whereas for both Khomeini and Qutb, *al-Shari'a* forms the basis of government, Qutb views the right to rule as a matter of delegation from the people, and Khomeini, directly and indirectly from the *Imam*.

Most fundamentalists reject any allusion to the Islamic government being a theocratic government because there is, to begin with, no class that can be properly endowed with religious rule. Furthermore, it is only by applying *al-Shari'a* that Islam can rule and be properly represented. Because Islam has created a society that is based on law, the fundamentalists' repudiation of theocracy stems from their opposition to the notion of the clergy's inherent authority. Qutb, al-Banna, Hasan al-Turabi, and Rashid al-Ghannushi (qq.v.) underscore the distinction between "men of religion," or clergy, and religious power; the first has no power, the second is invested in the people. The rule of clergy should not be taken as the ideal for an Islamic government, for neither theory nor practice supports this ideal and its consequences. *Ijma'* and *shura* (qq.v.), or consensus and consultation, are doctrines that provide authority to the people, and not to the clergy. See also GOVERNANCE; GOVERNMENT, FORMS OF; GOVERNMENT, FUNCTION OF; ISLAMIC STATE.

THEOLOGY (*'ILM AL-KALAM*). Although Islamic modernists and reformers have produced modern interpretations, they have not challenged the normative status of Islamic theological and juridical schools. Muhammad 'Abdu's rejection of man's complete understanding of divine things is traditional both in substance and method (q.v.) (*manhaj*). His *Risalat al-Tawhid* (*Treatise on Oneness*) is mainly a layman's reinterpretation of major works on medieval theology minus the hair-splitting argumentation and discussion about divine attributes. That science (q.v.) is congruent with religion (q.v.), or that they are not contradictory, is also an argument put forward by Abu Hamid al-Ghazali in his *Tahafut al-Falasifa* (*Incoherence of the Philosophers*). So is the case of the argument put against the futility of discussions about the divine attributes.

Again al-Kindi, Ibn Sina, and Ibn Rushd have introduced what was considered to be the science of the day into intellectual circles. In other words, the modernists have been very instrumental in opening up the closed intellectual circles to the need for rearguing tradition and for modernizing the interpretation (q.v.) of Islam (q.v.) as well as *tawhid* (q.v.) (Oneness of God) by using all possible tools at hand. From their point of view these disciplines are historically developed and as such have no universal values.

Though not aware of it the fundamentalists are indirect historicists. For almost all old, medieval, and even modern interpretations are viewed as nothing more than social and, at times, corrupt interpretations of the religious text (q.v.), or the imposition of different meanings by many readers into the religious text. The true interpretation of the text is only reserved to the author, and the reader, any reader, cannot make a claim to a universal reading of that text. Fundamentalists look at the divergent readings as the outcomes of a complex set of conditions that makes a reader read or interpret a text in one way or another.

The fundamentalists view differences between theological, juridical, philosophical, and political schools and sects as products of specific ways of living that may not necessarily fit contemporary societies and problems. Put differently, what is more important than the logic of an interpretation is its relevance to the conditions of the reader himself and its pragmatic outcome.

Sayyid Qutb, Hasan al-Turabi, Rashid al-Ghannushi (qq.v.), and other fundamentalists transfer their rejection of historical interpretations into the adoption of new interpretations that are relevant to the problems of this age. In general, the fundamentalists have produced a multitude of interpretations whose essential discourse converges on transformation, both intellectual and political, that could be either moderate or radical. See also APOSTASY; CALIPHATE; GOD; HISTORY; *HIZBULLAH*; *IJMA'*; IBN TAYMIYYA, TAQIY AL-DIN; INTERPRETATION; PAST; QUTB, SAYYID; RADICALISM; *TAWHID*.

AL-TIJANIYYA. *Al-Tijaniyya* is a Turkish Islamic Sufi movement whose existence goes back to 1801 and was founded in North Africa. It was weakened tremendously in 1925 and surfaced again after World War II. *Al-Tijaniyya* was run by Kamal Billo Oghlo, a Turkish businessman, who was tried along with others for destroying some idols. The *Tijanis* tried to revolt in 1952 in Minaman in Turkey, and the leaders of the revolt were executed.

TILMISANI, 'UMAR (1904–1986). Tilmisani was born in the neighborhood of Hawsh Qadam in Cairo to a family that came originally from Tilmisan in Algeria. He started studying law in 1924 and joined the *Wafd* party. In 1931, he received his B.A., and two years later he joined the Muslim Brotherhood (q.v.). He was repeatedly imprisoned during the ordeals of the Muslim Brotherhood and was released for good by Anwar al-Sadat in 1971. In 1973, after the death of Hasan al-Hudaybi (q.v.), Tilmisani became the General Guide of the Muslim Brotherhood until his death. See also the MUSLIM BROTHERHOOD.

TRADITIONALISM. See *TAQLID*.

TRADITIONS (*HADITH*). See FUNDAMENTALS; TEXT.

TREND FOR CHANGE. See *TAYYAR AL-TAGHYIR*.

TUFAYLI, SUBHI. Tufayli was the leader of *Hizbullah* (q.v.) in Lebanon during its radical period, that is until 1992 and the political changes in Iran that brought Hashimi Rafsanjani (q.v.) as President of Iran and reduced revolutionary fervor. He is from Biqa' region and now heads a local movement, *Majlis A 'yan Ba 'albak/al-Hirmil*, to lobby against the Lebanese government and its developmental policies. In 1998, and after military confrontations with the Lebanese army, he went underground to avoid arrest, and his council has been outlawed. Al-Tufayli is very radical in his political approach and is ready to clash with the authorities. See also *HIZBULLAH*.

TULAYS, 'ALI KHUDR (1962–   ). Tulays became a member of the Lebanese Parliament in 1992 and again in 1996 as a candidate for *Hizbullah* (q.v.) (Party of God) in the Biqa'. Tulays has been involved in the party's attempt to open up to Christians in Lebanon and has called for Muslim-Christian understanding.

TUNHAN, SULAYMAN HILMI. See *AL-SULAYMANIYYA.*

TUNISIAN RENAISSANCE MOVEMENT. See *HARAKAT AL-NAHDA AL-ISLAMIYYA IN TUNISIA.* See also *HARAKAT AL-ITIJAH AL-ISLAMI.*

AL-TURABI, HASAN (1932–   ). Hasan 'Abd Allah al-Turabi was born in the city of Ksla in Sudan. His family's interest in the traditions of learning and Sufism affected his personality. Al-Turabi graduated in 1955 with a B.A. in Law from the Faculty of Law at Khartoum University. In 1957, he obtained an M.A. in Law from the University of London and, in 1964, a doctorate in Law from the Sorbonne, Paris. In the mid-1960s he served as the Dean of the Faculty of Law at Khartoum University and was then appointed first Attorney General and later elected a member of the Sudanese Parliament.

Al-Turabi participated in the writing of the constitutions of Pakistan and the United Arab Emirates. During the period of 1964–1969, he headed the Islamic Charter, which came about by the unification of the Muslim Brotherhood (q.v.) and the Islamic Movement for Liberation. By the end of the 1970s, he became a cabinet minister.

In 1988, the National Islamic Front, al-Turabi's organization, joined a coalition government headed by Sadiq al-Mahdi, his brother-in-law. Al-Turabi was initially appointed Minister of Justice, then Minister of Foreign affairs and Deputy Prime Minister. He is assumed to be the ideologue for *Thawrat al-Inqadh* (Salvation Revolution) that was brought about by General 'Umar al-Bashir (q.v.) in 1989. Now, Dr. Hasan al-Turabi is the leading theoretician of Islamism in North Africa and the Middle East as well as being the leading ideologist and General Secretary of the Arab and Islamic Congress in the Sudan, who exerts tremendous influence over the Sudanese government. In 1996, he became Speaker of the Parliament.

Though his thought is not well known in the West (q.v.), his political role is widely acknowledged. In May 1992, he held a hearing at the United States Congress about Islamic fundamentalism (q.v.) in North Africa and the Sudan, Sudanese-Iranian relations, human rights, and minorities.

In al-Turabi's discourse, democracy (q.v.) occupies a major role because of his perception that it personifies Islam's (q.v.) capability of readoption and readaptation of modern doctrines. He argues that this adoptive and adaptive process makes democracy and *shura* (q.v.) (consultation) equivalent. Muslims cannot anymore turn a blind eye to the importance of democracy, introduced into Muslim areas by the dominant West and its discourses. It must now be reworked into modern Islamic thought, linked to Islamic political jurisprudence (q.v.) and, in particular, identified with *shura*. Although it is true that *shura* has not been solidly conceptualized or practiced as democracy, al-Turabi nevertheless has tried to conceptualize it as a synonym for democracy and has seen no religious or cultural obstacle for doing that.

Furthermore, al-Turabi advocates linking democracy to the two fundamentals (*usul*) of Islam (q.v.), namely the Qur'an (q.v.) and the *Sunna* (way) of the Prophet. In fact, *shura* as a general method (q.v.) (*manhaj*) of Islamic government (q.v.) can be read from and into the religious texts, if they are read in a specific way. For the religious text (q.v.) exhorts the community to take responsibility for its own affairs, which would include issues of rule and organization. The Islamization (q.v.) of democracy as *shura* needs only its linkage to *tawhid* (q.v.) (Oneness of God), which makes equality and freedom (qq.v.) universal religious doctrines instead of secular and human doctrines. In this sense, *shura* and its concomitant doctrines like human rights (q.v.) become actually more compelling and concrete. Al-Turabi explains that *shura* in Islam is a doctrine that is derived from the roots of religion (q.v.) and its general postulates and not specifically from any particular text. In other words, it must belong to the ways Muslims understand Islam. Textual references to *shura* relate to one aspect of life or another.

To al-Turabi, Islam has viewed the important issues of divinity, governance (qq.v.), and authority as being the domain of God (q.v.). It has also viewed all members of humanity equally, and therefore the vicegerency or caliphate (q.v.) belongs to them generally. The crisis of applying the Islamic system (q.v.) (*nizam*) of *shura* in Islamic countries cannot be resolved by just adding some sort of formalities or formal and cosmetic institutions to existing power structures. It must be reworked through the spirit of Islam where the entire community, not only an individual or a group of individuals, carries the responsibilities of government. *Shura* must be transformed into a system of living, not a limited political practice.

According to al-Turabi, a state that is not built on such a system does not lead its society to success but ends up being more an instrument of social and oppressive destruction. Modern national states of the Islamic world do not pay any regard to or possess similar rights because they are not founded on freedom but on the Sultanic conception of authority, which leaves no room for the community either to express its views or to develop a representative system. Contemporary realities call on Muslims to feel ashamed of their conditions and to recreate a discourse that reinstitutes the Islamic state (q.v.) and the Muslim society and not a mere *taqlid* (q.v.) (imitation) of the West. But Muslims must focus on the issues of freedom and *shura*, or democracy, and direct all of this toward developing as well a dialogue with the West.

Part of this dialogue and the new system being called for by al-Turabi is the relationship between *shura* and democracy, or, in fact, the Muslim world, and the West. Al-Turabi argues that the difference between Islamic democratic *shura* and Western democracy is not merely formal but also conceptual, because the former is based on and derived from the divine governance and, consequently, humanity's common *istikhlaf* (vicegerency). The latter, on the other hand, is based on concepts of nature. Thus, in Islam, freedom as well as what it entails is both metaphysical and doctrinal, that is, freedom is a religious doctrine whose violation goes beyond mere political violation to constitute a violation of something divine. Freedom in liberalism is, however, legal and political but never religious or divine.

Thus, the focus of Islamic discourse for al-Turabi is not only the interests of individuals or their fears of government but, in fact, their own consciousness (q.v.) (*wa'iy*), whose strengthening serves as a guarantee against any violation of political rule that has bestowed itself with powers usually reserved for the community. In this sense, *shura* becomes a religious doctrine of liberation (q.v.) that cannot be claimed by any authority as such, and any such authority must rule only contractually and in the service of the social structure.

Accepting the idea that *al-Shari'a* (q.v.) (Islamic Law) limits the powers of the state and frees society, he grounds it in the religious command "to enjoin good and to forbid evil." This command for al-Turabi becomes parallel to pluralism (q.v.), because its performance is obviously of a communal nature. Because the powers to exercise *shura* and *ijma'* (q.v.), or consultation and consensus, are the prerogatives of the people, this requires primarily the existence of many opinions, or *ijtihadat*, so that the community could choose one of the opinions circulated or what it considers to be the best opinion. This task is more urgent today because Muslims are beset by dire conditions and unprecedented challenges—a situation that demands a new understanding of religion that transcends mere addition and subtraction of particulars here and there to the need to provide new organizing principles appropriate for modernity (q.v.).

Al-Turabi theoretically justifies such a need by arguing that both the specifics and organizing principles of religion are historically developed and consequently subject to change in terms of the community's needs. Their historical nature means that no normative standing is attributed to them or that their replacement with new specifics and principles is not a violation of religion. Although this replacement does involve the Qur'an, and the *Sunna* (way) of the Prophet, the new *usul*, or organizing principles, must be the outcome of a new *ijma'*, itself the consequence of a popular choice in the form of contemporary *shura*, or democracy. See also AL-BASHIR, 'UMAR HASAN; DEMOCRACY; DIALOGUE; FREEDOM; HISTORY; *IJMA'*; INTERNATIONAL ORGANIZATION OF THE MUSLIM BROTHERHOOD; ISLAMIC FUNDAMENTAL- ISM; ISLAMIC STATE; ISLAMIZATION; JURISPRUDENCE; KNOWLEDGE; MODERNITY; MUSLIM BROTHERHOOD IN SUDAN; PAST; SCIENCE; SECOND ISLAMIC INTERNATIONAL; AL-*SHARI'A*; *SHURA*; SUPPORTERS OF MUHAMMADAN *SUNNA*; SYSTEM; TAHA, 'ALI 'UTHMAN; *TAQLID*; *TAWHID*; TEXT; THE- OCRACY; THEOLOGY.

TURKMEN, 'ALI. See *REFAH PARTISI*.

TWA HIJACKING. A TWA plane was hijacked in Lebanon in 1985 by pro-*Hizbullah* (q.v.) (Party of God) militants, *al-Jihad al-Islami* (Islamic *Jihad*) who took the passengers as hostages. One hostage, a U.S. service-man, was killed. This pushed the United States to impose a travel ban on Lebanon that lasted until early 1997. See also *HIZBULLAH*; ORGANI- ZATION OF THE ISLAMIC *JIHAD* IN LEBANON.

TYRANNY (*TAGHUT*). Tyranny from an Islamic point of view cannot be justified, according to fundamentalists. *Al-Shari'a* (q.v.) (Islamic Law) calls upon people to voice their views. But today's tyrannical rulers force the people to follow one ideology or another and one political program or another, thus contributing to the marginalization and oppression of their people and their aspirations. Therefore, most fundamentalists stand against the identification of the individual with the state, which can take away his freedom (q.v.) and impose tyranny over him.

The individual's original freedom cannot be given to institutions and to society, and any institutionalization of freedom means tyranny. The only normative individual commitment is to Islam (q.v.), which frees the individual from having to accept or yield to imposed principles or ideol-

ogies or tyranny. See also DEMOCRATIC ISLAMIC ARAB MOVE-
MENT; ISLAMIC SALVATION FRONT; *JIHAD*; *MUJAHIDIN*
MOVEMENT IN MOROCCO; *SHURA*; UNIVERSALISM.

-U-

'UBAYDI, ZUHAYR 'ABD AL-RAHMAN (1940–   ). 'Ubaydi won a
seat in the Lebanese Parliament in 1992 as a candidate for *al-Jama'a al-
Islamiyya* (q.v.) (Islamic Group). 'Ubaydi is a graduate of the Sorbonne
and works as professor at the Faculty of Economic Science and Business
Administration at the Lebanese University. He lost in the parliamentary
elections of 1996.

'ULAMA' SOCIETY. See *JAM'IYYAT AL-'ULAMA' AL-MUSLIMIN*; IS-
LAMIC SALVATION FRONT.

ULUHIYYA. See DIVINITY.

AL-UMAMIYYA AL-ISLAMIYYA. (ISLAMIC INTERNATIONAL). See
INTERNATIONAL ORGANIZATION OF THE MUSLIM BROTHER-
HOOD.

AL-UMAMIYYA AL-ISLAMIYYA AL-THANIYYA. See SECOND IS-
LAMIC INTERNATIONAL.

'UMAR, SHAYKH 'ABD AL-FATTAH. See *AL-SALAFIYYA*.

UMMA (NATION). For the fundamentalists, Islam (q.v.) aims at setting up
an *umma*, or nation, that is good in the sense that it has a message to
fulfill. It should be unified and self-sacrificing for the sake of God (q.v.).
It also aims at establishing a just and moral Islamic government (q.v.),
not a tyrannical and authoritarian one. Islam wants to establish a virtuous
nation with the government being its servant.

   That is why the Islamic nation, for the fundamentalists, is based on
four foundations: first, a pure creed that brings man closer to God; second, correct worship and good religious deeds such as praying and fast-
ing; third, unity, which completes faith and reduces tension between
sects and political tendencies; and fourth, legislation (q.v.) that is just
and good laws that are derived from the Qur'an (q.v.) and the *Sunna*

(way) of the Prophet. See also CALIPHATE; CALL; DEMOCRACY; *HIZB AL-HAQQ AL-ISLAMI*; *HIZBULLAH*; *HUDUD*; *IJMA'*; IS-LAMIC SOCIETY; ISLAMIC STATE; *JAHILI* SOCIETIES; *JIHAD*; JUSTICE; *MILLĪ SELAMET PARTISI*; PAST; RELIGION; RIDA, MU-HAMMAD RASHID; UNION OF POPULAR FORCES; VAN-GUARDS OF SACRIFICE.

UMMA **PARTY** (NATION'S PARTY) **IN MAURITANIA**. This party was set up in 1991 and is headed by Ould Siddi Yahyia. It is well connected with the Muslim Brotherhood (q.v.) in Mauritania. Its political orientations, like the Muslim Brotherhood, stress the need for a program of Islamization (q.v.), the implementation of *al-Shari'a* (q.v.) (Islamic Law), and an emphasis on Arab and Islamic identity.

UNBELIEF (*KUFR*). For most fundamentalists any deviation from *tawhid* (q.v.) (Oneness of God), be it theological, legal, political, or even personal, is considered *kufr*. For instance, the usurpation of political sovereignty is considered *kufr*. Sovereignty in both a strict and a general sense belongs only to God (q.v.) and not to the individual. Issues of legitimacy (q.v.) also revolve around divine governance (q.v.) (*hakimiyya*) and human paganism (q.v.) (*jahiliyya*). Whereas moderate fundamentalism (q.v.) leaves ample room for freedom of belief, expression, and movement, radical fundamentalism is very strict in terms of conceiving unbelief. Radical fundamentalism considers, for instance, any kind of submission to human, social, political, or individual pressures as *kufr*. However, moderate fundamentalism, although accepting the weakness of man and the existence of uncontrollable events and difficult conditions, gives more leeway in terms of interpreting the issue of sovereignty.

For both trends, however, the human programs and systems must not contradict the divine *Shari'a* (q.v.) (Islamic Law). Because divine sovereignty covers the mundane and the sublime, its implication is mostly related to politics, which orders man's and society's life. For the law of God (q.v.) is meaningful not only in terms of the beyond but more equally in terms of the here and now. It penetrates both the human conscience and, more significantly, man's political existence. Although the concern for the next life is part of religion (q.v.), the earthly existence is as important, because it is the bridge between the profane and the sacred. See also 'ABD AL-RAHMAN, 'UMAR; 'ABD AL-WAHHAB, MU-HAMMAD; *AL-DA'WA AL-ISLAMIYYA* IN IRAQ; APOSTASY; EX-TREMISM; AL-GHANNUSHI, RASHID; GOD; GOVERNANCE;

GROUP OF LEGITIMATE ISOLATION; *HIZBULLAH*; IBN TAYMI-YYA, TAQIY AL-DIN; ISLAMIC STATE; *JAMA'AT AL-JIHAD AL-ISLAMI*; *JIHAD*; PAGANISM; SCIENCE; SHAHIN, 'ABD AL-SABUR; *SHURA*; SIRRIYYA; TEXT.

UNION OF THE ISLAMIC ASSOCIATIONS AND GROUPS (*ITI-HAD AL-JAM'IYYAT WA AL-JAMA'AT AL-ISLAMIYYA*). This Union is considered to be the most radical model among Turkish Islamic movements. It was led by Shaykh Jamal al-Din Qabalan (q.v.), who died in 1995. Qabalan visited Iran and met Ayatollah Khomeini (q.v.) in 1984. He died in 1995, and his son, Matyan Oghlo, succeeded him. See also QABALAN, JAMAL AL-DIN.

UNION OF POPULAR FORCES (*ITIHAD AL-QIWA AL-SHA'BIYYA*). This Union was set up after the failure of the Yemeni revolution of 1948. It was first named *Hizb al-Shura* and *'Usbat al-Haqq* and was headed by 'Abd al-Raqib Hassan. Its Secretary-General was 'Ali 'Abd al-'Aziz, but Ibrahim Bin 'Ali al-Wazir represented the strong leadership. In 1960, it became *Itihad al-Qiwa al-Sha'biyya* and was licensed in 1962. After the revolution of 1962, it called for the establishment of the Islamic state (q.v.) and considered itself an international Islamic party that represented the interests of the Islamic *umma* (q.v.) (nation). It called for adherence to the Qur'an (q.v.) and the *Sunna* (way) of the Prophet as well as Islamic justice and *shura* (qq.v.) (consultation). It builds its ideological program on the need to realize justice, peace (q.v.), the truth, the good, and *shura*. It further accepts pluralism (q.v.) and freedom of choice.

UNION OF THE REVOLUTIONARY ISLAMIC FORCES (*ITIHAD AL-QIWA AL-ISLAMIYYA AL-THAWRIYYA*). This Union was established early in 1986 as an opposition party to the regime in North Yemen before the Unification. It aims at the implementation of *al-Shari'a* (q.v.) (Islamic Law) without compelling others to convert to Islam (q.v.) and calls for dialogue and freedom (qq.v.) of expression. Its political objective is to establish the Islamic state (q.v.) that is based on revolutionary justice, equality, and *shura* (qq.v.) (consultation). It opposes the government of Saudi Arabia and accepts the model of the Iranian Revolution of 1979 (q.v.).

UNIVERSALISM (*'ALAMIYYA*). The paganism (q.v.) (*jahiliyya*) of the world can be negated completely only when Islam's (q.v.) universalism has been spread all over the world. Universalism would be represented essentially by the submission of all people to God's divinity (q.v.) (*uluh-iyya*). Radical fundamentalists such as al-Hadi Mudarrisi, Sayyid Qutb (q.v.), and 'Abd al-Jawad Yasin do not view this dominance as a transgression against the freedom (q.v.) of humanity, because Islam (q.v.) raises it to its natural place as a final end in itself. For Islam constructed its relations on the respect of man for his fellow man in accordance with the general principles of *al-Shari'a* (q.v.) (Islamic Law).

Al-Mudarrisi explains this idea by expanding on human nature, which has a moral/spiritual aspect and a physical/material aspect. The latter aspect man holds in common with the animals; however, the former is unique to man. Islam strikes a balance (q.v.) between the two aspects and raises man above his material instincts by first linking value to what is right and to man qua man. Things are valued in terms of their service to man and not as things in themselves.

For Sayyid Qutb, Abu al-Hasan al-Nadawi, and Hasan al-Banna (qq.v.), one of these principles is the universalism of Islam ('*alamiyyat al-Islam*), which manifests itself in the rejection of privileges given to race, nationality, language, or land. It also manifests itself in its call (q.v.) (*da'wa*) to worship one God, justice (qq.v.) to all, brotherhood among all, and belief in all of the prophets, the divine books, and the Day of Judgment. Ayatollah Khomeini (q.v.) adds that Islam is the religion (q.v.) of those who fight for what is right and just and who call for freedom (q.v.) and independence.

But what makes the realization of universalism very important to the fundamentalists is their belief in Islam as the only system (q.v.) (*nizam*) that meets the needs of human *fitra* (q.v.) (intuition). In fact its universal character corresponds to its comprehensiveness (q.v.) (*al-shumuliyya*). For Islam first regulates all aspects of life and allows for renewed solutions to new problems. Second, it is a complete system, having social and political laws and regulations and laws for nations. Al-Nadawi dwells at length on the revolutionary changes that true Islam as a complete universal system can bring about. It eliminates the persuasive ritualistic paganism, including the pleasures of life and material things, and replaces it with self-sacrifice, love for humanity, and adherence to truth. It also leads to honesty and dignity, which make Muslims unyielding to any tyranny (q.v.) whether political or religious. Submission to power without proper political, moral, and legal objective is unacceptable. See also CALL; CALIPHATE; CIVILIZATION; DIALOGUE; GOVERNANCE; *JIHAD*; RELIGION; REVOLUTION; *TAWHID*.

'UQLA, 'ADNAN. See FIGHTING VANGUARDS; MUSLIM BROTHERHOOD IN SYRIA.

'USBAT AL-ANSAR AL-ISLAMIYYA. See ISLAMIC BAND OF HELPERS.

'USBAT AL-HAQQ (BAND OF RIGHT). See UNION OF POPULAR FORCES.

USRAT AL-JIHAD (FAMILY OF *JIHAD*). See *AL-JIHAD AL-ISLAMI* IN THE WEST BANK AND GAZA STRIP.

USUL. See FUNDAMENTALS.

USULIYYA. See FUNDAMENTALISM; FUNDAMENTALS; ISLAMIC FUNDAMENTALISM; REVOLUTION; VIOLENCE.

AL-'UTAYBI, JUHAYMAN BIN SAYF (?–1979). Al-'Utaybi is the leader of the group that stormed the Great Mosque in Mecca in 1979. Al-'Utaybi was killed in the aftermath, when the Saudi armed forces stormed the compound. The rise of al-'Utaybi was seen as the beginning of the spread of militant Islamic fundamentalism (q.v.) in Saudi Arabia. See also *HIZBULLAH* IN SAUDI ARABIA.

-V-

VALUE SOCIETY. See ISLAMIC SALVATION FRONT.

VANGUARD (*TALI'A*). A group of committed Muslims who are ready to sacrifice their comfort and, if necessary, their lives in order to lead their society to Islam and to bring about the establishment of an Islamic state. Many fundamentalists, especially Sayyid Qutb and Taqiy al-Din al-Nabahani (qq.v.), view the existence of a religious vanguard as essential for the development of Islamic activism (q.v.) (*harakiyya*). Thus, any ideological group or system (q.v.) (*nizam*) not based on Islam (q.v.) is not allowed to operate by radical fundamentalists. Minorities are included religiously in that they can keep their faith but are excluded politically because they are not given any right to form political parties (q.v.) or even a "vanguard."

For instance, Qutb, who is responsible for developing this concept, links valid free expression and association to the parameters of Islamic ideological understanding. All those societies and parties that do not conform to such an understanding are described as paganist, or *jahili* societies (q.v.). Thus, only an Islamic philosophy (q.v.) may be represented in a political party or the vanguard. Qutb's book *Ma'alim fi al-Tariq* is specific about the mission that this vanguard should carry out in an exclusive and uncompromising attitude toward all other ideologies, societies, and ways of life.

However, the establishment of an Islamic system permits the involvement of different institutions in political processes so that the will of the public is known in the context of an Islamic ideology and in exclusion of other ideologies. See also *JIHAD*; MUSTAPHA, SHUKRI; PARTIES.

VANGUARDS OF SACRIFICE (*TALA'I' AL-FIDA'*). Vanguards of Sacrifice is an armed Islamic group under the leadership of Muhammad Habib al-Aswad. In 1987, it was accused by the Tunisian authorities of planning to destroy the ruling regime and to establish an Islamic *umma* (q.v.) (nation). But when Zayn al-'Abidin Bin 'Ali became President of Tunisia, he set free the arrested members of *Tala'i' al-Fida'*.

VIOLENCE (*'UNF*). Continued intellectual disintegration, which the Arab world faced politically and socially, as well as the defeat of Arab regimes by the West (q.v.) contributed to the rise of Islamic groups among the masses. Many fundamentalist groups chose military and violent means and refused compromise, moderation, and step-by-step solutions. Furthermore, the tough positions of political regimes toward popular political participation and economic equality (q.v.) led many fundamentalist groups to believe that no common understanding could be achieved. Consequently, most regimes and fundamentalists of the Muslim world have been locked in a vicious circle of violent activities against each other. One might say the most profound causes for the use of violence by some few Islamic groups has been political repression, economic exploitation, and the lack of political understanding by the regimes of popular demands for freedom (q.v.).

Another factor that has contributed to the rise of violence of Islamic groups has been the continuous competition among various Islamic movements. This competition is fueled by divergent ideological beliefs and religious principles. Moreover, basic differences still exist among the various Islamic movements, although they unite when facing external pressures and persecution.

In the late 1960s and early 1970s while the Arab nationalist leftist trends were weakening, the fundamentalist trends started to spread, for instance, by the freeing of arrested people from the Egyptian Muslim Brotherhood (q.v.). Also, the establishment of Islamic groups in North Africa led to the emergence of the Moroccan Islamic Youth Organization (q.v.) in 1969, the Tunisian *Harakat al-Itijah al-Islami* (q.v.) (Islamic Tendency Movement) in 1970, and other organizations in Algeria and Libya. In the Arab East, many Islamic movements have been very active in their employment of political violence against either competitive political groups like the nationalists and socialists or their political regimes.

Violent actions have been especially connected with the rise of a few organizations, for example, *al-Takfir wa al-Hijra* or *Jama'at al-Muslimin* (q.v.), which attacked a military college in Cairo, Egypt; the Islamic Youth Organization, which assassinated 'Umar Bin Jallun in 1975; the Egyptian *al-Jihad* Movement (q.v.) that was responsible for the murder of the Egyptian President Anwar al-Sadat in 1981; the Armed Algerian Islamic Group, which mounted violent operations in 1982; as well *Hizbullah, Hamas*, and *al-Jihad al-Islami* (qq.v.) which all used violence from time to time.

Although these organizations express in an extremist fashion their demands, these demands, without violence, express generally the aspirations of most Muslim people. See also 'ABD AL-RAHMAN, 'UMAR; *AL-AFGHAN AL-'ARAB*; ANAS, 'ABD ALLAH; FADLALLAH, MUHAMMAD HUSAYN; AL-GHANNUSHI, RASHID; AL-GHAZALI, ZAYNAB; GROUP OF LEGITIMATE ISOLATION; ISLAMIC SALVATION FRONT; ISLAMIC YOUTH ORGANIZATION; JABAL-LAH, 'ABD ALLAH; *AL-JAMA'A AL-ISLAMIYYA*; *JAMA'AT AL-FANNIYYA AL-'ASKARIYYA*; *AL-JAMA'AT AL-ISLAMIYYA*; *JAMA'AT AL-MUSLIMIN*; *AL-JIHAD* ORGANIZATION; JUSTICE AND CHARITY GROUP; MUHAMMAD'S YOUTH; MUSLIM BROTHERHOOD; MUSLIM BROTHERHOOD, IDEOLOGY OF; NASRALLAH, SAYYID HASAN; ORGANIZATION OF SHAYKH 'ABD ALLAH AL-SIMAWI; PLURALISM; QUTB, SAYYID; RADICALISM.

-W-

AL-WAHHABIYYA. *Al-Wahhabiyya* movement was founded by Muhammad Ibn 'Abd al-Wahhab (q.v.), whose call (q.v.) (*da'wa*) was based on the comprehensive and eternal nature of Islam (q.v.). The movement and his *Ikhwan* (q.v.) revived the principle of reason (q.v.) (*ijtihad*) and its constitutive role in the life of the Muslims, condemned *taqlid* (q.v.) (traditionalism) and civil deterioration, and called on the believers to refer back to the fundamentals (q.v.) (*usul*): the Qur'an (q.v.) and the *Sunna* of the Prophet. *Al-Wahhabiyya* has been a modern interpretation (q.v.) of the *Salafi* Islam as interpreted by eminent scholars like Ibn Hanbal, Ibn Taymiyya (q.v.), and Ibn Qayyim al-Jawziyya.

Tawhid (q.v.) (Oneness of God) became the central concept by which every idea or action is measured. *Al-Wahhabiyya* refused the doctrine of predestination and adhered to strict *tawhid* and did not view Islamic legal schools as compulsory. Also, it called for political change by raising the banner of *jihad* (q.v.) (struggle). It was also against Sufi movements. All of these ideas are central doctrines that have been employed by modern fundamentalist movements in order to draw the basic outline of their ideologies.

Many Islamic movements, like *al-Sanusiyya* in Libya and *al-Mahdiyya* in Sudan and even the Muslim Brotherhood (q.v.), and many important figures, like Jamal al-Din Afghani, Muhammad 'Abdu, and Muhammad Iqbal (qq.v.), were affected by *al-Wahhabiyya* and adhered to the two basic doctrines of *ijtihad* and *jihad*. Also, great reformers like Muhammad Ibn 'Abd Allah al-Shawkani and 'Abd al-Qadir al-Jaza'iri followed the same line of thinking.

Politically, *al-Wahhabiyya* was a revolt against the Ottoman Caliphate (q.v.), and with the assistance of Ibn Saud, it tried to set up a new Islamic state (q.v.). It also opposed modern reforms suggested by European powers. However, the *Wahhabis* along with the followers of Ibn Saud tried to apply their doctrines strictly, which led to many fights with other tribal groups and religious schools. See also 'ABD AL-WAHHAB, MUHAMMAD IBN; IBN TAYMIYYA, TAQIY AL-DIN.

AL-WAHY (REVELATION). See FUNDAMENTALS; AL-QUR'AN; TEXT.

AL-WA'IY. See CONSCIOUSNESS.

WALIY AL-FAQIH (JURIST'S GUARDIAN). This title is given to the supreme authority, *Murshid al-Thawra* (Revolution's Guide), in the Iranian system. The Council of Experts (q.v.) positioned *waliy al-faqih* at the head of all authorities in Iran as the first guide in the absence of the

Mahdi, according to the Twelvers' understanding. The guide is to be elected by the Council of Experts by a secret ballot.

The guide also supervises the institutions of military forces, including the regular army and the Revolutionary Guards (q.v.). He declares war and calls for referendums as well as approves the election of the President by the people. The guide also appoints the highest six religious clerks in the Constitutional Council, which supervises electoral processes. He can be removed by the Council of Experts if he deviates from the course of the Iranian Revolution of 1979 (q.v.) or if he loses some quality of leadership. The first guide was Ayatollah Khomeini (q.v.), who was succeeded by Ayatollah Khamene'i (q.v.). See also CONSTITUTION; COUNCIL OF EXPERTS; *HIZBULLAH*; *HOJJATIYEH* ORGANIZATION; ISLAMIC ACTION ORGANIZATION; ISLAMIC REPUBLICAN PARTY; ISLAMIC REVOLUTION OF IRAN; KHAMENE'I, 'ALI; KHOMEINISM; *MAJLIS AL-SHURA* IN IRAN; *MARJI' AL-TAQLID*; MUNTAZARI, HUSAYN; MUSLIM PEOPLE'S REPUBLICAN PARTY.

WAR (*AL-HARB*). See *DAR AL-HARB*.

WARRIORS OF ISLAM SOCIETY (*SAZMANE-E MOJAHEDIN-E ISLAM*). This Iranian society, which was created in 1940, was led by Shams al-Din Qanatabadi, a clerical *Majlis* member allied to Ayatollah Kashani (q.v.). The society was used by Kashani in his confrontations with Prime Minister Musaddaq after the two leaders went their separate ways, especially after the events of 20 July 1952. The society sometimes aligned itself with the Devotees of Islam in opposition to what it claimed was the drift toward secularism in Iranian public life. The society was so closely identified with Kashani that it did not survive his political eclipse after the coup of August 1953.

AL-WARTALANI, FUDAYL. Al-Wartalani was born in Costantiniyya in Algeria and studied at al-Zaytuna Mosque under 'Abd al-Hamid Ibn Badis (q.v.). He joined *Jam'iyyat al-'Ulama' al-Muslimin* (q.v.) (the Association of Muslim Scholars) in 1930 and became its representative in France. Al-Wartalani was persecuted by the French authorities and fled to Cairo where he sat up the Committee for the Defense of Algeria in 1942 and participated in setting up the Front for the Defense of Africa. Al-Wartalani met Hasan al-Banna (q.v.) and worked with the Muslim Brotherhood (q.v.) in Egypt.

Al-Wartalani went to Yemen in 1947 to reform the political system there and was received by the ruler, the *Imam*, and his lieutenants. His program for reform was rejected by the authorities, and he returned to Cairo to report to Hasan al-Banna. However, his program was adopted by some tribal leaders and other groups. The Brotherhood supported the takeover of 1948, and al-Wartalani became very influential. He produced a *fatwa* (q.v.) (legal opinion) permitting the killing of the *Imam* in 1948. The Brotherhood recognized the new regime of 'Abd Allah al-Wazir. Al-Wartalani became a general advisor to the state with the rank of minister. The regime, however, collapsed after 26 days, when al-Wartalani was in Saudi Arabia. He escaped first to Lebanon and then to Turkey, where he died. See also *AL-TAJAMMU' AL-YEMENI LI AL-ISLAH*.

AL-WASAT. See MADI, ABU AL-'ULA.

AL-WAZIR, IBRAHIM BIN 'ALI. See UNION OF POPULAR FORCES.

WEST (*AL-GHARB*). The humiliation, whether political, ideological, or economic, that the Islamic world has experienced throughout the last two centuries because of Western imperialism and colonialism has led to the demoralization of the Muslim world and made numerous Muslims skeptical about the role of Islam (q.v.), its civilization (q.v.), and its values. Some Muslims reacted by wholesale adoption of the West, its benefits, and problems. Others totally rejected the West, including its benefits.

However, most fundamentalists view that the adoption or imposition of Western political systems has not resulted in any real benefit and has caused, instead, the emergence of military or semimilitary repressive regimes in most Islamic countries. These regimes only serve the interests of the ruling classes and their colonialist mentors, and the Muslim masses suffer from poverty, ignorance, and disease.

Radical fundamentalists blame generally the West and Western colonization (q.v.) for the current miseries of the Islamic world. They attribute to it the structural changes and economic transformation that deprived the Muslims of their wealth and authentic civilization. The West is not seen to be a model to be followed or imitated. It is materialistic, antireligious, and exploitative. Furthermore, the West will not leave the Islamic world alone, because it is a huge source of raw material and an extensive market for the surplus of Western capitalist production. Radical fundamentalists want to develop a categorical separation from the West, which includes all disciplines of knowledge and walks of life.

Moderate fundamentalists, however, do not want to break altogether with the West, although they acknowledge the long troublesome history the Muslim world has had with it. They want the West to treat the Muslim world equally. Through Islamization (q.v.) they are and have been adopting many Western disciplines like science (q.v.) and doctrines like democracy (q.v.). They do not see any inherent contradiction with the West and value its benefits and warn against its shortcomings. Many call for a new dialogue (q.v.), world order (q.v.), and form of relations with the West and are in favor of borrowing Western science, technology, and disciplines that are needed for the revival of the Islamic world. See also *AL-AFGHAN AL-'ARAB*; AUTHENTICITY; AL-'AWWA, MUHAMMAD SALIM; CALL; DEMOCRACY; DIALOGUE; FUNDAMENTALISM; *HARAKAT AL-NAHDA AL-ISLAMIYYA*; *HIZB AL-TAHRIR AL-ISLAMI*; INTERPRETATION; ISLAMIC FUNDAMENTALISM; ISLAMIC SOCIETY; ISLAMIC STATE; KHOMEINI, AYATOLLAH; LEGITIMACY; MODERNISM; MODERNITY; MONOTHEISTIC RELIGIONS; MUSLIM BROTHERHOOD IN PALESTINE; MUTAHHARI, MURTAZA; PAGANISM; PLURALISM; QUTB, SAYYID; RUSHDIE, SALMAN; SCIENCE; *SHURA*; AL-TURABI, HASAN; VIOLENCE; WESTERN CIVILIZATION; WESTERN COLONIZATION.

WESTERN CIVILIZATION (*AL-HADARA AL-GHARBIYYA*). The fundamentalists, especially the radicals like Sayyid Qutb (q.v.), argue that one of the basic components of Western civilization, Greek thought, suffers from the following defects: belief in the material and the insensitivity to what is not, lack of emphasis on the spiritual, dependence on worldly life and its pleasures, and devotion to nationalistic tendencies. All these points can be subsumed under the term *materialism*, and this is why the characteristics of God (q.v.) have been embodied in idols and temples. The Greek could not abstract the characteristics of God; thus, they invented a god for beauty, another for power, and so on. Such materialistic views led ultimately to a materialistic kind of living (sculpture, dancing, music), which negatively effected the morals of the Greeks and led to the spread of moral looseness and political anarchy.

Moreover, Abu al-Hasan al-Nadawi (q.v.) criticizes the Roman heritage, the second component of Western Civilization. Although less philosophical and poetical than the Greeks, the Romans depended on power and organization; in fact, power was added to materialism. The Romans were preoccupied with the idea of dominating the world. In politics, however, they overstepped their gods because they did not have any political weight. Ultimately, the Roman Empire collapsed because of luxury and moral degradation. This coincided with the Christianization of the Empire by Emperor Constantine. But Christianity (q.v.) lost in fact, because Greek paganism (q.v.) (*jahiliyya*) and Roman veneration of power triumphed over the true spirit of Christianity. Finally, materialism triumphed over all forms of thought, which is still to the present a main feature of Western thought.

Many fundamentalists like Abu al-A'la al-Mawdudi (q.v.), Qutb, and al-Nadawi argue that the distinctive divide between Western philosophical methods and the Islamic religious method (q.v.) (*manhaj*) is that the philosophic originates in the human mind but the religious originates from the divinely inspired and relates to consciousness (q.v.) (*wa'iy*). The divine origin of the Islamic discourses is what gives them their basic credibility insofar as they do not suffer from human imperfection, ignorance, and desire—which are common features of human discourses. Although other religions, especially Christianity and Judaism (q.v.), were originally like Islam (q.v.), nonetheless, the interference of human elements, such as paganism (q.v.) and materialism, in their interpretations took away their credibility.

For radical fundamentalists, Western civilization could not be the basis of the regeneration of the Islamic world because the West (q.v.) lacks the essential ingredient for setting up a just, moral, and equal civilization. Islamic regeneration should be based on Islamic authenticity (q.v.). On the contrary, Western colonization (q.v.) and the destruction of the Muslim world is the responsibility of the West. See also CIVILIZATION; ISLAMIC CULTURAL HERITAGE SOCIETY; ISRAEL; METHOD; MODERNITY; PAGANISM; RIDA, MUHAMMAD RASHID.

WESTERN COLONIZATION (*AL-ISTI'MAR AL-GHARBI*). Islamic movements, like the Muslim Brotherhood (q.v.), have been concerned with, and directed many of their reactions to, Western colonization and its related issues, like missionary schools. These movements tried to set up institutes that strengthen the education of Islam (q.v.) as a force that can withstand the perceived Western attempts to destroy the relevance of Islam to modern living. This is why Western colonization as well as the secular regimes that were created by it has been a target of Islamic movements in the past and the present. Many ills are blamed on the West (q.v.)

and its colonial period in the Muslim world, which has been seen as a hindrance to the natural development that could have occurred there.

At the least, Western colonization is blamed for fracturing the Islamic world into small secular states, cannibalizing local natural resources, and creating selfish elites whose allegiance is neither to their people nor to Islam but to one of the Western countries. Colonialism did not allow the indigenous forces, including an Islamic one, to take their proper places. Modern governments of the Islamic world are identified intellectually, politically, and economically with Western forces and their imperialist ambitions. See also WEST; WESTERN CIVILIZATION.

WILAYAT AL-FAQIH (GUARDIANSHIP OF THE JURIST). See *WALIY AL-FAQIH*.

WORLD ORDER (*AL-NIZAM AL-'ALAMI*). The legitimacy (q.v.) of any world power must stem, for the fundamentalists, from its adherence to Islam (q.v.). But such a situation cannot be brought about except by an Islamic state (q.v.) that positions itself as a guide to other states. Islam has postulated the superiority of Islamic sovereignty and the necessity of power-building so that the just should hold power. An Islamic world order must revolve around the principles of justice, equality, and morality (qq.v.).

Furthermore, the fundamentalists provide an *aya* (verse) that guarantees the rights of non-Muslims in an Islamic state or a world order, for instance: "God forbids you not, with regard to those who fight you not for (your) Faith nor drive you out of your homes, from dealing kindly and justly with them: For God loveth those who are just" (LX: 8).

In fact, the fundamentalists believe in the duty of the governing world authority to uphold the liberation (q.v.) of other peoples and to guide without compulsion other nations into Islam. Thus, an Islamic world order would be established in order to further and not to hinder the progress of nations; nations and people should be free to adopt the creed they choose. However, radical fundamentalists want to force all nations and peoples to adopt Islam and to establish the Islamic state. They uphold the doctrines of divine governance and human paganism (qq.v.) as universal points of reference. See also CHRISTIANITY; CIVILIZATION; DIALOGUE; ISLAMIZATION; JUSTICE; MONOTHEISTIC RELIGIONS; AL-NADAWI, ABU AL-HASAN; WEST.

-Y-

YAGHI, MUHAMMAD HUSAYN (1958–). Yaghi became a member of the Lebanese Parliament in 1992 and 1996 as a candidate for *Hizbullah* (q.v.) (Party of God) in the Biqaʻ. Yaghi did not finish the requirements for a law degree from the Lebanese University. He was a member of the first nucleus that set up *Hizbullah* in 1982. Today, he is head of the Executive *Majlis al-Shura* (q.v.) (*Shura* Council). Yaghi believes that sectarianism should be abolished in Lebanon and that cooperation between the Lebanese should be based on a national agenda.

YAKAN, FATHI (1933–). Yakan is the leader of *al-Jamaʻa al-Islamiyya* (q.v.) (Islamic Group) in Lebanon. Yakan was brought up in Tripoli in a religious family and studied Islamic sciences with well-known scholars like Shaykh Anwar al-Mawlawi. In 1953, he worked at *Makarim al-Akhlaq al-Islamiyya* Association. Yakan later joined *'Ibad al-Rahman* Association that was set up during 1948 and was much concerned with the events that were taking place in Palestine. He accepts and contributes to the political ideology of the Muslim Brotherhood (q.v.). Yakan was elected in the Lebanese parliamentary elections in 1992 but lost his seat in 1996. See also *AL-JAMAʻA AL-ISLAMIYYA*.

YASIN, ʻABD AL-JAWAD. See *AL-JAMAʻAT AL-ISLAMIYYA*.

YASIN, ʻABD AL-SALAM. See JUSTICE AND CHARITY GROUP.

YASIN, AHMAD (1936–). Yasin is the spiritual leader of the Islamic Resistance Movement, *Hamas* (q.v.), in Palestine. Shaykh Ahmad Yasin was born in ʻAsqalan, Palestine. His middle-class family left for the Gaza District in 1948. Yasin was paralyzed at the age of 12, but this fact did not stop him from accomplishing his secondary years at Gaza. He worked as a teacher in public schools at Gaza from 1958 until 1964, then he studied the English language in Ayn Shams University in Egypt. But the authorities prohibited him from leaving Gaza because he belonged to the Muslim Brotherhood (q.v.); therefore he went back to teaching until his retirement.

Ahmad Yasin was one of the most dedicated in working to establish and protect the Muslim movement in Gaza in 1973. He was held in jail in 1948 because he openly belonged to the Muslim Brethren. He was accused of possessing weapons and bombs as well as belonging to organizations that opposed the Israeli occupying forces. He was sentenced to 12 years of prison but was released after 11 months in a prisoner exchange between the Israeli government and a Palestinian organization, *al-Jabha al-Sha'biyya: al-Qiyada al-'Amma* in 1985.

In 1987, during the outburst of the Palestinian uprising, Yasin declared his foundation of the Islamic Resistance Movement (*Hamas*). He was arrested by the Israeli forces in May 1989, accused of instigating violence (q.v.) and murder, and sentenced to life imprisonment in 1991. He was released in 1997 after King Hussein of Jordan struck a deal with the Israeli government in the wake of a failed assassination attempt on Khalid Mash'al (q.v.) in Amman by the Israeli Mossad. See also *HAMAS*; MUSLIM BROTHERHOOD IN PALESTINE; AL-SHIQAQI, FATHI.

YATIM, MUHAMMAD. See AL-KHATIB, 'ABD AL-KARIM.

YAWM AL-QUDS. See JERUSALEM DAY.

YEMENI ASSOCIATION FOR REFORM. See *AL-TAJAMMU' AL-YEMENI LI AL-ISLAH.*

YUSUF, AHMAD RAMZI (1968–   ). Yusuf was accused of bombing the World Trade Center in New York in 1993 and was sentenced to life imprisonment in January 1998. Yusuf holds the United States responsible for the "crimes of Jewish settlements" in Palestine and the plight of unconditional U.S. support to Israel (q.v.). He rejected the accusation of being the mastermind of the World Trade Center bombing but acknowledged his relations with the Islamic Salvation Front, Armed Islamic Group, and *al-Jama'a al-Islamiyya* (qq.v.) (Islamic Group).

Yusuf was tried and convicted in absentia in 1995 and arrested later that year in Pakistan. In 1996, he was also convicted in the United States on charges of planning to blow up 12 American airliners as punishment for U.S. support to Israel. Yusuf was convicted as well of planting an explosive device on a Philippine airliner on a flight from Manila to Tokyo in 1994, which killed one Japanese passenger and wounded many others.

Yusuf, who was born in Kuwait, holds an Iraqi passport and Pakistani nationality and claims that he is of Pakistani origin and Palestinian identity. Yusuf is an electronics engineer who graduated from a school in

Wales in 1989. His real name is 'Abd al-Basit Bulushi. See also *AL-AFGHAN AL-'ARAB*.

YAYA, OULD SIDDI. See *UMMA* PARTY IN MAURITANIA.

-Z-

ZAHHAR, MAHMUD. Zahhar is a member of the political bureau of *Hamas* (q.v.): *Harakat al-Muqawama al-Islamiyya* (Islamic Resistance Movement) and its spokesman in Gaza District. See also *HAMAS*; MUSLIM BROTHERHOOD IN PALESTINE.

ZALLUM, 'ABD AL-QADIM. See *HIZB AL-TAHRIR AL-ISLAMI*.

ZANDANI, SHAYKH 'ABD AL-MAJID. Zandani is a very controversial figure in Yemen and represents a model for the Yemeni fundamentalists. Zandani was a staunch enemy of the Socialist Party, and in 1993 he became a member of the Presidential Council. He led the "constitutional battle" and was able to secure a place for the fundamentalists in the state system by having *al-Shari'a* (q.v.) (Islamic Law) recognized as the primary source of legislation (q.v.).

Earlier Zandani spent nine years in Mecca where he taught and wrote on Islamic topics. During the revolution and the civil war in Yemen, he became a close friend of 'Abd Allah al-Ahmar, currently head of *Hizb al-Tajammu' al-Yemeni li al-Islah* (q.v.) (The Party of the Yemeni Association for Reform). He was a member of the Muslim Brotherhood (q.v.) but quit it in the late 1970s. Currently, Zandani is the head of the *Shura* Council at *Hizb al-Tajammu'*. See also *HIZB AL-TAJAMMU' AL-YEMENI LI AL-ISLAH*; *AL-TAJAMMU' AL-YEMENI LI AL-ISLAH*.

AL-ZAWABRI, 'ANTAR. See ARMED ISLAMIC GROUP.

AL-ZAWAHIRI, AYMAN. See *AL-JIHAD AL-ISLAMI*; AL-MAGHRIBI, NABIL 'ABD AL-MAJID.

AL-ZAWAHRA, 'ABD AL-BARI 'ABD AL-KARIM (1945–). Al-Zawahra is a member of the executive bureau of *Hizb Jabhat al-'Amal al-Islami* (q.v.) (Islamic Action Front Party). Al-Zawahra was born and received his elementary and secondary education in al-Zarqa, Jordan. He became the Deputy Mayor of al-Zarqa.

AL-ZAYAT, MUNTASIR. Al-Zayat is the lawyer of the fundamentalists who have been tried for some years in Egypt, especially those of *al-Jama'a al-Islamiyya*, who were convicted of assassinating President Anwar al-Sadat. Al-Zayat, a moderate fundamentalist lawyer, is considered to be an expert on human rights (q.v.). Al-Zayat was arrested in 1994 on charges of contacting radical fundamentalist leaders living outside of Egypt.

Al-Zayat's initiative to make a deal between the Egyptian government and radical fundamentalist organizations like *al-Jama'at al-Islamiyya* and *al-Jihad al-Islami* (qq.v.), or Islamic Groups and Islamic *Jihad*, to give up violence (q.v.) and to allow more political participation has failed. He accused the leadership of these organizations abroad of aborting the initiative because of their internal divisions. Al-Zayat is considering leaving political life. See also RUSHDI, USAMA; TAHA, AHMAD.

AL-ZAYN, AHMAD. See MUSLIM SCHOLARS' ASSOCIATION.

ZIONISM. See ISRAEL.

ZUBAYRI, MUHAMMAD MAHMUD. See *AL-TAJAMMU' AL-YEMENI LI AL-ISLAH.*

ZUHDI, KARAM. See *JAMA'AT AL-JIHAD.*

AL-ZUMAR, 'ABBUD. 'Abbud al-Zumar was an army intelligence officer and the military leader of *Tanzim al-Jihad* (*Al-Jihad* Organization [q.v.]) as well as the leader and one of the founders of *Jama'at al-Jihad al-Islami* (q.v.) (Group of Islamic *Jihad*). He follows Sayyid Qutb's (q.v.) rationalization in stressing the importance of active involvement in total opposition to the state. The program of action should focus on an applicable Islamic vision that contributes to uniting Islamic movements within one framework and that leads to giving up individual and public differences. By employing a Qutbian political key term, *ma'alim al-tariq* (signpost of the road), al-Zumar urges the Islamic movement to concentrate on its basic objective, the Islamic state (q.v.). This requires an uncompromising and exclusive attitude toward the *jahili* societies (q.v.) and systems in all aspects of life. The alternative is to employ a radical transformation or total Islamization (q.v.) of all facets of life and the unwavering rejection of secularism, nationalism, and parliamentary life. All this change has to start, however, by dethroning current rulers who do not adhere to *al-Shari'a* (q.v.) (Islamic Law). In line with his exclusive radical ideology, al-Zumar failed first to kill President Anwar al-Sadat but succeeded later in aiding members of *Tanzim al-Jihad* to do the job. He is serving a life sentence in an Egyptian prison. See also *AL-JAMA'AT AL-ISLAMIYYA*; *JAMA'AT AL-JIHAD AL-ISLAMI*; AL-MAGHRIBI, NABIL 'ABD AL-MAJID.

Selected Bibliography

The literature on Islamic fundamentalism is quantitatively massive and qualitatively diverse. This bibliography cites written material on movements, groups, leaders, ideologues, and events throughout the Arab world, Iran, and Turkey. It covers the primary and secondary writings on and by the Islamic fundamentalist movements in the Arab world, Iran, and Turkey that are primarily written in English and Arabic. It includes bibliographical entries from all of the social sciences, including history, philosophy, religion, political science, anthropology, and sociology. Thus, introducing this material is by no means an easy task and requires accounting for all the necessary readings. Instead, the introduction here focuses on the more recent writings of a general importance and without references to specific fields of specialization.

Two aspects are delineated: the theoretical, which is understudied and skeletal, and the practical, which is overstudied and massive. On theoretical studies, one can find very little literature because many scholars have assumed that Islamic fundamentalism is of an ephemeral nature and will, sooner or later, disappear. A few writings have, however, looked more seriously at Islamic fundamentalism and have tried to reach its deepest intellectual meaning. Included in this category are Ibrahim Abu Rabi's *Intellectual Origins of Islamic Resurgence in the Modern Arab World*, Akbar S. Ahmad's *Postmodernism and Islam: Predicament and Promise*, Said Amir Arjomand's *The Shadow of God and the Hidden Imam* and *Authority and Political Culture in Shi'ism*, and Aziz Al-Azmeh's *Islam and Modernity*. At a higher and more comparative level, one can find Sadik Al-Azm's "Islamic Fundamentalism Reconsidered: A Critical Outline of Problems, Ideas and Approaches," and Leonard Binder's *Islamic Liberalism: A Critique of Development Ideologies* and Charles E. Butterworth's *Political Islam* and "State and Authority in Arabic Political Thought."

This category also includes Dale Eickelman's "Changing Interpretations of Islamic Movements," Bruce Lawrence's *Religious Fundamentalism* and *Defenders of God: The Fundamentalist Revolt Against the Modern Age* and

Ahmad S. Moussalli's *Islamic Fundamentalism: Myths and Realities* and *Moderate and Radical Fundamentalism: The Quest for Modernity, Legitimacy and the Islamic State* as well as "Discourses on Human Rights and Pluralistic Democracy." Though of a different focus, other important theoretical studies could be looked at, and these include Seyyed Hossein Nasr's *Ideals and Realities of Islam* and *Traditional Islam in the Modern World*, Fazlur Rahman's *Islam and Modernity: The Transformation of an Intellectual Tradition*, Bryan Turner's *Orientalism, Postmodernism and Globalism* and W. Montgomery Watt's *Islamic Fundamentalism and Modernity*.

More general writings that focus on general important issues or case studies on the diverse aspects of the Middle East from multiple scholarly disciplines include Muhammad Ayoob's *The Politics of Islamic Reassertion*, Nazih Ayubi's *Political Islam: Religion and Politics in the Arab World* and *Over-Stating the Arab State: Politics and Society in the Middle East*, Hrair H. Dekmejian's *Islam in Revolution*, John L. Esposito's *The Oxford Encyclopedia of the Modern Islamic World* as well as *Islam: The Straight Path*. Also included are John L. Esposito and James P. Piscatori's "Democratization and Islam," John L. Esposito and John Voll's *Islam and Democracy*, and Fuad Khuri's *Imams and Emirs: State, Religion and Sects in Islam*. However, Graham E. Fuller's *Islamic Fundamentalism in the Northern Tier Countries: An Integrative View* and Graham E. Fuller and Iran Lesser's *A Sense of Siege: The Geopolitics of Islam and the West* are a good introduction to current political issues that are written specifically for a Western audience. Also included in this category as reference works are R. East and T. Joseph's *Political Parties of Africa and the Middle East: A Reference Guide* and Frank Tachau's *Political Parties of the Middle East and North Africa*.

More comprehensive writings include Laura Guazzone's *The Islamist Dilemma: The Political Role of Islamist Movements in the Contemporary Arab World* and Yvonne Haddad's *Contemporary Islam and the Challenge of History*, Yvonne Y. Haddad, Byron Haynes, and Ellison Finfly's *The Islamic Impact*, Michael Hudson's "Arab Regimes and Democratization: Responses to the Challenge of Political Islam," Gudrun Kramer's "Islamist Notions of Democracy" and "Liberalization and Democracy in the Arab World," Moojan Momen's *An Introduction to Shi'i Islam*, John Voll's *Islam: Continuity and Change in the Modern World*, John Waterbury's *Exposed to Innumerable Delusions: Public Enterprise and State Power in Egypt, India, Mexico, and Turkey*, Allan Richards and John Waterbury's *A Political Economy of the Middle East* and Sami Zubaida's *Islam, the People and the State: Essays on Political Ideas and Movements in the Middle East*.

Edited works that include multiple and diverse perspectives include Juan Cole and Nikki Keddie's *Shi'ism and Social Protest*, Ira Lapidus's *Contemporary Islamic Movements in Historical Perspective*, Seyyed Hossein Nasr, Hamid Dabashi, and Seyyed Vali Reza Nasr's *Expectation of the Millennium: Shi'ism in History* and *Shi'ism: Doctrines, Thought, and Spirituality*, Augustus R. Norton's *Civil Society in the Middle East*, and Ahmad S. Moussalli's *Islamic Fundamentalism: Myths and Realities* as well as Martin Marty and R. Scott Appleby's volumes: *Accounting for Fundamentalisms: The Dynamic Character of Movements*; *Fundamentalisms and Society: Reclaiming the Sciences, the Family, and Education*; *Fundamentalisms and the State: Remaking Polities, Economies, and Militance*; and *Fundamentalisms Observed*. Included also within the same category are Ghassan Salame's *Democracy without Democrats? The Renewal of Politics in the Muslim World*, A. S. Sidahmed and A. Ehteshami's *Islamic Fundamentalism*, and Barbara Stowasser's *The Islamic Impulse*.

On North Africa, primary readings include Lisa Anderson's "Liberalism, Islam, and the Arab State," "Remaking the Middle East: The Prospects for Democracy and Stability," and "The State in the Middle East and North Africa," François Burgat and William Dowell's *The Islamic Movement in North Africa*, François Burgat's *The Political Transition in Algeria: Elements for Analysis*, Emad Eldin Shahin's *Political Ascent: Contemporary Islamic Movements in North Africa*, John P. Entelis's *Comparative Politics of North Africa: Algeria, Morocco, and Tunisia*, Clement Henry Moore's "Political Parties" and *Politics in North Africa: Algeria, Morocco, and Tunisia*, John Ruedy's *Islamism and Secularism in North Africa*, and William I. Zartman and William Mark Habeeb's *Polity and Society in Contemporary North Africa*. Also important as a reference work is the *Cambridge Encyclopedia of the Middle East and North Africa*.

On the Gulf, readings include Fred Lawson's *Oppositional Movements and U.S. Policy toward the Arab Gulf States*, Khaldoun Naqeeb's *Society and State in the Gulf and Arab Peninsula: A Different Perspective*, James Piscatori's *Islamic Fundamentalisms and the Gulf Crisis* and J. E. Peterson's *The Arab Gulf States: Steps toward Political Participation* and *Historical Dictionary of Saudi Arabia*.

On Iran, the reader can consult Evand Abrahamian's *Khomeinism: Essays on the Islamic Republic*, Said Amir Arjomand's *The Turban for the Crown: The Islamic Revolution in Iran* and *From Nationalism to Revolutionary Islam*, Gerold D. Green's *Revolution in Iran: The Politics of Countermobilization*, Farhad Kazemi's "Civil Society and Iranian Politics" and "Models of Iranian Revolution, the Road to the Islamic Revolution, and the

Challenge of Civil Society" as well as Roy Mottahedeh's *The Mantle of the Prophet: Religion and Politics in Iran* and R. K. Ramazani's *Iran's Revolution: The Search for Consensus* and *Revolutionary Iran: Challenge and Response in the Middle East.*

On Turkey, selected readings include Feroz Ahmad's *The Making of Modern Turkey,* Nilufer Gole's "Authoritarian Secularism and Islamic Participation," "Towards an Autonomization of Politics and Civil Turkey" and "Secularism and Islamism in Turkey: The Making and Counter-Making of Elites and Counter-Elites," W. M. Hale's *Turkish Politics and the Military,* Jacob M. Landau's *The Politics of Pan-Islamism: Ideology and Organization,* and Jenny B. White's "Islam and Democracy: The Turkish Experience" as well as Serif Mardin's "The Nakshibendi Order of Turkey."

The most complete bibliographical works on Islamic fundamentalism are Yvonne Haddad and John L. Esposito's *The Islamic Revival since 1988: A Critical Survey and Bibliography* and Yvonne Haddad, John O. Voll, and John L. Esposito's *The Contemporary Islamic Revival: A Critical Survey and Bibliography.*

In this bibliography, titles of books in Arabic are treated in the same way as English titles: That is, they are classified alphabetically. The bibliography is not meant to include each and every item written on Islamic fundamentalism, but it includes most of the relevant material, especially the new, on Islamic fundamentalism in the Arab world, Iran, and Turkey. It aims at providing solid comprehensive bibliographical data for the relevant topics treated in the dictionary. The bibliography is structured in a way that allows the reader to pursue a specific topic. Although relatively few books and articles were used extensively in the writing of this dictionary, no individual acknowledgment is made because of the layout of the dictionary. Furthermore, some of the research material, which includes newspapers, pamphlets, magazines, and others, was not acknowledged. Also, since the dictionary as well as the bibliography is written for the benefit of the English-speaking audience, there was a deliberate attempt not to burden the bibliography with non-English sources. Nonetheless, almost all major writings in Arabic on Islamic fundamentalism and by Islamic fundamentalists have been incorporated.

The bibliography is divided along geographical lines. It provides two general sections on Islamic fundamentalism—the Middle East (the Arab world, Iran, and Turkey) and North Africa (Algeria, Libya, Morocco, and Tunisia). A more specific section covers the Arab world, and is classified alphabetically. The Gulf Arab states and Saudi Arabia are treated in one subsection since the information on the Gulf Arab states has been tied in one way or another to Saudi Arabia. There are also two sections on non-Arab fundamentalisms: one on Iran, and another on Turkey. A few titles are cited more than once because they may cover more than one region or country. Thus, a book that covers Islamic fundamentalism in Iran and Saudi Arabia is cited under both countries.

CONTENTS

I. THE MIDDLE EAST

Abaza, Mona. "The Discourse of Islamic Fundamentalism in the Middle East and Southeast Asia: A Critical Perspective." *Institute of Southeast Asian Studies, Singapore,* 6 (August 1991): 203–239.

'Abbud, Salih Ibn 'Abd Allah. *'Aqidat al-Shaykh Muhammad Ibn 'Abd al-Wahhab: al-Salafiyyah wa-Atharuha fi al-'Alam al-Islami.* Al-Madina al-Munawwarah, Saudi Arabia: Al-Jami'ah al-Islamiyah bi-al-Madinah al-Munawwarah, al-Majlis al-'Ilmi, 1987/1988.

'Abd Allah, Isma'il Sabri. *Al-Harakat al-Islamiyya al-Mu'asira fi al-'Alam al-'Arabi.* Beirut: Markaz Dirasat al-Wihda al-'Arabiyya, 1987.

'Abd al-Raziq, Ahmad Muhammad Jad. *Falsafat al-Mashru' al-Hadari: Bayna al-Ihya' al-Islami wa al-Tahdith al-Gharbi.* 2 vols. Herndon, VA: International Institute of Islamic Thought, 1995.

'Abd al-Sami', 'Umr. *Al-Islamiyyun: Hiwarat Hawla al-Mustaqbal.* Cairo: Maktabat al-Turath al-Islami, 1992.

Abdullah, Ahsan. *Pan-Islamism.* Leicester, UK: Islamic Foundation, 1992.

Abedin, Syed Z. "Islamic Fundamentalism, Islamic Ummah and the World Conference on Muslim Minorities." *Journal of the Institute of Muslim Minority Affairs,* 12 (July 1991): 1–21.

Abraham, Antoine J. *Khoumani and Islamic Fundamentalism: Contributions of Islamic Sciences to Modern Civilization.* 2nd ed. Cloverdale Library, 1989.

Abraham, Antoine J., and George Haddad. *The Warriors of God and Jihad and the Fundamentalists of Islam.* Bristol, IN: Wyndham Hall Press, 1990.

Abu Ghunaymah, Zayid. *Al-Haraka al-Islamiyya wa Qadiyyat Filistiyn.* Amman: Dar al-Furqan, 1985.

Abu Khalil, As'ad. "The Incoherence of Islamic Fundamentalism: Arab Islamic Thought at the End of the 20th Century." *The Middle East Journal,* 48 (Autumn 1994): 677–694.

———. "A Viable Partnership: Islam, Democracy, and the Arab World." *Harvard International Review,* 15 ii (Winter 1992–1993): 22–23 and 65.

Abul-Fadl, Mona. *Introducing Islam from Within.* Leicester, UK: Islamic Foundation, 1991.

Abu-Lughod, I. "Retreat from the Secular Path? Islamic Dilemmas of Arab Politics." *The Review of Politics,* 28 iv (1966): 447–476.

Abu Rabi', Ibrahim. *Intellectual Origins of Islamic Resurgence in the Modern Arab World.* Albany: State University of New York Press, 1996.

———. "A Note on Some Recent Western Writing on Islamic Resurgence." *Al-Tawhid,* 11 iii–iv (1994): 233–246.

———. "Islamic Resurgence and the 'Problematic of Tradition' in the Modern Arab World." The Contemporary Academic Debate. *Islamic Studies* (Islamabad), 34 i (1995): 43–66.

———, ed. *Islamic Resurgence: Challenges, Directions and Future Perspectives. A Round Table with Ahmad Kurshad.* Tampa, FL: World and Islam Studies Enterprise, 1994.

Abuljobain, Ahmad. *Radical Islamic Terrorism or Political Islam?* Annadale, VA: Association for Studies and Research, 1993.

AbuSulayman, 'Abdul Hamid. *The Islamic Theory of International Relations: New Directions for Islamic Methodology and Thought.* Herndon, VA: International Institute of Islamic Thought, 1987.

Addi, Lhouari. "Islamist Utopia and Democracy." *Political Islam. The Annals of the American Academy of Political and Social Sciences,* 542 (November 1992).

Adelowo, Dada. "The Concept of Tauhid in Islam: A Theological Review." *Islamic Quarterly,* 35 i (1991).

Al-Afghani, Jamal al-Din. *Al-A'mal al-Kamila.* Part II, Political Writings. Introduced and edited by Muhammad 'Amara. Beirut: Al-Mu'assasa al-'Arabiyya li al-Dirasat wa al-Nashr, 1980.

———. *Al-'Urwa al-Wuthqa.* Cairo: Dar al-'Arab, 1957.

Afshary, Reza. "An Essay on Islamic Cultural Relativism in the Discourse of Human Rights." *Human Rights Quarterly,* 16 (May 1994): 235–276.

Ahady, Anwar-ul-Haq. "The Decline of Islamic Fundamentalism." *Journal of Asian and African Studies,* 27 iii–iv (1992): 229–243.

Ahmad, Rif'at Sayyid. *Al-Bawwaba al-Sawda': Al-Tarikh al-Sirri li Mu'taqal.* Cairo: al-Zahra' li al-I'lam al-'Arabi, 1986.

———. *Al-Din wa al-Dawla wa al-Thawra.* Cairo: Dar al-Hilal, 1985.

———. *Al-Nabiy al-Musallah: Al-Rafidun.* London: Riad al-Rayyes Books, 1991.

———. *Al-Nabiy al-Musallah: Al-Tha'irun.* London: Riad al-Rayyes Books, 1991.

———. *Tanzimat al-Ghadab al-Islami fi al-Sab'inat.* Cairo: Maktabat Madbuli, 1989.

Ahmad Khalafallah, Muhammad. *Al-Qur'an wa al-Dawla.* Cairo: Maktabat al-Anglo al-Misriyya, 1973.

Ahmed, Akbar S. *Postmodernism and Islam: Predicament and Promise.* New York: Routledge, 1992.

Ahrari, M. E. "Islam as a Source of Conflict and Change in the Middle East." *Security Dialogue,* 25 ii (1994): 177–192.

Ajami, Fouad. *The Arab Predicament: Arab Political and Practice since 1967.* Cambridge, UK: Cambridge University Press, 1981.

Akhtar, Karm B., and Ahmad H. Sakr. *Islamic Fundamentalism.* Cedar Rapids, IA: Igram Press, 1982.

'Ali, Haydar Ibrahim. *Al-Tayyarat al-Islamiyya wa Qadiyyat al-Ta'addudiyya.* Beirut: Center for the Studies of Arab Unity, 1996.

Allen, Richard. *Imperialism and Nationalism in the Fertile Crescent: Sources and Prospects of the Arab-Israeli Conflict.* London: Oxford University Press, 1975.

'Amara, Muhammad. *Abu al-A'la al-Mawdudi wa al-Sahwa al-Islamiyya.* Beirut: Dar al-Wahda, 1986.

———. *Al-Islam wa al-Hurub al-Diniyya.* Cairo: Dar al-Thaqafa al-Jadida, 1996.

———. *Al-Khilafa wa Nash'at al-Ahzab al-Siyasiyya.* Beirut: Al-Mu'assasa al-'Arabiyya li al-Dirasat al-Nashir, 1977.

———. *Muslimun Thuwwar.* Beirut: Al-Mu'assasa al-'Arabiyya li al-Dirasat wa al-Nashr, 1981.

Amuzegar, Jahangir. "The Truth and Illusion of Islamic Fundamentalism." *SAIS Review,* 13 (Summer-Fall 1993): 127–139.

Anderson, Gerald, ed. "Challenge of Islam for Christian Missions." *International Bulletin of Missionary Research*, 17 (1993): 160–173.

Anderson, Lisa. "Liberalism, Islam, and the Arab State." *Dissent,* 41 (Fall 1994): 439–444.

———. "Remaking the Middle East: The Prospects for Democracy and Stability." *Ithacas and International Affairs,* 6 (1992): 163–178.

———. "The State in the Middle East and North Africa." *Comparative Politics*, 20 i (1987): 1–18.

Anderson, Sean, and Stephen Sloan. *Historical Dictionary of Terrorism.* Metuchen, NJ and London: Scarecrow Press, 1995.

Antoun, Richard, and Mary Elaine Hegland, eds. *Religious Resurgence: Contemporary Cases in Islam, Christianity, and Judaism.* Syracuse, NY: Syracuse University Press, 1987.

Appleby, R. Scott. *Spokesmen for the Despised: Fundamentalist Leaders of the Middle East.* Chicago, IL: University of Chicago Press, 1996.

Arjomand, Said Amir. *The Shadow of God and the Hidden Imam.* Chicago, IL: University of Chicago Press, 1984.

———, ed. *Authority and Political Culture in Shi'ism.* Albany: State University of New York Press, 1988.

'Ata, 'Abd al-Khabir Mahmud. "Al-Haraka al-Islamiyya wa Qadiyat al-Ta'addudiyya." *Al-Majalla al-'Arabiyya li al-'Ulum al-Siyasiyya,* 5 and 6 (April 1992).

Avinery, Shlomo. "Beyond Saddam: The Arab Trauma." *Dissent,* 38 (Spring 1991): 149–152.

———. "The Return to Islam (Fighting Islamic Fundamentalism)." *Dissent,* 40 (Fall 1993): 410–412.

'Awwa, Muhammad. *Fi al-Nizam al-Siyasi al-Islami li al-Dawla al-Islamiyya.* Cairo: Dar al-Shuruq, 1989.

———. "Al-Ta'addudiyya min Manzur Islami." *Minbar Al-Hiwar,* 6 (Winter 1991).

Ayalon, Ami, ed. *Middle East Contemporary Survey.* Boulder, CO: Westview Press, 1989.

Ayoob, Mohammad. *The Politics of Islamic Reassertion.* New York: St. Martin's Press, 1981.

Ayubi, Nazih. *Over-Stating the Arab State: Politics and Society in the Middle East.* London: I. B. Tauris, 1995.

———. *Political Islam: Religion and Politics in the Arab World.* New York: Routledge, 1991.

Al-Azm, Sadik. "Islamic Fundamentalism Reconsidered: A Critical Outline of Problems, Ideas and Approaches." *South Asia Bulletin.* Comparative Studies of South Asia, Africa, and the Middle East, Part I in Vol. 13, Nos. 1 & 2 (1993), pp. 93–131, Part II in Vol. 14, No. 1 (1994), pp. 73–98.

———. *Naqd al-Fikr al-Dini.* 6th ed. Beirut: Dar al-Tali'a, 1988.

Al-Azmeh, Aziz. *Islam and Modernity.* London: Verso, 1993.

Al-Azmi, Tarik Hamid. "Religion, Identity, and State in Modern Islam." *Muslim World,* 84 iii–iv (1994): 334–341.

Azzam, Maha. "The Gulf Crisis: Perceptions in the Muslim World." *International Affairs,* 67 (July 1991): 473–485.

Babeair, Abdulwahab Saleh. "Contemporary Islamic Revivalism: A Movement or a Moment?" *Islamic Quarterly,* 37 i (1993): 5–23.

Badawi, M. A. Zaki. *The Reformers of Egypt.* London: Croom Helm, 1967.

Al-Balihi, Ibrahim Ibn 'Abd al-Rahman. *Sayyid Qutb wa-Turathuhu al-Adabi wa al-Fikri.* Riyad: n.p., 1972.

Bangura, Yusuf. *The Search for Identity: Ethnicity, Religion and Political Violence.* Geneva: United Nations Research Institute for Social Development, 1994.

Barakat, Halim. *Al-Mujtama' al-'Arabi al-Mu'asir.* 3rd ed. Beirut: Center for the Studies of Arab Unity, 1986.

Barakat, Muhammad T. *Sayyid Qutb: Khulasat Hayatih, Minhajuhuh fi al-Haraka wa al-Naqd al-Muwajjah ilayh.* Beirut: Dar al-Da'wa, 197?

Barghouty, Iyad. "Al-Islam Bayna al-Sulta wa al-Mu'arada." *Qadaya Fikriyya: Al-Islam al-Siyasi, al-Usus al-Fikriyya wa al-Ahdaf al-'Amalliyya.* Cairo: Dar al-Thaqafa al-Jadida, 1989.

Barut, Muhammad Jamal. *Yathrib al-Jadida: Al-Harakat al-Islamiyya al-Rahina.* London and Beirut: Riad Al-Rayyes Books, 1994.

Beeley, B. "Global Options: Islamic Alternatives." *A Global World? Re-Ordering Political Space.* Ed. J. Anderson et al. Oxford: Oxford University Press, 1995.

Bill, J. A., and R. Springborg. *Politics in the Middle East.* 4th ed. New York: HarperCollins, 1994.

Binder, Leonard. *The Ideological Revolution in the Middle East.* New York: John Wiley and Sons, 1964.

———. *Islamic Liberalism: A Critique of Development Ideologies.* Chicago, IL: University of Chicago Press, 1988.

Bizri, Dalal. *Akhawat al-Zill wa al-Yaqin. Islamiyyat bayna al-Hadatha wa al-Taqlid.* Beirut: Dar al-Nahar li al-Nashr, 1996.

Brumberg, Daniel. "Islamic Fundamentalism, Democracy, and the Gulf War." *Islamic Fundamentalisms and the Gulf Crisis.* Ed. James Piscatori, 155–185. Chicago, IL: American Academy of Arts and Sciences, 1991.

Bulliet, Richard W. "The Israeli-PLO Accord: The Future of the Islamic Movement." *Foreign Affairs,* 72 (November-December 1993): 38–44.

Burke, Edmond. *Struggle for Survival in the Modern Middle East.* London: I. B. Tauris, 1994.

Burrows, Bernard. *Footnotes in the Sand: The Gulf in Transition.* London: Michael Russell, 1991.

Busool, Assad N. *Islamic Fundamentalism?* American Islamic Education, 1993.

Butterworth, Charles. "State and Authority in Arabic Political Thought." *The Foundations of the Arab State.* Ed. Ghassan Salame, 91–111. London: Croom Helm, 1987.

Butterworth, Charles, ed. *Political Islam. The Annals of the American Academy of Political and Social Sciences,* 524 (November 1992).

Cambridge Encyclopedia of the Middle East and North Africa. Ed. Trevor Mostyn. Cambridge, UK: Cambridge University Press, 1988.

Cantouri, Louis J. "Democratization in the Middle East." *American-Arab Affairs,* 36 (Spring 1991): 1–51.

Carré, Olivier. *Les Frères Musulmans: Egypte et Syrie: 1928–1982.* Paris: Gallimard, Dulliard, 1983.

Chafri, Farida Faouzia. "When Galileo Meets Allah (Islam: The Politics of Monotheism)." *New Perspectives Quarterly,* 11 (Spring 1994): 30–32.

Charnayl, Jean Paul. *Islamic Culture and Socio-Economic Change.* Leiden: Brill, 1971.

Chelkowski, Peter, and Robert J. Pranger. *Ideology and Power in the Middle East: Studies in Honor of George Lenczowski.* Durham, NC: Duke University Press, 1988.

Choudhury, Golam W. *Islam and the Modern Muslim World.* London: Scorpion, 1993.

Choueiri, Youssef M. *Islamic Fundamentalism.* Boston: Twayne, 1990.

———. "Theoretical Paradigms of Islamic Movements." *Political Studies,* 41 i (1993): 108–116.

Cleveland, W. L. *A History of the Middle East*. Boulder, CO: Westview Press, 1994.

Cole, Juan R. I., and Nikki R. Keddie, eds. *Shi'ism and Social Protest*. New Haven, CT: Yale University Press, 1986.

Cox, W. S. "The Politics of Violence: Global Relations, Social Structure, and the Middle East." *Beyond Positivism: Critical Reflections on International Relations*. Eds. C. Turenne Solander and W. S. Cox. Boulder, CO: Lynne Rienner Publishers, 1994.

Cragg, Kenneth. *Counsels in Contemporary Islam*. Edinburgh: Edinburgh University Press, 1965.

Crone, P., and M. Hinds. *God's Caliph*. Cambridge, UK: Cambridge University Press, 1986.

Curtis, Michael, ed. *Religion and Politics in the Middle East*. Boulder, CO: Westview Press, 1981.

Dallal, Ahmad. "The Origins and Objectives of Islamic Revivalist Thought, 1750–1850." *The Journal of the American Oriental Society*, 113 (July-September 1993): 341–359.

Daly, M. W. "Islam, Secularism, and Ethnic Identity in the Sudan." *Religion and Political Power*. Eds. Gustavo and M. W. Daly Benavides. Albany: State University of New York Press, 1989.

Deegan, H. "Democratization in the Middle East." *The Middle East in the New World Order*. Ed. Haifa A. Jawad. Basingstoke, UK; Macmillan, NY: St. Martin's Press, 1994.

Dekmejian, Hrair R. "The Arab Anatomy of Islamic Revival: Legitimacy Crisis, Ethnic Conflict and the Search for Islamic Alternatives." *The Middle East Journal*, 34 (Winter 1980): 1–12.

——— . *Islam in Revolution: Fundamentalism in the Arab World*. 2nd ed. Syracuse, NY: Syracuse University Press, 1995.

Dessouki, Ali E. Hillal. "The Impact of Islamism on the Arab System." *The Islamist Dilemma: The Political Role of Islamist Movements in the Contemporary Arab World*. Ed. Laura Guazzone, 247–264. Reading, UK: Ithaca Press, 1995.

———. ed. *Islamic Resurgence in the Arab World*. New York: Praeger, 1982.

Dietl, Wilhelm. *Holy War*. New York: Macmillan, 1984.

Al-Din fi al-Mujtama' al-'Arabi. Beirut: Center for the Studies of Arab Unity, 1990.

Donohue, John, and John L. Esposito, eds. *Islam in Transition: Muslim Perspectives*. New York: Oxford University Press, 1982.

Dunn, Michael C. "Islamic Activists in the West: A New Issue Produces Backlashes." *Middle East Policy*, 3 (Winter 1994): 137–145.

Durrani, K. S. *Impact of Islamic Fundamentalism*. Bangalore, India: ISPCK, Delhi, 1993.

East, R., and T. Joseph. *Political Parties of Africa and the Middle East: A Reference Guide*. Harlow, UK: Longman, 1993.

Ehteshami, Anoushiravan. *Islamic Fundamentalism*. Boulder, CO: Westview Press, 1996.

Eickelman, Dale F. "Changing Interpretations of Islamic Movements." *Islam and the Political Economy of Meaning*. Ed. William R. Roff, 13–30. London: Croom Helm, 1987.

———. "Islamic Liberalism Strikes Back." *Middle East Studies Association Bulletin*, 27 ii (1993): 163–168.

El Affendi, Abel Wahab. *Who Needs an Islamic State?* London: Grey Seal, 1991.

Enayat, Hamid. *Modern Islamic Political Thought*. Austin: University of Texas Press, 1982.

The Encyclopedia of Islam, eds. M. T. Houtsma, A. J. Wensinck, et al. Leiden: E. J. Brill, 1911–38. New Edition, 1960– .

The Encyclopedia of Islam, eds. Bernard Lewis and V. L. Menage, et al. Leiden: E. J. Brill, 1971.

El-Erian, Mohamad A. *Jamjoom: A Profile of Islam, Past, Present, and Future: A Resource Book of Islam and the Muslim World*. Melbourne: Islamic Publications, 1990.

Esack, Farid. *Qur'an, Liberation and Pluralism: An Islamic Perspective of Interreligious Solidarity against Oppression*. Oxford, UK: Oneworld Publications, 1996.

Esposito, John L. *Islam: The Straight Path*. Expanded ed. New York: Oxford University Press, 1994.

———. *Islam and Development: Religion and Sociopolitical Change*. Syracuse, NY: Syracuse University Press, 1980.

———. *Islam and Politics*. 3rd ed. Syracuse, NY: Syracuse University Press, 1991.

———. "Islamic Movements, Democratization and U.S. Foreign Policy." *Riding the Tiger: The Middle East Challenge After the Cold War*. Eds. Phebe Marr and William Lewis. Boulder, CO: Westview Press, 1993.

———. *The Islamic Threat: Myth or Reality?* New York: Oxford University Press, 1992.

———. *The Oxford Encyclopedia of the Modern Islamic World*. New York: Oxford University Press, 1995.

———. "The Persian Gulf War, Islamic Movements and the New World Order." *Iranian Journal of International Affairs*, 5 ii (1993): 340–365.

———. "Political Islam: Beyond the Green Menace." *Current History,* 93 (January 1994): 19–24.

Esposito, John L., and James P. Piscatori. "Democratization and Islam." *The Middle East Journal,* 45 (Summer 1991): 427–440.

Esposito, John, and John Voll. *Islam and Democracy.* Oxford, UK: Oxford University Press, 1996.

Esposito, John L., ed. *Voices of Resurgent Islam.* New York: Oxford University Press, 1983.

Fadlallah, Sayyid Muhammad Hussein. *Fiqh al-Hayat.* Beirut: Mu'assasat al-Arif li al-Matbu'at, 1997.

———. *Al-Islam wa Filistin.* Beirut: Mu'assasat al-Dirasat al-Filistiniyya, 1995.

———. *Al-Islam wa Muntiq al-Quwwa.* Beirut: Al-Dar al-Islamiyya, 1986.

———. *Ma' al-Hikma fi Khatt al-Islam.* Beirut: Mu'assasat al-Wafa', 1985.

Falk, Richard. "In Search of a New World Model (The Emerging World Order after the Cold War)." *Current History,* 92 (April 1993): 145–149.

Farah, Caesar. "Political Dimensions of Islamic Fundamentalism." *Digest of Middle East Studies,* 5 (Spring 1996): 1–14.

Al-Fasi, Allal. *Durus fi al-Haraka al-Salafiyyah.* Dayda: Manshurat 'Uyun, 1986.

Filali-Ansari, A. "Islam and Liberal Democracy: The Challenge of Secularization." *Journal of Democracy,* 7 ii (1996): 76–80.

Flores, Alexander. "Secularism, Integralism and Political Islam." *Middle East Report,* 183 (July-August 1993).

Fuller, Graham E. *Islamic Fundamentalism in the Northern Tier Countries: An Integrative View.* Santa Monica, CA: Rand Corporation, 1991.

Fuller, Graham and Iran Lesser. *A Sense of Siege: The Geopolitics of Islam and the West.* Boulder, CO: Westview Press, 1995.

Gause, F. Gregory. "Sovereignty, Statecraft and Stability in the Middle East." *Journal of International Affairs,* 45 ii (Winter 1992): 441–469.

Gellner, Earnest. *Culture, Identity and Politics.* Cambridge, MA: Cambridge University Press, 1988.

Gerami, Shahim. *Women and Fundamentalism.* Oxford, UK: Garland Publishers, 1996.

Ghadbian, Najib. *Democratization and Islamist Challenge in the Arab World.* Boulder, CO: Westview Press, 1997.

Ghalun, Burhan. *Al-Dawla wa al-Din: Naqd al-Siyasa.* Beirut: Al-Mu'assasa al-'Arabiyya li al-Dirasat wa al-Nashr, 1991.

Al-Ghannushi, Rashid. *Al-Hurriyyat al-'Amma fi al-Dawla al-Islamiyya.* Beirut: Markaz Dirasat al-Wahda al-'Arabiyya, 1993.
———. "Al-Islam wa al-Gharb." *Al-Ghadir,* 10–11 (December, 1990).
———. "Ma'alim fi Istratijiyya al-Da'wa al-Islamiyya." *Al-Hiwar,* 19 (Autumn 1990).
———. *Mahawir Islamiyya.* Cairo: Matabi' al-Zahra', 1989.
———. "Mustaqbal al-Haraka al-Islamiyya." *Al-Huda* [Fez], 23 (1991).
———. "Mustaqbal al-Tayyar al-Islami." *Minbar al-Sharq,* 1 (March 1992).
———. "Tahlil li al-'Anasir al-Mukawwina li al-Zahira al-Islamiyya fi Tunis." *Al-Harakat al-Islamiyya fi al-Watan al-'Arabi.* Ed. I. S. 'Abd Allah and others. Beirut: Markaz Dirasat al-Wahda al-'Arabiyya, 1987.
Al-Ghazali. *Tahafut al-Falasifa.* Translated by Sabih Ahmad Kamali. Lahore: Pakistan Philosophical Congress, 1963.
Gibb, Hamilton A. R. *Modern Trends in Islam.* Chicago, IL: University of Chicago Press, 1947.
———. *Whither Islam? A Survey of Modern Movements in the Moslem World.* New York: AMS Press, 1973.
Gilsenan, Michael. *Recognizing Islam: Religion and Society in the Modern Middle East.* London: I. B. Tauris, 1994.
Glasse, Cyril. *The Concise Encyclopedia of Islam.* London: Stacey International, 1989.
Green, Jerrold D. "Islam, Religiopolitics, and Social Change." *Comparative Studies in Society and History,* 27 (April 1985): 312–322.
Guazzone, Laura. "Islamism and Islamists in the Contemporary Arab World." *The Islamist Dilemma: The Political Role of Islamist Movements in the Contemporary Arab World,* ed. Laura Guazzone, 3–38. Reading, UK: Ithaca Press, 1995.
Guazzone, Laura, ed. *The Islamist Dilemma: The Political Role of Islamist Movements in the Contemporary Arab World.* Reading, UK: Ithaca Press, 1995.
Guolo, R. *Il partito di dio: l'Islam radicale contro l'Occidente.* Milano: Guerini e Associati, 1994.
Hadar, Leon T. "What Green Peril (Fear of Islam)." *Foreign Affairs,* 72 (Spring 1993): 27–42.
Haddad, Yvonne Y. *Contemporary Islam and the Challenge of History.* Albany, NY: State University of New York Press, 1982.
———. "The Qur'anic Justification for an Islamic Revolution: The View of Sayyid Qutb." *The Middle East Journal,* 37 i (1983).
———. "Islamists and the 'Problem of Israel': The 1967 Awakening." *The Middle East Journal,* 46 (Spring 1992): 266–285.

Haddad, Yvonne Y., and John L. Esposito. *The Islamic Revival since 1988: A Critical Survey and Bibliography.* Westport, CT: Greenwood Press, 1998.

Haddad, Yvonne Y., John L. Esposito, and John Voll. *The Contemporary Islamic Revival: A Critical Survey and Bibliography.* Westport, CT: Greenwood Press, 1991.

Haddad, Yvonne Y., Byron Haynes, and Ellison Finfly, eds. *The Islamic Impact.* Syracuse, NY: Syracuse University Press, 1984.

Haider, Gulzar. "An 'Islamic Future' without a Name (Islam and the Future)." *Futures,* 23 (April 1991): 311–316.

Halliday, Fred. *Islam and the Myth of Confrontation: Religion and Politics of the Middle East.* London: I. B. Tauris, 1995.

———. "Review Article: The Politics of 'Islam'—A Second Look." *British Journal of Political Science,* 25 (July 1995): 399–417.

Halliday, Fred, and Hamza Alavi. *State and Ideology in the Middle East and Pakistan.* New York: Monthly Review Press, 1988.

Halpern, Manfred. *The Politics of Change in the Middle East and North Africa.* 4th ed. Princeton: Princeton University Press, 1970.

Hamad, Wadood. "The Dialectics of Revolutionary Islamic Thought and Action." *Arab Review,* 2 iii (1994): 35–41.

Hamadani, Abbas. "Islamic Fundamentalism." *Mediterranean Quarterly,* 4 iv (1993): 38–47.

Hamdi, M. E. "Islam and Liberal Democracy: The Limits of the Western Model." *Journal of Democracy,* 7 ii (1996): 81–85.

Al-Hamidi, Muhammad al-Hashimi. "Awlawiyyat Muhimma fi Daftar al-Harakat al-Islamiyya: Nahwa Mithaq Islami li al-'Adl wa al-Shura wa Huquq al-Insan." *Al-Mustaqbal al-Islami,* 2 (November 1991).

Hammuda, Husayn M. *Asrar Harakat al-Dubbat al-Ahrar wa al-Ikhwan al-Muslimun.* Cairo: Al-Zahra' li al-I'lam al-'Arabi, 1985.

Hanafi, Hasan. *Al-Yamin wa al-Yasar fi al-Fikr al-Dini.* Cairo: Dar al-Thaqafa al-Jadida, 1996.

Hanafi, Jamil M. *Islam and the Transformation of Culture.* New York: Asia Publication House, 1974.

Al-Harakat al-Islamiyya fi Muwajahat al-Taswiya. Beirut: Center for Strategic Studies, 1995.

Harik, Iliya. "Rethinking Civil Society: Pluralism in the Arab World." *Journal of Democracy,* 5 iii (July 1994): 43–56.

Harris, Christina P. *Nationalism and Revolution in Egypt: The Role of the Muslim Brotherhood.* Westport, CT: Hyperion Press, 1981.

Al-Hassan, Badr. *Milestones.* Karachi: International Islamic Publishers, 1981.

Hawwa, Sa'id. *Al-Madkhal ila Da'wat al-Ikhwan al-Muslimin bi-Munasabat Khamsin 'Aman 'ala Ta'sisiha*. 2nd ed. Amman: Dar al-Arqam, 1979.

Herichow, A., and J. B. Simonson, eds. *Islam in a Changing World: Europe and the Middle East*. Richmond, UK: Curzon Press, 1997.

Hermassi, Mohamed Abdelbaki. "Islam, Democracy, and the Challenge of Political Change." *Democracy in the Middle East: Defining the Challenge*. Eds. Yehuda Mirsky and Matt Abres, 41–52. Washington, DC: 1993.

Heywoth-Dunne, J. *Religions and Political Trends in Modern Egypt*. Washington, DC: n.p., 1950.

Al-Hibri, Azizah Y. *Islamic Constitutionalism and the Concept of Democracy*. New York and Washington, DC: American Muslim Foundation, 1992.

Hilal, 'Ali al-Din Hilal. *Al-Siyasa wa al-Hukm fi Misr: 1923–52*. Cairo: Maktabat Nahdat al-Sharq, 1977.

Hiro, Dilip. *Holy Wars: The Rise of Islamic Fundamentalism*. New York: Routledge, 1989.

———. *Inside the Middle East*. London: Routledge and Kegan Paul, 1981.

———. *Islamic Fundamentalism*. London: Paladin Grafton Books, 1988.

Hodgson, Marshall. *Venture of Islam*. Chicago, IL: University of Chicago Press, 1961.

Hottinger, A. "How Dangerous Is Islamism?" *Swiss Review of World Affairs*, 1 (1994): 10–12.

Hourani, Albert. *History of the Arab Peoples*. Cambridge, MA: Harvard University Press, 1990.

Hourani, George. *Essays on Islamic Philosophy and Science*. New York: State University of New York Press, 1975.

Hovsepian, Nubar. "Competing Identities in the Arab World." *Journal of International Affairs*, 49 (Summer 1995): 1–24.

Huband, Mark. *Warriors of the Prophet: The Challenge of Islamic Fundamentalism*. Boulder, CO: Westview, 1998.

Hudson, Michael. "After the Gulf War: Prospects for Democratization in the Arab World." *The Middle East Journal*, 45 iii (1991).

———. *Arab Politics*. New Haven, CT: Yale University Press, 1977.

———. "Arab Regimes and Democratization: Responses to the Challenge of Political Islam." *The Islamist Dilemma: The Political Role of Islamist Movements in the Contemporary Arab World*. Ed. Laura Guazzone, 217–245. Reading, UK: Ithaca Press, 1995.

Huergensmeyer, M. *The New Cold War? Religious Nationalism Confronts the Secular State*. Berkeley and Los Angeles: University of California Press, 1994.

Hunter, Shireen T. "Islamic Fundamentalism: What It Really Is and Why It Frightens the West." *SAIS Review,* 6 (Winter-Spring 1986): 189–200.

———. "The Rise of Islamist Movements and the Western Response: Clash of Civilizations or Clash of Interests?" *The Islamist Dilemma: The Political Role of Islamist Movements in the Contemporary Arab World.* Ed. Laura Guazzone, 317–350. Reading, UK: Ithaca Press, 1995.

———, ed. *The Politics of Islamic Revivalism: Diversity and Unity.* Bloomington: Indiana University Press, 1988.

Husain, Mir Zohair. *Global Islamic Politics.* New York: HarperCollins College Publishers, 1995.

Hussain, Asaf. *Islamic Movements in Egypt, Pakistan, and Iran: An Annotated Bibliography.* New York: Mansell, 1983.

Huwaydi, Fahmi. *Al-Islam wa al-Dimuqratiyya.* Cairo: Markaz al-Ahram li al-Tarjama wa al-Nashr, 1993.

———. "Al-Islam wa al-Dimuqratiyya." *al-Mustaqbal al-'Arabi,* 166 (December 1992).

———. *Al-Qur'an wa al-Sultan. Humum Islamiyya Mu'asira.* Cairo: Dar al-Shuruq, 1982.

———. "Al-Sahwa al-Islamiyya wa al-Muwatana wa al-Musawat." *Al-Hiwar,* 7 (Fall 1987).

Hyman, Anthony. "Islamic Bogeymen." *The World Today,* 46 (August-September 1990): 160–161.

———. "The Muslim Fundamentalism." *Conflict Studies,* 174 (1985): 1–27.

Ibn, Taymiyya. *Al-Siyasa al-Shar'iyya.* Beirut: Dar al-Fikr al-Hadith, n.d.

Ibrahim, Anwar. "The Ummah and Tomorrow's World (Koranic Moral Concept of How Muslims Should Relate to Each Other and the Communities of the World)." *Futures,* 23 (April 1991): 302–310.

Ibrahim, Saad Eddin. *Domestic Politics and Regional Security: Jordan, Syria and Israel.* London: Gower, International Institute for Strategic Studies, 1989.

———. "Islamic Activism: A Rejoinder." *Security Dialogue,* 25 ii (1994): 193–198.

'Ilwani, Taha. *Islah al-Fikr al-Islami.* Herndon, VA: International Institute of Islamic Thought, 1991.

'Imad, 'Abd al-Ghani. *Hakimiyyat Allah wa Sultan al-Faqih.* Beirut: Dar al-Tali'a, 1997.

Iqbal, Muhammad. *The Reconstruction of Religious Thought in Islam.* Lahore: Ashraf, 1960.

Islamic Fundamentalism and Islamic Radicalism: Jihad as a Global Concern. Diane Publishers, 1987.

Isma'il, Mahmud. *Sociologia al-Fikr al-Islami.* Cairo: Maktabat Madbuli, 1988.

Isma'il, Sabri. *Al-Harakat al-Islamiyya al-Mue'asira fi al-Watan al-'Arabi.* Beirut: Markaz Dirasat al-Wahda al-'Arabiyya, 1987.

Israeli, Raphael. *Fundamentalist Islam and Israel: Essays in Interpretation.* Lanham, MD: University Press of America, 1993.

'Izzat, Hiba Ra'uf. *Al-Mar'a wa al-'Amal al-Siyasi: Ru'ya Islamiyya.* Herndon, VA: International Institute of Islamic Thought, 1995.

Jabir, Husayn. *Al-Tariq ila Jama'at al-Muslimin.* Al-Mansura, Egypt: Dar Al-Wafa, 1987.

Ja'far, Hashim Ahmad 'Awad. *Al-Ab'ad al-Siyasiyya li Mafhum al-Hakimiyya: Ru'ya Ma'rifiyya.* Herndon, VA: International Institute of Islamic Thought, 1996.

Jalabi, Khalis. *Fi al-Naqd al-Dhati: Darura al-Naqd al-Dhati li al-Haraka al-Islamiyya.* Beirut: Mu'assasat al-Risala, 1985.

Al-Janhani, Al-Habib. "Al-Sahwa al-Islamiyya fi Bilad al-Sham: Mithal Surya." *Al-Harakat al-Islamiyya al-Mu'asira fi al-Watan al-'Arabi.* 2nd ed. Beirut: Center for the Studies of Arab Unity, 1989.

Jansen, Johannes J. G. *The Dual Nature of Islamic Fundamentalism.* Ithaca, NY: Cornell University Press, 1997.

———. *The Neglected Duty: The Creed of Sadat's Assassins and Islamic Resurgence in the Middle East.* New York: Macmillan Publishing Company, 1986.

Jawad, Haifaa. "Pan-Islamism in the Middle East: Prospects and Future." *Islamic Quarterly,* 37 iii (1993): 207–222.

Al-Jawjari, Adil. *Al-Hizb al-Islami.* Cairo: The Arabic Center for Journalism and Publications, 1993.

Jindi, Anwar. *Qadaya al-'Asr wa Mushkilat al-Fikr tahta Daw' al-Islam.* Beirut: Mu'assasat al-Risala, 1981.

Judy, Ronald A. T. "Islamiyya and the Construction of Human Being" *Islamic Fundamentalism: Myths and Realities.* Ed. Ahmad S. Moussalli, 103–122. Reading, UK: Ithaca Press, 1998.

Jum'a, Muhammad 'Ali. *Nazariyyat al-Dawla fi al-Fikr al-'Arabi al-Mu'asir.* Damascus: Dar 'Ala' al-Din, 1994.

Kabuli, Niaz Faizi. *Democracy According to Islam.* Pittsburgh, PA: Dorrance Publication Co., 1994.

Kaplan, Lawrence, ed. *Fundamentalism in Comparative Perspective.* Amherst: University of Massachusetts Press, 1992.

Karabell, Zachary. "The Wrong Threat: The United States and Islamic Fundamentalism." *World Policy Journal*, 12 (Summer 1995): 37–48.

Karpat, Kemal H. *Political and Social Thought in the Contemporary Middle East*. London: Pall Mall Press, 1968.

Kawtharani, Wajih. *Mashru' al-Nuhud*. Beirut: Dar al-Tali'a, 1995.

Keddie, Nikki R. *An Islamic Response to Imperialism: Political and Religious Writings of Sayyid Jamal ad-Din "al-Afghani."* Berkeley: University of California Press, 1968.

———. "Pan-Islam as Protonationalism." *The Journal of Modern History*, 41 i (1969): 17–28.

Kedourie, Elie. *Afghani and Abduh*. London: Frank Cass, 1966.

Kelidar, Abbas. "States without Foundations: The Political Evolution of State and Society in the Arab East." *Journal of Contemporary History*, 28 ii (1993): 315–338.

Kerr, David A. "The Challenge of Islamic Fundamentalism for Christians." *International Bulletin of Missionary Research*, 17 (October 1993): 169–173.

Kerr, Malcolm. *Islamic Reform: The Political and Legal Theories of Muhammad 'Abduh and Rashid Rida*. Berkeley: University of California Press, 1966.

Khadouri, M. *Political Trends in the Arab World*. Baltimore, MD: Johns Hopkins Press, 1970.

Khalafallah, Ahmad. *Al-Fikr al-Tarbawi lada Jama'at al-Ikhwan al-Muslimin*. Cairo: Maktabat Wahba, 1984.

Al-Khalidi, Mahmud. *Al-Dimuqratiyya al-Gharbiyya fi Daw' al-Shari'a al-Islamiyya*. Amman: Maktabat al-Risala al-Haditha, 1986.

Khalidi, Salah 'Abd al-Fattah. *Nazariyyat al-Taswir al-Fanni 'inda Sayyid Qutb*. Amman: Dar al-Furqan, 1983.

Al-Khumayni, Ayatollah. *Al-Hukuma al-Islamiyya*. Kuwait: n.p., n.d.

Khuri, Fuad. *Imams and Emirs: State, Religion and Sects in Islam*. London: Saqi Books, 1990.

Kilani, Najib. *Lamahat min Hayati*. Beirut: Mu'assasat al-Risala, 1985–88.

Koloctronis, Jamilah. *Islamic Jihad: An Historical Perspective*. American Trust Publications, 1990.

Korbani, A. G. *The Political Dictionary of Modern Middle East*. Lanham, MD: University Press of America, 1995.

Kramer, Gudrun. "Cross-Links and Double Talk? Islamist Movements in the Political Process." *The Islamist Dilemma: The Political Role of Islamist Movements in the Contemporary Arab World*. Ed. Laura Guazzone, 39–67. Reading, UK: Ithaca Press, 1995.

———. "Islamist Notions of Democracy." *Middle East Report*, 23 iv/183 (July-August 1993): 2–8.

———. "Liberalization and Democracy in the Arab World." *Middle East Report*, 174 (January-February 1992).

Kramer, Martin. *Arab Awakening and Islamic Revival*. New Brunswick, NJ: Transaction Publishers, Rutgers University, 1996.

———. *Islam Assembled: The Advent of the Muslim Congresses*. New York: Columbia University Press, 1986.

———. "Islam in the New World Order." *Middle East Contemporary Survey*, 15/1991 (1993): 172–205.

———. "Islam versus Democracy (Future of Islamic Fundamentalism)." *Commentary*, 95 (January 1993): 35–42.

———. *Political Islam*. Beverly Hills, CA: Sage Publications, 1980.

Kramer, Martin, ed. *Shi'ism, Resistance, and Revolution*. Boulder, CO: Westview Press, 1987.

Kucukcan, Talip. "The Nature of Islamic Resurgence in Near and Middle Eastern Muslim Societies." *Hamdard Islamicus*, 14 (Summer 1991): 65–104.

Kurdi, Rajih 'Abd al-Hamid. *Al-Ittijah al-Salafi: Bayna al-Asala wa-al-Mu'asara*. Amman: Dar 'Ammar, 1989.

Laffin, John. *Holy War, Islam Fights*. London: Grafton, 1988.

Lambton, Ann. *State and Government in Medieval Islam*. Oxford: Oxford University Press, 1981.

Lamchaichi, Abderrahim. *Islam: islamisme et modernité*. Paris: l'Harmattan, 1994.

Landau, Jacob M. *The Politics of Pan-Islamism: Ideology and Organization*. Oxford: Oxford University Press, 1992.

Lapidus, Ira. *Contemporary Islamic Movements in Historical Perspective*. Berkeley, CA: Institute of International Studies, University of California, 1983.

———. *A History of Islamic Societies*. Cambridge, UK: Cambridge University Press, 1989.

Lawrence, Bruce. *Defenders of God: The Fundamentalist Revolt against the Modern Age*. San Francisco, CA: Harper and Row, 1989.

———. *Religious Fundamentalism*. Durham, NC: Duke University Press, 1993.

Leach, Hugh. "Observing Islam from Within and Without." *Asian Affairs*, 21 (February 1991).

Lee, Robert D. *Overcoming Tradition and Modernity: The Search for Islamic Authenticity*. Boulder, CO: Westview Press, 1997.

Leiden, Karl, ed. *The Conflict of Traditionalism and Modernism in the Muslim Middle East.* Austin: Texas University Press, 1969.

Lemu, Aisha B. Laxity, *Moderation and Extremism in Islam.* London: International Institute of Islamic Thought, 1993.

Leveau, Remy. "Youth Culture and Islamism in the Middle East." *The Islamist Dilemma: The Political Role of Islamist Movements in the Contemporary Arab World.* Ed. Laura Guazzone, 265–287. Reading, UK: Ithaca Press, 1995.

Lewis, Bernard. *Islam in History: Ideas, People, and Events in the Middle East.* New ed., rev. and expanded. Chicago, IL: Open Court, 1993.

———. "Islam and Liberal Democracy." *The Atlantic Monthly,* 271 (February 1993): 89–94.

———. *Islam and the West.* New York: Oxford University Press, 1993.

———. *The Political Language of Islam.* Chicago, IL: University of Chicago Press, 1988.

———. "The Roots of Muslim Rage: Why So Many Muslims Deeply Resent the West, and Why Bitterness Will Not Be Easily Mollified." *The Atlantic Monthly,* 266 (September 1990): 47–57.

———. *The Shaping of the Modern Middle East.* New York: Oxford University Press, 1994.

Lowrie, Arthur L. "The Campaign against Islam and American Foreign Policy." *Middle East Policy,* 4 (September 1995): 210–219.

MacEain, Denis. *Islam in the Modern World.* London: Croom Helm, 1983.

Maddy-Weitzman, Bruce, and Efraim Inbar, eds. *Religious Radicalism in the Greater Middle East.* London, UK and Portland, OR: Frank Cass, 1997.

Mahdi, Muhsin, trans. *Al-Farabi's Philosophy of Plato and Aristotle.* Ithaca, NY: Cornell University Press, 1969.

Mahfuz, Muhammad. *Alladhina Zulimu.* London: Riad al-Rayyis Books Ltd., 1988.

Mallat, Chibli. "On Islam and the Democracy." *Islam and Public Law: Classical and Contemporary Studies.* Ed. Chibli Mallat. London: Graham and Trotman, 1993.

Maqsood, Ruqaiyyah Waris. *Islam: A Dictionary.* Cheltenham, UK: Thornes Ltd., 1996.

Mardini, Zuhayr. *Al-Ladudan: Al-Wafd wa al-Ikhwan.* Beirut: Dar Iqra', 1984.

Marr, Phebe. "The Islamic Revival: Security Issues." *Mediterranean Quarterly,* 3 (Fall 1992).

Marr, P., and W. Lewis, eds. *Riding the Tiger: The Middle East Challenge for the Cold War.* Boulder, CO: Westview Press, 1993.

Marshall, P. "Bookwatch: Islamic Activism in the Middle East." *International Socialism*, 60 (1993): 157–171.

Martin, Malachi. *The Encounter*. New York: Farrar Straus and Giroux, 1970.

Marty, Martin, and R. Scott Appleby, eds. *Fundamentalisms and Society: Reclaiming the Sciences, the Family, and Education*. Chicago, IL: University of Chicago Press, 1993.

———. *Fundamentalisms and the State: Remaking Polities, Economies, and Militance*. Chicago, IL: University of Chicago Press, 1993.

———. *Accounting for Fundamentalisms: The Dynamic Character of Movements*. Chicago, IL: University of Chicago Press, 1994.

———. *Fundamentalisms Observed*. Chicago, IL: University of Chicago Press, 1991.

Al-Mawardi, *Al-Ahkam al-Sultaniyya*. Beirut: Dar al-Kitab al-Lubnani al-'Arabi, 1990.

Al-Mawdudi, Abul al-A'la. *The Islamic Way of Life*. Lahore: Markazi Maktaba Jama'at-i-Islami, n.d.

———. *Al-Jihad fi-Sabilillah*. Beirut: Mu'assasat al-Risala, 1983.

———. *Jihad in Islam*. Beirut: The Holy Koran Publishing House, 1980.

———. *Mafahim Islamiyya*. Kuwait: Dar al-Qalam, 1977.

———. *Minhaj al-Inqilab al-Islami*. 3rd ed. Beirut: Mu'assasat al-Risala, 1981.

———. *Nahnu wa al-Hadara al-Gharbiyya*. Beirut: Mu'assasat al-Risala, 1983.

———. *Nizam al-Hayat fi al-Islam*. Beirut: Mu'assasat al-Risala, 1983.

———. *The Process of Islamic Revolution*. Lahore: Islamic Publications, 1977.

———. *A Short History of Revivalist Movements in Islam*. Lahore: Islamic Publications Limited, 1963.

———. *Towards Understanding Islam*. 8th ed. Lahore: Islamic Publications Limited, 1960.

Mayer, Ann E. *Islam and Human Rights: Tradition and Politics*. Boulder, CO: Westview Press, 1991.

Mazrui, Ali A. "Islam at War and Communism in Retreat: What Is the Connection?" *The Gulf War and the New World Order: International Relations of the Middle East*. Eds. Tareq Y. Ismael and J. S. Ismael. Gainesville: University Press of Florida, 1994.

Menashri, David, ed. *The Iranian Revolution and the Muslim World*. Boulder, CO: Westview Press, 1990.

Mernissi, Fatima. *Islam and Democracy: Fear of the Modern World*. New York: Addison-Wesley, 1993.

Miller, Judith. "The Challenge of Radical Islam." *Foreign Affairs,* 72 ii (1993): 43–56.

Moghadam, V. M., ed. *Gender and National Identity: Women and Politics in Muslim Societies.* London: Zed; Karachi: Oxford University Press, 1994.

Mohaddessin, Mohammad. *Islamic Fundamentalism: The New Global Threat.* Washington, DC: Seven Locks Press, 1993.

Mohamed, Yasien. "Islamization: A Revivalist Response to Modernity." *Muslim Education Quarterly,* 10 ii (1993): 12–23.

Momen, Moojan. *An Introduction to Shi'i Islam.* New Haven, CT: Yale University Press, 1985.

Monshipour, Mahmood, and C. G. Kukla. "Islam, Democracy and Human Rights: The Continuing Debate in the West." *Middle East Policy,* 2 ii (1994): 22–39.

Moosa, Matti. *Extremist Shiites: The Ghulat Sects.* Syracuse, NY: Syracuse University Press, 1988.

Mortimer, Edward. *Faith and Power: The Politics of Islam.* London: Faber and Faber, 1982.

Moten, Abdul Rashid. *Political Science—An Islamic Perspective.* Basingstoke, UK: Macmillan Press, 1996.

Mottahedeh, Roy. *The Mantle of the Prophet: Religion and Politics in Iran.* New York: Pantheon Books, 1988.

Moussalli, Ahmad S. "Discourses on Human Rights and Pluralistic Democracy." *Islam in a Changing World: Europe and the Middle East.* Eds. A. Herichow and J. B. Simonson. Richmond, UK: Curzon Press, 1997.

———. "Hasan al-Banna's Islamist Discourse on Constitutional Rule and Islamic State." *Journal of Islamic Studies,* 4 ii (1993): 161–174.

———. "Hasan al-Turabi's Discourse on Democracy and Shura." *Middle Eastern Studies,* 30 (January 1994): 52–61.

———. "Islamic Fundamentalism and Other Monotheistic Religions." *Religious Mutual Perceptions.* Ed. Jacque Waardenburgh. Lausanne, Switzerland: University of Lausanne, 1998.

———. "Islamic Fundamentalism and Pluralism." *Euro-Islam.* Eds. Thomas Lunden. Stockholm: Swedish Institute, 1996.

———. "Islamism and Modernity or Modernization of Islam." *The Future of Cosmopolitanism in the Middle East.* Amsterdam: Cultural Foundation, University of Amsterdam, 1998.

———. "Islamist Perspectives of Regime Political Response: The Case of Lebanon and Palestine." *Arab Studies Quarterly* (Summer 1996): 55–65.

————. *Moderate and Radical Fundamentalism: The Quest for Modernity, Legitimacy and the Islamic State.* Gainesville: University Press of Florida, 1999.

————. "Modern Islamic Fundamentalist Discourses on Civil Society, Pluralism and Democracy." *Civil Society in the Middle East.* Ed. Augustus Richard Norton. 79–119. Leiden: E. J. Brill, 1995.

————. "Modern Islamic Fundamentalist Discourses on Civil Society, Pluralism and Democracy." *Toward Civil Society in the Middle East.* Ed. Jillian Schwedler. Boulder, CO: Lynne Rienner Publishers, 1995.

————. *Radical Islamic Fundamentalism: The Ideological and Political Discourse of Sayyid Qutb.* Beirut: American University of Beirut, 1992 and 1995.

————. "Sayyid Qutb: The Ideologist of Islamic Fundamentalism." *Al-Abhath,* 38 (1990): 42–73.

————. "Sayyid Qutb's View of Knowledge." *The American Journal of Islamic Social Sciences,* 7 iii (1990): 315–334.

————. "Two Tendencies in Modern Islamic Political Thought: Modernism and Fundamentalism." *Hamdard Islamicus* 16 ii (1993): 51–78.

————. *Al-Usuliyya al-Islamiyya wa al-Nizam al-'Alami.* Beirut: Center for Strategic Studies, 1992.

————. "The Views of Islamic Fundamentalism on Epistemology and Political Philosophy." *Islamic Quarterly,* 37 iii (1993): 175–189.

————, ed. *Islamic Fundamentalism: Myths and Realities.* Reading, UK: Ithaca Press, 1998.

Al-Mudarrisi, Hadi. *Al-Islam wa al-Idiolojiyyat al-Munawi'a ila Ayn.* Beirut: Mu'assasat al-Balagh, 1987.

Muhammad, Muhsin. *Man Qatala Hasan al-Banna.* Cairo: Dar al-Shuruq, 1987.

Munson, Henry. *Islam and Revolution in the Middle East.* New Haven, CT: Yale University Press, 1988.

Musa, Kaval. "Politique et théologie: L'impact sur les mouvements islamistes." (Political Power and Theological Doctrine in Islam: The Impact on the Islamist Movements.) *Les Cahiers de l'Orient,* 34 (1994): 9–32.

Muslih, Muhammad, and Augustus Richard Norton. "The Need for Arab Democracy." *Foreign Policy,* 83 (Summer 1991): 3–19.

Mutahhari, Mohammad S. *Jihad: The Holy War of Islam and Its Legitimacy in the Qur'an.* Tehran: Islamic Propagation Organization, 1985.

Al-Mutalib, Hussein, and Taj ul-Islam Hashmi. *Islam, Muslims and the Modern State: Case Studies of Muslims in Thirteen Countries.* Basingstoke, UK; Macmillan, New York: St. Martin's Press, 1994.

Mutalib, H. "Islamic Resurgence and the Twenty-First Century: Redefining the Old Agendas in a New Age." *American Journal of Islamic Social Sciences*, 13 i (1996): 88–99.

Al-Nabahani, Taqiy al-Din. *Nizam al-Hukm*. Jerusalem: Matba'at al-Thiryan, 1952.

―――. *Al-Takatul al-Hizbi*. 2nd ed. Jerusalem: n.p., 1953.

Nacos, B. L. *Terrorism and the Media: From the Iran Hostage Crisis to the World Trade Center Bombing*. New York: Columbia University Press, 1994.

Al-Nadawi, Abu al-Hasan. *Madha Khasira al-'Alam bi-Inhitat al-Muslimin*. 8th ed. Beirut: Dar al-Kitab al-Lubnani, 1984.

Nadvi, Syed Habib ul Huque. *Islamic Fundamentalism: A Theology of Liberation and Renaissance*. Westville, S. Africa: Academia, Arabic-Persian-Urdu Department, University of Durban, 1995.

Nafi, Basheer. "Contemporary Islamic Political Forces: Traditional or Modern." *Arab Review*, 3 i (1994): 29–33.

Al-Najjar, Abd al-Majid. *Fi Fiqh al-Tadayyun*. 2 vols. Qatar: Kitab al-Umma, n.d.

―――. *Khilafat al-Insan bayna al-Wahy wa al-'Aql*. 2nd ed. Herndon, VA: International Institute of Islamic Thought, 1993.

Nasr, Seyyed Hossein. *Ideals and Realities of Islam*. London: Unwin Hyman, 1988.

―――. *Islamic Life and Thought*. London: Allen and Unwin, 1981.

―――. *Traditional Islam in the Modern World*. London: KPI, 1987.

Nasr, Seyyed Hossein, Hamid Dabashi, and Seyyed Vali Reza Nasr, eds. *Expectation of the Millennium: Shi'ism in History*. Albany: State University of New York Press, 1989.

―――. *Shi'ism: Doctrines, Thought, and Spirituality*. Albany: State University of New York Press, 1988.

Nasr, Seyyed Vali Reza. "Religious Modernism in the Arab World, India and Iran: The Perils and Prospects of a Discourse." *The Muslim World*, 83 i (January 1993): 20–47.

Nettler, Ronald, and Suha Taji-Farouki, eds. *Muslim-Jewish Encounters: Intellectual Traditions and Modern Politics*. Reading, UK: Harwood, 1997.

Niblock, Tim, and Emma Murphy. *Economic and Political Liberalism in the Middle East*. London: British Academic Press, 1993.

Nielsen, J. S. "Will Religious Fundamentalism Become Increasingly Violent?" *International Journal on Group Rights*, 2 (1994): 197–209.

Nielsen, Niels C. *Fundamentalism, Mythos, and World Religions*. Albany: State University of New York, 1993.

Nisrin, Taslima. "On Islamic Fundamentalism." *The Humanist*, 56 (July-August 1996): 24–27.

Noorozi, Touraj. "The Ideological Encounter between Shi'i Islam and Marxism: The Impact of Sadr al-Din al-Shirazi's Philosophy on the Polemics of Islamic Revolution." *Civilizations*, 43 i (1994): 39–54.

Norton, Augustus Richard. "Breaking through the Wall of Fear in the Arab World." *Current History,* 91 (January 1992): 37–41.

———. "The Challenge of Inclusion in the Middle East." *Current History,* 94 (January 1995): 1–6.

———. "The Future of Civil Society in the Middle East." *The Middle East Journal* 47, (Spring 1993).

———, ed. *Civil Society in the Middle East.* 2 vols. Leiden: E. J. Brill, 1995 & 1996.

O'Ballance, Edgar. *Islamic Fundamentalist Terrorism, 1979–95: The Iranian Connection.* New York: New York University Press, 1996.

Ogutco, Mehmet. "Islam and the West: Can Turkey Bridge the Gap?" *Futures,* 26 (October 1994): 811–829.

Paris, Jonathan S. "When to Worry in the Middle East (Threat from Islamic Fundamentalism)." *Orbis,* 37 (Fall 1993): 553–545.

Peretz, Don. *Islam: Legacy of the Past, Challenge of the Future.* New York: New Horizon Press, 1984.

Peters, F. E. *Allah's Commonwealth.* New York: Simon and Schuster, 1973.

Peters, Rudolph. *Jihad in Classical and Modern Islam.* Princeton: Princeton University Press, 1995.

Pietersee, J. N. "Fundamentalism Discourse: Enemy Images." *Women against Fundamentalism Journal*, 1 v (1994): 2–6.

Pipes, Daniel. *In the Path of God: Islam and Political Power.* New York: Basic Books, 1983.

———. "Islam's Intramural Struggle." *The National Interest*, 35 (Spring 1994): 84–86.

Piscatori, James. "Accounting for Islamic Fundamentalisms." *Accounting for Fundamentalisms: The Dynamic Character of Movements.* Eds. Martin E. Marty and R. Scott Appleby, 361–373. Chicago, IL: University of Chicago Press, 1994.

———. *Islam in a World of Nation-States.* Cambridge, UK: Cambridge University Press, 1986.

———. *Islam in the Political Process.* New York: Cambridge University Press, 1983.

———. "Religion and Realpolitik: Islamic Responses to the Gulf War." *Islamic Fundamentalisms and the Gulf Crisis.* Ed. James Piscatori, 1–27. Chicago, IL: American Academy of Arts and Sciences, 1991.

Piscatori, James and John Esposito. "Democratization and Islam." *The Middle East Journal,* 45 (Summer 1991).

Piscatori, James, ed. *Islamic Fundamentalisms and the Gulf Crisis.* Chicago, IL: American Academy of Arts and Sciences, 1991.

Al-Qaradawi, Yusuf. *Al-Hall al-Islami Farida wa Darura.* Cairo: Maktabat Wahba, 1977.

———. *Al-Sahwa al-Islamiyya bayna al-Juhud wa al-Tatarruf.* Qatar: Matba'at al-Dawha al-Haditha, 1982.

Qarqar, Muhammad. *Dawr al-Haraka al-Islamiyya fi Tasfiyyat al-Iqta'.* Kuwait: Dar al-Buhuth al-'Ilmiyya, 1980.

Rahman, Fazlur. *Islam and Modernity: The Transformation of an Intellectual Tradition.* Chicago, IL: University of Chicago Press, 1982.

Ramazani, R. K. "Shi'ism in the Persian Gulf." *Shi'ism and Social Protest.* Eds. Juan R. I. Cole and Nikki R. Keddie, 30–53. New Haven, CT: Yale University Press, 1986.

Rapoport, David C. "Comparing Militant Fundamentalist Movements and Groups." *Fundamentalisms and the State: Remaking Polities, Economies, and Militance.* Eds. Martin E. Marty and R. Scott Appleby, 429–461. Chicago, IL: University of Chicago Press, 1993.

Regan, D. "Islamic Resurgence: Characteristics, Causes, Consequences and Implications." *Journal of Political and Military Sociology,* 21 ii (1993): 259–266.

Rezun, Miron, ed. *Iran at the Crossroads: Global Relations in a Turbulent Decade.* Boulder, CO: Westview Press, 1990.

Richards, Alan and John Waterbury. *A Political Economy of the Middle East.* Boulder, CO: Westview Press, 1990.

Rizq, Jabir. *Al-Dawla wa al-Siyasa fi Fikr Hasan al-Banna.* Al-Mansura, Egypt: Dar al-Wafa, 1985.

Roberson, B. A. "Islam and Europe: An Enigma of a Myth?" *The Middle East Journal,* 48 (Spring 1994): 288–308.

Robinson, Francis, ed. *Islamic World: Cambridge Illustrated History.* Cambridge, UK: Cambridge University Press, 1996.

Rodinson, Maxim. *Islam and Capitalism.* Austin: University of Texas Press, 1981.

Roff, William. "Islamic Movements: One or Many?" *Islam and the Political Economy of Meaning.* Ed. William R. Roff, 31–52. London: Croom Helm, 1987.

Roff, William, ed. *Islam and the Political Economy of Meaning: Comparative Studies of Muslim Discourse.* London: Croom Helm, 1987.

Rondot, Pierre. *The Militant Radical Current in the Muslim Community.* Brussels: Pro Mundi Vita, 1982.

Roy, Olivier. *The Failure of Political Islam*. London: Tauris; Cambridge, MA: Harvard University Press, 1994.

Rudkin, Antony, and Irene Butcher. *A World Book Directory of the Arab Countries, Turkey and Iran*. Detroit, MI: Gale Research, 1981.

Sachedina, Abdulaziz A. *Islamic Messianism: The Idea of the Mahdi in Twelver Shi'ism*. Albany: State University of New York Press, 1981.

Sadowski, Yahya. "The New Orientalism and the Democracy Debate." *Middle East Report*, 183 (July-August 1993): 14–21 and 40.

Safi, Louay. *The Challenge of Modernity: The Quest for Authenticity in the Arab World*. Lanham, MD: University Press of America, 1994.

Said, Abdul Aziz. "Islamic Fundamentalism and the West." *Mediterranean Quarterly*, 3 (Fall 1992): 21–36.

Saif, Walid. "Human Rights and Islamic Revivalism." *Islam and Christian-Muslim Relations*, 5 i (1994): 57–65.

Salame, Ghassan. "Islam and the West." *Foreign Policy*, 90 (Spring 1993): 22–37.

———, ed. *Democracy without Democrats? The Renewal of Politics in the Muslim World*. London: Tauris, 1994.

Salvatore, Armando. "Discursive Contentions in Islamic Terms: Fundamentalism versus Liberalism?" *Islamic Fundamentalism: Myths and Realities*. Ed. Ahmad S. Moussalli, 75–102. Reading, UK: Ithaca Press, 1998.

Sami', Hasan. *Azmat al-Hurriyya al-Siyasiyya fi al-Watan al-'Arabi*. Cairo: Al-Zahra' li al-I'lam al-'Arabi, 1988.

Saqr, A. *Islamic Fundamentalism*. Chicago, IL: Kazi Publications, 1987.

Satloff, R. B., ed. *The Politics of Change in Saudi Arabia*. Boulder, CO: Westview Press, 1993.

Al-Sayyid, Ridwan. *Siyasat al-Islam al-Mu'asir*. Beirut: Dar al-Kitab al-'Arabi, 1997.

Schliefer, S. Abdullah. "Jihad: Modernist Apologies, Modern Apologetics." *Islamic Quarterly*, 28 i (1984): 25–46.

Schmid, E. "Turkey: Rising Power of Islamic Fundamentalism." *Women against Fundamentalism Journal*, 1 vi (1994): 57–67.

Schwedler, J., ed. *Toward Civil Society in the Middle East? A Primer*. London: Lynne Rienner Publishers, 1996.

Semaan, Wanis A. "The Double-Edged Challenge of Islamic Fundamentalism." *Mission Studies*, 11 ii (1994): 173–180.

Shafiq, Munir. "Awlawiyyat Amam al-Ijtihad wa al-Tajdid." *Al-Ijtihad wa Tajdid fi al-Fikr al-Islami al-Mu'asir*. Malta: Center for the Studies of the Muslim World, 1991.

———. *Al-Fikr al-Islami al-Mu'asir wa al-Tahaddiyat*. Beirut: Al-Nashir, 1991.

———. *Al-Islam fi Ma'rakat al-Hadara*. Beirut: Al-Nashir, 1991.

———. *Al-Islam wa Muwajahat al-Dawla al-Haditha*. 3rd ed. Beirut: Al-Nashir, 1992.

———. *Al-Nizam al-Dawli al-Jadid wa Khiyar al-Muwajaha*. Beirut: Al-Nashir, 1992.

Sharabi, Hisham. *Nationalism and Revolution in the Arab World*. Princeton: D. Van Nostrand and Co., 1966.

———, ed. *The Next Arab Decade: Alternative Futures*. Boulder, CO: Westview Press, 1988.

Sharaf al-Din, Rislan. "Al-Din wa al-Ahzab al-Siyasiyya al-Diniyya." *Al-Din fi al-Mujtama' al-'Arabi*. Beirut: Center for the Studies of Arab Unity, 1990.

Shari'ati, Ali. *On the Sociology of Islam*. Berkeley, CA: Mizan Press, 1979.

Sidahmed, A. S. and A. Ehteshami, eds. *Islamic Fundamentalism*. Boulder, CO: Westview Press, 1996.

Sid-Ahmed, Mohamed. "Cybernetic Colonialism and the Moral Search (Resurrection of the Religious Imagination)." *New Perspectives Quarterly*, 11 (Spring 1994): 15–19.

Siddiq, Ali. *Al-Ikhwan al-Muslimun Bayna Irhab Faruq wa 'Abd al-Nasir*. Cairo: Dar al-I'tisam, 1987.

Sihbudi, Riza. "Islamic 'Fundamentalism' and Democratization in the Middle East." *Iranian Journal of International Affairs*, 6 (Spring-Summer 1994): 119–128.

Silverburg, Sanford R. *Middle East Bibliography*. Metuchen, NJ and London, UK: Scarecrow Press, 1992.

Sisi, Abbas. *Hasan al-Banna: Mawqif fi al-Da'wa wa al-Tarbiyya*. Alexandria, Egypt: Dar al-Da'wa, 1981.

Sisk, Timothy. *Islam and Democracy*. Washington, DC: United States Peace Institute Press, 1992.

Sivan, Emmanuel. *Interpretations of Islam: Past and Present*. Princeton: Darwin Press, 1985.

———. *Islamic Fundamentalism and Anti-Semitism*. Jerusalem: Shazar Library, Institute of Contemporary Jewry, Hebrew University of Jerusalem, 1985.

———. *Radical Islam: Medieval Theology and Modern Politics*. New Haven, CT: Yale University Press, 1990.

Sivan, Emmanuel, and Menachem Friedman, eds. *Religious Radicalism and Politics in the Middle East*. Albany: State University of New York Press, 1990.

Smith, Wilfred C. *Islam in Modern History.* Princeton: Princeton University Press, 1957.

Solh, Ragid. "Islamist Attitudes towards Democracy: A Review of the Ideas of Al-Ghazali, Al-Turabi and 'Amara." *British Journal of Middle Eastern Studies*, 20 (1993): 57–63.

Stowasser, Barbara. "Women's Issues in Modern Islamic Thought." *Arab Women: Old Boundaries, New Frontiers.* Ed. J. E. Tucker. Bloomington: Indiana University Press, 1993.

―――, ed. *The Islamic Impulse.* Washington, DC: Georgetown University Center for Contemporary Arab Studies, 1987.

Tachau, Frank, ed. *Political Parties of the Middle East and North Africa.* Westport, CT: Greenwood Press, 1994.

Taheri, Amir. *Holy Terror: The Inside Story of Islamic Terrorism.* London: Hutchinson, 1987.

Tamadonfar, Mehran. *The Islamic Polity and Political Leadership: Fundamentalism, Sectariansim and Pragmatism.* Boulder, CO: Westview Press, 1989.

Tamimi, Azzam, ed. *Power-Sharing Islam?* London: Liberty for Muslim World Publications, 1993.

Taji-Farouki, Suha. "A Case-Study in Contemporary Political Islam and the Palestine Question: The Perspective of Hizb al-Tahrir." *Studies in Muslim-Jewish Relations*, 2 (1995): 35–58.

―――. "From Madrid to Washington: Palestinian Islamist Response to Israeli-Palestinian Peace Settlement." *World Faiths Encounter*, 9 (November 1994): 49–58.

―――. *A Fundamental Quest: Hizb al-Tahrir and the Search for the Islamic Caliphate.* London: Grey Seal, 1996.

―――. "Hizb al-Tahrir." *Encyclopedia of the Modern Islamic World.* New York: Oxford University Press, 1995.

―――. "Islamic Discourse and Modern Political Methods: An Analysis of al-Nabahani's Reading of the Canonical Text Sources of Islam." *American Journal of Islamic Social Sciences*, 11 iii (Fall 1994): 365–393.

―――. "Islamic State—Theories and Contemporary Realities." *Islamic Fundamentalism in Perspective.* Eds. Sid Ahmad and Ehteshemi. Boulder, CO: Westview, 1995.

―――. "Nazariyyat al-Dawla al-Islamiyya wa al-Waqi 'al-Mu'asir: Hala Dirasiyya." *Qira'at Siyasiyya*, 5 (Spring 1995): 83–99.

Taylor, Alan R. *The Islamic Question in the Middle East Politics.* Boulder, CO: Westview Press, 1988.

Taylor, P. *States of Terror: Democracy and Political Violence*. London: Penguin and BBC Books, 1993.

Tessler, Mark, and J. Jesse. "Gender and Support for Islamist Movements: Evidence from Egypt, Kuwait and Palestine." *Muslim World*, 86 ii (1996): 200–228.

Tetreault, Mary Ann. "Gulf Winds: Inclement Political Weather in the Arabian Peninsula." *Current History*, 95 (January 1996): 23–27.

Tibi, Bassam. *The Crisis of Modern Islam in a Pre-Industrial Culture in the Scientific-Technological Age*. Salt Lake City: University of Utah, 1988.

————. *Religious Fundamentalism and Ethnicity in the Crisis of the Nation-State in the Middle East: Subordinate Islamic and Pan-Arab Identities and Subordinate Islamic and Sectarian Identities*. Berkeley, CA: Center for German and European Studies, European Studies, 1992.

————. "The Renewed Role of Islam in the Political and Social Development of the Middle East." *The Middle East Journal*, 37 i (1983): 3–13.

Al-Turabi, Hasan. "Awlawiyyat al-Haraka al-Islamiyya." *Minbar al-Sharq*, 1 (March 1992).

————. *Al-Haraka al-Islamiyya fi al-Sudan: Al-Tatawwur wa al-Kasb wa al-Manhaj*. Khartoum: n.p., 1989.

————. *Al-Haraka al-Islamiyah fi al-Sudan*. Kuwait: Dar al-Qalam, 1988.

————. *Al-Iman wa Atharuhu fi Hayat al-Insan*. Jeddah: Al-Dar al-Su'udiyya li al-Nashr wa al-Tawzi', 1984.

————. *Al-Islam, Hiwarat fi al-Dimucratiyya, al-Dawla, al-Gharb*. Beirut: Dar al-Jadid, 1995.

————. "The Islamic Awakening's New Wave." *New Perspective Quarterly*, 10 (Summer 1993): 42–45.

————. *Al-Itijah al-Islami Yuqadim al-Mar'a bayna Ta'alim al-Din wa Taqalid al-Mujtama'*. Jeddah: Al-Dar al-Su'udiyya li al-Nashr wa al-Tawzi', 1984.

————. *Qadaya al-Hurriyya wa al-Wahda, al-Shura wa al-Dimuqratiyya, al-Din wa al-Fan*. Jeddah: Al-Dar al-Su'udiyya li al-Nashr wa al-Tawzi', 1987.

————. *Al-Salat 'Imad al-Din*. Beirut: Dar al-Qalam, 1971.

————. "Al-Shura wa al-Dimuqratiyya: Ishkalat al-Mustala wa al-Mafhum." *al-Mustaqbal al-'Arabi*, 75 (May 1985).

————. *Tajdid al-Fikr al-Islami*. 2nd ed. Jeddah: Al-Dar al-Su'udiyya li al-Nashr wa al-Tawzi', 1987.

————. *Tajdid Usul al-Fiqh*. Jeddah: Al-Dar al-Su'udiyya li al-Nashr wa al-Tawzi', 1984.

————. "Utruhat al-Haraka al-Islamiyya fi Majal Al-Hiwar Ma'a al-Gharb." *Shu'un al-Awsat*, 36 (December 1994).

Turner, Bryan. *Orientalism, Postmodernism and Globalism.* London and NY: Routledge, 1994.

Al-'Unf al-Usuli: Al-Ibda' min Nawafiz Jahannam. London and Beirut: Riad al-Rayyes Books, 1995.

Al-'Unf al-Usuli: Muwajahat al-Sayf wa al-Qalam. London and Beirut: Riad al-Rayyes Books, 1995.

Al-'Unf al-Usuli: Nuwwab al-Ard wa al-Sama'. London and Beirut: Riad al-Rayyes Books, 1995.

United States Congress-House Committee on Foreign Affairs, Sub-Committee on Europe and the Middle East. *Islamic Fundamentalism and Islamic Radicalism.* Hearing, June 24, July 15, and September 30, 1985, Washington, DC.

Uthman, Fathi. *Al-Salafiyyah fi al-Mujtama'at al-Mu'asira.* Cairo: Dar Afaq al-Ghad, 1982.

Voll, John. *Islam: Continuity and Change in the Modern World.* 2nd ed. Syracuse, NY: Syracuse University Press, 1994.

Von Grunebaun, Gustave. *Modern Islam: The Search for Cultural Identity.* Westport, CT: Greenwood Press, 1983.

Waal, A. "Rethinking Ethiopia." *Conflict and Peace in the Horn of Africa: Federalism and Its Alternative.* Eds. P. Woodward and M. Forsyth. Aldershot, UK: Dartmouth, 1994.

Waterbury, John. "Corruption, Political Stability, and Development: Comparative Evidence from Egypt and Morocco." *Government and Opposition,* 11 iv (Autumn 1976).

———. "Democracy without Democrats? The Potential for Political Liberalization in the Middle East." *Democracy without Democrats? The Renewal of Politics in the Muslim World.* Ed. Ghassan Salame. London: Tauris, 1994.

———. *Exposed to Innumerable Delusions: Public Enterprise and State Power in Egypt, India, Mexico, and Turkey.* Cambridge, UK: Cambridge University Press, 1993.

Watt, W. Montgomery. "Islamic Fundamentalism." *Studia Missionalia.* 41 (1992): 241–252.

———. *Islamic Fundamentalism and Modernity.* London: Routledge, 1988.

Weiner, M., and Ali Banuazizi, eds. *The Politics of Social Transformation in Afghanistan, Iran and Pakistan.* New York: Syracuse University Press, 1994.

Wolf, Kristin. *"New* New Orientalism." *Islamic Fundamentalism: Myths and Realities.* Ed. Ahmad S. Moussalli, 42–74. Reading, UK: Ithaca Press, 1998.

Woodward, P., and M. Forsyth, eds. *Conflict and Peace in the Horn of Africa: Federalism and Its Alternative.* Aldershot, UK: Dartmouth, 1994.

Wright, Robin. "Islam's New Political Face." *Current History,* 90 (January 1991): 25–30.

———. *Sacred Rage: The Crusade of Modern Islam.* New York: Simon & Schuster, 1985.

Yakan, Fathi. *Abjadiyyat al-Tasawwur al-Haraki li al-'Amal al-Islami.* 11th ed. Beirut: Mu'assasat al-Risala, 1993.

———. *Harakat wa Madhahib fi Mizan al-Islam.* 10th ed. Beirut: Mu'assasat al-Risala, 1992.

———. *Al-Mawsu'a Al-Harakiyya.* Amman: Dar al-Bashir, 1983.

———. *Nahwa Haraka Islamiyya 'Alamiyya.* 10th ed. Beirut: Mu'assasat al-Risala, 1993.

Yousef, Michael. *Revolt against Modernity: Muslim Zealots and the West.* Leiden: E. J. Brill, 1985.

Zafarul Islam, Khan. "Hukumat-e Islami: Imam Khumayni's Contribution to Islamic Political Thought." *Al-Tawhid,* 10 ii-iii (1992–1993): 237–247.

Zahmul, Ibrahim. *Al-Ikhwan al-Muslimin: Awraq Tarikhiyya.* France: s.n., 1985.

Zartman, I. William. "Democracy and Islam: The Cultural Dialectic." *Annals of the American Academy of Political and Social Sciences,* 524 (November 1992).

Zartman, I. William, and William Mark Habeeb, eds. *Polity and Society in Contemporary North Africa.* Boulder, CO: Westview Press, 1993.

Zebiri, Kate. *Mahmud Shaltut and Islamic Modernism.* Oxford: Oxford University Press, 1995.

Zubaida, Sami. *Islam, the People and the State: Essays on Political Ideas and Movements in the Middle East.* 2nd ed. London: Tauris, 1993.

II. NORTH AFRICA

Abramson, Gary. "Rise of the Crescent (Islamic Fundamentalism in North Africa)." *Africa Report,* 37 (March-April 1992): 18–21.

Anderson, Lisa. "Obligation and Accountability: Islamic Politics in North Africa." *Daedalus,* 120 (Summer 1991): 93–112.

———. "Liberalism in Northern Africa." *Current History,* 89 (April 1990): 145–148.

Brace, R. M. *Morocco, Algeria, Tunisia.* Englewood Cliffs, NJ: Prentice-Hall, 1964.

Burgat, François, and William Dowell. *The Islamic Movement in North Africa.* Austin: Center for Middle Eastern Studies, University of Texas, 1993.

Cambridge Encyclopedia of the Middle East and North Africa. Ed. Trevor Mostyn. Cambridge, UK: Cambridge University Press, 1988.

Deeb, Mary-Jane. "Militant Islam and the Politics of Redemption." *Annals of the American Academy of Political and Social Sciences,* 524 (November 1992): 52–65.

East, R., and T. Joseph. *Political Parties of Africa and the Middle East: A Reference Guide.* Harlow, UK: Longman, 1993.

Entelis, John P. *Comparative Politics of North Africa: Algeria, Morocco, and Tunisia.* Syracuse, NY: Syracuse University Press, 1980.

Farley, Jonathan. "The Maghreb's Islamic Challenge." *The World Today,* 47 (August-September 1991): 148–151.

Haireche, Abdel-Kader, and Azzedine Layachi. "National Development and Political Protest: Islamists in the Maghreb Countries." *Arab Studies Quarterly,* 14 (Spring-Summer 1992): 69–92.

Halpern, Manfred. *The Politics of Change in the Middle East and North Africa.* 4th ed. Princeton: Princeton University Press, 1970.

Hermassi, Mohamed Abdelbaki. *Leadership and National Development in North Africa.* Berkeley: University of California Press, 1970.

———. *Society and State in the Arab Maghreb.* Beirut: Center for Arab Unity Studies, 1987.

Hermida, Alfred. "The State and Islam." *Africa Report* 39 (September-October 1994): 55–58.

Hiskett, Marvyn. *The Course of Islam in Africa.* Edinburgh: Edinburgh University Press, 1994.

Joffe, G., and C. R. Pennell, eds. *Tribe and State: Essays in Honor of David Montgomery Hart.* Lincolnshire, UK: Middle East and North Africa Press, 1991.

Joffe, G., ed. *North Africa: Nation, State and Region.* London: Routledge, 1993.

Lamchiachi, Abderrahman. *Islam et contestation au Maghreb.* Paris: L'Harmattan, 1989.

Langewiesche, William. "The World in Its Extreme (Sahara Desert)." *The Atlantic,* 268 (November 1991): 105–128.

Moore, Clement Henry. "Political Parties." *Polity and Society in Contemporary North Africa.* Eds. I. William Zartman and William Mark Habeeb, 42–67. Boulder, CO: Westview Press, 1993.

———. *Politics in North Africa: Algeria, Morocco, and Tunisia.* Boston: Little, Brown, 1970.

Porteous, Tom. "The Islamisation of Modernity." *The Middle East,* 220 (February 1993): 19–22.

Ruedy, John, ed. *Islamism and Secularism in North Africa.* New York: St. Martin's Press, 1994.

Sara, Fayiz. *Al-Haraka al-Islamiyya fi al-Magrib al-'Arabi.* Beirut: Markaz al-Dirasat al-Istratijiyya, 1995.

Seddon, David. "Riot and Rebellion in North Africa." *Power and Stability in the Middle East.* Ed. Berch Berberoglu. London: Zed Books, 1989.

Shahin, Emad. *Political Ascent, Contemporary Islamic Movements in North Africa.* Boulder, CO: Westview Press, 1997.

III. THE ARAB WORLD

Algeria

Abdelmoula, Adam M. "The 'Fundamentalist' Agenda for Human Rights: The Sudan and Algeria." *Arab Studies Quarterly,* 18 (Winter 1996): 1–28.

Addi, Lahouari. "The Islamist Challenge: Religion and Modernity in Algeria." *Journal of Democracy,* 3 (October 1992): 75–84.

Arkoun, Mohammad. "Algeria." *The Politics of Islamic Revivalism: Diversity and Unity.* Ed. Shireen T. Hunter, 171–186. Bloomington: Indiana University Press, 1988.

'Ayyashi, Ahmida. *Al-Haraka al-Islamiyya fi al-Jaza'ir.* 2nd ed. Casablanca: 'Uyun al-Maqalat, 1993.

Ben Bella, Ahmed. "A Time for Peace in Algeria." *The World Today,* 51 (November 1995): 208–210.

Bennoune, Karima. "Algerian Women Confront Fundamentalism." *Monthly Review,* 46 (September 1994): 26–39.

Bilhaj, 'Ali. *Fasl al-Kalam fi Muwajahat al-Hukkam.* Beirut: n.p., 1994.

Bin Nabiy, Malik. *Dawr al-Muslim Rislatahu.* Damascus: Dar al-Fikr, 1989.

———. *Milad Mujtama'.* Damascus: Dar al-Fikr, 1989.

———. *Mushkilat al-Thaqafa.* 4th ed. Damascus: Dar al-Fikr, 1984.

———. *Shurut al-Nahda.* 4th ed. Damascus: Dar al-Fikr, 1987.

Brace, R. M. *Morocco, Algeria, Tunisia.* Englewood Cliffs, NJ: Prentice-Hall, 1964.

Brumberg, Daniel. "Islam, Elections and Reform in Algeria." *Journal of Democracy,* 2 (Winter 1992).

———. *L'Islamism au Maghreb—La voix du Sud.* Paris: Karthala. 1988.

———. "Prospects for a Democratic Bargain in Algeria." *American Arab Affairs,* 36 (1991).

Burgat, François. *The Political Transition in Algeria: Elements for Analysis.* Amsterdam: MERA (Middle East Research Associates), 1994.

Burgat, Francois, and William Dowell. *The Islamic Movement in North Africa.* Austin, Texas, Center for Middle East Politics, 1993.

Christelow, Allan. "Ritual, Culture and Politics of Islamic Reformism in Algeria." *Middle Eastern Studies,* 26 (July 1987): 255–273.

Deeb, M. J. "Islam and the State in Algeria and Morocco: A Dialectical Model." *Islamism and Secularism in North Africa.* Ed. J. Ruedy. Basingstoke, UK: Macmillan, 1994.

Dunn, Michael Collins. "Revivalist Islam and Democracy: Thinking About the Algerian Quandary." *Middle East Policy,* 1 (Spring 1992): 16–22.

Eickelman, Dale F. *Knowledge and Power in Morocco: The Education of a Twentieth-Century Notable.* Princeton: Princeton University Press, 1985.

———. *Moroccan Islam: Tradition and Society in a Pilgrimage Center.* Austin: University of Texas Press, 1976.

———. "Re-Imaging Religion and Politics: Moroccan Elections in the 1990s." *Islamism and Secularism in North Africa.* Ed. J. Ruedy. Basingstoke, UK: Macmillan, 1994.

Eickelman, Dale F., and James Piscatori, eds. *Muslim Travellers: Pilgrimage, Migration, and the Religious Imagination.* London: Routledge, 1990.

Entelis, John P. *Algeria: The Revolution Institutionalized.* Boulder, CO: Westview Press, 1986.

———. *Culture and Counterculture in Moroccan Politics.* Boulder, CO: Westview Press, 1989.

———. "Islam, Democracy and the State: The Reemergence of Authoritarian Politics in Algeria." *Islamism and Secularism in North Africa.* Ed. J. Ruedy. Basingstoke, UK: Macmillan, 1994.

———. "Political Islam in Algeria: The Nonviolent Dimension." *Current History,* 94 (January 1995): 13–17.

Haireche, Abdel-Kader, and Azzedine Layachi. "National Development and Political Protest: Islamists in the Maghreb Countries." *Arab Studies Quarterly,* 14 (Spring-Summer 1992): 69–92.

Halpern, Manfred. *The Politics of Change in the Middle East and North Africa.* 4th ed. Princeton: Princeton University Press, 1970.

Hermassi, Mohamed Abdelbaki. *Leadership and National Development in North Africa*. Berkeley: University of California Press, 1970.

———. *Society and State in the Arab Maghreb*. Beirut: Center for Arab Unity Studies, 1987.

Hermida, Alfred. "Algeria: Taking Responsibility." *The Middle East*, 222 (April 1993): 17–18.

———. "The State and Islam." *Africa Report*, 39 (September-October 1994): 55–58.

Hiskett, Marvyn. *The Course of Islam in Africa*. Edinburgh: Edinburgh University Press, 1994.

Iratni, Belkacem, and Mohand Salah Tahi. "The Aftermath of Algeria's First Free Local Elections." *Government and Opposition*, 26 (Autumn 1991): 466–479.

Islamic Movements in North Africa: The Algerian Experience and Its Future under Zeroual. London: Gulf Centre for Strategic Studies, 1994.

Isma'il, Sayf al-Din 'Abd al-Fattah. "Al-Tayyarat al-Islamiyya wa al-Qadiyya al-Dimuqratiyya: Ru'ya min Khilal al-Hadath al-Jaza'iri." *Al-Mustaqbal al-'Arabi*, 170 (April 1993).

Jackson, Henry F. *The FLN in Algeria: Party Development in a Revolutionary Society*. Westport, CT: Greenwood Press, 1977.

Jelloun, Tahar Ben. "Laughing at God in North Africa." *New Perspectives Quarterly*, 11 (Spring 1994): 26–29.

Joffe, G., ed. *North Africa: Nation, State and Region*. London: Routledge, 1993.

Joffe, G., and C. R. Pennell, eds. *Tribe and State: Essays in Honor of David Montgomery Hart*. Lincolnshire, UK: Middle East and North Africa Press, 1991.

Kapil, A. "Algeria." *Political Parties in the Middle East and North Africa*. Ed. F. Tachau. London: Mansell, 1994.

Kepel, Gilles. "Islamists versus the State in Egypt and Algeria." *Daedalus*, 124 (Summer 1995): 109–127.

Lamchichi, Abderrahman. *L'Islamisme an Algerie*. Paris: L'Harmattan, 1992.

Layachi, Azzadine. "Government, Legitimacy and Democracy in Algeria." *Maghreb Report*, 1 i (January-February 1992): 69–92.

Leca, Jean. "Algerie: Sur quelques aspects de la violence politique." *Maghreb-Machrek*, 141 (July-September 1993).

Madani, 'Abbassi. *Azmat al-Fikr al-Hadith wa Mubarrirat al-Hal al-Islami*. Algiers: Impr. Meziane, 1989.

———. *Mushkila Tarbawiyya fi Bilad al-Islamiyya*. Algeria: Batna: Dar al-Chihab, 1968.

Maghraoui, Abdeslam. "Problems of Transition to Democracy: Algeria's Short-Lived Experiment with Electoral Politics." *Middle East Insight,* 8 (July-October 1992): 20–26.

Mahfoud, Bennoune. "Algeria's Facade of Democracy." *MERIP Reports,* 20 ii (1990).

Moore, Clement Henry. "Political Parties." *Polity and Society in Contemporary North Africa.* Eds. I. William Zartman and William Mark Habeeb, 42–67. Boulder, CO: Westview Press, 1993.

———. *Politics in North Africa: Algeria, Morocco, and Tunisia.* Boston: Little, Brown, 1970.

Mortimer, Robert. "Algeria: The Clash between Islam, Democracy, and the Military." *Current History,* 92 (January 1993): 37–41.

———. "Islam and Multiparty Politics in Algeria." *The Middle East Journal,* 45 (Autumn 1991): 575–593.

Moussalli, Ahmad S. "Discourses on Human Rights and Pluralistic Democracy." *Islam in a Changing World: Europe and the Middle East.* Eds. A. Herichow and J. B. Simonson. Surrey, UK: Curzon Press, 1997.

———. "Islamic Fundamentalism and Other Monotheistic Religions." *Religious Mutual Perceptions.* Ed. Jacque Waardenburgh. Lausanne, Switzerland: University of Lausanne, 1998.

———. "Islamic Fundamentalism and Pluralism." *Euro-Islam.* Ed. Thomas Lunden. Stockholm: Swedish Institute, 1996.

———. "Islamism and Modernity or Modernization of Islam." *The Future of Cosmopolitanism in the Middle East.* Amsterdam: Cultural Foundation, University of Amsterdam, 1998.

———. "Modern Islamic Fundamentalist Discourses on Civil Society, Pluralism and Democracy." *Civil Society in the Middle East.* Ed. Augustus Richard Norton, 79–119. Leiden: E. J. Brill, 1995.

———. "Modern Islamic Fundamentalist Discourses on Civil Society, Pluralism and Democracy." *Toward Civil Society in the Middle East.* Ed. Jillian Schwedler. Boulder, CO: Lynne Rienner Publishers, 1995.

Naylor, Phillip Chiviges, and Alf Andrew Heggoy. *Historical Dictionary of Algeria.* Metuchen, NJ and London: Scarecrow Press, 1994.

Quandt, William. *Revolution and Political Leadership in Algeria, 1954–1968.* Cambridge, MA: MIT Press, 1969.

Al-Rasi, George. *Al-Islam al-Jaza'iri.* Beirut: Dar al-Jadid, 1997.

Roberts, Hugh. "The Algerian State and the Challenge to Democracy." *Government and Opposition,* 27 iv (Autumn 1992).

———. "Dictionaire Economics and Political Opportunism in the Strategy of Algerian Islamism." *Islamism and Secularism in North Africa.* Ed. John Ruedy. New York: St. Martin's Press, 1994.

————. "From Radical Mission to Equivocal Ambition: The Expansion of Manipulation of Algerian Islamism, 1979–1992." *Accounting for Fundamentalisms: The Dynamic Character of Movements.* Eds. Martin E. Marty and R. Scott Appleby, 428–489. Chicago, IL: University of Chicago Press, 1994.

————. "Radical Islamism and the Dilemma of Algerian Nationalism: The Embattled Arians of Algiers." *Third World Quarterly,* 10 ii (1988).

————. "A Trial of Strength: Algerian Islamism." *Islamic Fundamentalisms and the Gulf Crisis.* Ed. James Piscatori, 131–153. Chicago, IL: American Academy of Arts and Sciences, 1991.

Rouadjia, Ahmed. "Discourse and Strategy of the Algerian Islamist Movement (1986–1992)." *The Islamist Dilemma: The Political Role of Islamist Movements in the Contemporary Arab World.* Ed. Laura Guazzone, 69–103. Reading, UK: Ithaca Press, 1995.

Ruedy, John. *Modern Algeria. The Origins and Development of a Nation.* Bloomington: Indiana University Press, 1992.

Sara, Fayiz. *Al-Haraka al-Islamiyya fi al-Magrib al-'Arabi.* Beirut: Markaz al-Dirasat al-Istratijiyya, 1995.

Sherman, Alfred. "A New Algerian War?" *The World Today,* 48 (March 1992): 37–38.

Shirley, Edward G. "Is Iran's Present Algeria's Future?" *Foreign Affairs,* (May-June 1995): 28–44.

Stone, M. *The Agony of Algeria.* London: Hurst, 1997.

Tahi, M. S. "The Arduous Democratisation Process in Algeria." *Journal of Modern African Studies,* 30 (September 1992): 397–419.

Tzschaschel, Joachim. "Algeria Torn between Fundamentalism and Democracy." *Aussenpolitik,* 44 i (1993): 23–34.

Vatin, Jean Claude. "Religious Resistance and State Power in Algeria." *Islam and Power.* Eds. Cudsi and Dessouki, 119–157. Baltimore, MD: Johns Hopkins University Press, 1981.

Willis, Michael. *The Islamist Challenge in Algeria: A Political History.* Reading, UK: Ithaca Press, 1996.

Zebiri, Kate. "Islamic Revival in Algeria: An Overview." *The Muslim World,* 83 (July-October 1993).

Zoubir, Yahia H. "Algeria's Multi-Dimensional Crisis: The Story of a Failed State-Building Process." *Journal of Modern African Studies,* 32 (December 1994).

————. "Stalled Democratization of an Authoritarian Regime: The Case of Algeria." *Democratization,* 2 (January 1995).

————. "State, Civil Society and the Question of Radical Fundamentalism

in Algeria" in *Islamic Fundamentalism: Myths and Realities*. Ed.
Ahmad S. Moussalli, 123–168. Reading, UK: Ithaca Press, 1998.

Djibouti

Fukui, K., and J. Markakis. *Ethnicity and Conflict in the Horn of Africa*.
London: Currey; Athens, OH: Ohio University Press, 1994.
Gudrun, C., ed. *The Horn of Africa*. London: UCL Press, 1994.
Omar, Ahmed. "Quelques aspects de la sismicité de République de Dji-
bouti, années 1991 et 1992." *Sciences et Environnement*, 9 (1994):
15–32.
Omar, Ahmed, P. Carmagnolle, and Abdillahi Abar. "La crise sismique du
mois d'avril 1990." *Sciences et Environnement*, 9 (1994): 55–61.
Schraeder, P. J. "Ethnic Politics in Djibouti: From 'Eye of the Hurricane'
to 'Boiling Cauldron'." *African Affairs*, 92/367 (1993): 203–322.
Singh, D. "Djibouti: The Enigma of the Horn of Africa." *Africa Quarterly*,
9 (1994): 211–229.
Woodward, P., and M. Forsyth, eds. *Conflict and Peace in the Horn of Africa: Federalism and Its Alternative*. Aldershot, UK: Dartmouth, 1994.

Egypt

'Abbas, Ahmad. *Al-Ikhwan al-Muslimin fi Rif Misr*. Cairo: Dar al-Tawzi'
wa al-Nashir, 1987.
Abd al-Fattah, Nabil, ed. *Taqrir al-Haraka al-Diniyya fi Misr*. Cairo: Cen-
ter for Political and Strategic Studies, 1995.
———. *Al-Mushaf wa al-Sayf*. Cairo: Maktabat Madbuli, 1984.
'Abdallah, Ahmad. "Egypt's Islamists and the State." *Middle East Report*,
183 (July-August 1993): 28–31.
'Abdu, Muhammad. *Risalat al-Tawhid*. 2nd ed. Beirut: Al-Mu'assasa al-
'Arabiyya li-Dirasat al-Nashr, 1981.
Adams, Charles C. *Islam and Modernism in Egypt: A Study of the Modern
Reform Movement Inaugurated by Muhammad Abduh*. New York: Rus-
sel and Russel, 1968.
Ahmad, 'Abd al-Mu'ti Muhammad. *Al-Harakat al-Islamiyya fi Misr*.
Cairo: Markaz al-Ahram, 1995.
Ahmad, Rif'at Sayyid. *Al-Harakat al-Islamiyya fi Misr wa Iran*. Cairo:
Sina li al-Nashir, 1989.
———. *Hasan al-Banna: Mu'assis Harakat al-Ikhwan al-Muslimin*. Bei-
rut: Dar al-Tali'a, 1980.

———. *Al-Nabiy al-Musallah: Al-Rafidun.* London: Riad El-Rayyes Books, 1991.

———. *Al-Nabiy al-Musallah: Al-Tha'irun.* London: Riad El-Rayyes Books, 1991.

———. *Tanzimat al-Ghadab al-Islami fi al-Sab'inat.* Cairo: Maktabat Madbuli, 1989.

Ajami, Fouad. "The Sorrows of Egypt." *Foreign Affairs,* 74 (September-October 1995): 72–88.

Akhavi, Shahrough. "The Impact of the Iranian Revolution on Egypt." *The Iranian Revolution: Its Global Impact.* Ed. John L. Esposito, 138–155. Miami: Florida International University Press, 1990.

Alrawi, Karim. "Goodbye to the Enlightenment (Religious Intolerance in Egypt)." *Index on Censorship,* 23 (May-June 1994): 112–116.

Altman, Israel. "Islamic Movements in Egypt." *Jerusalem Quarterly,* 10 (Winter 1979): 87–105.

'Amara, Muhammad. *Al-Sahwa al-Islamiyya wa al-Tahaddi al-Hadari.* Beirut: Dar al-Shuruq, 1991.

———. *Tayyarat al-Fikr al-Islami.* Beirut: Dar al-Shuruq, 1991.

'Amir, 'Isam. *Al-Islam al-Siyasi wa Zahirat al-Irhab.* Cairo: Khulud li al-Nashr wa al-Tawzi', 1995.

Al-Ansari, Hamied. "The Islamic Militants in Egyptian Politics." *International Journal of Middle East Studies,* 16 (1984): 123–144.

Aoude, Ibrahim G. "From National Bourgeois Development to Infitah: Egypt 1952–1992." *Arab Studies Quarterly,* 16 (Winter 1994): 1–23.

Armajani, Yahya. *Middle East: Past and Present.* Englewood Cliffs, NJ: Prentice-Hall, 1979.

Auda, Gehad. "The 'Normalization' of the Islamic Movement in Egypt from the 1970s to the Early 1990s." *Accounting for Fundamentalisms: The Dynamic Character of Movements.* Eds. Martin E. Marty and R. Scott Appleby, 374–412. Chicago, IL: University of Chicago Press, 1994.

———. "An Uncertain Response: The Islamic Movement in Egypt." *Islamic Fundamentalisms and the Gulf Crisis.* Ed. James Piscatori, 109–130. Chicago, IL: American Academy of Arts and Sciences, 1991.

Audah, Abdul Qader. *Islam between Ignorant Followers and Incapable Scholars.* Kuwait: International Islamic Federation of Student Organizations, 1977.

———. *Al-Islam wa Awda'una al-Qanuniyya.* Kuwait: IIFSO, 1982.

'Awwa, Muhammad. *Fi al-Nizam al-Siyasi al-Islami li al-Dawlah al-Islamiyya.* Cairo: Dar al-Shuruq, 1989.

————. "Al-Ta'aduddiyya min Manzur Islami." *Minbar Al-Hiwar,* 6 (Winter 1991).

Ayubi, Nazih N. M. "The Political Revival of Islam: The Case of Egypt." *International Journal of Middle East Studies,* 12 (1980): 481–499.

Badawi, M. A. Zaki. *The Reformers of Egypt.* London: Croom Helm, 1967.

Badran, M. "Gender Activism: Feminists and Islamists in Egypt." *Identity Politics and Women: Cultural Reassertions and Feminisms in International Perspective.* Ed. V. M. Moghadam: 202–227. Boulder, CO: Westview Press, 1994.

Baker, Raymond William. "Afraid of Islam: Egypt's Muslim Centrists between Pharaohs and Fundamentalists." (Religion and Politics) *Daedalus,* 120 (Summer 1991): 41–68.

————. *Sadat and After: Struggles for Egypt's Political Soul.* Cambridge, MA: Cambridge University Press, 1990.

Al-Balihi, Ibrahim Ibn 'Abd al-Rahman. *Sayyid Qutb wa-Turathuhu al-Adabi wa-al-Fikri.* Riyad: n. p., 1972.

Al-Banna, Hasan. *Din wa-Siyasa.* Beirut: Maktabat Hittin, 1970.

————. *Five Tracts of Hasan Al-Banna (1906–1949).* Trans. and ann. Charles Wendell. Berkeley: University of California Press, 1978.

————. *Al-Imam Yatahadath ila Shabab al-'Alam al-Islami.* Beirut: Dar al-Qalam, 1974.

————. *Majmu'at Rasa'il al-Shahid Hasan al-Banna.* Beirut: Dar al-Qalam, 1984.

————. *Memoirs of Hasan al-Banna Shaheed.* Trans. M. N. Shaikh. Karachi, Pakistan: International Islamic Publishers, 1981.

————. *Minbar al-Jum'a.* Alexandria, Egypt: Dar al-Da'wa, 1978.

————. *Rasa'il al-Shahid Hasan al-Banna.* Beirut: Dar al-Qur'an al-Karim, 1984.

————. *Nazarat fi Islah al-Nafs wa al-Mujtama'.* Cairo: Maktabat al-I'tizam, 1969.

————. *Al-Salam fi al-Islam.* 2nd ed. Beirut: Manshurat al-'Asr al-Hadith, 1971.

————. *What Is Our Message?* Lahore: Islamic Publications Ltd., 1974.

Al-Bayyumi Ghanim, Ibrahim. *Al-Fikr al-Siyasi li al-Imam Hassan al-Banna.* Cairo: Dar al-Tawzi' wa al-Nashr al-Islamiyya, 1992.

Benin, J. "Terrorism, Class and Democracy in Egypt." *Middle East Report* 24 v/190 (1994): 28–29.

Berger, Morroe. *Islam in Egypt Today: Social and Political Aspects of Popular Religion.* Cambridge, UK: Cambridge University Press, 1970.

Berque, Jacques. *Egypt's Imperialism and Revolution.* Trans. Jean Steward. London: Faber and Faber, 1972.

Binder, Leonard. *In a Moment of Enthusiasm: Political Power and the Second Stratum in Egypt.* Chicago, IL: University of Chicago Press, 1978.

Al-Bishri, Tariq. *Al-Haraka al-Siyasiyya fi Misr: 1945–1952.* 2nd ed. Cairo: Dar al-Shuruq, 1983.

Brown, N. J., and T. J. Prio. "Egypt." *Political Parties of the Middle East and North Africa.* Ed. F. Tachau, 93–132. London: Mensell, 1994.

Campo, Juan Eduardo. "The Ends of Islamic Fundamentalism: Hegemonic Discourse and the Islamic Question in Egypt." *Contention: Debates in Society, Culture, and Science,* 4 (Spring 1995): 167–194.

Carré, Olivier. *Les Frères Musulmans: Egypte et Syrie: 1928–1982.* Paris: Gallimard, Dulliard, 1983.

Cassandra. "The Impending Crisis in Egypt." *The Middle East Journal,* 49 (Winter 1995): 9–27.

Cole, Juan R. *Colonialism and Revolution in the Middle East: Social and Cultural Origins of Egypt's 'Ubrabi Movement.* Princeton: Princeton University Press, 1993.

Davis, Joyce M. *Between Jihad and Salaam.* Basingstoke, UK: Macmillan, England, 1997.

Deeb, Marius. *Party Politics in Egypt: The Waft and Its Rivals 1919–1939.* London: Ithaca University Press, 1979.

Deng, Francis M. "Egypt's Dilemmas on the Sudan." *Middle East Policy,* 4 (September 1995): 50–56.

Dunn, Michael Collins. "Fundamentalism in Egypt." *Middle East Policy,* 2 (Summer 1993): 68–77.

Fandi, Mamoun. "Egypt's Islamic Group: Regional Revenge?" *The Middle East Journal,* 48 (Autumn 1994): 607–625.

Farah, Nadia. "Civil Society and Freedom of Research." *Academic Freedom in Africa.* Ed. Mahmood Mamdani and Mamandou Diouf, 262–273. [Dakar] CODESRIA, 1994.

Flores, Alexander. "Secularism, Integralism and Political Islam." *Middle East Report,* 183 (July-August 1993): 32–38.

Gallager, Nancy. "Islam vs. Secularism in Cairo: An Account of the Dar al-Hikma Debate." *Middle Eastern Studies,* 25 (1987): 208–215.

Gauch, Sarah. "Terror on the Nile (Analysis of Islamic Extremists' Attacks)." *Africa Report,* 38 (May-June 1993): 32–35.

Al-Ghazali, Shaykh Muhammad. *Azmat al-Shura fi al-Mujtama'at al-'Arabiyya wa al-Islamiyya.* Cairo: Dar al-Tawzi' wa al-Nashr al-Islamiyya, 1990.

———. *Al-Ta'assub wa al-Tasamuh bayna al-Masihiyya wa al-Islam.* 3rd ed. Cairo: Dar al-Fikr al-Haditha, 1965.

Goldberg, Ellis. "Smashing Idols and the State: The Protestant Ithaca and Egyptian Sunni Radicalism." *Comparative Studies in Society and History,* 33 (January 1991): 3–35.

Goldschmidt, Arthur Jr. *Historical Dictionary of Egypt.* Metuchen, NJ and London: Scarecrow Press, 1994.

Gordan, Joel. *Nasser's Blessed Movement: Egypt's Free Officers and the July Revolution.* Oxford: Oxford University Press, 1991.

Guenena, Nemat. *The 'Jihad': An Islamic Alternative.* Cairo: American University of Cairo, 1986.

Haddad, Yvonne Y. "Islamic 'Awakening' in Egypt." *Arab Studies Quarterly,* 9 (Summer 1987): 234–259.

———. "The Qur'anic Justification for an Islamic Revolution: The View of Sayyid Qutb." *The Middle East Journal,* 37 i (1983).

———. "Sayyid Qutb Ideologue of Islamic Revival." *Voices of Resurgent Islam.* Ed. John L. Esposito, 67–98. New York: Oxford University Press, 1983.

Hammoud, Miran. "Causes of Fundamentalist Popularity in Egypt." *Islamic Fundamentalism: Myths and Realities.* Ed. Ahmad S. Moussalli, 303–336. Reading, UK: Ithaca Press, 1998.

Harris, Christina P. *Nationalism and Revolution in Egypt: The Role of the Muslim Brotherhood.* Westport, CT: Hyperion Press, 1981.

Hatem, Mervat F. "Egyptian Discourses on Gender and Political Liberalization: Do Secularist and Islamist Views Really Differ?" *Middle East Journal,* 48 (1994): 661–676.

Holt, P. M., ed. *Political and Social Change in Modern Egypt.* London: Oxford University Press, 1968.

Hudaybi, Hasan. *Du'awat La Qudat.* Kuwait: IISFO, 1985.

Humphreys, R. Stephen. "Islam and Political Values in Saudi Arabia, Egypt and Syria." *Middle East Journal,* 30 (1979): 1–19.

Al-Husayni, Ishak M. *The Moslem Brethren: The Greatest of Modern Islamic Movements.* Beirut: Khayat's College Cooperative, 1956.

Hussain, Asaf. *Islamic Movements in Egypt, Pakistan and Iran: An Annotated Bibliography.* London: Mensell Publication, 1983.

Al-Huwaydi, Fahmi. *Al-Islam wa al-Dimocratiyya.* Cairo: Markaz al-Ahram li al-Tarjama wa al-Nashir, 1993.

———. *Al-Qur'an wa al-Sultan.* Beirut: Dar al-Shuruq, 1981.

Ibrahim, Saad Eddin. "Anatomy of Egypt's Militant Islamic Groups: Methodological Notes and Preliminary Findings." *International Journal of Middle East Studies,* 12 (1980): 423–453.

———. "Egypt's Islamic Activism in the 1980s." *Third World Quarterly,* 10 (April 1988): 632–657.

————. "Egypt's Islamic Militants." *MERIP Reports*, 103 (1982).

————. "An Islamic Alternative in Egypt: The Muslim Brotherhood and Sadat." *Arab Studies Quarterly*, 4 (Spring 1982).

————. "Islamic Militancy as a Social Movement: The Case of Two Groups in Egypt." *Islamic Resurgence in the Arab World.* Ed. Ali E. Hillal Dessouki, 117–137. New York: Praeger, 1982.

Hanafi, Hasan. *Al-Din wa al-Thawra fi Misr. Al-Harakat al-Diniyya al-Mu'asira.* Vol. 5. Cairo: Maktabat Madbuli, 1988.

Jameelah, Maryam. *Islam in Theory and Practice.* Lahore: Matbaat-ul-Maktab al-Ilmiyyah, 1973.

Jankowski, James P. *Egypt's Young Rebels, "Young Egypt": 1933–1952.* Stanford, CA: Hoover Institution Press, 1975.

Jansen, Johannes. *The Neglected Duty: The Creed of Sadat's Assassins and Islamic Resurgence in the Middle East.* New York: Macmillan, 1986.

Kaplan, Robert D. "Eaten from Within." *The Atlantic Monthly,* 274 (November 1994): 26–31.

Karam, Azza M. *Women, Islamisms and the State: Contemporary Feminisms in Egypt.* Basingstoke, UK: Macmillan, 1997.

Kepel, Gilles. "Islamists Versus the State in Egypt and Algeria." *Daedalus,* 124 (Summer 1995): 109–127.

————. *Muslim Extremism in Egypt: The Prophet and the Pharaoh.* Berkeley: University of California Press, 1984.

————. *The Prophet and the Pharaoh: Muslim Extremism in Contemporary Egypt.* London: Al-Saqi Books, 1985.

Khalafallah, Ahmad. *Al-Fikr al-Tarbawi lada Jama'at al-Ikhwan al-Muslimin.* Cairo: Maktabat Wahba, 1984.

Khalidi, Salah 'Abd al-Fattah. *Nazariyyat al-Taswir al-Fanni 'inda Sayyid Qutb.* Amman: Dar al-Furqan, 1983.

Kramer, Gudrun. "The Change of Paradigm: Political Pluralism in Contemporary Egypt." *Peuples Méditerranéens,* (October 1987-March 1988) 41–42.

————. "Liberalization and Democracy in the Arab World." *Middle East Report,* 144/33 i (1992): 22–24.

Mahfouz, Muhammad. *The Persecuted: Islamic Organizations in Egypt.* London: Riad El-Rayyes Books, 1988.

Malik, Hafeez. "Islamic Political Parties and Mass Politicisation." *Islam and the Modern Age,* 3 ii (1972): 26–64.

Malti-Douglas, Fedwa. "A Literature of Islamic Revival?: The Autobiography of Shaykh Kishk." *Cultural Transitions in the Middle East.* Ed. Serif Mardin, 116–129. Leiden: E. J. Brill, 1994.

Mashhur, Mustapha. *Zad 'Ala al-Tariq.* Kuwait: IIFSO, 1983.

Matthee, Rudi. "The Egyptian Opposition on the Iranian Revolution." *Shi'ism and Social Protest.* Eds. Juan R. I. Cole and Nikki R. Keddie, 247–274. New Haven, CT: Yale University Press, 1986.

Mattoon, Scott. "Egypt: A Sense of Foreboding." *The Middle East,* 219 (January 1993): 36–37.

Mitchell, Richard. *The Society of the Muslim Brothers.* London: Oxford University Press, 1969.

Moore, Clement Henry. *Images of Development: Egyptian Engineers in Search of Industry.* 2nd ed. Cairo: American University of Cairo, 1994.

Moussalli, Ahmad S. "Hasan al-Banna's Islamist Discourse on Constitutional Rule and Islamic State." *Journal of Islamic Studies,* 4 ii (1993): 161–174.

———. *Radical Islamic Fundamentalism: The Ideological and Political Discourse of Sayyid Qutb.* Beirut: American University of Beirut, 1992 and 1995.

———. "Sayyid Qutb: The Ideologist of Islamic Fundamentalism." *Al-Abhath,* 38 (1990): 42–73.

———. "Sayyid Qutb's View of Knowledge." *The American Journal of Islamic Social Sciences,* 7 iii (1990): 315–334.

———. "Two Tendencies in Modern Islamic Political Thought: Modernism and Fundamentalism." *Hamdard Islamicus,* 16 ii (1993): 51–78.

———. *Al-Usuliyya al-Islamiyya wa al-Nizam al-'Alami.* Beirut: Center for Strategic Studies, 1992.

Mubarak, Hisham. *Al-Irhabiyyun Qadimun!* Cairo: Kitab al-Mahrusa, 1995.

Muhammad, Muhsin. *Man Qatala Hasan al-Banna.* Cairo: Dar al-Shuruq, 1987.

Murphy, Caryle. "The Business of Political Change in Egypt." *Current History,* 94 (January 1995): 18–22.

Musallam, Adnan. "Sayyid Qutb and Social Justice, 1945–1948." *Journal of Islamic Studies,* 4 (1993): 52–70.

Mustafa, Hala. *Al-Dawla wa al-Harakat al-Islamiyya al-Mu'arida.* Cairo: Markaz al-Mahrusa, 1995.

———. "The Islamist Movements under Mubarak." *The Islamist Dilemma: The Political Role of Islamist Movements in the Contemporary Arab World.* Ed. Laura Guazzone, 161–185. Reading, UK: Ithaca Press, 1995.

Piscatori, James P. and R. K. Ramazani. "The Middle East." *Comparative Regional Systems.* Eds. W. J. Field and G. Boyd. New York: Pergamon Press, 1980.

Al-Nifaysi, 'Abd Allah Fahd, ed. *Al-Haraka al-Islamiyya: Ru'ya Mustaq-baliyya; Awraq fi al-Naqd al-Dhati.* Cairo: Maktabat Madbuli, 1989.

Peters, Rudolph. "Divine Law or Man-Made Law? Egypt and the Application of the Shari'a." *Arab Law Quarterly,* 3 iii (1988).

Qaradawi, Yusuf. *Awlawiyyat al-Haraka al-Islamiyya.* 13th ed. Beirut: Mu'assasat al-Risala, 1992.

———. *Al-Hall al-Islami Farida wa Darura.* Cairo: Maktabat Wahba, 1977.

———. *Al-Marja'iyya al-'Ulya fi al-Islam li al-Qur'an wa al-Sunna.* Beirut: Mu'assasat al-Risala, 1993.

———. *Al-Sahwa al-Islamiyya bayna al-Juhud wa al-Tatarruf.* Qatar: Matba'at al-Dawha al-Haditha, 1982.

———. *Wajib al-Shabab al-Muslim.* Beirut: Mu'assasat al-Risala, 1993.

Qutb, Muhammad. *Hal Nahnu Muslimun.* 3rd ed. Beirut: Dar al-Shuruq, 1991.

———. *Islam—The Misunderstood Religion.* 6th ed. Kuwait: IIFSO, 1986.

Qutb, Sayyid. *Al-'Adala al-Ijtima'iyya fi al-Islam.* 10th ed. Cairo: Dar al-Shuruq, 1980.

———. *Basic Principles of Islamic World View.* Berkeley: Mizan Press, 1993.

———. *Dirasat Islamiyya.* Beirut: Dar al-Suruq, 1978.

———. *Fi al-Tarikh: Fikra wa-Minhaj.* Cairo: Dar al-Shuruq, 1974.

———. *Fiqh al-Da'wa: Mawdu'at fi al-Da'wa wa al-Haraka.* Beirut: Mu'assasat al-Risala, 1970.

———. *Hadha al-Din.* 4th ed. Cairo: Maktabat Wahba, n.d.

———. *In the Shades of the Qur'an.* London: MWH, 1979.

———. *Islam and Universal Peace.* Indianapolis, IN: American Trust Publications, 1977.

———. *Islam: The Religion of the Future.* Chicago, IL: Kazi Publications, 1988.

———. *Al-Islam wa-Mushkilat al-Hadara.* 8th ed. Beirut: Dar al-Shuruq, 1983.

———. *Khasa'is al-Tasawwur al-Islami wa Muqawwimatu.* Cairo: 'Isa al-Halabi, n.d.

———. *Ma'alim fi al-Tariq.* 7th ed. Beirut: Dar al-Shuruq, 1980.

———. *Mar'rakat al-Islam wa al-Ra'simaliyya.* 4th ed. Beirut: Dar al-Shuruq, 1975.

———. *Muqawwimat al-Tasawwur al-Islami.* Cairo: Dar al-Shuruq, 1986.

———. *Al-Mustaqbal li-Hadha al-Din.* 2nd ed. Cairo: Maktabat Wahba, 1965.

————. *Nahwa Mujtama' Islami.* 6th ed. Beirut: Dar al-Shuruq, 1983.

————. *Al-Salam al-'Alami wa al-Islam.* 7th ed. Beirut: Dar al-Shuruq, 1983.

————. *Al-Shahada wa al-Istishhad fi Dhil al-Qur'an li al-Shaykh Sayyid Qutb.* Cairo: Maktabat al-Turath al-Islami, 1994.

————. *Tafsir Ayat al-Riba.* Beirut: Dar al-Shuruq, 1970.

————. *Tafsir Surat al-Shura.* Beirut: Dar al-Shuruq, n.d.

Ramadan, Abdel Azim. "Fundamentalist Influence in Egypt: The Strategies of the Muslim Brotherhood and the Takfir Groups." *Fundamentalisms and the State: Remaking Polities, Economies, and Militance.* Eds. Martin E. Marty and R. Scott Appleby, 152–183. Chicago, IL: University of Chicago Press, 1993.

————. *Al-Ikhwan al-Muslimin wa al-Tanzim al-Sirri.* Cairo: Al-Hay'a al-Misriyya al-'Amma li al-Kitab, 1993.

Reed, Stanley. "The Battle for Egypt." *Foreign Affairs,* 72 (September-October 1993): 94–107.

Rizq, Jabir. *Al-Asrar al-Haqiqiyya li-Ightiyal al-Imam Hasan al-Banna.* Alexandria, Egypt: Dar al-Da'wa, 1984.

Rubin, Barry. *Islamic Fundamentalism in Egyptian Politics.* New York: St. Martin's Press, 1990.

Saeed, Javaid. *Islam and Modernization: A Comparative Analysis of Pakistan, Egypt, and Turkey.* Westport, CT: Praeger, 1994.

Safran, Nadav. *Egypt in Search of Political Identity.* Cambridge, MA: Harvard University Press, 1961.

Sagiv, David. "Judge Ashmawi and Militant Islam in Egypt." *Middle Eastern Studies,* 28 (July 1992): 531–546.

Sa'id, Rif 'at. *Hasan al-Banna: Mu'assis Harakat al-Ikhwan al-Muslimin.* 4th ed. Beirut: Dar al-Tali'a, 1986.

Samman, Muhammad. *Hasan al-Banna al-Rajul wa al-Fikra.* Tunis: Dar Bu Salamah, 1982.

Al-Sayyid Marsot, Afaf Lutfi. *Egypt's Liberal Experiment, 1922–1936.* Berkeley: University of California Press, 1983.

————. *A Short History of Modern Egypt.* Cambridge, UK: Cambridge University Press, 1985.

Siddiq, Ali. *Al-Ikhwan al-Muslimun bayna Irhab Faruq wa 'Abd al-Nasir.* Cairo: Dar al-I'tisam, 1987.

Sivan, Emmanuel. "The Islamic Republic of Egypt." *Orbis,* 31 (1987): 43–53.

Smith, Charles D. *Islam and the Search for Social Order in Modern Egypt.* Albany: State University of New York Press, 1983.

Sonbol, Amira El-Azhary. "Egypt." *The Politics of Islamic Revivalism: Diversity and Unity.* Ed. Shireen T. Hunter, 23–38. Bloomington: Indiana University Press, 1988.

Sullivan, Denis J. *Private Voluntary Organization in Egypt: Islamic Development, Private Initiative and State Control.* Gainesville: University Press of Florida, 1994.

Vandenbroucke, Lucien S. "Why Allah's Zealots? A Study of the Causes of Islamic Fundamentalism in Egypt and Saudi Arabia." *Middle East Review,* 16 (Fall 1983): 30–41.

Vatikiotis, P. J. *The History of Egypt.* Baltimore, MD: Johns Hopkins University Press, 1980.

Vogt, Kari. "Militant Islam in Egypt: A Survey." *Egypt under Pressure.* Ed. Marianne Laanatza and others, 27–43. Uppsala, Sweden: Scandinavian Institute of African Studies, 1986.

Voll, John O. "Fundamentalism in the Sunni Arab World: Egypt and the Sudan." *Fundamentalisms Observed.* Eds. Martin E. Marty and R. Scott Appleby, 345–402. Chicago, IL: University of Chicago Press, 1991.

Warburg, Gabriel R. *Islam, Nationalism & Radicalism in Egypt and the Sudan.* New York: Greenwood Press, 1983.

Waterbury, John. *The Egypt of Nasser and Sadat: The Political Economy of Two Regimes.* Princeton: Princeton University Press, 1983.

———. *Exposed to Innumerable Delusions: Public Enterprise and State Power in Egypt, India, Mexico, and Turkey.* Cambridge, UK: Cambridge University Press, 1993.

"Wisdom of the Mosque (Islamic Fundamentalism in Egypt.)." *Index on Censorship,* 23 (May-June 1994): 122–126.

Yasin, 'Abd al-Jawad. *Muqaddima fi Fiqh al-Jahiliyya al-Mu'asira.* Cairo: Al-Zahra' li al-Il'am al-'Arabi, 1986.

Yusuf, al-Sayyid. *Al-Ikhwan al-Muslimun: Hal Hiya Sahwa Islamiyya?* 4 vols. Cairo: Kitab al-Mahrusa, 1994–95.

Zubaida, Sami. "The Quest for the Islamic State: Islamic Fundamentalism in Egypt and Iran." *Studies in Religious Fundamentalism.* Ed. Lionel Kaplan, 25–50. Albany: State University of New York Press, 1987.

Iraq

Baram, Amatzia. "From Radicalism to Radical Pragmatism: The Shi'ite Fundamentalist Opposition Movements in Iraq." *Islamic Fundamentalisms and the Gulf Crisis.* Ed. James Piscatori, 28–50. Chicago, IL: American Academy of Arts and Sciences, 1991.

————. "Two Roads to revolutionary Shi'ite Fundamentalism in Iraq." *Accounting for Fundamentalisms: The Dynamic Character of Movements.* Eds. Martin E. Marty and R. Scott Appleby, 531–589. Chicago, IL: University of Chicago Press, 1994.

Batatu, Hanna. "Iraq's Underground Shi'a Movements: Characteristics, Causes and Prospects." *The Middle East Journal,* 35 (Autumn 1981): 578–594.

————. "Shi'i Organizations in Iraq: Al-Da'wah al-Islamiyah and al-Mujahidin." *Shi'ism and Social Protest.* Eds. Juan R. I. Cole and Nikki R. Keddie, 179–200. New Haven, CT: Yale University Press, 1986.

Farouk-Sluglett, Marion, and Peter Sluglett. *Iraq since 1958: From Revolution to Dictatorship.* London: I. B. Tauris, 1990.

Hudson, Michael. "The Islamic Factor in Syrian and Iraqi Politics." *Islam in the Political Process.* Ed. James Piscatori. New York: Cambridge University Press, 1983.

Kedourie, Elie. "The Iraqi Shi'is and Their Fate." *Shi'ism, Resistance, and Revolution.* Ed. Martin Kramer, 135–157. Boulder, CO: Westview Press, 1987.

Khadduri, Majid. *Socialist Iraq.* Washington, DC: Middle East Institute, 1978.

Makiya, Kanan. *Cruelty and Silence: War, Tyranny and Uprising in the Arab World.* New York: Norton, 1992.

Mallat, Chibli. "Religious Militancy in Contemporary Iraq: Muhammad Baqer as-Sadr and the Sunni-Shia Paradigm." *Third World Quarterly,* 10 (April 1988): 699–729.

————. *The Renewal of Islamic Law: Muhammad Baqer as-Sadr, Najaf and the Shi'i International.* Cambridge, UK: Cambridge University Press, 1993.

Marr, Phebe. *The Modern History of Iraq.* Boulder, CO: Westview Press, 1985.

Al-Mudarrisi, Hadi. *Al-Islam wa al-Idiolojiyyat al-Munawi'a ila Ayn.* Beirut: Mu'assasat al-Balagh, 1987.

————. *Li alla Yakun Sidam Hadarat.* Beirut: Dar al-Jadid, 1996.

Robins, Philip. "Iraq: Revolutionary Threats and Regime Responses." *The Iranian Revolution: Its Global Impact.* Ed. John L. Esposito, 83–98. Miami: Florida International University Press, 1990.

Sachedina, Abdulaziz A. "Activist Shi'ism in Iran, Iraq, and Lebanon." *Fundamentalisms Observed.* Eds. Martin E. Marty and R. Scott Appleby, 403–456. Chicago, IL: University of Chicago Press, 1991.

Shariati, Ali. *Marxism and Other Western Fallacies: An Islamic Critique.* Trans. R. Campbell. Berkeley: Mizan Press, 1980.

————. *On the Sociology of Islam.* Trans. Hamid Algar. Berkeley: Mizan Press, 1979.

Simon, Reeva S. *Iraq between the Two World Wars: The Creation and Implementation of a Nationalist Ideology.* New York: Columbia University Press, 1986.

Sluglett, Peter. *Britain in Iraq: 1914–1932.* Oxford: Oxford University Press, 1976.

Wiley, Joyce. *The Islamic Movement of Iraqi Shi'as.* Boulder, CO: Lynne Rienner Publishers, 1992.

Jordan

Abidi, Aqil Hyder Hasan. *Jordan: A Political Study, 1948–1954.* London: Asia Publishing House, 1965.

Amawi, Abla. "Democracy Dilemmas in Jordan." *Middle East Report,* 174 (January-February 1992): 26–29.

Aruri, Naseer H. *Jordan: A Study in Political Development (1932–1965).* The Hague, Netherlands: Martinus Nijhoff, 1972.

Ayyad, Ranad al-Khatib. *Al-Tayyarat al-Siyasiyya fi al-Urdun.* Amman: n. p., 1991.

Barghouty, Iyad. "The Islamists in Jordan and the Palestinian Occupied Territories." *The Islamist Dilemma: The Political Role of Islamist Movements in the Contemporary Arab World.* Ed. Laura Guazzone, 129–159. Reading, UK: Ithaca Press, 1995.

Brand, Laurie A. *Jordan's Inter-Arab Relations: The Political Economy of Alliance Making.* New York: Columbia University Press, 1994.

Dunn, Collins M. "Islamist Parties in Democratizing States: A Look at Jordan and Yemen." *Middle East Policy,* 2 ii (1993): 16–27.

Gharayba, Ibrahim. *Jama'at al-Ikhwan al-Muslimin fi al-Urdun: 1946–1996.* Amman: Dar al-Sindibad, 1997.

Gubser, Peter. *Historical Dictionary of the Hashemite Kingdom of Jordan.* Metuchen, NJ and London: Scarecrow Press, 1991.

Hourani, Hani, and others. *Islamic Action Party.* Amman: Al-Urdun al-Jadid Research Center, 1993.

Jordanian Political Parties, Civil Society and Political Life in Jordan. Amman: New Jordan Research Center, 1993.

Al-Kaylani, Musa Zayd, ed. *Al-Haraka al-Islamiyya fi al-Urdun.* Amman: Dar al-Bashir, 1990.

Madi, Munib, and Sulayman Musa. *Ta rikh al-Urdun fi al-Qarn al-'Ishrin.* Amman: 1991.

"Malaf al-Ahzab al-Siyasiyya fi al-Urdun." *Al-Urdun al-Jadid* (Fall 1990): 17–18.

Milton-Edwards, Beverley. "A Temporary Alliance with the Crown: The Islamic Response in Jordan." *Islamic Fundamentalisms and the Gulf Crisis.* Ed. James Piscatori, 88–108. Chicago, IL: American Academy of Arts and Sciences, 1991.

Moussalli, Ahmad S. "Discourses on Human Rights and Pluralistic Democracy." *Islam in a Changing World: Europe and the Middle East.* Eds. A. Herichow and J. B. Simonson. Surrey, UK: Curzon Press, 1997.

———. "Islamic Fundamentalism and Other Monotheistic Religions." *Religious Mutual Perceptions.* Ed. Jacque Waardenburgh. Lausanne, Switzerland: University of Lausanne, 1998.

———. "Islamic Fundamentalism and Pluralism." *Euro-Islam.* Ed. Thomas Lunden. Stockholm: Swedish Institute, 1996.

———. "Islamism and Modernity or Modernization of Islam." *The Future of Cosmopolitanism in the Middle East.* Amsterdam: Cultural Foundation, University of Amsterdam, 1998.

———. "Modern Islamic Fundamentalist Discourses on Civil Society, Pluralism and Democracy." *Civil Society in the Middle East.* Ed. Augustus Richard Norton, 79–119. Leiden: E. J. Brill, 1995.

———. "Modern Islamic Fundamentalist Discourses on Civil Society, Pluralism and Democracy." *Toward Civil Society in the Middle East.* Ed. Jillian Schwedler. Boulder, CO: Lynne Rienner Publishers, 1995.

Al-Nabahani, Taqiy al-Din. *Nizam al-Hukm.* Jerusalem: Matba'at al-Thiryan, 1952.

———. *Al-Takatul al-Hizbi.* 2nd ed. Jerusalem: n.p., 1953.

Piro, Timothy. "Parliament, Politics, and Pluralism in Jordan: Trends at a Difficult Time." *Middle East Insight,* 8 i (July-October 1992): 39–44.

Rashid, Kamal. "Al-Islamiyyun wa al-Nizam fi al-Urdun." *Filastiyn al-Muslima* 10 (October 1992).

Rath, K. "The Process of Democratization in Jordan." *Middle Eastern Studies,* 30 iii (1994): 530–557.

Roberts, John. "Prospects for Democracy in Jordan." *Arab Studies Quarterly,* 13 (Summer-Fall 1991): 119–138.

Robins, Philip. "Jordan's Elections: A New Era?" *Middle East Report,* (May-August 1990): 164–165.

Robinson, Glenn E. "Islamists under Liberalization in Jordan." *Islamic Fundamentalism: Myths and Realities.* Ed. Ahmad S. Moussalli, 169–196. Reading, UK: Ithaca Press, 1998.

Satloff, Robert B. *From Abdallah to Hussein: Jordan in Transition.* Oxford: Oxford University Press, 1994.

————. "Jordan Looks Inward." *Current History*, 89 (February 1990): 57–60 .

————. *They Cannot Stop Our Tongues: Islamic Activism in Jordan*. Washington, DC: Washington Institute for Near East Policy, 1988.

Shafiq, Munir. "Awlawiyyat Amam al-Ijtihad wa al-Tajdid." *Al-Ijtihad wa Tajdid fi al-Fikr al-Islami al-Mu'asir*. Malta: Center for the Studies of the Muslim World, 1991.

————. *Al-Fikr al-Islami al-Mu'asir wa al-Tahaddiyat*. Beirut: Al-Nashir, 1991.

————. *Al-Islam wa Muwajahat al-Dawla al-Haditha*. 3rd ed. Beirut: Al-Nashir, 1992.

————. *Al-Nizam al-Dawli al-Jadid wa Khiyar al-Muwajaha*. Beirut: Al-Nashir, 1992.

Taji-Farouki, Suha. "A Case-Study in Contemporary Political Islam and the Palestine Question: The Perspective of Hizb al-Tahrir." *Studies in Muslim-Jewish Relations*, 2 (1995): 35–58.

————. "From Madrid to Washington: Palestinian Islamist Response to Israeli-Palestinian Peace Settlement." *World Faiths Encounter*, 9 (November 1994): 49–58.

————. *A Fundamental Quest: Hizb al-Tahrir and the Search for the Islamic Caliphate*. London: Grey Seal, 1996.

————. "Hizb al-Tahrir." *Encyclopedia of the Modern Islamic World*. New York: Oxford University Press, 1995.

————. "Islamic Discourse and Modern Political Methods: An Analysis of al-Nabahani's Reading of the Canonical Text Sources of Islam." *American Journal of Islamic Social Sciences*, 11 iii (Fall 1994): 365–393.

————. "Islamic State—Theories and Contemporary Realities." *Islamic Fundamentalism in Perspective*. Eds. Sid Ahmad and Ehteshemi. Boulder, CO: Westview Press, 1995.

Al-Talha, Zaki. *Al-Islam al-Siyasi fi al-Urdun wa al-Dimocratiyya*. Amman: Al-Urdun al-Jadid Research Center, 1996.

Tal, Lawrence. "Is Jordan Doomed? The Israeli-PLO Accord." *Foreign Affairs*, 72 (November-December 1993): 45–58.

————. "Dealing with Radical Islam: The Case of Jordan." *Survival*, 37 (Autumn 1995): 139–156.

Lebanon

Aboujaoude, Joseph. *Les partis politiques au Liban*. Kaslik, Lebanon: Bibliothéque de l'Université Saint-Esprit, 1985.

Abu Khalil, As'ad. "Ideology and Practice of Hizballah in Lebanon: Islamization of Leninist Organizational Principles." *Middle Eastern Studies* 27 (July 1991): 390–403.

———. "Lebanon." *Political Parties of the Middle East and North Africa.* Ed. F. Tachau, 297–368. London: Mansell, 1994.

Ajami, Fouad. *The Vanished Imam: Musa al Sadr and the Shia of Lebanon.* Ithaca, NY: Cornell University Press, 1986.

Allah, A. "The Discovery of Lebanese Shi'a." *Third World Quarterly,* 10 (April 1988): 1047–1051.

———. "The Islamic Resistance in Lebanon and the Palestinian Uprising: The Islamic Jihad Perspective." *Middle East Insight,* 5 (1988): 4–12.

Bailey, Clinton. "Lebanon's Shi'is after the 1982 War." *Shi'ism, Resistance, and Revolution.* Ed. Martin Kramer, 219–235. Boulder, CO: Westview Press, 1987.

Cobban, Helena. "The Growth of Shi'i Power in Lebanon and Its Implications for the Future." *Shi'ism and Social Protest.* Ed. J. R. I. Cole and N. R. Keddie, 137–155. New Haven, CT: Yale University Press, 1986.

Deeb, Marius. *Militant Islamic Movements in Lebanon: Origin, Social Basis and Ideology.* Washington, DC: Center for Contemporary Arab Studies, Georgetown University, 1986.

———. "Shia Movements in Lebanon: Their Formation, Ideology, Social Basis, and Links with Iran and Syria." *Third World Quarterly,* 10 (April 1988): 683–698.

Dinnawi, Muhammad 'Ali. *Muqaddimat fi Fahm al-Hadara al-Islamiyya.* Kuwait: IIFSO, 1983.

Fadlallah, Sayyid Muhammad Hussein. *Fiqh al-Hayat.* Beirut: Mu'assasat al-'Arif li al-Matbu'at, 1997.

———. *Al-Islam wa Filistin.* Beirut: Mu'assasat al-Dirasat al-Filistiniyya, 1995.

———. *Al-Islam wa Muntiq al-Quwwa.* Beirut: Al-Dar al-Islamiyya, 1986.

———. *The Islamic Movement: Problems and Causes.* Beirut: Dar al-Malak, 1991.

———. *Ma' al-Hikma fi Khatt al-Islam.* Beirut: Mu'assasat al-Wafa', 1985.

Al-Habashi, Shaykh Abd Allah. *Sarih al-Bayan.* Beirut: Islamic Studies and Research Section, Jami'yyat al-Mashari' al-Khayriyya al-Islamiyya, 1990.

Hamzeh, A. Nizar. "The Future of Islamic Movements in Lebanon." *Islamic Fundamentalism: Myths and Realities.* Ed. Ahmad S. Moussalli, 249–274. Reading, UK: Ithaca Press, 1998.

———. "Lebanon's Hizbullah: From Islamic Revolution to Parliamentary Accommodation." *Third World Quarterly,* 14 ii (1993): 321–337.

Hamzeh, A. Nizar, and H. Dekmejian. "The Islamic Spectrum of Lebanese Politics." *Journal of South Asian and Middle Eastern Studies* 15, 3 (1993): 25–42.

———. "A Sufi Response to Political Islamism: Al-Ahbash of Lebanon." *International Journal of Middle East Studies,* 28 (May 1996): 217–229.

Hanf, Theodor. *Coexistence in Wartime Lebanon: Decline of a State and Rise of a Nation.* London: Centre for Lebanese Studies and I. B. Tauris, 1993.

Hudson, Michael C. *The Precarious Republic.* New York: Random House, 1972.

Jaber, Hala. *Hezbollah: Born with a Vengence.* New York: Columbia University Press, 1997.

Khashan, Hilal. "The Development Programs of Islamic Fundamentalist Groups in Lebanon as a Source of Popular Legitimation." *Islam and the Modern Age,* 25 ii (1994): 116–142.

———. "The Development Programmes of Islamic Fundamentalist Groups in Lebanon as a Source for Popular Legitimation." *Islamic Fundamentalism: Myths and Realities.* Ed. Ahmad S. Moussalli, 221–248. Reading, UK: Ithaca Press, 1998.

Kramer, Martin. "Hizbullah: The Calculus of Jihad." *Fundamentalisms and the State: Remaking Polities, Economies, and Militance.* Eds. Martin E. Marty and R. Scott Appleby, 539–556. Chicago, IL: University of Chicago Press, 1993.

———. *The Moral Logic of Hizballah.* Occasional Paper, no. 101. Tel Aviv: The Dayan Center for Middle Eastern and African Studies, The Shiloah Institute, Tel Aviv University, 1987.

Mallat, Chibli. *Shi'i Thought from the South of Lebanon.* Oxford: Centre for Lebanese Studies, 1988.

Miller, Judith. "Faces of Fundamentalism: Hassan al-Turabi and Muhammad Fadlallah." *Foreign Affairs,* 73 (November-December 1994): 123–142.

Moussalli, Ahmad S. "Islamist Perspectives of Regime Political Response: The Cases of Lebanon and Palestine." *Arab Studies Quarterly,* 18 iii (Summer 1996): 53–63.

Norton, Augustus Richard. *Amal and the Shia: Struggle for the Soul of Lebanon.* Austin: University of Texas Press, 1987.

———. "Changing Actors and Leadership among the Shiites of Lebanon." *Annals of the American Academy of Political and Social Sciences,* 482 (November 1985): 109–121.

————. "Lebanon: The Internal Conflict and the Iranian Connection." *The Iranian Revolution: Its Global Impact.* Ed. John L. Esposito, 116–136. Miami: Florida International University Press, 1990.

————. "The Origins and Resurgence of Amal." *Shi'ism, Resistance, and Revolution.* Ed. Martin Kramer, 203–218. Boulder, CO: Westview Press, 1987.

————. "Shi'ism and Social Protest in Lebanon." *Shi'ism and Social Protest.* Eds. Juan R. I. Cole and Nikki R. Keddie, 156–178. New Haven, CT: Yale University Press, 1986.

Olmert, Joseph. "The Shi'is and the Lebanese State." *Shi'ism, Resistance, and Revolution.* Ed. Martin Kramer, 189–201. Boulder, CO: Westview Press, 1987.

Perthes, Volker. "Problems with Peace: Post-War Politics and Parliamentary Elections in Lebanon." *Orient,* 33 iii (1992).

Ranstrop, M. *Hizballah in Lebanon: The Politics of the Western Hostage Crisis.* London: Macmillan, 1996.

Sachedina, Abdulaziz A. "Activist Shi'ism in Iran, Iraq, and Lebanon." *Fundamentalisms Observed.* Eds. Martin E. Marty and R. Scott Appleby, 403–456. Chicago, IL: University of Chicago Press, 1991.

Shrara, Wadah. *Dawlat Hizballah: Lubnan Mujtama'an Islamiyyan.* 2nd ed. Beirut: Dar al-Nahar li al-Nashr, 1997.

Shruru, Fadl. *Al-Ahzab wa al-Tandhimat wa al-Qiwa al-Siyasiyya fi Lubnan, 1930–1980.* Beirut: Dar al-Masira, 1981.

Srur, Ali H. *Al-'Alama Fadlallah and the Challenge of the Forbidden.* Beirut: Public Company for Development Services, 1992.

Suleiman, Michael. *Political Parties in Lebanon: The Challenge of a Fragmented Political Culture.* Ithaca, NY: Cornell University Press, 1967.

Yakan, Fathi. *Abjadiyyat al-Tasawwur al-Haraki li al-'Amal al-Islami.* 11th ed. Beirut: Mu'assasat al-Risala, 1993.

————. *Harakat wa Madhahib fi Mizan al-Islam.* 10th ed. Beirut: Mu'assasat al-Risala, 1992.

————. *Al-Mawsu'a Al-Harakiyya.* Amman: Dar al-Bashir, 1983.

————. *Nahwa Haraka Islamiyya 'Alamiyya.* 10th ed. Beirut: Mu'assasat al-Risala, 1993.

————. *Problems Faced by the Da'wa and the Da'iya.* Kuwait: IIFSO, 1985.

Libya

Abdrabboh, Bob, ed. *Libya in the 1980s: Challenges and Changes.* Washington, DC: International Economics and Research, 1985.

Ahmida, Ali Abdullatif. *The Making of Modern Libya: State Formation, Colonization, and Resistance 1830–1932.* Albany: State University of New York, 1994.

Allen, J. A. *Libya since Independence: Economic and Political Development.* London: Croom Helm, 1982.

Anderson, Lisa. "Qadhdhafi and His Opposition." *Middle East Journal,* 40 ii (Spring 1986): 225–237.

———. *The State and Social Transformation in Tunisia and Libya, 1830–1980.* Princeton: Princeton University Press, 1986.

———. "Tunisia and Libya: Responses to the Islamic Impulse." *The Iranian Revolution: Its Global Impact.* Ed. John L. Esposito, 157–175. Miami: Florida International University Press, 1990.

Christman, Henry M., ed. *Qaddafi's Green Book: An Unauthorized Edition.* Buffalo, NY: Prometheus Books, 1988.

Cooley, John K. *Libyan Sandstorm: The Complete Account of Qaddafi's Revolution.* New York: Holt, Rinehart and Winston, 1982.

Davis, John. *Libyan Politics: Tribe and Revolution.* London: I. B. Tauris, 1987.

Deeb, M. K. "Libya: Internal Developments and Regional Politics." *The Middle East: Annual Issues and Events.* Ed. D. V. Partinton, vol. 4. Boston: G. K. Hall, 1985.

———. "Libya." *Political Parties of the Middle East and North Africa.* Ed. F. Tachau, 369–379. London: Mensell, 1994.

———. "Militant Islam and Its Critics: The Case of Libya." *Islamism and Secularism in North Africa.* Ed. J. Ruedy. Basingstoke, UK: Macmillan, 1994.

———. "Radical Political Ideologies and Concepts of Property in Libya and South Yemen." *Middle East Journal,* 40 iii (Summer 1986): 445–461.

Deeb, Marius, and Mary-Jane Deeb. *Libya since the Revolution: Aspects of Social and Political Development.* New York: Praeger, 1982.

Deeb, Mary-Jane. "New Thinking in Libya." *Current History,* 89 (April 1990): 149–152 and 177–178.

Harris, Lillian Craig. *Libya: Qadhafi's Revolution and the Modern State.* Boulder, CO: Westview Press, 1986.

Joffe, E. G. H., and K. S. McLachlan, eds. *Social and Economic Development of Libya.* Wesbach, UK: Middle East and North Africa Studies Press, 1982.

Khadduri, Majid. *Modern Libya: A Study in Political Development.* Baltimore, MD: Johns Hopkins University Press, 1968.

Kucukcan, Talip. "Some Reflections on the Wahhabiya and the Sanusiya Movements: A Comparative Approach." *The Islamic Quarterly,* 37 iv (1993): 237–251.

Lawless, Richard. *Libya.* World Bibliographical Series, vol. 79. Oxford: CLIO Press, 1987.

Penneli, R. "Libya and Morocco: Consensus on the Past." *North Africa: Nation State, and Region.* Ed. G. Goffe, 203–220. London: Routledge, 1993.

Ronen, Y. "Libya (al-Jumahiriyya al-'Arabiyya al-Libiyya al-Sha'biyya al-Ishtrakiyya al-'Uzma)." *Middle East Contemporary Survey, 15/1991* (1993): 577–594.

Sammut, Dennis. "Libya and the Islamic Challenge." *The World Today,* 50 (October 1994): 198–200.

St. John, Ronald Bruce. *Historical Dictionary of Libya.* 2nd ed. Lanham, MD, and London: Scarecrow Press, 1998.

Zartman, I. William. *Government and Politics in North Africa.* New York: Frederick A. Praeger, 1963.

Mauritania

Barron, M. "Mauritania." *Middle East Review,* 20/1995 (1994): 65–67.

Cronje, S. "Mauritania." *Middle East Review,* 19/1993–94 (1993): 66–68.

Diallo, Garba. *Mauritania, the Other Apartheid.* Uppsala, Sweden: Nordiska Afrikainstitutet, 1993.

Morocco

Ashford, Douglas E. *Political Change in Morocco.* Princeton: Princeton University Press, 1961.

Brace, R. M. *Morocco, Algeria, Tunisia.* Englewood Cliffs, NJ: Prentice-Hall, 1964.

Burgat, François. *The Islamic Movement in North Africa.* Austin: Center for Middle Eastern Studies, University of Texas, 1993.

Deeb, M.J. "Islam and the State in Algeria and Morocco: A Dialectical Model." *Islamism and Secularism in North Africa.* Ed. J. Ruedy. Basingstoke, UK: Macmillan, 1994.

East, R., and T. Joseph. *Political Parties of Africa and the Middle East: A Reference Guide.* Harlow, UK: Longman, 1993.

Eickelman, Dale F. *Knowledge and Power in Morocco: The Education of a Twentieth-Century Notable.* Princeton: Princeton University Press, 1985.

————. *Moroccan Islam: Tradition and Society in a Pilgrimage Center.* Austin: University of Texas Press, 1976.

————. "Re-Imaging Religion and Politics: Moroccan Elections in the 1990s." *Islamism and Secularism in North Africa.* Ed. J. Ruedy. Basingstoke, UK: Macmillan, 1994.

Eickelman, Dale, and James Piscatori, eds. *Muslim Travellers: Pilgrimage, Migration, and the Religious Imagination.* London: Routledge, 1990.

Entelis, John P. *Comparative Politics of North Africa: Algeria, Morocco, and Tunisia.* Syracuse, NY: Syracuse University Press, 1980.

————. *Culture and Counterculture in Moroccan Politics.* Boulder, CO: Westview Press, 1989.

Farley, Jonathan. "The Maghreb's Islamic Challenge." *The World Today,* 47 (August-September 1991): 148–151.

Haireche, Abdel-Kader, and Azzedine Layachi. "National Development and Political Protest: Islamists in the Maghreb Countries." *Arab Studies Quarterly,* 14 (Spring-Summer 1992): 69–92.

Halpern, Manfred. *The Politics of Change in the Middle East and North Africa.* 4th ed. Princeton: Princeton University Press, 1970.

Hermassi, Mohamed Abdelbaki. *Leadership and National Development in North Africa.* Berkeley: University of California Press, 1970.

————. *Society and State in the Arab Maghreb.* Beirut: Center for Arab Unity Studies, 1987.

Hermida, Alfred. "The State and Islam." *Africa Report,* 39 (September-October 1994): 55–58.

Hiskett, Marvyn. *The Course of Islam in Africa.* Edinburgh: Edinburgh University Press, 1994.

Moore, Clement Henry. "Political Parties." *Polity and Society in Contemporary North Africa.* Eds. I. William Zartman and William Mark Habeeb, 42–67. Boulder, CO: Westview Press, 1993.

————. *Politics in North Africa: Algeria, Morocco, and Tunisia.* Boston: Little, Brown, 1970.

Munson, Henry Jr. "Morocco's Fundamentalists." *Government and Opposition,* 26 (Summer 1991): 331–344.

————. *Religion and Power in Morocco.* New Haven, CT: Yale University Press, 1993.

————. "The Social Base of Islamic Militancy in Morocco." *The Middle East Journal* 40 (Spring 1986): 267–284.

Nelson, Harold. D., ed. *Morocco: A Country Study.* 5th ed. Washington, DC: (Government Printing Office for Foreign Area Studies, American University), 1985.

Parker, Richard B. *North Africa: Regional Tensions and Strategic Concerns.* New York: Praeger, 1984.

Penneli, R. "Libya and Morocco: Consensus on the Past." *North Africa: Nation, State, and Region.* Ed. G. Goffe, 203–220. London: Routledge, 1993.

Sara, Fayiz. *Al-Haraka al-Islamiyya fi al-Magrib al-'Arabi.* Beirut: Markaz al-Dirasat al-Istratijiyya, 1995.

Shahin, Emad Eldin. "Secularism and Nationalism: The Political Discourse of 'Abd al-Salam Yassin." *Islam and Secularism in North Africa.* Ed. J. Ruedy. Basingstoke, UK: Macmillan, 1994.

Waterbury, John. *The Commander of the Faithful: The Moroccan Political Elite—A Study in Segmented Politics.* New York: Columbia University Press, 1970.

Zartman, I. William. "Opposition as Support of the State," *The Arab State.* Ed. Giacomo Luciani. Berkeley: University Press of California, 1990.

———. *The Political Economy of Morocco.* New York: Praeger, 1987.

Palestine

Abu Amr, Ziad. "*Hamas*: A Historical and Political Background." *Journal of Palestine Studies,* 12 (Winter 1993).

———. *Islamic Fundamentalism in the West Bank and Gaza: Muslim Brotherhood and Islamic Jihad.* Bloomington: Indiana University Press, 1994.

Abu Ghunaymah, Zayid. *Al-Haraka al-Islamiyya wa Qadiyyat Filistiyn.* Amman: Dar al-Furqan, 1985.

Al-'Asli, Bassam. *Thawrat 'Izz al-Din al-Qassam.* Beirut: Al-Nashir, 1991.

Badawi, M. A. Zaki. *The Reformers of Egypt.* London: Croom Helm, 1967.

Al-Balihi, Ibrahim Ibn 'Abd al-Rahman. *Sayyid Qutb wa-Turathuhu al-Adabi wa-al-Fikri.* Riyad: n.p., 1972.

Barghouty, Iyad. "The Islamists in Jordan and the Palestinian Occupied Territories." *The Islamist Dilemma: The Political Role of Islamist Movements in the Contemporary Arab World.* Ed. Laura Guazzone, 129–159. Reading, UK: Ithaca Press, 1995.

Brand, Laurie A. *Palestinians in the Arab World: Institution Building and the Search for State.* Boulder, CO: Lynne Rienner Publishers, 1988.

Budeiri, Musa K. "The Nationalist Dimension of Islamic Movements in Palestinian Politics." *Journal of Palestine Studies,* 24 (Spring 1995): 89–95.

Bulliet, Richard W. "The Israeli-PLO Accord: The Future of the Islamic Movement." *Foreign Affairs,* 72 (November-December 1993): 38–44.

Cohen, Amnon. *Political Parties in the West Bank under the Jordanian Regime, 1949–1967.* Ithaca, NY: Cornell University Press, 1982.

Haddad, Yvonne Y. "Islamists and the 'Problem of Israel': The 1967 Awakening." *The Middle East Journal,* 46 (Spring 1992): 266–285.

Al-Harub, Khalid. *Hamas: Al-Fikr wa al-Mumarasa.* Beirut: Mu'assasat al-Dirasat al-Falastiniyya, 1996.

Al-Hout, Bayan Nuwayhid. *Al-Shaykh al-Mujahid 'Izz al-Din al-Qassam.* Beirut: Dar al-Istiqlal, 1987.

Israeli, Raphael. *Fundamentalist Islam and Israel: Essays in Interpretation.* Lanham, MD: University Press of America, 1993.

———. *Muslim Fundamentalism in Israel.* London: Brassey's, 1993.

Jensen, Michael Irving. "Islamism and Civil Society in the Gaza Strip." *Islamic Fundamentalism: Myths and Realities.* Ed. Ahmad S. Moussalli, 197–220. Reading, UK: Ithaca Press, 1998.

Jubran, Michel, and Laura Drake. "The Islamic Fundamentalist Movement in the West Bank and Gaza Strip." *Middle East Policy,* 2 (Spring 1993): 1–15.

Kjorlien, Michele L. "Hamas: In Theory and Practice." *The Arab Studies Journal,* 1 (Fall 1993): 4–7.

Kodmani-Darwish, Bassma. "Arafat and the Islamists: Conflict or Cooperation?" *Current History,* 95 (January 1996): 28–32.

Lee, Jeffrey. "Islam Cements the Bonds of Resistance (Hamas Islamist Resistance Movement)." *The Middle East,* 224 (June 1993): 43–44.

Legrain, Jean-François. "A Defining Moment: Palestinian Islamic Fundamentalism." *Islamic Fundamentalisms and the Gulf Crisis.* Ed. James Piscatori, 70–86. Chicago, IL: The American Academy of Arts and Sciences, 1991.

———. "Palestinian Islamisms: Patriotism as a Condition of Their Expansion." *Accounting for Fundamentalisms: The Dynamic Character of Movements.* Eds. Martin E. Marty and R. Scott Appleby, 413–427. Chicago, IL: University of Chicago Press, 1994.

Lesch, Ann Mosely. *Arab Politics in Palestine, 1917–1939: The Frustration of a Nationalist Movement.* Ithaca, NY: Cornell University Press, 1982.

Milton-Edwards, Beverly. *Islamic Politics in Palestine.* London: Tauris Academic Studies, 1996.

Moussalli, Ahmad S. "Discourses on Human Rights and Pluralistic Democracy." *Islam in a Changing World: Europe and the Middle East.* Eds. A. Herichow and J. B. Simonson. Surrey, UK: Curzon Press, 1997.

————. "Islamic Fundamentalism and Other Monotheistic Religions." *Religious Mutual Perceptions*. Ed. Jacque Waardenburgh. Lausanne, Switzerland: University of Lausanne, 1998.

————. "Islamic Fundamentalism and Pluralism." *Euro-Islam*. Ed. Thomas Lunden. Stockholm: Swedish Institute, 1996.

————. "Islamism and Modernity or Modernization of Islam." *The Future of Cosmopolitanism in the Middle East*. Amsterdam: Cultural Foundation, University of Amsterdam, 1998.

————. "Islamist Perspectives of Regime Political Response: The Cases of Lebanon and Palestine." *Arab Studies Quarterly*, 18 iii (Summer 1996): 53–63.

————. "Modern Islamic Fundamentalist Discourses on Civil Society, Pluralism and Democracy." *Civil Society in the Middle East*. Ed. Augustus Richard Norton, 79–119. Leiden: E. J. Brill, 1995.

————. "Modern Islamic Fundamentalist Discourses on Civil Society, Pluralism and Democracy." *Toward Civil Society in the Middle East*. Ed. Jillian Schwedler. Boulder, CO: Lynne Rienner Publishers, 1995.

Muslih, Muhammad. "Arafat's Dilemma." *Current History*, 94 (January 1995): 23–27.

————. *The Origins of Palestinian Nationalism*. New York: Columbia University Press, 1990.

Al-Nabahani, Taqiy al-Din. *Nizam al-Hukm*. Jerusalem: Matba'at al-Thiryan, 1952.

————. *Al-Shakhsiyya al-Islamiyya*. 4th ed. Beirut: Dar al-Umma, 1994.

————. *Al-Takatul al-Hizbi*. 2nd ed. Jerusalem: n.p., 1953.

Peretz, Don. *Intifada: The Palestinian Uprising*. Boulder, CO: Westview Press, 1990.

Robinson, Glenn E. "The Role of Professional Middle Class in Mobilization of Palestinian Society: The Medical and Agricultural Committees." *International Journal of Middle East Studies*, 25 ii (May 1993): 301–326.

Sahliyeh, Emile. *In Search of Leadership: West Bank Politics since 1967*. Washington, DC: Brookings Institution, 1988.

Shadid, Mohammed K. "The Muslim Brotherhood Movement in the West Bank and Gaza." *Third World Quarterly*, 10 (April 1988): 658–682.

Shafiq, Munir. *Al-Fikr al-Islami al-Mu'asir wa al-Tahaddiyat*. Beirut: Al-Nashir, 1991.

————. *Al-Islam wa Muwajahat al-Dawla al-Haditha*. 3rd ed. Beirut: Al-Nashir, 1992.

————. *Al-Nizam al-Dawli al-Jadid wa Khiyar al-Muwajaha*. Beirut: Al-Nashir, 1992.

Taji-Farouki, Suha. "A Case-Study in Contemporary Political Islam and the Palestine Question: The Perspective of Hizb al-Tahrir." *Studies in Muslim-Jewish Relations*, 2 (1995): 35–58.

———. "From Madrid to Washington: Palestinian Islamist Response to Israeli-Palestinian Peace Settlement." *World Faiths Encounter*, 9 (November 1994): 49–58.

———. *A Fundamental Quest: Hizb al-Tahrir and the Search for the Islamic Caliphate*. London: Grey Seal, 1996.

———. "Hizb al-Tahrir." *Encyclopedia of the Modern Islamic World*. New York: Oxford University Press, 1995.

———. "Islamic Discourse and Modern Political Methods: An Analysis of al-Nabahani's Reading of the Canonical Text Sources of Islam." *American Journal of Islamic Social Sciences*, 11 iii (Fall 1994): 365–393.

———. "Islamic State—Theories and Contemporary Realities." *Islamic Fundamentalism in Perspective*. Eds. Sid Ahmad and Ehteshemi. Boulder, CO: Westview Press, 1995.

Zallum, 'Abd al-Qadir. *Kayfa Hudimat al-Khilafa*. 3rd ed. Beirut: Dar al-Umma, 1990.

———. *Nizam al-Hukm fi al-Islam*. Beirut: Dar al-Umma, 1996.

Saudi Arabia and the Gulf States

Aba Namay, Rahshe. "Constitutional Reform: A Systemization of Saudi Politics." *Journal of South Asian and Middle Eastern Studies*, 16 (Spring 1993): 70–88.

Abir, M. *Saudi Arabia: Government, Society and the Gulf Crisis*. London: Routledge, 1993.

Ahrari, M. E., and J. H. Noyes, eds. *The Persian Gulf after the Cold War*. Westport, CT: Praeger, 1993.

Allen, Calvin H. Jr. *Oman: The Modernization of the Sultanate*. Boulder, CO: Westview Press, 1987.

Bill, James A. "Resurgent Islam in the Persian Gulf." *Foreign Affairs*, 63 (Fall 1984): 108–127.

Buchan, James. "Secular and Religious Opposition in Saudi Arabia." *State, Society and Economy in Saudi Arabia*. Ed. Tim Niblock. London: Croom Helm, 1982.

Burrows, Bernard. *Footnotes in the Sand: The Gulf in Transition*. London: Michael Russell, 1991.

Chubin, Shahram. "The Islamic Republic's Foreign Policy in the Gulf."

Shi'ism, Resistance, and Revolution. Ed. Martin Kramer, 159–171. Boulder, CO: Westview Press, 1987.

Dahlan, Ahmad H., ed. *Politics, Administration and Development in Saudi Arabia.* Jeddah: Dar al-Shuruq, 1990.

Dekmejian, R. Hrair. *Islam in Revolution.* Syracuse, NY: Syracuse University Press, 1982.

———. "The Rise of Political Islamism in Saudi Arabia." *The Middle East Journal,* 48 (Autumn 1994): 627–643.

Al-Farsy, Fouad. *Saudi Arabia: A Country Study in Development.* London: Kegan Paul, 1986.

Gause, F. G. *Oil Monarchies: Domestic and Security Challenges in the Arab Gulf States.* New York: Council on Foreign Relations Press, 1994.

———. "Saudi Arabia: Desert Storm and After." *The Middle East after the Iraq's Invasion of Kuwait.* Ed. R. O. Freedman. Gainesville: University Press of Florida. 1993.

———. "Sovereignty, Statecraft and Stability in the Middle East." *Journal of International Affairs,* 45 ii (Winter 1992): 441–469.

Gavrielidides, Nicholas. "Tribal Democracy: The Anatomy of Parliamentary Democracy in Kuwait." *Elections in the Middle East.* Ed. L. Layne. Boulder, CO: Westview Press, 1987.

Ghabra, Shafeeq. "Democratization in a Middle Eastern State: Kuwait/1993." *Middle East Policy,* 3 i (1994): 102–119.

———. "Kuwait: Elections and Issues of Democratization in a Middle Eastern State." *Digest of Middle East Studies,* 3 i (Winter 1992): 495–510.

Goldberg, Jacob. "The Shi'i Minority in Saudi Arabia." *Shi'ism and Social Protest.* Eds. Juan R. I. Cole and Nikki R. Keddie, 230–246. New Haven, CT: Yale University Press, 1986.

Graham, Douglas. *Saudi Arabia Unveiled.* Dubuque, IA: Kendall/Hunt Publishing, 1991.

Habib, John. *Ibn Saud's Warriors of Islam: The Ikhwan of Najd and Their Role in the Creation of the Saudi Kingdom 1910–1930.* Leiden: E. J. Brill, 1978.

Halliday, Fred. *Arabian without Sultans.* Baltimore, MD: Penguin Books, 1974.

Helms, Christine M. *The Cohesion of Saudi Arabia.* London: Croom Helm, 1981.

Hooglund, Eric. "Iranian Populism and Political Change in the Gulf." *Middle East Report,* 194 (January-February 1992): 19–21.

Howarth, David. *The Desert King: Ibn Saud and His Arabia.* New York: Mc-Graw-Hill, 1964.

Kechichian, Joseph A. "Islamic Revivalism and Change in Saudi Arabia: Juhayman al-'Utaybi's 'Letters' to the Saudi People." *The Muslim World*, 80 (January 1990): 1–16.

Khury, Fuad. *Tribe and State in Bahrain*. Chicago, IL: University Press of Chicago, 1980.

Kostiner, Joseph. "Shi'i Unrest in the Gulf." *Shi'ism, Resistance, and Revolution*. Ed. Martin Kramer, 173–187. Boulder, CO: Westview Press, 1987.

Kramer, M. "Tragedy in Mecca." *Sandstorm: Middle East Conflicts and America*. Ed. Daniel Pipes. Lanham, MD: University Press of America, 1993: 241–267.

Kucukcan, Talip. "Some Reflections on the Wahhabiya and the Sanusiya Movements: A Comparative Approach." *The Islamic Quarterly*, 37 iv (1993): 237–251.

Lackner, Helen. *A House Built on Sand*. London: Ithaca Press, 1978.

Lawson, Fred. *Bahrain: The Modernization of Autocracy*. Boulder, CO: Westview Press, 1989.

———. *Oppositional Movements and U.S. Policy toward the Arab Gulf States*. New York: Council on Foreign Relations, 1992.

Long, David. "The Impact of the Iranian Revolution on the Arabian Peninsula and the Gulf States." *The Iranian Revolution: Its Global Impact*. Ed. John L. Esposito, 100–115. Miami: Florida International University Press, 1990.

McMillan, Joseph. "Saudi Arabia: Culture, Legitimacy, and Political Reform." *Global Affairs*, 7 (Spring 1992): 56–75.

Mohtahed-Zadeh, Pirouz. "A Geopolitical Triangle in the Persian Gulf: Actions and Reactions among Iran, Bahrain and Saudi Arabia." *Iranian Journal of International Affairs*, 6 i–ii (1994): 47–59.

Nakhleh, E. A. "Regime Stability and Change in the Gulf: The Case of Saudi Arabia." *The Politics of Change in Saudi Arabia*. Ed. R. B. Satloff. Boulder, CO: Westview Press, 1993.

Naqeeb, Khaloun. *Society and State in the Gulf and Arab Peninsula: A Different Perspective*. London: Routledge, 1990.

Naqib, Khaldun Hasan. *Al-Mujtama' wa al-Dawla fi al-Khalij wa al-Jazira al-'Arabiyya*. Beirut: Center for the Studies of Arab Unity, 1987.

Nehme, Michel G. "The Islamic-Capitalist State of Saudi Arabia: The Surfacing of Fundamentalism." *Islamic Fundamentalism: Myths and Realities*. Ed. Ahmad S. Moussalli, 275–302. Reading, UK: Ithaca Press, 1998.

———. "Islamic Constraints on the Capitalist State of Saudi Arabia." *East West Review*, 2 iv (June 1995).

———. "Saudi Arabia 1950–1980: Between Nationalism and Religion." *Middle Eastern Studies*, 30 iv (1994): 930–943.

———. "Saudi Development Plans between Capitalist and Islamic Value." *Middle Eastern Studies*, 30 iii (July 1994).

———. "The Shifting Sand of Political Participation in Saudi Arabia." *Orient*, 36 i (1995).

Ochsenwald, William. "Saudi Arabia and the Islamic Revival." *International Journal of Middle East Studies,* 13 (August 1981).

Openshaw, M. "Religion and Regime Legitimacy: The Al-Saud, Wahhabism, and Saudi Arabian Politics." *Journal of Arabic, Islamic and Middle Eastern Studies*, 1 ii (1994): 76–89.

Pasha, A. K. "Demography, Political Reforms and Opposition in GCC States." *The Political Economy of West Asia: Demography, Democracy and Economic Reforms.* Ed. G. Pant. Delhi: Mank, 1994.

Peterson, J. E. *The Arab Gulf States: Steps toward Political Participation.* New York: Praeger, 1988.

———. *Historical Dictionary of Saudi Arabia.* Metuchen, NJ and London: Scarecrow Press, 1993.

Piscatori, James, ed. *Islamic Fundamentalisms and the Gulf Crisis.* Chicago, IL: American Academy of Arts and Sciences, 1991.

Al-Rasheed, Madawi. "Saudi Arabia's Islamic Opposition." *Current History,* 95 (January 1996): 16–22.

Al-Rumaihi, Mohammad. "Kuwait: Oasis of Liberalism?" *Middle East Quarterly,* 1 (September 1994): 31–35.

Said Zahlan, Rosemarie. *The Making of the Modern Gulf States.* London: Unwin Hyman, 1989.

Salame, Ghassan. "Islam and Politics in Saudi Arabia." *Arab Studies Quarterly,* 9 (Summer 1987): 306–326.

Salih, Kamal Osman. "Kuwait's Parliamentary Elections: 1963–1985: An Appraisal." *Journal of South Asian and Middle Eastern Studies,* 16 ii (1992).

Satloff, R. B., ed. *The Politics of Change in Saudi Arabia.* Boulder, CO: Westview Press, 1993.

Sours, Martin H. "Saudi Arabia's Role in the Middle East: Regional Stability within the New World Order." *Asian Affairs*, 18 (Spring 1991).

Tachau, Frank, ed. *Political Parties of the Middle East and North Africa.* Westport, CT: Greenwood Press, 1994.

Tetreault, Mary Ann. "Gulf Winds: Inclement Political Weather in the Arabian Peninsula." *Current History,* 95 (January 1996): 23–27.

Vandenbroucke, Lucien S. "Why Allah's Zealots? A Study of the Causes of Islamic Fundamentalism in Egypt and Saudi Arabia." *Middle East Review,* 16 (Fall 1983): 30–41.

Yamani, Mai. "Saudi Arabia and Central Asia: The Islamic Connection." *From the Gulf to Central Asia: Players in the New Great Game.* Ed. Anoushiravan Ehteshami. Exeter, UK: University of Exeter Press, 1994.

Al-Yassini, Ayman. *Religion and State in the Kingdom of Saudi Arabia.* Boulder, CO: Westview Press, 1985.

Zahlan, Rosemarie. *The Making of the Modern Gulf States.* London: Unwin Hyman, 1989.

Somalia

Adid, Muhammad Farah, and P. S. Ruhela. *Somalia: From the Dawn of Civilization to Modern Times.* Delhi: Vikas, 1994.

Ahmed, Akbar S., and David M. Hart. *Islam in Tribal Society: From the Atlas to the Indus.* London: Routledge and Kegan Paul, 1984.

Andrzejewski, B. W. "The Survival of National Culture in Somalia during and after the Colonial Era." *The Decolonization of Africa: Southern Africa and the Horn of Africa.* New York: UNIPUB, 1982.

Castagno, Alphonso A. "The Republic of Somalia: Africa's Most Homogenous State?" *Africa,* 5 (July 1960): 2–15.

———. "Somali Republic." *Political Parties and National Integration in Tropical Africa.* Ed. James S. Coleman, et al., 512–519. Berkeley: University of California Press, 1964.

Drysdale, J. *Whatever Happened to Somalia?* London: Haan, 1994.

Dualeh, Hussein Ali. *From Barre to Aideed: Somalia: The Agony of a Nation.* Nairobi, Kenya: Stellagraphics, 1994.

Galydh, Ali Khalif. "Democratic Practice and Breakdown in Somalia." *Democracy and Pluralism in Africa.* Ed. Dov Ronen. Boulder, CO: Lynne Rienner Publishers, 1986.

Gilkes, P. *Conflict in Somalia and Ethiopia.* Parsippany, NJ: Silver Burdett Press, 1994.

Hanley, G. *Warriors: Life and Death among the Somalis.* London: Eland, 1993.

Hassan, Mohamed Yusuf, and R. Balducci. *Somalia: le radici del futuro.* Rome: II Passaggio, 1993.

Healy, Sally, and Mark Delancey. "Somali Democratic Republic." *World Encyclopedia of Political Systems and Parties,* Vol. 2. Eds. George E. Delury and Marc Arnson, 974–978. New York: Facts on File, 1987.

Lewis, I. M. "Modern Political Movements in Somaliland." *Africa,* 28 iii (July 1958): 244–261, and 28 iv (October 1958): 244–263.

———. "Nationalism and Particularism in Somalia." *Tradition and Transition in East Africa: Studies of the Tribal Element in the Modern Era.* Ed. P. H. Gulliver, 339–361. Berkeley and Los Angeles: University of California Press, 1969.

———. *Religion in Context: Cult and Charisma.* Cambridge, UK: Cambridge University Press, 1986.

Lewis, I. M., ed. *Islam in Tropical Africa.* Bloomington, IN; London: International Africa Institute and Indiana University Press, 1964.

———. *Nationalism and Self-Determination in the Horn of Africa.* London: Ithaca Press, 1982.

Markakis, John. *National and Class Conflict in the Horn of Africa.* Cambridge, UK: Cambridge University Press, 1987.

Martin, Bradford G. *Muslim Brotherhoods in 19th Century Africa.* Cambridge, UK: Cambridge University Press, 1976.

Sheik-Abdi Abdi. "Ideology and Leadership in Somalia." *Journal of Modern African Studies,* 19 i (1981): 163–172.

Trimingham, J. Spencer. *The Influence of Islam upon Africa.* 2nd ed. London and New York: Longman, 1980.

———. *Islam in East Africa.* Oxford, UK: Clarendon Press, 1964.

Sudan

Abdelmoula, Adam M. "The 'Fundamentalist' Agenda for Human Rights: The Sudan and Algeria." *Arab Studies Quarterly,* 18 (Winter 1996): 1–28.

Afaf, Abdel Majid Abu Hasabu. *Factional Conflict in the Sudanese Nationalist Movement,* 1918–1948. Khartoum, Sudan: Graduate College, 1985.

'Ali, Hayder Ibrahim. *Azmat al-Islam al-Siyasi: Al-Jabha al-Islamiyya al-Qawimiyya fi al-Sudan.* Cairo: Car al-Nil li al-Nashr, 1991.

———. "Islamism in Practice: The Case of Sudan." *The Islamist Dilemma: The Political Role of Islamist Movements in the Contemporary Arab World.* Ed. Laura Guazzone, 187–214. Reading, UK: Ithaca Press, 1995.

Chiriyankandath, J. "The Policies of Religious Identity: A Comparison of Hindu Nationalism and Sudanese Islamism." *Journal of Commonwealth and Comparative Politics,* 23 i (1994): 31–53.

Daly, M. W. *Imperial Sudan: The Anglo-Egyptian Condominium, 1934–1965.* Cambridge, UK: Cambridge University Press, 1991.

———. "Islam, Secularism, and Ethnic Identity in the Sudan." *Religion and Political Power.* Eds. Gustavo and M. W. Daly Benavides. Albany: State University of New York Press, 1989.

Duran, Khalid. "Islamism and Power Politics: The Case of Sudan." *Aussenpolitik* (English Edition), 45 ii (1994): 189–198.

El-Affendi, Abdelwahab. "Discovering the South: Sudanese Dilemmas for Islam in Africa." *African Affairs,* 89 (July 1990): 371–389.

———. *Turabi's Revolution: Islam and Power in Sudan.* London: Grey Seal, 1991.

Esposito, John L. "Sudan." *The Politics of Islamic Revivalism: Diversity and Unity.* Ed. Shireen T. Hunter, 187–203. Bloomington: Indiana University Press, 1988.

Flint, Julie. "In the Name of Islam." *Africa Report,* 40 (May-June 1995): 34–37.

Fluehr-Lobban, Carolyn. *Islamic Law and Society in the Sudan.* London: Frank Cass, 1987.

———. "Islamization of the Law in the Sudan." *Legal Studies Forum,* 10 ii (1987): 189–204.

———. "Islamization in Sudan: A Critical Assessment." *The Middle East Journal,* 44 iv 4 (1990).

Fluehr-Lobban, Carolyn, Richard A. Lobban Jr., and John O. Voll. *Historical Dictionary of the Sudan.* 2nd ed. Metuchen, NJ: Scarecrow Press, 1992.

Gurdon, Charles. *Sudan at the Crossroads.* Cambridgeshire, UK: Menas Press Limited, 1994.

———. "Sudan's Political Future." *The Horn of Africa.* Ed. Charles Cudrun. London: UCL Press, 1994.

Hale, Sondra. "Gender Politics and Islamization in Sudan." *South Asia Bulletin,* 14 ii (1994): 51–66.

———. "Gender, Religious Identity, and Political Mobilization in Sudan." *Identity, Politics and Women: Cultural Reassertions and Feminisms in International Perspective.* Ed. V. M. Moghadam. Boulder, CO: Westview Press, 1994.

———. "The Rise of Islam and Women of the National Front in Sudan." *Review of African Political Economy,* 554 (1992).

Higueras, G. "Hasan al-Turabi: Islamism Will Engulf North Africa." *Middle East Quarterly,* 1 vi (1994): 88–91.

Holt, P. M., and M. W. Daly. *A History of the Sudan.* 4th ed. London: Longman, 1988.

Jacobs, Scott H. "The Sudan's Islamization." *Current History,* 84 (May 1985): 205–208.

382 • SELECTED BIBLIOGRAPHY

Khalid, Mansour. *The Government They Deserve: The Role of the Elite in Sudan's Political Evolution.* London: Kegan Paul, 1990.

Lefebvre, Jeffrey A. "Post-Cold War Clouds on the Horn of Africa: The Eritrea-Sudan Crisis." *Middle East Policy,* 4 (September 1995): 34–49.

Lesch, Ann Mosely. "A Review from Khartoum." *Foreign Affairs,* 65 iv (1987): 807–826.

Mahmoud, Ushari. "The Cultural Question in the New Sudan Discourse." *Perspectives and Challenges in the Development of Sudanese Studies.* Ed. Ismail H. Abdallah with D. Sconyers, 239–264. Lewiston, Queenston, and Lampeter, UK: Edwin Mellen Press, 1993.

Makinda, Samuel M. "Iran, Sudan and Islam." *The World Today,* 49 (June 1993): 108–111.

Makki, Hassan. *Haraka al-Ikhwan al-Muslimin fi al-Sudan 1944–69.* Khartoum: Khartoum University Press, 1982.

———. *Al-Haraka al-Islamiyya fi al-Sudan.* Khartoum: Bayt al-Mar'ifa, 1990.

Marchal, Roland. "Le Soudan entre islamisme et dictature militaire." *Maghreb-Machrek,* 137 (July-September 1992).

Miller, Judith. "Faces of Fundamentalism: Hassan al-Turabi and Muhammad Fadlallah." *Foreign Affairs,* 73 (November-December 1994): 123–142.

Mohamed, Omer Beshir. *Revolution and Nationalism in the Sudan.* London: Rex Collings, 1974.

Mohammed, Nadir A. L. "Militarization in Sudan: Tends and Determinants." *Armed Forces and Society,* 19 iii (1993): 411–433.

Moussalli, Ahmad S. "Discourses on Human Rights and Pluralistic Democracy." *Islam in a Changing World: Europe and the Middle East.* Eds. A. Herichow and J. B. Simonson. Surrey, UK: Curzon Press, 1997.

———. "Hasan al-Turabi's Islamist Discourse on Democracy and Shura." *Middle Eastern Studies,* 30 i (1994): 52–63.

———. "Islamic Fundamentalism and Other Monotheistic Religions." *Religious Mutual Perceptions.* Ed. Jacque Waardenburgh. Lausanne, Switzerland: University of Lausanne, 1998.

———. "Islamic Fundamentalism and Pluralism." *Euro-Islam.* Ed. Thomas Lunden. Stockholm: Swedish Institute, 1996.

———. "Islamism and Modernity or Modernization of Islam." *The Future of Cosmopolitanism in the Middle East.* Amsterdam: Cultural Foundation, University of Amsterdam, 1998.

———. "Modern Islamic Fundamentalist Discourses on Civil Society, Pluralism and Democracy." *Civil Society in the Middle East.* Ed. Augustus Richard Norton, 79–119. Leiden: E. J. Brill, 1995.

————. "Modern Islamic Fundamentalist Discourses on Civil Society, Pluralism and Democracy." *Toward Civil Society in the Middle East.* Ed. Jillian Schwedler. Boulder, CO: Lynne Rienner Publishers, 1995.

————, ed. *Islamic Fundamentalism: Myths and Realities.* Reading, UK: Ithaca Press, 1998.

Muddathir, Abd al-Rahim. *Imperialism and Nationalism in the Sudan.* London: Oxford University Press, 1969.

Na'im, Abdullahi Ahmed. "Constitutionalism and Islamization in the Sudan." *Africa Today,* 36 iii–iv (1989): 11–29.

Na'im, Abdullahi Ahmed, and Peter N. Kok. *Fundamentalism and Militarism: A Report on Root Causes of Human Rights Violations in the Sudan.* New York: Fund for Peace, 1991.

Niblock, Tim. *Class and Power in the Sudan: The Dynamics of Sudanese Politics, 1898–1985.* Albany: State University of New York, 1987.

Ronen, Y. "Sudan (Jumhuriyyat al-Sudan)." *Middle East Contemporary Survey,* 15 1991 (1993): 641–663.

Simone, T. Abdou Maliqalim. *In Whose Image? Political Islam and Urban Practices in Sudan.* Chicago, IL: University of Chicago Press, 1994.

Al-Turabi, Hasan. "Awlawiyyat al-Haraka al-Islamiyya." *Minbar al-Sharq,* 1 (March 1992).

————. *Al-Haraka al-Islamiyah fi al-Sudan.* Kuwait: Dar al-Qalam, 1988.

————. *Al-Iman wa Atharuhu fi Hayat al-Insan.* Jeddah: Al-Dar al-Su'udiyya li al-Nashr wa al-Tawzi', 1984.

————. *Al-Islam, Hiwarat fi al-Dimucratiyya, al-Dawla, al-Gharb.* Beirut: Dar al-Jadid, 1995.

————. "The Islamic Awakening's New Wave." *New Perspective Quarterly,* 10 (Summer 1993): 42–45.

————. *Al-Itijah al-Islami Yuqaddim al-Mar'a bayna Ta'alim al-Din wa Taqalid al-Mujtama'.* Jeddah: Al-Dar al-Su'udiyya li al-Nashr wa al-Tawzi', 1984.

————. *Qadaya al-Hurriyya wa al-Wahda', al-Shura wa al-Dimuqratiyya, al-Din wa al-Fan.* Jeddah: Al-Dar al-Su'udiyya li al-Nashr wa al-Tawzi', 1987.

————. *Al-Salat 'Imad al-Din.* Beirut: Dar al-Qalam, 1971.

————. "Al-Shura wa al-Dimuqratiyya: Ishkalat al-Mustalah wa al-Mafhum." *Al-Mustaqbal al-'Arabi,* 75 (May 1985).

————. *Tajdid al-Fikr al-Islami.* 2nd ed. Jeddah: Al-Dar al-Su'udiyya li al-Nashr wa al-Tawzi', 1987.

————. *Tajdid Usul al-Fiqh.* Jeddah: Al-Dar al-Su'udiyya li al-Nashr wa al-Tawzi', 1984.

————. "Utruhat al-Haraka al-Islamiyya fi Majal Al-Hiwar Ma'a al-Gharb." *Shu'un al-Awsat*, 36 (December 1994).

Viorst, Milton. "Sudan's Islamic Experiment." *Foreign Affairs,* 74 (May-June 1995): 45–58.

Voll, John O. "Fundamentalism in the Sunni Arab World: Egypt and the Sudan." *Fundamentalisms Observed.* Eds. Martin E. Marty and R. Scott Appleby, 345–402. Chicago, IL: University of Chicago Press, 1991.

————. "Islamization in the Sudan and the Iranian Revolution." *The Iranian Revolution: Its Global Impact.* Ed. John L. Esposito, 283–300. Miami: Florida International University Press, 1990.

————. "Political Crisis in Sudan." *Current History,* 89 (1990): 153–156 and 178–180.

————. *The Political Impact of Islam in the Sudan.* Washington, DC: Department of State, 1984.

————. "The Sudanese Mahdi: Frontier Fundamentalist." *International Journal of Middle East Studies,* 10 (1979): 145–166.

————, ed. *Sudan: State and Society in Crisis.* Bloomington: Indiana University Press, 1991.

Voll, John O., and Sarah Potts Voll. *The Sudan: Unity and Diversity in a Multicultural State.* Boulder, CO: Westview Press, 1985.

Warburg, Gabriel R. *Egypt and the Sudan: Studies in History and Politics.* London: Frank Cass, 1985.

————. "From Revolution to Conservatism: Some Aspects of Mahdist Ideology and Politics in the Sudan." *Der Islam,* 70 i (1993): 88–111.

————. *Islam, Nationalism and Radicalism in Egypt and the Sudan.* New York: Greenwood Press, 1983.

————. "The Sharia in Sudan: Implementation and Repercussions, 1983–1989." *Middle East Journal,* 4 (1990): 624–637.

Woodward, Peter. "Sudan and Africa: A Political Analysis." *Perspectives and Challenges in the Development of Sudanese Studies.* Ed. Ismail H. Abdalla with D. Sconyers, 171–187. Lewiston, Queenston, and Lampeter, UK: Edwin Mellen Press, 1993.

————. *Sudan, 1898–1989: The Unstable State.* Boulder, CO: Lynne Rienner Publishers, 1990.

Syria

Abdallah, Umar F. *The Islamic Struggle in Syria.* London: Mizan Press, 1983.

Batatu, Hanna. "Syria's Muslim Brethren." *State and Ideology in the Mid-*

dle East and Pakistan. Eds. Fred Halliday and Hamza Alavi, 112–132. London: Macmillan, 1988.

Carré, Olivier. Les Frères Musulmans: Egypte et Syrie: 1928–1982. Paris: Gallimard, Dulliard, 1983.

Chizik, I. "Political Parties in Syria." Journal of the Royal Central Asian Society, 22 i (October 1935): 556–565.

Hawwa, Saeed. The Muslim Brotherhood. Kuwait: IISFO, 1985.

Hawwa, Sa'id. Jundullah: Thaqafatan wa Akhlakan. Cairo: Dar al-Tiba'a al-Haditha, 1977.

———. Al-Madkhal ila Da'wat al-Ikhwan al-Muslimin bi-Munasabat Khamsin 'Aman 'ala Ta'sisiha. 2nd ed. Amman: Dar al-Arqam, 1979.

Hinnebusch, Raymond A. "The Islamic Movement in Syria: Sectarian Conflict and Urban Rebellion in an Authoritarian-Populist Regime." Islamic Resurgence in the Arab World. Ed. Ali E. Hillal Dessouki. New York: Praeger, 1982.

———. "Liberalization in Syria: The Struggle of Economic and Political Rationality." Contemporary Liberalization between Cold War and Cold Peace. Ed. E. Kienle. London: British Academic Press, 1994.

———. "Syria." The Politics of Islamic Revivalism: Diversity and Unity. Ed. Shireen T. Hunter. Bloomington: Indiana University Press, 1988.

Hudson, Michael. "The Islamic Factor in Syrian and Iraqi Politics." Islam in the Political Process. Ed. James Piscatori. New York: Cambridge University Press, 1983.

Al-Janhani, Al-Habib. "Al-Sahwa al-Islamiyya fi Bilad al-Sham: Mithal Surya." Al-Harakat al-Islamiyya al-Mu'asira fi al-Watan al-'Arabi. 2nd ed. Beirut: Center for the Studies of Arab Unity, 1989.

Khoury, Philip S. Syria and the French Mandate. Princeton: Princeton University Press, 1987.

———. Urban Notables and Arab Nationalism. Cambridge, UK: Cambridge University Press, 1983.

Knudsen, Erik L. "Hafiz al-Assad, Islamic Fundamentalism and the Syrian State: An Analysis of Fundamentalist Opposition to the Bathist-Alawite Political/Military Complex." Current World Leaders, 37 (April 1994): 71–85.

Kramer, Martin. "Syria's Alawis and Shi'ism." Shi'ism, Resistance, and Revolution. Ed. Martin Kramer, 237–255. Boulder, CO: Westview Press, 1987.

Lawson, Fred H. "Domestic Pressure and the Peace Process: Fillip or Hindrance?" Contemporary Syria: Liberalization between Cold War and Cold Peace. Ed. E. Kienle. London: British Academic Press, 1994.

————. "Social Basis of the Hama Revolt." *MERIP Reports,* 12 (November-December 1982).

————. "Syria." *Political Parties in the Middle East and North Africa.* Ed. F. Tachau. London: Mansell, 1994.

Lobmeyer, H. G. "Al-Dimocratiyya Hiyya al-Hall? The Syrian Opposition at the Den of the Asad Ear." *Contemporary Syria: Liberalization between Cold War and Cold Peace.* Ed. E. Kienle. London: British Academic Press, 1994.

Moussalli, Ahmad S. "Discourses on Human Rights and Pluralistic Democracy." *Islam in a Changing World: Europe and the Middle East.* Eds. A. Herichow and J. B. Simonson. Surrey, UK: Curzon Press, 1997.

————. "Islamic Fundamentalism and Other Monotheistic Religions." *Religious Mutual Perceptions.* Ed. Jacque Waardenburgh. Lausanne, Switzerland: University of Lausanne, 1998.

————. "Islamic Fundamentalism and Pluralism." *Euro-Islam.* Ed. Thomas Lunden. Stockholm: Swedish Institute, 1996.

————. "Islamism and Modernity or Modernization of Islam." *The Future of Cosmopolitanism in the Middle East.* Amsterdam: Cultural Foundation, University of Amsterdam, 1998.

————. "Modern Islamic Fundamentalist Discourses on Civil Society, Pluralism and Democracy." *Civil Society in the Middle East.* Ed. Augustus Richard Norton, 79–119. Leiden: E. J. Brill, 1995.

————. "Modern Islamic Fundamentalist Discourses on Civil Society, Pluralism and Democracy." *Toward Civil Society in the Middle East.* Ed. Jillian Schwedler. Boulder, CO: Lynne Rienner Publishers, 1995.

Rabu, Annka. "Nation-State Building in Syria: Ba'th and Islam—Conflict or Accommodation?" *Islam: State and Society.* Eds. Klaus Ferdinand and Mehdi Mozaffari, 117–126. London: Curzon Press, 1988.

Roberts, David. *The Ba'th and the Creation of the Modern Syria.* New York: St. Martin's Press, 1987.

Siba'i, Mustapha. *'Uzama'una fi al-Tarikh.* Beirut: Al-Maktab al-Islami, n.d.

Tunisia

Anderson, Lisa. *The State and Social Transformation in Tunisia and Libya, 1830–1980.* Princeton: Princeton University Press, 1986.

————. "Tunisia and Libya: Responses to the Islamic Impulse." *The Iranian Revolution: Its Global Impact.* Ed. John L. Esposito, 157–175. Miami: Florida International University Press, 1990.

Brace, R. M. *Morocco, Algeria, Tunisia.* Englewood Cliffs, NJ: Prentice-Hall, 1964.

Burgat, François. *The Islamic Movement in North Africa.* Austin: Center for Middle Eastern Studies, University of Texas at Austin, 1993.

Collins Dunn, M. "The Al-Nahda Movement in Tunisia: From Renaissance to Revolution." *Islamism and Secularism in North Africa.* Ed. J. Ruedy. Basingstoke, UK: Macmillan, 1994.

Deeb, Mary-Jane. "Militant Islam and the Politics of Redemption." *Annals of the American Academy of Political and Social Science,* 521 (November 1992): 52–65.

Eickelman, Dale F., and James Piscatori, eds. *Muslim Travellers: Pilgrimage, Migration, and the Religious Imagination.* London: Routledge, 1990.

Al-Ghannushi, Rashid. *Harakat al-Itijah al-Islami fi Tunis.* Kuwait: Dar al-Qalam, 1989.

———. *Huquq al-Muwatana: Huquq Ghayr al-Muslim fi al-Mujtama' al-Muslim.* 2nd ed. Herndon, VA: International Institute of Islamic Thought, 1993.

———. *Al-Hurriyyat al-'Amma fi al-Dawla al-Islamiyya.* Beirut: Markaz Dirasat al-Wahda al-'Arabiyya, 1993.

———. "Al-Islam wa al-Gharb." *Al-Ghadir,* nos. 10–11 (December 1990).

———. "Ma'alim fi Istratijiyya al-Da'wa al-Islamiyya." *Al-Hiwar,* 19 (Autumn 1990).

———. *Mahawir Islamiyya.* Cairo: Matabi' al-Zahra, 1989.

———. "Mustaqbal al-Haraka al-Islamiyya." *Al-Huda* (Fez), 23 (1991).

———. "Mustaqbal al-Tayyar al-Islami." *Minbar al-Sharq,* 1 (March 1992).

———. "Tahlil li al-'Anasir al-Mukawwina li al-Zahira al-Islamiyya fi Tunis." *Al-Harakat al-Islamiyya fi al-Watan al-'Arabi.* Eds. I. S. 'Abd Allah and others. Beirut: Markaz Dirasat al-Wahda al-'Arabiyya, 1987.

Haliday, Fred. "The Politics of Islamic Fundamentalism in Iran, Tunisia and the Challenge to the Secular State." *Islam, Globalization and Postmodernity.* Eds. Ekbar S. Ahmad and H. Donn. London: Routledge, 1994.

Al-Hamidi, Muhammad al-Hashimi. *Ashwaq al-Huriyya: Qisat al-Haraka al-Islamiyya fi Tunis.* 2nd ed. Kuwait, Dar al-Qalam, 1990.

Al-Harmassi, 'Abd al-Latif. *Al-Haraka al-Islamiyya fi Tunis.* Tunis: Bayram li al-Nashr, 1985.

Hermassi, Abdelbaki. "The Rise and Fall of the Islamist Movement in Tunisia." *The Islamist Dilemma: The Political Role of Islamist Movements in the Contemporary Arab World*. Ed. Laura Guazzone, 105–127. Reading, UK: Ithaca Press, 1995.

Hermassi, Mohamed Abdelbaki. *Leadership and National Development in North Africa*. Berkeley: University of California Press, 1972.

————. *Society and State in the Arab Maghreb*. Beirut: Center for Arab Unity Studies, 1987.

————. *Leadership and National Development in North Africa*. Berkeley: University of California Press, 1970.

Hermida, Alfred. "The State and Islam." *Africa Report* 39 (September-October 1994): 55–58.

Hiskett, Marvyn. *The Course of Islam in Africa*. Edinburgh: Edinburgh University Press, 1994.

Joffe, G., ed. *North Africa: Nation, State and Region*. London: Routledge, 1993.

Joffe, G., and C. R. Pennell, eds. *Tribe and State: Essays in Honor of David Montgomery Hart*. Lincolnshire, UK: Middle East and North Africa Press, 1991.

Jourshi, Salah al-Din. *Al-Muqaddimat al-Nazariyya li al-Islamiyyin al-Taqaddumiyyin*. Tunis: Dar al-Barraq li al-Nashr, 1989.

Leveau, Remy. "Tunisie: Equilibre interne et environnement arabe." *Maghreb-Machrek*, 124 (April 1989): 4–17.

Magnuson, Douglas K. "Islamic Reform in Contemporary Tunisia." *Tunisia: The Political Economy of Reform*. Ed. I. William Zartman. Boulder, CO: Lynne Rienner Publishers, 1991.

Moore, Clement Henry. "Political Parties." Eds. I. William Zartman and William Mark Habeeb. *Polity and Society in Contemporary North Africa*. Boulder, CO: Westview Press, 1993.

————. *Politics in North Africa: Algeria, Morocco, and Tunisia*. Boston: Little, Brown, 1970.

————. *Tunisia since Independence*. Berkeley: University of California Press, 1972.

Moussalli, Ahmad S. "Discourses on Human Rights and Pluralistic Democracy." *Islam in a Changing World: Europe and the Middle East*. Eds. A. Herichow and J. B. Simonson. Surrey, UK: Curzon Press, 1998.

————. "Islamic Fundamentalism and Other Monotheistic Religions." *Religious Mutual Perceptions*. Ed. Jacque Waardenburgh. Lausanne, Switzerland: University of Lausanne, 1998.

————. "Islamic Fundamentalism and Pluralism." *Euro-Islam*. Ed. Thomas Lunden. Stockholm: Swedish Institute, 1996.

———. "Islamism and Modernity or Modernization of Islam." *The Future of Cosmopolitanism in the Middle East.* Amsterdam: Cultural Foundation, University of Amsterdam, 1998.

———. "Modern Islamic Fundamentalist Discourses on Civil Society, Pluralism and Democracy." *Civil Society in the Middle East.* Ed. Augustus Richard Norton, 79–119. Leiden: E. J. Brill, 1995.

———. "Modern Islamic Fundamentalist Discourses on Civil Society, Pluralism and Democracy." *Toward Civil Society in the Middle East.* Ed. Jillian Schwedler. Boulder, CO: Lynne Rienner Publishers, 1995.

Munson, Henry Jr. "Islamic Revivalism in Morocco and Tunisia." *Muslim World,* 76 (1986): 203–218.

Nelson, Harold D., ed. *Tunisia: A Country Study.* Washington, DC: U.S. Government Printing Office, 1987.

Rowland, Jacky. "Tunisia: 'More Repressive Than Ever'." *Africa Report,* 37 (September-October 1992): 50–51.

Salem, Norma. *Habib Bourguiba, Islam, and the Creation of Tunisia.* London: Croom Helm, 1984.

Sara, Fayiz. *Al-Haraka al-Islamiyya fi al-Magrib al-'Arabi.* Beirut: Markaz al-Dirasat al-Istratijiyya, 1995.

Vandewalle, Dirk. "From the New State to the New Era: Toward a Second Republic in Tunisia." *The Middle East Journal,* 42 iv (1988).

Waltz, Susan. "The Islamist Appeal in Tunisia." *The Middle East Journal,* 40 (Autumn 1986): 651–670.

Ware, Louis. "The Role of the Tunisian Military in the Post-Bourguiba Era." *The Middle East Journal,* 39 (1984): 27–47.

Zartman, I. William, ed. *Tunisia: The Political Economy of Reform.* Boulder, CO: Lynne Rienner Publishers, 1991.

Yemen

Burrowes, Robert. *The Yemen Arab Republic.* Boulder, CO: Westview Press, 1987.

Carapico, Sheila. "Elections and Mass Politics in Yemen." *Middle East Report,* 23 vi/185 (1993): 2–6.

———. "From Ballot Box to Battlefield: The War of the Two 'Alis." *Middle East Report,* 24 v/190 (1994): 24–27.

Carapico, Sheila, and J. Rone. *Yemen: Human Rights in Yemen during and after the 1994 War.* New York: Human Rights Watch/Middle East, [1994].

Cigar, Norman. "Islam and the State in South Yemen: The Uneasy Coexistence." *Middle Eastern Studies,* 26 (April 1990): 185–203.

Collins Dunn, M. "Islamist Parties in Democratizing States: A Look at Jordan and Yemen." *Middle East Policy,* 2 ii (1993): 16–27.

Douglas, J. Leigh. *The Free Yemeni Movement 1935–1962.* Beirut: American University of Beirut, 1987.

Dresch, Paul, and Bernard Haykel. "Stereotypes and Political Styles: Islamists and Tribesfolk in Yemen." *International Journal of Middle East Studies,* 27 (November 1995): 405–431.

Glosemeyer, Iris. "The First Yemeni Parliamentary Elections in 1993: Practicing Democracy." *Orient,* 34 iii (1993).

Halliday, Fred. *Arabia without Sultans.* Harmandsworth, UK: Penguin Books, 1974.

Hudson, Michael. "Unhappy Yemen: Watching the Slide Toward Civil War." *Middle East Insight,* 10 (May-August 1994).

Ismael, Tareq Y., and Jacqueline S. Ismael. *PDR Yemen.* London: Frances Pinter, 1986.

Kostiner, Joseph. *The Struggle for South Yemen.* London: Croom Helm, 1984.

Lackner, Helen. *P.D.R. Yemen.* London: Ithaca Press, 1985.

Latta, Rafiq. *Yemen: Unification and Modernization.* London: Gulf Centre for Strategic Studies, 1994.

Lefresne, Bernard. "Les islamistes yemenites et les élections." *Maghreb-Machrek,* 141 (July-September 1993).

Pridham, Brian, ed. *Contemporary Yemen: Politics and Historical Background.* London: Croom Helm, 1984.

Saeed, Javaid. *Islam and Modernization: A Comparative Analysis of Pakistan, Egypt, and Turkey.* Westport, CT: Praeger, 1994.

Sa'id, Abd al-Karim Qasim. *Al-Ikhwan al-Muslimin wa al-Harakat al-Usuliyya fi al-Yaman.* Cairo: Maktabat Madbuli, 1995.

Stookey, Robert W. *South Yemen: A Marxist Republic in Arabia.* Boulder, CO: Westview Press, 1982.

———. *Yemen: The Politics of Yemen Arab Republic.* Boulder, CO: Westview Press, 1978.

Wenner, Manfred. *Modern Yemen 1918–1966.* Baltimore, MD: Johns Hopkins University Press, 1968.

Zandani, 'Abd al-Majid. *Tariq al-'Iman.* Kuwait: IIFSO, 1983.

IV. IRAN

Abrahamian, Envand. *Iran between Two Revolutions.* Princeton: Princeton University Press, 1982.

––––––. *Khomeinism: Essays on the Islamic Republic*. Berkeley: University of California Press, 1993.

––––––. *Radical Islam: The Iranian Mojahidin*. London: I. B. Tauris, 1989.

Afkhami, Gholam R. *The Iranian Revolution: Thanatos on a National Scale*. Washington, DC: Middle East Institute, 1985.

Afray, Janet. *The Iranian Constitutional Revolution of 1906–1911*. New York: Columbia University Press, 1996.

Afshar, Helen. *Iran: A Revolution in Turmoil*. Basingstoke, UK: Macmillan, 1985.

Ahmad, Rif'at Sayyid. *Al-Harakat al-Islamiyya fi Misr wa Iran*. Cairo: Sina li al-Nashir, 1989.

Akhavi, Shahrough. *Religion and Politics in Contemporary Iran*. Albany: State University of New York Press, 1980.

Algar, Hamid. *Imam Khomeini, Islam and Revolution*. Berkeley: Mezan Press, 1981.

––––––. *The Islamic Revolution in Iran*. London: The Muslim Institute, 1980.

––––––. *The Islamic Revolution in Iran*. London: Open Press, 1980.

Algar, Hamid. Trans. *Draft Constitution of the Islamic Republic of Iran*. London: The Muslim Institute, 1979.

Amirahamadi, Hooshang, and Manoucher Parvin, eds. *Post-Revolutionary Iran*. Boulder, CO: Westview Press, 1988.

Amjad, Mohammed. *Iran: From Royal Dictatorship to Theocracy*. Westport, CT: Greenwood Press, 1989.

Amuzegar, Jahangir. "Islamic Fundamentalism in Action: The Case of Iran." *Middle East Policy,* 4 (September 1995): 22–33.

Arjomand, Said Amir. "Shi'ite Jurisprudence and Constitution Making in the Islamic Republic of Iran." *Fundamentalisms and the State: Remaking Polities, Economies, and Militance*. Eds. Martin E. Marty and R. Scott Appleby, 88–109. Chicago, IL: University of Chicago Press, 1993.

––––––. "A Victory for the Pragmatists: The Islamic Fundamentalist Reaction in Iran." *Islamic Fundamentalisms and the Gulf Crisis*. Ed. James Piscatori, 52–68. Chicago, IL: American Academy of Arts and Sciences, 1991.

––––––. *The Turban for the Crown: The Islamic Revolution in Iran*. Oxford: Oxford University Press, 1988.

Arjomand, Said Amir, ed. *From Nationalism to Revolutionary Islam*. Albany: State University of New York, 1984.

Askari, Hasan. "Khomeini and Non-Muslims." *Encounter*. Rome: Pontificio di Studi Arabi, no. 7, January 1981.

Ayoob, Mohammad. "The Revolutionary Thrust of Islamic Political Traditions." *Third World Quarterly,* 3 ii (April 1981): 269–276.

———. "Two Faces of Political Islam: Iran and Pakistan Compared." *Asian Survey,* 19 vi (June 1979): 535–556.

Ayyubi, Mohiuddin. *Khumeini Speaks Revolution.* Karachi: International Islamic Publishers, 1981.

Bakhash, Shaul. *The Reign of Ayatollahs.* New York: Basic Books, 1984.

Bakhiari, Bahman. *Parliamentary Politics in Revolutionary Iran: The Institutionalization of Factional Politics.* Gainesville: University Press of Florida, 1996.

Banisadr, Abolhassan. *Islamic Government.* Lexington, KY: Mazda Publishers, 1981.

Bashiriyeh, Hossein. *The State and Revolution in Iran, 1962–1982.* London: Croom Helm, 1984.

Bazargan, Mehdi. *The Inevitable Victory.* Trans. M. Yusefi. Bedford, OH: Free Islamic Literature, Inc., 1978.

Beheshti, Ayatollah. "Autobiography." *Echo of Islam,* 1 vi (September 1981): 11–14.

Behn, Wofgang. *Islamic Revolution or Revolution in Islam: A Selected Bibliography.* Berlin: Adiyok, 1980.

Bernard, Cheyl, and Zalmay Khalilzad. *"The Government of God"—Iran's Islamic Republic.* New York: Columbia University Press, 1984.

Bill, James A. "Power and Religion in Revolutionary Iran." *The Middle East Journal,* 36 i (1982).

Binder, Leonard. *Iran.* Berkeley: University of California Press, 1962.

Boroujerdi, Mehrzad. *Iranian Intellectuals and the West.* Syracuse, NY: Syracuse University Press, 1996.

The Cambridge History of Iran. 7 vols. Cambridge, UK: Cambridge University Press, 1968–1991.

Carlsen, Robin Wordsworth. *The Imam and His Islamic Revolution.* Victoria, British Columbia, Canada: Snowman Press, 1982.

Chehabi, Houchang E. *Iranian Politics and Religious Modernism.* Ithaca, NY: Cornell University Press, 1990.

———. "Religion and Politics in Iran: How Theocratic Is the Islamic Republic." *Daedalus,* 120 (Summer 1991): 69–91.

Cottam, Richard. "The Iranian Revolution." *Shi'ism and Social Protest.* Eds. Juan R. I. Cole and Nikki R. Keddie, 55–86. New Haven, CT: Yale University Press, 1986.

———. *Nationalism in Iran.* Pittsburgh, PA: University of Pittsburgh Press, 1979.

Dabashi, Hamid. *Theology of Discontent: The Ideological Foundations of the Islamic Revolution in Iran.* New York: New York University Press, 1993.

Encyclopedia Iranica, ed. Ehsan Yar-Shater. Cambridge and London, Routledge and Kegan Paul, 1982.

Esposito, John, ed. *The Iranian Revolution: Its Global Impact.* Miami: Florida International University Press, 1990.

Ezzati, Abul-Fazl. *The Revolutionary Islam and the Islamic Revolution.* Tehran: The Ministry of Islamic Guidance, 1981.

———. "The Spirit of Islamic Revolution: Government and Constitution." *Islamic Defence Review,* VI: 3 (1980): 26–31.

Fisher, Michael. *Iran: From Religious Dispute to Revolution.* Cambridge, MA: Harvard University Press, 1980.

Fuller, Graham E. *The Center of the Universe: The Geopolitics of Iran.* Boulder, CO: Westview Press, 1991.

Ghaffari, Reza. "The Economic Consequences of Islamic Fundamentalism in Iran." *Capital and Class,* 56 (Summer 1995): 91–115.

Ghods, M. Reza. *Iran in the Twentieth Century.* Boulder, CO: Lynne Rienner Publishers, 1989.

Green, Gerold D. *Revolution in Iran: The Politics of Countermobilization.* New York: Praeger, 1982.

Haghayeghi, Mehrdad. "Politics and Ideology in the Islamic Republic of Iran." *Middle Eastern Studies,* 29 (January 1993): 36–52.

Halliday, Fred. *After the Shah.* Washington, DC: Institute for Policy Studies (Issue Paper Series), 1980.

———. *Iran: Revolution and Dictatorship.* Baltimore, MD: Penguin Books, 1979.

———. "Iranian Foreign Policy Since 1979: Internationalism and Nationalism in the Islamic Revolution." *Shi'ism and Social Protest.* Eds. Juan R. I. Cole and Nikki R. Keddie, 88–106. New Haven, CT: Yale University Press, 1986.

Heikal, Mohammed. *The Return of the Ayatollah: The Iranian Revolution from Mossadeq to Khomieni.* London: Andre Deutsch, 1981.

Hiro, Dilip. *Iran under the Ayatollahs.* London: Routledge and Kegan Paul, 1985.

Hunter, Shireen T. *Iran after Khomeini.* New York: Praeger Publishers, 1992.

———. *Iran and the World: Continuity in a Revolutionary Decade.* Bloomington: Indiana University Press, 1990.

Hussain, Asaf. *Islamic Iran: Revolution and Counter Revolution.* New York: St. Martin's Press, 1995.

Hussain, Asaf. *Islamic Movements in Egypt, Pakistan, and Iran: An Annotated Bibliography.* New York: Mansell, 1983.

Jabbari, Ahmad, and Robert Oslon, eds. *Iran: Essays on a Revolution in the Making.* Lexington, KY: Mazda Publishers, 1981.

Kamrava, Mehran. *Revolution in Iran: The Roots of Turmoil.* New York: Routledge, 1990.

Katouzian, Homa. *Musaddiq and the Struggle for Power in Iran.* London: I. B. Tauris, 1990.

Katzman, Kenneth. *The Warriors of Islam.* Boulder, CO: Westview Press, 1993.

Kazemi, Farhad. "Civil Society and Iranian Politics." *Civil Society in the Middle East.* Ed. Augustus Richard Norton. Leiden: E. J. Brill, 1995.

———. "Models of Iranian Revolution, the Road to the Islamic Revolution, and the Challenge of Civil Society." *World Politics,* 47 (1995).

Keddie, Nikki R. *Roots of Revolution: An Interpretive History of Modern Iran.* New Haven, CT and London: Yale University Press, 1981.

Keddie, Nikki R., and Farah Monian. "Militancy and Religion in Contemporary Iran." *Fundamentalisms and the State: Remaking Polities, Economies, and Militance.* Eds. Martin E. Marty and R. Scott Appleby, 511–538. Chicago, IL: The University of Chicago Press, 1993.

Keddie, Nikki R., and Eric Hoogland, eds. *The Iranian Revolution and the Islamic Republic.* Washington, DC: 1982.

Khamene'i, Sayyid Ali. *Al-Imama wa al-Dawla fi al-Islam.* Beirut: Dar al-Furat, 1990.

Khomeini, Ayatollah Ruhallah. *Imam's Final Discourse.* Tehran: Ministry of Guidance and Islamic Culture, n.d.

———. *Islamic Government.* New York: Manor Books, 1979.

———. *Sayings of the Ayatollah Khomeini.* Trans. Jean-Marie Xaviere. New York: Bantam Books, 1980

———. *Selected Messages and Speeches of Imam Khomeini.* Tehran: The Hamadani Foundation Publishers, n.d.

"Khomeini's Leaden Legacy (Islamic Fundamentalists Rule Iran's Politics)." *The Middle East,* 221 (March 1993): 13–15.

Khoury, Enver, and Charles MacDonald, eds. *Revolution in Iran: A Reappraisal.* Hyattsville, MD: Institute of Middle Eastern and North African Affairs, 1982.

Lambton, Ann K. S. "A Reconsideration of the Position of the Marja al-Taqlid and the Religious Institution." *Studia Islamica,* VI: 20 (1964): 115–135.

Looney, Robert. *Origins of the Iranian Revolution.* New York: Pergamon Press, 1982.

Lorentz, John H. *Historical Dictionary of Iran*. Lanham, MD and London: Scarecrow Press, 1995.

Makinda, Samuel M. "Iran, Sudan and Islam." *The World Today,* 49 (June 1993): 108–111.

Mayer, Ann Elizabeth. "The Fundamentalist Impact on Law, Politics, and Constitutions in Iran, Pakistan, and the Sudan." *Fundamentalisms and the State: Remaking Polities, Economies, and Militance*. Eds. Martin E. Marty and R. Scott Appleby, 110–151. Chicago, IL: University of Chicago Press, 1993.

McDaniel, Tim. *Autocracy, Modernization, and Revolution in Russia and Iran*. Princeton: Princeton University Press, 1991.

Milani, Mohsen M. "Harvest of Shame: Tudeh and the Bazargan Government." (Mehdi Bazargan's Provisional Revolutionary Government in Iran) *Middle Eastern Studies*, 29 (April 1993): 307–320.

———. *The Making of Iran's Islamic Revolution*. Boulder, CO: Westview Press, 1988.

Moallem, Minoo. "Ethnicité et rapports de sexes: le fondamentalisme islamique en Iran." (Ethnicity and Gender Relations: Islamic Fundamentalism in Iran) *Sociologie et Sociétés,* 24 (Autumn 1992): 59–71.

———. "The Ethnicity of an Islamic Fundamentalism: The Case of Iran." *South Asia Bulletin,* 12 (Fall 1992): 25–34.

Moosa, Matti. *Extremist Shiites: The Ghulat Sects*. Syracuse, NY: Syracuse University Press, 1988.

Mottahedeh, Roy. *The Mantle of the Prophet: Religion and Politics in Iran*. New York: Pantheon Books, 1988.

Mutahery, M. *Islamic Movements in the Twentieth Century*. Tehran: Great Islamic Library, 1979.

———. *The Martyr*. Tehran: Great Islamic Library, 1980.

Mutahhari, Ayatollah Murtaza. *Fundamentals of Islamic Thought: God, Man and the Universe*. Berkeley: Mizan Press, 1985.

Nasr, Seyyed Hossein. *The Islamic Intellectual Traditions in Persia*. London: Curzon Press, 1996.

Navabpour, Reza. *Iran*. World Bibliographical Series, vol. 81. Oxford, UK: Clio Press, 1988.

Noorbaksh, Mehdi. "The Middle East, Islam and the United States: The Special Case of Iran (U.S. and the Threat of Islamic Fundamentalism)." *Middle East Policy,* 2 (Summer 1993): 78–97.

O'Ballance, Edgar. *The Iranian Connection*. New York, NY: New York University Press, 1997.

Parsa, Misagh. *Social Origins of the Iranian Revolution*. New Brunswick, NJ: Rutgers University Press, 1989.

Pipes, Daniel. "There Are No Moderates: Dealing with Fundamentalist Iran." *The National Interest,* 41 (Fall 1995): 48–57.

Precht, H. "Ayatollah Realpolitik." *Foreign Policy,* 70 (Spring 1988).

Rajaee, Farhang. "Iranian Ideology and Worldview: The Cultural Export of Revolution." *The Iranian Revolution: Its Global Impact.* Ed. John L. Esposito, 63–81. Miami: Florida International University Press, 1990.

Ramazani, R. K. "Church and State in Modernising Society: The Case of Iran." *The American Behavioral Scientist,* VII: 7 (January 1964): 26–28.

———. "Constitution of the Islamic Republic of Iran." *Middle East Journal,* 34, ii (Spring 1980): 181–204.

———. "Iran's Export of the Revolution: Politics, Ends, and Means." *The Iranian Revolution: Its Global Impact.* Ed. John L. Esposito, 40–62. Miami: Florida International University Press, 1990.

———. *Revolutionary Iran: Challenge and Response in the Middle East.* Baltimore, MD: Johns Hopkins University Press, 1986.

Ramazani, R. K., ed. *Iran's Revolution: The Search for Consensus.* Bloomington: Indiana University Press, 1990.

Ritcheson, Philip L. "Iranian Military Resurgence: Scope, Motivations, and Implications for Regional Security." *Armed Forces and Society: An Interdisciplinary Journal,* 21 (Summer 1995): 573–592.

Sachedina, Abdulaziz A. "Activist Shi'ism in Iran, Iraq, and Lebanon." *Fundamentalisms Observed.* Eds. Martin E. Marty and R. Scott Appleby, 403–456. Chicago, IL: University of Chicago Press, 1991.

———. *Islamic Messianism: The Idea of the Mahdi in Twelver Shi'ism.* Albany: State University of New York Press, 1981.

———. *The Just Ruler in Shi'ite Islam: The Comprehensive Authority of the Jurist in Imamite Jurisprudence.* New York: Oxford University Press, 1988.

Saikal, Amin. "The West and Post-Khomeini Iran." *The World Today,* 49 (October 1993): 197–200.

Salehi, M. M. *Insurgency through Culture and Revolution: The Islamic Revolution of Iran.* New York: Praeger, 1988.

Sarraf, Tahmoores. *Cry of a Nation: The Saga of Iranian Revolution.* New York: Peter Lang Publishing, 1990.

Shirley, Edward G. "Is Iran's Present Algeria's Future?" *Foreign Affairs,* (May-June 1995): 28–44.

Sick, Gary. "Iran: The Adolescent Revolution." *Journal of International Affairs,* 49 (Summer 1995): 145–166.

Simpson, John. *Inside Iran: Life under Khomeini's Regime.* New York: St. Martin's Press, 1988.

Stempel, J. *Inside the Iranian Revolution.* Bloomington: Indiana University Press, 1982.

Tabar, A., and N. Yeganeh, eds. *In the Shadow of Islam.* London: Zed Press, 1982.

Tabatab'i, Hossein Modarresi. *An Introduction to Shi'i Law: A Bibliographical Study.* London: Ithaca Press, 1984.

Taheri, Amir. *The Spirit of Allah: Khomeini and the Islamic Revolution.* London: Hutchinson, 1985.

Weiner, M., and Ali Banuazizi, eds. *The Politics of Social Transformation in Afghanistan, Iran and Pakistan.* Syracuse, NY: Syracuse University Press, 1994.

Wright, Robin. *In the Name of God: The Khomeini Decade.* New York: Simon and Schuster, 1989.

Zubaida, Sami. "The Quest for the Islamic State: Islamic Fundamentalism in Egypt and Iran." *Studies in Religious Fundamentalism.* Ed. Lionel Kaplan, 25–50. Albany: State University of New York Press, 1987.

V: TURKEY

Abramowitz, Morton. "Dateline Ankara: Turkey After Ozal." *Foreign Policy,* 91 (Summer 1993): 164–181.

Ahmad, Feroz. *The Making of Modern Turkey.* London: Routledge, 1993.

———. "Politics and Islam in Modern Turkey." *Middle Eastern Studies,* 27 (January 1991): 3–21.

———. *The Turkish Experiment with Democracy, 1950–1975.* London: C. Hurst, 1977.

Ahmed, Feroz. "Islamic Reassertion in Turkey." *Third World Quarterly,* 10 (April 1988): 750–769.

Akarli, E. D., and G. Ben-Dor, eds. *Political Participation in Turkey.* Istanbul: Bogazici University Publications, 1975.

Alkan, Turker. "The National Salvation Party in Turkey." *Islam and Politics in the Modern Middle East.* Eds. M. Heper and R. Israeli, 79–102. New York: St. Martin's Press.

Arat, Yesim. "Islamic Fundamentalism and Women in Turkey." *The Muslim World,* 80 i (1990): 17–23.

Ayat, Sencer. "Patronage, Party and State: The Politicization of Islam in Turkey." *The Middle East Journal,* 50 (Winter 1996): 41–56.

Birtek, Faruk, and Binnaz Toprak. "The Conflictual Agendas of Neo-Liberal Reconstruction and the Rise of Islamic Politics in Turkey: The Hazards of Rewriting History." *Praxis International*, 13 ii (1993): 123–129, 227.

Dodd, C. H. *The Crisis of Turkish Democracy*. 2nd ed. Walkington, UK: Eothen Press, 1990.

———. *Democracy and Development in Turkey*. Walkington, UK: Eothen Press, 1983.

———. "Revolution in the Ottoman Empire and Modern Turkey." *Revolutionary Theory and Political Reality*. Ed. N. K. Sullivan. Brighton, UK: Harvester, 1983.

Finkel, Andrew, and Nuket Sirman. *Turkish State, Turkish Society*. London: Routledge, 1990.

Gole, Nilufer. "Authoritarian Secularism and Islamic Participation." *Civil Society in the Middle East*. Ed. Augustus Richard Norton. Leiden: E. J. Brill, 1995.

———. "Secularism and Islamism in Turkey: The Making and Counter-Making of Elites and Counter-Elites." *The Middle East Journal*, 51 i (Winter 1997): 46–79.

———. "Towards an Autonomization of Politics and Civil Turkey." *Politics in the Third Turkish Republic*. Eds. Metin Heper and Ahmet Evin. Boulder, CO: Westview Press, 1994.

Hale, W. M. *Turkish Politics and the Military*. London: Routledge, 1994.

Heper, Metin. *Historical Dictionary of Turkey*. Metuchen, NJ and London: Scarecrow Press, 1994.

———. "Islam and Democracy in Turkey: Toward a Reconciliation?" *The Middle East Journal*, 51 i (Winter 1997): 32–45.

———. "Islam, Polity and Society in Turkey: A Middle Eastern Perspective." *The Middle East Journal*, 35 (Summer 1981): 345–363.

Heper, Metin, and Ahmet Evin. *Politics in the Third Turkish Republic*. Boulder, CO: Westview Press, 1994.

Heper, Metin, and Jacob M. Landau, eds. *Political Parties and Democracy in Turkey*. London: I. B. Tauris, 1991.

Kadioglu, Ayse. "Women's Subordination in Turkey: Is Islam Really the Villain." *The Middle East Journal*, 48 (Autumn 1994): 645–660.

Karpat, K. H. *Turkey's Politics: The Transition to a Multi-Party System*. Princeton: Princeton University Press, 1959.

Karpat, K. H., et al. *Social Change and Politics in Turkey: A Structural-Historical Analysis*. Leiden: E. J. Brill, 1973.

Kazancigil, Ali. "Democracy in Muslim Lands: Turkey in Comparative Perspective." *International Social Science Journal*, 43 (May 1991): 343–360.

Kedourie, S., ed. *Turkey: Identity, Democracy and Politics*. London: Frank Cass, 1997.

Kopanski, A. Bogdan. "Namik Kemal: A Pioneer of Islamic Revival." *The Muslim World League Journal*, 15 (1988): 38–40.

Kushner, David. "Turkish Secularists and Islam." *Jerusalem Quarterly*, 38 (1986): 89–106.

Landau, Jacob M. "The National Salvation Party in Turkey." *Asian and African Studies*, 11 (1976): 1–57.

———. *The Politics of Pan-Islam: Ideology and Organization*. Oxford, UK: Oxford University Press, 1990.

———. *Politics and Islam: The National Salvation Party in Turkey*. Research Monograph, no. 5. Salt Lake City: Middle East Center, University of Utah, 1976.

Landau, Jacab, et al. *Electoral Politics in the Middle East: Issues, Voters, and Elites*. London: Croom Helm, 1980.

Lewis, Bernard. *The Emergence of Modern Turkey*. London: Oxford University Press, 1966.

Mardin, Serif. "The Nakshibendi Order of Turkey." *Fundamentalisms and the State: Remaking Polities, Economies, and Militance*. Eds. Martin E. Marty and R. Scott Appleby, 204–232. Chicago, IL: University of Chicago Press, 1993.

Milter, Louis. *Contemporary Turkish Writers: A Critical Bibliography of Leading Writers of the Turkish Republican Period up to 1980*. Bloomington: Indiana University Press, 1988.

Muhammad, Samir R. *Nursi, Badi' al-Zaman Sa'id*. Cairo: Al-Mu'assasa al-Su'udiyya, 1995.

Nur al-Din, Muhammad. *Quba'a wa 'Amama: Madkhal ila al-Harakat al-Islamiyya fi Turkiyya*. Beirut: Dar al-Nahar li al-Nashr, 1997.

———. *Turkiyya fi al-Zaman al-Mutahawil: Qalaq al-Hawiyya wa Sira' al-Khiyyarat*. London and Beirut: Riad al-Rayyes Books, 1997.

Ortayli, Ilber, ed. *Liberal Elements in the Programmes of Turkish Political Parties*. Ankara: TES-AR, 1992.

Saeed, Javaid. *Islam and Modernization: A Comparative Analysis of Pakistan, Egypt, and Turkey*. Westport, CT: Praeger, 1994.

Salt, Jeremy. "Nationalism and the Rise of Muslim Sentiment in Turkey." *Middle Eastern Studies*, 31 (January 1995): 13–27.

Shaw, Stanford H., and Ezel Kural Shaw. *History of the Ottoman Empire and Modern Turkey, Volume II: Reform, Revolution and Republic—The Rise of Modern Turkey, 1808–1975*. New York: Cambridge University Press, 1977.

Shrewood, W. B. "The Rise of Justice Party in Turkey." *World Politics,* 20 (1967–68): 54–65.

Tachau, Frank. *Turkey: The Politics of Authority, Democracy and Development.* New York: Praeger, 1984.

Toprak, Binnaz. *Islam and Political Development in Turkey.* Leiden: E. J. Brill, 1981.

———. "The Religious Right." *The Modern Middle East: A Reader.* Eds. A. Hourani et al. London: Tauris, 1993.

Turan, Ilter. "Political Parties and Party System in Post-1983 Turkey," *State, Democracy and the Military: Turkey in the 1980s.* Ed. M. Helper and A. Evin. Berlin: Walter De Gruyter, 1988.

U.S. Library of Congress. *Turkey: A Selected List of References.* Comp. Grace Hadley Fuller. Washington, DC: Library of Congress, 1959.

Waterbury, John. *Exposed to Innumerable Delusions: Public Enterprise and State Power in Egypt, India, Mexico, and Turkey.* Cambridge, UK: Cambridge University Press, 1993.

Welker, W. F. *The Modernization of Turkey from Ataturk to the Present Day.* New York: Holmes and Meier, 1981.

———. *Political Tutelage and Democracy in Turkey: The Free Party and Its Aftermath.* Leiden: E. J. Brill, 1973.

White, Jenny B. "Islam and Democracy: The Turkish Experience." *Current History,* 94 (January 1995): 7–12.

Yavuz, M. Hakan. "Turkey's 'Imagined Enemies': Kurds and Islamists." *The World Today,* 52 (April 1996): 99–101.

Ziring, Lawrence. *Iran, Turkey, and Afghanistan: A Political Chronology.* New York: Praeger, 1981.

About the Author

Ahmad S. Moussalli is Associate Professor of Political Science at the American University of Beirut. He received a B.A. from the University of Al-Azhar, Cairo, Egypt; an M.A. from St. John's College, Santa Fe, New Mexico; and a Ph.D. from the University of Maryland, College Park, Maryland. His interests include ideologies, political theories, and histories of Islamic movements. He has written, lectured, and traveled extensively all over the Islamic and Western worlds. His book *Radical Islamic Fundamentalism: The Ideological and Political Discourse of Sayyid Qutb*, published by the American University of Beirut in 1993, was selected as Outstanding Academic Book by *Choice* in 1994. He received the 'Abdul Hamid Shuman Prize for Young Arab Scholars in 1993.

His writings include numerous articles and seven books, the latest of which are *Islamic Fundamentalism: Myths and Realities* (Ithaca Press, 1998) and *Moderate and Radical Islamic Fundamentalism: The Quest for Modernity, Legitimacy and the Islamic State* (University Press of Florida, 1999).